Rodale's
FLOWER GARDEN
PROBLEM SOLVER

Rodale's FLOWER GARDEN PROBLEM SOLVER

Annuals, Perennials, Bulbs, and Roses

by Jeff and Liz Ball

Illustrations by Pamela and Walter Carroll and Robin Brickman

 Rodale Press, Emmaus, Pennsylvania

Printed in the United States of America

Editor in Chief: Willliam Gottlieb
Managing Editor: Margaret Lydic Balitas
Editor: Barbara W. Ellis
Research Associate: Heidi A. Stonehill
Editorial/Administrative Assistant: Stacy Brobst
Copy Editor: Lisa D. Andruscavage

Cover Design: Denise Mirabello
Cover Photography: Jerry Pavia
Book Design: Denise Mirabello
Book Layout: Lisa Farkas

If you have any questions or comments concerning this book, please
write:
    Rodale Press
    Book Reader Service
    33 East Minor Street
    Emmaus, PA 18098

Library of Congress Cataloging-in-Publication Data

Ball, Jeff.
    Rodale's flower garden problem solver : annuals, perennials,
bulbs, and roses / by Jeff and Liz Ball ; illustrations by Pamela
and Walter Carroll and Robin Brickman.
       p.   cm.
    ISBN 0-87857-868-4
    1. Flowers—Diseases and pests—Control. 2. Flowers. 3. Flower
gardening. 4. Organic gardening. I. Ball, Liz. II. Carroll, Pamela.
III. Carroll, Walter. IV. Brickman, Robin. V. Title.
SB608.07B348 1990
635.9—dc20   89-10992
                                   CIP

Distributed in the book trade by St. Martin's Press

2 4 6 8 10 9 7 5 3 1 hardcover

Contents

Acknowledgments

This is the third book in the Rodale problem-solving series. Again it has been a team effort. Mike Wisniewski was our data traffic manager, making sure everyone's work got organized in the master data base and generally supervising the flow of the work load as floppy discs moved from person to person. Pete Johnson and Kim Wilson did much of the collection and organization of the basic data for the plants. Jim Janczewski helped us with the complex task of checking horticultural nomenclature and verifying facts. Much of the valuable information about roses was offered by Jack Potter and Maggie Oster. Many of the tips for growing plants in the flower garden came from Charles Cresson, our good friend and mentor.

We also depended on many fine reference books for information about the plants discussed in this book, as well as the symptoms and life cycles of the insect pests and diseases that affect them. For plant information, the primary sources we used were *Wyman's Gardening Encyclopedia* by Donald Wyman and the three volumes of the Taylor's Guides —*Taylor's Guide to Annuals, Taylor's Guide to Perennials,* and *Taylor's Guide to Bulbs.* For insect and disease information, the *Gardener's Bug Book* by Cynthia Wescott and *Diseases and Pests of Ornamental Plants* by Pascal P. Pirone were most helpful. We depended on Barbara J. Barton's book *Gardening by Mail 2* for much of the information in the source list. The publications of Bio-Integral Resource Center (BIRC) were a major source of information about safe techniques for pest control. Helga and Bill Olkowlski and Sheila Daar performed a tremendous service to us all in pulling together such helpful information in a usable and readable form. We also are very much indebted to Niles Kinerk for his help and for the very informative catalog from his Natural Gardening Research Center. To all these folks, we give our thanks.

Special thanks to our top-notch editor, Barbara Ellis, who always kept the backyard gardener in mind as she edited this book. Her sharp eye and vast horticultural knowledge ensured that the information was both correct and helpful.

From our own experience, we realize that there are basically three kinds of gardening problems. First, there are cultural problems, meaning those related to plant care, the site in which the plant is growing, or the environment. Second, there are those caused by insects, and third, those caused by disease organisms. The problems discussed in this book under each plant entry are organized accordingly— Most Common Cultural Problems, Most Common Insect Pests, and Most Common Diseases. In part 1, for each problem we've tried to describe the symptoms, identify the causes, and provide basic solutions. For insects or diseases that you may only encounter occasionally, we've mentioned them at the beginning of the section. Part 2, which contains discussions of common insect, disease, and animal pest problems, provides even more information about symptoms and solutions. Here, you'll find a wide range of methods for dealing with the most common problems that affect your flower garden.

Obviously, the individual gardener normally confronts only a small percentage of the problems we discuss, especially if he or she follows the basic good gardening practices that we suggest throughout this book. We offer this book as a resource for those times when you discover that a flowering plant is not thriving and may be showing signs of insect attack or illness. It will help you identify the cause of the problem and then give you a safe and practical solution. From among the hundreds and hundreds of wonderful flowering plants that grow in the United States, we have selected some of the most familiar, versatile, and sturdy to discuss in detail. We hope that with this book to back you up, you will confidently try even more flowering plants in the years to come.

Introduction

Once again, this third volume in Rodale's problem-solving series contains a wealth of information about the insects, diseases, and other problems that can occur in the garden. As you page through this book, though, take note of a thread that has been woven through all three of the books in this series—problem prevention. *Rodale's Flower Garden Problem Solver* contains extensive information about what to do to prevent these very problems before they occur. From cultural recommendations to suggestions for good garden maintenance techniques, we've collected everything you need to know about how to prevent serious problems in the garden. Then, if problems do crop up, you'll also find hundreds of suggestions for dealing with them in an effective manner that is also safe for the environment.

Of course, it is easier to prevent problems in the flower garden than it is to handle them once they appear. The best way to have a healthy, trouble-free flower garden is to locate each plant in a site that meets its cultural needs—a site with the right soil and the right amount of light, for example—and then provide it with its basic food and water requirements. Healthy, vigorous plants are much less vulnerable to pest and disease problems, and they are better able to fight off any infections or infestations that do occur. With this in mind, we have included extensive information on the cultural requirements each plant requires for healthy, vigorous growth. There are other steps you can take to keep your plants healthy: Follow good garden cleanup practices, protect your plants from injury from wind and freezing temperatures, keep your eye out for potential problems—such as some of the symptoms we've described in this book for the major pests of the plants you grow. Prevention is an essential part of normal gardening activities and will become second nature to you. So, while this book is dedicated to helping you identify and solve problems, its real story is about how to prevent those problems in the first place.

When problems do occur, you'll be able to solve them more quickly and effectively if you have the necessary supplies on hand. We have listed some basic products for insect and disease control that we like to have available just in case:

1. A generous pile of finished compost.
2. A bottle of seaweed or kelp extract to supply micronutrients. (You'll need a fresh supply each year.)
3. A bottle of liquid fertilizer such as fish emulsion. (This will keep for two to three years.)
4. A bottle of insecticidal soap concentrate. (This will last indefinitely.)
5. A bottle of liquid Bt (*Bacillus thuringiensis*). (You'll need a fresh supply each year.)
6. A bottle of pyrethrum or a mix of pyrethrum and rotenone. (This will keep for three to four years.)
7. A bottle of flowable sulfur fungicide. (This will keep for one year.)
8. A good sprayer with a capacity of at least 1 gallon.
9. Sufficient organic mulching material to cover the area around plants that need mulch.
10. If you have roses, a bottle of dormant oil. (This will last indefinitely.)

These supplies will enable you to respond effectively to just about any problem that presents itself in your backyard. In addition, consider installing at least one bird feeder and one birdhouse to attract insect-eating birds to your yard. Enjoy your flowers!

How to Use This Book

This book has been designed so that you can discover solutions to your flower garden problems within seconds. Because it is so easy to use, you could sit down and figure it out yourself, but we'd like to save you even that bit of trouble. In addition, we'd like to direct you to some areas of general information that will help you use the text most effectively.

FOR IMMEDIATE CONTROL OF PROBLEMS

If a problem develops on one of your flower garden plants—holes in the blossoms, yellow spots on the leaves—follow these steps to identify it and to find a quick solution.

1. Locate the entry for that plant in part 1 of the book.

2. Scan that entry to find the symptom that matches the one you've discovered on your plant. Here you'll find the cause of the problem (cultural, insect, or disease), a more complete description of the symptoms, and the best method for immediate control.

FOR GENERAL CONTROL

This book doesn't stop at the one quick solution to any given plant problem. Turn to part 2 for an in-depth discussion of the control of insect pests, diseases, and animal pests. There you'll read about the many different control measures you can consider. You'll learn the best ways to use insecticides such as pyrethrum and rotenone, how to make pest-repellent sprays of garlic and other natural substances, how to set traps, and much more. You'll learn the details of disease control and how to keep animal pests away from your plants. Detailed descriptions of insects and diseases will help you identify these problems accurately, and prepare you to handle them more effectively.

FOR PROBLEM PREVENTION

Each entry in part 1 contains loads of information about the cultural requirements of each plant. Take time to read through the entries on plants you are considering or ones you've had problems with in the past. Not only will you learn what to do once you find a problem in your backyard, but you'll discover techniques that will help you prevent insects and diseases from attacking your plants in the first place. Give your plants the right environment from the start, and they'll give you a beautiful backyard that you can enjoy for years.

Part 3 continues the discussion of problem prevention. There, you'll find details on caring for the soil, what fertilizers to use, and other tips for success. At the end of the book, you'll find a USDA plant hardiness zone map so you can determine which species and cultivars will grow in your part of the country. You'll also find a recommended reading section and a list of sources for all the products mentioned throughout the book.

You probably already have a stock of tools, sprays, and dusts to help you fight the insects and diseases that show up in the flower garden around your home. This book is another powerful tool to help you manage a pest-free and disease-free garden. So keep this book near the back door, where it's readily at hand. As the years go by, you'll need it less and less as you perfect your techniques for preventing plant problems . . . then you can move it to the bookshelf.

PART 1

Problem Solver for Plants

CHAPTER 1

Annuals

No garden is complete without at least a few annuals. These flexible and adaptable plants will cheerfully provide weeks and often months of bloom in return for very little day-to-day care. There are annuals for every part of the garden: Use them as edgings in front of shrubs or perennials; combine them in beds for summer-long displays of color; or plant them in tubs, pots, or window boxes to decorate porches, front stoops, or patios. Annuals are especially useful in flower gardens as fillers because they can easily be slipped into place between perennials that have stopped blooming or bulbs that are dying back for the season. They also can be used to dress up a vegetable garden. An edging of marigolds, for example, will not only add summer color but can also be tilled under the soil at the end of the season to discourage nematodes. Nasturtiums have bright orange or yellow flowers and peppery-tasting foliage that adds spice to salads. So, try planting some annuals anywhere a bright spot of color would add to your garden's appeal. Because they are relatively inexpensive and easy to grow, you can hardly go wrong.

Because they are selected and planted anew each year, annuals provide plenty of opportunity to try new color combinations and new growing techniques. Many gardeners routinely replace some of their annuals between spring and summer or summer and fall to create different color combinations and continuous color in their gardens. Another advantage is that annuals make it easy to practice one of the best methods of preventing insect and disease problems—crop rotation. If a particular annual has problems one year, grow it in another part of the garden the following year. Or if the problem is severe, don't grow it at all for a season or two.

You'll notice that the individual plant entries in this chapter contain a great deal of information about cultural conditions that each plant prefers—soil, light, water, planting, and feeding. That's because the best time to start your garden problem solving isn't when you first notice symptoms of disease or insect infestation, it's when you select a site for a plant and when you care for it. Many of the problems covered in this book can be controlled by following the basic cultural information discussed in the individual plant entries. Parts 2 and 3 also contain a great deal of information about preventing problems in the flower garden.

Finally, you'll notice that we've included in this chapter a category often not associated with annuals —hardiness. Annuals differ in their ability to withstand cold weather. Tender annuals, such as ageratums and zinnias, can't tolerate frost at all and are best planted out after danger of frost has passed and the soil has warmed up a bit. Half-hardy annuals, such as salvia, can withstand a few degrees of frost, provided the seedlings are conditioned, or hardened off, properly. Seedlings or purchased bedding plants of hardy annuals, such as pansies, will survive temperatures that fall below 25°F, provided they are properly hardened off. Hardy annual seed can also be sown outdoors in fall for germination the following spring. There are also a number of plants commonly grown as annuals that are actually tender perennials. Wax begonias, four-o'clocks, and geraniums fall into this category. We've provided details for overwintering these plants so that you can enjoy them in your garden year after year without having to buy new plants each year.

Ageratum

Ageratum houstonianum

DESCRIPTION

Ageratums, also known as flossflowers, are small, stocky annuals native to Mexico and Central America. Members of the daisy family, Compositae, they bear distinctive clusters of puffy flowers from summer until the first frost of autumn. Blooms are generally purplish blue to purple, but sometimes white or pink. These extremely versatile annuals are ideal for edging, bedding, borders, cut flowers, and containers. Many fine hybrids are available, including dwarf forms.

Height

6 to 15 inches; dwarf cultivars, 3 to 5 inches

Spread

9 to 12 inches

Blossoms

Ageratums bear many-flowered clusters of fluffy, ¼- to ½-inch blossoms from summer to fall. Each bloom is nearly spherical in shape and actually is a daisylike head of tiny, tightly packed individual flowers called disc florets. The blooms lack the showy "petals," called ray florets, of the common daisy. Blooms are chiefly pale lilac, lavender, or purplish blue, but there are pink- and white-flowered cultivars, too. The flowers have only a slight fragrance.

Foliage

The leaves are oval or heart-shaped and are generally borne opposite each other on the stem. The medium to dark green foliage has a moderately coarse or hairy texture.

ENVIRONMENT

Hardiness

Ageratums are tender, heat-loving annuals that will be killed if exposed to even a light frost.

Light

Plants generally perform best in full sun but also will tolerate light shade. However, they dislike excessive heat and humidity, so where summers are long and hot, such as in the South and Southwest, grow ageratums in light shade or plant them for spring or fall bloom. Dwarf cultivars prefer light shade, even in the North.

Soil

Ageratums prefer moist, fertile, well-drained soil with a pH between 6 and 7.

PLANTING AND PROPAGATION

Planting

Sow seed indoors six to eight weeks before the last frost date. Ageratum seeds are very fine and require light to germinate, so scatter them on the surface of the soil, and do not cover them. Sow seeds in individual pots, or sow them in flats and transplant the seedlings to pots when the first set of true leaves appears. Germination will take place in 7 to 10 days. For germination, soil temperatures between 70° and 80°F are ideal. Transplant seedlings to the garden two to three weeks *after* the last frost date, once night temperatures remain above 60°F, to avoid exposing them to a late frost. Seed also can be sown outdoors in a prepared seedbed after danger of frost has passed, but the seedlings are very tiny and are easily lost among the weeds. When transplanting to the garden, space plants about a foot apart; 9 inches for dwarf cultivars. To encourage compact growth, pinch the seedlings back when they are moved to the garden. Plants should begin blooming about 65 days after sowing seed.

Propagation

Ageratums can be propagated from softwood cuttings taken anytime during the growing season.

Container Gardening

Ageratums are excellent plants for growing in containers or in window boxes. They also can be dug up in the fall and grown as houseplants in a sunny, south-facing window.

PLANT MANAGEMENT

General Care

Pinch taller cultivars several times during the growing season to encourage compact growth. Plants that have become leggy can be sheared back. Ageratums also benefit from occasional deadheading, so remove spent flowers.

Water

Ageratums require a well-drained soil that remains evenly moist throughout the growing season. Water when the soil begins to dry out but before the leaves wilt.

Feeding

Fertilize ageratum seedlings with a slow-acting, general-purpose fertilizer in spring when they are transplanted to the garden. Monthly applications of a dilute fertilizer, such as a foliar spray, are optional but will help plants perform at their peak.

Cutting Fresh Flowers

Taller ageratum cultivars make fine cut flowers. Pick the flowers in early morning and place them directly in water for the longest vase life.

Drying Flowers

Blooms can be air dried or dried in silica gel. To air dry, cut the stems when the flowers are in full bloom, strip off the leaves, bundle the stems, and hang them upside down in a dark, well-ventilated place. To dry in silica gel, cut flowers in full bloom, leaving 1-inch stems. Place flower cluster, stems down, in a coffee can or other sealable container partially filled with silica gel. Carefully sift silica gel over blooms until they are completely covered.

MOST COMMON CULTURAL PROBLEMS

Scorched Foliage; Plants Die Out in Summer

Hot, Dry Weather
Drought or extremely hot weather will occasionally kill entire plants or will kill the center branches and foliage of plants. Foliage wilts and appears yellowed or scorched. To avoid this condition, keep plants evenly moist during the hot season. If temperatures are consistently in the nineties, water daily at noon, if possible, to help cool the roots. In the South and Southwest, plant ageratums in light shade to protect them from high temperatures.

Tall, Spindly Plants

Unpinched Plants; Improper Planting Location
Plants will get tall and spindly if they are not pinched back two or three times early in the growing season. They also will become leggy and produce few, if any, flowers when planted in a location that is too shady. Pinching encourages branching, more compact growth, and flower production. Extremely leggy plants can be sheared.

MOST COMMON INSECT PESTS

Holes in Leaves

Caterpillars
Ageratums that have holes in the leaves, but lack the slime trails that indicate the prescence of slugs or snails, are infested with caterpillars. Various caterpillars may attack these plants, but two pests are most common: corn earworm (*Heliothis zea*) and tobacco budworm (*H. virescens*). Corn earworms are 2-inch-long caterpillars that are yellowish, green, or brown with stripes running lengthwise. They eat leaves and flower buds and tunnel into the stems. The adults are small, grayish brown moths. Tobacco budworms are tiny, rust-colored or green-striped caterpillars that also attack flower buds and foliage. Adults are light green, 1½-inch-long moths. There may be several generations per year.

Mild infestations are easily controlled by hand-picking caterpillars and dropping them in a jar of soapy water. To control serious infestations, apply Bt (*Bacillus thuringiensis*) at three- to five-day intervals until symptoms disappear. Dust or spray both sides of the leaves, and reapply after rain. Also, regularly clean up and dispose of garden debris throughout the season to reduce future generations. A thorough end-of-season cleanup is also beneficial.

Leaves Stuck Together with Silk; Foliage Ragged and Discolored

Leaftiers
Leaves that are fastened together with strands of silk, followed by foliage that becomes ragged and unsightly, turns brown, and dies are signs that your plants are infested with greenhouse or celery leaftier (*Udea rubigalis*). It is the larval stage that damages plants by feeding on the undersides of the leaves and binding the leaves together. The larvae are ⅜- to ¾-inch-long caterpillars that are light green or cream to yellow in color with a white stripe down their backs and a green line down the center of the stripe. Adult leaftier moths, which are active only at night, are brown or gray and ¼ to ½ inch long. They lay eggs that resemble fish scales on the undersides of leaves.

Handpicking of eggs and larvae is usually an effective way to control this pest, since infestations are usually light. Remove any rolled or folded leaves, for they shelter caterpillars. Infested leaves should be destroyed, since the pests pupate and overwinter in them. Bt (*Bacillus thuringiensis*) also is an effective control. Apply as a powder or spray every two weeks until leaftiers disappear.

Ragged Holes in Leaves; Trails of Slime on Plants

Slugs and Snails

Plants that have large, ragged holes in the leaves and stems are probably infested with slugs and/or snails. Trails of slime on the foliage and around the plants are further confirmation of the presence of these pests. Slugs and snails are active only at night, when they feast on plants by rasping holes in the foliage with their filelike tongues. During the day, they hide under boards, mulch, or leaf litter. Slugs are similar to snails except that they have no shells. Both are generally 1 to 2 inches long, although some species of slugs grow up to 8 inches in length. Either pest may be white, gray, yellow, or brown-black in color. They are attracted to moist, well-mulched gardens and are most destructive in shaded gardens and during rainy spells. During winter and in dry seasons, slugs burrow into the ground to wait for more favorable weather.

A multifaceted approach to control is best. Remove boards, rocks, clippings, and other debris to cut down on the places where these pests hide during the day. Or, check daily under favorite hiding places, handpick snoozing slugs, crush them or seal them into a jar full of water and kerosene or insecticidal soap, and discard them. Inverted flowerpots, pieces of grapefruit peel, and cabbage leaves will lure slugs and can be used to trap them. Handpicking at night with a flashlight can be effective if started early in the spring. Traps baited with beer or yeast and water are also effective. To make an effective trap, cut a 2-inch hole in the lid of a coffee can or a small plastic container and bury the container flush with the soil. Slugs are attracted to the yeast in the beer, climb down through the hole in the lid, and drown. The key is to begin trapping very early in the season in order to prevent the population from building up. Surrounding plants with barriers of sand, ashes, or copper sheeting will discourage slugs from invading your plantings.

Leaves Stippled with Tiny Yellow Dots; Webby Foliage

Spider Mites

Leaves that are dry and stippled with tiny yellow dots are a sign that your ageratums are infested with spider mites, tiny pests that suck chlorophyll out of the leaves. They also inject toxins into the foliage; this causes distorted or discolored growth. Leaves, stems, and flowers also may be swathed in fine webbing. As their name suggests, spider mites are related to spiders. These tiny creatures, which are about $\frac{1}{50}$ inch long and barely visible to the naked eye, may be yellow, green, red, or brown. Both cyclamen mites (*Steneotarsonemus pallidus*) and two-spotted spider mites (*Tetranychus urticae*) attack ageratums. Spider mites reproduce most rapidly during hot, dry weather. They are especially a problem on greenhouse-grown ageratum plants; inspect purchased bedding plants carefully to avoid bringing home infested specimens.

Severely infested plants should be destroyed, since infestations are difficult to control once they are well under way. Spider mites can be controlled by washing the plants, especially the undersides of the leaves. For best results, use a forceful spray of water once every other day to knock the mites off the plants; wash the plants at least three times. If that is not effective, spray the plants with insecticidal soap every three to five days for two weeks. To avoid spreading the mites from plant to plant, don't touch healthy plants after examining infested ones.

Weakened Plants; Leaves Yellowed

Whiteflies

Plants that are infested with whiteflies are weakened and undersized with leaves that begin to turn yellow and die. The undersides of the leaves of infested plants may be covered with a sooty, black fungus, which grows on the shiny, sticky honeydew secreted by the whiteflies. Adults are white, mothlike insects about the size of the head of a pin and are clearly visible on the undersides of ageratum leaves. Whitefly infestation is sometimes referred to as flying dandruff because when an infested plant is bumped or brushed, the adults flutter out in clouds, somewhat resembling dandruff flying off the leaves. Nymphs, which are yellowish, legless, flat, and oval, resemble scale at certain stages. Both nymphs and adults suck juices from plant leaves, buds, and stems. These pests, which are particular problems in greenhouses, are often brought home on purchased bedding plants or vegetable transplants. (Greenhouse whitefly, *Trialeurodes vaporariorum,* the most common species found in gardens, does not overwinter outdoors in the North.) Inspect purchased bedding plants carefully to avoid bringing home infested specimens.

Whiteflies are difficult to control once they have infested your garden. Destroy infected plants as soon as you detect the problem, for whiteflies will quickly spread throughout the garden if infestations are not controlled. To control infestations, spray plants with insecticidal soap every two to three days for two weeks. Be sure to spray the undersides of the leaves. Also, use insecticidal soap early in the season to prevent infestations. Pyrethrum may be used as a last resort. Spray once every five days, making three applications. Isolate and destroy severely infested plants.

MOST COMMON DISEASES

White Powder Covering Leaves

Powdery Mildew

If your ageratum leaves are covered with a white or ash gray powdery mold, they probably have powdery mildew. Badly infected ageratum leaves become discolored and distorted, then drop off. Powdery mildew is caused by fungi that live primarily on the surface of the leaves, flowers, and stems of plants, not inside them.

Powdery mildew most commonly develops on plants grown close together where air circulation is restricted, especially on the lower leaves where humidity is higher and moisture is more abundant. Allow ample spacing between plants, and collect and discard all aboveground refuse in the fall. Spray affected plants thoroughly with wettable sulfur once or twice at weekly intervals starting as soon as the whitish coating of the fungus is visible.

Plants Wilt; Leaves Turn Yellow

Root Rot

Plants that turn yellow, wilt, and die, despite the fact that the soil is damp, have probably been stricken by one of the fungi that cause root rot. Usually, the root systems rot, causing plants to topple over, and plant stems are attacked at or near the soil level.

Plants growing in heavy, wet soil are most susceptible to root rot. To avoid this problem, select a location with moist but well-drained soil, and do not overwater. Avoid overcrowding plants to encourage air circulation. Remove and discard infected plants, or cut away affected plant parts with a clean, sharp knife or razor blade. Disinfect tools after use. Keep the garden free of old plant debris, and keep mulch away from stem bases. For long-term prevention, lighten heavy soil to improve drainage with a mixture of perlite, vermiculite, and/or peat moss. Crop rotation is also beneficial.

Leaves with Pale Areas Above, Powdery Orange Spots Beneath

Rust

A rust disease caused by the fungus *Puccinia conoclinii* occasionally attacks ageratum. It causes pale areas to appear on upper leaf surfaces, with powdery orange pustules or spots directly beneath on the undersides of the leaves.

Remove infected leaves as soon as possible, and destroy severely diseased plants. Clean up and destroy all plant material at the end of the season to avoid reinfecting the garden the following year. Rust can be prevented by periodic applications of wettable sulfur, begun several weeks before rust normally appears. To ensure good ventilation, space plants far enough apart so that air can circulate between them. Also, avoid wetting foliage when watering.

Alyssum, Sweet *Lobularia maritima*

DESCRIPTION

Sweet alyssum is a low-growing, mounding or sprawling plant that produces abundant quantities of small flowers from spring until frost. An ideal bedding or edging plant, it is often the last plant killed by frost in fall. Although grown as an annual throughout most of the country, it is actually a perennial and can be grown as one in USDA Zones 9 and 10. In the North, it will often reseed itself from year to year. It makes a fine informal ground cover and grows well in rock gardens, between paving stones, in pots, and in hanging baskets. If planted in bulb beds, it will help obscure the unattractive foliage that remains after bulbs finish blooming. Many cultivars are available, including several dwarf selections. Sweet alyssum is in the mustard or cabbage family and is subject to many of the same diseases and insects as cabbage, broccoli, turnips, and other cole crops.

Height

1 foot; dwarf cultivars, 3 to 8 inches

Spread

Up to 10 inches

Blossoms

Sweet alyssum bears globe-shaped clusters of tiny, ¾-inch-wide flowers that may be white, pink, or purple. Blooms have a sweet, honeylike fragrance. Like all mustard family members, its flowers have four petals arranged in a crosslike fashion. Blooms appear from spring to frost.

Foliage

Leaves are narrow, lance shaped, and light green in color. The foliage, borne on heavily branched, mound-shaped plants, has a fine, delicate texture.

ENVIRONMENT

Hardiness

Although sweet alyssum is a perennial that will bloom year-round in Zones 9 and 10, in most parts of the country it is grown as an annual. Plants will tolerate mild frost. They bloom best in cool weather, but also will tolerate some heat.

Light

For best results, grow sweet alyssum in full sun. Plants also will bloom well in a site with good light that receives direct sun only in the morning.

Soil

Sweet alyssum likes well-drained soil but otherwise is not particular. Alkaline soil helps prevent club root in this species, but plants will thrive in soils with a wide pH range.

PLANTING AND PROPAGATION

Planting

Seed can be sown indoors or out. Outdoors, sow sweet alyssum seed in a prepared seedbed several weeks before the last expected frost. Or for earlier bloom, sow indoors four to six weeks before last frost date. For indoor germination, maintain soil temperatures between 70° and 75°F. Use a sterile growing mix (peat moss, perlite, and vermiculite, with a topping of milled sphagnum moss), and water plants from below to avoid problems with damping-off. Do not cover the seeds with soil; they require light for germination. Sow seed thinly because the germination rate is high. Seed will germinate in 8 to 15 days. Thin mature seedlings to about 5 inches. To thin, cut seedlings down with scissors rather than pulling them out to avoid damaging the roots of remaining seedlings. Transplant seedlings sown indoors to their permanent site after four weeks, spacing them 6 to 8 inches apart. A second sowing outdoors in June where the plants are to grow will ensure plenty of flowers for fall. Sweet alyssum will reseed itself and come back from year to year. Small plants are easy to transplant, so if seedlings appear where they are unwanted, use them to fill empty spots in beds and borders.

Propagation

Sweet alyssum will reseed itself from year to year.

Container Gardening

Sweet alyssum is attractive when grown alone in shallow (2- to 3-inch) containers or combined in larger containers with other annuals. You also can pot up plants to bring indoors in the fall as frost nears. Carefully lift them with as much earth as possible adhering to the roots and reset in pots large enough to accommodate the roots. Shear plants after moving them to encourage new growth and blossoms. Sweet alyssum also may be started from seed in pots for winter bloom. It will begin flowering about a month after sowing.

PLANT MANAGEMENT

General Care

Shearing alyssum back a few inches in midsummer encourages more compact growth and better bloom later in the season.

Water

While alyssum, like most plants, prefers about 1 inch of water each week, established plants can withstand temporary drought.

Feeding

A light feeding of compost or a slow-acting, general-purpose fertilizer in the spring will serve sweet alyssum's basic needs all season. Sweet alyssum is a light feeder and too much fertilizer spurs an abundance of foliage at the expense of blossoms.

Drying Flowers

Alyssum does not air dry well, but it can be dried using silica gel. To dry in silica gel, cut flowers in full bloom, leaving 1-inch stems. Place flower cluster, stems down, in a coffee can or other sealable container partially filled with silica gel. Carefully sift silica gel over blooms until they are completely covered.

MOST COMMON CULTURAL PROBLEMS

Plants Stop Blooming

Weather Too Hot
In very hot weather, sweet alyssum can become ragged looking, and plants may even stop blooming completely. Watering the plants at noon to cool the roots can help prevent this problem. Shearing or cutting plants back by half their height will encourage new growth and new blooms.

MOST COMMON INSECT PESTS

Various caterpillars, as well as slugs and snails, may attack sweet alyssum and eat foliage and flowers, but for the most part they are not seriously bothered by insect pests.

Seedlings Severed at Base

Cutworms
If your alyssum seedlings look as though they have been leveled by a lawn mower, you may have cutworms. These pests sever the stems of seedlings and transplants at or below the soil surface, leaving the tops to die. (In contrast, slugs and snails completely consume seedlings, leaving only their slimy trails.) Cutworms are most active at night. They also can harm plant root systems, damage that causes the plant to wilt and collapse. Cutworms are generally plump, soft-bodied caterpillars that are dull grayish or brownish and measure 1 to 2 inches long. They feed at night and hide in the soil during the day. The adults are night-flying moths.

Prevention is the only way to fight cutworms, for once they have cut down a seedling, there is nothing you can do to save it. Since alyssum seedlings are so small, protecting individual seedlings with stiff paper or plastic collars, or making cornmeal traps, probably is not practical. Instead, thoroughly till the seedbed to expose these pests to birds and other predators. Beneficial nematodes added to the soil are an effective, long-term control measure.

Plants Stunted; Leaves Yellowed and Small; Knots on Roots

Nematodes
Nematode-infested plants look sickly, wilted, or stunted and have yellowed or bronzed foliage. Their root systems are poorly developed, may have tiny galls or knots on them, and can even be partially decayed. Plants decline slowly and die. The effects of nematode activity are most apparent in hot weather, when plants recover poorly from the heat. Southern root knot nematodes (*Meloidogyne incognita*) attack sweet alyssum. Nematodes are not insects, but slender, unsegmented roundworms that are barely visible to the unaided eye.

Prevention is the best way to deal with nematodes when growing annuals in infested soil, since severely infested annuals are best dug up and destroyed; do not compost. Organic matter in the soil helps to control nematodes because it not only benefits the fungi and bacteria that feed on them, it also keeps plants healthy and better able to withstand mild infestations. Add lots of compost, especially leaf mold, to the bed before planting. Turn severely infested plots over to a thick planting of French marigolds for an entire season and dig the plant remains into the soil at season's end to discourage these pests. Crop rotation is also a good idea; don't grow susceptible plants on the same plot year after year.

MOST COMMON DISEASES

Flowers and Foliage Greenish Yellow; Plants Stunted

Aster Yellows

If the leaves of your sweet alyssum are greenish yellow and spindly, and growth is stunted or dwarfed, they may be infected with aster yellows, a disease caused by a viruslike organism spread by leafhoppers. It is primarily carried by the aster leafhopper (*Macrosteles fascifrons*). Flowers of infected plants turn yellow and may be smaller than they should be. They may also be aborted entirely. Shoot tips branch abnormally and tend to develop into witches'-brooms.

There is no cure for infected plants; remove and destroy them. Spray remaining plants with a mixture of insecticidal soap and isopropyl alcohol. Make this mix by adding 1 tablespoon of alcohol to each pint of insecticidal soap solution. Spray every three to five days, for three applications, to kill the leafhoppers that carry the disease. The virus overwinters in various perennials and weeds such as daisies, plantain, and gaillardia. Infected plants are not necessarily killed by the disease, but should be dug up and destroyed, since they continue to infect nearby plants via leafhoppers.

Plants Wilt and Die

Club Root

Club root (*Plasmodiophora brassicae*) is a fungal disease that prevents plant root systems from developing, causing plants to wilt and die. There is no cure for infected plants, which should be dug and destroyed. Move remaining healthy alyssum plantings to other parts of the landscape, for the fungus enters the soil from decayed abnormal growths of infected plants. Avoid planting where cabbage, turnips, and other cole crops have been grown previously unless the soil is first pasteurized or well limed. Dig and destroy weeds in the mustard family, such as shepherd's purse and wild mustard, which also can be infected.

Seedlings Rot at Base, Fall Over

Damping-Off

Seedling stems that are water soaked and blackened at the soil line have been afflicted with damping-off. Affected stems are unable to support the plants, which fall over and die. Usually, the foliage is still green and healthy looking when the plants collapse. Stems of older plants show tan to reddish brown lesions that eventually girdle stems. Damping-off is caused by soil-dwelling fungi such as *Pythium*, *Fusarium*, *Sclerotium*, and *Rhizoctonia*, and it usually occurs in seedlings in greenhouses or on windowsills. Germinating alyssum seeds may be attacked before they emerge from the soil, or shortly thereafter.

Cultural controls are effective in preventing damping-off. Sow seed in well-drained soil, do not overcrowd plants, and keep soil on the dry side. Thin seedlings so they are far enough apart to allow air to circulate between them, which will carry away excessive moisture and reduce humidity. When thinning, use scissors instead of pulling up plants to avoid damaging the roots and stems of remaining plants, which might open them up to infection. In the greenhouse, a fan will promote air circulation. Avoid feeding seedlings too much nitrogen, for it causes lank, weak growth. Routinely disinfect garden tools in boiling water or household bleach solution (1 part bleach to 3 parts water) to discourage disease problems.

Leaves with Pale Patches Above, Mildew Beneath; Foliage Wilts

Downy Mildew

A downy mildew caused by the fungus *Peronospora parasitica* occasionally causes pale areas on upper leaf surfaces and gray, white, or purplish "downy" patches on undersides. Leaves eventually wilt and die. The fungus spreads most quickly on moist leaf and stem surfaces and is especially active in periods of cool, wet nights and warm, humid days.

Cultural controls are very effective. Plant alyssum on well-drained, fertile soil, water early on sunny days, avoid overcrowding, and try to avoid wetting the foliage when watering. Dig up heavily infected plants, together with adjacent soil, and discard them; do not compost. Spray lightly infected plants with wettable sulfur, or apply bordeaux mixture or another copper fungicide when downy mildew first appears on leaves. (Watch for leaf discoloration when using the bordeaux mixture.) Several applications may be needed to stop the spread of the fungus.

Leaves with Pale Yellow Spots Above, Powdery Spots Beneath

White Rust

Plants infected with white rust, caused by the fungus *Albugo candida,* have pale yellow spots on upper leaf surfaces. Smooth, white pustules or spots develop beneath the leaves and produce white clouds of spores. The fungus causes stems and flowers to be seriously deformed.

In mild cases, pick and destroy infected leaves. Remove and destroy heavily infected plants. If rust is a severe problem in your garden, start several weeks before rust normally appears and apply wettable sulfur to vulnerable plants every four to five days for three applications. Preventive measures

are helpful in avoiding this problem. Before plants start to grow in the spring, clean up all garden debris from the previous season. Control weeds in and around the yard, especially mustard family members, such as shepherd's purse and wild mustard, which also can be infected. To ensure good ventilation, space plants far enough apart so that air can circulate between them. Also, avoid wetting the foliage when watering.

Lower Leaves Rot; Stem Tips Die

Wilt

If the lower leaves on your sweet alyssum plants wilt during wet weather, they are probably infected with a wilt disease caused by the fungus *Pellicularia filamentosa.* A telltale cobweblike mycelium develops between the leaves, which then shrivel and die. Stems above the site of the infection wilt and die.

Remove and discard infected plants, together with the soil immediately adjacent to them. Do not grow alyssum year after year in the same soil; rotate plantings and change seedbeds, if possible. Sterilize tools between cuts with 70 percent rubbing alcohol to avoid spreading the fungus.

ANNUAL *Aster, Annual*   *Callistephus chinensis*

DESCRIPTION

These showy flowers from the Orient, also called China asters, belong to the daisy family, Compositae. They produce single or double blooms that may resemble daisies, fully double chrysanthemums, or small pompons and come in a wide range of colors.

All make fine, long-lasting cut flowers. Dwarf cultivars, useful for pot culture or as edging plants, also are available. In addition, annual asters are used in beds or borders and can be grown in greenhouses. Annual asters have a reputation for being difficult to grow, but new disease-resistant cultivars have been developed, making them excellent plants to consider for the garden.

Height

3 feet; dwarf cultivars, 6 to 12 inches

Spread

12 to 15 inches

Blossoms

Annual asters bear flowers in a wide variety of colors, including pale and deep pink, rose red, lavender-blue, purple, white, yellow, and cream. Many have contrasting yellow centers. Depending on the cultivar, flower heads are 2 to 5 inches across. Asters do not bloom continuously throughout the season. Instead, each plant usually flowers for about a month and then does not bloom again. Since there are early-, midseason, and late-blooming cultivars, however, it is possible to have asters in bloom from early to late summer. Select cultivars from each bloom period or sow seed at two-week intervals for the longest season of bloom. Plants will not rebloom once cut.

Foliage

Annual asters have somewhat oval, dark green leaves that are irregularly toothed.

ENVIRONMENT

Hardiness

Asters are tender annuals that will not tolerate frost.

Light

Plants perform best in full sun, but will tolerate light shade.

Soil

Asters prefer deep, sandy, fertile soil, but are fairly tolerant and will grow in most soils, provided they are well drained. The pH can range from mildly acidic to mildly alkaline.

PLANTING AND PROPAGATION

Planting

Seed can be sown indoors or out. Outdoors, sow

seed in a prepared seedbed where the plants are to grow after danger of frost has passed. For earlier bloom, sow seed indoors six to eight weeks before the last frost date. Seedlings sown indoors will appear in 10 to 14 days, and 70°F is the best soil temperature for germination. Don't be upset with a low germination rate; a 70 percent germination rate is common. Transplant seedlings to the garden when all danger of frost has passed and night temperatures remain warm. Space transplants 6 to 18 inches apart, depending on the height of the plants at maturity. Pinch them back in June to encourage bushiness. Asters do not transplant well; avoid moving them. Do not plant annual asters in the same place two years in a row to avoid disease problems. Do not grow asters near pot marigolds (*Calendula* spp.) for the same reason. To extend the blooming season, sow seed every other week for two or three weeks.

Container Gardening

Asters are only marginally successful in containers because they need cool soil. Use deep containers and cool, airy locations—indoors or out. Choose dwarf cultivars such as 'Pinocchio' for best success in containers.

PLANT MANAGEMENT

General Care

Once annual aster blooms are cut, the plants will not flower again, so make successive plantings about every two weeks to provide cut flowers over a long season. They are also shallow-rooted plants that prefer cool soil. Mulch plants to keep the soil cool and retain moisture. Plant asters in different locations in consecutive years to discourage soil-borne fungus diseases.

Water

Annual asters need at least 1 inch of water every week from rain or by watering.

Feeding

A spring application of compost or a slow-acting, general-purpose fertilizer will serve the basic needs of annual asters all season. For exceptional performance, give plants supplemental, light feedings (side-dressings or foliar spray) monthly throughout the growing season.

Cutting Fresh Flowers

Annual asters make fine, long-lived cut flowers.

Drying Flowers

Annual asters air dry well if they are fresh when the drying process begins.

MOST COMMON INSECT PESTS

In addition to the pests listed below, annual asters are sometimes infested with thrips, which cause flowers and foliage that are silvery or covered with whitish flecks, as well as whiteflies, caterpillars, and leafrollers.

Pale or Yellow Spots on Leaves, Leaves Curled and Distorted

Aphids

Plants infested with aphids have distorted growth that may be curled, puckered, or stunted. Leaves may turn yellow or brown, and feeding can seriously damage flower buds or cause distorted flowers. Plants may also wilt under bright sunlight. Aphids are soft-bodied, pear-shaped sucking insects about the size of the head of a pin; they may be brown, green, yellow, or nearly black. They are often found clustered under leaves, and flower buds and stem tips may be covered with dense colonies of these insects. Ants, attracted by the aphids' honeydew secretions, wander over the plants, and black, sooty mold can develop on the honeydew as well. In addition to the damage they cause by feeding, aphids are important vectors of virus diseases. Several species of aphids infest annual asters, including potato aphid (*Macrosiphum euphorbiae*), crescent-marked lily aphid (*Neomyzus circumflexus*), green peach aphid (*Myzus persicae*), and melon aphid (*Aphis gossypii*). Several beneficial insects feed on aphids, including ladybugs and lacewings.

Light infestations of aphids can be controlled by washing the plants, especially the undersides of the leaves. For best results, use a forceful spray of water once every other day to knock the aphids off the plants; wash the plants at least three times. If that is not effective, spray the plants with insecticidal soap every three to five days for two weeks. If these pests become a very serious problem, make two applications of pyrethrum, three to five days apart.

Holes in Leaves and/or Flowers

Beetles

Several species of beetles chew holes in aster foliage and flowers. Japanese beetles (*Popillia japonica*), which skeletonize aster leaves and destroy their flowers, are ½-inch-long beetles that are shiny, metallic green with copper-colored wing covers. Asiatic garden beetles (*Maladera castanea*), which also attack asters, are ½-inch-long, cinnamon brown beetles that feed only at night. Black blister beetles (*Epicauta pennsylvanica*) are black, ½-inch-long insects that also feed on flowers and leaves. The larvae of these three beetles are C-shaped, grayish white grubs with dark brown heads that can eat plant roots. Fully grown grubs are ¾ to 1 inch long.

Aster leaves perforated with dozens or hundreds of tiny holes may be victims of the potato flea beetle (*Epitrix cucumeris*). These shiny black or brown pests are only $1/16$ inch long and very active, jumping like fleas when disturbed. Flea beetles, which are especially a problem on younger plants, transmit viral and bacterial diseases. They overwinter as adults and generally feed on weeds in early spring, then move to the garden. The larvae are tiny grubs that feed on plant roots.

For the most part, all beetles are controlled the same way. Where possible, handpick and crush them or drop them into a pail of soapy water. (Wear gloves if you suspect you have blister beetles, for they can cause blisters if they are crushed on skin.) If the infestation is light, this is all you will need to do. For heavier infestations, spray infested plants with a solution of pyrethrum and isopropyl alcohol, mixing 1 tablespoon of alcohol with every pint of diluted pyrethrum mixture. Apply this solution every three to five days until the problem is corrected. Barriers such as floating row covers, like Reemay, can also be used to prevent beetles from gaining access to asters. For long-term control, apply milky spore disease (*Bacillus popilliae*) to lawns and garden. It will kill the larvae of most beetles. Beneficial nematodes introduced into the soil will take care of the flea beetle larvae.

Japanese beetles can also be controlled by pheromone traps. Set up traps a week before the beetles are expected to emerge in your area, making sure traps are no closer than 50 feet from the asters or any other plant vulnerable to beetle attack, such as roses.

Sawdust Exudes from Stems; Stems Break Off; Leaves Wilt

Borers

If aster stems break and leaves wilt, look closely for small, round holes in the stems, from which borers may have expelled their castings. Stalk borer (*Papaipema nebris*) and European corn borer (*Ostrinia nubilalis*) both attack asters. Stalk borer is a long, slender caterpillar marked with a dark brown or purple band around the middle and several conspicuous stripes running the length of the body. Adults are grayish brown moths. European corn borer larvae are pinkish caterpillars with two rows of dark spots down the sides. Adults are yellow-brown moths with dark wavy bands on the wings.

Preventive measures are most effective when dealing with these pests, since by the time symptoms occur, it is usually too late to save the plant.

Clean up all weeds, and cut and burn any plant stalks that may harbor overwintering eggs or pupae. Rotating the location of your aster plantings can also help control this pest. Bt (*Bacillus thuringiensis*) is effective if applied early in the season just as the borers are entering the plants. Borer infestations also can be controlled by slitting each affected stem lengthwise, removing the borers, and binding the stems together, but this is tedious work if you have a large planting.

Seedlings Severed at Base

Cutworms

If your aster seedlings look as though they have been leveled by a lawn mower, you may have cutworms. These pests sever the stems of seedlings and transplants at or below the soil surface, leaving the tops to die. (In contrast, slugs and snails completely consume seedlings, leaving only their slimy trails.) They are most active at night. Cutworms also can harm plant root systems, damage that causes the plant to wilt and collapse. Cutworms are generally plump, soft-bodied caterpillars that are dull grayish or brownish and measure 1 to 2 inches long. They feed at night and hide in the soil during the day. The adults are night-flying moths.

Prevention is the only way to fight cutworms, for once they have cut down a young plant, there is nothing you can do to save it. Protect individual seedlings with a 3-inch collar made from stiff paper or plastic. Push the collar an inch or so into the ground. Or make a trap by sprinkling ½ teaspoon of cornmeal or bran meal around each plant. Spread it in a circle leading away from the stem of the plant. The cutworm eats the meal and dies. Beneficial nematodes added to the soil are an effective long-term control measure.

Leaves Discolored, Distorted

Leafhoppers

Suspect aster leafhoppers (*Macrosteles fascifrons*) if aster leaves are finely mottled with white or yellow spots and the leaves eventually shrivel and drop off. Leafhoppers are tiny, ⅛-inch-long insects that are greenish yellow marked with six black spots. Nymphs are grayish. These pests spread aster yellows disease, which they pick up in spring when feeding on infected wild plants.

To control serious infestations, spray infested plants with a mixture of insecticidal soap and isopropyl alcohol. Make this mix by adding 1 tablespoon of alcohol to each pint of insecticidal soap solution. Spray at three- to five-day intervals, making three applications. If leafhoppers are a common problem in your backyard, place a barrier such as floating row covers, like Reemay, over plants in early spring. Also, apply preventive sprays of insecticidal soap solution or pyrethrum at four- or five-day intervals for the first month of growth.

Plants Stunted;
Leaves Yellowed and Small;
Knots on Roots

Nematodes

Plants infested with nematodes look sickly, wilted, or stunted and have yellowed or bronzed foliage. Their root systems are poorly developed, may have tiny galls or knots on them, and can even be partially decayed. Plants decline slowly and die. Southern root knot nematodes (*Meloidogyne incognita*) attack annual asters. Nematodes are not insects, but slender, unsegmented roundworms that are barely visible to the unaided eye.

Prevention is the best way to deal with nematodes when growing annuals in infested soil, since severely infested annuals are best dug up and destroyed; do not compost. Organic matter in the soil helps to control nematodes because it not only benefits the fungi and bacteria that feed on them, it also keeps plants healthy and better able to withstand mild infestations. Add lots of compost, especially leaf mold, to the bed before planting. Turn severely infested plots over to a thick planting of French marigolds for an entire season and dig the plant remains into the soil at season's end to discourage these pests. Crop rotation is also a good idea; don't grow susceptible plants on the same plot year after year.

Plants Stunted and Wilted; Foliage Yellowed

Root Aphids

If your annual asters seem to stop growing and leaves mysteriously turn yellow and wilt under bright sunlight, suspect root aphids. Root aphids are soft-bodied, pear-shaped insects about the size of the head of a pin. They are generally white or blue-green in color. The corn root aphid (*Aphis maidi-radicis*) is the most serious root aphid attacking annual asters. Small, brown ants collect aphid eggs in fall and carry young aphids to plants to feed in spring. Throughout the summer, the ants carry aphids from plant to plant while feeding on the honeydew produced by the aphids.

The only way to effectively control root aphids is to control the ants that shepherd them. Root aphids can sometimes be prevented by adding a small amount of wood ashes in the planting holes when you set the asters out in the spring. Thorough spading in the fall disturbs ant nests that house caches of aphid eggs. Once a bed has been infested with root aphids, replant the following year with plants that are not as susceptible.

Flowers Deformed and Dwarfed

Tarnished Plant Bugs

If the young shoots, and especially buds, of your asters are deformed or the flowers are dwarfed, look for tarnished plant bugs (*Lygus rugulipennis*). These active, ¼-inch-long bugs are green to brown in color and mottled with white, yellow, and black. On either side of the insect near the back is a yellow triangle with a black dot at one corner. Tarnished plant bugs appear in early spring, and, if left uncontrolled, become increasingly numerous toward the end of summer. They feed by sucking sap from plants and also release a toxin when feeding that can deform foliage and shoots.

Preventive measures are the best way to con-trol this pest. Adults overwinter in weeds, as well as under leaves and other garden debris. Thoroughly clean up the garden in spring and fall to discourage overwintering adults. Handpicking adults and nymphs and dropping them into a jar of soapy water is also effective if the infestation isn't too great. If that is not effective, spray the plants with insecticidal soap every three to five days for two weeks, or try three applications of pyrethrum laced with isopropyl alcohol, one every three days. Spray early in the morning when bugs are least active. If the infestation is heavy, dust plants with sabadilla.

MOST COMMON DISEASES

In addition to the diseases listed below, annual asters are occasionally infected with rust, which causes bright yellow spots on young growth. They can also develop cankers, which cause stems to fall over.

Flowers and Foliage Greenish Yellow, Deformed; Shoots Spindly

Aster Yellows

If the leaves of your asters are greenish yellow and spindly, and growth is stunted or dwarfed, they may be infected with aster yellows, a disease caused by a viruslike organism primarily spread by the aster leafhopper (*Macrosteles fascifrons*). Next to wilt, aster yellows is the most destructive disease of asters. Young plants that are infected show a slight yellowing along leaf veins. As the disease becomes more severe, the entire plant is stunted and yellowed, and the unusual number of shoots that develop cause the plant to become very bushy and upright. Shoot tips branch abnormally and tend to develop into witches'-brooms; secondary shoots are usually spindly. Flowers are curiously deformed and may be aborted entirely. Regardless of the normal bloom color of the cultivar, flowers are often sickly yellow green.

There is no cure for infected plants; remove

and destroy them. Spray remaining plants with a mixture of insecticidal soap and isopropyl alcohol. Make this mix by adding 1 tablespoon of alcohol to each pint of insecticidal soap solution. Spray at three- to five-day intervals, making three applications, to kill the leafhoppers that carry the disease. The virus overwinters in various perennials and weeds such as daisies, plantain, and gaillardia. Infected plants are not necessarily killed by the disease, but should be dug up and destroyed, since they continue to infect nearby plants via leafhoppers.

Seedlings Rot at Base, Fall Over

Damping-Off

Seedling stems that are water soaked and blackened at the soil line have been afflicted with damping-off. Affected stems are unable to support the plants, which fall over and die. Usually, the foliage is still green and healthy looking when the plants collapse. Stems of older plants show tan to reddish brown lesions that eventually girdle stems. Damping-off is caused by soil-dwelling fungi such as *Pythium*, *Fusarium*, *Sclerotium*, and *Rhizoctonia*, and it usually occurs in seedlings in greenhouses or on windowsills. Germinating aster seeds may be attacked before they emerge from the soil, or shortly thereafter.

Cultural controls are effective in preventing damping-off. Sow seed in well-drained soil, do not overcrowd plants, and keep soil on the dry side. Outdoors, plant your asters in well-drained soil or raised beds. Indoors, sow seed in sterile growing mix (peat moss, perlite, and vermiculite, with a topping of milled sphagnum moss), and water plants from below by setting pots in water and allowing the water to soak up to just beneath the soil surface. Thin seedlings so they are far enough apart to allow air to circulate between them, which will carry away excessive moisture and reduce humidity. When thinning, use scissors instead of pulling up plants to avoid damaging the roots and stems of remaining plants, which might open them up to infection. In the greenhouse, a fan will promote air circulation. Avoid feeding seedlings too much nitrogen, for it

causes lank, weak growth. Routinely disinfect garden tools in boiling water or a household bleach solution (1 part bleach to 3 parts water) to discourage disease problems.

Plants Covered with Tangled Mass of Thin Stems

Dodder

If your asters seem to be choked by a mass of thin, leafless stems that climb or twine and are pale yellowish or yellow in color, they are probably infested with dodder (*Cuscuta* spp.). Although it looks something like a fungus, dodder actually is a parasitic seed plant related to morning-glories. It feeds entirely off the host plant by means of tiny suckers and covers its victims with twining stems.

Dodder cannot be controlled by hand-pulling; infested plants must be dug and destroyed. If you see dodder early in the season, before seeds form, cut out and destroy affected plant parts along with the dodder. Seed can ripen as early as April. Dodder overwinters in fields, often on members of the daisy (Compositae) or pea (Leguminosae) families. Cultivate open ground repeatedly over several weeks to allow dodder seeds to sprout and die.

Leaves Covered with Dark Spots or Blotches

Leaf Spot

Several different kinds of fungi cause unsightly spots on aster foliage. Leaves may have transparent or brown or black spots. Some fungal spots are surrounded by flecks or black dots, which are the spore-bearing fruiting bodies. Often spots come together to form larger patches of dead tissue. These fungi thrive on moist leaf surfaces.

To control leaf spot, pick off and destroy infected leaves. Also, regularly clean up and destroy dead plant debris in the garden to reduce spore populations. These fungi overwinter as spores in such debris, so an end-of-season cleanup is especially important. Pull up and discard seriously infected plants, together with the soil in which they are growing. A layer of mulch helps prevent spores from splashing from the soil onto plants. If leaf spot is a particular problem in your area, spray at weekly to ten-day intervals with wettable sulfur or bordeaux mixture, particularly in rainy seasons. (Watch for leaf discoloration with the latter.)

Moldy Coating on Leaves and/or Flowers

Molds or Mildews

Several different fungi cause grayish or white molds or powdery coverings on aster flowers and foliage. As its name suggests, gray mold (caused by the fungus *Botrytis cinerea*) causes a gray coating on leaves and flowers. Infected plant parts give off a cloud of white spores when picked. Gray mold generally attacks petals first, but quickly rots the entire flower and spreads to leaves and stems. Primarily a problem in cool, wet weather, it is further encouraged by poor ventilation or insufficient light.

A downy mildew caused by the fungus *Basidiophora entospora* occasionally causes pale areas on upper leaf surfaces and gray, white, or purplish "downy" patches on undersides. Unlike powdery mildew (below), which causes a white, powderlike growth on the surface of the leaves, downy mildew grows deep into plant tissue and only sticks its spore-bearing stalks above the leaf surface. This fungal disease, most common in the Deep South, spreads most quickly on moist leaf and stem surfaces and is especially active in periods of cool, wet nights and warm, humid days. Leaves eventually wilt and die.

A powdery mildew caused by the fungus *Erysiphe cichoracearum* causes a whitish dust or bloom that is primarily on the surface of leaves but can also infect flowers. Infected leaves are often curled or distorted, and the growth of severely infected plants can be stunted. Powdery mildew most commonly develops on asters grown close together in ornamental plantings, especially on the lower leaves where moisture is more abundant.

Cultural controls are a very effective way to deal with molds and mildews. Plant asters in a location that affords plenty of ventilation and sunlight. Choose a location with well-drained, fertile soil, water early on sunny days, allow ample spacing between plants, and try to avoid wetting the foliage when watering. Unless the season is unusually humid, these precautions should save you from most problems with molds and mildews. Pick and destroy infected leaves and stems; dig up heavily infected plants, together with adjacent soil, and discard them; do not compost. Collect and discard all aboveground refuse in the fall. Spray infected plants once or twice at weekly intervals with wettable sulfur, bordeaux mixture, or another copper fungicide when molds or mildews first appear on leaves. (Watch for leaf discoloration when using bordeaux mixture.) Several applications may be needed to stop the spread of the fungus.

Plants Either Wilt Suddenly or Turn Yellow and Wilt Slowly

Wilt

Young aster plants that wilt suddenly and seem to have rotted roots have been stricken with wilt, caused by the fungus *Fusarium oxysporum* forma *callistephi*. Older, flowering-size plants first turn pale yellow-green and then wilt slowly, beginning with the lower leaves. The fungus attacks and rots plant roots, which causes wilting of the plant above. A close examination of the stems of afflicted plants will reveal pale pink fungal spores covering the stem at or below ground level. The fungus overwinters as spores in the soil.

Similar symptoms are caused by another fungus, *Phytophthora cryptogea*. Commonly called root rot, this disease not surprisingly rots roots and stems, giving them a black, water-soaked appearance. Infected plants are not covered with the pink spores characterized by wilt.

Wilt-resistant annual asters are now available, and these cultivars are able to grow and bloom even in infected soil. Since even these cultivars are not completely immune, and they are not generally resistant to root rot, preventive measures to combat these diseases are in order. They are essential for success with any cultivars that are not resistant to wilt. Remove and discard plants showing any sign of infection, along with the nearby soil. Discard the debris; do not compost. Do not grow asters continuously in the same soil; rotate plantings and change seedbeds, if possible. Control weeds in and around the garden. If space is limited and the same soil must be used yearly, steam pasteurize infested soil before reusing, or plant resistant aster selections. Do not propagate from infected plants. The fungus is even carried on seed. Sterilize tools between cuts with 70 percent rubbing alcohol.

ANNUAL *Bachelor's Buttons*

Centaurea spp.

DESCRIPTION

The popular bachelor's button or cornflower, *Centaurea cyanus,* is an annual grown for its brilliant blue blossoms, although it comes in other colors as well. Native to southern Europe, it is an old-fashioned favorite used in nosegays, bouquets, and as cut flowers. Basket flower (*C. americana*), also an annual, is native to North America. Both species are grown in beds, borders, and wildflower meadows, especially in areas with cool summers. *Centaurea* spp. are members of the daisy family, Compositae.

Height

C. americana (basket flower), 4 to 6 feet

C. cyanus (bachelor's button or cornflower), 1 to 2½ feet

Spread

1 to 2 feet

Blossoms

Centaurea spp. bloom for much of the summer, roughly from June to September, performing best in areas with cool summers. Both bear daisylike heads of flowers that consist of a row or rows of showy petal-like ray florets that are notched at the tip, giving the blooms a somewhat shaggy appearance, surrounding smaller disc florets. Bachelor's button most commonly has bright blue flowers (they are the flowers for which the color "cornflower blue" is named), but cultivars with pink, purplish red, or white flowers also are available. There are both single- and double-flowered forms, and blooms are about 1½ inches wide. Basket flower, whose rose or lilac ray florets surround center disc florets, gets its name because its blooms resemble baskets. Its flower heads are from 4 to 5 inches wide.

Foliage

Both species have green to gray-green leaves that are borne alternately on the stem. The leaves of bachelor's buttons are soft and hairy. Lower leaves, which are divided in a featherlike fashion, are up to 6 inches long; upper leaves are narrow and entire. Basket flowers have narrow to somewhat oval leaves that are about 4 inches long.

ENVIRONMENT

Hardiness

Both species are hardy annuals that will tolerate cool temperatures. They can both reseed themselves annually throughout much of North America.

Light

Both species prefer full sun.

Soil

Both species prefer rich, moist, well-drained soil, but will tolerate poor to ordinary soil. These plants tolerate a pH range from 6 to 8.

PLANTING AND PROPAGATION

Planting

Centaurea spp. are difficult to transplant and are best sown directly in the garden where the plants are to grow. North of USDA Zone 5, sow seed in spring two to three weeks before the last frost date. South of that, seed can be sown in late summer or fall, or in early spring. Cover the seed completely; it requires darkness for germination. Seed will germinate in one to two weeks with soil temperatures of 60° to 70°F. Thin seedlings to 8 to 12 inches apart.

PLANT MANAGEMENT

General Care

These plants are easy to grow and require little care once established. To prolong the blooming period, especially in areas with warm summers, make successive plantings by sowing a few seeds every two to three weeks for a few weeks in early spring. Removing spent flowers will help prolong the blooming period. *Centaurea* spp. are best planted in clumps because they tend to flop over if they are spaced too far apart. Plants arranged in clumps will help hold each other up. Plants grown in less than full sun will need staking.

Water

Both species will grow in dry soils, but regular moisture should help prolong their bloom period. Make sure the plants get a total of 1 inch of water every week from rain or by watering. Water early in the day and avoid overwatering.

Feeding

A single application of compost or a slow-acting, general-purpose fertilizer worked into the seedbed before sowing will serve the basic needs of these annuals all season. They can tolerate poor soils, and heavy feeding results in weak plants with few flowers.

Cutting Fresh Flowers

Centaurea spp. make attractive additions to informal bouquets. Their stems tend to be a bit too flexible and weak for formal arrangements.

Drying Flowers

Freshly opened blooms can be air dried. Cut the stems when the blooms have just opened, remove the leaves, and hang bunches upside down in a dark, dry, warm place. Drying bachelor's buttons in borax or silica gel prevents shrinkage and provides brighter color. The calyxes—the parts remaining after the petals and seeds have dropped—are pretty and starlike, too. Harvest them late in the season by which time they will have dried naturally.

MOST COMMON CULTURAL PROBLEMS

Leggy Plants; Insufficient Flowering

Planted Too Late

Centaurea spp. are happiest in cool weather. Seed sown too late in the season will not develop into sturdy plants because of the hot summer temperatures. Plants will be leggy and generally unhealthy looking, and blooming may be reduced. Plants that are not receiving enough sun also will be leggy.

Seedlings Appear Where They Are Not Wanted

Reseeding

Centaurea spp. can reseed prolifically from year to year, and unexpected seedlings can become a nuisance. Removing the spent flowers before the seed ripens can reduce this problem.

MOST COMMON INSECT PESTS

Centaurea spp. are bothered by few pests and are generally trouble-free additions to the sunny garden. In addition to the insects discussed below, they are occasionally attacked by borers, which cause stems to break and leaves to wilt. If you suspect this pest, look for small, round holes in the stems, from which borers may have expelled their castings. Aster leafhoppers, which cause small white or yellow spots on the leaves, also sometimes infest *Centaurea* spp.

Pale or Yellow Spots on Leaves, Leaves Curled and Distorted

Aphids

Plants infested with aphids have distorted growth that may be curled, puckered, or stunted. Leaves may turn yellow or brown, and feeding can seriously damage flower buds or cause distorted flowers. Plants may also wilt under bright sunlight. Aphids are soft-bodied, pear-shaped sucking insects about the size of the head of a pin; they may be brown, green, yellow, or nearly black. They are often found clustered under leaves, and flower buds and stem tips may be covered with dense colonies of these insects. Ants, attracted by the aphids' honeydew secretions, wander over the plants, and black, sooty mold can develop on the honeydew as well. In addition to the damage they cause by feeding, aphids are important vectors of virus diseases. Several species of aphids infest *Centaurea* spp., including leaf-curl plum aphid (*Brachycaudus helichrysi*). Several beneficial insects feed on aphids, including ladybugs and lacewings.

Light infestations of aphids can be controlled by washing the plants, especially the undersides of the leaves. For best results, use a forceful spray of water once every other day to knock the aphids off the plants; wash the plants at least three times. If that is not effective, spray the plants with insecticidal soap every three to five days for two weeks. If these pests become a very serious problem, make two applications of pyrethrum, three to five days apart.

Seedlings Severed at Base

Cutworms

If your seedlings look as though they have been leveled by a lawn mower, you may have cutworms. These pests sever the stems of seedlings and transplants at or below the soil surface, leaving the tops to die. (In contrast, slugs and snails completely consume seedlings, leaving only slimy trails.) They are most active at night. Cutworms also can harm plant root systems, damage that causes the plant to wilt and collapse. Cutworms are generally plump, soft-bodied caterpillars that are dull grayish or brownish and measure 1 to 2 inches long. They feed at night and hide in the soil during the day. The adults are night-flying moths.

Prevention is the only way to fight cutworms, for once they have cut down a seedling, there is nothing you can do to save it. Protect individual seedlings with a 3-inch collar made from stiff paper or plastic. Push the collar an inch or so into the ground. Or make a trap by sprinkling ½ teaspoon of cornmeal or bran meal around each plant. Spread it in a circle leading away from the stem of the plant. The cutworm eats the meal and dies. Beneficial nematodes added to the soil are an effective long-term control measure.

MOST COMMON DISEASES

Leaves Greenish Yellow, Deformed; Shoots Spindly

Aster Yellows

If the leaves of your plants are greenish yellow and spindly, and growth is stunted or dwarfed, they may be infected with aster yellows, a disease caused by a viruslike organism primarily spread by the aster leafhopper (*Macrosteles fascifrons*). Young plants that are infected show a slight yellowing along leaf veins. As the disease becomes more severe, the entire plant is stunted and yellowed, and the unusual number of shoots that develop cause the plant to become very bushy and upright. Shoot tips branch abnormally and tend to develop into witches'-brooms; secondary shoots are usually spindly. Flowers are deformed and may be aborted entirely. Regardless of the normal bloom color of the cultivar, flowers are often sickly yellow-green.

There is no cure for infected plants; remove and destroy them. Spray remaining plants with a mixture of insecticidal soap and isopropyl alcohol. Make this mix by adding 1 tablespoon of alcohol to each pint of insecticidal soap solution. Spray at three- to five-day intervals, making three applications, to kill the leafhoppers that carry the disease. The virus overwinters in various perennials and weeds such as daisies, plantain, and gaillardia. Infected plants are not necessarily killed by the disease, but should be dug up and destroyed, since they continue to infect nearby plants via leafhoppers.

Leaves with Pale Patches Above, Mildew Beneath; Foliage Wilts

Downy Mildew

A downy mildew caused by the fungus *Bremia lactucae* occasionally causes pale greenish or reddish spots on upper leaf surfaces and gray moldy or "downy" patches on undersides. Leaves eventually wilt and die. The fungus spreads most quickly on moist leaf and stem surfaces and is especially active in periods of cool, wet nights and warm, humid days.

Cultural controls are very effective. Plant *Centaurea* spp. in well-drained, fertile soil, water early on sunny days, avoid overcrowding, and try to avoid wetting the foliage when watering. Dig up heavily infected plants, together with adjacent soil, and discard them; do not compost. Spray lightly infected plants with wettable sulfur, or apply bordeaux mixture or another copper fungicide when downy mildew first appears on leaves. (Watch for leaf discoloration when using the bordeaux mixture.) Several applications may be needed to stop the spread of the fungus.

Foliage Turns Yellow; Plants Wilt and/or Fall Over

Root and Stem Rots

Centaurea spp. infected with stem rot turn yellow, wilt, and die. Root systems and stems rot, causing the plants to topple over. Stem and root rots are caused by a variety of soil-dwelling fungi (including *Pellicularia filamentosa, Phytophthora cactorum, Phymatotrichum omnivorum,* and *Sclerotinia sclerotiorum*) that typically attack stems at or near the soil level.

Preventive measures are the best way to control root and stem rots. Plant *Centaurea* spp. in well-drained soil, avoid overwatering, keep the garden clear of old plant debris, avoid overcrowding the plants, and keep mulch away from the base of plant stems. Remove and discard infected plants, together with the surrounding soil, or cut away affected plant parts with a clean, sharp knife or razor blade. Disinfect these tools with a solution of 1 part household bleach and 3 parts water or 70 percent rubbing alcohol to avoid spreading the disease. For long-term prevention, lighten heavy soil with a mixture of perlite, vermiculite, and/or peat moss, and provide good drainage.

Leaves Pale Yellow Above with Powdery Orange Spots Beneath

Rust

Centaurea spp. that have bright yellow-orange pustules on the undersides of the leaves are infected with rust, a fungal disease caused primarily by *Puccinia cyani* and *P. irrequisita*. In severe cases, leaves and stems can be completely covered by these yellow-orange spots, which contain spores that are spread by the wind.

Remove and destroy infected leaves, or in severe cases entire plants, as soon as possible. Collect and destroy all infected garden debris before growth starts in the spring. Control weeds in and around the garden, for they may also harbor rust fungi. To ensure good ventilation, space plants far enough apart so that air can circulate between them. Also, avoid wetting the foliage when watering. Rust can be prevented by periodic applications of wettable sulfur, begun several weeks before the problem normally appears.

Plants Either Wilt Suddenly or Turn Yellow and Wilt Slowly

Wilt

Young plants that wilt suddenly and seem to have rotted roots have been stricken with wilt, caused by the same fungus that attacks annual asters, *Fusarium oxysporum* forma *callistephi*. Older, flowering-size plants first turn pale yellow-green and then wilt slowly, beginning with the lower leaves. The fungus attacks and rots plant roots, which causes wilting of the plant above. A close examination of the stems of afflicted plants will reveal pale pink fungal spores covering the stem at or below ground level. The fungus overwinters as spores in the soil.

Preventive measures to combat this disease are in order. Remove and discard plants showing any sign of infection, along with the nearby soil. Discard the debris; do not compost. Do not grow *Centaurea* spp. continuously in the same soil; rotate plantings and change seedbeds, if possible. Control weeds in and around the garden. If space is limited and the same soil must be used yearly, steam pasteurize infested soil before reusing, or plant resistant bachelor's button selections. Do not propagate from infected plants. The fungus is even carried on seed. Sterilize tools between cuts with a solution of 1 part household bleach and 3 parts water or 70 percent rubbing alcohol.

Begonia, Wax

Begonia × semperflorens-cultorum

DESCRIPTION

The waxy, succulent leaves and colorful flowers of the popular wax begonia are familiar to beginning and advanced gardeners alike. Adaptable and forgiving plants, they combine a neat, compact habit, attractive flowers and foliage, and trouble-free cultural requirements. Wax begonias are ideal for beds, borders, or containers in sun or shade and are commonly used as edging plants or massed in groups. They also make very satisfactory houseplants, bringing color to your home in the dead of winter.

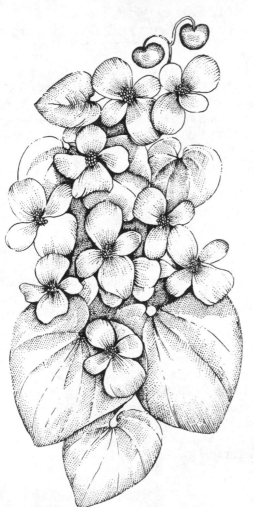

Height

6 to 12 inches

Spread

6 to 12 inches

Blossoms

Wax begonias can have pink, white, or red flowers, and blooms may be single or double. If you look closely, you'll notice that they bear two kinds of flowers on each plant; male blooms sport a bright tuft of yellow pollen at the center, and female flowers have a three-sided ovary behind the petals. The flowers, which have no scent, are about 1 inch across and appear from early summer continuously through to fall frost.

Foliage

Leaves are heart shaped, shiny, and succulent and usually 2 to 4 inches long. The foliage may be bright green, bronzy green, maroon, or variegated with green and white.

ENVIRONMENT

Hardiness

Wax begonias are tender perennials usually grown

as annuals. They will not survive frost. Do not move seedlings to the garden until night temperatures remain above 50°F.

Light

Begonias do best in light shade but will tolerate deep shade, although they may become leggy and will not bloom as vigorously. They will also grow in full sun if the soil is kept moist. Many of the new heat-resistant hybrids are quite tolerant of sunny situations, especially in areas with cool summers. Wax begonias prefer 65°F nights and 75° to 85°F days in summer. Indoors, grow them in a south-facing window in winter for best blooming.

Soil

Begonias like rich, well-drained soil with a pH range of 6 to 8.

PLANTING AND PROPAGATION

Planting

Wax begonia seed must be sown indoors four to six months before the last spring frost date. Sow the very fine, almost powderlike seeds in a sterile growing mix (peat moss, perlite, and vermiculite, with a topping of milled sphagnum moss), and water plants from below to avoid problems with damping-off. Press the seeds into the soil but do not cover them with soil; they require light to germinate. Cover the seed flat with glass or plastic to maintain high humidity. Allow 14 to 20 days for germination. Soil temperatures between 70° and 75°F are ideal.

Because wax begonias take so long to grow from seed, most gardeners prefer to purchase them as bedding plants from local nurseries or garden centers. Do not move begonias to the garden until nighttime temperatures stay above 50°F. Space transplants or nursery stock 8 to 10 inches apart.

Propagation

Wax begonias are easy to propagate by softwood cuttings. Take cuttings from plants brought indoors for winter bloom and root them to produce spring transplants.

Container Gardening

Begonias take to containers. Outdoors, they are staples in window boxes and patio planters.

PLANT MANAGEMENT

General Care

Although a variety of insects and diseases have been found on these popular annuals, few are serious, for wax begonias are virtually trouble-free, easy-to-grow plants that require only minimum attention. Plants in shady spots occasionally become leggy and benefit from pinching back. Under most conditions, insects and diseases that may infest these lovely plants will not hamper their performance.

Overwintering

To move wax begonias indoors, dig and pot them up just before the first fall frost. To promote bushy growth and new flowers and help plants ajust to the shock of transplanting, pinch back the stems by at least half. Or, take cuttings of the best plants in your garden and root them. Give them full winter sun, water when the soil becomes dry, and keep temperatures on the cool side, but above 50°F for best growth.

Water

Make sure the plants get 1 inch of water every week from rain or by watering, but try to allow the soil to dry out slightly between waterings for best results.

Feeding

A single application of compost or a slow-acting, general-purpose fertilizer worked into the soil before planting will serve the basic needs of these annuals all season. For exceptional performance, give your plants supplemental, light feedings (side-dressings or foliar spray) monthly throughout the growing season.

Cutting Fresh Flowers

Although not commonly used as cut flowers, stems are attractive in small vases. Remove any leaves that would be below the water line. These stems will often root in water.

MOST COMMON CULTURAL PROBLEMS

Buds Drop Off

Poor Drainage; High Temperatures
If flower buds drop off before they open, it is usually a sign that the plants are growing in poorly drained soil, or that they have received too much rain or watering. This does not mean that the soil should not be watered, for dried out soil also can cause dropped buds. The best way to prevent such problems is to add plenty of well-composted organic material to the soil. This vital addition will allow the soil to soak up more water and nutrients while enabling it to drain well.

Begonias exposed to high temperatures for extended periods of time also will sometimes drop flower buds. For this reason, begonias grow best if they are not exposed to hot, midday sun. During hot spells, mist plants in the late morning and, if possible, water at noon to cool the roots. Mulch also helps keep the roots cool.

Excessive Foliage; Few Flowers

Too Much Nitrogen; Improper Planting Location
Begonias that have many more leaves than flowers may have received too much nitrogen, which encourages foliage growth at the expense of flowers. This is especially common if plants are growing along the edge of a lawn that has been fed with a high-nitrogen lawn fertilizer. Water generously for a few days to wash through excess fertilizer. Do not fertilize for the rest of the season.

Wax begonias that are growing in deep shade also will produce foliage at the expense of flowers. Under such conditions, they also will become leggy and may flop over.

MOST COMMON INSECT PESTS

Begonias are seldom seriously bothered by insect pests. Slugs and snails occasionally may eat the foliage. Plants grown indoors, in greenhouses, or in the Deep South or Southwest can be infested with mealybugs, spider mites, scale, and thrips.

MOST COMMON DISEASES

Wax begonias are nearly as disease-free as they are insect-free. In addition to the two problems listed below, various fungi may cause leaf spots, which can be controlled by handpicking infected foliage, and in very humid areas, powdery mildew may occur. Neither problem is particularly serious, however.

Seedlings Rot at Base, Fall Over

Damping-Off
Seedling stems that are water soaked and blackened at the soil line have been afflicted with damping-off. Affected stems are unable to support the plants, which fall over and die. Usually, the foliage is still green and healthy looking when the plants collapse. Stems of older plants show tan to reddish brown lesions that eventually girdle stems. Damping-off is caused by soil-dwelling fungi such as *Pythium, Fusarium, Sclerotium,* and *Rhizoctonia,* and it usually occurs in seedlings in greenhouses or on windowsills. Germinating begonia seeds may be attacked before they emerge from the soil, or shortly thereafter.

Cultural controls are effective in preventing damping-off. Sow seed in well-drained soil, do not overcrowd plants, and keep soil on the dry side. Use a sterile growing mix (peat moss, perlite, and vermiculite, with a topping of milled sphagnum moss), and water plants from below by setting pots in water and allowing the water to soak up to just beneath the soil surface. Thin seedlings so they are far enough apart to allow air to circulate between them, which will carry away excessive moisture and reduce humidity. When thinning, use scissors instead of pulling up plants to avoid damaging the roots and stems of remaining plants, which might open them up to infection. In the greenhouse, a fan will promote air circulation. Avoid feeding seedlings too much nitrogen, for it causes lank, weak growth. Routinely disinfect garden tools in boiling water or household bleach solution (1 part bleach to 3 parts water) to discourage disease problems.

Roots and Stems Turn Black and Rot

Stem Rot

Wax begonias are occasionally attacked by a stem rot caused by *Pythium ultimum*. Stems of infected plants rot at the base and subsequently collapse.

Preventive measures are very helpful in controlling this problem. Plant wax begonias in well-drained soil, avoid overwatering, avoid overcrowding the plants, and keep mulch away from the base of plant stems. Remove and discard infected plants, together with the surrounding soil, or cut away affected plant parts with a clean, sharp knife or razor blade. (Cuttings taken from the tops of afflicted stems are generally healthy and can be used to propagate plants stricken with stem rot.) Do not compost infected plants or soil; discard them. Disinfect tools with a solution of 1 part household bleach and 3 parts water or 70 percent rubbing alcohol after use to avoid spreading the disease. For long-term prevention, lighten heavy soil with a mixture of perlite, vermiculite, and/or peat moss, and provide good drainage.

ANNUAL *Black-Eyed Susan* *Rudbeckia hirta*

DESCRIPTION

The black-eyed Susans grown in gardens today are descendants of midwestern wildflowers. They are biennials or short-lived perennials that bloom so reliably the first year from seed that they are often treated as annuals. The traditional black-eyed Susans bear charming, daisylike flowers with the brown centers and a single row of orange-yellow petals. The blooms of 'Gloriosa Daisy' and 'Double Gloriosa Daisy' bear orange-yellow petals marked with bronze red or maroon at the center. Black-eyed Susans are a staple of summer borders and look best planted in masses behind groups of smaller flowers. They are stunning in a bed all by themselves and are excellent candidates for cutting.

Height

2 to 3 feet

Spread

2 to 2½ feet

Blossoms

Black-eyed Susans bear 2- to 3-inch flowers that are golden yellow and often marked with bronze, deep orange, or mahogany. Blooms have brown centers, and there are semidouble- and double-flowered cultivars available. The plants will bloom from summer into the fall.

Foliage

Leaves and stems are coarse, somewhat hairy, and green in color. Leaves at the top of the plant are narrow and pointed; the basal leaves are somewhat oval shaped and may be toothed toward the tip.

ENVIRONMENT

Hardiness

Black-eyed Susans are heat-loving biennials or perennials grown as half-hardy annuals. They will withstand some frost.

Light

For best bloom, grow black-eyed Susans in full sun, although they will tolerate light shade.

Soil

Although black-eyed Susans will tolerate poor, dry soil, they grow best in rich, well-drained soil high in organic matter. The pH can range from 6 to 8.

PLANTING AND PROPAGATION

Planting

For flowers the first year from seed, sow seed indoors in late winter six to eight weeks before the last frost date. Seeds will germinate in five to ten days. Transplant seedlings to the garden after danger of frost has passed, spacing them 1 to 2 feet apart. Seed can also be sown outdoors in very early spring as soon as the soil can be worked where the plants are to grow or in late summer or fall for bloom the following year. These plants self-sow heavily, so you can expect them to return year after year.

PLANT MANAGEMENT

General Care

Once established, black-eyed Susans require little regular care to keep them performing at their peak. Tall cultivars, or those grown singly instead of in large clumps, may need some staking. Remove faded blooms to encourage continuous bloom.

Water

Black-eyed Susans will withstand drought, but for best bloom, keep the soil moderately moist. Make sure the plants get 1 inch of water every week from rain or by watering.

Feeding

An application of compost or a slow-acting, general-purpose fertilizer in the spring will serve the basic needs of black-eyed Susans all season long.

Cutting Fresh Flowers

Black-eyed Susans make excellent cut flowers. They are standouts in informal bouquets.

Drying Flowers

Blooms can be air dried. To air dry, cut the blooms when they are at their peak, remove the foliage, and hang them upside down in a warm, dark, dry place.

MOST COMMON CULTURAL PROBLEMS

Seedlings Appear Where They Are Not Wanted

Reseeding

Black-eyed Susans can reseed prolifically from year to year, and unexpected seedlings can become a nuisance. Picking or deadheading the flowers before they go to seed can reduce this problem.

MOST COMMON INSECT PESTS

Black-eyed Susans are seldom bothered by insect pests, and infestations seldom affect the color they lend to massed displays. If you are trying to grow perfect specimens for use as cut flowers, however, watch for and take precautions to prevent insect attacks. Aphids can infest black-eyed Susans; they gather on stem tips to suck juices from buds and new leaves. Beetles and caterpillars also chew holes in flowers and foliage.

MOST COMMON DISEASES

Black-eyed Susans are as disease-free as they are insect-free. Although fungi occasionally cause leaf spots or rust on the foliage, these diseases are seldom serious enough to warrant control measures. In addition to the disease listed below, these plants are also sometimes afflicted by stem or crown rot. These fungal diseases are especially a problem when plants are grown in soil that is not well-drained.

White Powder Covering Leaves

Powdery Mildew

In late summer, black-eyed Susan foliage can become covered with powdery mildew, a whitish dust or bloom on leaves and flowers. Caused by the fungus *Erysiphe cichoracearum*, powdery mildew develops in hot, humid weather. It is especially a problem on the lower leaves of plants grown close together. Badly infected leaves become discolored, distorted, and drop off.

Powdery mildew most commonly develops on plants grown close together where air circulation is restricted, especially on the lower leaves where humidity is higher and moisture is more abundant. Allow ample spacing between plants, and collect and discard all aboveground refuse in the fall. Spray affected plants thoroughly with wettable sulfur once or twice at weekly intervals starting as soon as the whitish coating of the fungus is visible.

ANNUAL Cockscomb *Celosia cristata*

DESCRIPTION

Cockscomb, a showy annual from the tropics, is a species that produces two different types of unique-looking flowers in a variety of brilliant colors. At first glance, the blooms of the two different forms of cockscomb look completely unrelated. Crested or true cockscomb, *Celosia cristata,* bears crested or rolled blooms that resemble roosters' combs. Plumed or feather cockscomb (*C. argentea plumosa*), as its name suggests, bears fluffy, plumelike flower clusters. Both provide a long season of color in the garden and can be used in beds or borders. *C. cristata,* because of its unusual blooms, is used as an accent plant as well. Both make excellent cut or dried flowers.

Height

15 to 36 inches; dwarf cultivars, 6 to 10 inches

Spread

10 to 18 inches

Blossoms

Cockscombs bloom from early summer through to fall frost, or roughly June to October. Their spectacular blooms actually consist of thousands of minute flowers packed onto dense spikes. The blooms of *C. cristata* are rounded and compact, often with convoluted indentations on the velvety surfaces. These unusual blossoms can be as much as 6 inches wide and 12 inches long. *C. argentea plumosa* have plume-shaped blooms with a silky or featherlike texture. Plumes are from 6 to 12 inches tall. Both forms come in yellow, orange, red, apricot, pink, and maroon.

Foliage

Cockscomb has oval green leaves that taper to a point. Plants are generally bushy and compact.

ENVIRONMENT

Hardiness

Cockscombs are tender annuals, and young plants are especially vulnerable to cold. Seedlings may be stunted when night temperatures drop below 60°F.

Light

Cockscombs require full sun to perform at their best. Plants with too little sun will be leggy and will not bloom as well, if at all.

Soil

For best results, grow cockscombs in rich, well-drained soil that is high in organic matter. The pH can range from 6 to 8. These plants also will grow in poor, dry soil.

PLANTING AND PROPAGATION

Planting

Outdoors, sow cockscomb seed where the plants are to grow as soon as the soil warms in spring, all danger of frost has passed, and nighttime temperatures remain above 60°F. Indoors, sow seed four weeks before the last frost date and move seedlings to the garden once the weather conditions would permit outdoor sowing. Barely cover the seed, and germinate at soil temperatures between 70° and

75°F. Cockscomb can be difficult to transplant, so start seeds indoors in individual peat pots for best results. The seed is very fine and prone to drying out, but it requires light to germinate, so cover it with a very thin dusting of milled sphagnum moss. Seeds germinate in 8 to 14 days, and seedlings can be transplanted in four to five weeks. Plant seedlings or thin seed sown outdoors to a spacing of 6 to 12 inches.

Container Gardening

Cockscomb can be grown in pots that are a minumun of 5 to 6 inches deep. Do not crowd the plants or allow them to become potbound.

PLANT MANAGEMENT

General Care

The flowers of *C. cristata* develop from terminal buds, so do not pinch these plants, for it will prevent the development of large blooms. Pinched plants will often develop small blooms from sideshoots, however. *C. argentea plumosa* can be pinched to encourage bushiness and improve the shape of the plant, if desired. However, it also will develop the largest flowers if left unpinched.

Water

Make sure the plants get 1 inch of water every week from rain or by watering. Cockscombs are drought and heat tolerant, but severe dry spells can cause permanent stunting, especially of young plants.

Feeding

A single application of compost or a slow-acting, general-purpose fertilizer will serve the basic needs of these plants all season. For exceptional performance, provide supplemental, light feedings (side-dressings or foliar spray) monthly throughout the growing season.

Cutting Fresh Flowers

Both types of cockscomb add color and drama to arrangements of fresh flowers and are long-lasting when cut.

Drying Flowers

Cockscombs are exceptional dried flowers, for they hold their brilliant color when dried. To air dry, cut the blooms when they are at their peak, remove the foliage, and hang them upside down in a warm, dark, dry place.

MOST COMMON CULTURAL PROBLEMS

Plants Fail to Flower or Only Produce Several Small Blooms

Terminal Bud Damaged; Drought

If several small flower heads arise from the side branches, especially on *C. cristata,* and no main blossom develops, then it is possible that the terminal bud has been damaged. This can happen as a result of careless transplanting, which will check the growth of the plant. Handle transplants carefully and be sure to keep the soil evenly moist, especially while they are becoming established, to avoid this problem.

Extended drought can permanently stunt plants and prevent blooming. Be sure plants receive adequate water throughout the growing season.

MOST COMMON INSECT PESTS

Plants Stunted; Leaves Yellowed and Small; Knots on Roots

Nematodes

Cockscomb plants infested with nematodes look sickly, wilted, or stunted and have yellowed or bronzed foliage. Their root systems are poorly developed, even partially decayed, and may have tiny galls or knots on them. Plants decline slowly and die. The effects of nematode activity are most apparent in hot weather, when plants recover poorly from the heat. Southern root knot nematodes (*Meloidogyne incognita*) attack cockscomb. Nematodes are not insects, but slender, unsegmented roundworms that are barely visible to the unaided eye.

Prevention is the best way to deal with nema-todes when growing annuals in infested soil, since severely infested annuals are best dug up and destroyed; do not compost. Organic matter in the soil helps to control nematodes because it not only benefits the fungi and bacteria that feed on them, it also keeps plants healthy and better able to withstand mild infestations. Add lots of compost, especially leaf mold, to the bed before planting. Turn severely infested plots over to a thick planting of French marigolds for an entire season and dig the plant remains into the soil at season's end to discourage these pests. Crop rotation is also a good idea; don't grow susceptible plants on the same plot year after year.

Leaves Stippled with Tiny Yellow Dots; Webby Foliage

Spider Mites

Leaves that are dry and stippled with tiny yellow dots are a sign that your cockscombs are infested with spider mites, tiny pests that suck chlorophyll out of the leaves. They also inject toxins into the foliage; this causes distorted or discolored growth. Leaves, stems, and flowers also may be swathed in fine webbing. As their name suggests, spider mites are related to spiders. These tiny creatures, which are about 1/50 inch long and barely visible to the naked eye, may be yellow, green, red, or brown. Two-spotted spider mites (*Tetranychus urticae*) attack cockscombs. Spider mites reproduce most rapidly during hot, dry weather. They are especially a problem on greenhouse-grown cockscomb plants; inspect purchased bedding plants carefully to avoid bringing home infested specimens.

Severely infested plants should be destroyed, since infestations are difficult to control once they are well under way. Spider mites can be controlled by washing the plants, especially the undersides of the leaves. For best results, use a forceful spray of water once every other day to knock the mites off the plants; wash the plants at least three times. If that is not effective, spray the plants with insecticidal soap every three to five days for two weeks. To avoid spreading the mites from plant to plant, don't touch healthy plants after examining infested ones.

MOST COMMON DISEASES

Leaves Curled and Distorted; Plants Stunted

Curly Top Virus

If your cockscomb plants produce curled, thickened, or otherwise distorted foliage, they may be infected with the viral disease that causes beet curly top, which causes excessive cell growth and thus distorted growth. The virus is spread by leafhoppers. Infected plants may be stunted or dwarfed.

There is no cure for infected plants. Pull and destroy them; do not compost. Clean up garden debris in the fall to prevent the virus from overwintering, and control weeds that may serve as hosts for the leafhopper vector. Shield young, vulnerable plants from leafhoppers with floating row covers, like Reemay. Plant cockscomb away from the vegetable garden to prevent the virus from being transmitted to food plants.

Seedlings Rot at Base, Fall Over

Damping-Off

Seedling stems that are water soaked and blackened at the soil line have been afflicted with damping-off. Affected stems are unable to support the plants, which fall over and die. Usually, the foliage is still green and healthy looking when the plants collapse. Stems of older plants show tan to reddish brown lesions that eventually girdle stems. Damping-off is caused by soil-dwelling fungi such as *Pythium, Fusarium, Sclerotium,* and *Rhizoctonia,* and it usually occurs in seedlings in greenhouses or on windowsills. Germinating cockscomb seeds may be attacked before they emerge from the soil, or shortly thereafter.

Cultural controls are effective in preventing damping-off. Sow seed in well-drained soil, do not overcrowd plants, and keep soil on the dry side. Outdoors, plant your cockcomb in well-drained soils or raised beds. Indoors, sow seed in sterile growing mix (peat moss, perlite, and vermiculite, with a topping of milled sphagnum moss), and water plants from below by setting pots in water and allowing the water to soak up to just beneath the soil surface. Thin seedlings so they are far enough apart to allow air to circulate between them, which will carry away excessive moisture and reduce humidity. When thinning, use scissors instead of pulling up plants to avoid damaging the roots and stems of remaining plants, which might open them up to infection. In the greenhouse, a fan will promote air circulation. Avoid feeding seedlings too much nitrogen, for it causes lank, weak growth. Routinely disinfect garden tools in boiling water or household bleach solution (1 part bleach to 3 parts water) to discourage disease problems.

Leaves Covered with Dark Spots or Blotches

Leaf Spot

Several different kinds of fungi cause unsightly spots on cockscomb foliage. Leaves may have transparent or brown or black spots. Some fungal spots are surrounded by flecks or black dots, which are the spore-bearing fruiting bodies. Often spots come together to form larger patches of dead tissue. These fungi thrive on moist leaf surfaces.

To control leaf spot, pick off and destroy infected leaves. Also, regularly clean up and destroy dead plant debris in the garden to reduce spore populations. These fungi overwinter as spores in such debris, so an end-of-season cleanup is especially important. Rogue out and discard seriously infected plants, together with the soil in which they are growing. A layer of mulch helps prevent spores from splashing from the soil onto plants. If leaf spot is a particular problem in your area, spray at weekly to ten-day intervals with wettable sulfur or bordeaux mixture, particularly in rainy seasons. (Watch for leaf discoloration with the latter.)

<small>ANNUAL</small> Cosmos <small>*Cosmos* spp.</small>

DESCRIPTION

Cosmos are heat-loving, summer-blooming plants that bear brilliantly colored flowers atop tall, delicate stems. The two species commonly grown as annuals are native to Mexico, and hence sometimes called Mexican aster. Cosmos aren't well suited for formal plantings because they have a somewhat sprawling habit and tend to tangle with neighboring plants. These sturdy, trouble-free plants are best planted at the back of an informal mixed bed or border, or in a sunny wild garden or meadow. A variety of cultivars are available. Cut blooms are lovely in informal arrangements.

Height

Cosmos bipinnatus (common or garden cosmos), 4 to 6 feet; dwarf cultivars, 3 to 3½ feet

C. sulphureus (yellow cosmos), 2 to 6 feet; dwarf cultivars, 1 to 2 feet

Spread

1 to 3 feet

Blossoms

Cosmos belong to the daisy family, Compositae, and both species bear typical daisylike flowers with yellow centers of tightly packed disc florets surrounded by showy "petals," called ray florets. Blooms may be single, semidouble, or double and can be up to 4 inches across. The ray florets are commonly notched or toothed at the tips, giving the blooms a lacy appearance. *C. bipinnatus* and its cultivars bear blooms that are magenta, deep pink, pale pink, and white. *C. sulphureus* produces blooms that are gold, yellow, orange-red, or orange. Both species flower from early summer to first frost.

Foliage

The leaves, which are medium green and borne opposite on the stem, are deeply cut into threadlike segments giving the foliage a fine, lacy texture.

ENVIRONMENT

Hardiness

Cosmos are tender, heat-loving annuals that will not withstand frost.

Light

Cosmos grow best in full sun, but will tolerate light shade. They are heat-loving plants, but need a spot protected from wind.

Soil

For best results, grow cosmos in dry, infertile soil that is very well drained; rich, fertile soil leads to plants with plenty of foliage but few flowers. The pH can range from 6 to 8.

PLANTING AND PROPAGATION

Planting

Outdoors, sow cosmos seed where the plants are to grow after all danger of frost has passed. Seed can also be started indoors to encourage earlier bloom, and seedlings transplant easily. To start seeds indoors, sow four to six weeks before the last spring frost date and move seedlings to the garden when danger of frost has passed. Barely cover the seed with soil, and germinate at soil temperatures between 70° and 85°F. Seeds germinate in five to ten days. Space plants 9 to 24 inches apart, depending on their height at maturity.

Propagation

Cosmos will reseed itself from year to year.

PLANT MANAGEMENT

General Care

Cosmos are care-free plants that will grow and flower well if left relatively undisturbed. To encourage compact, well-branched plants, pinch young plants at least twice early in the growing season but before the flower buds form. Plants may need staking to keep them erect. Plants arranged in clumps will provide some support for each other by twining together. Remove spent flowers to keep plants neat looking and encourage new blooms to form. Cosmos will reseed prolifically from year to year; if desired, flowers can be removed to prevent plants from self-seeding.

Water

These Mexican natives are suited to dry soil and should not be overwatered. They require about 1 inch of water per week from rain or by watering.

Feeding

A single application of compost or a slow-acting, general-purpose fertilizer will serve the basic needs of these plants all season. Additional fertilizer will reduce bloom.

Cutting Fresh Flowers

Cosmos make excellent, long-lasting cut flowers.

Drying Flowers

Cosmos do not air dry well, but can be dried in silica gel. To dry in silica gel, cut flowers in full bloom, leaving 1-inch stems. Place flower cluster, stems down, in a coffee can or other sealable container partially filled with silica gel. Carefully sift gel over blooms until they are completely covered.

MOST COMMON CULTURAL PROBLEMS

Seedlings Appear Where They Are Not Wanted

Reseeding

Cosmos can reseed prolifically from year to year,

and unexpected seedlings can become a nuisance. Picking or deadheading the flowers before they go to seed can reduce this problem.

Plants Fall Over

Unpinched plants; Improper Planting Location

Cosmos can become top-heavy, sprawl onto nearby plants, or flop over entirely. To avoid this condition, pinch seedlings back at least twice before the flower buds begin to form to encourage well-branched, compact plants or select dwarf cultivars to grow. Also, plant cosmos in a location that has dry, infertile soil; is protected from wind; and is in full sun. Staking is the only solution for plants that have fallen over.

MOST COMMON INSECT PESTS

Cosmos plants are bothered by few insects and can easily withstand attacks by most pests. In addition to the insects listed below, they occasionally are infested with leafhoppers, which cause small white or yellow spots on the leaves and can transmit virus diseases; root aphids, which cause plants that are stunted or stop growing altogether; and tarnished plant bugs, which cause deformed growth on young shoots.

Pale or Yellow Spots on Leaves, Leaves Curled and Distorted

Aphids

Plants infested with aphids have distorted growth that may be curled, puckered, or stunted, especially at the tips of the shoots. Leaves may turn yellow or brown, and feeding can damage flower buds or cause distorted flowers. Aphids are soft-bodied, pear-shaped sucking insects about the size of the head of a pin; they may be brown, green, yellow, or nearly black. They are often found clustered under leaves, and flower buds and stem tips may be covered with dense colonies of these insects. Ants, attracted by the aphids' honeydew secretions, wander over the plants, and black, sooty mold can develop on the honeydew as well. Several species of aphids will infest cosmos, including melon aphid (*Aphis gossypii*), potato aphid (*Macrosiphum euphorbiae*), and coreopsis aphid (*A. coreopsidis*).

Light infestations of aphids can be controlled by washing the plants, especially the undersides of the leaves. For best results, use a forceful spray of water once every other day to knock the aphids off the plants; wash the plants at least three times. If that is not effective, spray the plants with insecticidal soap every three to five days for two weeks. If these pests become a very serious problem, make two applications of pyrethrum, three to five days apart.

Holes in Leaves and/or Flowers

Beetles

Several species of beetles chew holes in the foliage and flowers of cosmos. Japanese beetles (*Popillia japonica*), which eat leaves and destroy flowers, are shiny, ½-inch-long beetles that are metallic green with copper-colored wing covers. Asiatic garden beetles (*Maladera castanea*), which also attack cosmos, are ½-inch-long, cinnamon brown beetles that feed only at night. The larvae of both beetles are C-shaped, grayish white grubs with dark brown heads that can eat plant roots. Fully grown grubs are ¾ to 1 inch long.

Spotted cucumber beetle (*Diabrotica undecimpunctata*) is a slender, ¼-inch-long insect that is greenish yellow with 12 black spots on its back. It feasts on petals, buds, and leaves and seems especially drawn to light-colored flowers in late summer. Adults overwinter at the base of weeds or other plants and lay eggs in spring. This pest is also commonly called southern corn rootworm because the yellowish, wormlike, ½- to ¾-inch-long larvae feed on roots.

For the most part, all beetles are controlled the same way. Where possible, handpick and crush them or drop them into a pail of soapy water. If the infestation is light, this is all you will need to do. For heavier infestations, spray infested plants with a solution of pyrethrum and isopropyl alcohol, mixing 1 tablespoon of alcohol with every pint of diluted pyrethrum mixture. Apply this solution every three to five days until the problem is corrected. For long-term control, apply milky spore disease (*Bacillus popilliae*) to lawns and garden. It will kill the larvae of most beetles.

Japanese beetles can also be controlled by pheromone traps. Set up traps a week before the beetles are expected to emerge in your area, making sure traps are no closer than 50 feet from the cosmos or any other plant vulnerable to beetle attack, such as roses.

Sawdust Exudes from Stems; Stems Break Off; Leaves Wilt

Borers

If cosmos stems break and leaves wilt, look closely for small, round holes in the stems, from which borers may have expelled their castings. Stalk borer and European corn borer (*Papaipema nebris* and *Ostrinia nubilalis*) both attack cosmos. Stalk borer is a long, slender caterpillar marked with a dark brown or purple band around the middle and several conspicuous stripes running the length of the body. Adults are grayish brown moths. European corn borer larvae are pinkish caterpillars with two rows of dark spots down the sides. Adults are yellow-brown moths with dark wavy bands on the wings.

Preventive measures are most effective when dealing with these pests, since by the time symptoms occur, it is usually too late to save the plant. Clean up all weeds, and cut and burn any plant stalks that may harbor overwintering eggs or pupae. Rotating the location of your cosmos in the garden can also help control this pest. Bt (*Bacillus thuringiensis*) is effective if applied early in the season just as the borers are entering the plants.

MOST COMMON DISEASES

Cosmos are generally as disease-free as they are insect-free, and plantings are seldom bothered, provided their few cultural requirements are met. In addition to the diseases listed below, cosmos are occasionally attacked by fungal leaf spot, which causes brown or black blotches on leaves, and powdery mildew, which causes a powdery white or gray coating on the leaves. Removing afflicted leaves and stems followed by a thorough fall cleanup provides adequate control.

Leaves Greenish Yellow, Deformed; Shoots Spindly

Aster Yellows

If the leaves of your plants are greenish yellow and spindly, and growth is stunted or dwarfed, they may be infected with aster yellows, a disease caused by a viruslike organism primarily spread by the aster leafhopper (*Macrosteles fascifrons*). Young plants that are infected show a slight yellowing along leaf veins. As the disease becomes more severe, the entire plant is stunted and yellowed, and the unusual number of shoots that develop cause the plant to become very bushy and upright. Shoot tips branch abnormally and tend to develop into witches'-brooms; secondary shoots are usually spindly. Flowers are deformed and may be aborted entirely. Regardless of the normal bloom color of the cultivar, flowers are often sickly yellow-green.

There is no cure for infected plants; remove and destroy them. Spray remaining plants with a mixture of insecticidal soap and isopropyl alcohol. Make this mix by adding 1 tablespoon of alcohol to each pint of insecticidal soap solution. Spray at three- to five-day intervals, making three applications, to kill the leafhoppers that carry the disease. The virus overwinters in various perennials and weeds such as daisies, plantain, and gaillardia. Infected plants are not necessarily killed by the disease, but should be dug up and destroyed, since they continue to infect nearby plants via leafhoppers.

Plants Wilt Suddenly; Stems Rot at Soil Line

Bacterial Wilt

Plants that turn yellow and then wilt suddenly and die may be infected with bacterial wilt. Afflicted plants may at first wilt during the day and appear to recover at night, but they usually die within a few days of the onset of symptoms. The stems are often rotted at ground level. The disease is caused by the bacteria *Pseudomonas solanacearum,* which also infects potatoes, eggplant, and tomatoes.

Remove and discard severely infected plants and garden debris. Do not compost this material to avoid spreading the bacteria. Disinfect all tools that come in contact with infected plants with 70 percent rubbing alcohol. The bacteria overwinter in the soil and can be destroyed by steam pasteurization. Don't plant cosmos near solanaceous vegetables such as potatoes, tomatoes, eggplant, and other plants subject to the same disease.

Brown to Gray Lesions on Stems; Foliage Wilts

Canker
Stems that develop dark brown spots that turn ash gray indicate the presence of stem canker, which is caused by a fungus. The infected areas eventually girdle the stem, which wilts, breaks off, and dies.

Remove and destroy infected plants or plant parts as soon as you notice them because prompt pruning of canes is the best control. Clean cuts made just above a bud heal most quickly, but be sure to cut off all infected tissue. Disinfect clippers or other tools with 70 percent rubbing alcohol after use to avoid spreading the disease. A thorough fall cleanup can help keep the fungus from overwintering.

Leaves Curled and Distorted; Plants Stunted

Curly Top Virus
If your cosmos produce curled, thickened, or otherwise distorted foliage, they may be infected with the viral disease that causes beet curly top, which causes excessive cell growth and thus distorted growth. The virus is spread by leafhoppers. Infected plants may be stunted or dwarfed.

There is no cure for infected plants. Pull and destroy them; do not compost. Clean up garden debris in the fall to prevent the virus from overwintering, and control weeds that may serve as hosts for the leafhopper vector. Shield young, vulnerable plants from leafhoppers with floating row covers, like Reemay. Plant cosmos away from the vegetable garden to prevent the virus from being transmitted to food plants.

Foliage Turns Yellow; Plants Wilt and/or Fall Over

Root and Stem Rots
Cosmos infected with root or stem rots turn yellow, wilt, and die. The soil-dwelling fungi that cause this affliction rot root systems and stems, which causes the plants to topple over. Stem and root rots are caused by a variety of soil-dwelling fungi including *Pellicularia filamentosa, Phytophthora cactorum,* and *Sclerotinia sclerotiorum.* All typically attack stems at or near the soil level, especially during very wet seasons, on overwatered plants, or plants grown in soil that is too moist. Root and stem rots are particular problems in the South where summers are humid.

Preventive measures are very helpful in controlling this problem. Plant cosmos in well-drained soil, avoid overwatering, keep the garden clear of old plant debris, avoid overcrowding the plants, and keep mulch away from the base of plant stems. Remove and discard infected plants, together with the surrounding soil, or cut away affected plant parts with a clean, sharp knife or razor blade. Disinfect these tools with a solution of 1 part household bleach and 3 parts water or 70 percent rubbing alcohol to avoid spreading the disease. For long-term prevention, lighten heavy soil with a mixture of perlite, vermiculite, and/or peat moss, and provide good drainage.

Foliage Marked with Round Lesions

Tomato Spotted Wilt Virus
Cosmos plants that have leaves marked with round lesions that turn brown may be infected with tomato spotted wilt virus, also called ring spot. Stems, leaves,

and flowers may also be streaked or marked with brown, and growth of infected plants is stunted. Flowering may be reduced. The virus is spread by thrips and aphids. This virus is especially a problem on the West Coast and in Texas.

There is no cure for infected plants. Pull and destroy them; do not compost. Clean up garden debris in the fall to prevent the virus from over-wintering, and control weeds that may serve as hosts for the vectors. Plant cosmos and other host plants away from the vegetable garden to prevent the virus from being transmitted to tomatoes, potatoes, lettuce, peas, and other vegetables. Spray with insecticidal soap every three days for two weeks to control aphids and thrips. For serious infestations, use pyrethrum.

ANNUAL *Forget-Me-Not* *Myosotis sylvatica*

DESCRIPTION

Annual forget-me-nots, sometimes also called woodland forget-me-nots, are low-growing plants that produce small clusters of tiny flowers on fragile, many-branched stems. Although the individual flowers are small, they are borne prolifically and are a welcome source of spring color in the garden. Most bear blue flowers. Plants are weak-stemmed and tend to be prostrate. They grow best in cool weather. Forget-me-nots reseed themselves generously and look their best when used in clumps among spring bulbs, in meadows, or as edgings. They provide temporary ground cover for unplanted spaces early in the season.

Height

6 to 12 inches

Spread

10 to 12 inches

Blossoms

Forget-me-nots bear clusters of tiny, five-petaled blooms that are 1/3 inch wide. The small blossoms are usually blue with a contrasting yellow eye, but cultivars with pink or white flowers are also available. The flowers have a slight sweet scent and appear from late spring to early summer.

Foliage

Leaves are narrow to somewhat oval and are borne alternately on the stem. Stems and leaves are hairy.

ENVIRONMENT

Hardiness

Forget-me-nots are hardy annuals or biennials that perform best in regions with long, cool springs. Seedlings are cold tolerant, and in most areas, seed can be sown outdoors in fall for germination in early spring. Once established, plants will reseed themselves each year.

Light

For the longest season of bloom, grow forget-me-nots in light shade where they will be protected from hot sun. Where summers are cool, they can tolerate full sun.

Soil

Plant forget-me-nots in fertile soil that is moist but well drained. They perform best in soil that is rich in organic matter with a pH between 6 and 8.

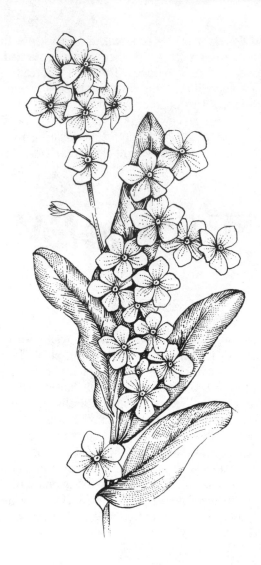

PLANTING AND PROPAGATION

Planting

In most parts of the country, forget-me-not seed either can be sown outdoors in early spring or in late summer or fall for bloom the following spring. Where winters are harsh, sow seed outdoors in early spring. Spring-sown seedlings will bloom in late summer or fall, but may not perform well in areas with hot summers. Seed can be sown indoors six weeks before planting out in early spring, but must be kept at 55°F during germination. Darkness is required for germination, so cover the seeds when sowing. When transplanting, space plants 8 to 12 inches apart.

Propagation

Forget-me-nots will reseed themselves from year to year, especially in areas with light shade and rich soil.

PLANT MANAGEMENT

General Care

Forget-me-nots are care-free plants that are seldom bothered by pests or diseases. They will die out in hot weather, however. Shear them back once they begin to look ragged and use them with plants such as impatiens, which can tolerate summer heat, so you don't end up with empty spots in the garden.

Water

For best results, make sure plants receive 1 inch of water per week from rain or by watering.

Feeding

Forget-me-nots grow best in rich soil, so work compost into the soil at planting time, but they do not require additional fertilizing in order to bloom at their best. Or, apply a slow-acting, general-purpose fertilizer in spring.

Cutting Fresh Flowers

Although their flowers are tiny, forget-me-nots make

beautiful additions to miniature bouquets and nose-gays. Pick the flowers in early morning and place them directly in water for the longest vase life.

Drying Flowers

Forget-me-nots do not air dry well, but can be dried in silica gel. To dry in silica gel, cut flowers in full bloom, leaving 1-inch stems. Place flower cluster, stems down, in a coffee can or other sealable container partially filled with silica gel. Carefully sift silica gel over blooms until they are completely covered.

MOST COMMON CULTURAL PROBLEMS

Seedlings Appear Where They Are Not Wanted

Reseeding
Forget-me-nots can reseed prolifically from year to year, and unexpected seedlings can become a nuisance. Picking the flowers or shearing back the plants before seed ripens can reduce this problem. Otherwise, pull out unwanted seedlings when they arise.

Plants Have Yellow Leaves, Few Flowers, and Die Out in Midsummer

Hot, Dry Weather
Forget-me-nots do not tolerate summer heat and will normally get spindly, ragged looking, turn yellow, and then die out completely as the temperatures rise. They will either stop flowering completely or bloom only sporadically. Once warm weather arrives, shear plants back when they begin to look untidy. Grow forget-me-nots as a spring and early summer annual and then replace them with more heat-tolerant plants. Summer-blooming annuals can be interplanted with the forget-me-nots as soon the latter begin to show signs of dying out.

MOST COMMON INSECT PESTS

Pale or Yellow Spots on Leaves, Leaves Curled and Distorted

Aphids
Plants infested with aphids have distorted growth that may be curled, puckered, or stunted, especially at the tips of the shoots. Leaves may turn yellow or brown, and feeding can damage flower buds or cause distorted flowers. Aphids are soft-bodied, pear-shaped sucking insects about the size of the head of a pin; they may be brown, green, yellow, or nearly black. They are often found clustered under leaves, and flower buds and stem tips may be covered with dense colonies of these insects. Ants, attracted by the aphids' honeydew secretions, wander over the plants, and black, sooty mold can develop on the honeydew as well. Green peach aphid (*Myzus persicae*) infests forget-me-nots.

Light infestations of aphids can be controlled by washing the plants, especially the undersides of the leaves. For best results, use a forceful spray of water once every other day to knock the aphids off the plants; wash the plants at least three times. If that is not effective, spray the plants with insecticidal soap every three to five days for two weeks. If these pests become a very serious problem, make two applications of pyrethrum, three to five days apart.

Leaves and/or Flowers Riddled with Tiny Holes

Flea Beetles
Forget-me-not leaves perforated with dozens or hundreds of tiny holes may be victims of the potato flea beetle (*Epitrix cucumeris*). These shiny black or brown pests are only $1/16$ inch long and very active, jumping like fleas when disturbed. Flea beetles, which are especially a problem on younger plants, transmit viral and bacterial diseases. They overwinter as adults and generally feed on weeds in early spring, then move to the garden. The larvae are tiny grubs that feed on plant roots.

Flea beetles are too small to handpick and

crush, but severe infestations can be controlled with an application of pyrethrum and isopropyl alcohol, made by mixing 1 tablespoon of alcohol with every pint of diluted pyrethrum mixture. Apply this solution every three to five days until the beetles are controlled. Barriers such as floating row covers, like Reemay, can also be used to prevent beetles from gaining access to forget-me-nots in early spring. Beneficial nematodes introduced into the soil will take care of the flea beetle larvae.

Leaves Stuck Together with Silk; Foliage Ragged and Discolored

Leaftiers

Leaf surfaces that are fastened together with strands of silk, followed by foliage that becomes ragged and unsightly, turns brown, and dies are signs that your plants are infested with greenhouse or celery leaftier (*Udea rubigalis*). It is the larval stage that damages plants by feeding on the undersides of the leaves and binding the leaves together. The larvae are ⅜- to ¾-inch-long caterpillars that are light green or cream to yellow in color with a white stripe down their backs and a green line down the center of the stripe. Adult leaftier moths, which are active only at night, are brown or gray and ¼ to ½ inch long. They lay eggs that resemble fish scales on the undersides of leaves.

Handpicking of eggs and larvae is usually an effective way to control this pest, since infestations are usually light. Remove any rolled or folded leaves, for they shelter caterpillars. Infested leaves should be destroyed, since the pests pupate and overwinter in them. Bt (*Bacillus thuringiensis*) also is an effective control. Apply as a powder or spray every two weeks until leaftiers disappear.

MOST COMMON DISEASES

Forget-me-nots are seldom bothered by diseases. In addition to the problems listed below, they are occasionally attacked by a fungus-caused rust disease, which covers leaf undersides with powdery spots. Rust is seldom serious enough to warrant treatment.

Plants grown under very high humidity that are also overcrowded or grown in too little light are occasionally afflicted with a blight that causes gray fuzzy spots on leaves and dead or blackened flowers. Pick off and destroy blighted flowers and remove and destroy infected shoots if this occurs.

Leaves Greenish Yellow, Deformed; Shoots Spindly

Aster Yellows

If the leaves of your forget-me-nots are greenish yellow and spindly, and growth is stunted or dwarfed, they may be infected with aster yellows, a disease caused by a viruslike organism primarily spread by the aster leafhopper (*Macrosteles fascifrons*). Young plants that are infected show a slight yellowing along leaf veins. As the disease becomes more severe, the entire plant is stunted and yellowed, and the unusual number of shoots that develop cause the plant to become very bushy and upright. Shoot tips branch abnormally and tend to develop into witches'-brooms; secondary shoots are usually spindly. Flowers are deformed and may be aborted entirely. Regardless of the normal bloom color of the cultivar, flowers are often sickly yellow-green.

There is no cure for infected plants; remove and destroy them. Spray remaining plants with a mixture of insecticidal soap and isopropyl alcohol. Make this mix by adding 1 tablespoon of alcohol to each pint of insecticidal soap solution. Make three applications at three- to five-day intervals to kill the leafhoppers that carry the disease. The virus overwinters in various perennials and weeds such as daisies, plantain, and gaillardia. Infected plants are not necessarily killed by the disease, but should be dug up and destroyed, since they continue to infect nearby plants via leafhoppers.

Leaves with Pale Patches Above, Mildew Beneath; Foliage Wilts

Downy Mildew

Several different kinds of fungi cause pale greenish or reddish spots on upper leaf surfaces and gray moldy or "downy" patches on undersides. Leaves eventually wilt and die. The fungus spreads most quickly on moist leaf and stem surfaces and is especially active in periods of cool, wet nights and warm, humid days.

Cultural controls are very effective. Plant forget-me-nots in well-drained soil, water early on sunny days, avoid overcrowding, and try to avoid wetting the foliage when watering. Dig up heavily infected plants, together with adjacent soil, and discard them; do not compost. Spray lightly infected plants with wettable sulfur, or apply bordeaux mixture or another copper fungicide when downy mildew first appears on leaves. (Watch for leaf discoloration when using bordeaux mixture.) Several applications may be needed to stop the spread of the fungus.

Lower Leaves Rot; Stem Tips Die

Wilt

A wilt disease caused by the fungus *Sclerotinia sclerotiorum* attacks forget-me-nots. The disease works its way up from the base of the plant and, for this reason, is also called crown rot. Leaves and branches of afflicted plants wilt, turn brown, and die.

Remove and discard infected plants, together with the surrounding soil. Do not grow forget-me-nots year after year in the same soil; rotate plantings and change seedbeds, if possible. Sterilize tools between cuts with 70 percent rubbing alcohol to avoid spreading the fungus.

ANNUAL *Four-O'clock* *Mirabilis jalapa*

DESCRIPTION

The common four-o'clock is a perennial from tropical America that is most often grown in this country as an annual. Also called beauty-of-the-night and marvel-of-Peru, this plant comes into its own in the late afternoon when its trumpet-shaped flowers open. Blooms remain open through the night and fade early the following morning. Although each bloom lasts only a day, plants flower prolifically and often bear flowers of several different colors on the same plant. The blooms are fragrant and attract night-flying moths. Four-o'clocks are so easy to grow, they are perfect for a child's first garden. The plants are also lush enough to be useful as screening or small hedge plants, or they can be used at the back of beds and borders.

Height

1½ to 3 feet

Spread

2 to 3 feet

Blossoms

Four-o'clocks have trumpet-shaped flowers that are from 1 to 2 inches across. Blooms open daily in late afternoon and close the next morning. On cloudy days, they may remain open all day. The flowers may be white, yellow, gold, orange, red, or pink and are often striped or mottled with more than one color.

Most forms have fragrant, lemon-scented flowers. The plants bloom continuously from summer to first fall frost.

Foliage

Leaves are shaped like elongated hearts and are borne opposite on the stem. The foliage is lush, light green, and smooth in texture.

ENVIRONMENT

Hardiness

Four-o'clocks are tender perennials usually grown as annuals. They cannot withstand any frost. Do not move seedlings to the garden until night temperatures remain above 50°F.

Light

For best results, grow four-o'clocks in full sun. They will tolerate light shade, but may produce fewer flowers under these conditions.

Soil

Although four-o'clocks will grow in almost any soil, they grow best in one that is light and well drained.

PLANTING AND PROPAGATION

Planting

Outdoors, sow seed where the plants are to grow after all danger of frost has passed. It can also be sown indoors four to six weeks before the last frost date, but can be difficult to transplant and should be sown in individual peat pots. Seeds will germinate in seven to ten days. Soil temperatures between 70° and 75°F are ideal. Transplant seedlings sown indoors to their permanent site after all danger of frost has passed and the soil has warmed. Space seedlings 2 to 3 feet apart when planting.

Propagation

Four-o'clocks have fleshy, tuberous roots similar to dahlias that can be lifted in fall, stored in a frost-free place, and divided in spring. When dividing, be sure to cut through the stem of the plant, leaving a portion of stem and root on each division. Four-o'clocks will also reseed themselves from year to year.

PLANT MANAGEMENT

General Care

Four-o'clocks are tough, easy-to-grow plants that can withstand high humidity, heat, drought, and air pollution. They will reseed themselves freely from year to year.

Overwintering

The fleshy, tuberous roots can be dug before the first fall frost. Dig the roots, shake the soil off them, and cut back the tops of the plants. Then dry them in the sun for a few hours and store them over winter in a cool, dry but frost-free place, such as an unheated basement or root cellar. Roots overwintered indoors can be divided, if necessary. Replant in spring when all danger of frost has passed. Four-o'clocks will also reseed themselves from year to year, but plants grown from overwintered roots will bloom earlier in the season.

Water

For best growth, four-o'clocks should get 1 inch of water per week from rain or by watering. However, they are very drought tolerant once established.

Feeding

A single application of compost or a slow-acting, general-purpose fertilizer in the spring will satisfy the basic needs of four-o'clocks all season long. For exceptional performance, give plants supplemental, light feedings (side-dressings or foliar spray) monthly throughout the growing season.

MOST COMMON CULTURAL PROBLEMS

Seedlings Appear Where They Are Not Wanted

Reseeding

Four-o'clocks can reseed prolifically from year to year, and unexpected seedlings can become a nuisance. Removing the spent flowers before the seed ripens can reduce this problem.

MOST COMMON INSECT PESTS

Although Japanese beetles occasionally skeletonize leaves of four-o'clocks, these plants are not seriously bothered by any insect pests.

Plants Stunted; Leaves Yellowed and Small; Knots on Roots

Nematodes

Four-o'clocks are sometimes infested with nematodes, which can cause sickly, wilted, or stunted growth and yellowed or bronzed foliage. Infested root systems are poorly developed, even partially decayed, and may have tiny galls or knots on them. The effects of nematode activity are most apparent in hot weather, when plants recover poorly from the heat. Southern root knot nematodes (*Meloidogyne incognita*) occasionally attack four-o'clocks, although they do not generally cause serious problems when the plants are grown as annuals. Nematodes are not insects, but slender, unsegmented roundworms that are barely visible to the unaided eye.

Do not save and overwinter the roots of infested four-o'clocks. Dig and destroy them; do not compost. Prevention is the best way to deal with nematodes when growing annuals in infested soil, since severely infested annuals are best dug up and destroyed. Organic matter in the soil helps to control nematodes because it not only benefits the fungi and bacteria that feed on them, it also keeps plants healthy and better able to withstand mild infestations. Add lots of compost, especially leaf mold, to the bed before planting. Turn severely infested plots over to a thick planting of French marigolds for an entire season and dig the plant remains into the soil at season's end to discourage these pests. Crop rotation is also a good idea;

don't grow susceptible plants on the same plot year after year.

MOST COMMON DISEASES

Leaves Curled and Distorted; Plants Stunted

Curly Top Virus

If your four-o'clocks produce curled, thickened, or otherwise distorted foliage, they may be infected with the viral disease that causes beet curly top, which causes excessive cell growth and thus distorted growth. The virus is spread by leafhoppers. Infected plants may be stunted or dwarfed.

There is no cure for infected plants. Pull and destroy them; do not compost. Do not save and overwinter the roots of infected plants. Clean up garden debris in the fall to prevent the virus from overwintering, and control weeds that may serve as hosts for the leafhopper vector. Shield young, vulnerable plants from leafhoppers with floating row covers, like Reemay. Plant four-o'clocks away from the vegetable garden to prevent the virus from being transmitted to food plants. Do not overwinter the roots of infected plants. Dig and destroy them; do not compost.

Leaves Covered with Dark Spots or Blotches

Leaf Spot

The fungus *Cercospora mirabilis* causes unsightly spots on four-o'clock foliage. Leaves may have transparent or brown or black spots. Some fungal spots are surrounded by flecks or black dots, which are the spore-bearing fruiting bodies. Often spots come together to form larger patches of dead tissue. These fungi thrive on moist leaf surfaces.

To control leaf spot, pick off and destroy infected leaves. Also, regularly clean up and destroy dead plant debris in the garden to reduce spore populations. These fungi overwinter as spores in such debris, so an end-of-season cleanup is especially important. Rogue out and discard seriously infected plants, together with the soil in which they are growing. Do not compost infected plant material; discard it. A layer of mulch helps prevent spores from splashing from the soil onto plants. If leaf spot is a particular problem in your area, spray at weekly to ten-day intervals with wettable sulfur or bordeaux mixture, particularly in rainy seasons. (Watch for leaf discoloration with the latter.)

Foliage Turns Yellow; Plants Wilt and/or Fall Over

Root Rot

A root rot caused by the soil-dwelling fungus *Phymatotrichum omnivorum* attacks four-o'clock stems at or near the soil level. The foliage of afflicted plants turns yellow, wilts, and dies. Root systems rot, causing plants to topple over.

Preventive measures are very helpful in controlling this problem. Plant four-o'clocks in well-drained soil, avoid overwatering, keep the garden clear of old plant debris, avoid overcrowding the plants, and keep mulch away from the base of plant stems. Remove and discard infected plants, together with the surrounding soil. Disinfect tools with a solution of 1 part household bleach and 3 parts water or 70 percent rubbing alcohol to avoid spreading the disease. *P. omnivorum* is most common on heavy, alkaline soil, so for long-term prevention, lighten heavy soil with a mixture of perlite, vermiculite, and/or peat moss, and provide good drainage. Adjust pH to neutral or slightly acid levels.

Leaves with Pale Areas Above, Powdery Spots Beneath

Rust

Three different rust diseases occasionally attack four-o'clocks, causing pale areas on upper leaf surfaces with powdery, rusty or whitish pustules directly beneath. On four-o'clocks, *Aecidium mirabilis* and *Puccinia aristidae* cause rusts, and *Albugo platensis* causes a white rust.

Remove and destroy infected leaves, or in severe

cases entire plants, as soon as possible. Collect and destroy all infected garden debris before growth starts in the spring. Control weeds in and around the garden, for they may also harbor rust fungi. To ensure good ventilation, space plants far enough apart so that air can circulate between them. Also, avoid wetting the foliage when watering. Rust can be prevented by periodic applications of wettable sulfur, begun several weeks before the problem normally appears.

ANNUAL Geraniums *Pelargonium* spp.

DESCRIPTION

The showy, brightly colored flowers of geraniums are a traditional sign of summer. Familiar to all gardeners, they are loved for their easy cultivation and the red, white, pink, or salmon blooms they produce in abundance all season long. Although most often grown as annuals, geraniums are actually tender shrubs native to South Africa. In California, Florida, and similar climates, they can be grown outdoors year-round. In the North, many gardeners move plants indoors and grow them as houseplants in winter or all year round. The stems are fleshy or woody, and there are upright or trailing forms. Geraniums are ideal for window boxes and other containers, as well as in beds and borders. Keep in mind that the geraniums grown as annuals are actually *Pelargonium* spp., while the botanical name *Geranium* applies to a genus of popular hardy perennials.

Height

P. × *hortorum* (common, bedding, or zonal geranium), 1 foot when plants are grown as annuals. To 3 feet or more when grown as perennials.

P. peltatum (ivy or hanging geranium), 6 to 8 inches

Spread

P. × *hortorum* (common, bedding, or zonal geranium), 1 to 2 feet

P. peltatum (ivy or hanging geranium), trailing branches, 3 to 4 feet

Blossoms

Geraniums bear showy, ball-shaped clusters of flowers atop slim, leafless stems that arise from the leaf axils. Clusters range from 2 to 4 inches across and contain many individual flowers that open over a long period of time. Individual blooms are about 1 inch across and may be single or double. Single flowers have five petals. Geraniums come in shades of red from crimson to scarlet, as well as pink, salmon, orange, and white. There are also bicolored cultivars with contrasting colored "eyes." Most geraniums bloom from summer through to the first hard frost of autumn.

Foliage

Geraniums bear deep green, heart-shaped leaves ranging from 3 to 5 inches across. Many have scalloped margins and are softly hairy to smooth in texture. Leaves may be marked with a dark horseshoe-shaped zone or ring. The foliage of *P.* × *hortorum* has a characteristic scent that some gardeners find fishy and unpleasant. Although *P. peltatum* and *P.* × *hortorum* are grown primarily for their flowers, there are many different species and cultivars of geraniums grown for their intensely fragrant foliage. Scented-leaved geraniums may have deeply cut, lacy leaves that have apple-, rose-, peppermint-, nutmeg-, lemon-, or mint-scented foliage.

ENVIRONMENT

Hardiness

Although geraniums are actually perennials, in all but the warmest parts of this country (USDA Zone 10) they are most often grown as annuals. Although plants can withstand cool temperatures, they will be killed by hard frost. For best results, do not move seedlings to the garden until night temperatures remain above 50°F.

Light

Geraniums are sun-loving plants that bloom and grow best in full sun. They will, however, tolerate dappled shade. Although quite heat tolerant, prolonged high heat and humidity can cause them to stop producing new blooms. In the South and Southwest, where summer temperatures are high, grow geraniums in partial shade. A site with afternoon shade is best.

Soil

Although geraniums will grow in a wide variety of soil types, including poor, dry soil, for best results, grow them in a rich, moist, well-drained soil that is high in organic matter. The pH can range from 5 to 8, but they seem to grow best in slightly acidic soil, between 6 and 7.

PLANTING AND PROPAGATION

Planting

Until a few years ago, geraniums were always raised from cuttings, which were either taken from stock plants and raised in commercial greenhouses or from plants overwintered on windowsills by home gardeners. Today, gardeners can start or purchase cutting-grown plants, but they can also grow some cultivars of geraniums from seed or purchase seed-grown plants.

To grow geraniums from seed, sow the seed indoors in midwinter, 12 to 16 weeks before last spring frost. Cover the seed with about ¼ inch of potting medium and keep the medium at a temperature of about 75°F. Germination takes 7 to 15 days. When seedlings are about the size of a quarter, transplant them to individual 3-inch pots.

Seed or cutting-grown plants, whether homegrown or purchased, can be moved to the garden after all danger of frost has passed. Space plants about 1 foot apart. The leaves of geraniums moved outdoors too early in the spring may turn red when the plants are first out because of the cool night temperatures. To avoid this, wait to transplant until night temperatures remain reliably above 40°F.

Seed-grown plants have one advantage over their cutting-grown brethren; they start the growing season free of all viral diseases, which can weaken geraniums and reduce bloom.

Propagation

Geraniums can be propagated by cuttings taken in the fall and rooted indoors over the winter in 2½- or 3-inch pots. For best results, in mid- to late summer, cut back plants from which cuttings are to be taken to encourage the production of new shoots. Then a month later, in late summer or early fall, take cuttings from the new tip growth produced. Using a very sharp knife, cut straight across the stem just below where a leaf is attached to the main stem. Cuttings should be about 3 or 4 inches long. Never use pruning shears to avoid crushing the stem. Remove all but the top two or three leaves and any flower buds. Cuttings can be allowed to air dry for several hours before being rooted, but will root more quickly if they are immediately dipped in rooting powder and stuck in moistened vermiculite or sharp sand. Keep cuttings in bright light but out of direct sunlight until roots are formed, which usually takes four to five weeks. Keep the medium slightly dry, but don't allow the cuttings to wilt. On the other hand, too much water at this stage will lead to damping-off. To see if roots have developed, gently pull on a leaf or nudge the cuttings with a finger. If they seem firmly planted in the soil, they are ready to be moved to individual pots and placed in full sun. When potting, use a rich potting soil that does not contain too much nitrogen, which will cause rank growth.

Container Gardening

Geraniums thrive in containers, including window boxes, hanging baskets, and pots. They bloom best if slightly potbound, however. Container-grown specimens should be allowed to dry out slightly between waterings.

PLANT MANAGEMENT

General Care

Once they are established in the garden, geraniums require little care and will bloom profusely with little more than occasional attention. To encourage flower production, remove spent blooms regularly. Also remove any yellowed leaves promptly, and pinch or trim back stems to encourage branching. Another way to encourage well-branched plants is to occasionally remove the largest leaves to allow sunlight to filter in toward the center of the plant. When removing leaves, pinch them off at the end of their stalks, leaving the leaf stalks on the plant. This prevents damage to the fleshy stem and reduces the chances of disease organisms entering through the wound. When watering, avoid wetting the leaves and soaking blossoms to prevent fungal diseases.

Overwintering

Since geraniums are actually tender perennials, they can be grown outdoors year-round in Zone 10. However, for gardeners who don't want to start or buy them anew each year, there are two basic ways to carry them through northern winters: They can be potted up and grown indoors or stored dry in a cool but frost-free area. Pot-grown geraniums can be brought indoors with little disturbance, but you can also cut back plants grown in the ground and pot them up and bring them indoors before the first fall frost. Grow them in a very sunny window through the winter in a cool (preferably 60°F) room.

If you have a cool but frost-free spot, such as a root cellar, protected garage, or unheated basement, you can hold your geraniums over winter by digging them up and storing them without soil. To do this, dig the plants and cut off almost all of the top growth. Allow the plants to dry for an hour or two, shake the soil off the roots, and cut the roots back by about two-thirds. Place the trimmed plants in a brown paper bag, seal the bag shut, and set it in a dark, cool place for the winter. Check the plants periodically to make sure they haven't shriveled completely. If they begin growing while still in the bags, either the temperature is too high (40°F is ideal) or they are not dry enough. Pot the plants up in late winter and move them to a bright window to start them growing again. Water very sparingly at first, letting them dry out between waterings, until they show signs of growth.

Water

For best bloom, geraniums should receive 1 inch of water every week from rain or by watering. When watering by hand, avoid sprinkling the leaves and flowers, which will encourage fungal diseases.

Feeding

A single application of compost or a slow-acting, general-purpose fertilizer at planting time will serve the basic needs of these plants all season. For exceptional performance, give plants supplemental, light feedings (side-dressings or foliar spray) monthly throughout the growing season.

Cutting Fresh Flowers

Geraniums make a colorful addition to arrangements of cut flowers.

MOST COMMON CULTURAL PROBLEMS

Excessive Foliage; Few Flowers

Too Much Nitrogen; Improper Planting Location

Geraniums that produce many more leaves than flowers may have received too much nitrogen, or may have been overwatered or planted in too little sun. Under such conditions, plants often produce spindly, lank growth and few, if any, flowers. Geraniums grown in shade also will produce foliage at the expense of flowers. Under such conditions they also will become leggy and may flop over. Overwatering will also produce these symptoms. Prolonged periods of high temperatures in summer can also cause plants to stop blooming.

Restrict the amount of nitrogen these plants receive. Nitrogen encourages foliage growth at the expense of flowers. Geraniums grown along the edge of a lawn that has been fed with a high-nitrogen lawn fertilizer often exhibit these symptoms. Water generously for a few days to wash through excess fertilizer, and do not fertilize for the rest of the season.

MOST COMMON INSECT PESTS

Geraniums are bothered by few insects and can easily withstand attacks by most pests, provided the plants are healthy and vigorous. In addition to the pests listed below, slugs, snails, and caterpillars may eat holes in the foliage. Plants grown indoors, in greenhouses, or in the Deep South or Southwest can be infested with mealybugs, spider mites, and scale. Be sure to inspect purchased plants carefully to avoid bringing home infested specimens.

Pale or Yellow Spots on Leaves, Leaves Curled or Distorted

Aphids

Plants infested with aphids have distorted growth

that may be curled, puckered, or stunted. Leaves may turn yellow or brown, and feeding can seriously damage flower buds or cause distorted flowers. Plants may also wilt under bright sunlight. Aphids are soft-bodied, pear-shaped sucking insects about the size of the head of a pin; they may be brown, green, yellow, or nearly black. They are often found clustered under leaves, and flower buds and stem tips may be covered with dense colonies of these insects. Ants, attracted by the aphids' honeydew secretions, wander over the plants, and black, sooty mold can develop on the honeydew as well. In addition to the damage they cause by feeding, aphids are important vectors of virus diseases. Several species of aphids infest geraniums, including foxglove aphid (*Acyrthosiphon solani*), geranium aphid (*A. pelargonii*), green peach aphid (*Myzus persicae*), and potato aphid (*Macrosiphum euphorbiae*).

Light infestations of aphids can be controlled by washing the plants, especially the undersides of the leaves. For best results, use a forceful spray of water once every other day to knock the aphids off the plants; wash the plants at least three times. If that is not effective, spray the plants with insecticidal soap every three to five days for two weeks. If these pests become a very serious problem, make two applications of pyrethrum, three to five days apart.

Leaves Stuck or Rolled Together with Silk; Foliage Ragged or Discolored

Leafrollers or Leaftiers

Aptly named, leafrollers protect themselves while feeding by rolling terminal leaves into tubes and binding them with strands or webs of silk. Leaftiers feed in a similar manner, by fastening leaves together with strands of silk. Both cause foliage that is ragged or skeletonized, turns brown, and dies. Oblique-banded leafroller (*Choristoneura rosaceana*) and red-banded leafroller (*Argyrotaenia velutinana*) attack geraniums. Adult leafrollers are brown or gray, ¼- to ½-inch-long moths. The larvae are dark to light green or cream to yellow and ⅜ inch to 1¾

inches long. Greenhouse or celery leaftier (*Udea rubigalis*) also infests geraniums. The larvae are ⅜- to ¾-inch-long caterpillars that are light green or cream to yellow in color with a white stripe down their backs and a green line down the center of the stripe. Adult leaftier moths, which are active only at night, are brown or gray and ¼ to ½ inch long. They lay eggs that resemble fish scales on the undersides of leaves. It is the larval stage of all three insects that damages plants by feeding on the undersides of the leaves and binding the leaves together.

Handpicking of eggs and larvae is usually an effective way to control this pest, since infestations are usually light. Remove any rolled or folded leaves, for they shelter caterpillars. Infested leaves should be destroyed, since the pests pupate and overwinter in them. Bt (*Bacillus thuringiensis*) also is an effective control. Apply as a powder or spray every two weeks until the larvae disappear.

Plants Stunted; Leaves Yellowed and Small; Knots on Roots

Nematodes

Geraniums are sometimes infested with nematodes, which can cause sickly, wilted, or stunted growth and yellowed or bronzed foliage. Infested root systems are poorly developed, even partially decayed, and may have tiny galls or knots on them. The effects of nematode activity are most apparent in hot weather, when plants recover poorly from the heat. Southern root knot nematodes (*Meloidogyne incognita*) and northern root knot nematodes (*M. hapla*) occasionally attack geraniums, although they do not generally cause serious problems when the plants are grown as annuals. Nematodes are not insects, but slender, unsegmented roundworms that are barely visible to the unaided eye.

Do not save and overwinter infested geraniums. Dig and destroy them; do not compost. Prevention is the best way to deal with nematodes when growing annuals in infested soil, since severely infested annuals are best dug up and destroyed. Organic matter in the soil helps to control nematodes because it not only benefits the fungi and bacteria that feed on them, it also keeps plants healthy and better able to withstand mild infestations. Add lots of compost, especially leaf mold, to the bed before planting. Turn severely infested plots over to a thick planting of French marigolds for an entire season and dig the plant remains into the soil at season's end to discourage these pests. Crop rotation is also a good idea; don't grow susceptible plants on the same plot year after year.

Plants Turn Yellow and Die

Termites
Surprisingly, termites occasionally tunnel through the woody stems of geraniums, causing the plants to turn yellow and die for no apparent reason. Dig up and destroy infested plants, and check wooden structures nearby for termite infestations.

Weakened Plants; Leaves Yellowed

Whiteflies
Plants that are infested with whiteflies are weakened and undersize with leaves that begin to turn yellow and die. The undersides of the leaves of infested plants may be covered with a sooty, black fungus, which grows on the shiny, sticky honeydew secreted by the whiteflies. Adults are white, mothlike insects about the size of the head of a pin and are clearly visible on the undersides of geranium leaves. Whitefly infestation is sometimes referred to as flying dandruff because when an infested plant is bumped or brushed, the adults flutter out in clouds, somewhat resembling dandruff flying off the leaves. Nymphs, which are yellowish, legless, flat, and oval, resemble scale at certain stages. Both nymphs and adults suck juices from plant leaves, buds, and stems. These pests, which are particular problems in greenhouses, are often brought home on purchased bedding plants or vegetable transplants. (Greenhouse whitefly, *Trialeurodes vaporariorum,* the most common species found in gardens, does not overwinter outdoors in the North.) Inspect purchased bedding plants carefully to avoid bringing home infested specimens.

Whiteflies are difficult to control once they have infested your garden. Destroy infected plants as soon as you detect the problem, for whiteflies will quickly spread throughout the garden if infestations are not controlled. To control infestations, spray plants with insecticidal soap spray every two to three days for two weeks. Be sure to spray the undersides of the leaves. Also, use insecticidal soap early in the season to prevent infestations. Pyrethrum may be used as a last resort. Make three applications five days apart. Isolate and destroy severely infested plants.

MOST COMMON DISEASES

Leaves Covered with Spots or Blotches

Bacterial or Fungal Leaf Spot
Both bacteria and fungi cause leaf spot in geraniums. These diseases are primarily problems of greenhouse-grown plants, but can become a problem in very warm, humid weather or when plants are overcrowded or leaves are moistened frequently with water.

Two bacteria, *Pseudomonas erodii* and *Xanthomonas pelargonii,* cause spots on geranium leaves. At first, bacterial leaf spots are tiny, dispersed, and translucent. They enlarge to form papery brown blotches that are sunken and irregular in shape. Leaves may wilt and drop, and branches can turn black, collapse, and rot.

Many kinds of fungi that thrive on moist leaf surfaces cause leaf spots on geraniums. Leaves may have transparent or brown or black spots. Some fungal spots are surrounded by flecks or black dots, which are the spore-bearing fruiting bodies. Often spots come together to form larger patches of dead tissue.

Cultural controls are effective ways to combat both bacterial and fungal leaf spot. Pick off and destroy any infected leaves as soon as they appear. Also, regularly clean up and destroy dead plant debris in the garden. Do not compost plant material you suspect to be infected. Rogue out and discard seriously infected plants, together with the soil in which they are growing. A layer of mulch helps prevent fungal spores from splashing from the soil onto plants. If fungal leaf spot is a particular problem in your area, spray at weekly to ten-day intervals with wettable sulfur or bordeaux mixture, particularly in rainy seasons. (Watch for leaf discoloration with the latter.)

If you suspect bacterial leaf spot, disinfect garden tools with 70 percent denatured alcohol or liquid bleach after working with each plant to avoid transmitting bacteria from plant to plant. Spray afflicted plants weekly during rainy spells with a copper-based bactericide. Control insects (such as aphids) that may transmit disease organisms. Increase air circulation by spacing plants so air can move between them, and remove the lower 4 to 6 inches of foliage to avoid contact with wet soil.

Leaves Spotted, Crinkled

Crinkle
Geraniums that have crinkled or dwarfed younger leaves marked with irregular or circular spots are infected with the viral disease crinkle. Symptoms are visible only during the spring months and disappear during summer. Even though plants have apparently recovered, cuttings taken from them will show viral symptoms the following spring. Rogue out and destroy infected plants.

Leaves Curled and Distorted; Plants Stunted

Curly Top Virus
If your geraniums produce curled, thickened, or otherwise distorted foliage, they may be infected with the viral disease that causes beet curly top, which causes excessive cell growth and thus dis-torted growth. The virus is spread by leafhoppers. Infected plants may be stunted or dwarfed.

There is no cure for infected plants. Pull and destroy them; do not compost. Do not save and overwinter the roots of infected plants. Clean up garden debris in the fall to prevent the virus from overwintering, and control weeds that may serve as hosts for the leafhopper vector. Shield young, vulnerable plants from leafhoppers with floating row covers, like Reemay. Plant geraniums away from the vegetable garden to prevent the virus from being transmitted to food plants. Do not overwinter the roots of infected plants. Dig and destroy them; do not compost.

Stems Turn Black at Base; Leaves Wilt

Root and Stem Rots
If the stems of your geraniums turn black from the base upward, and water-soaked, discolored lesions eventually girdle the plants, they are probably infected with one of the soil-borne fungi that cause root or stem rot. Once these fungi have girdled the stems, the plants wilt and die. Root rots that attack geraniums at or near the soil level may not cause the stem to turn black, but instead cause the foliage to turn yellow, wilt, and die. In this case, the root system rots and the plants topple over. These diseases primarily attack greenhouse-grown plants or plants that are overcrowded or overwatered.

Remove and discard infected plants, together with the surrounding soil, or cut away affected plant parts with a clean, sharp knife or razor blade. (Cuttings taken from the tops of afflicted stems are generally healthy and can be used to propagate plants stricken with stem rot.) Also, regularly clean up and destroy dead plant debris in the garden. Do not compost infected plants or soil; discard them. Disinfect tools with a solution of 1 part household bleach and 3 parts water or 70 percent rubbing alcohol after use to avoid spreading the disease. For long-term prevention, replace infected soil, improve drainage, and avoid overwatering.

ANNUAL Impatiens

Impatiens spp.

DESCRIPTION

Impatiens are among the most popular bedding plants in the United States. The shade-loving common impatiens, *Impatiens wallerana*, has many common names, including busy Lizzie, patient Lucy, patience plant, and sultana. Its brightly colored, single or double blooms bring color to shade gardens everywhere. Garden balsam, *I. balsamina*, is an old-fashioned, somewhat more sun-loving relative that has spikes of single or double flowers borne close to the stem. Newest on the gardening scene are the New Guinea impatiens, a group of hybrids that boast variegated foliage and colorful flowers. All of these colorful and versatile plants are ideal for bedding, borders, containers, and for color under trees.

Height

I. balsamina (garden balsam), 1 to 2½ feet
I. wallerana (common impatiens), 6 to 24 inches
New Guinea impatiens, 1 to 2 feet

Spread

1 to 2 feet

Blossoms

Both *I. wallerana* and *I. balsamina* bear both single and double flowers that have a thin spur in the back. While the former carries its blooms on short stalks at the ends of the stems, *I. balsamina* bears its blooms against the stem in a spike along the top third of the plant. Single blooms are five-petaled and may be up to 2 inches across; double flowers can have so many petals that they resemble camellias. New Guinea impatiens, which are grown as much for their attractive foliage as their flowers, generally have single blooms. *I. wallerana, I. balsamina,* and New Guinea impatiens come in many colors including scarlet, purple, pink, salmon, white, orange, and mauve. In addition, some cultivars of *I. balsamina* bear yellow flowers. Blooms appear continuously from early summer to the first fall frost.

Foliage

The stems, foliage, and flowers of these tropical plants are very succulent. The leaves of most impatiens are green, however, New Guinea impatiens have leaves that are green, bronze, maroon, or variegated with cream or yellow.

ENVIRONMENT

Hardiness

I. wallerana, I. balsamina, and New Guinea impatiens are tender plants that will not survive frost. Do not move seedlings to the garden until night temperatures remain above 50°F. *I. wallerana* is actually a tender perennial usually grown as an annual.

Light

Impatiens are tropical natives that thrive in the hot temperatures of summer. In most parts of the country, *I. wallerana* grows best in partial to deep shade, although it can handle full sun in coastal areas or where summers are cool. *I. balsamina* will grow well in full sun, especially in the North where temperatures remain cool, although it will tolerate light shade. The New Guinea impatiens are a little trickier to keep happy because they need full sun but dislike heat.

Soil

Grow all types of impatiens in fertile, well-drained

56

soil rich in organic matter. A pH range between 6.0 and 7.5 is ideal.

PLANTING AND PROPAGATION

Planting

Sow seed of *I. wallerana* indoors 10 to 12 weeks before the last spring frost date. Do no cover the

seeds, which need light to germinate, but cover the flats with plastic to provide high humidity. Germinate at temperatures between 70° and 75°F. Seeds will sprout in 15 to 20 days. Do not overwater, as seedlings are subject to damping-off. *I. balsamina* can be sown outdoors where plants are to grow after all danger of frost has passed. Or, sow indoors 6 to 8 weeks before the last frost date. Germination takes 8 to 14 days at temperatures of 70° to 75°F.

Move seedlings of either species outdoors after all danger of frost has passed. Impatiens are heat-loving plants that will not grow well until the soil has warmed in spring. Space seedlings or purchased bedding plants 8 to 18 inches apart, depending on the cultivar.

Propagation

Impatiens are easy to propagate by softwood cuttings. Take cuttings from plants brought indoors for winter bloom and root them to produce spring transplants.

Container Gardening

I. wallerana will do well in planters, window boxes, and hanging baskets in lightly shaded spots on the porch or patio.

PLANT MANAGEMENT

General Care

Impatiens are essentially care-free and require little day-to-day maintenance once they are established in the garden. In late summer, plants that have become leggy can be pinched back to encourage a compact, bushy appearance.

Overwintering

I. wallerana can be overwintered as a houseplant indoors. Dig and pot up plants just before the first fall frost. To promote bushy growth and new flowers and help plants adjust to the shock of transplanting, pinch back the stems by at least half when you bring them indoors. Give them full winter sun, water when the soil becomes dry, and keep temperatures on the cool side, but above 50°F for best growth. Take cuttings in late winter to produce plants for the following year.

Water

Impatiens appreciate moist soil, but should not be overwatered, for constantly moist soil can lead to root rot. Make sure the plants get 1 inch of water every week from rain or by watering. Plants located in full sun should be watered regularly. Impatiens stems are succulent and wilt dramatically when the plants are dry; this saps the plant's strength, so water before wilting occurs. Avoid watering in mid-afternoon when temperatures are very high.

Feeding

A single application of compost or a slow-acting, general-purpose fertilizer worked into the soil before planting will serve the basic needs of these annuals all season. Excessive fertilization will cause leggy growth and the production of foliage at the expense of flowers.

MOST COMMON INSECT PESTS

Pale or Yellow Spots on Leaves, Leaves Curled and Distorted

Aphids

Plants infested with aphids have distorted growth that may be curled, puckered, or stunted. Leaves may turn yellow or brown, and feeding can seriously damage flower buds or cause distorted flowers. Plants may also wilt under bright sunlight. Aphids are soft-bodied, pear-shaped sucking insects about the size of the head of a pin; they may be brown, green, yellow, or nearly black. They are often found clustered under leaves, and flower buds and stem tips may be covered with dense colonies of these insects. Ants, attracted by the aphids' honeydew secretions, wander over the plants, and black, sooty mold can develop on the honeydew as well. In addition to the damage they cause by feeding, aphids are important vectors of virus diseases. Three species, all known as impatiens aphids, infest these plants: *Aphis impatientis, Macrosiphum impatiensicolens,* and *M. impatientis.*

Light infestations of aphids can be controlled by washing the plants, especially the undersides of the leaves. For best results, use a forceful spray of water once every other day to knock the aphids off the plants; wash the plants at least three times. If that is not effective, spray the plants with insecticidal soap every three to five days for two weeks. If these pests become a very serious problem, make two applications of pyrethrum, three to five days apart.

Plants Stunted; Leaves Yellowed and Small; Knots on Roots

Nematodes

Especially in the southern states, impatiens are sometimes infested with nematodes, which can cause sickly, wilted, or stunted growth and yellowed or bronzed foliage. Infested root systems are poorly developed, even partially decayed, and may have tiny galls or knots on them. The effects of nematode activity are most apparent in hot weather, when plants recover poorly from the heat. Southern root knot nematodes (*Meloidogyne incognita*) occasionally attack impatiens, although they do not generally cause serious problems when the plants are grown as annuals. Nematodes are not insects, but slender, unsegmented roundworms that are barely visible to the unaided eye.

Do not try to save and overwinter impatiens infested with nematodes. Dig and destroy them; do not compost. Prevention is the best way to deal with nematodes when growing annuals in infested soil, since severely infested annuals are best dug up and destroyed. Organic matter in the soil helps to control nematodes because it not only benefits the fungi and bacteria that feed on them, it also keeps plants healthy and better able to withstand mild infestations. Add lots of compost, especially leaf mold, to the bed before planting. Turn severely infested plots over to a thick planting of French marigolds for an entire season and dig the plant remains into the soil at season's end to discourage these pests. Crop rotation is also a good idea; don't grow susceptible plants on the same plot year after year.

Leaves Stippled with Tiny Yellow Dots; Webby Foliage

Spider Mites

Leaves that are dry and stippled with tiny yellow dots are a sign that your impatiens are infested with spider mites, tiny pests that suck chlorophyll out of the leaves. They also inject toxins into the foliage; this causes distorted or discolored growth. Leaves, stems, and flowers also may be swathed in fine webbing. As their name suggests, spider mites are related to spiders. These tiny creatures, which are about $\frac{1}{50}$ inch long and barely visible to the naked eye, may be yellow, green, red, or brown. Two-spotted spider mites (*Tetranychus urticae*) attack impatiens, especially those brought indoors for overwintering or in greenhouses. Spider mites reproduce most rapidly during hot, dry weather. Inspect purchased bedding plants carefully to avoid bringing home infested specimens.

Severely infested plants should be destroyed, since infestations are difficult to control once they are well under way. Spider mites can be controlled by washing the plants, especially the undersides of the leaves. For best results, use a forceful spray of water once every other day to knock the mites off the plants; wash the plants at least three times. If

that is not effective, spray the plants with insecticidal soap every three to five days for two weeks. To avoid spreading the mites from plant to plant, don't touch healthy plants after examining infested ones.

Flowers Deformed and Dwarfed

Tarnished Plant Bugs

If the young shoots, and especially buds, of your impatiens are deformed or the flowers are dwarfed, look for tarnished plant bugs (*Lygus rugulipennis*). These active, ¼-inch-long bugs are green to brown in color and mottled with white, yellow, and black. On either side of the insect near the back is a yellow triangle with a black dot at one corner. Tarnished plant bugs appear in early spring, and, if left uncontrolled, become increasingly numerous toward the end of summer. They feed by sucking sap from plants and also release a toxin when feeding that can deform foliage and shoots.

Preventive measures are the best way to control this pest. Adults overwinter in weeds, as well as under leaves and other garden debris. Thoroughly clean up the garden in spring and fall to discourage overwintering adults. Handpicking adults and nymphs and dropping them into a jar of soapy water is also effective if the infestation isn't too great. If that is not effective, spray the plants with insecticidal soap every three to five days for two weeks, or try three applications of pyrethrum laced with isopropyl alcohol, one every three days. Spray early in the morning when bugs are least active. If the infestation is heavy, dust plants with sabadilla.

MOST COMMON DISEASES

Seedlings Rot at Base, Fall Over

Damping-Off

Seedling stems that are water soaked and blackened at the soil line have been afflicted with damping-off. Affected stems are unable to support the plants, which fall over and die. Usually, the foliage is still green and healthy looking when the plants collapse. Stems of older plants show tan to reddish brown lesions that eventually girdle stems. Damping-off is caused by a variety of soil-dwelling fungi such as *Pythium, Fusarium, Sclerotium,* and *Rhizoctonia,* and germinating seeds may be attacked before they emerge from the soil, or shortly thereafter.

Cultural controls are effective in preventing damping-off. Sow seed in well-drained soil, do not overcrowd plants, and keep soil on the dry side. Use a sterile growing mix (peat, perlite, and vermiculite, with a topping of milled sphagnum moss), and water plants from below by setting pots in water and allowing the water to soak up to just beneath the soil surface. For *I. balsamina* sown outdoors, plant in well-drained soil or raised beds. Thin seedlings so they are far enough apart to allow air to circulate between them, which will carry away excessive moisture and reduce humidity. When thinning, use scissors instead of pulling up plants to avoid damaging the roots and stems of remaining plants, which might open them up to infection. In the greenhouse, a fan will promote air circulation. Avoid feeding seedlings too much nitrogen, for it causes lank, weak growth. Routinely disinfect garden tools in boiling water or a household bleach solution (1 part bleach to 3 parts water) to discourage disease problems.

Leaves Covered with Small Brown Spots

Fungal Leaf Spot
A variety of fungi cause small, circular brown leaf spots on the foliage of these plants.

To control leaf spot, pick off and destroy infected leaves. Also, regularly clean up and destroy dead plant debris in the garden to reduce spore populations. These fungi overwinter as spores in such debris, so an end-of-season cleanup is especially important. Weed out and discard seriously infected plants, together with the soil in which they are growing. Do not compost infected plant material; discard it. A layer of mulch helps prevent spores from splashing from the soil onto plants. If leaf spot is a particular problem in your area, spray at weekly to ten-day intervals with wettable sulfur or bordeaux mixture, particularly in rainy seasons. (Watch for leaf discoloration with the latter.)

Roots and Stems Turn Black and Rot

Stem Rot
Impatiens are occasionally attacked by stem rot caused by a variety of soil-dwelling fungi. Stems of infected plants rot at the base. The fungi girdle the stem, and plants subsequently turn yellow, wilt, and die. If your impatiens rot suddenly at the ground level and stems fall over, cut an afflicted stem and check for a yellowish ooze. This indicates the presence of a bacterial wilt caused by *Pseudomonas solanacearum.*

Preventive measures are very helpful in controlling stem rot. Plant impatiens in well-drained soil, avoid overwatering, avoid overcrowding the plants, and keep mulch away from the base of plant stems. Remove and discard infected plants, together with the surrounding soil, or cut away affected plant parts with a clean, sharp knife or razor blade. (Cuttings taken from the tops of afflicted stems are generally healthy and can be used to propagate plants stricken with stem rot.) Also, regularly clean up and destroy dead plant debris in the garden. Do not compost infected plants or soil; discard them. Disinfect tools with a solution of 1 part household bleach and 3 parts water or 70 percent rubbing alcohol after use to avoid spreading the disease. For long-term prevention, lighten heavy soil with a mixture of perlite, vermiculite, and/or peat moss, and provide good drainage. A thorough end-of-season cleanup is also helpful in controlling this problem.

Larkspur *Consolida ambigua*

DESCRIPTION

Annual larkspur offers all the elegance and beauty of its perennial relatives, the true *Delphinium* species, plus a longer blooming period and easier cultivation. In fact, once these hardy, care-free annuals are established, they will reseed themselves annually and fill the garden from late spring to early

summer with their spikes of flowers. Annual larkspur is also commonly called rocket larkspur or annual delphinium and is sometimes sold under the name of *Delphinium ajacis*. They are very effective when used at the back of beds or borders and are most attractive when planted in groups. They also make lovely cut flowers.

Height

1 to 5 feet

Spread

1 to 2 feet

Blossoms

Annual larkspur bears many-flowered spikes of 1- to 1¼-inch-long blooms. Flowers most commonly come in shades of violet to pale lilac, light to dark blue, deep to pale pink, and white. These plants prefer cool temperatures and bloom in late spring to early summer throughout most of the country. However, blooms will persist into September in areas with cooler summers if dead flowers are faithfully removed to encourage further bloom.

Foliage

Larkspur foliage is finely divided and feathery or lacy in texture. The leaves are deep green.

ENVIRONMENT

Hardiness

Annual larkspur is a hardy annual that performs best in regions with long, cool springs. Seedlings are cold tolerant, and throughout much of the country, seed can be sown outdoors in fall for germination in early spring. Once established, plants will reseed themselves each year.

Light

Annual larkspur prefers full sun but will tolerate very light shade.

Soil

For best results, grow annual larkspur in rich, well-drained soil with a neutral to slightly alkaline pH. A range from 6.5 to 8.0 is fine.

PLANTING AND PROPAGATION

Planting

Sow seed outdoors where the plants are to grow in very early spring. In USDA Zones 7 through 10, sow seed in early fall for germination the following spring. Cover the seed completely, as it requires darkness to germinate. Seed can be sown indoors, but sow in individual peat pots, since the seedlings can be difficult to transplant. Sow seed six to eight weeks before planting outside in early spring, and germinate at temperatures between 65° and 70°F. Germination takes 10 to 20 days. When transplanting seeds sown indoors, set peat pots directly into the ground with the seedlings to minimize disturbance. Space plants 10 to 12 inches apart.

PLANT MANAGEMENT

General Care

Annual larkspurs are easy-to-grow plants that are seldom bothered by pests or diseases. They will die out in hot weather, however. Provide a thick layer of mulch once the plants are about a foot tall to keep the roots cool. Shear them back once they begin to look ragged, and plan on using them with heat-tolerant annuals so you don't end up with empty spots in the garden. Remove spent blooms to prolong the flowering season, but be sure to allow enough to go to seed for next year's crop. Taller forms may need staking, especially in areas that are windy or suffer heavy summer storms.

Water

Make sure larkspur plants get 1 inch of water every week from rain or by watering. On especially hot days, water at midday to help keep their roots cool.

Feeding

Annual larkspurs grow best in soil that is rich in organic matter, so work compost into the soil at planting time. This will serve the basic needs of the plants all season long. Or, apply a slow-acting, general-purpose fertilizer in spring. For exceptional performance, give plants supplemental, light feedings (side-dressings or foliar spray) monthly throughout the growing season.

Cutting Fresh Flowers

Larkspurs make excellent cut flowers. For longest vase life, cut flowers early in the day and when the flowers are not yet fully open. Keep them away from pets and children, however, since these plant are poisonous if ingested.

Drying Flowers

Cut larkspur flower spikes when the blooms are only partially open and some are even still in the bud stage. Strip off the leaves so that you have bare stems. Air dry them by hanging them upside down in a warm, dry room. They can also be preserved in silica gel. To dry in silica gel, cut flowers in full bloom, leaving 1-inch stems. Place flower cluster, stems down, in a coffee can or other sealable container partially filled with silica gel. Carefully sift silica gel over blooms until they are completely covered.

MOST COMMON CULTURAL PROBLEMS

Plants Fail to Flower

Planted Too Late

Larkspur plants die out once summer heat arrives, and if seed is sown too late in the year, plants may not attain flowering size before that time. Sow seed in fall or very early spring, as soon as the soil can be worked. Seedlings are quite hardy and can handle light frosts.

Seedlings Appear Where They Are Not Wanted

Reseeding

Larkspurs can reseed prolifically from year to year, and unexpected seedlings can become a nuisance. Picking the flowers or shearing back the plants before seed ripens can reduce this problem. Otherwise, pull out unwanted seedlings when they arise.

MOST COMMON INSECT PESTS

Pale or Yellow Spots on Leaves, Leaves Curled and Distorted

Aphids

Plants infested with aphids have distorted growth that may be curled, puckered, or stunted. Leaves may turn yellow or brown, and feeding can seriously damage flower buds or cause distorted flowers. Plants may also wilt under bright sunlight. Aphids are soft-bodied, pear-shaped sucking insects about the size of the head of a pin; they may be brown, green, yellow, or nearly black. They are often found clustered under leaves, and flower buds and stem tips may be covered with dense colonies of these insects. Ants, attracted by the aphids' honeydew secretions, wander over the plants, and black, sooty mold can develop on the honeydew as well. In addition to the damage they cause by feeding, aphids are important vectors of virus diseases. Delphinium aphid (*Brachycaudus rociadae*), green peach aphid (*Myzus persicae*), and crescent-marked lily aphid (*Neomyzus circumflexus*) all are found on annual larkspur.

Light infestations of aphids can be controlled by washing the plants, especially the undersides of the leaves. For best results, use a forceful spray of water once every other day to knock the aphids off the plants; wash the plants at least three times. If that is not effective, spray the plants with insecticidal soap every three to five days for two weeks. If these pests become a very serious problem, make two applications of pyrethrum, three to five days apart.

Leaves Covered with Tan to Brown Blotches; Foliage Appears Blighted

Leafminers

If large areas of the leaves of your annual larkspur plants turn brown or tan, and the foliage looks discolored and diseased, they may be infested with larkspur leafminers (*Phytomyza* spp.). The larvae of these species feed in small groups, sharing a single mine or tunnel within the leaf. Careful observation will reveal dark flecks of excrement within the mines. The larvae feed inside the leaves and then pupate in brown, seedlike cases that often are attached to the infested foliage. There are several generations per year.

Pick off and destroy all infested leaves. If necessary, prune back stems until healthy growth remains. Larvae can sometimes be repelled by spraying plants with several weekly applications of insecticidal soap in late June or early July.

Leaves Stippled with Tiny Yellow Dots; Webby Foliage

Spider Mites

Leaves that are dry and stippled with tiny yellow dots are a sign that your annual larkspurs are infested with spider mites, tiny pests that suck chlorophyll out of the leaves. They also inject toxins into the foliage; this causes distorted or discolored growth. Leaves, stems, and flowers also may be swathed in fine webbing. As their name suggests, spider mites are related to spiders. These tiny creatures, which are about $\frac{1}{50}$ inch long and barely visible to the naked eye, may be yellow, green, red, or brown. Both cyclamen mites (*Steneotarsonemus pallidus*) and two-spotted spider mites (*Tetranychus urticae*) attack annual larkspur. Spider mites reproduce most rapidly during hot, dry weather.

Severely infested plants should be destroyed, since infestations are difficult to control once they are well under way. Spider mites can be controlled by washing the plants, especially the undersides of the leaves. For best results, use a forceful spray of water once every other day to knock the mites off the plants; wash the plants at least three times. If that is not effective, spray the plants with insecticidal soap every three to five days for two weeks. To avoid spreading the mites from plant to plant, don't touch healthy plants after examining infested ones.

MOST COMMON DISEASES

Stems Turn Black at Base; Leaves Wilt

Crown and Stem Rots
Annual larkspur are subject to crown and stem rots caused by both bacteria and fungi. If your plants rot at the base and eventually wilt, suspect one of these diseases. Stems may also turn black from the base upward, and foliage may turn brown. Root rots that attack annual larkspurs at or near the soil level may not cause the stem to turn black, but instead cause the foliage to turn yellow, wilt, and die. In this case, the root system rots and the plants topple over.

These diseases primarily attack larkspurs grown for several years in the same spot, or in very hot or very wet weather. Bacterial rots are characterized by a strong, unpleasant odor and masses of oozing bacteria from cut stems; fungal rots by the tiny fruiting bodies of the fungi themselves.

Control measures for both types of rots are the same. Remove and discard infected plants, together with the surrounding soil, or cut away affected plant parts with a clean, sharp knife or razor blade. Also, regularly clean up and destroy dead plant debris in the garden. Do not compost infected plants or soil; discard them. Disinfect tools with a solution of 1 part household bleach and 3 parts water or 70 percent rubbing alcohol after use to avoid spreading the disease. For long-term prevention, replace infected soil, improve drainage, and avoid overwatering. Rotate plantings by collecting ripened seed in summer and sowing it in a new location.

White Powder Covering Leaves

Powdery Mildew
If your annual larkspur leaves are covered with a white or ash gray powdery mold they probably have powdery mildew. Badly infected leaves become discolored and distorted, then drop off. Powdery mildew is caused by fungi that live primarily on the surface of the leaves, flowers, and stems of plants, not inside them.

Powdery mildew most commonly develops on plants grown close together where air circulation is restricted, especially on the lower leaves where humidity is higher and moisture is more abundant. Allow ample spacing between plants, and collect and discard all aboveground refuse in the fall. Spray afflicted plants thoroughly with wettable sulfur once or twice at weekly intervals starting as soon as the whitish coating of the fungus is visible.

ANNUAL **Marigolds** *Tagetes* spp.

DESCRIPTION

Marigolds are popular members of the daisy family, Compositae, that will provide summer-long color for even the most inexperienced gardener, provided a few basic cultural conditions are met. They pro-

duce showy, single or double flower heads all summer long in shades of orange, yellow, maroon, and white. Foliage is deeply cut and aromatic—some gardeners find the odor unpleasant. There are several species and many cultivars of marigolds from which to choose, but the vast majority of marigolds available fall into two groups: French marigolds, cultivars of *Tagetes patula*, which are small plants that bear small flowers, and African or American marigolds, cultivars of *T. erecta*, which are taller plants with larger flowers than the French marigolds. Marigolds are undemanding, easy-to-grow plants that can be used in borders, as bedding plants, or in containers. They also make fine cut flowers.

Height

T. erecta (African or American marigold), 2 to 3 feet

T. patula (French marigold), 1 to 2 feet

Spread

10 to 24 inches

Blossoms

As members of the daisy family, marigold blooms consist of small individual flowers arranged in dense heads. Heads may be single—with a tufted center composed of tiny, tightly packed individual flowers called disc florets surrounded by a ring of more showy "petals," called ray florets—or double—with densely packed petals throughout. *T. patula* produces 2- to 3-inch blooms; *T. erecta* bears flower heads that range from 2 to 6 inches across. Flowers range from ivory to gold, orange, yellow, and maroon. Many are marked with two colors. Marigolds bloom from early summer to first fall frost.

Foliage

Marigolds have deeply cut, feathery-looking leaves. Most cultivars have strongly scented foliage, although some cultivars are odorless. The leaves are dark green and shiny.

ENVIRONMENT

Hardiness

Marigolds are half-hardy annuals that will withstand cool temperatures, but for best results, plant them in the garden after danger of frost has passed.

Light

For best bloom, grow marigolds in full sun—a hot, sunny, southern exposure is ideal. They will tolerate a site that is shaded in early morning or late afternoon if they are in full sun the rest of the day. In the South and Southwest, afternoon shade will prolong bloom.

Soil

Grow marigolds in well-drained soil that is well-tilled, but not overly rich. They will tolerate most soil types.

PLANTING AND PROPAGATION

Planting

Outdoors, sow seed where the plants are to grow after all danger of frost has passed. Indoors, sow four to six weeks before the last frost date. Seeds germinate in about seven days. Temperatures of 70° to 75°F are ideal. Move seedlings and purchased bedding plants to the garden after all danger of frost has passed. Space plants 8 to 18 inches apart depending on the ultimate height of the cultivar. For earliest bloom, sow seed of *T. erecta* indoors.

Container Gardening

Marigolds will grow well in window boxes, pots, and tubs.

PLANT MANAGEMENT

General Care

Marigolds require very little day-to-day maintenance once they are established in the garden. Removing faded flowers helps encourage new flowers to form.

Water

Make sure the plants get 1 inch of water every week from rain or by watering, but do not overwater. When watering, water thoroughly and then let the plants nearly dry out between waterings. Avoid spraying water on the blooms of large-flowered cultivars, for it can cause flowers to become waterlogged and turn brown. Water early in the day to allow foliage to dry before nightfall.

Feeding

A single application of compost or a slow-acting, general-purpose fertilizer worked into the soil before planting will serve the basic needs of these annuals all season. For exceptional performance, give plants supplemental, light feedings (side-dressings or foliar spray) monthly throughout the growing season.

Cutting Fresh Flowers

For those gardeners who do not object to the strong scent of the foliage, marigolds make fine additions to cut flower arrangements.

Drying Flowers

Marigolds can be air dried. To air dry, cut the blooms when they are at their peak, remove the foliage, and hang them upside down in a warm, dark, dry place.

MOST COMMON CULTURAL PROBLEMS

Plants Stop Blooming

Excessive Heat
High summer temperatures may slow or stop flower production. Keep plants well watered and mulched to help them withstand summer heat.

MOST COMMON INSECT PESTS

Marigolds are bothered by few insects, and can easily withstand attacks by most pests, provided the plants are healthy and vigorous. In addition to the pests listed below, slugs, snails, and caterpillars occasionally eat holes in the foliage. Stalk borers may bore holes in the stems and spider mites may cause yellowed foliage stuck together by silken webs. Be sure to inspect purchased plants carefully to avoid bringing home infested specimens.

Pale or Yellow Spots on Leaves, Leaves Curled and Distorted

Aphids
Plants infested with aphids have distorted growth that may be curled, puckered, or stunted. Leaves may turn yellow or brown, and feeding can seriously damage flower buds or cause distorted flowers. Plants may also wilt under bright sunlight. Aphids are soft-bodied, pear-shaped sucking insects about the size of the head of a pin; they may be brown, green, yellow, or nearly black. They are often found clustered under leaves, and flower buds and stem tips may be covered with dense colonies of these insects. Ants, attracted by the aphids' honeydew secretions, wander over the plants, and black, sooty mold can develop on the honeydew as well. In addition to the damage they cause by feeding, aphids are important vectors of virus diseases. The most common species of aphids infesting marigolds are green peach aphid (*Myzus persicae*) and melon aphid (*Aphis gossypii*).

Light infestations of aphids can be controlled by washing the plants, especially the undersides of the leaves. For best results, use a forceful spray of water once every other day to knock the aphids off the plants; wash the plants at least three times. If that is not effective, spray the plants with insecticidal soap every three to five days for two weeks. If these pests become a very serious problem, make two applications of pyrethrum, three to five days apart.

Holes in Leaves and/or Flowers

Beetles
T. erecta is a particular favorite of Japanese beetles (*Popillia japonica*), which will skeletonize leaves and destroy flowers. Adults are ½-inch-long beetles that are shiny, metallic green with copper-colored wing covers. The larvae are C-shaped, grayish white grubs with dark brown heads that can eat plant roots. Fully grown grubs are ¾ to 1 inch long.

Where possible, handpick and crush Japanese beetles or drop them into a pail of soapy water. If the infestation is light, this is all you will need to do. For heavier infestations, spray infested plants with a solution of pyrethrum and isopropyl alcohol, mixing 1 tablespoon of alcohol with every pint of diluted pyrethrum mixture. Apply this solution every three to five days until the problem is corrected. For long-term control, apply milky spore disease (*Bacillus popilliae*) to lawns and garden. It will kill the larvae of most beetles.

Japanese beetles can also be controlled by pheromone traps. Set up traps a week before the beetles are expected to emerge in your area, making sure traps are no closer than 50 feet from the marigolds or any other plant vulnerable to beetle attack, such as roses.

Leaves Discolored, Distorted

Leafhoppers
Several species of leafhoppers feed on marigold foliage, causing cupped or rolled leaf margins, which fold over the midrib. Severely infested leaves twist

on their stalks and are finely mottled with white or yellow spots. Leaves eventually shrivel and drop off; branch tips may wilt. Leafhoppers are often strikingly colored, ⅛- to ¼-inch-long insects that are wedge-shaped with wings held in a rooflike position above their bodies. They're very active, moving sideways or hopping suddenly when disturbed. Nymphs and adults suck juices from leaves, buds, and stems. Some species may spread virus diseases such as aster yellows, which they pick up in spring when feeding on infected wild plants. Potato leafhopper (*Empoascus fabae*), red-banded leafhopper (*Graphocephala coccinea*), and aster leafhopper (*Macrosteles fascifrons*) all attack marigolds.

To control serious infestations, spray infested plants with a mixture of insecticidal soap and isopropyl alcohol. Make this mix by adding 1 tablespoon of alcohol to each pint of insecticidal soap solution. Make three applications, spraying once every three to five days. If leafhoppers are a common problem in your backyard, place a barrier such as floating row covers, like Reemay, over plants in early spring. Also, apply preventive sprays of insecticidal soap solution or pyrethrum at four- to five-day intervals for the first month of growth.

Leaves Stuck Together with Silk; Foliage Ragged and Discolored

Leaftiers

Leaves that are fastened together with strands of silk, followed by foliage that becomes ragged and unsightly, turns brown, and dies are signs that your plants are infested with greenhouse or celery leaftier (*Udea rubigalis*). It is the larval stage that damages plants by feeding on the undersides of the leaves and binding the leaves together. The larvae are ⅜- to ¾-inch-long caterpillars that are light green or cream to yellow in color with a white stripe down their backs and a green line down the center of the stripe. Adult leaftier moths, which are active only at night, are brown or gray and ¼ to ½ inch long. They lay eggs that resemble fish scales on the undersides of leaves.

Handpicking of eggs and larvae is usually an effective way to control this pest, since infestations are usually light. Remove any rolled or folded leaves, for they shelter caterpillars. Infested leaves should be destroyed, since the pests pupate and overwinter in them. Bt (*Bacillus thuringiensis*) also is an effective control. Apply as a powder or spray every two weeks until leaftiers disappear.

Flowers Deformed and Dwarfed

Tarnished Plant Bugs

If the young shoots, and especially buds, of your marigolds are deformed or the flowers are dwarfed, look for tarnished plant bugs (*Lygus rugulipennis*). These active, ¼-inch-long bugs are green to brown in color and mottled with white, yellow, and black. On either side of the insect near the back is a yellow triangle with a black dot at one corner. Tarnished plant bugs appear in early spring, and, if left uncontrolled, become increasingly numerous toward the end of summer. They feed by sucking sap from plants and also release a toxin when feeding that can deform foliage and shoots.

Preventive measures are the best way to control this pest. Adults overwinter in weeds, as well as under leaves and other garden debris. Thoroughly clean up the garden in spring and fall to discourage overwintering adults. Handpicking adults and nymphs and dropping them into a jar of soapy water is also effective if the infestation isn't too great. If that is not effective, spray the plants with insecticidal soap every three to five days for two weeks, or try three applications of pyrethrum laced with isopropyl alcohol, one every three days. Spray early in the morning when bugs are least active. If the infestation is heavy, dust plants with sabadilla.

MOST COMMON DISEASES

Marigolds grown with proper cultural conditions—well-drained soil and full sun—are subject to few diseases. In addition to the ones listed below, they can be infected with the virus disease aster yellows, which causes deformed growth and greenish yellow leaves and flowers.

Flowers Turn Brown and Rot

Blight

During wet weather, a fungus disease caused by *Botrytis cinerea* can cause marigold flowers to turn brown and decay. The fungi also cause ashy gray spots to develop on bud scales and stems and may cause the tips of plant stems to die.

Pick off and destroy blighted flowers as soon as you spot them; do not compost.

Leaves Covered with Spots or Blotches

Leaf Spot

Marigold foliage marked with irregular gray or black spots that are speckled with tiny fungal fruiting bodies are probably infected with the fungal leaf spot disease caused by *Septoria tageticola*. The disease starts on lower leaves and progresses upward. *Tagetes erecta* is very susceptible to leaf spot, but *T. patula* is either resistant or immune.

Cultural controls are effective ways to combat leaf spot in marigolds. Pick off and destroy any infected leaves as soon as they appear. Also, regularly clean up and destroy dead plant debris in the garden. Do not compost plant material you suspect to be infected. Rogue out and discard seriously infected plants, together with the soil in which they are growing. A layer of mulch helps prevent fungal spores from splashing from the soil onto plants. If fungal leaf spot is a particular problem in your area, spray at weekly to ten-day intervals with wettable sulfur or bordeaux mixture, particularly in rainy seasons. (Watch for leaf discoloration with the latter.)

Plants Wilt Suddenly; Stems Rot at Soil Line

Wilt and Stem Rot

Marigolds can be afflicted with a variety of diseases that cause plants to wilt suddenly or to rot at or below the soil line. Plants may wilt suddenly and/or leaves may turn yellow and then wilt. *Phytophthora* spp. fungi rot marigold roots and cause stems to turn brown and shrivel at the soil line, followed shortly by wilting and death. *T. erecta* is susceptible to this disease, while *T. patula* is not. A fungal stem rot causes dark lesions on stems at or near the soil line and sometimes causes root decay. A wilt disease caused by *Fusarium* spp. fungi attacks *T. patula* primarily, which is immune to the wilt and stem rot diseases caused by *Phytophthora* spp. The disease works its way up from the base of the plant, causing leaves and branches to wilt and die. Several soil-dwelling fungi, including *Pellicularia filamentosa, P. rolfsii, Sythium ultimum,* and *Sclerotinia sclerotiorum*, can rot marigold roots and crowns. Finally a bacterial wilt caused by *Pseudomonas solanacearum* causes sudden wilting and collapse of plants and stems rotted at ground level. Yellowish masses of bacteria ooze out when the stems are cut.

Preventive measures are very helpful in controlling these diseases. Plant marigolds in well-drained soil, avoid overwatering and overcrowding, and keep mulch away from the base of plant stems. Remove and discard infected plants, together with the surrounding soil, or cut away affected plant parts with a clean, sharp knife or razor blade. Discard infected plant material; do not compost. Disinfect tools with a solution of 1 part household bleach and 3 parts water or 70 percent rubbing alcohol to avoid spreading the disease. Keep the garden clear of old plant debris. For long-term prevention, lighten heavy soil with a mixture of perlite, vermiculite, and/or peat moss, and provide good drainage.

Nasturtium

Tropaeolum majus

DESCRIPTION

The common garden nasturtium is a succulent-leaved annual native to the cool highlands of South and Central America. It is such an easy-to-grow, trouble-free plant, that it is often included in gardens for children. Nasturtiums are fast-growing plants

that bear a multitude of vibrantly colored, single or double flowers. Plant breeders have developed many cultivars of this popular annual, which can be roughly divided into three different types of plant habits: dwarf cultivars, which feature bushy, compact growth; semitrailing cultivars, which are compact but trail somewhat; and climbing or vining cultivars. Vining forms climb by wrapping their fleshy leaf stalks around supports, although they generally will need to be tied to a trellis for support as well. Depending on the cultivar selected, nasturtiums are suitable for growing against a trellis or wall, covering a bank, trailing from hanging baskets or window boxes, and for beds and borders. The foliage and flowers of nasturtiums contain mustard oil and have a peppery watercress-like flavor (the common name, nasturtium, is also the botanical name of watercress). Both make fine additions to salads. Young seed heads can be pickled like capers.

Height

Dwarf cultivars, 10 to 12 inches; semitrailing cultivars, 1½ to 2 feet; climbing cultivars, 8 to 10 feet

Spread

Dwarf cultivars, 1 to 2 feet; semitrailing and climbing cultivars, 2 to 3 feet

Blossoms

Nasturtiums bear single or double blooms that are trumpet-shaped with a long spur behind the flower. Colors range from yellowish white to deep yellow, light to dark orange, and scarlet-orange to deep reddish brown. Blooms often are spotted or streaked with contrasting colors and range from 2 to 3 inches across. Many cultivars have a somewhat spicy fragrance. The plants will bloom continuously from summer through fall, although they may stop blooming during prolonged heat spells.

Foliage

Nasturtiums have somewhat succulent, nearly round leaves that are brilliant green in color and smooth in texture. Leaves range from 2 to 7 inches in diameter. Climbing types have fleshy leaf stalks that twine around supports, plants, and any other object with which they come in contact. The leaves release a peppery scent when bruised.

ENVIRONMENT

Hardiness

Nasturtiums are tender annuals that are quite susceptible to frost. They grow best in regions with dry, cool summers.

Light

Grow nasturtiums in full sun where summers are cool; in light shade where summers are hot. Plants will produce lush leaves, but few flowers when grown in the shade.

Soil

For best results, grow nasturtiums in sandy, dry, well-drained soil that is not too fertile. Rich soil will lead to the production of lush foliage but few flowers. Soil pH can range from 6 to 8.

PLANTING AND PROPAGATION

Planting

Nasturtiums are best sown outdoors where the plants are to grow after danger of frost has passed. Plant seeds ¼ inch deep, for they require darkness to germinate. Seedlings will emerge in 7 to 14 days. Seed sown too early in spring may not germinate because the soil has not warmed sufficiently. For best results, wait until the soil temperature is at least 65°F before sowing seed. Seed can be sown indoors, but nasturtiums are difficult to transplant, so outdoor sowing is best. For sowing indoors, plant seeds in individual peat pots six to eight weeks before the last frost date, and germinate at 65°F. Transplant seedlings—pot and all to minimize disturbance—after danger of frost has passed.

Propagation

Plants can be propagated from stem cuttings taken from young shoots in fall, which are rooted in vermiculite and grown indoors over winter. Double-flowered cultivars are often propagated in this manner.

Container Gardening

Nasturtiums will grow well in pots, window boxes, and hanging baskets.

PLANT MANAGEMENT

General Care

Nasturtiums require very little day-to-day maintenance once they are established in the garden. Vining or climbing forms must be tied to supports, although they can also be allowed to clamber over the ground as well.

Water

Plants should receive 1 inch of water per week from rain or by watering. Nasturtiums tolerate drought, but only in areas with cool summers; they should be kept moist where summers are hot.

Feeding

A single application of compost or a slow-acting, general-purpose fertilizer worked into the soil before planting will serve the basic needs of these annuals all season. Excessive fertilization will result in leaves at the expense of flowers. Container-grown plants should receive monthly applications of a mild-strength fertilizer.

Cutting Fresh Flowers

Flowers make attractive and edible additions to salads and can also be used as garnishes.

MOST COMMON CULTURAL PROBLEMS

Excessive Foliage; Few Flowers

Soil Too Rich; Improper Planting Location

Nasturtiums that produce many more leaves than flowers may be growing in soil that is too rich, or in a location that receives too little sun. Under such conditions, plants often produce abundant foliage and few, if any, flowers.

Plant nasturtiums in sandy, somewhat infertile soil that is well drained. Choose a location in full sun. Plants grown along the edge of a lawn that has been fed with a high-nitrogen lawn fertilizer often exhibit these symptoms. Water generously for a few days to wash through excess fertilizer, and do not fertilize for the rest of the season.

MOST COMMON INSECT PESTS

Nasturtiums are bothered by few insects and can easily withstand attacks by most pests, provided the plants are healthy and vigorous. In addition to the pests listed below, leaftiers, which fasten leaves together with silk and then devour foliage, and nematodes, which can attack roots, causing stunted growth, both attack nasturtiums. If you plan to use the foliage or flowers in salads, you'll need to control infestations of caterpillars, leafminers, and slugs and snails, all of which are listed below.

Pale or Yellow Spots on Leaves, Leaves Curled and Distorted

Aphids

Plants infested with aphids have distorted growth that may be curled, puckered, or stunted. Leaves may turn yellow or brown, and feeding can seriously damage flower buds or cause distorted flowers. Plants may also wilt under bright sunlight. Aphids are soft-bodied, pear-shaped sucking insects about the size of the head of a pin; they may be brown, green, yellow, or nearly black. They are often found clustered under leaves, and flower buds and stem tips may be covered with dense colonies of these insects. Ants, attracted by the aphids' honeydew secretions, wander over the plants, and black, sooty mold can develop on the honeydew as well. In addition to the damage they cause by feeding, aphids are important vectors of virus diseases. Several species of aphids infest nasturtiums, including bean aphid (*Aphis fabae*), buckthorn aphid (*Aphis nasturtii*), crescent-marked lily aphid (*Neomyzus circumflexus*), and green peach aphid (*Myzus persicae*). Several beneficial insects feed on aphids, including ladybugs and lacewings.

Light infestations of aphids can be controlled by washing the plants, especially the undersides of the leaves. For best results, use a forceful spray of water once every other day to knock the aphids off the plants; wash the plants at least three times. If that is not effective, spray the plants with insecticidal soap every three to five days for two weeks. If these pests become a very serious problem, make two applications of pyrethrum, three to five days apart.

Holes in Leaves; Chewed Edges

Caterpillars

Nasturtiums that have holes in the leaves or chewed leaf edges, but lack the slime trails that indicate the presence of slugs or snails, are infested with caterpillars. Various caterpillars may attack these plants, including cabbage looper (*Trichoplusia ni*), imported cabbageworm (*Pieris rapae*), and corn earworm

(*Heliothis zea*). Cabbage loopers are greenish, 1¼-inch-long caterpillars with three white or yellowish stripes down their backs; they walk with a looping motion. The adult is a night-flying, mottled, grayish or brownish moth with a silvery spot in the middle of each wing. Cabbage loopers overwinter as pupae in brown cocoons attached to plant foliage. The larvae of imported cabbageworms are green with darker stripes and are about 1 inch long at maturity. Adults are white butterflies that lay yellowish, bullet-shaped eggs. There may be five or more generations of imported cabbageworms per year. Corn earworms are 2-inch-long caterpillars that are yellowish, green, or brown with stripes running lengthwise. They eat leaves and flower buds and tunnel into the stems. The adults are small, grayish brown moths.

Mild infestations are easliy controlled by hand-picking caterpillars and dropping them in a jar of soapy water. To control serious infestations, apply Bt (*Bacillus thuringiensis*) at three- to five-day intervals until the caterpillars disappear. Dust or spray both sides of the leaves, and reapply after rain. Also, regularly clean up and dispose of garden debris throughout the season to reduce future generations. A thorough end-of-season cleanup is also beneficial.

Leaves and/or Flowers Riddled with Tiny Holes

Flea Beetles
Nasturtium leaves perforated with dozens or hundreds of tiny holes may be victims of flea beetles, including the western black flea beetle (*Phyllotreta pusilla*). These shiny black or brown pests are only ¹⁄₁₆ inch long and very active, jumping like fleas when disturbed. Flea beetles transmit viral and bacterial diseases. They overwinter as adults and generally feed on weeds in early spring, then move to the garden. The larvae are tiny grubs that feed on plant roots.

Barriers such as floating row covers, like Reemay, can be used to prevent flea beetles from gaining access to nasturtiums. For heavier infestations, spray infested plants with a solution of pyrethrum and isopropyl alcohol, mixing 1 tablespoon of alcohol with every pint of diluted pyrethrum mixture. Apply this solution every three to five days until the problem is corrected. For long-term control, beneficial nematodes introduced into the soil will take care of the flea beetle larvae.

Leaves Covered with Tan to Brown Blotches, or Mines in Leaves

Leafminers
Nasturtium leaves with yellow and white to brown tunnels or blotches between upper and lower leaf surfaces are probably infested with leafminers. Careful observation will reveal dark flecks of excrement within the mines, and larvae are often visible through leaf tissue. Leaves may later blister or curl, turn brown, and die. The larvae feed inside the leaves and then pupate in the mines or the soil. Adults are minute black-and-yellow flies. There are several generations per year. Leafminer infestations can give entry to fungal rots and other diseases.

Pick off and destroy all infested leaves. If necessary, prune back stems until only healthy growth remains. Larvae can sometimes be repelled by spraying plants with several weekly applications of insecticidal soap in late June or early July.

Ragged Holes in Leaves; Trails of Slime on Plants

Slugs and Snails
Plants that have large, ragged holes in the leaves and stems are probably infested with slugs and/or snails. Trails of slime on the foliage and around the plants are further confirmation of the presence of these pests. Slugs and snails are active only at night, when they feast on plants by rasping holes in the foliage with their filelike tongues. During the day, they hide under boards, mulch, or leaf litter. Slugs are similar to snails except that they have no shells. Both are generally 1 to 2 inches long, although some species of slugs grow up to 8 inches in length. Either pest may be white, gray, yellow, or brown-

black in color. They are attracted to moist, well-mulched gardens and are most destructive in shaded gardens and during rainy spells. During winter and in dry seasons, slugs burrow into the ground to wait for more favorable weather.

A multifaceted approach to control is best. Remove boards, rocks, clippings, and other debris to cut down on the places where these pests hide during the day. Or, check daily under favorite hiding places, handpick snoozing slugs, crush them or seal them into a jar full of water and kerosene or insecticidal soap, and discard them. Inverted flowerpots, pieces of grapefruit peel, and cabbage leaves will lure slugs and can be used to trap them. Handpicking at night with a flashlight can be effective if started early in the spring. Traps baited with beer or yeast and water are also effective. To make an effective trap, cut a 2-inch hole in the lid of a coffee can or a small plastic container and bury the container flush with the soil. Slugs are attracted to the yeast in the beer, climb down through the hole in the lid, and drown. The key is to begin trapping very early in the season in order to prevent the population from building up. Surrounding plants with barriers of sand, ashes, or copper sheeting will discourage slugs from invading your plantings.

Leaves Stippled with Tiny Yellow Dots; Webby Foliage

Spider Mites
Leaves that are dry and stippled with tiny yellow or red dots are a sign that your nasturtiums are infested with spider mites, tiny pests that suck chlorophyll out of the leaves. They also inject toxins into the foliage; this causes distorted or discolored growth. Leaves, stems, and flowers also may be swathed in fine webbing. As their name suggests, spider mites are related to spiders. These tiny creatures, which are about $1/50$ inch long and barely visible to the naked eye, may be yellow, green, red, or brown. Two-spotted spider mites (*Tetranychus urticae*) attack nasturtiums. Spider mites reproduce most rapidly during hot, dry weather.

Severely infested plants should be destroyed, since infestations are difficult to control once they are well under way. Spider mites can be controlled by washing the plants, especially the undersides of the leaves. For best results, use a forceful spray of water once every other day to knock the mites off the plants; wash the plants at least three times. If that is not effective, spray the plants with insecticidal soap every three to five days for two weeks. To avoid spreading the mites from plant to plant, don't touch healthy plants after examining infested ones.

Flowers Deformed and Dwarfed

Tarnished Plant Bugs
If the young shoots, and especially buds, of your nasturtiums are deformed or the flowers are dwarfed, look for tarnished plant bugs (*Lygus rugulipennis*). These active, $1/4$-inch-long bugs are green to brown in color and mottled with white, yellow, and black. On either side of the insect near the back is a yellow triangle with a black dot at one corner. Tarnished plant bugs appear in early spring, and, if left uncontrolled, become increasingly numerous toward the end of summer. They feed by sucking sap from plants and also release a toxin when feeding that can deform foliage and shoots.

Preventive measures are the best way to control this pest. Adults overwinter in weeds, as well as under leaves and other garden debris. Thoroughly clean up the garden in spring and fall to discourage overwintering adults. If tarnished plant bugs become a problem, try three applications of pyrethrum laced with isopropyl alcohol, one every three days. Spray early in the morning when bugs are least active. If the infestation is heavy, dust plants with sabadilla.

MOST COMMON DISEASES

Leaves Covered with Spots or Blotches

Bacterial or Fungal Leaf Spot
One species of bacteria and several species of fungi

cause leaf spots on nasturtiums. These diseases generally do not threaten the life of the plant, but do make the leaves unsightly. The bacteria *Pseudomonas aptata* causes spots on the leaves, which eventually rot completely. Fungi that thrive on moist leaf surfaces, including *Heterosporium tropaeoli, Cercospora tropaeoli,* and *Pleospora* spp., also cause leaf spots on nasturtiums. Leaves may have transparent, brown or black spots. Some fungal spots are surrounded by flecks or black dots, which are the spore-bearing fruiting bodies. Often spots come together to form larger patches of dead tissue.

Cultural controls are effective ways to combat both bacterial and fungal leaf spot. Pick off and destroy any infected leaves as soon as they appear. Also, regularly clean up and destroy dead plant debris in the garden. Do not compost plant material you suspect to be infected. Rogue out and discard seriously infected plants, together with the soil in which they are growing. A layer of mulch helps prevent fungal spores from splashing from the soil onto plants.

If fungal leaf spot is a particular problem in your area, spray at weekly to ten-day intervals with wettable sulfur or bordeaux mixture, particularly in rainy seasons. (Watch for leaf discoloration with the latter.) If you suspect bacterial leaf spot, disinfect garden tools with 70 percent denatured alcohol or liquid bleach after working with each plant to avoid transmitting bacteria from plant to plant. Spray afflicted plants weekly during rainy spells with a copper-based bactericide. Control insects (such as aphids) that may transmit disease organisms. Increase air circulation by spacing plants far enough apart for air to move between them, and remove the lower 4 to 6 inches of foliage to avoid contact with wet soil.

Plants Turn Yellow and Wilt; Stems Rot at Soil Line

Bacterial Wilt

A bacterial wilt caused by *Pseudomonas solanacearum* causes nasturtium plants to turn yellow, wilt, and die. Decaying stems become water soaked and have dark streaks; roots also decay and turn black. Grayish masses of bacteria ooze out when the stems are cut.

Preventive measures are helpful in controlling bacterial wilt. Plant nasturtiums in well-drained soil, avoid overwatering or overcrowding plants, and keep the garden clear of old plant debris. Plants can become infected through damaged roots, so avoid cultivating around nasturtium plants. Remove and discard infected plants, together with the surrounding soil, or cut away affected plant parts with a clean, sharp knife or razor blade. Discard infected plant material; do not compost. Disinfect tools with a solution of 1 part household bleach and 3 parts water or 70 percent rubbing alcohol to avoid spreading the disease. The bacterium overwinters in the soil, so avoid planting susceptible plants in heavily infested soil. Also avoid planting vulnerable plants near solanaceous vegetables such as potatoes, tomatoes, eggplant, and other plants subject to the same disease.

Leaves Greenish Yellow or Curled and Deformed; Shoots Spindly or Stunted

Virus Diseases

Nasturtiums are susceptible to a few virus diseases, including aster yellows, beet curly top, and tomato spotted wilt virus. Aster yellows causes leaves that are greenish yellow and spindly, along with stunted or dwarfed growth. The disease is caused by a virus-like organism primarily spread by the aster leafhopper (*Macrosteles fascifrons*). Young plants that are infected show a slight yellowing along leaf veins. As the disease becomes more severe, the entire plant is stunted and yellowed, and the unusual number of shoots that develop cause the plant to become very bushy and upright. Shoot tips branch abnormally and tend to develop into witches'-brooms; secondary shoots are usually spindly. Flowers are deformed and may be aborted entirely. Regardless of the normal bloom color of the cultivar, flowers are often sickly yellow-green.

Nasturtiums that produce curled, thickened,

or otherwise distorted foliage, may be infected with the viral disease that causes beet curly top, which causes excessive cell growth and thus distorted growth. The virus is spread by leafhoppers. Infected plants may be stunted or dwarfed.

Tomato spotted wilt virus causes ring spots, lines, pale areas, mottling, or dead areas to appear on the foliage of infected plants. Afflicted plants eventually wilt and die.

There is no cure for virus-infected plants. Remove and destroy them; do not compost. Small stem-tip cuttings can be made from infected plants if necessary because the virus does not move readily toward the growing tips. Disinfect garden tools with a solution of 1 part household bleach and 3

parts water or 70 percent rubbing alcohol to avoid spreading virus diseases from plant to plant. Also, wash your hands after handling infected plants. To control the insects that transmit the disease, spray remaining plants with a mixture of insecticidal soap and isopropyl alcohol. Make the mix by adding 1 tablespoon of alcohol to each pint of insecticidal soap solution. Spray at three- to five-day intervals, making three applications. The virus overwinters in various perennials and weeds such as daisies, plantain, and gaillardia. Infected plants are not necessarily killed by the disease, but should be dug up and destroyed, since they continue to infect nearby plants via leafhoppers.

ANNUAL Pansy   *Viola × wittrockiana*

DESCRIPTION

Pansies are colorful, dainty annuals or short-lived perennials that provide much-welcomed spring color in garden beds and borders. Their flat-faced blooms come in a multitude of colors; many have as many as three colors per flower. Perhaps the most popular characteristic of the flowers are the facelike markings. Also commonly called heartsease, pansies can be grown as winter-flowering plants in mild climates. They are ideal for use as bedding or edging plants, or in rock gardens and containers. They also make fine cut flowers.

Height

4 to 9 inches

Spread

5 to 6 inches

Blossoms

Pansies bear 2- to 5-inch-wide flowers, each of which has five petals that overlap to form nearly circular blooms. The flowers are flat and often feature blotches of contrasting colors that make them resemble faces. They have a slight sweet and peppery fragrance. Flowers come in many colors and combinations of colors, including yellow, gold, blue, purple, lavender, rust, red, pink, orange, bronze, and white. There are cultivars with single-color blooms and those marked with two and three colors. Pansies bloom from midspring to early summer, but in areas with cool summers, they can bloom throughout the growing season. New cultivars bred for heat-resistance will lengthen the blooming season. To lengthen bloom time, keep picking the flowers, or removing spent flowers, to prevent seed formation.

Foliage

The foliage is dark green with smooth, small, scalloped leaves.

ENVIRONMENT

Hardiness

Pansies are hardy annuals that grow best in cool-summer regions. Seedlings can handle light frosts, and plants kept over the winter will survive temperatures down to 15°F if covered with a mulch of hay or dry leaves.

Light

Pansies will grow in full sun or light shade, but since they do not tolerate heat well, keep them out of hot sun. A location in dappled shade will also help lengthen the blooming season.

Soil

For best results, grow pansies in rich, moist, well-drained soil high in organic matter. An ideal mix is 2 parts loam to 1 part peat moss. They will grow well in soils with pH ranging from 6 to 8.

PLANTING AND PROPAGATION

Planting

Since pansies bloom best in spring before summer heat sends them into decline, it's important to have large, well-grown plants in early spring. Many gardeners rely on purchased bedding plants from the nursery, but in most areas, pansies can be sown outdoors where they are to grow in late summer or winter. A mulch of straw or a thick snow cover is all they require for protection. Seeds should be covered with soil, as they require darkness for germination. About the only thing that will keep pansies from overwintering safely, even in the North, is rot, caused by standing water in spring and fall. To prevent this, be sure to plant them in well-drained soil—a slightly raised bed that is mounded so it is higher in the middle is ideal. Seed sown in late fall will germinate the following spring. Or, seed sown in late summer will germinate in fall and seedlings will begin establishing themselves during the cool weeks of autumn. They can also be sown in late summer and overwintered in a cold frame.

To start pansies indoors, sow seed in late winter, 10 to 12 weeks before the last spring frost date. Sow seeds in a moist flat, $\frac{1}{16}$ inch deep, chill in the refrigerator for 4 to 5 days, and then germinate at temperatures between 60° and 70°F. Germination takes 8 to 20 days. Seedlings can be grown at temperatures between 50° and 60°F. It is safe to set out hardened transplants a month before your frost-free date; they can also be transferred to a cold frame.

If you buy your pansy plants, insist on short, bushy plants with deep green, healthy-looking leaves. Plants with flowers that are fully open will have a harder time establishing themselves than ones with tight buds. Pick flowers before planting. Be sure to inspect purchased plants carefully to avoid bringing home infested specimens.

Container Gardening

Pansies are attractive in window boxes or pots.

PLANT MANAGEMENT

General Care

Because pansies are so vulnerable to the heat, mulch the soil around them to keep their roots cool. Choose heat-resistant cultivar, especially if you live in an area where the temperatures exceed 85°F in summer. Many of the newer cultivars are heat resistant. For biggest blooms, trim your plants after they start flowering, leaving from four to six shoots. To encourage early fall bloom, shear the plants in July. Even though it can be time consuming, deadheading—or better yet picking pansies for indoor bouquets—will increase the number of blossoms and will extend the bloom period. Pansies also can be rejuvenated in August for fall bloom by a form of division called Irishman's cuttings, which means teasing out and replanting the loosely growing shoots that are produced at the base of the plant. By leaving these basal shoots attached to the plant for a time, they form new roots, and then can be gently pulled away from the plant and set out as new plants for fall bloom. Pinch plants from time to time throughout the season to help them keep their bushy shape.

Water

As with most annuals, pansies grow best with evenly moist soil. They should not be allowed to dry out to the point where their leaves wilt. As a general guide, make sure your pansies get ½ to 1 inch of water every week from rain or by watering.

Feeding

A single application of compost or a slow-acting, general-purpose fertilizer worked into the soil before planting will serve the basic needs of these annuals all season. Pansies are considered heavier than average feeders, so for exceptional performance, give your plants supplemental, light feedings (side-dressings or foliar spray) monthly throughout the growing season.

Cutting Fresh Flowers

Although they are somewhat short-stemmed for formal arrangements, pansies make fine cut flowers in small bouquets.

Drying Flowers

Pansies do not air dry well, but can be dried in silica gel. To dry in silica gel, cut flowers in full bloom, leaving 1-inch stems. Place flowers, stems down, in a coffee can or other sealable container partially filled with silica gel. Carefully sift silica gel over blooms until they are completely covered.

MOST COMMON CULTURAL PROBLEMS

Short Bloom Period

Weather Too Hot

Pansies resent temperatures much above 75°F for any length of time, so in most parts of the country, they die out in hot weather. For the longest season of bloom, sow seed in summer or fall for bloom the following spring, or start with well-grown plants in early spring, and transplant them to the garden up to four weeks before the expected last frost. (You can cover the plants with straw or floating row covers, like Reemay, to protect them from hard frosts.) Most cultivars are very hardy and will survive moderate frosts. Shearing will also prolong bloom. To do this, cut plants back by 50 percent—leaves and flowers. Shearing plants will temporarily set them back, but once rid of the burden of producing so many flowers, they will green up and start blooming all over again. Deadheading or picking flowers will prevent the formation of seeds and prolong bloom.

Warty or Corky Growths on Leaves and Flower Stalks

Edema

If your pansy leaves and flower stalks are covered with warty, ⅛-inch-long growths that cause the afflicted tissue to become dry and brittle, they probably have been stricken with edema, sometimes called wart disease. Although wounds made by insects sometimes lead to these growths, this condition is not disease- or insect-related; it is a physiological condition caused by improper water conditions in the plants' environment. Overwatering, an excessively thick layer of mulch that keeps the soil too wet, or high humidity due to stagnant air or overcrowding can all lead to edema. Plant pansies in well-drained soil, don't overcrowd, and to ensure good ventilation, space plants far enough apart so that air can circulate between them.

MOST COMMON INSECT PESTS

Pale or Yellow Spots on Leaves, Leaves Curled and Distorted

Aphids

Plants infested with aphids have distorted growth that may be curled, puckered, or stunted, especially at the tips of the shoots. Leaves may turn yellow or brown, and feeding can damage flower buds or cause distorted flowers. Aphids are soft-bodied, pear-shaped sucking insects about the size of the head of a pin; they may be brown, green, yellow, or nearly black. They are often found clustered under leaves, and flower buds and stem tips may be covered with dense colonies of these insects. Ants, attracted by the aphids' honeydew secretions, wander over the plants, and black, sooty mold can develop on the honeydew as well. Foxglove aphid (*Acyrthosiphon solani*) infests pansies.

Light infestations of aphids can be controlled by washing the plants, especially the undersides of the leaves. For best results, use a forceful spray of water once every other day to knock the aphids off the plants; wash the plants at least three times. If that is not effective, spray the plants with insecticidal soap every three to five days for two weeks. If these pests become a very serious problem, make two applications of pyrethrum, three to five days apart.

Seedlings Severed at Base

Cutworms

If your pansy seedlings look as though they have been leveled by a lawn mower, you may have cutworms. These pests sever the stems of seedlings and transplants at or below the soil surface, leaving the tops to die. (In contrast, slugs and snails completely consume seedlings, leaving only their slimy trails.) They are most active at night. Cutworms also can harm plant root systems, damage that causes the plant to wilt and collapse. Cutworms are generally plump, soft-bodied caterpillars that are dull grayish or brownish and measure 1 to 2 inches long. They feed at night and hide in the soil during the day. The adults are night-flying moths.

Prevention is the only way to fight cutworms, for once they have cut down a young plant, there is nothing you can do to save it. Protect individual seedlings with a 3-inch collar made from stiff paper or plastic. Push the collar an inch or so into the ground. Or make a trap by sprinkling ½ teaspoon of cornmeal or bran meal around each plant. Spread it in a circle leading away from the stem of the plant. The cutworm eats the meal and dies. Beneficial nematodes added to the soil are an effective long-term control measure.

Leaves Stuck Together with Silk; Foliage Ragged and Discolored

Leaftiers

Leaves that are fastened together with strands of silk, followed by foliage that becomes ragged and unsightly, turns brown, and dies are signs that your plants are infested with greenhouse or celery leaftier (*Udea rubigalis*). It is the larval stage that damages plants by feeding on the undersides of the leaves and binding the leaves together. The larvae are ⅜- to ¾-inch-long caterpillars that are light green or cream to yellow in color with a white stripe down their backs and a green line down the center of the stripe. Adult leaftier moths, which are active only at night, are brown or gray and ¼ to ½ inch long. They lay eggs that resemble fish scales on the undersides of leaves.

Handpicking of eggs and larvae is usually an effective way to control this pest, since infestations are usually light. Remove any rolled or folded leaves, for they shelter caterpillars. Infested leaves should be destroyed, since the pests pupate and overwinter in them. Bt (*Bacillus thuringiensis*) also is an effective control. Apply as a powder or spray every two weeks until leaftiers disappear.

Dwarfed, Distorted Leaves; Aborted Flowers; Root Lesions

Nematodes

Several types of nematodes can attack pansies. Fern nematodes (*Aphelenchoides olesistus*) can attack the new growth around the growing point. They cause dwarfed and distorted foliage and flowers that fail to develop. Leaf stalks are shortened and may be swollen at the base, often with a cauliflower-like appearance. Infestations of root knot nematodes (including *Meloidogyne incognita* and *M. hapla*) are characterized by small, wartlike swellings on the roots. Meadow nematodes (*Pratylenchus pratensis*) cause lesions on the roots that are brown and sunken. Plants infested with root knot or meadow nematodes are sickly and wilted and have stunted growth and yellowed or bronzed foliage. Infested root systems are poorly developed, even partially decayed, and may have tiny galls or knots on them. The effects of nematode activity are most apparent in hot weather, when plants recover poorly from the heat. Nematodes are not insects, but slender, unsegmented roundworms that are barely visible to the unaided eye. Most are soil dwellers, less than 1/20 inch long, and have piercing-sucking mouthparts.

Prevention is the best way to deal with nematodes when growing annuals in infested soil, since severely infested annuals are best dug up and destroyed; do not compost. Organic matter in the soil helps to control nematodes because it not only benefits the fungi and bacteria that feed on them, it also keeps plants healthy and better able to withstand mild infestations of them. Add lots of compost, especially leaf mold, to the bed before planting. Turn severely infested plots over to a thick planting of French marigolds for an entire season and dig the plant remains into the soil at season's end to discourage these pests. Crop rotation is also a good idea; don't grow susceptible plants on the same plot year after year.

Ragged Holes in Leaves; Trails of Slime on Plants

Slugs and Snails

Plants that have large, ragged holes in the leaves and stems are probably infested with slugs and/or snails. Trails of slime on the foliage and around the plants are further confirmation of the presence of these pests. Slugs and snails are active only at night, when they feast on plants by rasping holes in the foliage with their filelike tongues. During the day, they hide under boards, mulch, or leaf litter. Slugs are similar to snails except that they have no shells. Both are generally 1 to 2 inches long, although some species of slugs grow up to 8 inches in length. Either pest may be white, gray, yellow, or brown-black in color. They are attracted to moist, well-mulched gardens and are most destructive in shaded gardens and during rainy spells. During winter and in dry seasons, slugs burrow into the ground to wait for more favorable weather.

A multifaceted approach to control is best. Remove boards, rocks, clippings, and other debris to cut down on the places where these pests hide during the day. Or, check daily under favorite hiding places, handpick snoozing slugs, crush them or seal them into a jar full of water and kerosene or insecticidal soap, and discard them. Inverted flowerpots, pieces of grapefruit peel, and cabbage leaves will lure slugs and can be used to trap them. Handpicking at night with a flashlight can be effective if started early in the spring. Traps baited with beer or yeast and water are also effective. To make an effective trap, cut a 2-inch hole in the lid of a coffee can or a small plastic container and bury the container flush with the soil. Slugs are attracted to the yeast in the beer, climb down through the hole in the lid, and drown. The key is to begin trapping very early in the season in order to prevent the population from building up. Surrounding plants with barriers of sand, ashes, or copper sheeting will discourage slugs from invading your plantings.

Leaves Stippled with Tiny Yellow Dots; Webby Foliage

Spider Mites

Lower leaves that are dry and stippled with tiny yellow dots are a sign that your pansies are infested with spider mites, tiny pests that suck chlorophyll out of the leaves. They also inject toxins into the foliage; this causes distorted or discolored growth. Leaves, stems, and flowers also may be swathed in fine webbing. As their name suggests, spider mites are related to spiders. These tiny creatures, which are about $\frac{1}{50}$ inch long and barely visible to the naked eye, may be yellow, green, red, or brown. Two-spotted spider mites (*Tetranychus urticae*) attack pansies. They reproduce most rapidly during hot, dry weather.

Severely infested plants should be destroyed, since infestations are difficult to control once they are well under way. Spider mites can be controlled by washing the plants, especially the undersides of the leaves. For best results, use a forceful spray of water once every other day to knock the mites off the plants; wash the plants at least three times. If that is not effective, spray the plants with insecticidal soap every three to five days for two weeks. To help discourage spider mites, keep the soil evenly moist at all times, for moist soil counteracts the hot, dry conditions they prefer. To avoid spreading the mites from plant to plant, don't touch healthy plants after examining infested ones.

Undersides of Leaves Skeletonized; Holes Chewed through Leaves

Violet Sawfly

Pansies whose leaves have been skeletonized on the undersides are probably infested with violet sawfly. This pest later eats holes entirely through the leaves and eventually defoliates the entire plant. The violet sawfly is a bluish black or olive green, $\frac{1}{2}$-inch-long larva marked with white spots. It feeds at night and is found in the eastern United States. The adult is a four-winged, black, $\frac{3}{8}$-inch-long fly. The larvae pupate in plant stalks. Adults lay eggs on the lower sides of leaves; the egg-laying operation causes blisters on foliage. There may be several generations per year.

Mild infestations are easily controlled by handpicking the larvae and dropping them in a jar of soapy water, however, the larvae are primarily active at night and finding them during the daytime will require diligent searching. If that is not effective, spray the plants with insecticidal soap every three to five days for two weeks. If these pests become a very serious problem, make two applications of pyrethrum, three to five days apart.

MOST COMMON DISEASES

Leaves Have Brown Blotches with Black Margins

Anthracnose

Pansies whose leaves are marked with brown blotches

surrounded by distinct black margins are infected with the fungal disease anthracnose, caused by *Colletotrichum violae-tricoloris* and *C. violae-rotundifoliae*. The petals of infected plants also develop abnormally, and seriously infected plants may die of the disease.

Cultural controls can be used to combat anthracnose. Dig up and destroy infected plants. Disinfect garden tools with liquid bleach solution (1 part bleach to 3 parts water) or 70 percent rubbing alcohol to avoid spreading the fungus. Pick off and destroy any infected leaves as soon as they appear. Also, regularly clean up and destroy dead plant debris in the garden. Do not compost plant material you suspect to be infected. Rogue out and discard seriously infected plants, together with the soil in which they are growing. A layer of mulch helps prevent fungal spores from splashing from the soil onto plants. If anthracnose is a particular problem in your area, spray at weekly to ten-day intervals with wettable sulfur or bordeaux mixture, particularly in rainy seasons. (Watch for leaf discoloration with the latter.)

Leaves Covered with Dark Spots or Blotches

Leaf Spot

Quite a few species of fungi can cause unsightly spots on pansy foliage. Leaves may have transparent or brown or black spots. Some fungal spots are surrounded by flecks or black dots, which are the spore-bearing fruiting bodies. Often spots come together to form larger patches of dead tissue. These fungi thrive on moist leaf surfaces.

To control leaf spot, pick off and destroy infected leaves. Also, regularly clean up and destroy dead plant debris in the garden to reduce spore populations. These fungi overwinter as spores in such debris, so an end-of-season cleanup is especially important. Rogue out and discard seriously infected plants, together with the soil in which they are growing. A layer of mulch helps prevent spores from splashing from the soil onto plants. If leaf spot is a particular problem in your area, spray at weekly to

ten-day intervals with wettable sulfur or bordeaux mixture, particularly in rainy seasons. (Watch for leaf discoloration with the latter.)

Moldy Coating on Leaves and/or Flowers

Molds or Mildews

Several different fungi cause grayish or white molds or powdery coverings on pansy flowers and foliage. As its name suggests, gray mold (caused by the fungus *Botrytis cinerea*) causes a gray coating on leaves and flowers. Infected plant parts give off a cloud of white spores when picked. Gray mold generally attacks petals first, but quickly rots the entire flower and spreads to leaves and stems, causing a soft, slimy rot. Primarily a problem in cool, wet weather, it is further encouraged by poor air circulation due to overcrowding or insufficient light.

A downy mildew caused by the fungus *Bremiella megasperma* occasionally causes irregular spots on upper leaf surfaces and grayish "downy" or feltlike patches on undersides. Downy mildew attacks the lower leaves of the plant first and then spreads upward. Plants may wilt and die without developing dead areas on the foliage. This fungal disease is most common under damp conditions.

Powdery mildew is also found on pansies, although it is seldom serious enough to warrant control measures. It causes a whitish dust or bloom that is primarily on the surface of leaves but can also infect flowers. Infected leaves are often curled or distorted, and the growth of severely infected plants can be stunted.

Cultural controls are a very effective way to deal with molds and mildews. Plant pansies in a location that affords plenty of ventilation and sunlight. Choose a location with well-drained, fertile soil, water early on sunny days, allow ample spacing between plants, and try to avoid wetting the foliage when watering. Unless the season is unusually humid, these precautions should save you from most problems with molds and mildews. Pick and destroy infected leaves and stems. Dig up heavily infected plants, together with adjacent soil, and discard them;

do not compost. Collect and discard all aboveground refuse in the fall. If these are serious problems in your area, spray infected plants once or twice at weekly intervals with wettable sulfur, bordeaux mixture, or another copper fungicide when molds or mildews first appear on leaves. (Watch for leaf discoloration when using bordeaux mixture.) Several applications may be needed to stop the spread of the fungus.

Leaves with Yellowish Pustules Above; Pale Green Spots Beneath

Rust
Pansies with pale green spots on the undersides of the leaves and yellowish pustules of spores on the upper surfaces are probably infected with a rust disease caused by the fungus *Puccinia violae*. The stems and leaf stalks of severely infected plants may also develop pustules. Later in the season, the pustules turn brown as the spores ripen. Although common, rust is not generally serious enough to do much damage to plants.

Remove infected leaves as soon as possible. Remove and destroy severely infected plants and discard infected plant material; do not compost. To ensure good ventilation, space plants far enough apart so that air can circulate between them. Also, avoid wetting foliage. A thorough fall cleanup is also helpful in controlling this disease. In severe cases, make periodic applications of wettable sulfur, begun several weeks before rust normally appears and repeated at weekly to ten-day intervals.

Stems and Leaf Stalks Spotted

Scab
Pansies that have oval or nearly round lesions up to ¼ inch diameter on leaves, stems, buds, blossoms, or seed capsules may be infected with scab, a disease caused by the fungus *Sphaceloma violae*. The lesions may be yellow-brown, pinkish brown, or whitish. The centers of spots fall out eventually, giving the leaves a "shothole" appearance. Lesions eventually girdle the stems, causing wilt and death.

Dig up and discard infected plants or plant parts as soon as they appear; do not compost. In severe cases, make periodic applications of wettable sulfur, begun several weeks before rust normally appears and repeated at weekly to ten-day intervals. This disease also infects wild violets, so controlling them can also help avert this problem. Remove and discard plant debris in the fall. Do not save or plant seed from infected plants.

Leaves Have Raised Blisters That Discharge Powdery Spores

Smut
Pansies are occasionally infected with a smut disease caused by the fungus *Urocystis violae*. Leaves, leaf stalks, and flowers of infected plants develop raised, somewhat calluslike blisters or pustules. Afflicted growth is deformed and the pustules eventually break open to discharge dark spores.

Dig up and discard or burn infected plants or plant parts as soon as they appear; do not compost. In severe cases, make periodic applications of wettable sulfur or a copper-based fungicide, such as bordeaux mixture, starting several weeks before rust normally appears and repeated at weekly to ten-day intervals. (Watch for leaf discoloration when using bordeaux mixture.) This disease also infects wild violets, so controlling them can also help avert this problem. Remove and discard plant debris in the fall. Do not save or plant seed from infected plants. If possible, change the location of the planting in future years.

Stems Turn Black at Base; Leaves Turn Yellow and Wilt; Plants Topple Over

Stem, Root, and Crown Rots
A variety of soil-dwelling fungi attack pansies at the base of the plant, causing stems to turn black from the base upward and rotting the crowns or roots of the plants. Discolored, water-soaked lesions eventually girdle the stems, and leaves turn yellow and wilt. Once these fungi have girdled stems or rotted crowns or roots, the stems or plants topple over, and

the plants eventually die. *Pellicularia rolfsii* and *Sclerotium delphinii* are both fungi that cause crown rot in pansies by attacking them at the soil line. The fungi *Myrothecium roridum* also attacks pansy stems at the soil line, causing a stem rot characterized by dry, brittle stem tissue that is covered with black fungal spores. Leaves of afflicted plants develop purplish black spots or streaks, and infected tissue eventually dries up. A number of fungi cause pansy root rot, including *Ciborinia violae, Fusarium* spp., *Pellicularia filamentosa,* and *Phymatotrichum omnivorum.*

These diseases attack greenhouse-grown bedding plants as well as plants grown outdoors, especially those that are overcrowded or overwatered. Although steam pasteurization is the only surefire way to destroy the fungi, preventive measures are very helpful in controlling these diseases. Plant pansies in well-drained soil, avoid overwatering and overcrowding, and keep mulch away from the base of plant stems. Remove and discard infected plants, together with the surrounding soil, or cut away affected plant parts with a clean, sharp knife or razor blade. Discard infected plant material; do not compost. Disinfect tools with a solution of 1 part household bleach and 3 parts water or 70 percent rubbing alcohol to avoid spreading the disease. Keep the garden clear of old plant debris. For long-term prevention, lighten heavy soil with a mixture of perlite, vermiculite, and/or peat moss, and provide good drainage.

Leaves Greenish Yellow or Curled and Deformed; Shoots Spindly or Stunted

Virus Diseases

Pansies are susceptible to a few virus diseases, including aster yellows and beet curly top. Aster yellows causes leaves that are greenish yellow and spindly, along with stunted or dwarfed growth. The disease is caused by a viruslike organism primarily spread by the aster leafhopper (*Macrosteles fascifrons*). Young plants that are infected show a slight yellowing along leaf veins. As the disease becomes more severe, the entire plant is stunted and yellowed, and the unusual number of shoots that develop cause the plant to become very bushy and upright. Shoot tips branch abnormally and tend to develop into witches'-brooms; secondary shoots are usually spindly. Flowers are deformed and may be aborted entirely. Regardless of the normal bloom color of the cultivar, flowers are often sickly yellow-green.

Pansies that produce curled, thickened, or otherwise distorted foliage, may be infected with the viral disease that causes beet curly top, which causes excessive cell growth and thus distorted growth. Infected plants are stunted and form dense "rosettes" and small flowers. The virus is spread by leafhoppers.

There is no cure for virus-infected plants. Remove and destroy them; do not compost. Disinfect garden tools with a solution of 1 part household bleach and 3 parts water or 70 percent rubbing alcohol to avoid spreading virus diseases from plant to plant. Also, wash your hands after handling infected plants. To control the insects that transmit the disease, spray remaining plants with a mixture of insecticidal soap and isopropyl alcohol. Make the mix by adding 1 tablespoon of alcohol to each pint of insecticidal soap solution. Spray at three- to five-day intervals, making three applications. The virus overwinters in various perennials and weeds such as daisies, plantain, and gaillardia. Infected plants are not necessarily killed by the disease, but should be dug up and destroyed, since they continue to infect nearby plants via leafhoppers.

ANNUAL

Petunia

Petunia × hybrida

DESCRIPTION

The colorful, trumpet-shaped blooms of petunias are a common sight in gardens all across the country. These popular plants belong in the nightshade family, Solanaceae, and thus are closely related to tomatoes, peppers, and potatoes. The common garden petunia (*Petunia × hybrida*) is the result of extensive breeding and hybridization, but the primary species from which it was developed are native to Argentina. Petunias come in a wide variety of solid colors, as well as with blooms marked with blotches or stripes of contrasting colors. Gardeners can also choose from cultivars with single or double blooms and those with smooth, ruffled, or fringed petals. There are three basic classes of plants: Grandiflora, multiflora, and floribunda. Grandiflora petunias bear single or double flowers up to 5 inches in diameter; multiflora petunias bear smaller, 2- to 3-inch single or double blooms and are more disease resistant than grandifloras. Floribunda petunias combine the size of grandiflora blooms with the disease resistance and weather tolerance of multifloras. They bear single blooms. Petunias, extremely adaptable annuals, are verstile, colorful, and easy to grow. They can be used as bedding plants, along beds or borders, or in containers and hanging baskets.

Height

6 to 18 inches

Spread

1½ to 2 feet

Blossoms

Petunias bear showy, trumpet-shaped blooms with a single petal that flairs into a flat, five-lobed face. There are also double-flowered petunias with blossoms quite like carnations or camellias. Flowers may have ruffled, fringed, or frilled edges. Petunias come in solid or a variety of bicolor combinations, including flowers with contrasting veins, stripes, or centers. Blooms may be deep purple, lilac, pink, salmon, red, yellow, and white. Some cultivars have blossoms with a sweet fragrance, which is often most evident after dark. Petunias bloom from early summer through to the first fall frost. Flowers are borne at the tips of the stems, which means that pinching increases flower production by encouraging branching.

Foliage

The leaves of petunias are medium green, oval, hairy, and small.

ENVIRONMENT

Hardiness

Petunias are half-hardy annuals that will withstand cool temperatures, but for best results, plant them in the garden after danger of frost has passed.

Light

For best bloom, plant petunias in a location that receives full sun for at least half the day. Too much shade will discourage them from flowering.

Soil

Grow petunias in average, well-drained soil, although they will also grow well in light, sandy soil. The single-flowered cultivars are best for gardens with somewhat heavy, alkaline soil. Petunias prefer a pH range of between 6 and 8.

PLANTING AND PROPAGATION

Planting

Sow seed indoors 10 to 12 weeks before the last frost date. The seeds are dustlike, so handle them with care. They require light to germinate, so do not cover them with soil. Press the seeds into the soil, and water flats from below. Cover the seed flat with glass or plastic to maintain high humidity.

Germination takes about ten days, and soil temperatures between 70° and 75°F are ideal. Transplant seedlings to the garden after all danger of frost has passed, spacing plants 1 foot apart. When selecting seedlings for transplanting, don't necessarily reject the smaller ones, for they are likely to produce double flowers or have the most vivid flowers.

When purchasing petunia plants from a nursery or garden center, look for young, compact plants that have good foliage color but few flowers. Plants in full bloom are often root bound and will take longer to recover from transplant shock when set out in the garden.

Propagation

Take cuttings of, or pot up healthy plants of, desirable cultivars in late or early fall. Grow them over the winter in a cool but frost-free place to supply cuttings in late winter for next season.

PLANT MANAGEMENT

General Care

Pinch out the growing tips when the plants are about 6 inches tall to encourage branching and bushy growth. Pinch again after the first flush of bloom to encourage branching and more abundant flowering. If plants become leggy and stop blooming during the hottest part of summer, shear them back, feed them, and keep them well watered to promote the development of new flowers.

Water

Make sure the plants get about 1 inch of water every week from rain or by watering, but avoid overwatering, for petunias do not like soggy soil. Use a soaker hose or watering wand to apply water at ground level without wetting the flowers.

Feeding

A single application of compost or a slow-acting,

general-purpose fertilizer worked into the soil before planting will serve the basic needs of these annuals all season. However, feed plants after each pinching, and for exceptional performance, give your plants supplemental, light feedings (side-dressings or foliar spray) monthly throughout the growing season.

MOST COMMON CULTURAL PROBLEMS

Bicolor Petunias Change Color

Changing Growing Conditions
The flowers of bicolor petunias sometimes change as the season progresses. For example, a white edge may become wider or disappear altogether, or stripes may change width. These changes occur in reaction to the plants' growing conditions. When the colored areas in the flowers gradually expand while white zones diminish, it is a sign that moisture and nutrients are ample and temperatures have been low. When white areas expand while the colored zones shrink, it is usually because temperatures are too high, soil is too dry, and soil nutrients are depleted.

Plants Get Leggy and Stop Flowering

Hot Temperatures and Shorter Days
During the hot summer months, petunia plants can get leggy and stop blooming. This is because they are thermophotoperiodic, which means that both temperature and day length influence growth and flowering. When temperatures remain below 62°F, the plants are compact, branch well, and flower profusely. When days are short (less than 12 hours of light) and temperatures are between 62° and 75°F, plants stop flowering or develop only a single flower per stem. When temperatures soar above 75°F, regardless of the day length, the plants become leggy and stop flowering or develop only a single flower per stem.

For best results, plant petunias in spring while it's still cool, and pinch the plants to stimulate maximum branching. If temperatures are already above 70°F at planting time, the flower stem will elongate rapidly and should be pinched often. In early summer, the plants can be rejuvenated by pinching again, cutting back each stem 3 to 4 inches above the soil line. This will result in a fine flower display about two weeks later. Cutting back the older stems once more in late summer as temperatures start to become cooler will force more branching and heavy flowering until frost. Also keep the spent blooms and seedpods picked off, and pinch back the sideshoots frequently.

MOST COMMON INSECT PESTS

Petunias are relatively care-free, easy-to-grow plants that are not seriously bothered by many insect pests. In addition to the pests listed below, slugs, snails, and caterpillars may chew holes in the foliage. Leafhoppers, which transmit aster yellows, may cause leaves that are finely mottled with yellowish or whitish spots.

Holes in Leaves and/or Flowers

Beetles
Several species of beetles chew holes in the foliage and flowers of petunias. Asiatic garden beetles (*Maladera castanea*) are ½-inch-long, cinnamon brown beetles that feed only at night. The larvae are C-shaped, grayish white grubs with dark brown heads that can eat plant roots. Fully grown grubs are ¾ to 1 inch long. Spotted cucumber beetle (*Diabrotica undecimpunctata*) is a slender, ¼-inch-long insect that is greenish yellow with 12 black spots on its back. It feasts on petals, buds, and leaves and seems especially drawn to light-colored flowers in late summer. Adults overwinter at the base of weeds or other plants and lay eggs in spring. This pest is also commonly called southern corn rootworm because the yellowish, wormlike, ½- to ¾-inch-long larvae feed on roots. Colorado potato beetle (*Leptinotarsa*

decemlineata) adults and larvae attack the foliage of petunias. Adults are ⅜ inch long by ¼ inch wide with black and yellow stripes running lengthwise along the shiny wing covers. The grubs are plump and red, with black spots and black heads.

Petunia leaves and flowers perforated with dozens or hundreds of tiny holes may be victims of flea beetles, including the potato flea beetle (*Epitrix cucumeris*). These shiny black or brown pests are only ¹⁄₁₆ inch long and very active, jumping like fleas when disturbed. Flea beetles transmit viral and bacterial diseases. They overwinter as adults and generally feed on weeds in early spring, then move to the garden. The larvae are tiny grubs that feed on plant roots.

For the most part, all beetles are controlled the same way. Where possible, handpick and crush them or drop them into a pail of soapy water. If the infestation is light, this is all you will need to do. Barriers such as floating row covers, like Reemay, can be used to prevent flea beetles from gaining access to petunias. For heavier infestations, spray infested plants with a solution of pyrethrum and isopropyl alcohol, mixing 1 tablespoon of alcohol with every pint of diluted pyrethrum mixture. Apply this solution every three to five days until the problem is corrected. For long-term control, apply milky spore disease (*Bacillus popilliae*) to lawns and garden. It will kill the larvae of most beetles. Beneficial nematodes introduced into the soil will take care of the flea beetle larvae.

Leaves Encrusted with Small, Whitish Bumps; Growth Discolored; Leaves Drop

Greenhouse Orthezia

Petunia plants whose upper leaf surfaces are discolored or are covered with waxy, whitish bumps are probably infested with greenhouse orthezia (*Orthezia insignis*). This scalelike insect, which can infest purchased bedding plants, causes leaf drop, reduced growth, and stunted plants. Heavy infestations kill plants. Greenhouse orthezia is about ⅓ inch long,

light brown or dark green in color with a whitish, waxy fringe around the edge of its body. Nymphs are dark green, wingless, and pinhead-size.

Inspect purchased bedding plants to avoid bringing home infested specimens. Control minor infestations with a cotton swab dipped in rubbing alcohol. Destroy heavily infested plants or spray them with a mixture of alcohol and insecticidal soap every three days for two weeks. Mix 1 cup of isopropyl alcohol and 1 tablespoon of commercial insecticidal soap concentrate in 1 quart of water. If you have soap already mixed with water, add 1 tablespoon of alcohol to a pint of your dilute soap spray.

Plants Stunted; Leaves Yellowed and Small; Knots on Roots

Nematodes

Petunia plants are sometimes infested with nematodes, which can cause sickly, wilted, or stunted growth and yellowed or bronzed foliage. Infested root systems are poorly developed, even partially decayed, and may have tiny galls or knots on them. The effects of nematode activity are most apparent in hot weather, when plants recover poorly from the heat. Southern root knot nematodes (*Meloidogyne incognita*) occasionally attack petunias, although they do not generally cause serious problems when the plants are grown as annuals. Nematodes are not insects, but slender, unsegmented roundworms that are barely visible to the unaided eye.

Do not save and overwinter infested petunia plants, dig and destroy them; do not compost. Prevention is the best way to deal with nematodes when growing annuals in infested soil, since severely infested annuals are best dug up and destroyed. Organic matter in the soil helps to control nematodes because it not only benefits the fungi and bacteria that feed on them, it also keeps plants healthy and better able to withstand mild infestations. Add lots of compost, especially leaf mold, to the bed before planting. Turn severely infested plots over to a thick planting of French marigolds for an entire season and dig the plant remains into the soil at season's end to discourage these pests. Crop rotation is also a good idea; don't grow susceptible plants on the same plot year after year.

Leaves Appear Bronzed or Stippled with Tiny Yellow Dots; Webby Foliage

Spider Mites

Tomato russet mites (*Aculops lycopersici*) cause stems and leaves of infested plants to turn bronze or russet in color. Signs of injury appear suddenly, as mites multiply very quickly. These pests spread mosaic virus. Lower leaves that are dry and stippled with tiny yellow dots are a sign that your petunias are infested with two-spotted spider mites (*Tetranychus urticae*), tiny pests that suck chlorophyll out of the leaves. They also inject toxins into the foliage; this causes distorted or discolored growth. Leaves, stems, and flowers also may be swathed in fine webbing. As their name suggests, spider mites are related to spiders. These tiny creatures, which are about 1/50 inch long and barely visible to the naked eye, may be yellow, green, red, or brown. They reproduce most rapidly during hot, dry weather.

Severely infested plants should be destroyed, since infestations are difficult to control once they are well under way. Carefully inspect purchased bedding plants to avoid bringing home infested specimens. Spider mites can be controlled by washing the plants, especially the undersides of the leaves. For best results, use a forceful spray of water once every other day to knock the mites off the plants; wash the plants at least three times. If that is not effective, spray the plants with insecticidal soap every three to five days for two weeks. To help discourage spider mites, keep the soil evenly moist at all times, for moist soil counteracts the hot, dry conditions they prefer. To avoid spreading the mites from plant to plant, don't touch healthy plants after examining infested ones.

MOST COMMON DISEASES

Seedlings Rot at Base, Fall Over

Damping-Off

Seedling stems that are water soaked and blackened at the soil line have been afflicted with damping-off. Affected stems are unable to support the plants, which fall over and die. Usually, the foliage is still green and healthy looking when the plants collapse. Stems of older plants show tan to reddish brown lesions that eventually girdle stems. Damping-off is primarily caused by the soil-dwelling fungus *Rhizoctonia solani*, and it usually occurs in seedlings in greenhouses or on windowsills. Germinating seeds may be attacked before they emerge from the soil, or shortly thereafter.

Cultural controls are effective in preventing damping-off. Sow seed in well-drained soil, do not overcrowd plants, and keep soil on the dry side. Use a sterile growing mix (peat moss, perlite, and vermiculite, with a topping of milled sphagnum moss), and water plants from below by setting pots in water and allowing the water to soak up to just beneath the soil surface. Thin seedlings so they are far enough apart to allow air to circulate between them, which will carry away excessive moisture and reduce humidity. When thinning, use scissors instead of pulling up plants to avoid damaging the roots and stems of remaining plants, which might open them up to infection. In the greenhouse, a fan will promote air circulation. Avoid feeding seedlings too much nitrogen, for it causes lank, weak growth. Routinely disinfect garden tools in boiling water or household bleach solution (1 part bleach to 3 parts water) to discourage disease problems.

Roots and Stems Turn Black and Rot

Stem Rot

Petunias are occasionally attacked by a stem rot caused by a variety of fungi. Stems of infected plants rot at the base and subsequently collapse.

Preventive measures are very helpful in controlling this problem. Plant petunias in well-drained soil, avoid overwatering, avoid overcrowding the plants, and keep mulch away from the base of plant stems. Remove and discard infected plants, together with the surrounding soil, or cut away affected plant parts with a clean, sharp knife or razor blade. (Cuttings taken from the tops of afflicted stems are generally healthy and can be used to propagate plants stricken with stem rot.) Do not compost infected plants or soil; discard them. Disinfect tools with a solution of 1 part household bleach and 3 parts alcohol or 70 percent rubbing alcohol after use to avoid spreading the disease. For long-term prevention, lighten heavy soil with a mixture of perlite, vermiculite, and/or peat moss, and provide good drainage.

Leaves Greenish Yellow or Curled and Deformed; Shoots Spindly or Stunted

Virus Diseases

Petunias are susceptible to a number of virus diseases, including mosaic, ring spot, tomato spotted wilt virus, beet curly top, and aster yellows. Virus-infected plants have spindly, stunted shoots and yellowed foliage. Leaves may be marked with ring spots, lines, pale areas, or mottling, and dead spots may appear on the foliage of infected plants. Petunias that produce curled, thickened, or otherwise distorted foliage may be infected with the viral disease that causes beet curly top, which causes excessive cell growth and thus distorted growth. Infected plants are stunted and form dense "rosettes" and small flowers.

Aster yellows causes leaves that are greenish yellow and spindly, along with stunted or dwarfed growth. Young plants that are infected show a slight yellowing along leaf veins. Shoot tips branch abnormally and tend to develop into witches'-brooms; secondary shoots are usually spindly. Flowers are deformed and may be aborted entirely. Regardless of the normal bloom color of the cultivar, flowers are often sickly yellow-green.

Petunias that have crinkled, dwarfed, and cupped leaves that are mottled with green are probably infected with a mosaic virus, which can be transmitted to plants from infected smoking or chewing tobacco. Virus diseases are spread by sucking insects such as leafhoppers. Afflicted plants eventually wilt and die.

There is no cure for virus-infected plants. Remove and destroy them; do not compost. To control the insects that transmit these diseases, spray remaining plants with a mixture of insecticidal soap and isopropyl alcohol. Make this mix by adding 1 tablespoon of alcohol to each pint of insecticidal soap solution. Spray at three- to five-day intervals, making three applications. The virus overwinters in various perennials and weeds such as daisies, plantain, and gaillardia. Infected plants are not necessarily killed by the disease, but should be dug up and destroyed, since they continue to infect nearby plants via leafhoppers. Disinfect garden tools with a solution of 1 part household bleach and 3 parts water or 70 percent rubbing alcohol to avoid spreading virus diseases from plant to plant. Also, wash your hands after handling infected plants. Do not smoke or use tobacco products when working with plants susceptible to tobacco mosaic. Do not plant petunias too close to tomatoes, flowering tobacco, potatoes, eggplant, or peppers.

ANNUAL *Phlox* *Phlox drummondii*

DESCRIPTION

Commonly called annual phlox, Drummond Phlox, or Texas-pride, *Phlox drummondii,* is the only member of this genus of showy perennial flowers that is commonly grown as an annual. Its loose clusters of

brightly colored flowers, care-free habit, and long blooming season make it a popular plant for bedding. Annual phlox grows best in areas with cool summers, but will bloom in spring in warm climates. It can also be used for edging, in containers, or in rock and wall gardens.

Height

6 to 20 inches; dwarf cultivars, 6 to 8 inches

Spread

8 to 10 inches

Blossoms

Annual phlox bears terminal clusters of showy flowers in a wide variety of colors, including pure white, purple, crimson, yellow, and lavender. Many cultivars are available, some with contrasting centers. Individual blooms are trumpet- or funnel-shaped, 1 to 1½ inches across, and have five petals that open into a flat face.

Foliage

Phlox leaves are about 3 inches long, lance-shaped, and light green in color.

ENVIRONMENT

Hardiness

Annual phlox is a hardy annual that performs best in regions with long, cool springs. Seedlings are cold tolerant, so seed can be sown in very early spring. In areas with mild winters, it can be sown outdoors in fall for germination in early spring.

Light

Annual phlox grows best in full sun, but it will tolerate light shade. These plants prefer areas with cool summers, and although they can tolerate some heat, they will generally stop flowering during the hottest part of the summer. A location with protection from sun during the hottest part of the day may help prolong bloom.

Soil

Grow annual phlox in rich, well-drained soil that is moist, sandy, and high in organic matter. They will not grow well in heavy clay soil, but will tolerate a broad pH range from 6 to 8.

PLANTING AND PROPAGATION

Planting

Annual phlox resents transplanting, so for best results, sow seed outdoors in the garden where the plants are to grow in early spring as soon as the soil can be worked. Plant seeds at a depth of ⅛ inch, for they require darkness to germinate. Germination takes 6 to 15 days. Or, in areas with mild winters, sow seed outdoors from late summer to fall for germination the following spring. To start seed indoors, sow in individual peat pots, since the seedlings can be difficult to transplant. Sow seed eight to ten weeks before the last frost date, and germinate at temperatures between 55° and 65°F. Transplant hardened seedlings to the garden two to three weeks *before* the last frost date. When transplanting seed sown indoors, set peat pots directly into the ground with the seedlings to minimize disturbance. Space seedlings 6 to 10 inches apart. When thinning phlox, keep in mind that the weakest seedlings often develop the strongest color. For the greatest color range, sow seed thinly to reduce the amount of thinning required.

Container Gardening

Annual phlox can be grown in containers or in window boxes. For best results, sow seed directly in the containers where the plants are to grow.

PLANT MANAGEMENT

General Care

Annual phlox require very little day-to-day maintenance once they are established in the garden. Removing faded flowers helps encourage new flowers to form.

Water

As a general guide, annual phlox should receive ½ to 1 inch of water per week from rain or by watering. As with most annuals, a steady level of moisture in the soil promotes vigor and continuous bloom. Do not allow plants to dry out to the point that the leaves wilt.

Feeding

Fertilize annual phlox seedlings with compost or a slow-acting, general-purpose fertilizer in spring at planting time, and provide monthly applications of a dilute fertilizer, such as a side-dressing or foliar spray, to help plants perform at their peak.

MOST COMMON CULTURAL PROBLEMS

Plants Stop Blooming

Weather Too Hot

In areas with very hot summers, annual phlox will stop flowering once warm temperatures arrive. When the plants stop producing new flowers and start to get leggy, cut them halfway back to promote new growth and flowers. Cutting off the main flower head after it fades will promote the production of sideshoots with smaller flower clusters and extend the blooming season. Annual phlox can be grown as a spring-flowering annual and can be replaced with more heat-tolerant species once warm temperatures arrive.

MOST COMMON INSECT PESTS

Annual phlox plants are bothered by few insects and can easily withstand attacks by most pests, provided the plants are healthy and vigorous. They are subject to attacks by the same insects that infest perennial phlox, including beetles, phlox plant bug, spider mites, and nematodes. For more information on these pests, turn to the entry on perennial phlox, beginning on page 189.

MOST COMMON DISEASES

Annual phlox plants are subject to many of the diseases that infect perennial phlox, including crown rot, leaf spot, and virus diseases, but for the most

part are trouble-free, easy-to-grow annuals. For more information on diseases of phlox, see the entry on perennial phlox, beginning on page 189.

White Powder Covering Leaves

Powdery Mildew

Phlox leaves that are covered with a white or ash gray powdery mold probably have powdery mildew. Badly infected leaves become discolored and distorted, then drop off. Powdery mildew is caused by fungi that live primarily on the surface of the leaves, flowers, and stems of plants, not inside them.

Powdery mildew most commonly develops on plants grown close together where air circulation is restricted, especially on the lower leaves where humidity is higher and moisture is more abundant. Allow ample spacing between plants, and collect and discard all aboveground refuse in the fall. Spray affected plants thoroughly with wettable sulfur once or twice at weekly intervals starting as soon as the whitish coating of the fungus is visible.

ANNUAL Salvias *Salvia* spp.

DESCRIPTION

The salvias are mint family members that bear many-flowered spikes of two-lipped, somewhat tube-shaped flowers. The annual salvias most often grown in gardens are actually shrubs or perennials in their native habitats. Of these, scarlet sage (*Salvia splendens*) and mealy-cup sage (*S. farinacea*) are probably most popular. (There are also salvias grown as hardy perennials.) Their brightly colored, spiked-shaped blooms make them excellent subjects for using with lower-growing, rounded, or ground-hugging plants. Try planting salvia as a backdrop for clumps of ageratums, begonias, or petunias. Salvias tolerate

both sun and part shade and can be used in massed plantings, borders, or containers. They also make fine cut flowers.

Height

S. farinacea (mealy-cup sage), 2 to 3 feet
S. splendens (scarlet sage), 2½ to 3 feet; dwarf cultivars, 10 to 12 inches

Spread

1½ to 2 feet

Blossoms

S. farinacea bears tall, many-flowered spikes covered with tiny, ½-inch-long, violet-blue or sometimes white blossoms. Spikes can reach 8 inches in length. The calyx, the cupped part of the flower that holds the petals, is covered with tiny white hairs, hence the common name of mealy-cup sage. Gardeners are probably most familiar with the scarlet-flowered cultivars of *S. splendens,* but this species also comes in white and pastel shades of rose, purple,

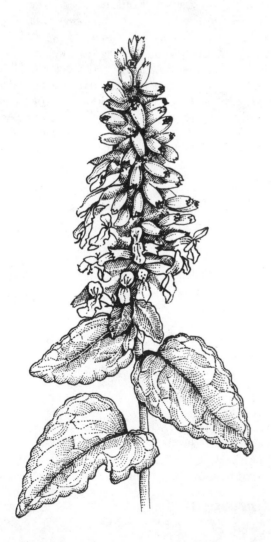

and salmon. Both species bloom from early summer until the first fall frost.

Foliage

The leaves of salvia are narrow, lance- or oval-shaped. They are borne in pairs and are slightly gray-green.

ENVIRONMENT

Hardiness

Salvias are grown as half-hardy annuals and will die with the first hard frost. *S. farinacea,* which is native to Texas and New Mexico, can be grown as a perennial in the South and Southwest and will often reseed itself in areas with mild winters. *S. splendens,* which is native to Brazil, is less hardy, but can be grown as a perennial where winters are warm.

Light

Grow annual salvias in full sun or light shade. Cultivars with pastel- or cream-colored flowers tend to fade in full sun and are best grown in partial shade. Salvias are heat tolerant, but perform best under such conditions if kept evenly watered. In the South and Southwest, grow salvias in light shade to protect them from excessive heat and sun.

Soil

Plant salvias in well-drained soil that is moist, loamy, and rich in organic matter. They tolerate a pH range from 6 to 8.

PLANTING AND PROPAGATION

Planting

Sow seed of *S. splendens* indoors 8 to 10 weeks before the last frost date; *S. farinacea* should be sown 12 weeks before the last frost. Seeds of *S. splendens* are not long-lived, so be sure to use fresh seeds. Don't cover the seeds of red-flowered salvias; they need light to germinate. Germination takes 12 to 15 days, and temperatures of 70°F are ideal. Damping-off can be a problem, so use sterile medium (peat moss, perlite, and vermiculite, with a topping of milled sphagnum moss), water from below, and grow the seedlings in a well-ventilated area. When it's time to transfer them into the garden, try to do so before the plants come into bloom, as they do much better if planted before flowers form. The same is true with purchased bedding plants; buy healthy-looking plants that have not yet begun to flower.

Space transplants 8 to 12 inches apart, depending on the cultivar. A good rule of thumb is to space plants equal to one-half their expected mature height. When the transplants are about 8 inches high, pinch them back an inch or so to encourage a bushy look.

Container Gardening

Dwarf cultivars of salvia will do quite well in window boxes and other containers.

PLANT MANAGEMENT

General Care

Salvias require very little day-to-day maintenance once they are established in the garden. Pinching off faded flower spikes will encourage branching and give plants a more bushy form.

Water

As a general rule, salvia should receive ½ to 1 inch of water per week from rain or by watering. As with most annuals, a steady level of moisture in the soil promotes vigor and continuous bloom. Do not allow plants to dry out to the point that the leaves wilt.

Feeding

Fertilize salvia seedlings with compost or a slow-acting, general-purpose fertilizer in spring at transplant time, and provide monthly applications of a dilute fertilizer, such as a side-dressing or foliar spray, to help plants perform at their peak.

Cutting Fresh Flowers

Salvias make fine cut flowers.

Drying Flowers

Salvias make exceptional dried flowers. To air dry, cut the blooms when they are at their peak, remove the foliage, and hang them upside down in a warm, dark, dry place. The scarlet-flowered cultivars may not hold their color well, but the violet-flowered ones dry very well.

MOST COMMON CULTURAL PROBLEMS

Plants Stop Blooming

Weather Too Hot

In areas with very hot summers, salvias may stop flowering or slow down their flower production during periods with very high heat and humidity. When the plants stop producing new flowers and start to get leggy, cut them halfway back to promote new growth and flowers. Cutting off the main flower head after it fades will promote the production of sideshoots with smaller flower clusters and extend the blooming season. A thick layer of mulch will help keep salvia roots cool. Sluggish bloomers will start blooming again in the early fall as the temperatures moderate.

MOST COMMON INSECT PESTS

Although quite a few insects will infest salvias, they are basically trouble-free, easy-to-grow plants that are seldom seriously threatened by insect infestations. In addition to the insects listed below, slugs, snails, and beetles occasionally chew holes in the foliage. Stalk borers, tarnished plant bugs, leafhoppers, and leaftiers also may infest these plants.

Pale or Yellow Spots on Leaves, Leaves Curled and Distorted

Aphids

Plants infested with aphids have distorted growth that may be curled, puckered, or stunted. Leaves may turn yellow or brown, and feeding can seriously damage flower buds or cause distorted flowers. Plants may also wilt under bright sunlight. Aphids are soft-bodied, pear-shaped sucking insects about the size of the head of a pin; they may be brown, green, yellow, or nearly black. They are often found clustered under leaves, and flower buds and stem tips may be covered with dense colonies of these insects. Ants, attracted by the aphids' honeydew secretions, wander over the plants, and black, sooty mold can develop on the honeydew as well. In addition to the damage they cause by feeding, aphids are important vectors of virus diseases. The most common species of aphids infesting salvias are crescent-marked lily aphid (*Neomyzus circumflexus*) and foxglove aphid (*Acyrthosiphon solani*).

Light infestations of aphids can be controlled by washing the plants, especially the undersides of the leaves. For best results, use a forceful spray of water once every other day to knock the aphids off the plants; wash the plants at least three times. If that is not effective, spray the plants with insecticidal soap every three to five days for two weeks. If these pests become a very serious problem, make two applications of pyrethrum, three to five days apart.

Leaves Stippled with Tiny Yellow Dots; Webby Foliage

Spider Mites

Leaves that are dry and stippled with tiny yellow dots are a sign that your salvias are infested with spider mites, tiny pests that suck chlorophyll out of the leaves. They also inject toxins into the foliage; this causes distorted or discolored growth. Leaves, stems, and flowers also may be swathed in fine webbing. As their name suggests, spider mites are related to spiders. These tiny creatures, which are about $\frac{1}{50}$ inch long and barely visible to the naked eye, may be yellow, green, red, or brown. Spider mites reproduce most rapidly during hot, dry weather. They are especially a problem on greenhouse-grown plants; inspect purchased bedding plants carefully to avoid bringing home infested specimens.

Severely infested plants should be destroyed, since infestations are difficult to control once they are well under way. Spider mites can be controlled by washing the plants, especially the undersides of the leaves. For best results, use a forceful spray of water once every other day to knock the mites off the plants; wash the plants at least three times. If that is not effective, spray the plants with insecticidal soap every three to five days for two weeks. To avoid spreading the mites from plant to plant, don't touch healthy plants after examining infested ones.

Weakened Plants, Leaves Yellowed

Whiteflies

Plants that are infested with whiteflies are weakened and undersized with leaves that begin to turn yellow and die. The undersides of the leaves of infested plants may be covered with a sooty, black fungus, which grows on the shiny, sticky honeydew secreted by the whiteflies. Adults are white, mothlike insects about the size of the head of a pin and are clearly visible on the undersides of salvia leaves. Whitefly infestation is sometimes referred to as flying dandruff because when an infested plant is bumped or brushed, the adults flutter out in clouds, somewhat resembling dandruff flying off the leaves. Nymphs, which are yellowish, legless, flat, and oval, resemble scale at certain stages. Both nymphs and adults suck juices from plant leaves, buds, and stems. These pests, which are particular problems in greenhouses, are often brought home on purchased bedding plants or vegetable transplants. (Greenhouse whitefly, *Trialeurodes vaporariorum*, the most common species found in gardens, does not overwinter outdoors in the North.) Inspect purchased bedding plants carefully to avoid bringing home infested specimens.

Whiteflies are difficult to control once they have infested your garden. Destroy infected plants as soon as you detect the problem, for whiteflies will quickly spread throughout the garden if infestations are not controlled. To control infestations, spray plants with insecticidal soap spray every two to three days for two weeks. Be sure to spray the undersides of the leaves. Also, use insecticidal soap early in the season to prevent infestations. Pyrethrum may be used as a last resort. Spray once every five days, making three applications. Isolate and destroy severely infested plants.

MOST COMMON DISEASES

Annual salvias are not seriously bothered by diseases. They are occasionally afflicted with leaf spot, which is caused by a variety of fungi; by downy and powdery mildew, which cause powdery white or gray mold on the foliage; rust; and stem rot. They can also harbor the aster yellows virus.

Seedlings Rot at Base, Fall Over

Damping-Off
Seedling stems that are water soaked and blackened at the soil line have been afflicted with damping-off. Affected stems are unable to support the plants, which fall over and die. Usually, the foliage is still green and healthy looking when the plants collapse. Stems of older plants show tan to reddish brown lesions that eventually girdle stems. Damping-off is caused by soil-dwelling fungi, including *Pythium debaryanum* and *Pellicularia filamentosa*. Germinating seeds may be attacked before they emerge from the soil, or shortly thereafter.

Cultural controls are effective in preventing damping-off. Sow seed in well-drained soil, do not overcrowd plants, and keep soil on the dry side. Use a sterile growing mix (peat moss, perlite, and vermiculite, with a topping of milled sphagnum moss), and water plants from below by setting pots in water and allowing the water to soak up to just beneath the soil surface. Thin seedlings so they are far enough apart to allow air to circulate between them, which will carry away excessive moisture and reduce humidity. When thinning, use scissors instead of pulling up plants to avoid damaging the roots and stems of remaining plants, which might open them up to infection. In the greenhouse, a fan will promote air circulation. Avoid feeding seedlings too much nitrogen, for it causes lank, weak growth. Routinely disinfect garden tools in boiling water or a household bleach solution (1 part bleach to 3 parts water) to discourage disease problems.

ANNUAL *Snapdragon* *Antirrhinum majus*

DESCRIPTION

Common or garden snapdragon features tall spikes of various-colored flowers that would make a dramatic statement in any garden. These cool weather-loving plants are actually perennials, but are usually grown as annuals. Plant breeders have developed many different cultivars, which vary in size, flower form, and color. Use snapdragons in beds or borders. Dwarf cultivars make excellent edging plants; tall cultivars are better for the rear of the border. They also make fine cut flowers.

Height

Tall cultivars, 3 to 4 feet; medium cultivars, 1½ to 2 feet; dwarf cultivars, 6 to 9 inches

Spread

12 to 15 inches

Blossoms

Snapdragon flowers are densely clustered along tall stems or spikes. In addition to the familiar two-lipped "dragons" that snap open when pressed, there are double-flowered forms and those with open, trumpet-shaped blooms. They have a light fragrance and come in a wide range of colors, including maroon, red, white, pink, yellow, and orange. Snapdragons bloom best when the weather is cool and are at their best in early summer. They can be cut back and will bloom again in fall. Or in areas with long growing seasons, they can be sown in late summer for fall bloom.

Foliage

Snapdragon foliage is dark green. The narrow, lance-shaped leaves may be up to 3 inches long.

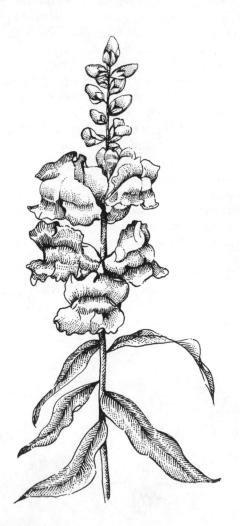

ENVIRONMENT

Hardiness

Snapdragons are perennials grown as half-hardy annuals, and most cultivars will stand some frost. If protected, they will survive the winter in many parts of the country, but bloom best when grown as annuals.

Light

For best bloom, grow snapdragons in full sun, although they will tolerate light shade.

Soil

Grow snapdragons in light, well-drained soil that is somewhat sandy and rich in organic matter. Because of their very fine roots, they do not grow well in heavy clay soils; so add organic materials to improve clay soil. The pH can range from slightly acidic to alkaline, pH 6.5 to 8.0.

PLANTING AND PROPAGATION

Planting

For best results, sow snapdragons indoors six to

eight weeks before the last frost date, and transplant hardened seedlings to the garden after danger of frost has passed. Sow seeds on the surface of the soil because they require light for germination. Germinate at temperatures between 70° and 75°F. Or sow seed outdoors where the plants are to grow after danger of frost has passed and the soil has warmed. Germination takes 10 to 14 days. Space the plants 6 to 12 inches apart in the garden.

Container Gardening

Snapdragons grow well in containers.

PLANT MANAGEMENT

General Care

Pinch the young plants back a few inches a month or so after they have been set out in the garden to encourage branching, bushy growth, and more flowers. Snapdragons will die out if the seed heads are not sheared off, so remove the spent blossoms to improve the bloom throughout the season. When warm temperatures arrive and plants stop blooming, cut them back to encourage repeat flowering in fall.

Taller cultivars will require staking. The stems are brittle and will tear off at the base, so stake them with care. Install stakes around the perimeter of each clump when plants are less than a foot high, and string twine around and between the stakes. Train the plants up through the twine.

Water

As a general rule, snapdragons should receive ½ to 1 inch of water per week from rain or by watering. As with most annuals, a steady level of moisture in the soil promotes vigor and continuous bloom. Do not allow plants to dry out to the point that the leaves wilt.

Feeding

A spring application of compost or a slow-acting, general-purpose fertilizer will serve the basic needs of snapdragons all season. For exceptional performance, give plants supplemental, light feedings (side-dressings or foliar spray) monthly throughout the growing season.

Cutting Fresh Flowers

Snapdragons make superior cut flowers for bouquets and arrangements.

Drying Flowers

Snapdragons don't air dry well, but can be dried using silica gel. To dry in silica gel, cut flowers in full bloom, leaving 1-inch stems. Place flower cluster, stems down, in a coffee can or other sealable container partially filled with silica gel. Carefully sift gel over blooms until they are completely covered.

MOST COMMON INSECT PESTS

In addition to the pests listed below, slugs, snails, caterpillars, and beetles can chew holes in the foliage, flowers, and flower buds of snapdragons. Greenhouse or celery leaftiers can chew leaves and fasten them together with their silken webs. Handpicking is the best control for all of these pests.

Pale or Yellow Spots on Leaves, Leaves Curled and Distorted

Aphids

Plants infested with aphids have distorted growth that may be curled, puckered, or stunted. Leaves may turn yellow or brown, and feeding can seriously damage flower buds or cause distorted flowers. Plants may also wilt under bright sunlight. Aphids are soft-bodied, pear-shaped sucking insects about the size of the head of a pin; they may be brown, green, yellow, or nearly black. They are often found clustered under leaves, and flower buds and stem tips may be covered with dense colonies of these insects. Ants, attracted by the aphids' honeydew secretions, wander over the plants, and black, sooty mold can develop on the honeydew as well. Green peach aphid (*Myzus persicae*) and melon aphid (*Aphis gossypii*) both attack snapdragons.

Light infestations of aphids can be controlled by washing the plants, especially the undersides of the leaves. For best results, use a forceful spray of water once every other day to knock the aphids off the plants; wash the plants at least three times. If that is not effective, spray the plants with insecticidal soap every three to five days for two weeks. If these pests become a very serious problem, make two applications of pyrethrum, three to five days apart.

Sawdust Exudes from Stems; Stems Break Off; Leaves Wilt

Borers

If snapdragon stems break and leaves wilt, look closely for small, round holes in the stems, from which borers may have expelled their castings. Stalk borer (*Papaipema nebris*) attacks snapdragons. It is a long, slender caterpillar marked with a dark brown or purple band around the middle and several conspicuous stripes running the length of the body. Adults are grayish brown moths.

Preventive measures are most effective when dealing with these pests, since by the time symptoms occur, it is usually too late to save the plant. Clean up all weeds, and cut and burn any plant stalks that may harbor overwintering eggs or pupae. Rotating the location of your snapdragon planting can also help control this pest. Bt (*Bacillus thuringiensis*) is effective if applied early in the season just as the borers are entering the plants. Borer infestations also can be controlled by slitting each affected stem lengthwise, removing the borers, and binding the stems together, but this is tedious work if you have a large planting.

Leaves and Flowers Deformed, Dwarfed, or Marked with Small Spots

Bugs

Several of the true bugs (order Hemiptera) infest snapdragons. Their feeding can cause deformed growth and young shoots and buds that are dwarfed. Leaves and flowers may be marred with tiny yellow or brown spots. Damage is the result of the bugs feeding with their piercing-sucking mouthparts. Red-and-black stink bugs (*Cosmopepla bimaculata*), tarnished plant bugs (*Lygus rugulipennis*), and four-lined plant bugs (*Poecilocapsus lineatus*) all infest snapdragons.

As their name suggests, red-and-black stink bugs are shiny, red and black in color, and have a foul odor. They are ¼ to ⅓ inch long.

Tarnished plant bugs are active, ¼-inch-long bugs that are green to brown in color and mottled with white, yellow, and black. On either side of the insect near the back is a yellow triangle with a black dot at one corner. Tarnished plant bugs appear in early spring, and, if left uncontrolled, become increasingly numerous toward the end of summer. They feed by sucking sap from plants and also release a toxin when feeding that can deform foliage and shoots.

Four-lined plant bugs, which are primarily a pest of early summer, are greenish yellow with four wide black stripes down their backs. Their nymphs are bright red with black dots.

Preventive measures are helpful in controlling these pests. Thoroughly clean up the garden in spring and fall to discourage overwintering adults and eggs. Handpicking adults and nymphs and dropping them into a jar of soapy water is also effective if the infestation isn't too great. If that is not effective, spray the plants with insecticidal soap every three to five days for two weeks. In severe cases, try three applications of pyrethrum laced with isopropyl alcohol, one every three days. Spray early in the morning when bugs are least active. If the infestation is heavy, dust plants with sabadilla.

Leaves Stippled with Tiny Yellow Dots; Webby Foliage

Spider Mites

Leaves that are dry and stippled with tiny yellow

dots are a sign that your snapdragons are infested with spider mites, tiny pests that suck chlorophyll out of the leaves. They also inject toxins into the foliage; this causes distorted or discolored growth. Leaves, stems, and flowers also may be swathed in fine webbing. Inspect lower leaves for evidence of these pests, especially during hot, dry weather, when these pests reproduce most rapidly. As their name suggests, spider mites are related to spiders. These tiny creatures, which are about ¹/₅₀ inch long and barely visible to the naked eye, may be yellow, green, red, or brown. Two-spotted spider mites (*Tetranychus urticae*), broad mites (*Polyphagotarsonemus latus*), and cyclamen mites (*Steneotarsonemus pallidus*) attack snapdragons.

Severely infested plants should be destroyed, since infestations are difficult to control once they are well under way. Spider mites can be controlled by washing the plants, especially the undersides of the leaves. For best results, use a forceful spray of water once every other day to knock the mites off the plants; wash the plants at least three times. If that is not effective, spray the plants with insecticidal soap every three to five days for two weeks. To avoid spreading the mites from plant to plant, don't touch healthy plants after examining infested ones.

MOST COMMON DISEASES

Leaves Have Pale Blotches with Brown Margins

Anthracnose

In late summer, snapdragon leaves and stems may become marked with pale yellow-green or gray blotches surrounded by distinct brown margins. Tiny black spore pustules appear in the spots. These symptoms indicate your snapdragons are infected with the fungal disease anthracnose, caused by *Colletotrichum antirrhini*. The petals of infected plants also develop abnormally, and seriously infected plants may die of the disease.

Cultural controls can be used to combat anthrac-

nose. Pick off and destroy any infected leaves as soon as they appear. Also, regularly clean up and destroy dead plant debris in the garden. Do not compost plant material you suspect to be infected. Rogue out and discard seriously infected plants, together with the soil in which they are growing. Disinfect garden tools with liquid bleach solution (1 part bleach to 3 parts water) or 70 percent rubbing alcohol to avoid spreading the fungus from plant to plant. When watering, avoid wetting the foliage. A layer of mulch helps prevent fungal spores from splashing from the soil onto plants. If anthracnose is a particular problem in your area, spray at weekly to ten-day intervals with wettable sulfur or bordeaux mixture, particularly in rainy seasons. (Watch for leaf discoloration with the latter.)

Round Spots on Leaves and Stems; Plants Wilt

Blight

Snapdragons infected with blight develop round, cream or light brown spots on leaves and stems. The spots are sometimes ringed with other colors, and black fungal spores develop in the middle. Spots that develop on stems, are grayish black at first, but rapidly turn dark brown. As they enlarge, they eventually girdle the stem, and the plants wilt and die. The disease is caused by the fungus *Phyllosticta antirrhini*.

Weed out and discard seriously infected plants, together with the soil in which they are growing. At the end of the season, dig and destroy all parts of the plants growing in infected beds; do not compost. Regularly clean up and destroy dead plant debris in the garden. Do not compost plant material you suspect to be infected. Disinfect garden tools with liquid bleach solution (1 part bleach to 3 parts water) or 70 percent rubbing alcohol to avoid spreading the fungus from plant to plant. When watering, avoid wetting the foliage. If blight is a particular problem in your area, spray at weekly to ten-day intervals with wettable sulfur or bordeaux mixture, particularly in rainy seasons. (Watch for leaf discoloration with the latter.)

Moldy Coating on Leaves and/or Flowers

Gray Mold

As its name suggests, gray mold causes a gray coating on leaves and flowers. Caused by the fungus *Botrytis cinerea,* it attacks flowers first, wilting and then rotting them. It then spreads downward into the stem, and afflicted plants often break off about 2 feet from the ground where the fungus has damaged the tissue. Primarily a problem in cool, wet weather, it is further encouraged by poor ventilation or insufficient light.

Cultural controls are a very effective way to deal with molds and mildews. Plant snapdragons in a location that affords plenty of ventilation and sunlight, as well as well-drained, fertile soil. Water early on sunny days, and try to avoid wetting the foliage when watering. Allow ample spacing between plants. Unless the season is unusually humid, these precautions should save you from most problems with molds and mildews. Pick and destroy infected flowers as soon as they appear. Dig up heavily infected plants, together with adjacent soil, and discard them; do not compost. Collect and discard all aboveground refuse in the fall. If gray mold is a particular problem in your area, spray infected plants once or twice at weekly intervals with wettable sulfur, bordeaux mixture, or another copper fungicide when molds or mildews first appear on leaves. (Watch for leaf discoloration with the bordeaux mixture.)

Leaves Pale Yellow Above with Powdery Spots Beneath

Rust

Rust-infected snapdragons develop brown pustules on leaves, stems, and flowers. The pustules are surrounded by a yellowish area, and plants quickly wilt and die. Infected plants may fail to bloom or may only produce small flowers. Rust is caused by the fungus *Puccinia antirrhini,* which is most active during cool (below 60°F) weather.

Remove and destroy any infected leaves, stems, or flowers as soon as they appear; do not compost. Collect and discard all aboveground refuse in the fall. When planting, to ensure good ventilation, space plants far enough apart so that air can circulate between them. Also, avoid wetting the foliage when watering. If rust is a particular problem in your area, make weekly applications of wettable sulfur starting in early spring, before rust normally appears.

Stems Turn Black at Base; Leaves Turn Yellow and Wilt; Plants Topple Over

Stem, Root, and Crown Rots

A variety of soil-dwelling fungi attack snapdragons at the base of the plant, causing stems to turn black from the base upward and rotting the crowns or roots of the plants. Discolored, water-soaked lesions eventually girdle the stems, and leaves turn yellow and wilt. Once these fungi have girdled stems or rotted crowns or roots, the stems or plants topple over, and the plants eventually die.

These diseases attack greenhouse-grown snapdragons as well as plants grown outdoors, especially those that are overcrowded or overwatered. Although steam pasteurization is the only surefire way to destroy the fungi, preventive measures are very helpful in controlling these diseases. Plant snapdragons in well-drained soil, avoid overwatering and overcrowding, and keep mulch away from the base of plant stems. Remove and discard infected plants, together with the surrounding soil, or cut away affected plant parts with a clean, sharp knife or razor blade. Discard infected plant material; do not compost. Disinfect tools with a solution of 1 part household bleach and 3 parts water or 70 percent rubbing alcohol to avoid spreading the disease. Keep the garden clear of old plant debris. For long-term prevention, lighten heavy soil with a mixture of perlite, vermiculite, and/or peat moss, and provide good drainage.

Strawflower *Helichrysum bracteatum*

DESCRIPTION

Strawflowers have been favorites for the annual garden since Victorian times because their flower heads are perfect for drying and will add brilliant color to winter bouquets. Members of the daisy family, Compositae, they produce colorful flowers from summer until the first frost of autumn. Straw-

flowers are often grown in a cutting garden because the plants are not particularly attractive. However, they can be planted at the back of a border or combined with other annuals. Dried and wired, their blooms make wonderful additions to wreaths, bouquets, and other dried-flower arrangements.

Height

15 to 48 inches

Spread

12 to 15 inches

Blossoms

The flowers of strawflowers are about 2½ inches across and come in many colors including white, yellow, orange, red, salmon, pink, and purple. Although they resemble double daisies, the flowers actually consist of a daisylike head of tiny, tightly packed, individual flowers called disc florets surrounded by many brightly colored bracts, which are actually modified leaves. The bracts resemble petals, but are stiff and glossy. Blossoms appear in the early summer and continue until fall frost.

Foliage

Strawflowers have narrow leaves that are rough in texture and medium green in color.

ENVIRONMENT

Hardiness

Strawflowers are actually perennials grown as half-hardy annuals. They will often self-seed in sandy soil.

103

Light

Strawflowers grow best in full sun and appreciate long, hot, dry summers.

Soil

Plant strawflowers in light, well-drained soil. They will tolerate soil pH ranging from 6.5 to 8.0. Very rich or heavily fertilized soil will cause rampant foliage growth and few flowers.

PLANTING AND PROPAGATION

Planting

For best results, sow seed indoors four to six weeks before the last frost date, and germinate at temperatures around 70°F. Do not cover the seeds with soil; They require light to germinate. Seedlings sown indoors or purchased bedding plants can be transplanted to the garden after danger of frost has passed. Or sow seed in the garden where the plants are to grow after danger of frost has passed. Germination takes seven to ten days.

PLANT MANAGEMENT

General Care

Strawflowers require very little day-to-day maintenance once they are established in the garden. The plants will need staking, however, so start staking them when they are about 1 foot tall.

Water

As a general rule, make sure your strawflowers get ½ to 1 inch of water every week from rain or by watering. Do not allow them to dry out to the point that the leaves wilt.

Feeding

A spring application of compost or a slow-acting, general-purpose fertilizer will serve the basic needs of strawflowers all season. For exceptional performance, give plants supplemental, light feedings (side-dressings or foliar spray) monthly throughout the growing season.

Drying Flowers

Strawflowers are one of the best flowers for drying, but you need to pick the blooms before the bracts open enough to reveal the center disc florets. If the flowers dry with open fuzzy centers, you waited too long to pick them; ideally, the centers should be covered by petals. Strawflowers are wired rather than dried with their stems, so snip each bloom at its base, leaving the remaining plant to continue blooming until frost. Wire the blossom immediately so the base of the bud doesn't dry out; otherwise you won't be able to insert the wire up through the center of the bloom. To wire, use florist's wire, sticking it up through the base of each flower and out its center. Make a small hook in the tip of the wire and pull it back down into the bloom to anchor the wire in place.

MOST COMMON CULTURAL PROBLEMS

Plants Weak, Spindly

Not Enough Sun

If your strawflower plants look weak, spindly, and lack vigor, they may not be receiving enough sun. These plants thrive in hot weather and need at least 6 hours of direct sun daily. They can be transplanted to a better spot. Rich, overly fertilized soil will also cause lank growth and the production of foliage at the expense of flowers.

MOST COMMON INSECT PESTS

Strawflowers are bothered by few insects and can easily withstand attacks by most pests, provided the plants are healthy and vigorous. They are occasionally infested by aster leafhopper (*Amcrosteles fascifrons*), which sucks sap from plants, leaving tiny yellow spots on foliage as evidence. This pest also carries aster yellows.

MOST COMMON DISEASES

Strawflowers grown with proper cultural conditions—well-drained soil and full sun—are subject to few diseases. They can be infected with the virus disease aster yellows, which causes greenish yellow leaves and flowers and deformed growth. They are also occasionally attacked by stem rot and nematodes.

ANNUAL *Sunflowers* *Helianthus* spp.

DESCRIPTION

Sunflowers are native North-American plants most often grown for their enormous flower heads that resemble the sun. Common annual sunflower (*Helianthus annuus*), which provides the edible seeds coveted by both birds and gardeners, is best known, but there are both perennial and annual species of sunflowers. There are smaller-flowered forms of common sunflower that are more ornamental than the giant types, and many of the species also bear graceful flowers that are attractive in flower gardens. Jerusalem artichoke (*H. tuberosus*) is a perennial species of sunflower grown for its starchy, edible tubers. Depending on their height, sunflowers can be used as background plants, in borders, or as screens. Dwarf cultivars can be planted in beds. Many of the native species are perfect for meadow gardens. All will attract birds, but giant cultivars grown for their edible seeds are especially attractive to the smaller seed-eating birds such as goldfinches and chickadees, which will harvest the seeds themselves.

Height

H. annuus (common sunflower), 6 to 12 feet
H. × *multiflorus* (perennial sunflower), 5 to 6 feet
H. petiolaris (prairie sunflower), 6 feet
H. tuberosus (Jerusalem artichoke), 9 to 12 feet

Spread

1 to 3 feet

Blossoms

Sunflowers belong to the daisy family, Compositae, and bear typical daisylike flowers. *H. annuus* bears centers of tightly packed disc florets surrounded by showy yellow "petals," called ray florets. Ornamental forms may have single, semidouble, or double blooms with ray florets in yellow, white, orange, maroon, or bicolored. Centers may be yellow, dark brown, or purplish. Flower heads of seed-producing cultivars can be up to 1 foot across, however most ornamental forms have 3- to 5-inch flowers. Sunflowers bloom from midsummer to fall.

Foliage

Most sunflowers have rough, coarse, green leaves that are generally alternate on the stem and usually have toothed margins.

ENVIRONMENT

Hardiness

Annual species of sunflowers are hardy annuals that will tolerate some frost. Perennial species such as *H. × multiflorus* and *H. tuberosus* are hardy to USDA Zone 5.

Light

Sunflowers are quite tolerant of heat and drought and will grow best in full sun.

Soil

Sunflowers will grow in almost any soil, but they grow best in light, well-drained, somewhat dry soil. The pH can range from 6 to 8.

PLANTING AND PROPAGATION

Planting

Although sunflower seeds can be started indoors, they grow so quickly and are so aggressive—crowding out all nearby weeds—indoor sowing isn't necessary. Sow seed outdoors, after danger of frost has passed, where the plants are to grow. Sow seed at a depth of ½ to 1 inch. Seeds will germinate in three to ten days. Plants should eventually be spaced about 2 to 3 feet apart, so space seeds carefully when sowing and thin seedlings so the plants will have enough room to grow and develop.

PLANT MANAGEMENT

General Care

Sunflowers are care-free, easy-to-grow plants that require little maintenance once established. Tall cultivars will require staking or some other form of support, such as wiring to a wall or fence. Sunflowers grown for seeds will need to be covered with netting or cheesecloth as soon the heads begin to ripen.

Water

As a general rule, make sure your sunflowers get ½ to 1 inch of water per week from rain or by watering. Although tolerant of drought once established, for best bloom, don't allow sunflowers to dry out to the point that the leaves wilt.

Feeding

A spring application of compost or a slow-acting, general-purpose fertilizer will serve the basic needs of sunflowers all season. For exceptional performance, give plants supplemental, light feedings (side-dressings or foliar spray) monthly throughout the growing season.

Drying Flowers

Sunflowers can be harvested as soon as the backs of the seed heads are brown and dry. At this time, the inner seed rows are ripe but need drying. To harvest, cut off the heads with about a foot of the stalk attached. Tie the stalks together and hang the heads in an airy attic or loft to dry. When they are thoroughly dry, remove the seeds by rubbing the heads lightly. If stored in airtight containers, the seeds will retain their nutritional value for a long time.

MOST COMMON INSECT PESTS

Although a variety of insects infest sunflowers, as a general rule, they can withstand attacks by most pests. Beetles and caterpillars may chew holes in foliage, but most infestations can be controlled by handpicking.

Pale or Yellow Spots on Leaves, Leaves Curled and Distorted

Aphids

Plants infested with aphids have distorted growth that may be curled, puckered, or stunted. Leaves may turn yellow or brown, and feeding can seriously damage flower buds or cause distorted flowers. Plants may also wilt under bright sunlight. Aphids are soft-bodied, pear-shaped sucking insects about the size of the head of a pin; they may be brown, green, yellow, or nearly black. They are often found clustered under leaves, and flower buds and stem tips may be covered with dense colonies of these insects. Ants, attracted by the aphids' honeydew secretions, wander over the plants, and black, sooty mold can develop on the honeydew as well. Dogwood or sunflower aphid (*Aphis helianthi*), hop aphid (*Phorodon humuli*), leafcurl plum aphid (*Brachycaudus helichrysi*), and melon aphid (*Aphis gossypii*) all attack sunflowers.

In addition, root aphids can also attack sunflowers, causing plants that are stunted or that stop growing completely. The leaves of sunflowers infested with these pests may turn yellow and wilt under bright sunlight, and in some cases, they curl and pucker. White aster root aphid (*Prociphilus erigeronensis*) is carried by ants to the plant's roots. Ants also nurse the aphids' eggs through the winter.

Light infestations of aphids can be controlled by washing the plants, especially the undersides of the leaves. For best results, use a forceful spray of water once every other day to knock the aphids off the plants; wash the plants at least three times. If that is not effective, spray the plants with insecticidal soap every three to five days for two weeks. If these pests become a very serious problem, make two applications of pyrethrum, three to five days apart.

The only way to effectively control root aphids is to control the ants that shepherd them, however, root aphids can sometimes be prevented by adding a small amount of wood ashes to the planting holes when you plant seed in spring. Thorough spading of the garden soil in the fall disturbs ant nests that house caches of aphid eggs.

Leaves and Flowers Deformed, Dwarfed, or Marked with Small Spots

Bugs

Several of the true bugs (order Hemiptera) infest sunflowers. Their feeding can cause deformed growth and young shoots and buds that are dwarfed. Leaves and flowers may be marred with tiny yellow or brown spots. Damage is the result of the bugs feeding with their piercing-sucking mouthparts. Four-lined plant bugs (*Poecilocapsus lineatus*), harlequin bugs (*Mugantia histrionica*), leaf-footed bugs (*Leptoglossus phyllopus*), and tarnished plant bugs (*Lygus rugulipennis*) all infest sunflowers.

Four-lined plant bugs, which are primarily a pest of early summer, are greenish yellow with four wide black stripes down their backs. Their nymphs are bright red with black dots.

Harlequin bugs are a serious pest of cabbage and its relatives that also attack other plants. Adults are black with bright red markings and are about ⅜ inch in length. The eggs of this pest are very distinctive—they look like tiny white cylinders with black bands and are arranged in rows. Nymphs can suck large amounts of sap from infested plants.

Leaf-footed bugs are brown with a yellow stripe and have rear legs with flattened leaflike projections. Adults are about ¾ inch long and nymphs are small-size versions of the adults.

Tarnished plant bugs are active, ¼-inch-long bugs that are green to brown in color and mottled with white, yellow, and black. On either side of the insect near the back is a yellow triangle with a black dot at one corner. Tarnished plant bugs appear in early spring, and, if left uncontrolled, become increasingly numerous toward the end of summer. They feed by sucking sap from plants and also release a toxin when feeding that can deform foliage and shoots.

Preventive measures are helpful in controlling these pests, several of which overwinter in garden refuse. Thoroughly clean up the garden in spring and fall to discourage overwintering adults and eggs. Handpicking adults, nymphs, or eggs and dropping them into a jar of soapy water is also effective if the infestation isn't too great. If that is not effective, spray the plants with insecticidal soap every three to five days for two weeks. In severe cases, try three applications of pyrethrum laced with isopropyl alcohol, one every three days. Spray early in the morning when bugs are least active. If the infestation is heavy, dust plants with sabadilla.

Flower Heads Covered with Webbing; Seeds Destroyed

Sunflower Moth

If the flower heads of your sunflowers are covered with masses of webbing and frass, and the seeds are destroyed, they are probably infested with the larvae of the sunflower moth (*Homoeosoma electellum*). The adult of this pest is a gray moth that lays its eggs in the florets that make up the sunflowers' huge heads. The larvae are greenish yellow striped with brown. These pests pupate in the heads of the sunflowers.

Take preventive measures to control these pests because severe infestations will destroy the seed heads. Spray sunflowers with Bt (*Bacillus thuringiensis*) when the flowers first appear. Handpicking the larvae can be an effective way to control these pests if you carefully monitor the plants and catch infestations as soon as they occur.

MOST COMMON DISEASES

Sunflowers are generally as disease-free as they are insect-free, for they are subject to few serious diseases. In addition to the diseases listed below, the foliage may occasionally be marked by powdery mildew or leaf spot, but control measures for these problems are seldom warranted.

Leaves with Brown Spots Above, Powdery Spots Beneath

Rust

Sunflowers are attacked by fungi that cause rust

disease. These fungi cause powdery brown spots or pustules, which contain the spores, to appear on the undersides of the leaves. Afflicted leaves dry up and fall prematurely. Severely infected sunflower stems and flowers may be seriously deformed. These fungi most often spread from wild sunflower relatives to infect cultivated ones.

Remove infected leaves as soon as possible, and destroy severely diseased plants. Clean up and destroy all plant material at the end of the season to avoid reinfecting the garden the following year. Rust can be prevented by periodic applications of wettable sulfur, begun several weeks before rust normally appears. To ensure good ventilation, space plants far enough apart so that air can circulate between them. Also, avoid wetting foliage when watering.

Plants Wilt Suddenly; Stems Rot

Wilt and Stem Rot

Sunflowers can be afflicted with a variety of diseases that rot stems or cause plants to wilt suddenly.

Plants may wilt suddenly and leaves may turn yellow or develop a mottled pattern and then wilt. Plants afflicted with stem rot, caused by the fungi *Sclerotinia sclerotiorum*, have a thick, feltlike growth on the stems. Stem rot is a particular problem during wet weather, and afflicted stems wilt and then fall over.

Preventive measures are very helpful in controlling these diseases. Plant sunflowers in well-drained soil, avoid overwatering and overcrowding, and keep mulch away from the base of plant stems. Remove and discard infected plants, together with the surrounding soil, or cut away affected plant parts with a clean, sharp knife or razor blade. Discard infected plant material; do not compost. Disinfect tools with a solution of 1 part household bleach and 3 parts water or 70 percent rubbing alcohol to avoid spreading the disease. Keep the garden clear of old plant debris. For long-term prevention, lighten heavy soil with a mixture of perlite, vermiculite, and/or peat moss, and provide good drainage. Rotating sunflowers to other parts of the garden will also help control these diseases.

ANNUAL # Verbena   *Verbena × hybrida*

DESCRIPTION

This popular annual, which is commonly called garden verbena, is grown for its colorful clusters of flowers, which are borne at the ends of the stems. Most are low-growing plants with a trailing habit, and for that reason, verbena makes an excellent ground cover. It also is at home in beds, rock gardens, containers, and hanging baskets and can also be used as a cut flower. Since verbena is actually a tender perennial grown as an annual, it can be brought indoors for winter bloom, propagated, and planted outside the following year.

Height

8 to 18 inches

Spread

1 to 2 feet

Blossoms

The individual flowers of garden verbena are tube-shaped with flat, five-lobed or petaled "faces." They are borne in dense, 2- to 3-inch clusters. Blossom colors include red, white, pink, purple, lavender, and yellow. Flowers are often marked with a contrasting white eye in the center. The plants bloom from early summer to fall frost.

Foliage

Verbena has small, hairy leaves that are bluntly toothed and deep green in color. They are from 2 to 4 inches long.

ENVIRONMENT

Hardiness

Garden verbenas are tender perennials usually grown as tender annuals. They will not tolerate frost and do not grow well when temperatures are cool. Move plants to the garden only after temperatures remain over 50°F at night.

Light

Verbenas need full sun to grow and bloom well. In the Deep South and desert Southwest, however, select a location with light shade to protect plants from extreme heat and drought.

Soil

Although verbenas will tolerate poor soil, for best results plant them in rich, well-drained, soil. Plants will tolerate a pH range from 6 to 8.

PLANTING AND PROPAGATION

Planting

Sow seed indoors 12 to 14 weeks before the last frost date. Verbena seeds are very small and can be difficult to germinate, although seed of newer hybrids is more reliable. For best results, fill flats of pots with sterilized potting medium and moisten it 24 hours before you plan to sow. Press the tiny seeds into the surface, but do not cover them with soil, for they are sensitive to dampness. Since the seeds require darkness to germinate, cover the flats or pots with black plastic until seeds germinate. Germination takes 20 to 25 days, and germination temperatures from 70° to 75°F are ideal. Germination percentages are normally quite low, around 40 to 50 percent, so plant at least twice as many seeds as you'll need plants.

Because garden verbenas take so long to grow from seed, most gardeners prefer to purchase them as bedding plants from local nurseries or garden centers. Do not move purchased bedding plants or home-grown seedlings to the garden until night-time temperatures stay above 50°F and danger of frost has passed. Space plants 1 to 1½ feet apart to ensure good air circulation.

Propagation

Garden verbenas are easy to propagate by stem cuttings. Take cuttings in summer or early fall to bring plants indoors for overwintering or from plants that have been dug and brought indoors for winter bloom. This is an excellent way to perpetuate desirable colors and plant habits.

Container Gardening

These plants make attractive additions to window boxes, hanging baskets, and planters.

PLANT MANAGEMENT

General Care

Garden verbenas are quite heat tolerant, but may temporarily stop flowering during very hot weather. A layer of mulch helps keep the roots cooler and may delay or prevent this problem. Remove the seed heads as the flowers fade to encourage the production of new blooms.

Overwintering

To move garden verbenas indoors, dig and pot them up just before the first fall frost. To promote bushy growth and new flowers and help plants adjust to the shock of transplanting, pinch back the stems by at least half. Or, take cuttings of the best plants in your garden and root them. Give them full winter sun, water when the soil becomes dry, and keep temperatures on the cool side but above 50°F for best growth.

Water

As a general rule, make sure plants get ½ to 1 inch of water every week from rain or by watering. Do not allow them to dry out to the point that the leaves wilt.

Feeding

A single application of compost or a slow-acting, general-purpose fertilizer at planting time will serve the basic needs of these plants all season. For exceptional performance, give plants supplemental, light feedings (side-dressings or foliar spray) monthly throughout the growing season.

Cutting Fresh Flowers

Verbenas make fine cut flowers.

Drying Flowers

Verbenas do not air dry well, but can be dried in silica gel. To dry in silica gel, cut flowers in full bloom, leaving 1-inch stems. Place flower cluster, stems down, in a coffee can or other sealable container partially filled with silica gel. Carefully sift gel over blooms until they are completely covered.

MOST COMMON INSECT PESTS

Once established, garden verbenas are not seriously bothered by many insect pests. In addition to the insects listed below, caterpillars and leafrollers can chew holes in the foliage and flowers. Spider mites can cause tiny yellow dots on foliage and encase leaves with their silken webs. Carefully inspect purchased bedding plants to avoid bringing home infested specimens.

Pale or Yellow Spots on Leaves, Leaves Curled and Distorted

Aphids
Plants infested with aphids have distorted growth that may be curled, puckered, or stunted. Leaves may turn yellow or brown, and feeding can seriously damage flower buds or cause distorted flowers. Plants may also wilt under bright sunlight. Aphids are soft-bodied, pear-shaped sucking insects about

the size of the head of a pin; they may be brown, green, yellow, or nearly black. They are often found clustered under leaves, and flower buds and stem tips may be covered with dense colonies of these insects. Ants, attracted by the aphids' honeydew secretions, wander over the plants, and black, sooty mold can develop on the honeydew as well. In addition to the damage they cause by feeding, aphids are important vectors of virus diseases. Several species of aphids infest garden verbenas, including foxglove aphid (*Acyrthosiphon solani*), geranium aphid (*A. pelargonii*), green peach aphid (*Myzus persicae*), and melon aphid (*Aphis gossypii*). Several beneficial insects feed on aphids, including ladybugs and lacewings.

Light infestations of aphids can be controlled by washing the plants, especially the undersides of the leaves. For best results, use a forceful spray of water once every other day to knock the aphids off the plants; wash the plants at least three times. If that is not effective, spray the plants with insecticidal soap every three to five days for two weeks. If these pests become a very serious problem, make two applications of pyrethrum, three to five days apart.

Holes in Leaves and/or Flowers

Clematis Blister Beetles
Clematis blister beetles (*Epicauta cinerea*) occasionally infest verbenas. Adults are yellowish gray and exude a liquid that can cause blisters when it touches bare skin. The larvae are C-shaped, grayish white grubs.

Clematis blister beetles can be controlled by handpicking, but wear gloves for they can cause blisters if they are crushed on skin. Crush the beetles or drop them into a pail of soapy water. If the infestation is light, this is all you will need to do. For heavier infestations, spray infested plants with a solution of pyrethrum and isopropyl alcohol, mixing 1 tablespoon of alcohol with every pint of diluted pyrethrum mixture. Apply this solution every three

to five days until the problem is corrected. For long-term control, apply milky spore disease (*Bacillus popilliae*) to lawns and garden. It will kill the larvae.

Leaves Covered with Tan to Brown Blotches; Foliage Appears Blighted

Leafminers
If large areas of the leaves of your garden verbena plants develop brown or tan blisters or blotchy-looking mines, they may be infested with verbena leafminers (*Agromyza artemisiae*). The foliage of infested specimens has a discolored and diseased appearance. The adult is a small midge, but it is the larvae that do the damage to the foliage. The larvae feed singly, but mines of several individuals join together, which makes the foliage very unsightly.

Pick off and destroy all infested leaves as they appear. If necessary, prune back stems until only healthy growth remains. Clean up all plant material in fall to prevent the leafminers from overwintering. Larvae can sometimes be repelled by spraying plants with several weekly applications of insecticidal soap in late June or early July.

MOST COMMON DISEASES

Although verbenas are occasionally attacked by wilt, stem rot, and powdery mildew, these diseases are primarily problems when the plants are grown too close together or in soil that is not well-drained or during unusually damp weather.

Seedlings Rot at Base, Fall Over

Damping-Off
Seedling stems that are water soaked and blackened at the soil line have been afflicted with damping-off. Affected stems are unable to support the plants, which fall over and die. Usually, the foliage is still green and healthy looking when the plants collapse. Stems of older plants show tan to reddish brown

lesions that eventually girdle stems. Damping-off is caused by soil-dwelling fungi such as *Pythium, Fusarium, Sclerotium,* and *Rhizoctonia,* and can attack plants before they emerge from the soil or shortly thereafter.

Cultural controls are effective in preventing damping-off. Sow seed in well-drained soil, do not overcrowd plants, and keep soil on the dry side. Use a sterile growing mix (peat moss, perlite, and vermiculite, with a topping of milled sphagnum moss), and water plants from below by setting pots in water and allowing the water to soak up to just beneath the soil surface. Thin seedlings so they are far enough apart to allow air to circulate between them, which will carry away excessive moisture and reduce humidity. When thinning, use scissors instead of pulling up plants to avoid damaging the roots and stems of remaining plants, which might open them up to infection. In the greenhouse, a fan will promote air circulation. Routinely disinfect garden tools in boiling water or household bleach solution (1 part bleach to 3 parts water) to discourage disease problems.

ANNUAL **Zinnia** *Zinnia elegans*

DESCRIPTION

The common garden zinnia, which is also sometimes called youth-and-old-age, belongs to the daisy family, Compositae, and is native to Mexico. These popular annuals bear showy flowers atop stiff stems, and plant breeders have developed many cultivars from which to choose. Blooms come in a wide variety of sizes and forms; they may be single or double and come in every color except blue. Plants range in size from diminutive dwarfs to tall plants for the back of the border. Because of their bright colors and tolerance for summer heat, zinnias are invaluable additions to the summer flower garden, where they are used for bedding, borders, edging, and in containers. They also make excellent cut flowers.

Height

Tall cultivars, 30 inches; medium cultivars, 20 inches; semidwarf cultivars, 14 to 16 inches; dwarf cultivars, 6 to 12 inches

Spread

8 to 24 inches, depending on height at maturity

Blossoms

Zinnias bear single or double flowers that range in size from 5 or 6 inches across down to dainty, buttonlike blooms no more than 1½ inches across. Flowers most often come in red, orange, yellow, pink, and white and appear from early summer until first fall frost.

Foliage

Zinnias have medium green leaves with a rough or coarse texture.

Soil

Zinnias will tolerate poor soil, but for best results, plant them in fertile, well-drained soil rich in organic matter. The pH can range from 6 to 8.

PLANTING AND PROPAGATION

Planting

For best results, sow zinnias outdoors where the plants are to grow after all danger of frost has passed and nighttime temperatures remain above 50°F. Zinnias also can be started indoors four to six weeks before the last frost date. However, double-flowered forms often begin producing single blooms after transplanting, so outdoor sowing is recommended. In either case, plant the seeds about 1/16 inch deep and lightly cover the seeds. Germination takes four to seven days, and temperatures of 70° to 75°F are ideal. After the seedlings have developed their first true leaves, they may be thinned to stand 4 or 5 inches apart. A final thinning should leave the plants spaced 6 to 10 inches apart for dwarf cultivars, 10 to 12 inches apart for semidwarf cultivars, and 15 to 20 inches apart for medium and tall cultivars.

Container Gardening

Dwarf zinnias do well in containers such as tubs, pots, and window boxes.

PLANT MANAGEMENT

General Care

Zinnias require very little care once they are established in the garden. Pinch young plants to encourage branching, bushy growth, and more blooms. Cutting flowers also encourages branching and flower production, as does removing dead flowers.

Water

As a general rule, make sure your zinnias get ½ to

ENVIRONMENT

Hardiness

Zinnias are tender annuals that will not survive frost. Do not plant seed outdoors or move seedlings to the garden until night temperatures remain above 50°F.

Light

Grow zinnias in full sun. They thrive in hot, dry climates with long summers.

1 inch of water per week from rain or by watering. Established plants tolerate some drought, but a steady supply of moisture promotes vigor and continuous bloom. Do not allow zinnias to dry out to the point that the leaves wilt. To avoid problems with powdery mildew, never water zinnias late in the day, and avoid getting water on the foliage. It is best to soak or flood zinnias when watering them.

Feeding

A single application of compost or a slow-acting, general-purpose fertilizer worked into the soil before planting will serve the basic needs of these annuals all season. For exceptional performance, give your plants supplemental, light feedings (side-dressings or foliar spray) monthly throughout the growing season.

Cutting Fresh Flowers

Zinnias make excellent, long-lasting cut flowers.

Drying Flowers

For best results, dry zinnias in silica gel. To dry in silica gel, cut flowers in full bloom, leaving 1-inch stems. Place flower cluster, stems down, in a coffee can or other sealable container partially filled with silica gel. Carefully sift gel over blooms until they are completely covered.

MOST COMMON
CULTURAL PROBLEMS

Double-Flowered Plants Produce Only Single Flowers

Transplant Stress
Zinnias can be difficult to transplant, and if sown indoors, should be handled with care. Double-flowered cultivars will revert to producing single blooms as a result of transplant stress. Either direct-sow zinnias where the plants are to grow or sow indoors in individual peat pots or large pots to avoid stressing plants at transplant time.

Plants Get Leggy and/or Fall Over

Unpinched plants;
Improper Planting Location
Zinnias can become top-heavy and sprawl onto nearby plants or flop over entirely. To avoid this condition, pinch seedlings back at least twice before the flower buds begin to form to encourage well-branched, compact plants. Or, select dwarf cultivars to grow. Also, plant zinnias in full sun. Tall cultivars need a location that is protected from wind. Staking is the only solution for plants that have fallen over.

MOST COMMON INSECT PESTS

Zinnias are very easy-to-grow plants that are seldom seriously bothered by insect pests, provided they are grown in a location that suits their taste. In addition to the insects listed below, they occasionally are infested with leafhoppers, which cause small white or yellow spots on the leaves and can transmit virus diseases; aphids, which cause curled and distorted growth; and tarnished plant bugs, which cause deformed growth on young shoots. Stalk borers also sometimes infest zinnias, drilling holes in stems and causing shoot tips to wilt and die.

Holes in Leaves and/or Flowers

Beetles
Several species of beetles chew holes in zinnia foliage and flowers. Japanese beetles (*Popillia japonica*), which skeletonize zinnia leaves and destroy their flowers, is the most serious pest. They are ½-inch-long beetles that are shiny, metallic green with copper-colored wing covers. Asiatic garden beetles (*Maladera castanea*), which also attack zinnias are ½-inch-long, cinnamon brown beetles that feed only at night. Black blister beetles (*Epicauta pennsylvanica*) are black, ½-inch-long insects that also feed on flowers and leaves. The larvae of these three beetles are

C-shaped, grayish white grubs with dark brown heads that can eat plant roots. Fully grown grubs are ¾ to 1 inch long.

For the most part, all beetles are controlled the same way. Where possible, handpick and crush them or drop them into a pail of soapy water. (Wear gloves if you suspect you have blister beetles, for they can cause blisters if they are crushed on skin.) If the infestation is light, this is all you will need to do. For heavier infestations, spray infested plants with a solution of pyrethrum and isopropyl alcohol, mixing 1 tablespoon of alcohol with every pint of diluted pyrethrum mixture. Apply this solution every three to five days until the problem is corrected. For long-term control, apply milky spore disease (*Bacillus popilliae*) to lawns and garden. It will kill the larvae of most beetles.

Japanese beetles can also be controlled by pheromone traps. Set up traps a week before the beetles are expected to emerge in your area, making sure traps are no closer than 50 feet from the zinnias or any other plant vulnerable to beetle attack, such as roses.

Leaves Stippled with Tiny Yellow Dots; Webby Foliage

Spider Mites

Leaves that are dry and stippled with tiny yellow dots are a sign that your zinnias are infested with spider mites, tiny pests that suck chlorophyll out of the leaves. They also inject toxins into the foliage; this causes distorted or discolored growth. Leaves, stems, and flowers also may be swathed in fine webbing. Inspect lower leaves for evidence of these pests, especially during hot, dry weather, when these pests reproduce most rapidly. As their name suggests, spider mites are related to spiders. These tiny creatures, which are about 1/50 inch long and barely visible to the naked eye, may be yellow, green, red, or brown. Two-spotted spider mites (*Tetranychus urticae*), broad mites (*Polyphagotarsonemus latus*),

and cyclamen mites (*Steneotarsonemus pallidus*) attack zinnias.

Severely infested plants should be destroyed, since infestations are difficult to control once they are well under way. Spider mites can be controlled by washing the plants, especially the undersides of the leaves. For best results, use a forceful spray of water once every other day to knock the mites off the plants; wash the plants at least three times. If that is not effective, spray the plants with insecticidal soap every three to five days for two weeks. To avoid spreading the mites from plant to plant, don't touch healthy plants after examining infested ones.

MOST COMMON DISEASES

Small, Red-Brown Spots on Flowers; Brown Cankers on Stems

Blight

Zinnias covered with small, red-brown spots that have gray centers may have blight, caused by the fungus *Alternaria zinniae*. The flowers of seriously infested plants can be completely covered with spots, and the disease also causes dark brown cankers to form on zinnia stems.

Pick off and destroy blighted flowers as soon as you spot them. Also, regularly clean up and destroy dead plant debris in the garden. Do not compost plant material you suspect to be infected. Rogue out and discard seriously infected plants. If blight is a particular problem in your area, spray at weekly to ten-day intervals with wettable sulfur or bordeaux mixture, particularly in rainy seasons. (Watch for leaf discoloration with the latter.)

White Powder Covering Leaves

Powdery Mildew

In late summer, zinnia foliage becomes covered with powdery mildew, a whitish or ash gray dust or bloom on leaves and flowers. Caused by the fungus

Erysiphe cichoracearum, powdery mildew develops in hot, humid weather. It is especially a problem on the lower leaves of plants grown close together. The flowers and foliage of badly infected plants become discolored, distorted, and drop off.

Powdery mildew most commonly develops on plants grown close together where air circulation is restricted, especially on the lower leaves where humidity is higher and moisture is more abundant. Allow ample spacing between plants, and collect and discard all aboveground refuse in the fall. Spray affected plants thoroughly with wettable sulfur once or twice at weekly intervals, starting as soon as the whitish coating of the fungus is visible.

Another excellent preventive is a monthly spray of an antitranspirant spray (about 3 to 4 teaspoons per gallon of water) starting a month after last frost time. Plant breeders have begun to develop mildew-resistant cultivars, produced by crossing mildew-immune *Zinnia angustifolia* with the common garden zinnia. The cultivar 'Rose Pinweel' was the first of the mildew-resistant releases.

Plants Wilt Suddenly; Stems Rot at Soil Line

Root and Stem Rots

Zinnias can be afflicted with a variety of diseases that cause plants to wilt suddenly or to rot at or below the soil line. Plants may wilt suddenly and/or leaves may turn yellow and then wilt. Stem and root rots are caused by several different soil-dwelling fungi, including *Phytophora, Fusarium,* and *Sclerotinia.*

Preventive measures are very helpful in controlling these diseases. Plant zinnias in well-drained soil, avoid overwatering and overcrowding, and keep mulch away from the base of plant stems. Remove and discard infected plants, together with the surrounding soil, or cut away affected plant parts with a clean, sharp knife or razor blade. Discard infected plant material; do not compost. Disinfect tools with a solution of 1 part household bleach and 3 parts water or 70 percent rubbing alcohol to avoid spread-

ing the disease. Keep the garden clear of old plant debris. For long-term prevention, lighten heavy soil with a mixture of perlite, vermiculite, and/or peat moss, and provide good drainage.

Leaves Greenish Yellow or Curled and Deformed; Shoots Spindly or Stunted

Virus Diseases

Zinnias are susceptible to a number of virus diseases. Plants that produce curled, thickened, or otherwise distorted foliage may be infected with the viral disease that causes beet curly top, which causes excessive cell growth and thus distorted growth. Viruses are spread by sucking insects such as leafhoppers. Infected plants may be stunted or dwarfed. Other virus diseases cause spots, lines, pale areas, mottling, or dead areas to appear on the foliage of infected plants. Afflicted plants may be stunted and yellowed, and eventually wilt and die. Shoot tips may branch abnormally and tend to develop into witches'-brooms; secondary shoots are usually spindly. Flowers are deformed and may be aborted entirely. Regardless of the normal bloom color of the cultivar, flowers are often sickly yellow-green.

There is no cure for virus-infected plants. Remove and destroy them; do not compost. Disinfect garden tools with a solution of 1 part household bleach and 3 parts water or 70 percent rubbing alcohol to avoid spreading virus diseases from plant to plant. Also, wash your hands after handling infected plants. To control the insects that transmit the disease, spray remaining plants with a mixture of insecticidal soap and isopropyl alcohol. Make this mix by adding 1 tablespoon of alcohol to each pint of insecticidal soap solution. Spray at three- to five-day intervals, making three applications. The virus overwinters in various perennials and weeds such as daisies, plantain, and gaillardia. Infected plants are not necessarily killed by the disease, but should be dug up and destroyed, since they continue to infect nearby plants via leafhoppers.

CHAPTER 2

Perennials

Perennials are the backbone of the flower garden. Unlike annuals, which need to be replaced each year, perennials go dormant over the winter and emerge again in spring. Many perennials will live for decades, among them peonies, daylilies, and hostas. Others live for only a few seasons and must be replaced every few years. Because they need to store up energy to return and bloom again, most perennials have shorter blooming seasons than annuals. Typically, they flower for only three to four weeks, sometimes less and sometimes more, and offer foliage and perhaps seedpods as interest for the rest of the growing season. However, when many perennials are used together in the garden—such as in beds or borders—the progression of different plants in bloom from spring through summer to fall can provide a fascinating array of combinations of colors, textures, and habits.

Perennials are often promoted as the perfect flowering plants for the low-maintenance garden. Since they return season after season, it's a good idea to spend some extra time getting them planted properly in a site that will allow them to thrive. Taking the extra time to dig the soil deeply and incorporate plenty of organic matter to increase fertility and improve drainage will pay off in the long run with healthy, vigorous plants. As with annuals, perennials that are thriving will be better able to withstand attacks by insects and diseases. In the individual entries that follow, you'll find plenty of information about the cultural conditions and care the plants prefer.

For best performance, many perennials also benefit from some basic maintenance throughout the season. As with all plants, a layer of mulch in the summer will discourage weeds, keep the roots cool, and help retain moisture in the soil. Mulch applied in late fall after the ground freezes will serve to keep soil temperatures more constant throughout the winter months, which will help prevent the crowns of the plants from heaving out of the soil due to repeated freezing and thawing. Many perennials also benefit from pinching, which encourages bushy growth, and deadheading—or removing spent flowers. Staking taller-growing perennials keeps the plants from flopping over, reduces stem breakage due to wind and rain, and helps the flowers show to best advantage. Finally, most perennials must be divided every few years in order to prevent overcrowding and to control their spread in the garden.

If you combine proper culture with a thorough fall cleanup, you'll be well on your way to solving many of the problems you may encounter in the perennial garden. By gathering up and discarding plant material such as stalks, leaves, spent flowers, and seedpods at the end of the season, you'll also be disposing of many of the fungal spores and overwintering insects that might infest your plants in future years.

PERENNIAL Asters, Perennial *Aster* spp.

DESCRIPTION

Aster spp., the true asters (as opposed to the annual China asters, *Callistephus* spp.), are a large group of mostly perennial plants that belong to the daisy family, Compositae. Also called Michaelmas daisies, many of them are wildflowers native to North America. They produce daisylike blooms that consist of a row of petal-like ray florets surrounding a center of yellow disc florets. All make fine, long-lasting cut flowers and are prized for their lavish, late-autumn bloom and easy care. For the most part, these are tall plants that are suitable for use at the back of perennial borders or in meadow gardens.

Height

A. novae-angliae (New England aster), 3 to 5 feet
A. novae-belgii (New York aster), 3 to 5 feet
A. tataricus (Tatarian aster), 6 to 8 feet

Spread

2 to 3 feet

Blossoms

Perennial asters bear showy flowers with yellow centers in a wide variety of colors, including pale and deep pink, rose red, blue-violet, purple, and white. Flower heads are about 1 inch across. Blooms appear from late August through late fall.

Foliage

Perennial asters have narrow, dark green leaves that are borne alternately on the stem.

ENVIRONMENT

Hardiness

A. novae-angliae, A. novae-belgii, and *A. tataricus* are all hardy to USDA Zone 4.

Light

For best results, grow perennial asters in full sun. They will tolerate very light shade as well.

Soil

Asters like most soils, provided they are well-drained, but will perform best in fertile, well-drained soil that remains moist during the growing season. They will not survive in soil that is wet in winter. The pH can range from 6 to 8.

PLANTING AND PROPAGATION

Planting

Most cultivars of perennial asters are produced by cuttings or division because the seed does not come true to type. However, if you want to grow the species, or if perpetuating a particular color or form isn't important, they are easy to grow from seed. Sow seed outdoors in a prepared seedbed where the plants are to grow from spring through summer up to about two months before the first frost of autumn. Or sow indoors in early spring, and germinate at temperatures between 70° and 75°F. Germination takes 15 to 20 days.

Purchased plants, whether from cuttings or divisions can be planted in spring for bloom the following autumn.

PLANT MANAGEMENT

General Care

Perennial asters should be dug, divided, and re-planted in spring every two to three years. Select the vigorous shoots at the outsides of the clumps for replanting, and discard the older, less vigorous growth at the center. Tall cultivars will require staking when grown in perennial borders, for they will tend to flop over and overwhelm nearby plants. However, asters grown in meadows, along the edge of woods, or in other natural settings can be left to spread as they will. In small gardens, try training the stems along the ground in spring when the stems are still pliant. By using wire wickets to hold the plants in a horizontal position you can create a low-growing mound of flowers that will be spread over a large area. It's also a good idea to prune away all but six or eight stalks from each clump every spring to control their somewhat rampant growth and to direct more of the plant's energy into fewer stems. Finally, since perennial asters can self-sow very easily, remove the flowers as they fade.

Water

Perennial asters will grow best if provided with at least 1 inch of water per week from rain or by watering.

Feeding

A spring application of compost or a slow-acting, general-purpose fertilizer will serve the basic needs of perennial asters all season.

Cutting Fresh Flowers

Perennial asters make fine, long-lived cut flowers.

MOST COMMON CULTURAL PROBLEMS

Seedlings Appear Where They Are Not Wanted

Reseeding
Perennial asters can reseed prolifically from year to year, and unexpected seedlings can become a nuisance. Picking or deadheading the flowers before they go to seed can reduce this problem.

MOST COMMON INSECT PESTS

Pale or Yellow Spots on Leaves, Leaves Curled and Distorted

Aphids
Plants infested with aphids have distorted growth

that may be curled, puckered, or stunted. Leaves may turn yellow or brown, and feeding can seriously damage flower buds or cause distorted flowers. Plants may also wilt under bright sunlight. Aphids are soft-bodied, pear-shaped sucking insects about the size of the head of a pin; they may be brown, green, yellow, or nearly black. They are often found clustered under leaves, and flower buds and stem tips may be covered with dense colonies of these insects. Ants, attracted by the aphids' honeydew secretions, wander over the plants, and black, sooty mold can develop on the honeydew as well. In addition to the damage they cause by feeding, aphids are important vectors of virus diseases. Several species of aphids infest perennial asters, including artemisia aphid (*Macrosiphum artemisiae*) and aster aphid (*Dactynotus anomalae*). Several beneficial insects feed on aphids, including ladybugs and lacewings.

Light infestations of aphids can be controlled by washing the plants, especially the undersides of the leaves. For best results, use a forceful spray of water once every other day to knock the aphids off the plants; wash the plants at least three times. If that is not effective, spray the plants with insecticidal soap every three to five days for two weeks. If these pests become a very serious problem, make two applications of pyrethrum, three to five days apart.

Holes in Leaves and/or Flowers

Beetles
Perennial asters are a particular favorite of Japanese beetles, which chew holes in foliage and flowers. Japanese beetles (*Popillia japonica*) are ½-inch-long beetles that are shiny, metallic green with copper-colored wing covers. Severe infestations can completely skeletonize plants. The larvae are C-shaped, grayish white grubs with dark brown heads that can eat plant roots. Fully grown grubs are ¾ to 1 inch long.

Japanese beetles can be controlled by handpicking, provided the infestation is not too large.

Where possible, handpick and crush them or drop them into a pail of soapy water. For heavier infestations, spray infested plants with a solution of pyrethrum and isopropyl alcohol, mixing 1 tablespoon of alcohol with every pint of diluted pyrethrum mixture. Apply this solution every three to five days until the problem is corrected. For long-term control, apply milky spore disease (*Bacillus popilliae*) to lawns and garden. It will kill the larvae of most beetles.

Japanese beetles can also be controlled by pheromone traps. Set up traps a week before the beetles are expected to emerge in your area, making sure traps are no closer than 50 feet from the asters or any other plant vulnerable to beetle attack, such as roses.

Leaves and Flowers Deformed, Yellowish, or Marked with Small Spots

Chrysanthemum Lace Bugs
Perennial asters infested with chrysanthemum lace bugs (*Corythucha marmorata*) will cause deformed growth and leaves that are marred with tiny yellow or brown spots. Damage is the result of the bugs feeding on the undersides of leaves with their piercing-sucking mouthparts. Adults have lacy-looking wings; both adult and juvenile stages feed on leaves and stems. They cause the foliage to develop a bleached appearance, damage stems, and leave resinous, dark droppings on the undersides of leaves.

Preventive measures are helpful in controlling these pests. Thoroughly clean up the garden in spring and fall to discourage overwintering adults and eggs. Handpicking adults, nymphs, or eggs and dropping them into a jar of soapy water is also effective if the infestation isn't too great. If that is not effective, spray the plants with insecticidal soap every three to five days for two weeks. Be sure to spray the undersides of the leaves where these insects feed. In severe cases, try three applications of pyrethrum laced with isopropyl alcohol, one every three days. Spray early in the morning when bugs are least active. If the infestation is heavy, dust plants with sabadilla.

MOST COMMON DISEASES

Leaves Covered with Dark Spots or Blotches

Leaf Spot

Several different kinds of fungi cause unsightly spots on aster foliage. Leaves may have transparent or brown or black spots. Some fungal spots are surrounded by flecks or black dots, which are the spore-bearing fruiting bodies. Often spots come together to form larger patches of dead tissue. These fungi thrive on moist leaf surfaces.

To control leaf spot, pick off and destroy infected leaves. Also, regularly clean up and destroy dead plant debris in the garden to reduce spore populations. These fungi overwinter as spores in such debris, so an end-of-season cleanup is especially important. Rogue out and discard seriously infected plants, together with the soil in which they are growing. A layer of mulch helps prevent spores from splashing from the soil onto plants. If leaf spot is a particular problem in your area, spray at weekly to ten-day intervals with wettable sulfur or bordeaux mixture, particularly in rainy seasons. (Watch for leaf discoloration with the latter.)

Moldy Coating on Leaves and/or Flowers

Molds or Mildews

Several different fungi cause grayish or white molds or powdery coverings on aster flowers and foliage. Downy mildew, which is caused by the fungus *Basidiophora entospora*, attacks asters in the Midwest and South. It causes pale areas on upper leaf surfaces and gray, white, or purplish "downy" patches on undersides. Unlike powdery mildew (below), which causes a white, powderlike growth on the surface of the leaves, downy mildew grows deep into plant tissue and only sticks its spore-bearing stalks above the leaf surface. It spreads most quickly on moist leaf and stem surfaces and is especially active in periods of cool, wet nights and warm, humid days. Leaves eventually wilt and die.

Asters are also susceptible to powdery mildew caused by the fungus *Erysiphe cichoracearum*, which causes a whitish dust or bloom on the surface of leaves. It can also infect flowers. Infected leaves are often curled or distorted, and the growth of severely infected plants can be stunted. Powdery mildew most commonly develops on asters grown close together in ornamental plantings, especially on the lower leaves where moisture is more abundant.

Cultural controls are a very effective way to deal with molds and mildews. Plant asters in a location that affords plenty of ventilation and sunlight. Choose a location with well-drained, fertile soil, water early on sunny days, allow ample spacing between plants, and try to avoid wetting the foliage when watering. Unless the season is unusually humid, these precautions should save you from most problems with molds and mildews. Pick and destroy infected leaves and stems. Dig up heavily infected plants, together with adjacent soil, and discard them; do not compost. Collect and discard all aboveground refuse in the fall. Spray infected plants once or twice at weekly intervals with wettable sulfur, bordeaux mixture, or another copper fungicide when molds or mildews first appear on leaves. (Watch for leaf discoloration when using bordeaux mixture.) Several applications may be needed to stop the spread of the fungus.

Leaves with Pale Areas Above; Powdery Orange Spots Beneath

Rust

Perennial asters are susceptible to several rust diseases caused by a variety of fungi. They cause pale areas to appear on upper leaf surfaces, with powdery orange pustules or spots directly beneath on the undersides of the leaves.

Remove infected leaves as soon as possible, and destroy severely diseased plants. Clean up and destroy all plant material at the end of the season to avoid reinfecting the garden the following year. Rust can be prevented by periodic applications of wettable sulfur, begun several weeks before rust normally appears. To ensure good ventilation, space plants far enough apart so that air can circulate between them. Also, avoid wetting foliage when watering.

PERENNIAL Astilbes *Astilbe* spp.

DESCRIPTION

Astilbes are perennials native to the Far East that bear fluffy spikes of flowers that are pink, white, red, or purplish. Although sometimes called spirea and false goatsbeard, they are not closely related to the true spireas, which are shrubs in the genus *Spiraea*, or true goatsbeards, which are native perennials in the genus *Aruncus*. Astilbes have been extensively hybridized, and cultivars of *Astilbe* × *arendsii* are most commonly available. Astilbes are versatile perennials that are easy to grow, provided their few cultural demands are met. They make fine additions to perennial borders and shady wild gardens.

Height

A. × *arendsii* (hybrid astilbe), 2 to 4 feet
A. chinensis 'Pumila' (Chinese astilbe), 6 to 12 inches

Spread

1 to 3 feet

Blossoms

The individual flowers of astilbes are actually very tiny, but they are arrayed in dense, plumelike clusters atop tall stems. Flowers are carried well above the foliage and are very showy. Blooms come in white, pink, red, or purple. Hybrid astilbes generally bloom in early summer, although there are species that bloom in summer and early fall.

Foliage

Astilbes bear delicate, fernlike leaves that are dark green or bronzed. Red-flowered astilbes usually have the darkest foliage. New, young leaves are glossy, but they gradually lose their shine as they mature.

ENVIRONMENT

Hardiness

Astilbes are fairly hardy perennials, and most are hardy to USDA Zone 5.

Light

Astilbes grow best in partial shade and rich, moist soil. They do not tolerate heat or drought well and need shade to protect them from the hot summer sun, especially in the South. In the North, they can handle full sun.

Soil

For best results, plant astilbes in a location with soil that is moist, rich in organic matter, and slightly acidic. They can grow in a spot that is wet during the growing season, but the soil should dry out in winter. Plants will tolerate pH ranging from 6 to 8.

PLANTING AND PROPAGATION

Planting

Astilbes can be grown from seed, but most cultivars must be propagated by division because they do not

come true from seed. Sow seed indoors or in a cold frame in early spring. Germination takes 20 to 30 days, and temperatures of 60° to 70°F are ideal. Dormant or actively growing plants can be planted in either spring or fall. Space them about 1 to 1½ feet apart. Astilbes have shallow roots, so take care not to plant them too deeply.

Propagation

Astilbes should be dug and divided every three to five years. Dig up the plants in spring or fall, and cut new plants at the outside of the clump away from the older plants at the center. Replant the divisions at the correct spacing.

Container Gardening

Astilbes can be grown in containers, but they must be large enough to keep the soil cool and moist—at least 1 to 2 feet in diameter and 1 foot deep. They also can be forced in pots in cool greenhouses.

PLANT MANAGEMENT

General Care

Astilbes are relatively care-free, provided they are planted in moist soil that is rich in organic matter. They need to be divided regularly to keep the clumps healthy, and regular mulching helps keep roots cool and moist. They don't need staking or much other regular care once established. The flowers don't need to be removed when they fade because they dry to attractive shades of brown that many gardeners consider ornamental.

Water

Astilbes are moisture lovers that grow best in soil that remains evenly moist at all times. They will need at least ½ to 1 inch of water per week from regular watering or rainfall. Mulch the plants to help keep the roots cool and damp, and watch them carefully during dry spells.

Feeding

Astilbes are heavy feeders. Work plenty of compost into the soil at planting time and provide established plants with a handful of slow-acting, general-purpose fertilizer in spring. Astilbes appreciate supplemental feedings during the summer, so for exceptional performance, give plants light feedings (side-dressings or foliar spray) monthly throughout the growing season.

Cutting Fresh Flowers

Astilbes make fine cut flowers, adding interesting texture to arrangements.

Drying Flowers

Astilbes are particularly useful and attractive in dried arrangements. Their feathery flower plumes shrink when air dried, but they can be dried in silica gel. To dry in silica gel, cut flowers in full bloom, leaving 1-inch stems. Place flower cluster, stems down, in a coffee can or other sealable container partially filled with silica gel. Carefully sift gel over blooms until they are completely covered.

MOST COMMON CULTURAL PROBLEMS

Plants Stunted; Leaves Have Brown Edges

Improper Planting Location

Astilbes that develop dry, brown leaf edges usually have been planted in a location that receives too much hot sun or have not received sufficient moisture. Plants that are grown in soil that is too dry or that receive too much sun will wilt frequently, and growth is often stunted. To correct this condition, add plenty of organic matter to the soil when planting, mulch plants to keep the roots cool, and select a location that is shaded, especially during the hottest part of the day.

MOST COMMON INSECT PESTS

Holes in Leaves and/or Flowers

Beetles

Astilbes are seldom bothered by insects, and Japanese beetles are their only serious pests. Japanese beetles (*Popillia japonica*), which often descend in hordes, chew holes in foliage and consume the flowers. They can completely skeletonize leaves. They are ½-inch-long beetles that are shiny, metallic green with copper-colored wing covers. The larvae are C-shaped, grayish white grubs with dark brown heads that can eat plant roots. Fully grown grubs are ¾ to 1 inch long.

Handpick beetles and crush them or drop them into a pail of soapy water. If the infestation is light, this is all you will need to do. For heavier infestations, spray infested plants with a solution of pyrethrum and isopropyl alcohol, mixing 1 tablespoon of alcohol with every pint of diluted pyrethrum mixture. Apply this solution every three to five days until the problem is corrected. For long-term control, apply milky spore disease (*Bacillus popilliae*) to lawns and garden.

Japanese beetles can also be controlled by pheromone traps. Set up traps a week before the beetles are expected to emerge in your area, making sure traps are no closer than 50 feet from the astilbes or any other plant vulnerable to beetle attack, such as roses.

MOST COMMON DISEASES

White Powder Covering Leaves

Powdery Mildew

Astilbe foliage can become covered with powdery mildew, a whitish or ash gray dust or bloom on leaves and flowers. Caused by the fungus *Erysiphe polygoni,* the problem develops in hot, humid weather, especially on the lower leaves of plants grown close together. The flowers and foliage of badly infected plants become discolored, distorted, and drop off.

Powdery mildew most commonly develops on plants grown close together where air circulation is restricted, especially on the lower leaves where humidity is higher and moisture is more abundant. Allow ample spacing between plants, and collect and discard all aboveground refuse in the fall. Spray affected plants thoroughly with wettable sulfur once or twice at weekly intervals starting as soon as the whitish coating of the fungus is visible.

Plants Wilt while Soil Is Still Moist

Wilt

Astilbes are occasionally afflicted by a wilt disease caused by *Fusarium* spp. fungi, which cause the plants to wilt and die, despite the fact that they have adequate soil moisture. Young plants wilt quickly; older ones first develop a pale green color and the lower leaves wilt. Brown streaks then appear on the stems, which eventually become darkened, and a grayish pink fungal growth sometimes appears.

Dig and discard infected plants, together with surrounding soil. Discard the debris; do not compost. If wilt is a problem in your area, don't grow vulnerable plants continuously in the same soil; rotate plantings and change seedbeds, if possible. Do not divide infected plants. Sterilize tools after use on infected plants by dipping them in 70 percent rubbing alcohol.

PERENNIAL Baby's-Breath *Gypsophila* spp.

DESCRIPTION

Baby's-breath is grown for its cloudlike clusters of delicate, white or pink flowers that add a soft, feathery texture to the garden. There are both annual and perennial species, but all bear heavily branched clusters of tiny flowers that may be single or double. The most common of the perennial species is *Gypsophila paniculata,* which is used as a filler in perennial borders. *G. repens,* creeping baby's-breath, is a creeping species used in rock gardens, as an edging plant, or as a ground cover in sunny spots. Baby's-breath makes a fine filler in cut flower arrangements.

Height

G. paniculata (baby's-breath), 2½ to 3 feet
G. repens (creeping baby's-breath), 6 to 8 inches

Spread

G. paniculata (baby's-breath), 3 to 4 feet
G. repens (creeping baby's-breath), 1½ to 2 feet

Blossoms

Although the individual flowers of baby's-breath are tiny—ranging from ¹⁄₁₆ to ⅓ inch across—they are borne in abundance. *G. paniculata* bears 1,000 or more flowers per feathery cluster. Flowers may be white or pink, as well as single or double. Perennial species bloom for about six weeks in June and July; annual baby's-breath flowers from mid-June until frost.

Foliage

Leaves are narrow, 1 to 3 inches long, and bluish to

gray-green. They are borne in pairs from swollen joints along thin stems. The foliage is so inconspicuous that plants in bloom seem to be all stems and flowers at first glance.

ENVIRONMENT

Hardiness

G. paniculata and *G. repens* are hardy to USDA Zone 4.

Light

Baby's-breath requires full sun for best performance.

Soil

Plant baby's-breath in light, well-drained soil that is not too rich. The soil should be neutral to slightly alkaline, pH 7 to 8. Add some ground dolomitic limestone to raise the soil pH, if necessary.

PLANTING AND PROPAGATION

Planting

Baby's-breath can be grown from seed, but double-flowered forms are usually purchased as grafted plants. Sow seed outdoors in spring or summer where the plants are to grow, or sow them indoors in individual peat pots. Germination takes 10 to 15 days, and temperatures around 70°F are ideal.

Spring is the best time to plant purchased plants. Plant grafted specimens with the graft union 1 inch below the soil level to encourage root development from the stems and to help support the plant. Plant baby's-breath 3 feet apart. Because of their long tap roots, baby's-breath does not like to be transplanted once established.

Propagation

Baby's-breath is easiest to propagate by seeds because established plants are best left undisturbed. *G. repens* can be propagated by division or cuttings.

PLANT MANAGEMENT

General Care

Baby's-breath plants need a bit more care than some perennials, but are generally well worth the effort. For best effect, plants over 1½ feet in height will require staking, especially when planted in a windy spot or if tight clusters of bloom are desired. When the first bloom period is over in midsummer, cut back the flowering branches before they go to seed to encourage a repeat performance. Mulch plants in the winter with a layer of organic material to protect them from cold. Keep the mulch away from the base of the plant because moisture at the crown can lead to rot.

Water

Baby's-breath does best with ½ to 1 inch of water per week from rainfall or by watering, but established plants will survive considerable drought.

Feeding

A spring application of compost or a slow-acting, general-purpose fertilizer will serve the basic needs of baby's-breath all season. Check soil pH every other year and scratch in some ground limestone if the pH has dropped below 7.

Cutting Fresh Flowers

Baby's-breath lasts well in water and is a valuable filler for bouquets and floral arrangements.

Drying Flowers

Baby's-breath is easy to air dry and is ideal for dried arrangements. To air dry, trim off broken stems and leaves and either hang plants upside down or place them in a large bucket or other container to support them upright. Dry in a warm, dry, well-ventilated space like an attic or large closet. Handle carefully, as the stems are fragile.

MOST COMMON INSECT PESTS

Leaves Discolored, Distorted

Leafhoppers
Suspect aster leafhoppers (*Macrosteles fascifrons*) if baby's-breath leaves are finely mottled with white or yellow spots and the leaves eventually shrivel and drop off. Leafhoppers are tiny, ⅛-inch-long insects that are greenish yellow marked with six black spots. Nymphs are grayish. These pests spread aster yellows disease, which they pick up in spring when feeding on infected wild plants.

To control serious infestations, spray infested plants with a mixture of insecticidal soap and isopropyl alcohol. Make this mix by adding 1 tablespoon of alcohol to each pint of insecticidal soap solution. Spray at three- to five-day intervals, making three applications. If leafhoppers are a common problem in your backyard, place a barrier such as floating row covers, like Reemay, over plants in early spring. Also, apply preventive sprays of insecticidal soap solution or pyrethrum at four- to five-day intervals for the first month of growth.

MOST COMMON DISEASES

Flowers and Foliage Greenish Yellow, Deformed; Shoots Spindly

Aster Yellows
If the leaves of your baby's-breath plants are greenish yellow and spindly, and growth is stunted or dwarfed, they may be infected with aster yellows, a disease caused by a viruslike organism primarily spread by the aster leafhopper (*Macrosteles fascifrons*). Young plants that are infected show a slight yellowing along leaf veins. As the disease becomes more severe, the entire plant is stunted and yellowed, and the unusual number of shoots that develop cause the plant to become very bushy and upright. Shoot tips branch abnormally and tend to develop into witches'-brooms; secondary shoots are usually spindly. Flowers are curiously deformed and may be aborted entirely. Regardless of the normal bloom color of the cultivar, flowers are often sickly yellow-green.

There is no cure for infected plants; remove and destroy them. Spray remaining plants with a mixture of insecticidal soap and isopropyl alcohol. Make this mix by adding 1 tablespoon of alcohol to each pint of insecticidal soap solution. Spray at three- to five-day intervals, making three applications, to kill the leafhoppers that carry the disease. The virus overwinters in various perennials and weeds such as daisies, plantain, and gaillardia. Infected plants are not necessarily killed by the disease, but should be dug up and destroyed, since they continue to infect nearby plants via leafhoppers.

Soft Galls at Graft Union on Grafted Plants

Crown Gall
Grafted specimens of baby's-breath occasionally develop soft galls, which can reach 1 inch in diameter, near the graft union. The galls can completely envelop the stem and kill the plants. The galls are caused by the bacteria *Agrobacterium gypsophilae*.

Inspect purchased plants carefully, if possible, to avoid buying infected specimens. Don't propagate plants infested with these galls. Remove and discard infected plants, together with the surrounding soil; do not compost. Disinfect tools with a solution of 1 part household bleach and 3 parts water or 70 percent rubbing alcohol to avoid spreading the disease.

Crowns and Roots Rot; Plants Fail to Sprout in Spring

Crown Rot
Although ultimately caused by fungi and bacteria that attack the crowns of the plants, crown rot is a cultural as much as a disease problem. Baby's-breath is susceptible to crown rot when grown in soil that is not well drained. This is especially a problem during the winter months; suspect it if no shoots appear in spring. Moist soil around the plants leads to attack by both bacteria and fungi. The roots may be blackened, rotten, and covered with white fungal threads. The whole plant dies in a few days.

Cultural practices are very helpful in preventing crown rot in baby's-breath. When planting, select a site with well-drained soil, or improve the drainage of the site by incorporating compost and other organic material into the soil. Keep winter mulch away from the crowns of the plants. This helps reduce moisture and prevents rotting during the winter dormant season. Thoroughly cultivating around plants also helps dry out the soil and discourages the spread of the organisms that cause this problem. Since baby's-breath emerges late in spring, be sure to mark plantings to avoid accidentally digging into them and damaging the crowns. Remove and discard afflicted plants and the soil immediately surrounding them; do not compost.

Moldy Coating on Leaves and/or Flowers

Gray Mold
Baby's-breath is occasionally attacked by a gray mold caused by *Botrytis cinerea*. These fungi cause a gray coating on buds and stems, and the stem tips of afflicted plants die back. Primarily a problem in cool, wet weather, it is further encouraged by poor ventilation or insufficient light.

Cultural controls are a very effective way to deal with gray mold on baby's-breath. Grow baby's-breath in a location that affords plenty of ventilation and sunlight. Choose a location with well-drained, fertile soil. Water early on sunny days, and try to avoid wetting the foliage when watering. Allow ample spacing between plants, and thin the stems to improve air circulation. Pick and destroy infected leaves and stems. Unless the season is unusually humid, these precautions should save you from most problems with molds and mildews. Dig up heavily infected plants, together with adjacent soil, and discard them; do not compost. Collect and discard all aboveground refuse in the fall. Spray infected plants once or twice at weekly intervals with wettable sulfur, bordeaux mixture, or another copper fungicide when molds or mildews first appear on leaves. (Watch for leaf discoloration when using the bordeaux mixture.) Several applications may be needed to stop the spread of the fungus.

Balloon Flower

Platycodon grandiflorus

DESCRIPTION

Balloon flowers are handsome, summer-blooming perennials that come to us from East Asia. They take their common name from their puffy, balloonlike buds that may be white, pink, or blue. Their open flowers are bell-shaped, an indication of their close relationship to the bellflowers, *Campanula* spp. Blooms may be single, semidouble, or double, and many forms are available; *Platycodon grandiflorus* var. *mariesii* is a dwarf form. Balloon flowers are easy to grow and will bloom year after year with little care. They make outstanding additions to perennial borders and beds and also make fine cut flowers.

Height

2 to 2½ feet; dwarf forms, about 1½ feet

Spread

1 to 1½ feet

Blossoms

The inflated, balloonlike buds expand into wide-spreading, bell-shaped flowers each having five petals with pointed tips. Each flower is 2 to 3 inches across with a white star-shaped pistil in the center. The flowers are usually a deep, rich, blue-violet, but cultivars with white, pale blue, or pink flowers are available. Flower color is strongest along the veins of the petals, which gives the blooms a pleasing textured or streaked effect. The flowers have no scent. Balloon flowers bloom from late June to August, sometimes into September.

Foliage

Leaves are 1 to 3 inches long and narrowly oval with toothed edges. They're blue-green or gray-green and have a strong, leathery texture.

ENVIRONMENT

Hardiness

Balloon flowers are hardy to USDA Zone 3 or 4.

Light

Balloon flowers grow and flower best when planted in full sun, but will also tolerate very light shade.

131

Soil

Grow balloon flowers in moist, well-drained, moderately fertile soil with a pH range of 6 to 8. They will not grow well in wet, poorly drained soil.

PLANTING AND PROPAGATION

Planting

Balloon flowers are easy to grow from seed, which can be sown indoors or outdoors. Do not cover the seed, as it requires light for germination. Indoors, sow seed in early spring, and germinate at 70°F; germination takes 10 to 15 days. Seedlings can be planted out after danger of frost has passed or grown in pots in a cold frame and set out the following year. Outdoors, sow seed where the plants are to grow in spring or summer, up to two months before the first frost of autumn. Sow the seeds and then thin so seedlings are 1 to 1½ feet apart.

Plant purchased specimens in spring, placing the crowns of the plants (the thick area where the roots meet the stem) barely below the soil surface. Space plants 1 to 1½ feet apart; 10 to 12 inches for dwarf types. The plants develop deep, carrotlike roots, so they are difficult to divide or transplant. Once established, they are best left undisturbed. Plants do not begin growing until late spring; mark plantings carefully so you won't injure the dormant crowns when preparing the soil in spring. Plants take two to three years to become established.

Propagation

Balloon flowers can be divided, but it is usually best not to disturb established plants. If you decide to divide a plant, dust the cut roots with wettable sulfur or a copper fungicide to prevent rot.

PLANT MANAGEMENT

General Care

Balloon flowers will return year after year with little or no special attention. Taller cultivars benefit from staking as they mature and come into bloom; it makes their flowers show to best advantage. Removing faded flowers will help prolong the blooming period. A layer of mulch in summer will help retain water in the soil. A heavier layer of mulch in winter, applied after the ground freezes, will protect the crowns from heaving out of the soil due to fluctuations in temperature. Spread mulch carefully to leave the crown of the plant uncovered. Be sure to mark the locations of your balloon flowers carefully; they sprout late in spring and are easily damaged.

Water

Balloon flowers will grow best when they receive ½ to 1 inch of water per week from rainfall or by watering. However, they tolerate dry soil and will do well with much less water.

Feeding

A spring application of compost or a slow-acting, general-purpose fertilizer will serve the basic needs of balloon flowers all season.

Cutting Fresh Flowers

Balloon flowers make outstanding additions to floral arrangements. Cut flowers last up to a week if the freshly cut stems are seared with a flame before being placed in water.

MOST COMMON INSECT PESTS

Balloon flowers are easy-to-grow plants that are seldom bothered by insect pests. Slugs and snails may chew holes in the foliage and flowers, especially during rainy weather or on plants grown in shade. Aphids may suck juices from stems and buds.

MOST COMMON DISEASES

In addition to crown rot (discussed below), balloon

flowers are subject to the same diseases that afflict their close relatives, the bellflowers (*Campanula* spp.). For information on other disease problems, see the entry on bellflowers below.

Crowns and Roots Rot; Plants Fail to Sprout in Spring

Crown Rot

Although ultimately caused by fungi and bacteria that attack the crowns of the plants, crown rot is a cultural as much as a disease problem. Balloon flowers are susceptible to crown rot when grown in soil that is not well drained. Damaging the crown of a plant by inadvertently digging into it, for example, can also lead to rot. Crown rot is especially a problem during the winter months; suspect it if no shoots appear in spring. Moist soil around the crowns of the plants leads to attack by both bacteria and fungi. The roots and crowns may be blackened, rotten, and covered with white fungal threads. The whole plant dies in a few days.

Cultural practices are very helpful in preventing crown rot in balloon flowers. When planting, select a site with well-drained soil, or improve the drainage of the site by incorporating compost and other organic material into the soil. Keep winter mulch away from the crowns of the plants. This helps reduce moisture and prevents rotting during the winter dormant season. Thoroughly cultivating around plants also helps dry out the soil and discourages the spread of the organisms that cause this problem. Since balloon flowers emerge late in spring, be sure to mark plantings to avoid accidentally digging into them and damaging the crowns. Remove and discard afflicted plants and the soil immediately surrounding them; do not compost.

PERENNIAL *Bellflowers* *Campanula* spp.

DESCRIPTION

Bellflowers belong to a large genus of perennials, biennials, and annuals. Also commonly called harebells or bluebells, they are grown for their delicate, bell-shaped flowers, which are generally purplish blue or white but also come in pink or deep violet. There are low-growing species suitable for use as edging plants or in rock gardens; these include tussock bellflower (*Campanula carpatica*) and Serbian bellflower (*C. poscharskyana*). Taller species such as peach-leaved bellflower (*C. persicifolia*) and the traditional bluebell or harebell (*C. rotundifolia*) make fine additions to perennial beds and borders. Canterbury-bells (*C. medium*) is a popular annual or biennial member of this group.

Height

C. carpatica (tussock bellflower), 4 to 12 inches

C. medium (Canterbury-bells), 2 to 4 feet

C. persicifolia (peach-leaved bellflower), 2 to 3 feet

C. poscharskyana (Serbian bellflower), 8 to 10 inches

C. rotundifolia (bluebell or harebell), 1 to 2 feet

Spread

1 to 2 feet

Blossoms

As their common names suggest, these species bear bell-shaped flowers. The flowers are wide-spreading and have five petals with pointed tips. Blooms range from 1 to 3 inches across and are usually blue-violet, but cultivars with white, sky blue, deep purple, or pink flowers are available. The flowers have no scent. Bellflowers bloom in late spring to summer; some species will rebloom in late summer or fall if flowers are removed as they fade.

Foliage

Leaves are borne alternately on the stem, are oval to lance-shaped, and often have toothed edges. Bellflowers have basal leaves that are different from the leaves borne along the stems. Foliage may be bright green or blue- to gray-green.

ENVIRONMENT

Hardiness

C. carpatica, C. poscharskyana, and *C. persicifolia* are hardy to USDA Zone 4; *C. rotundifolia* is hardy to Zone 3. *C. medium* is a biennial often grown as a hardy annual. Seedlings can handle light frosts, and plants kept over the winter will survive temperatures down to 15°F if covered with a mulch of hay or dry leaves.

Light

Bellflowers grow and flower best when planted in full sun, but will also tolerate very light shade.

Soil

Most bellflowers will grow in moist, well-drained, moderately fertile soil with a pH range of 6 to 8. They will not grow well in wet, poorly drained soil. *C. poscharskyana* is very drought tolerant and will tolerate drier sites than most bellflowers.

PLANTING AND PROPAGATION

Planting

Bellflowers are easy to grow from seed, which can be sown indoors or outdoors. Do not cover the seed, as it requires light for germination. Indoors, sow seed in early spring six to eight weeks before the last frost date, and germinate at temperatures between 70° and 80°F. Germination takes 15 to 20 days. Seedlings can be planted out after danger of frost has passed or grown in pots in a cold frame and set out the following year. Biennial bellflowers will bloom the first year from seed when grown in this manner; perennial species will bloom the second year. Outdoors, sow seed where the plants are to grow in spring or summer, up to two months before the first frost of autumn.

Plant purchased specimens in spring or fall.

Propagation

Bellflowers can be easily propagated by division as well as stem or root cuttings. Several species, including *C. rotundifolia,* will self-sow.

PLANT MANAGEMENT

General Care

Bellflowers will return year after year with little or no special attention. Taller species may require staking as they mature and come into bloom, for it makes their flowers show to best advantage. Removing faded flowers will help prolong the blooming period, and in some species encourage production of a second flush of blooms in fall. A layer of mulch in summer will help retain water in the soil. A layer of mulch in winter, applied after the ground freezes, will protect the plant's roots from heaving out of the soil due to fluctuations in winter temperatures. Spread mulch carefully to leave the crown of the plant uncovered.

Water

Bellflowers will grow best when they receive ½ to 1 inch of water per week from rainfall or by watering.

Feeding

A spring application of compost or a slow-acting, general-purpose fertilizer will serve the basic needs of bellflowers all season.

Cutting Fresh Flowers

The larger bellflowers make outstanding additions to floral arrangements.

MOST COMMON INSECT PESTS

Pale or Yellow Spots on Leaves, Leaves Curled and Distorted

Aphids

Plants infested with aphids have distorted growth that may be curled, puckered, or stunted. Leaves may turn yellow or brown, and feeding can seriously damage flower buds or cause distorted flowers. Plants may also wilt under bright sunlight. Aphids are soft-bodied, pear-shaped sucking insects about the size of the head of a pin; they may be brown, green, yellow, or nearly black. They are often found clustered under leaves, and flower buds and stem tips may be covered with dense colonies of these insects. Ants, attracted by the aphids' honeydew secretions, wander over the plants, and black, sooty mold can develop on the honeydew as well. Foxglove aphid (*Acyrthosiphon solani*) infests bellflowers.

Light infestations of aphids can be controlled by washing the plants, especially the undersides of the leaves. For best results, use a forceful spray of water once every other day to knock the aphids off the plants; wash the plants at least three times. If that is not effective, spray the plants with insecticidal soap every three to five days for two weeks. If these pests become a very serious problem, make two applications of pyrethrum, three to five days apart.

Ragged Holes in Leaves; Trails of Slime on Plants

Slugs and Snails

Plants that have ragged holes in the leaves, or leaves that have been completely eaten away, are probably infested with slugs or snails. Trails of slime on the foliage and around the plants are further confirmation of the presence of these pests. Slugs are active only at night, when they feast on plants by rasping holes in the foliage with their filelike tongues. During the day, they hide under boards, mulch, or leaf litter. Slugs are similar to snails except that they have no shells. Both are generally 1 to 2 inches long, although some species of slugs grow up to 8 inches in length. Either pest may be white, gray, yellow, or brown-black in color. They are attracted to moist, well-mulched gardens and are most destructive in shaded gardens and during rainy spells. During winter and dry seasons, slugs burrow into the ground to wait for more favorable weather.

A multifaceted approach to control is best. Remove boards, rocks, clippings, and other debris to cut down on the places where these pests hide during the day. Or, check daily under favorite hiding places, handpick snoozing slugs, crush them or seal them into a jar full of water and kerosene or insecticidal soap, and discard them. Inverted flowerpots, pieces of grapefruit peel, and cabbage leaves will lure slugs and can be used to trap them. Handpicking at night with a flashlight can be effective if started early in the spring. Traps baited with beer or yeast and water are also effective. To make an effective trap, cut a 2-inch hole in the lid of a coffee can or a small plastic container and bury the container flush with the soil. Slugs are attracted to the yeast in the beer, climb down through the hole in the lid, and drown. The key is to begin trapping very early in the season in order to prevent the population from building up. Surrounding plants with barriers of sand, ashes, or copper sheeting will discourage slugs from invading your plantings.

MOST COMMON DISEASES

Bellflowers are seldom seriously bothered by diseases, provided their basic cultural conditions are met. In addition to the problems listed below, they are occasionally afflicted with powdery mildew and leaf spot caused by a variety of fungi. They can also harbor the aster yellows virus.

Leaves with Pale Yellow Spots Above, Powdery Orange or Brown Spots Beneath

Rust
Bellflowers are subject to rust diseases caused by at least three species of fungi: *Coleosporium cam-*
panulae, Aecidium campanulastri, and *Puccinia campanulae.* Afflicted plants have pale yellow areas on upper leaf surfaces and powdery, orange or red-brown pustules beneath. The pustules on the undersides of the leaves are the fruiting bodies of the fungi. Infected leaves dry out and plant growth is stunted. Stems and flowers may be seriously deformed.

Remove infected leaves as soon as possible, and destroy severely diseased plants. Clean up and destroy all plant material at the end of the season to avoid reinfecting the garden the following year. Control weeds in and around the garden. Rust can be prevented by periodic applications of wettable sulfur, begun several weeks before rust normally appears. To ensure good ventilation, space plants far enough apart so that air can circulate between them. Also, avoid wetting foliage when watering.

Stems Turn Black at Base; Leaves Turn Yellow and Wilt; Plants Topple Over

Stem, Root, and Crown Rots
A variety of soil-dwelling fungi can attack bellflowers at the base of the plant, causing stems to turn black from the base upward, and rotting the crowns and roots of the plants. Grayish white mold may be present at the base of the plant, and discolored, water-soaked lesions eventually girdle the stems. Once these fungi have girdled stems or rotted crowns or roots, the leaves turn yellow and wilt, stems or plants topple over, and the plants eventually die. *Pellicularia rolfsii, Fusarium* spp., *Rhizoctonia solani,* and *Sclerotinia sclerotiorum* all cause rot diseases in bellflowers. Plants are most susceptible to rot when grown in soil that is not well drained. Damaging the crown of a plant, by inadvertently digging into it, for example, can also lead to rot.

Cultural practices are very helpful in preventing rot diseases in bellflowers. When planting, select a site with well-drained soil, or improve the drainage of the site by incorporating compost and other organic material into the soil. Avoid overwatering and overcrowding, and keep mulch away from the base of plant stems. Keep winter mulch away from the crowns to reduce moisture near the plants. Thoroughly cultivating around plants also helps dry out the soil and discourages the spread of the organisms that cause this problem. Keep plants carefully labeled to prevent accidental damage to the plants, especially during seasons when the plants are dormant. Remove and discard afflicted plants and the soil immediately surrounding them; do not compost. To avoid spreading the fungi that cause this problem, disinfect tools with a solution of 1 part household bleach and 3 parts water or 70 percent rubbing alcohol.

PERENNIAL Bleeding-Hearts *Dicentra* spp.

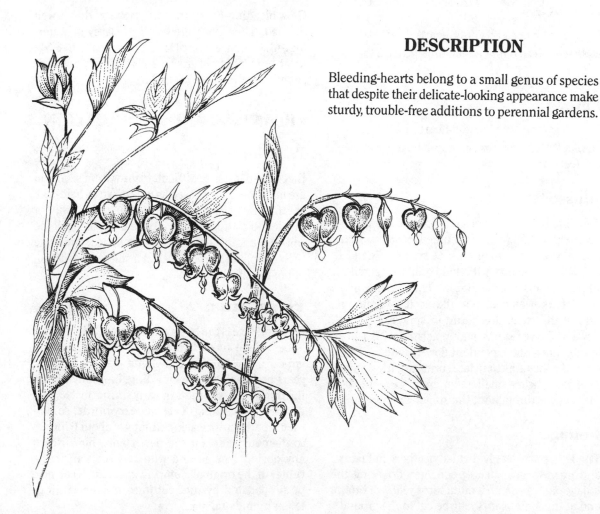

DESCRIPTION

Bleeding-hearts belong to a small genus of species that despite their delicate-looking appearance make sturdy, trouble-free additions to perennial gardens.

They offer attractive, feathery foliage texture and dependable flower displays year after year. Common bleeding-heart (*Dicentra spectabilis*), a native of Japan, is an old garden favorite. It bears arching stems of dangling pink flowers with reflexed white tips that resemble hearts. Fringed bleeding-heart (*D. eximia*) is a low-growing, North-American native that bears short, straight spikes of heart-shaped flowers that are mauve pink or white. Both make fine additions to perennial borders and excellent cut flowers. *D. eximia* can be used as a ground cover or edging plant as well.

Height

D. eximia (fringed bleeding-heart), 1 to 2 feet
D. spectabilis (common bleeding-heart), 2 to
    3 feet

Spread

D. eximia (fringed bleeding-heart), 1 to 1½ feet
D. spectabilis (common bleeding-heart), 2 to
    3 feet

Blossoms

Bleeding-hearts produce arching sprays of inflated, heart-shaped flowers. Plant breeders have selected a variety of cultivars of both *D. spectabilis* and *D. eximia*, and plants with light pink, rose red, or white blooms are available. The flowers of *D. spectabilis*, which dangle like lockets along one side of the stem, are borne in sprays of 8 to 12 flowers. Flower stems may reach 2 to 2½ feet in length. Each of the pendant flowers is about 1 inch long, and they appear in late spring to early summer. *D. eximia* bears smaller flowers on 1-foot spikes that appear throughout the summer.

Foliage

The leaves are deeply divided, feathery in texture, and are medium to deep green. After flowering, the foliage of *D. spectabilis* often turns yellow or brown, and at this time plants may be cut to the ground.

ENVIRONMENT

Hardiness

Both *D. spectabilis* and *D. eximia* are hardy to USDA Zone 3 or 4.

Light

Bleeding-hearts prefer light shade and will grow in full sun only in areas with cool summers. They do well in woodsy areas that are shaded.

Soil

Grow bleeding-hearts in moist, rich soil that is well drained. They won't grow well in clayey or waterlogged soils. An acidic pH ranging from 6.0 to 6.5 is ideal, but plants will grow in soils that are neutral or slightly alkaline (pH 7.0 to 7.5).

PLANTING AND PROPAGATION

Planting

Bleeding-hearts are difficult to grow from seed and are most often purchased as pot-grown or bare-root specimens. They can be planted in early spring or in fall and should be spaced 2 feet apart. Work the soil to a depth of at least a foot to accommodate their deep, fleshy roots. Select a sheltered location out of direct wind.

Propagation

Bleeding-hearts can be propagated by division, which is best done in early spring. Plants can develop large root systems, and dividing plants every five years or so will reduce crowding. Carefully dig up the thickly massed roots in early spring, just as new growth is beginning. They are very brittle, so pull them apart gently, leaving clumps of about 6 inches in diameter. Replant the new plants, but discard any obviously aged and withered roots near the center of the original clump. *D. spectabilis* can also be propagated by root cuttings or stem cuttings taken in midsummer.

PLANT MANAGEMENT

General Care

These charming plants are virtually care-free. Properly sited and planted, they require very little special attention from year to year. *D. spectabilis* should be cut back when the leaves yellow and the plants die back in summer. Clumps can be divided every five years or so. Since they prefer moist soil, a 1- or 2-inch layer of mulch will help hold moisture in the soil. A heavier layer of mulch in winter, applied after the ground freezes, will protect the crowns from heaving out of the soil due to fluctuations in temperature.

Water

Bleeding-hearts need ½ to 1 inch of water per week from rainfall or by watering. Evenly moist soil will extend the bloom period and keep the foliage from dying back. Bleeding-hearts won't grow in boggy soils, however.

Feeding

Bleeding-hearts are heavy feeders and should be planted in soil that is rich in organic matter. Give them an annual spring application of compost or a slow-acting, general-purpose fertilizer.

MOST COMMON CULTURAL PROBLEMS

Foliage Dies Back in Summer

Summer Dormancy
D. spectabilis usually dies back after flowering, especially in areas with hot, dry summers. If you keep the soil evenly moist, this may not happen, but if the leaves do turn yellow or die down, cut them back to the ground. Be sure to mark plantings carefully, so you won't disturb them accidentally after they die back. Combine bleeding-hearts with baby's-breath, hostas, or summer-blooming annuals that will fill in the gap once they die down for the summer.

MOST COMMON INSECT PESTS

Bleeding-hearts are not seriously bothered by any insect pests. Slugs and snails may occasionally chew holes in the foliage, and aphids may infest plants.

MOST COMMON DISEASES

Bleeding-hearts are as disease-free as they are insect-free. With the exception of wilt and stem rot, they are not seriously bothered by any diseases.

Stems Turn Black at Base; Leaves Turn Yellow and Wilt; Plants Topple Over

Wilt and Stem Rot
A variety of soil-dwelling fungi can attack bleeding-hearts at the base of the plants, causing stems to turn black from the base upward and rotting the crowns of the plants. Grayish white mold may be present at the base of the plant, and discolored, water-soaked lesions eventually girdle the stems. Once these fungi have girdled stems or rotted crowns or roots, the leaves turn yellow and wilt, stems or plants topple over, and the plants eventually die. Plants are most susceptible to rot when grown in soil that is not well drained.

Preventive measures are very helpful in controlling rot and wilt. Plant bleeding-hearts in well-drained soil, avoid overwatering and overcrowding, and keep mulch away from the base of plant stems. Remove and discard infected plants, together with the surrounding soil, or cut away affected plant parts with a clean, sharp knife or razor blade. Discard infected plant material; do not compost. Disinfect tools with a solution of 1 part household bleach and 3 parts water or 70 percent rubbing alcohol to avoid spreading the disease. Keep the garden clear of old plant debris. For long-term prevention, lighten heavy soil with a mixture of perlite, vermiculite, and/or peat moss, and provide good drainage.

Chrysanthemums

Chrysanthemum spp.

DESCRIPTION

Chrysanthemums are an important group of perennials belonging to the daisy family, Compositae, that are grown and loved for their showy flowers. There are many species and cultivars of this popular genus for gardeners to choose from, with blossoms that vary greatly in size and color. Flowers may be single and daisylike—with white petals surrounding yellow centers—or double. Double-flowered forms can range in size from tiny, buttonlike blooms to the traditional large chrysanthemums sold as cut flowers. Chrysanthemums are perfect for perennial borders, flower beds, and meadow gardens. Smaller types can be used as edging plants.

Height

Chrysanthemum coccineum (painted daisy), 1 to 3 feet

C. leucanthemum (oxeye daisy), 1 to 2 feet

C. × morifolium (hardy or garden chrysanthemum or florist's chrysanthemum), 9 to 48 inches

C. parthenium (feverfew), 1 to 3 feet

C. × superbum (Shasta daisy), 1 to 2 feet

Spread

C. coccineum (painted daisy), 1½ feet

C. leucanthemum (oxeye daisy), 1 to 1½ feet

C. × morifolium (hardy or garden chrysanthemum or florist's chrysanthemum), 1 to 2½ feet

C. parthenium (feverfew), 10 to 12 inches

C. × superbum (Shasta daisy), 1 to 1½ feet

Blossoms

C. × morifolium flowers come in many forms. Some examples include: singles, which look like daisies; doubles, which have large outer petals and smaller center petals; pompons, whose dense masses of petals curve in to form a globular shape; spiders, which have long, thin petals; spoons, whose tubular petals flare out into little spoons at the tips; and anemones, which have one or more rows of petals surrounding a raised central disc. Blooms of all other species are either single and daisylike or double. Flower colors include white, yellow, pink, orange, red, bronze, purple, and lavender. Flower size can range from 1 to 7 inches in diameter. *C. coccineum, C. leucanthemum, C. parthenium,* and *C. × superbum* all are summer-blooming perennials. *C. × morifolium* blooms in fall, and flower production is triggered by the shortening day length of autumn.

Foliage

Chrysanthemum leaves are oval or deeply lobed or toothed. They are up to 3 inches long and have a strong aromatic scent.

ENVIRONMENT

Hardiness

C. coccineum, USDA Zone 4

C. leucanthemum, Zone 3

C. × morifolium, Zone 5

C. parthenium and *C. × superbum,* Zones 4 to 5

Light

Most chrysanthemums should be grown in full sun. *C. parthenium* and *C. × superbum* will tolerate partial shade.

Soil

Plant chrysanthemums in slightly acid soil (pH 6.0 to 6.5) that is well drained. They do poorly in wet, clayey soils. Grow them in raised beds and add lots of organic matter, such as leaf mold or compost, to the soil to improve drainage, if necessary.

PLANTING AND PROPAGATION

Planting

Several species of chrysanthemums are easily raised from seed, but many of the cultivars of hardy chrysanthemums can only be propagated by cuttings or division. To grow *C. coccineum, C. leucanthemum, C. × morifolium,* or *C. × superbum* from seed, sow outdoors where the plants are to grow from early spring through summer, up to two months before the first frost of autumn. Or sow indoors eight to ten weeks before the last spring frost date and transplant seedlings to the garden after danger of frost has passed. Germination takes anywhere from 10 to 20 days, depending on the species, and germination temperatures of 70°F are ideal. Sow *C. parthenium* outdoors where the plants are to grow in early spring. Or, sow indoors eight to ten weeks before the last spring frost and transplant after danger of frost has passed. Germination takes 10 to 15 days, and temperatures of 70°F are ideal for germination. Do not cover the seed of *C. parthenium* or *C. × superbum,* as light aids germination.

Plant purchased greenhouse-grown bedding plants in a sunny location in spring after the weather has warmed up and nighttime temperatures remain above 50°F. Field-grown divisions can be planted out earlier. Both can be planted out in late summer or fall as well. Space plants about 1½ feet apart.

Propagation

Divide established garden mum plants once a year in early spring. Dig up the entire clump and carefully separate vigorously growing shoots from the outer portions of the clumps, taking care that they have roots attached. Discard older, woody, central parts of the clump.

Container Gardening

Hardy chrysanthemums do well in patio containers, window boxes, and planters outdoors. Use containers large enough to ensure that the soil does not dry out rapidly.

PLANT MANAGEMENT

General Care

To get compact, bushy plants with lots of flower buds, pinch the growing tips of *C. × morifolium* as soon as the plants are 6 to 8 inches high. This stimulates branching and the production of more flower buds. Pinch hardy chrysanthemums, which bloom in fall, at least once more before July 15, which is about the time the flower buds begin to form. To get fewer but larger flowers, nip all but one or two buds from each cluster. After the plants have finished flowering, cut the dried-out stems back to within a few inches of the ground.

Tall cultivars of hardy chrysanthemums may need staking to support their flowering stems. All mums need mulching for winter protection of their shallow roots.

C. × superbum is often grown as a biennial, since plants tend to die out after a few years.

Water

Chrysanthemums need regular watering because their roots are so shallow. Be sure they receive ½ to 1 inch of water per week, especially during the hot summer months. Drought will cause woody, stunted growth.

Feeding

Chrysanthemums are heavy feeders. Provide them with a spring application of compost or a slow-acting, general-purpose fertilizer, as well as supplemental, light feedings (side-dressings or foliar spray) monthly throughout the growing season. Stop feeding in late August.

Cutting Fresh Flowers

Chrysanthemums make excellent additions to bouquets and arrangements. For indoor display, cut flowers in the early morning with a clean, sharp knife. Plunge them into a pail of warm water for several hours or overnight. When you've arranged them in the container, add a teaspoon of sugar per quart of water to prolong freshness.

MOST COMMON CULTURAL PROBLEMS

Plants Fail to Flower

Florist Chrysanthemum Cultivars Planted Outdoors

If you have planted a pot-grown, gift chrysanthemum outdoors, you may find that it does not bloom before winter freezes kill the plant back to the ground. Although florist's chrysanthemums are classified as the same species as hardy chrysanthemums, *C. × morifolium,* the cultivars that florists force in greenhouses in pots require more weeks of short days to flower than hardy cultivars do. Florist's chrysanthemums generally require 11 to 14 weeks of long nights and short days; hardy cultivars need only 8 to 9 weeks. So, florist's chrysanthemums are often killed before they have a chance to bloom. Furthermore, florist's cultivars are often less hardy than garden or hardy cultivars and may not survive the winter from year to year.

Another reason that hardy chrysanthemums fail to bloom is also related to their need for long nights in order to initiate bud formation. Hardy chrysanthemums planted near an outdoor light that is always on may receive too much light at night to start forming buds and will therefore fail to flower. Plants purchased in bud or flower will not be affected by such lights, but may fail to flower in future years.

Seedlings Appear Where They Are Not Wanted

Reseeding

Both *C. leucanthemum* and *C. parthenium* can reseed prolifically from year to year, and unexpected seedlings can become a nuisance. Picking or deadheading the flowers before they go to seed can reduce this problem.

MOST COMMON INSECT PESTS

In addition to the pests listed below, chrysanthemums are sometimes infested with caterpillars, which chew holes in the foliage; leaftiers, which roll the leaves and fasten them with silken webs; and whiteflies, which cause tiny, yellow-green spots on the foliage and look like "flying dandruff" when disturbed. For information on controlling these pests, see chapter 5.

Pale or Yellow Spots on Leaves, Leaves Curled and Distorted

Aphids

Plants infested with aphids have distorted growth that may be curled, puckered, or stunted. Leaves may turn yellow or brown, and feeding can seriously damage flower buds or cause distorted flowers. Plants may also wilt under bright sunlight. Aphids are soft-bodied, pear-shaped sucking insects about the size of the head of a pin; they may be brown, green, yellow, or nearly black. They are often found clustered under leaves, and flower buds and stem tips may be covered with dense colonies of these insects. Ants, attracted by the aphids' honeydew secretions, wander over the plants, and black, sooty mold can develop on the honeydew as well. Several species of aphids infest chrysanthemums, including chrysanthemum aphid (*Macrosiphoniella sanborni*), foxglove aphid (*Acyrthosiphon solani*), green peach aphid (*Myzus persicae*), leafcurl plum aphid (*Brachycaudus helichrysi*), and melon aphid (*Aphis gossypii*).

Light infestations of aphids can be controlled by washing the plants, especially the undersides of the leaves. For best results, use a forceful spray of water once every other day to knock the aphids off the plants; wash the plants at least three times. If that is not effective, spray the plants with insecticidal soap every three to five days for two weeks. If these pests become a very serious problem, make two applications of pyrethrum, three to five days apart.

Holes in Leaves and/or Flowers

Beetles

Several species of beetles chew holes in chrysanthemum foliage and flowers. Asiatic garden beetles (*Maladera castanea*) are ½-inch-long, cinnamon brown beetles that feed only at night. Black blister beetles (*Epicauta pennsylvanica*) are black, ½-inch-long insects that also feed on flowers and leaves. Fuller rose beetles (*Pantomorus cervinus*) are ⅓-inch-long weevils with a broad snout and a white stripe on each wing cover. They are primarily a pest outdoors in the South and Southwest where they feed at night and drop to the ground during the day. Rose chafer (*Macrodactylus subspinosus*), often called rose bug although it is a beetle, also infests chrysanthemums. The adult is a tan, ⅓- to ½-inch-long insect with a reddish brown head.

For the most part, all beetles are controlled the same way. Where possible, handpick and crush them or drop them into a pail of soapy water. For night-feeding species, you'll need to use a flashlight and catch them when they're most active. (Wear gloves if you suspect you have blister beetles, for they can cause blisters if they are crushed on skin.) If the infestation is light, this is all you will need to do. For heavier infestations, spray infested plants with a solution of pyrethrum and isopropyl alcohol, mixing 1 tablespoon of alcohol with every pint of diluted pyrethrum mixture. Apply this solution every three to five days until the problem is corrected. Barriers such as floating row covers, like Reemay, can also be used to prevent beetles from gaining access to chrysanthemums. For long-term control, apply milky spore disease (*Bacillus popilliae*) to lawns and garden. It will kill the larvae of most beetles.

Sawdust Exudes from Stems; Stems Break Off; Leaves Wilt

Borers

If chrysanthemum stems break and leaves wilt, look closely for small, round holes in the stems, from which borers may have expelled their castings. Stalk borer (*Papaipema nebris*) and European corn borer

(*Ostrinia nubilalis*) both attack chrysanthemums. Stalk borer is a long, slender caterpillar marked with a dark brown or purple band around the middle and several conspicuous stripes running the length of the body. Adults are grayish brown moths. European corn borer larvae are pinkish caterpillars with two rows of dark spots down the sides. Adults are yellow-brown moths with dark, wavy bands on the wings.

Preventive measures are most effective when dealing with these pests. Clean up all weeds, and cut and burn any plant stalks that may harbor overwintering eggs or pupae. Rotating the location of your chrysanthemum planting can also help control this pest. Bt (*Bacillus thuringiensis*) is effective if applied early in the season just as the borers are entering the plants. Borer infestations also can be controlled by slitting each affected stem lengthwise, removing the borers, and binding the stems together, but this is tedious work if you have a large planting.

Leaves and Flowers Deformed, Dwarfed, or Marked with Small Spots

Bugs

Several of the true bugs (order Hemiptera) infest chrysanthemums. Their feeding can cause deformed growth and young shoots and buds that are dwarfed. Leaves and flowers may be marred with tiny yellow or brown spots. Damage is the result of the bugs feeding with their piercing-sucking mouthparts. Chrysanthemum lace bug (*Corythucha marmorata*) has lacy-looking wings; both adult and juvenile stages feed on the undersides of leaves and on the stems. They cause the foliage to develop a bleached appearance, damage stems, and leave resinous, dark droppings on the undersides of leaves. Four-lined plant bugs (*Poecilocapsus lineatus*), harlequin bugs (*Mugantia histrionica*), and tarnished plant bugs (*Lygus rugulipennis*) also infest chrysanthemums.

Four-lined plant bugs, which are primarily a pest of early summer, are greenish yellow with four wide black stripes down their backs. Their nymphs are bright red with black dots.

Harlequin bugs are a serious pest of cabbage and its relatives that also attack other plants. Adults are black with bright red markings and about ⅜ inch in length. The eggs of this pest are very distinctive—they look like tiny white cylinders with black bands and are arranged in rows. Nymphs can suck large amounts of sap from infested plants.

Tarnished plant bugs are active, ¼-inch-long bugs that are green to brown in color and mottled with white, yellow, and black. On either side of the insect near the back is a yellow triangle with a black dot at one corner. Tarnished plant bugs appear in early spring, and, if left uncontrolled, become increasingly numerous toward the end of summer. They feed by sucking sap from plants and also release a toxin when feeding that can deform foliage and shoots.

Preventive measures are helpful in controlling these pests, several of which overwinter in garden refuse. Thoroughly clean up the garden in spring and fall to discourage overwintering adults and eggs. Handpicking adults, nymphs, or eggs and dropping them into a jar of soapy water is also effective if the infestation isn't too great. If that is not effective, spray the plants with insecticidal soap every three to five days for two weeks. Especially with chrysanthemum lace bug, be sure to spray the undersides of the leaves. In severe cases, try three applications of pyrethrum laced with isopropyl alcohol, one every three days. Spray early in the morning when bugs are least active. If the infestation is heavy, dust plants with sabadilla.

Foliage and Buds Turn Brown

Chyrsanthemum Gall Midges

Chrysanthemum foliage that is covered with tiny, pimplelike galls is probably infested with chrysanthemum gall midges. These pests, which are common on greenhouse-grown plants but are also found in the garden, are tiny, gnatlike flies that have two wings. They are $1/14$ to ⅛ inch long and have long legs and antennae. The larvae cause the strange-looking galls on the upper leaf surfaces. Foliage is also generally distorted.

Control chrysanthemum gall midges by picking off and destroying leaves infected with galls. Thoroughly clean up all garden debris each fall and discard it to destroy overwintering midges. Do not compost soil or plant material that may be infested. Spray the entire plant with insecticidal soap in the evening at five-day intervals as soon as the galls are discovered. Make three applications altogether. The spray does not kill larvae in the leaves, but will be effective on emerging larvae, eggs, and adults.

Leaves Covered with Yellow-Brown Spots or Blotches; Leaves Die and Turn Brittle

Foliar Nematodes

Hardy chrysanthemums that develop yellow-brown spots starting on the lower leaves and gradually moving up the stems may be infested with foliar nematodes (*Aphelenchoides ritzema-bosi*). Nematodes are not insects, but slender, unsegmented roundworms that are barely visible to the unaided eye. Foliar nematodes overwinter in the soil, in infested leaves, or in the leaves of young plants. In spring or early summer, during rainy weather, they swim up the film of water on the plants and enter leaves through the stomata. As the season progresses, they move up the stems and can even infest the ray florets on the blooms. The yellow-brown spots eventually run together and cover the entire leaf, which dies, turns brittle, and falls. Serious infestations can kill the entire plant. Foliar nematodes are easily confused with leaf spot, discussed on page 146, but fungal leaf spots are most often black, not brown. Another way to distinguish the two is to use a hand lens and look closely at the leaves to see if fungal spores are present.

Remove infested leaves and stems, and dig up and destroy seriously infested specimens, along with the soil in which they are growing; do not compost. There is no cure once the plants are infested. If foliar nematodes have been a problem in your garden, do not propagate chrysanthemums by dividing clumps. Instead, take cuttings from the tops of tall, vigorous stems. Do not grow chrysanthemums in the same spot year after year. Thoroughly clean up all garden debris each fall and discard it to destroy overwintering nematodes. Do not compost soil or plant material that may be infested. (Soil that has been removed with infested plants can be heat pasteurized in an oven and then re-used, but this is a tedious process.) Mulch plants in spring to discourage nematodes from climbing up from the soil, and avoid spraying water on leaves when watering.

Leaves Covered with Tan to Brown Blotches, or Serpentine Mines in Leaves

Leafminers

Chrysanthemum leaves with light green to brown serpentine mines or tunnels between upper and lower leaf surfaces are probably infested with leafminers. About two weeks after the infestation begins, the afflicted leaves turn completely brown and collapse. Careful observation will reveal dark flecks of excrement within the mines, and the tiny white maggots, or larvae, are often visible through leaf tissue. The larvae feed inside the leaves and then pupate in small, seedlike cases often attached to the outside of the leaves. Adults are minute, two-winged flies.

Pick off and destroy all infested leaves. If necessary, prune back stems until only healthy growth remains. Thoroughly clean up all garden debris each fall and discard it to destroy overwintering leafminers. Do not compost soil or plant material that may be infested. The larvae can sometimes be repelled by spraying plants with several weekly applications of insecticidal soap in late June or early July.

Leaves Stippled with Tiny Yellow Dots; Webby Foliage

Spider Mites

Leaves that are dry and stippled with tiny yellow dots are a sign that your chrysanthemums are infested with spider mites, tiny pests that suck chlorophyll out of the leaves. They also inject toxins into the foliage; this causes distorted or discolored growth. Leaves, stems, and flowers also may be swathed in fine webbing. As their name suggests, spider mites are related to spiders. These tiny creatures, which are about ¹⁄₅₀ inch long and barely visible to the naked eye, may be yellow, green, red, or brown. Both cyclamen mites (*Steneotarsonemus pallidus*) and two-spotted spider mites (*Tetranychus urticae*) attack chrysanthemums. Spider mites reproduce most rapidly during hot, dry weather. They are especially a problem on greenhouse-grown chrysanthemum plants; inspect purchased bedding plants carefully to avoid bringing home infested specimens.

Severely infested plants should be destroyed, or infested portions cut and disposed of, since infestations are difficult to control once they are well under way. Spider mites can be controlled by washing the plants, especially the undersides of the leaves. For best results, use a forceful spray of water once every other day to knock the mites off the plants; wash the plants at least three times. If that is not effective, spray the plants with insecticidal soap every three to five days for two weeks. To avoid spreading the mites from plant to plant, don't touch healthy plants after examining infested ones.

MOST COMMON DISEASES

Leaves Covered with Dark Spots or Blotches

Leaf Spot

Several different kinds of fungi cause unsightly spots on chrysanthemum foliage. Leaves may have transparent or brown or black spots. Some fungal spots are surrounded by flecks or black dots, which are the spore-bearing fruiting bodies. Often spots come together to form larger patches of dead tissue. These fungi thrive on moist leaf surfaces.

To control leaf spot, pick off and destroy infected leaves. Also, regularly clean up and destroy dead plant debris in the garden to reduce spore popula-

tions. These fungi overwinter as spores in such debris, so an end-of-season cleanup is especially important. Rogue out and discard seriously infected plants, together with the soil in which they are growing. A layer of mulch helps prevent spores from splashing from the soil onto plants. If leaf spot is a particular problem in your area, spray at weekly to ten-day intervals with wettable sulfur or bordeaux mixture, particularly in rainy seasons. (Watch for leaf discoloration with the latter.)

Leaves with Pale Areas Above, Powdery Orange Spots Beneath

Rust

A rust disease caused by the fungus *Puccinia chrysanthemi* occasionally attacks chrysanthemums. It causes pale areas to appear on upper leaf surfaces, with powdery orange pustules or spots directly beneath on the undersides of the leaves.

Remove infected leaves as soon as possible, and destroy severely diseased plants. Clean up and destroy all plant material at the end of the season to avoid reinfecting the garden the following year. Rust can be prevented by periodic applications of wettable sulfur, begun several weeks before rust normally appears. To ensure good ventilation, space plants far enough apart so that air can circulate between them. Also, avoid wetting foliage when watering.

Leaves Greenish Yellow or Curled and Deformed; Shoots Spindly or Stunted

Virus Diseases

Chrysanthemums are susceptible to a number of virus diseases, including mosaic, chrysanthemum smut virus, tomato spotted wilt virus, and aster yellows. Virus-infected plants generally have spindly, stunted shoots and yellowed foliage. Leaves may be marked with ring spots, lines, pale areas, or mottling, and dead spots may appear on the foliage of infected plants. Infected plants are stunted, form dense "rosettes," and have small flowers. Virus diseases are spread by sucking insects such as aphids and leafhoppers.

There is no cure for virus-infected plants. Remove and destroy them; do not compost. To control the insects that transmit these diseases, spray remaining plants with a mixture of insecticidal soap and isopropyl alcohol. Make this mix by adding 1 tablespoon of alcohol to each pint of insecticidal soap solution. Spray at three- to five-day intervals, making three applications. Viruses overwinter in various perennials and weeds such as daisies, plantain, and gaillardia. Infected plants are not necessarily killed by the disease, but should be dug up and destroyed, since they continue to infect nearby plants. Disinfect garden tools with a solution of 1 part household bleach and 3 parts water or 70 percent rubbing alcohol to avoid spreading virus diseases from plant to plant. Also, wash your hands after handling infected plants.

PERENNIAL *Columbines* *Aquilegia* spp.

DESCRIPTION

Columbines are delicate-looking perennials that make lovely additions to perennial borders and wild gardens. Members of the buttercup family, Ranunculaceae, there are many species native to the United States. In cultivation, the long-spurred hybrids, classified as *Aquilegia* × *hybrida,* are most popular. They make fine additions to perennial borders. All columbines have attractive compound leaves and showy, five-petaled flowers that have long, hollow spurs in the back. *A. canadensis* is a popular native columbine that is commonly called wild columbine, meeting-houses, or honeysuckle. It is grown in wildflower gardens and borders. *A. flabellata* is a Japanese native commonly called fan columbine and has dwarf forms suitable for rock gardens, cut flowers, or the front of borders.

Height

A. canadensis (wild columbine, meeting-houses, or honeysuckle), 2 to 3 feet

A. flabellata (fan columbine), 1 to 1½ feet; dwarf forms, 6 to 10 inches

A. × *hybrida* (hybrid columbine), 1½ to 3 feet

Spread

Most species spread 1½ to 2 feet; dwarf forms, 6 to 8 inches

Blossoms

Columbine flowers get their distinctive appearance from the long, hollow spurs that sweep back from the point where the flowers are attached to the stems. The blooms have five petals and range from 1 to 2 inches wide and 1 to 4 inches long, depending on the length of the spurs, which contain nectar for attracting pollinating insects. These "granny bonnet"-shaped flowers also invite nectar-drinking hawk moths and hummingbirds. The flowers are scentless but come in many colors and combinations of colors. *A. canadensis* bears blooms that are red and yellow; *A. flabellata* has flowers that range from lilac to white. The blooms of hybrid columbines may be pink, red, yellow, lavender, purple, or white and also come in two-color combinations. Columbines bloom for two to four weeks in late spring and early summer. Removing the spent flowers before they set seed prolongs flowering.

Foliage

Columbine leaves are finely divided and somewhat fernlike in appearance. They are usually light green to gray-green.

ENVIRONMENT

Hardiness

A. canadensis and *A. flabellata* are hardy to USDA Zones 3 to 4. *A. × hybrida* is hardy to Zone 5.

Light

Columbines will grow in full sun, but will also grow well in partial shade, especially in the warmer southern climates. Partial shade prolongs their flowering season.

Soil

Plant columbines in well-drained, somewhat sandy soil with a pH between 6 and 7.

PLANTING AND PROPAGATION

Planting

Seed can be sown indoors or out. For best results, the seeds need a cool, moist period before they will germinate. To sow indoors, sow the seed and store it in the refrigerator for three weeks before germinating at temperatures between 70° and 75°F. Germination takes 20 to 25 days. Or, sow in pots in fall and hold them in a cold frame over winter. Outdoors, seed can be sown where the plants are to grow anytime from early spring through summer, up to two months before frost. Do not cover the seed as it needs light to germinate.

Propagation

Columbines are short-lived, so it is best to grow new plants from seed every three years or so. *A. canadensis* and many of the hybrids will self-sow right in the garden. Plants are difficult to transplant except when small.

PLANT MANAGEMENT

General Care

Pinch off dead flowers before they go to seed to encourage a longer bloom period and prevent self-

seeding. Since plants retain their vigor for only about three years, they will need to be replaced periodically. In the fall, cut back their foliage to near soil level and mulch after the ground is frozen to protect them from the heaving of the soil during the winter.

Water

Columbines need ½ to 1 inch of water per week from regular watering or from rainfall. They prefer soil that remains evenly moist, so try not to let the soil dry out to the point that the leaves wilt.

Feeding

A spring application of compost or a slow-acting, general-purpose fertilizer will serve the basic needs of these plants all season. For exceptional performance, give plants supplemental, light feedings (side-dressings or foliar spray) monthly from spring to midsummer.

Cutting Fresh Flowers

Columbine flowers and foliage make fine additions to cut flower arrangements.

MOST COMMON CULTURAL PROBLEMS

Flowers Change Color the Second Year or Over Several Seasons

Cultivars Don't Come True from Seed

Although species columbine such as *A. canadensis* will produce the same color flowers year after year, even if they are allowed to self-seed, hybrid forms may not be so consistent. Many of the cultivars of *A. × hybrida* are the result of specific crosses or complex breeding programs. The seed these plants produce may resemble one of the parent plants, not the cultivar you selected. If these plants are allowed to set seed and self-sow, the seedlings will take over and in subsequent years the flower form and/or color of your columbines will not look like the ones you planted. To prevent this, remove the flowers as they fade to prevent the seed from ripening.

Seedlings Appear Where They Are Not Wanted

Reseeding

Columbines can reseed prolifically from year to year, and unexpected seedlings can become a nuisance. Picking or deadheading the flowers before they go to seed can reduce this problem.

Plants Die Out after Several Seasons

Short-Lived Plants

Columbines are generally short-lived plants, and unless allowed to reseed naturally, they will disappear from the garden after two to three seasons. You can allow the plants to self-sow, or start new seedlings every two to three years so you'll always have vigorous plants in the garden.

MOST COMMON INSECT PESTS

Pale or Yellow Spots on Leaves, Leaves Curled and Distorted

Aphids

Plants infested with aphids have distorted growth that may be curled, puckered, or stunted. Leaves may turn yellow or brown, and feeding can seriously damage flower buds or cause distorted flowers. Plants may also wilt under bright sunlight. Aphids are soft-bodied, pear-shaped sucking insects about the size of the head of a pin; they may be brown, green, yellow, or nearly black. They are often found clustered under leaves, and flower buds and stem tips may be covered with dense colonies of these insects. Ants, attracted by the aphids' honeydew secretions, wander over the plants, and black, sooty mold can develop on the honeydew as well. Several species of aphids infest columbines, including columbine aphid (*Pergandeidia trirhoda*), which is a cream-colored species, crescent-marked lily aphid (*Neomyzus circumflexus*), foxglove aphid (*Acyrthosiphon solani*), and melon aphid (*Aphis gossypii*).

Light infestations of aphids can be controlled by washing the plants, especially the undersides of the leaves. For best results, use a forceful spray of water once every other day to knock the aphids off the plants; wash the plants at least three times. If that is not effective, spray the plants with insecticidal soap every three to five days for two weeks. If these pests become a very serious problem, make two applications of pyrethrum, three to five days apart.

Sawdust Exudes from Stems and Crown; Stems Break Off; Leaves Wilt

Borers

If the stems of your columbines break and leaves wilt, look closely for small, round holes in the crowns or the stems, from which borers may have expelled their castings. Columbine borer (*Papaipema purpurifascia*) is the larva of a moth that bores into the stalks and fleshy roots and crowns of columbine. The adult is a red-brown moth, and the larvae, which hatch in April or early May, are 1½-inch-long, salmon-colored caterpillars with a pale stripe down their backs. Stalk borer (*Papaipema nebris*) also attacks columbine. It is a long, slender caterpillar marked with a dark brown or purple band around the middle and several conspicuous stripes running the length of the body. Adults are grayish brown moths.

Clean up all weeds, and cut and destroy any plant stalks that may harbor overwintering eggs or pupae. The adult columbine borer scatters its eggs on the ground near the plants, so scraping the soil around the plants can destroy the eggs. Bt (*Bacillus thuringiensis*) is effective if applied early in the season just as the borers are entering the plants.

Holes Chewed in Leaves; Leaves Rolled and Fastened Together with Silk

Columbine Skipper

The columbine skipper is the larval stage of a purplish butterfly. The caterpillars are about ¾ inch long and green with black heads. They chew holes in columbine leaves and hide in rolled-up leaves.

The caterpillars can be handpicked and crushed or dropped in a pail of soapy water. Remove any rolled or folded leaves, for they shelter caterpillars. Bt (*Bacillus thuringiensis*) also is an effective control. Apply as a powder or spray every two weeks until the larvae disappear.

Leaves Covered with Tan to Brown Blotches, or Serpentine Mines in Leaves

Leafminers

Columbine leaves with light green to brown serpentine mines or tunnels between upper and lower leaf surfaces are probably infested with leafminers. About two weeks after the infestation begins, the afflicted leaves turn brown completely and collapse. Careful observation will reveal dark flecks of excrement within the mines, and the tiny white maggots, or larvae, are often visible through leaf tissue. The larvae feed inside the leaves and then pupate in small, seedlike cases often attached to the outside of the leaves. Adults are minute, two-winged flies. Columbine leafminer (*Phytomyza aquilegivora*) is the most common species that attacks this host.

Pick off and destroy all infested leaves. If necessary, prune back stems until only healthy growth remains. Thoroughly clean up all garden debris each fall and discard it to destroy overwintering leafminers. Do not compost soil or plant material that may be infested. The larvae can sometimes be repelled by spraying plants with several weekly applications of insecticidal soap in late June or early July.

MOST COMMON DISEASES

In addition to the diseases listed below, columbines are sometimes attacked by powdery mildew, which causes a whitish coating on the foliage; rust, which causes powdery, orangish spots on the undersides of the leaves; and the virus that causes cucumber mosaic.

Stems Turn Black at Base; Leaves Turn Yellow and Wilt; Plants Topple Over

Crown and Root Rots

Although ultimately caused by fungi and bacteria that attack the crowns and roots of the plants, these are a cultural as much as a disease problem. Columbines are susceptible to crown rot when grown in soil that is not well drained. Damaging the roots or crown of a plant, by inadvertently digging into them, for example, can also lead to rot. Crown rot is especially a problem during the winter months; suspect it if no shoots appear in spring. Moist soil around the crowns of the plants leads to attack by both bacteria and fungi.

Cultural practices are very helpful in preventing crown and root rots. When planting, select a site with well-drained soil, or improve the drainage of the site by incorporating compost and other organic material into the soil. Keep winter mulch away from the crowns of the plants. This helps reduce moisture and prevents rotting during the winter dormant season. Thoroughly cultivating around plants also helps dry out the soil and discourages the spread of the organisms that cause this problem. Be sure to mark plantings to avoid accidentally digging into them and damaging the crowns. Remove and discard afflicted plants and the soil immediately surrounding them; do not compost.

Leaves Covered with Dark Spots or Blotches

Leaf Spot

Several different kinds of fungi cause unsightly spots on columbine foliage, including *Ascochyta aquilegiae, Cercospora aquilegiae,* and *Septoria aquilegiae.* Leaves may develop transparent or brown or black spots that may have gray or nearly white centers. Some fungal spots are surrounded by flecks or black dots, which are the spore-bearing fruiting bodies. Often spots come together to form larger patches of dead tissue. These fungi thrive on moist leaf surfaces.

To control leaf spot, pick off and destroy infected leaves. Also, regularly clean up and destroy dead plant debris in the garden to reduce spore populations. These fungi overwinter as spores in such debris, so an end-of-season cleanup is especially important. Rogue out and discard seriously infected plants, together with the soil in which they are growing. A layer of mulch helps prevent spores from splashing from the soil onto plants. If leaf spot is a particular problem in your area, spray at weekly to ten-day intervals with wettable sulfur or bordeaux mixture, particularly in rainy seasons. (Watch for leaf discoloration with the latter.)

Coralbells

Heuchera sanguinea

DESCRIPTION

Coralbells are sturdy, low-growing perennial plants that year after year produce panicles of delicate, bell-shaped flowers atop stems that rise far above the leaves. Although the individual flowers are tiny, the many-flowered stems appear throughout much of the season. They are so delicate in texture that the flowers appear to float above the ground. The foliage of these easy-to-grow plants is basal, meaning borne at the base of the plant, so they make excellent ground covers, edging plants, or specimens for the front of the border.

Height

While the foliage of coralbells is 6 or 8 inches high, the flower stems reach nearly 2 feet.

Spread

1 to 1½ feet

Blossoms

Individual blooms are bell-shaped and only ¼ to ⅓ inch long. The tiny, nodding flowers are borne in abundance atop erect, 10- to 20-inch stems. Cultivars with pink, white, and red flowers are available. The plants begin to bloom in late May or early June and continue well into July and often even longer if the dead stalks are routinely cut off. Because cool summer temperatures help to prolong flowering, coralbells may bloom longer in the North than in warmer southern climates.

Foliage

Leaves are rounded with scalloped edges and range from ¾ to 2 inches across. They may be plain green or marbled with dark or silvery lines or patches. Usually they are evergreen. The foliage forms a tight, low-growing clump at the base of the plant.

ENVIRONMENT

Hardiness

Coralbells are hardy to USDA Zone 3 or 4.

Light

Coralbells grow and flower best in full sun in the North, but they will also do well in light shade. In the warmer southern climates, they do best in light shade.

Soil

Plant coralbells in fertile, well-drained soil that is rich in organic matter. Although moist soil will help these shallow-rooted plants survive drought, well-drained soil is essential for winter survival. The pH can range from 6.5 to 7.7.

PLANTING AND PROPAGATION

Planting

Coralbells can be grown from seed, but many of the cultivars that are available must be propagated by division or cuttings. Sow seed outdoors in late fall or in early spring. Seedlings will germinate in late spring or early summer. Seed can also be sown in pots in early spring or fall and germinated in a cold frame. Or sow indoors, and germinate at 55°F. Germination takes 12 to 15 days.

Plant purchased specimens in spring. The plants don't spread very much, so they can be spaced 1 to

1½ feet apart. Set the crowns (the point at the base of the plant where the leaves are attached and from which the roots grow) just at ground level.

Propagation

Coralbells are easy to propagate by divisions, which should be made in spring. They can also be propagated by leaf cuttings. Take a leaf that has a portion of stem attached to it and root it in moist sand or vermiculite. A dusting of rooting hormone and/or a dusting of wettable sulfur will improve results.

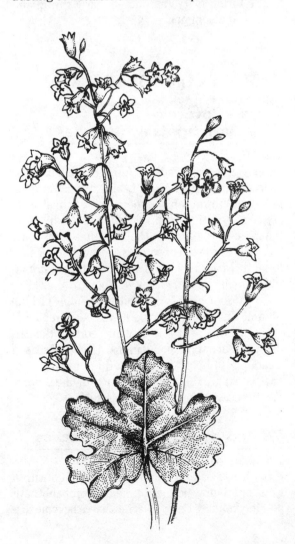

PLANT MANAGEMENT

General Care

These easy-to-grow perennials require very little care once established in the garden. After the soil freezes in fall, a winter mulch will help keep the plants from heaving out of the soil. Mulch in summer will help retain moisture in the soil.

Water

As a general rule, coralbells should receive ½ to 1 inch of water per week from rain or by watering. They are shallow-rooted and will require regular watering during droughts.

Feeding

A spring application of compost or a slow-acting, general-purpose fertilizer will serve the basic needs of coralbells all season.

Cutting Fresh Flowers

The panicles of delicate flowers make fine additions to cut flower arrangements.

MOST COMMON INSECT PESTS

Coralbells are easy-to-grow perennials that are not seriously bothered by many insects. In addition to the insects listed below, they are occasionally infested with four-lined plant bugs.

Leaves Covered with Yellow-Brown Spots or Blotches; Leaves Die and Turn Brittle

Foliar Nematodes

Coralbells that develop yellow-brown spots starting on the leaves may be infested with foliar nematodes (*Aphelenchoides ritzema-bosi*), which also infest chrysanthemums. Nematodes are not insects, but slender, unsegmented roundworms that are barely visible to the unaided eye. Foliar nematodes overwinter in the soil, in infested leaves, or in the leaves of young plants. In spring or early summer, during rainy weather, they swim up the film of water on the plants and enter leaves through the stomata. The yellow-brown spots that they cause eventually run together and cover the entire leaf, which dies, turns brittle, and falls. Serious infestations can kill the entire plant. Foliar nematodes are easily confused with leaf spot, discussed below. One way to distinguish the two is to use a hand lens and look closely at the leaves to see if fungal spores are present.

Remove infested leaves and stems, and dig up and destroy seriously infested specimens, along with the soil in which they are growing; do not compost. There is no cure once the plants are infested. Do not propagate from infested clumps. Thoroughly clean up all garden debris each fall and discard it to destroy overwintering nematodes. Do not compost soil or plant material that may be infested. (Soil that has been removed with infested plants can be heat pasteurized in an oven and then re-used, but this is a tedious process.)

Crowns of Plants Blacken and Die; Grubs Feeding on Roots and Crowns

Strawberry Root Weevil
If the crowns of your coralbells turn black and die, are very stunted, or have crowns that are eaten away, they may be infested with strawberry root weevils (*Brachyrhinus ovatus*) or rough strawberry root weevils (*B. rugostriatus*). The larvae are tiny, ⅜-inch-long, C-shaped grubs that are white with light brown heads. They feed on the crowns of the plants, beginning in early spring. The adults are black, ¼-inch-long beetles that cannot fly. Adults feed on foliage. These insects overwinter as adults and larvae in leaf litter and around the crowns of the plants. The adults lay tiny white eggs among the roots and near the crowns of the plants. There are probably two generations per year.

These pests are difficult to control once plants are infested, but since the adults are unable to fly,

moving healthy plants to another part of the garden is an effective way to keep them from spreading. Dig and discard infested specimens, together with the soil in which they are growing. Do not compost this material; discard it. Scraping the soil near the plants in very early spring to expose the eggs to birds may be effective. Also cleaning up plant debris and cutting away the foliage of infested plants may prevent the pests from overwintering. For heavier infestations, drench the crowns of infested plants with a solution of one of the botanical poisons such as pyrethrum or ryania once in early spring and again in midsummer.

MOST COMMON DISEASES

Leaves Covered with Dark Spots or Blotches

Leaf Spot
Several different kinds of fungi cause unsightly spots on coralbells foliage. Leaves may have transparent or brown or black spots. Some fungal spots are surrounded by flecks or black dots, which are the spore-bearing fruiting bodies. Often spots come together to form larger patches of dead tissue. These fungi thrive on moist leaf surfaces and are primarily a problem during rainy weather.

Leaf spot is easily controlled by simply picking off and destroying infected leaves. Also, regularly clean up and destroy dead plant debris in the garden to reduce spore populations. An end-of-season cleanup also helps discourage these fungi. If leaf spot is a particular problem in your area, spray plants occasionally with wettable sulfur.

White Powder Covering Leaves

Powdery Mildew
If the leaves of your coralbells are covered with a white or ash gray powdery mold they probably have powdery mildew. Badly infected leaves become dis-

colored and die. Powdery mildew is caused by fungi that live primarily on the surface of the leaves, not inside them. Although unsightly, it does not cause any permanent damage to the plants.

Seriously infected plants can be sprayed thoroughly with wettable sulfur once or twice at weekly intervals starting as soon as the whitish coating of the fungus is visible.

Stems Turn Black at Base; Leaves Turn Yellow and Wilt; Plants Collapse and Die

Stem Rot

Coralbells are also attacked by the stem rot fungus *Sclerotinia sclerotiorum*, which rots the crowns or roots of the plants. White fungal mycelia are apparent on the crowns, and discolored, water-soaked lesions eventually girdle the stems. Once these fungi have rotted the crowns or roots, the plants collapse and die.

Stem rot fungus primarily attacks plants that are overcrowded or overwatered. Although steam pasteurization of the soil is the only surefire way to destroy the fungi, preventive measures are very helpful in controlling stem rot. Plant coralbells in well-drained soil, avoid overwatering and overcrowding, and keep mulch away from the base of plant stems. Remove and discard infected plants, together with the surrounding soil, or cut away affected plant parts with a clean, sharp knife or razor blade. Discard infected plant material; do not compost. Disinfect tools with a solution of 1 part household bleach and 3 parts water or 70 percent rubbing alcohol to avoid spreading the disease. Keep the garden clear of old plant debris. For long-term prevention, lighten heavy soil with a mixture of perlite, vermiculite, and/or peat moss, and provide good drainage.

PERENNIAL # Coreopsis   *Coreopsis* spp.

DESCRIPTION

Coreopsis are prime examples of native American wildflowers that have made it to the big time. These members of the daisy family, Compositae, have been appreciated by gardeners for many years for their colorful flowers and easy care. There are both perennial and annual species, most of which bear yellow flower heads. *Coreopsis grandiflora*, sometimes called tickseed, is a popular perennial species that is generally grown as a biennial in gardens. *C. lanceolata* (lance coreopsis) and *C. verticillata* (threadleaf coreopsis) are the most popular perennial species. Many cultivars of all three are available. Coreopsis are somewhat weedy species that make excellent additions to sunny wildflower gardens and meadows. There are dwarf cultivars, including *C. auriculata* 'Nana', that can be used in rock gardens. They can also be used in perennial borders and make excellent cut flowers.

Height

- *C. auriculata* (eared coreopsis), 1 to 1½ feet; dwarf cultivar 'Nana', 9 inches
- *C. grandiflora* (tickseed), *C. lanceolata* (lance coreopsis), and *C. verticillata* (threadleaf coreopsis), 2 to 2½ feet; dwarf cultivars, 1 to 1½ inches

Spread

1 to 1½ feet

Blossoms

Coreopsis bears yellow or orange-yellow, daisy-shaped flowers from the middle of June until well into July. Flowers range from 1 to 3 inches across and may be single or double. The flowers attract beneficial insects such as hover flies (syrphids), whose larvae are great enemies of aphids.

Foliage

Coreopsis leaves are quite narrow and pointed and are 2 to 6 inches long with smooth margins. They are medium green and borne opposite on the stems.

ENVIRONMENT

Hardiness

C. auriculata, C. lanceolata, and *C. verticillata* are all hardy to USDA Zone 3 or 4. *C. grandiflora* is hardy to Zone 7, but it generally performs as a biennial in the garden, dying out after the second year. However, it reseeds readily.

Light

Coreopsis must have full sun for best performance.

Soil

Coreopsis grow in practically any soil, but prefer light, sandy, or ordinary, well-drained soils.

PLANTING AND PROPAGATION

Planting

Sow seed outdoors from early spring to summer, up to two months before the first frost of autumn. Or sow indoors, and germinate at temperatures between 55° and 70°F. Germination takes 20 to 25 days. Thin the seedlings so they have plenty of room to spread. Plant purchased, pot-grown plants in spring or fall.

Propagation

Coreopsis can be propagated by division. Dig the clumps in either spring or fall, divide by cutting through them with a sharp spade or knife, and replant. Coreopsis will also self-sow readily.

PLANT MANAGEMENT

General Care

Coreopsis need very little attention once they are

established. To prevent indiscriminant reseeding, be sure to cut off spent flowers. To keep the clumps healthy and control spreading, dig the plants up and divide them every three to four years.

Water

Coreopsis are very drought tolerant and will not grow well in soil that is always moist. However, newly planted specimens need regular watering—an inch of water a week from rain or by watering—until they become established.

Feeding

These plants do not require a highly fertile soil and will grow and bloom well without any regular feeding at all. In fact, too much fertilizer causes spindly, rank growth. A spring application of compost or a slow-acting, general-purpose fertilizer is all they will ever need.

Cutting Fresh Flowers

Coreopsis make excellent cut flowers. They are especially effective in informal arrangements of wildflowers.

MOST COMMON CULTURAL PROBLEMS

Seedlings Appear Where They Are Not Wanted

Reseeding
Coreopsis can reseed prolifically from year to year, and unexpected seedlings can become a nuisance. Picking or deadheading the flowers before they go to seed can reduce this problem.

MOST COMMON INSECT PESTS

Coreopsis are bothered by few insects and can easily withstand attacks by most pests, provided the plants are healthy and vigorous. In addition to the pests listed below, they are occasionally infested with leafhoppers, which carry the aster yellows virus.

Pale or Yellow Spots on Leaves, Leaves Curled and Distorted

Aphids
Plants infested with aphids have distorted growth that may be curled, puckered, or stunted. Leaves may turn yellow or brown, and feeding can seriously damage flower buds or cause distorted flowers. Plants may also wilt under bright sunlight. Aphids are soft-bodied, pear-shaped sucking insects about the size of the head of a pin; they may be brown, green, yellow, or nearly black. They are often found clustered under leaves, and flower buds and stem tips may be covered with dense colonies of these insects. Ants, attracted by the aphids' honeydew secretions, wander over the plants, and black, sooty mold can develop on the honeydew as well. In addition to the damage they cause by feeding, aphids are important vectors of virus diseases. Coreopsis aphid (*Aphis coreopsidis*) and potato aphid (*Macrosiphum euphorbiae*) both attack coreopsis.

Light infestations of aphids can be controlled by washing the plants, especially the undersides of the leaves. For best results, use a forceful spray of water once every other day to knock the aphids off the plants; wash the plants at least three times. If that is not effective, spray the plants with insecticidal soap every three to five days for two weeks. If these pests become a very serious problem, make two applications of pyrethrum, three to five days apart.

Leaves and Flowers Deformed, Yellowish, or Marked with Small Spots

Four-Lined Plant Bugs
Four-lined plant bugs (*Poecilocapsus lineatus*) infest coreopsis. Their feeding can cause leaves and flowers to be marred with small, sunken spots that may be tan, yellow, or brown. The shoot tips of severely infested plants can wilt. Damage is the result of the bugs feeding with their piercing-sucking mouthparts.

Four-lined plant bugs are primarily a pest of early summer. They are greenish yellow with four wide black stripes down their backs. Their nymphs are bright red with black dots.

Preventive measures are helpful in controlling these pests because they overwinter in garden refuse. Thoroughly clean up the garden in spring and fall to discourage overwintering adults and eggs. Hand-picking adults, nymphs, or eggs and dropping them into a jar of soapy water is also effective if the infestation isn't too great. If that is not effective, spray the plants with insecticidal soap every three to five days for two weeks. Be sure to spray the undersides of the leaves. In severe cases, try three applications of pyrethrum laced with isopropyl alcohol, one every three days. Spray early in the morning when bugs are least active. If the infestation is heavy, dust plants with sabadilla.

Holes in Leaves and/or Flowers

Spotted Cucumber Beetles

Spotted cucumber beetles (*Diabrotica undecimpunctata*) eat the leaves and flower petals of coreopsis, especially late in the summer. The adults are greenish yellow, ¼-inch-long insects with 12 black spots on their backs. The whitish, C-shaped grubs live in the soil and attack coreopsis roots.

Like most beetles, spotted cucumber beetles can be controlled by handpicking, provided the infestation is not too large. Where possible, hand-pick and crush them or drop them into a pail of soapy water. For heavier infestations, spray infested plants with a solution of pyrethrum and isopropyl alcohol, mixing 1 tablespoon of alcohol with every pint of diluted pyrethrum mixture. Apply this solution every three to five days until the problem is corrected. For long-term control, apply milky spore disease (*Bacillus popilliae*) to lawns and garden. It will kill the larvae of the beetles.

MOST COMMON DISEASES

Coreopsis are bothered by few diseases, provided their few basic cultural requirements are met. They grow best in sandy, well-drained soil and tolerate drought. Waterlogged soil, which prevents air from getting to the roots, will lead to crown rot. In addition, coreopsis can be infected with leaf spot disease, caused by several species of fungi and rust, another fungal disease that causes yellow-orange pustules on the leaves. These seldom warrant control measures. They can also harbor the virus diseases aster yellows and beet curly top. For information on controlling these diseases, see chapter 6.

PERENNIAL **Daylilies** *Hemerocallis* spp.

DESCRIPTION

Daylilies are wonderful, low-maintenance perennials that bear showy, funnel-shaped flowers, each of which opens only for a day. Fortunately, they bear their blooms in such abundance that healthy, established plants are seldom without open flowers during the blooming season. The flowers are borne on stalks held high above the foliage. Plant breeders have developed thousands of named cultivars from which to choose. Flower colors include cream, yellow, orange, orange-red, peach, salmon, and maroon. Daylilies are used in beds or borders and can also be massed along roadsides and on slopes.

Height

The foliage of most daylilies is low-growing, generally 2 to 2½ feet tall. Bloom stalks range from 2½ to 3½ feet tall. Dwarf forms are 1 to 2 feet tall.

Spread

Most gardeners divide their daylilies every few years, so clumps seldom spread more than 2 to 3 feet. Undivided specimens can spread 6 feet or more.

Blossoms

Daylily plants send up long stalks that bear 3 or 4 to 20 or more buds that open into funnel-shaped flowers. Blooms are generally about 5 inches long and 3½ to 6 inches wide. Most are not fragrant, but cultivars descended from *Hemerocallis citrina* often are. Almost all cultivars have single flowers, but 'Kwanso' has double flowers. There are cultivars that flower in late spring, summer, or early fall, as well as ever-blooming and repeat-blooming selections. Daylily flowers are edible; the buds can be eaten steamed, dried, or breaded and lightly fried.

Foliage

Daylilies have narrow, sword-shaped leaves that are medium green. They are 1 to 2 feet long and about ¾ inch wide. Some cultivars, most of which are hardy only in the South, have evergreen foliage.

ENVIRONMENT

Hardiness

Most daylilies are hardy in USDA Zone 2 or 3; evergreen cultivars are less hardy and generally won't survive winters north of Zone 7.

Light

For best bloom, grow daylilies in full sun. In the South, a location in partial shade may be preferable. Daylilies will not bloom in full shade, but the foliage will endure.

Soil

Daylilies can grow in almost any type of soil, but will perform at their best in moist, well-drained soil. They will tolerate a pH range of 6 to 8.

PLANTING AND PROPAGATION

Planting

Most gardeners grow daylilies from purchased bare-root plants or pot-grown specimens, for most cultivars do not come true from seed. If you'd like to grow your own from seed, sow outdoors in early spring or late fall for spring germination. The seed requires six weeks of cool temperatures in order to germinate, so indoors, sow seed and store it in the refrigerator, then germinate at temperatures between 60° and 70°F.

Purchased daylilies or divisions are best planted in spring or fall. Make sure the crown sits an inch or so below the soil surface. Space plants about 2 feet apart or plant in clumps with three plants within a 4-foot area.

Propagation

Daylilies are easy to propagate by division. In spring or fall, cut the foliage back by half and dig the clumps. Separate the plants into individual "fans," cutting through the tangled roots with a sharp spade or knife. Discard any old, woody, center sections. Then replant at the same depth as the original plant. Daylilies can survive for many years without being divided, but it's best to divide every three or four years.

Container Gardening

Daylilies can be grown in containers that are at least 18 inches in diameter and 16 inches deep. Dwarf cultivars are especially suitable for this purpose.

Water

Daylilies appreciate supplemental watering before and during the blooming season, as well as during periods of drought. Newly planted specimens also should be watered regularly. However, a severe drought will not permanently harm established plants.

Feeding

A spring application of compost or a slow-acting, general-purpose fertilizer will serve the basic needs of daylilies all season. For exceptional performance, give plants supplemental, light feedings (side-dressings or foliar spray) monthly from spring to midsummer.

Cutting Fresh Flowers

Although each flower opens for only one day, they can be cut and used in arrangements because the buds on each stem will open in succession for five or six days. If possible, cut flower stems for indoor display in the early morning; use a clean, sharp knife. Plunge them into a pail of warm water for several hours. Add a teaspoon of sugar per quart of water in the container in which they are to be displayed to prolong freshness.

PLANT MANAGEMENT

General Care

Once established, daylilies need virtually no care. In fact, they thrive with minimal attention. Attentive gardeners remove dead flowers each day and cut off the flowering spikes once all the buds have bloomed, but this is not essential. A fall cleanup to remove withered, dried foliage from the daylily bed helps keep plants disease-free.

MOST COMMON CULTURAL PROBLEMS

Leaves Have Brown Tips or Die in Summer

Normal Leaf Senescence
Many daylilies develop browned leaf tips and dead leaves in late summer after they have bloomed. The leaves of some may die back completely. Regular watering and mulch may reduce this problem. Pull out the brown leaves and trim browned leaf tips to make plants more attractive.

MOST COMMON INSECT PESTS

With the exception of flower thrips, daylilies are not bothered by many insect pests. Japanese beetles, slugs, and root knot nematodes sometimes infest these sturdy plants, but they are seldom serious problems.

Flower Buds Die; Corky Stems

Flower Thrips

Flower thrips (*Frankliniella tritici*) occasionally infest daylilies, feeding on buds, stem tips, and flowers. Infested plants have distorted blooms, and in severe cases, the flower stalks may fail to develop altogether. Stems also may develop corky lesions that extend over several inches. Adult thrips are tiny, slender insects that are $1/25$ inch long and variously colored pale yellowish, black, or brown. They have four long, narrow wings fringed with long hairs. The larvae are usually wingless.

Since thrips burrow deeply into the petals, they are difficult to control, and early identification is necessary. Set out yellow sticky traps about four weeks after the last frost, as early warning devices. As soon as you spot thrips on a trap, spray plants with insecticidal soap every three days for two weeks. Prune away affected flowers and dip them in soapy water to kill burrowing thrips.

MOST COMMON DISEASES

Daylilies are as disease-free as they are insect-free. Although susceptible to leaf spot caused by various species of fungi, they are not seriously bothered by any diseases.

PERENNIAL *Delphiniums* *Delphinium* spp.

DESCRIPTION

Despite their reputation for being difficult, delphiniums are relatively easy-to-grow perennials. Their tall, stately flower spikes dominate flower beds and borders in early summer. The individual blooms are packed along stiff stems and may have contrasting "eyes" or centers. Delphiniums are especially prized because they come in deep, rich blue, a color that is all too rare among perennials, as well as sky blue, white, pink, lilac, and purple. Plant breeders have developed many cultivars from which to choose. They vary in flower color, bloom and spike size, and height. Although they technically are perennials, many gardeners, especially in the South, grow delphiniums as annuals or biennials, for starting new seeds regularly ensures a show-stopping performance each year. Delphiniums make nice cut flowers.

Height

Delphinium × belladonna, sometimes listed as *D. formosum* (garland delphinium), reach 3 to 4 feet. *D. elatum* (candle larkspur, bee larkspur) and the Giant Pacific Hybrids, Blackmore and Langdon Hybrids, and King Arthur Series cultivars all grow from 4 to as much as 8 feet tall. Connecticut Yankee Series cultivars are dwarf in stature, ranging from 1½ to 2½ feet.

Spread

1 to 2 feet

Blossoms

Delphinium flowers are densely arrayed on tall spikes that tower over other plants in the garden. Each flower has five brightly colored, modified leaves that serve as petals, one of which has a long spur. Flowers may be single, semidouble, or double and are about 2 inches across. Although delphiniums are best known for their purple, lavender, and true blue colors, they also come in white and pink. There are also red- and yellow-flowered species.

Foliage

Delphinium leaves are large and divided into five or seven deeply toothed lobes. Most cluster near the base of the plant while a few branch off the flower stalks.

ENVIRONMENT

Hardiness

D. × belladonna and *D. elatum* are both hardy to USDA Zone 3. They prefer areas with cool summers and do not grow well south of Zone 7.

Light

For best results, grow delphiniums in full sun, although in warm climates, they benefit from a site protected from the hot afternoon sun.

Soil

Delphiniums do best in deep, rich, moist soil enriched with lots of organic matter and will not grow well in soil that is constantly wet or clayey. If drainage is a problem, they can be planted in beds that are higher than the surrounding soil surface. When planting, add lots of organic matter (such as chopped leaves, leaf mold, or peat moss) to the soil to improve drainage and moisture retention. If possible, loosen the soil 1 foot deep when preparing the bed for planting. Ideally, the soil should be slightly alkaline (pH 7.0 to 7.5).

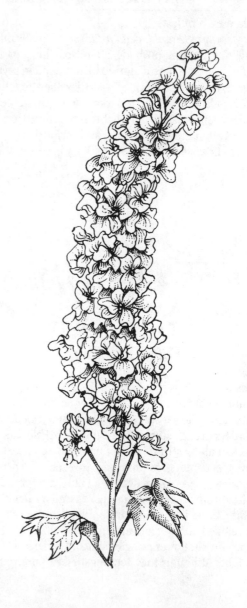

PLANTING AND PROPAGATION

Planting

To grow delphiniums from seed, sow seed outdoors where the plants are to grow in spring or summer, up to two months before the first frost of autumn. Cover the seed completely, as it requires darkness to germinate. Indoors, sow seed six to eight weeks before planting outside in early spring, and germinate at temperatures between 65° and 70°F. Germination takes 10 to 20 days.

Purchased delphinium plants can be planted in late spring. Do not select a spot where wind will be a problem. When setting the plants in their holes, be sure to keep their crowns (the thick place where the roots join the foliage) level with the soil surface. Space plants 1 to 3 feet apart, depending on their ultimate height and spread.

Propagation

Although they are perennials, after two or three years, most delphinium plants pass their peak, lose vigor, and die out. Replace them with new seed-grown or purchased plants. Delphiniums can also be propagated by division in spring. Dig them carefully and gently pull them apart to avoid damaging or bruising the plants, which can lead to fungal or bacterial infection.

PLANT MANAGEMENT

General Care

Delphiniums need staking to help support their hollow, flower-laden stems, which are quite brittle. Begin with 4-foot stakes when the plants are about a foot tall. Replace them with taller stakes as needed. (Stakes that are taller than the plants look unsightly.) Tie the plants to the stakes with soft cord or strips of fabric. It is important to cut off faded flower spikes before they go to seed. Later, when the foliage turns yellow, cut off the remaining stalks down at the crowns to encourage new flowering spikes to form.

Water

Delphiniums like moisture and need about 1 inch of water a week from rain or by watering—even more during hot, dry weather. Soak the soil at their roots to a depth of 10 to 12 inches. Overhead watering weights down their heavy bloom stalks and promotes mildew on their leaves, so try to water without wetting flowers or foliage.

Feeding

Delphiniums grow best in soil that is rich in organic matter, so work compost into the soil at planting time. Or, apply a slow-acting, general-purpose fertilizer in spring. For exceptional performance, give plants supplemental, light feedings (side-dressings or foliar spray) monthly from spring to midsummer.

Cutting Fresh Flowers

Because of their size, shape, and special blue color, delphiniums make splendid cut flowers. Their heavy stalks work best in large, formal arrangements combined with many other kinds of flowers. For indoor display, cut flowers in the early morning with a clean, sharp knife. Add a teaspoon of sugar per quart of water in the container to prolong freshness.

Drying Flowers

Delphiniums make fine dried flowers as well and can be air dried or dried in silica gel. Cut the flower spikes when the blooms are only partially open, and some are even still in the bud stage. Strip off the leaves so that you have bare stems. Air dry them by hanging them upside down in a warm, dry room. To dry in silica gel, cut flowers in full bloom, leaving 1-inch stems. Place flower cluster, stems down, in a coffee can or other sealable container partially filled with silica gel. Carefully sift silica gel over blooms until they are completely covered. The stems of the dried flowers will need to be wired for arrangements.

MOST COMMON CULTURAL PROBLEMS

Plants Die Out in Summer

Excessive Heat

Delphiniums do not like hot, humid weather and will simply die in the middle of summer heat waves. In areas with long, hot summers, try planting delphiniums on the north side of a building or where trees provide afternoon shade. In these areas, delphiniums are best grown as annuals or biennials. Start them in early winter indoors and set plants in the garden in early spring.

MOST COMMON INSECT PESTS

In addition to the pests listed below, Asiatic garden beetles and Japanese beetles occasionally chew holes in delphinium foliage. Slugs also damage foliage and flowers, and their presence can be identified by the slimy trails they leave behind.

Pale or Yellow Spots on Leaves, Leaves Curled and Distorted

Aphids

Plants infested with aphids have distorted growth that may be curled, puckered, or stunted. Leaves may turn yellow or brown, and feeding can seriously damage flower buds or cause distorted flowers. Plants may also wilt under bright sunlight. Aphids are soft-bodied, pear-shaped sucking insects about the size of the head of a pin; they may be brown, green, yellow, or nearly black. They are often found clustered under leaves, and flower buds and stem tips may be covered with dense colonies of these insects. Ants, attracted by the aphids' honeydew secretions, wander over the plants, and black, sooty mold can develop on the honeydew as well. In addition to the damage they cause by feeding, aphids are important vectors of virus diseases. Delphinium aphid (*Brachycaudus rociadae*), green peach aphid (*Myzus*

persicae), and crescent-marked lily aphid (*Neomyzus circumflexus*) all are found on delphiniums.

Although aphids can be controlled by washing the plants with a forceful spray of water, this method is not ideal for delphiniums because the flower spikes are brittle and water-laden flowers can be heavy enough to break the stems. So, spray the plants with insecticidal soap every three to five days for two weeks. If these pests become a very serious problem, make two applications of pyrethrum, three to five days apart.

Sawdust Exudes from Stems; Stems Break Off; Leaves Wilt

Borers

If delphinium stems break and leaves wilt, look closely for small, round holes in the stems, from which borers may have expelled their castings. Stalk borer (*Papaipema nebris*) and burdock borer (*Papaipema cataphracta*) both attack delphiniums. Stalk borer is a long, slender caterpillar marked with a dark brown or purple band around the middle and several conspicuous stripes running the length of the body. Adults are grayish brown moths. Burdock borer is a pale brown caterpillar with three white stripes. Adults are small moths.

Preventive measures are most effective when dealing with these pests, since by the time symptoms occur, it is usually too late to save the flower stalks. Clean up all weeds, and cut and burn any plant stalks that may harbor overwintering eggs or pupae. Rotating the location of your plantings can also help control this pest. Bt (*Bacillus thuringiensis*) is effective if applied early in the season just as the borers are entering the plants. Borer infestations also can be controlled by slitting each affected stem lengthwise, removing the borers, and binding the stems together, but this is tedious work if you have a large planting.

Seedlings Severed at Base

Cutworms

Newly transplanted seedlings or young plants that

look as though they have been leveled by a lawn mower have probably been attacked by cutworms. These pests sever the stems of seedlings and transplants at or below the soil surface, leaving the tops to die. (In contrast, slugs and snails completely consume seedlings, leaving only their slimy trails.) Cutworms are most active at night. They also can harm plant root systems, damage that causes the plant to wilt and collapse. Cutworms are generally plump, soft-bodied caterpillars that are dull grayish or brownish and measure 1 to 2 inches long. They feed at night and hide in the soil during the day. The adults are night-flying moths.

Prevention is the only way to fight cutworms, for once they have cut down a young plant, there is nothing you can do to save it. Protect individual seedlings with a 3-inch collar made from stiff paper or plastic. Push the collar an inch or so into the ground. Or make a trap by sprinkling ½ teaspoon of cornmeal or bran meal around each plant. Spread it in a circle leading away from the stem of the plant. The cutworm eats the meal and dies. Beneficial nematodes added to the soil are an effective long-term control measure.

Leaves Covered with Tan to Brown Blotches; Foliage Appears Blighted

Leafminers

If large areas of the leaves of your delphiniums turn brown or tan, and the foliage looks discolored and diseased, they may be infested with larkspur leafminers (*Phytomyza* spp.). The larvae of these species feed in small groups, sharing a single mine or tunnel within the leaf. Careful observation will reveal dark flecks of excrement within the mines. The larvae feed inside the leaves and then pupate in brown, seedlike cases that often are attached to the infested foliage. There are several generations per year.

Pick off and destroy all infested leaves. If necessary, prune back stems until only healthy growth remains. Larvae can sometimes be repelled by spraying plants with several weekly applications of insecticidal soap in late June or early July.

Plants Stunted; Leaves Yellowed or Covered with Yellow-Brown Spots; Knots on Roots

Nematodes

Delphiniums are attacked by both root knot nematodes and foliar nematodes. Plants infested with root knot nematodes look sickly, wilted, or stunted and have yellowed or bronzed foliage. Their root systems are poorly developed, may have tiny galls or knots on them, and can even be partially decayed. Plants decline slowly and die. Southern root knot nematodes (*Meloidogyne incognita*) attack delphiniums.

Foliar nematodes (*Aphelenchoides ritzema-bosi*) cause yellow-brown spots starting on the leaves at the base of the stalks. They overwinter in the soil, in infested leaves, or in the leaves of young plants. In spring or early summer, during rainy weather, they swim up the film of water on the plants and enter leaves through the stomata. The yellow-brown spots that they cause eventually run together and cover the entire leaf, which dies, turns brittle, and falls. Serious infestations can kill the entire plant. One way to distinguish the two is to use a hand lens and look closely at the leaves to see if fungal spores are present.

Nematodes are not insects, but slender, unsegmented roundworms that are barely visible to the unaided eye. Prevention is the best way to deal with them since severely infested plants are best dug up and destroyed. Do not propagate from infested clumps. Thoroughly clean up all garden debris each fall and discard it to destroy overwintering nematodes. Do not compost soil or plant material that may be infested. (Soil that has been removed with infested plants can be heat pasteurized in an oven and then re-used, but this is a tedious process.) Organic matter in the soil helps to control root knot nematodes because it not only benefits the fungi and bacteria that feed on them, it also keeps plants healthy and better able to withstand mild infestations. Add lots of compost, especially leaf mold, to the bed before planting. Turn severely infested plots over to a thick planting of French marigolds for an entire season and dig the plant remains into the soil at season's end to discourage these pests. Crop rotation is also a good idea; don't grow susceptible plants on the same plot year after year.

Remove leaves and stems infested with foliar nematodes, and dig up and destroy seriously infested specimens along with the soil in which they are growing; do not compost.

Leaves Stippled with Tiny Yellow Dots; Webby Foliage

Spider Mites

Leaves that are dry and stippled with tiny yellow dots are a sign that your delphiniums are infested with spider mites, tiny pests that suck chlorophyll out of the leaves. They also inject toxins into the foliage; this causes distorted or discolored growth. Leaves, stems, and flowers also may be swathed in fine webbing. As their name suggests, spider mites are related to spiders. These tiny creatures, which are about ¹⁄₅₀ inch long and barely visible to the naked eye, may be yellow, green, red, or brown. Both cyclamen mites (*Steneotarsonemus pallidus*) and two-spotted spider mites (*Tetranychus urticae*) attack delphiniums. Spider mites reproduce most rapidly during hot, dry weather.

Severely infested plants should be destroyed, since infestations are difficult to control once they are well under way. Although spider mites can be controlled by washing the plants with a forceful spray of water, this method is not ideal for delphiniums because the flower spikes are brittle; water-laden flowers can be heavy enough to break the stems. So spray infested plants with insecticidal soap every three to five days for two weeks beginning as soon as the mites appear. To avoid spreading the mites from plant to plant, don't touch healthy plants after examining infested ones.

MOST COMMON DISEASES

In addition to the diseases listed below, delphiniums can be afflicted with leaf spot and rust, both diseases caused by fungi.

Stems Turn Black at Base; Plants Wilt

Crown Rot

Delphiniums are subject to crown rot caused by both bacteria and fungi. If your plants wilt suddenly or rot at the base and wilt gradually, suspect one of these diseases. Stems may also turn black from the base upward, and foliage may turn brown. Bacterial rots are characterized by a strong, unpleasant odor and masses of oozing bacteria from cut stems; fungal rots by the tiny fruiting bodies of the fungi themselves.

Although ultimately caused by fungi and bacteria that attack the crowns of the plants, this is a cultural as much as a disease problem. Delphiniums are especially susceptible to crown rot when grown in soil that is too wet. Wounding crowns or roots, by inadvertently digging into them or during division, for example, can also lead to rot. Crown rot is especially a problem during the winter months; suspect it if no shoots appear in spring. Moist soil around the crowns of the plants leads to attack by both bacteria and fungi. The roots and crowns may be blackened, rotten, and covered with white fungal threads.

Cultural practices are helpful in preventing crown rot in delphiniums. When planting, select a site with soil that is moist but well drained, or improve the drainage of the site by incorporating compost and other organic material into the soil. Don't grow delphiniums or other susceptible plants in the same spot year after year. Keep winter mulch away from the crowns of the plants. This helps reduce moisture and prevents rotting during the winter dormant months. Thoroughly cultivating around plants also helps dry out the soil and discourages the spread of the organisms that cause this problem. Remove and discard infected plants, together with the surrounding soil, or cut away affected plant parts with a clean, sharp knife or razor blade. Also, regularly clean up and destroy dead plant debris in the garden. Do not compost infected plants or soil; discard them. Disinfect tools with a solution of 1 part household bleach and 3 parts water or 70 percent rubbing alcohol after use to avoid spreading the disease. For long-term prevention, replace infected soil, improve drainage, and avoid overwatering. Rotate plantings by collecting ripened seed in summer and sowing it in a new location.

Seedlings Rot at Base, Fall Over

Damping-Off

Seedling stems that are water soaked and blackened at the soil line have been afflicted with damping-off. Affected stems are unable to support the plants, which fall over and die. Usually, the foliage is still green and healthy looking when the plants collapse. Stems of older plants show tan to reddish brown lesions that eventually girdle stems. Damping-off is caused by soil-dwelling fungi such as *Pythium, Fusarium, Sclerotium,* and *Rhizoctonia,* and it usually occurs in seedlings in greenhouses or on windowsills. Germinating delphinium seeds may be attacked before they emerge from the soil, or shortly thereafter.

Cultural controls are effective in preventing damping-off. Sow seed in well-drained soil, do not overcrowd plants, and keep soil on the dry side. Outdoors, plant your delphiniums in well-drained soils or raised beds. Indoors, sow seed in sterile growing mix (peat moss, perlite, and vermiculite, with a topping of milled sphagnum moss), and water plants from below by setting pots in water and allowing the water to soak up to just beneath the soil surface. Thin seedlings so they are far enough apart to allow air to circulate between them, which will carry away excessive moisture and reduce humidity. When thinning, use scissors instead of pulling up plants to avoid damaging the roots and stems of remaining plants, which might open them up to infection. In the greenhouse, a fan will promote air circulation. Avoid feeding seedlings too much nitrogen, for it causes lank, weak growth. Routinely disinfect garden tools in boiling water or household bleach solution (1 part bleach to 3 parts water) to discourage disease problems.

White Powder Covering Leaves

Powdery Mildew

If your delphinium leaves are covered with a white or ash gray powdery mold, they probably have powdery mildew, which can be a serious problem in cool, moist weather. Badly infected leaves become discolored and distorted, then drop off. Powdery mildew is caused by fungi that live primarily on the surface of the leaves, flowers, and stems of plants, not inside them.

Powdery mildew most commonly develops on plants grown close together where air circulation is restricted, especially on the lower leaves where humidity is higher and moisture is more abundant. Allow ample spacing between plants, and collect and discard all aboveground refuse in the fall. Spray afflicted plants thoroughly with wettable sulfur once or twice at weekly intervals starting as soon as the whitish coating of the fungus is visible.

Leaves Greenish Yellow or Curled and Deformed; Shoots Spindly or Stunted

Virus Diseases

Delphiniums are susceptible to a number of virus diseases, including aster yellows, mosaic, delphinium ring spot, beet curly top, and stunt. Virus-infected plants generally have spindly, stunted shoots and yellowed foliage. Leaves may be marked with ring spots, lines, pale areas, or mottling, and dead spots may appear on the foliage of infected plants. Infected plants may also be stunted, form dense "rosettes," and have small flowers. Virus diseases are spread by sucking insects such as aphids and leafhoppers.

There is no cure for virus-infected plants. Remove and destroy them; do not compost. To control the insects that transmit these diseases, spray remaining plants with a mixture of insecticidal soap and isopropyl alcohol. Make this mix by adding 1 tablespoon of alcohol to each pint of insecticidal soap solution. Spray at three- to five-day intervals, making three applications. Viruses overwinter in various perennials and weeds such as daisies, plantain, and gaillardia. Infected plants are not necessarily killed by the disease, but should be dug up and destroyed, since they continue to infect nearby plants. Disinfect garden tools with a solution of 1 part household bleach and 3 parts water or 70 percent rubbing alcohol to avoid spreading virus diseases from plant to plant. Also, wash your hands after handling infected plants.

PERENNIAL *Dianthus*   *Dianthus* spp.

DESCRIPTION

The garden-grown relatives of the showy florist's carnation are commonly called pinks, and many of these plants are popular, old-fashioned garden favorites. There are annual, biennial, and perennial species from which to choose. One of the best known is sweet William (*Dianthus barbatus*), which although often grown as an annual or biennial, is actually a short-lived perennial. Flowers come in shades of pink, white, maroon, and red. Many have very fragrant blooms. These plants are ideal for edging, bedding, containers, and rock gardens. Many make fine cut flowers.

Height

D. × allwoodii (Allwood pink), 1 to 1½ feet
D. barbatus (sweet William), 1½ feet; dwarf cultivars, 4 to 8 inches
D. deltoides (maiden pink), 4 to 12 inches
D. gratianopolitanus (cheddar pink), 4 to 8 inches
D. plumarius (grass pink), 10 to 18 inches

Spread

1 to 2 feet

Blossoms

Flowers are borne singly or in dense clusters. The individual blossoms are single or double, and the edges are serrated or "pinked," hence the common name pinks. Most species have blooms with a spicy fragrance. Flowers come in white, pink, salmon, purple, and red, and blossoms are often patterned with more than one color. Most species bloom in spring.

Foliage

Pinks have narrow, deep green leaves.

ENVIRONMENT

Hardiness

D. × allwoodii, D. deltoides, and *D. plumarius* are hardy to USDA Zone 4. *D. barbatus* is hardy to Zone

6, but can be grown as an annual in the North. *D. gratianopolitanus* is hardy to Zone 5.

Light

For best results, grow pinks in full sun, although they will tolerate light shade. They tend to decline once summer temperatures arrive, although some of the newer hybrids are more heat resistant.

Soil

Pinks will grow in any ordinary garden soil that is very well drained. They grow best in slightly alkaline soils, ranging in pH from 7 to 8.

PLANTING AND PROPAGATION

Planting

To grow pinks from seed, sow outdoors in spring or summer where the plants are to grow. Or, sow indoors in spring six to eight weeks before the last frost date. Germination takes 10 to 20 days, and temperatures of 70°F are ideal. To grow *D. barbatus* as an annual, sow seed indoors; it will germinate in 5 to 10 days and can be moved outdoors on the last frost date.

Propagation

Pinks can be propagated by division, layering, or cuttings. *D. barbatus* will also self-sow readily.

PLANT MANAGEMENT

General Care

To prolong the blooming season, cut off flowers as they fade. At the end of the spring blooming season, cut plants back to encourage flowering later in the season. Perennial pinks should be propagated regularly, since they are inclined to die out after two or three seasons.

Water

As a general rule, make sure your pinks get ½ to 1 inch of water per week from rain or by watering. Do not allow plants to dry out to the point that the leaves wilt.

Feeding

A spring application of compost or a slow-acting, general-purpose fertilizer will serve the basic needs of pinks all season. For exceptional performance, give plants supplemental, light feedings (side-dressings or foliar spray) monthly throughout the growing season.

Cutting Fresh Flowers

The taller species of dianthus make fine cut flowers.

MOST COMMON CULTURAL PROBLEMS

Plants Die Out

Excessive Heat

Most pinks, and especially *D. barbatus*, prefer cool temperatures and bloom best in areas where summers are cool and damp. If plants die out before blooming, they may be in a location that is just too hot. In warmer regions, plant pinks in light shade or where plants will benefit from shade during the afternoon when the temperatures are highest.

MOST COMMON INSECT PESTS

Seedlings Severed at Base

Cutworms

Seedlings that look as though they have been leveled by a lawn mower have probably been attacked by cutworms. These pests sever the stems of seedlings and transplants at or below the soil surface, leaving the tops to die. (In contrast, slugs and snails completely consume seedlings, leaving only their slimy trails.) They are most active at night. Cutworms also sometimes climb the stems of pinks and feed just below the buds. They are generally plump, soft-bodied caterpillars that are dull grayish or brownish and measure 1 to 2 inches long. They feed at night and hide in the soil during the day. The adults are night-flying moths.

Prevention is the only way to fight cutworms, for once they have cut down a young plant, there is nothing you can do to save it. Protect individual seedlings with a 3-inch collar made from stiff paper or plastic. Push the collar an inch or so into the ground. Or make a trap by sprinkling ½ teaspoon of cornmeal or bran meal around each plant. Spread it in a circle leading away from the stem of the plant. The cutworm eats the meal and dies. Beneficial nematodes added to the soil are an effective long-term control measure.

Leaves Stippled with Tiny Yellow Dots; Webby Foliage

Spider Mites

Leaves that are dry and stippled with tiny yellow dots are a sign that your pinks are infested with spider mites, tiny pests that suck chlorophyll out of the leaves. They also inject toxins into the foliage; this causes distorted or discolored growth. Leaves, stems, and flowers also may be swathed in fine webbing. As their name suggests, spider mites are related to spiders. These tiny creatures, which are about $\frac{1}{50}$ inch long and barely visible to the naked eye, may be yellow, green, red, or brown. Spider mites reproduce most rapidly during hot, dry weather. Inspect purchased bedding plants carefully to avoid bringing home infested specimens.

Severely infested plants should be destroyed, since infestations are difficult to control once they are well under way. Spider mites can be controlled by washing the plants, especially the undersides of the leaves. For best results, use a forceful spray of water once every other day to knock the mites off the plants; wash the plants at least three times. If that is not effective, spray the plants with insecticidal soap every three to five days for two weeks. To avoid spreading the mites from plant to plant, don't touch healthy plants after examining infested ones.

MOST COMMON DISEASES

Leaves with Brown Spots Above, Powdery Spots Beneath

Rust

A rust disease caused by the fungus *Puccinia conoclinii* occasionally attacks *D. barbatus,* causing pale areas to appear on upper leaf surfaces, with powdery pustules directly beneath.

Remove infected leaves as soon as possible, and destroy severely diseased plants. Clean up and destroy all plant material at the end of the season to avoid reinfecting the garden the following year. Rust can be prevented by periodic applications of wettable sulfur, begun several weeks before rust normally appears. To ensure good ventilation, space plants far enough apart so that air can circulate between them. Also, avoid wetting foliage when watering.

Leaves Greenish Yellow or Curled and Deformed; Shoots Spindly or Stunted

Virus Diseases

Pinks are susceptible to a number of virus diseases, including mosaic, carnation streak virus, and ring spot. Virus-infected plants have spindly, stunted shoots and yellowed foliage. Leaves may be marked with ring spots, lines, pale areas, or mottling, and dead spots may appear on the foliage of infected plants. Infected plants are stunted, form dense "rosettes," and small flowers. Virus diseases are spread by sucking insects such as aphids.

There's no cure for infected plants. Remove and destroy them; do not compost. To control the insects that transmit these diseases, spray remaining plants with a mixture of insecticidal soap and isopropyl alcohol. Make this mix by adding 1 tablespoon of alcohol to each pint of insecticidal soap solution. Spray at three- to five-day intervals, making three applications. Viruses overwinter in various perennials and weeds such as daisies, plantain, and gaillardia. Infected plants are not necessarily killed by the disease, but should be dug up and destroyed, since they continue to infect nearby plants. Disinfect tools with a solution of 1 part household bleach and 3 parts water or 70 percent rubbing alcohol to avoid spreading virus diseases from plant to plant. Also, wash your hands after handling infected plants.

Plants Wilt Suddenly; Stems Rot at Soil Line

Wilt and Stem Rot

Pinks can be afflicted with a variety of diseases that cause plants to wilt suddenly or to rot at or below the soil line. Plants may wilt suddenly or leaves may turn yellow and then wilt.

Preventive measures are very helpful in controlling these diseases. Plant pinks in well-drained soil, avoid overwatering and overcrowding, and keep mulch away from the base of plant stems. Remove and discard infected plants, together with the surrounding soil, or cut away affected plant parts with a clean, sharp knife or razor blade. Discard infected plant material; do not compost. Disinfect tools with a solution of 1 part household bleach and 3 parts water or 70 percent rubbing alcohol to avoid spreading the disease. Keep the garden clear of old plant debris. For long-term prevention, lighten heavy soil with a mixture of perlite, vermiculite, and/or peat moss, and provide good drainage.

Hollyhock *Alcea rosea*

DESCRIPTION

Hollyhocks are familiar, old-fashioned flowers that have graced dooryards and gardens in Europe and America for hundreds of years. One glance at a plant in bloom, towering majestically over all the other flowers in the garden, tells why. Their tall spikes of large single or double flowers are striking. Hollyhocks are biennials, but are also commonly grown as annuals, for they tend to decline after about two years. In the garden, they reseed themselves so readily, they perform like perennials, returning year after year. The botanical name for this plant is also sometimes listed as *Althaea*.

Height

5 to 9 feet; dwarf cultivars, 3 to 4 feet

Spread

2 to 3 feet

Blossoms

Hollyhock flowers are single or double and range from 3 to 5 inches across. Blooms are borne along the top half of tall stalks and may be maroon, pink, red, white, yellow, or purplish red. Flowers generally develop the second year after seed is sown, although seed of some cultivars will bloom the first year if sown indoors in midwinter. Plants bloom from June to August or September. The lowest flowers on the stalks open first. The flowers, while unscented, attract bees.

Foliage

Hollyhock leaves are large and hairy or feltlike to the touch. They are medium green and have three, five, or seven deep lobes. They cluster at the base of the plant, but also grow on the flower stalk.

ENVIRONMENT

Hardiness

Hollyhocks are hardy to USDA Zone 3.

Light

Hollyhocks will grow best in full sun.

Soil

For best results, plant hollyhocks in moist, well-drained soil. They prefer soil that is moderately acidic (pH 6.0 to 6.5).

PLANTING AND PROPAGATION

Planting

Seed can be sown indoors or out. Outdoors, sow seed in spring or summer, up to two months before the first frost of autumn. Seed can be sown where the plants are to grow or in pots or flats, which can be held in a cold frame or other protected area and set out the following spring. They will flower the following season. Indoors, sow in midwinter for cultivars that can be grown as annuals; anytime for plants that are to be grown as biennials. Germination takes 10 to 15 days at temperatures of 70°F. Plant seedlings or purchased transplants in a sunny site with well-drained, rich soil, such as a border area in front of a wall. Space plants 2 to 3 feet apart to provide plenty of air circulation, which will reduce the risk of rust disease. Do not cover the seed, as it needs light to germinate.

Propagation

Hollyhocks are best propagated by seed. Since they are biennials, seed-grown plants generally will flower the second year after sowing. To develop a planting that blooms reliably every year, it's best to plant seedlings at least two years in a row, so you will have plenty of plants flowering and setting seed every year.

PLANT MANAGEMENT

General Care

Hollyhocks grow quickly and their flower stalks may need staking a month or six weeks into the growing season. Stake each stalk separately, tying the main stem with strips of cloth or other material to sturdy stakes that are set firmly in the ground.

Water

Hollyhocks should get 1 inch of water a week from rain or by watering. When watering, try to avoid wetting the foliage because hollyhocks are susceptible to fungus diseases that are encouraged by damp leaves.

Feeding

A spring application of compost or a slow-acting, general-purpose fertilizer will serve the basic needs of hollyhocks all season. For exceptional performance, give plants supplemental, light feedings (side-dressings or foliar spray) monthly from spring to midsummer.

MOST COMMON INSECT PESTS

In addition to the pests listed below, hollyhocks also can be attacked by various caterpillars, which can be controlled with periodic applications of Bt (*Bacillus thuringiensis*) as well as aphids, slugs, and leafminers.

Holes in Leaves and/or Flowers

Beetles

Hollyhocks are a particular favorite of Japanese beetles, which chew holes in foliage and flowers. Japanese beetles (*Popillia japonica*) are ½-inch-long beetles that are shiny, metallic green with copper-colored wing covers. Severe infestations can completely skeletonize plants. Several other species of beetles also chew holes in hollyhock foliage and flowers. Rose chafer (*Macrodactylus subspinosus*), often called rose bug although it is a beetle, is a tan, ⅓- to ½-inch-long insect with a reddish brown head. The larvae of these beetles are C-shaped, grayish white grubs with dark brown heads that can eat plant roots. Fully grown grubs can reach ¾ to 1 inch long. Spotted cucumber beetle (*Diabrotica undecim-*

punctata) is a slender, ¼-inch-long insect that is greenish yellow with 12 black spots on its back. It feasts on petals, buds, and leaves and seems especially drawn to light-colored flowers in late summer. Adults overwinter at the base of weeds or other plants and lay eggs in spring. This pest is also commonly called southern corn rootworm because the yellowish, wormlike, ½- to ¾-inch-long larvae feed on roots.

For the most part, all beetles are controlled the same way. Where possible, handpick and crush them or drop them into a pail of soapy water. If the infestation is light, this is all you will need to do. For heavier infestations, spray infested plants with a solution of pyrethrum and isopropyl alcohol, mixing 1 tablespoon of alcohol with every pint of diluted pyrethrum mixture. Apply this solution every three to five days until the problem is corrected. For long-term control, apply milky spore disease (*Bacillus popilliae*) to lawns and garden. It will kill the larvae of most beetles

Japanese beetles can also be controlled by pheromone traps. Set up traps a week before the beetles are expected to emerge in your area, making sure traps are no closer than 50 feet from the hollyhocks or any other plant vulnerable to beetle attack, such as roses.

Sawdust Exudes from Stems; Stems Break Off; Leaves Wilt

Borers

If hollyhock stems break and leaves wilt, look closely for small, round holes in the stems, from which borers may have expelled their castings. Burdock borer (*Papaipema cataphracta*), stalk borer (*Papaipema nebris*), and European corn borer (*Ostrinia nubilalis*) all attack hollyhocks. Burdock borer is a pale brown caterpillar with three white stripes. Adults are small moths. Stalk borer is a long, slender caterpillar marked with a dark brown or purple band around the middle and several conspicuous stripes running the length of the body. Adults are grayish brown moths. European corn borer larvae are pinkish caterpillars with two rows of dark spots

down the sides. Adults are yellow-brown moths with dark wavy bands on the wings.

Preventive measures are most effective when dealing with these pests. Clean up all weeds, and cut and burn any plant stalks that may harbor overwintering eggs or pupae. Rotating the location of your hollyhock plantings can also help control this pest. Bt (*Bacillus thuringiensis*) is effective if applied early in the season just as the borers are entering the plants. Borer infestations also can be controlled by slitting each affected stem lengthwise, removing the borers, and binding the stems together, but this is tedious work if you have a large planting.

Leaves and Flowers Deformed, Dwarfed, or Marked with Small Spots

Bugs

Several of the true bugs (order Hemiptera) infest hollyhocks. Their feeding can cause deformed growth and young shoots and buds that are dwarfed. Leaves and flowers may be marred with tiny yellow or brown spots. Damage is the result of the bugs feeding with their piercing-sucking mouthparts. Hollyhock plant bugs (*Lygocoris caryae*), tarnished plant bugs (*Lygus rugulipennis*), and species of lace bugs all infest hollyhocks. Tarnished plant bugs, which are the most serious of these pests, are active, ¼-inch-long bugs that are green to brown in color and mottled with white, yellow, and black. On either side of the insect near the back is a yellow triangle with a black dot at one corner. Tarnished plant bugs appear in early spring, and, if left uncontrolled, become increasingly numerous toward the end of summer. They feed by sucking sap from plants and also release a toxin when feeding that can deform foliage and shoots.

Preventive measures are helpful in controlling these pests, several of which overwinter in garden refuse. Thoroughly clean up the garden in spring and fall to discourage overwintering adults and eggs. Handpicking adults, nymphs, or eggs and dropping them into a jar of soapy water is also effective if the infestation isn't too great. If that is not effective, spray the plants with insecticidal soap every three to five days for two weeks. In severe cases, try three applications of pyrethrum laced with isopropyl alcohol, one every three days. Spray early in the morning when bugs are least active. If the infestation is heavy, dust plants with sabadilla.

Flower Buds Die or Petals Are Distorted

Flower Thrips

Thrips occasionally infest hollyhocks, feeding on buds, stem tips, and flowers. Infested plants have distorted blooms, petals and leaves are flecked with white, and leaf tips can wither, curl, and die. The undersides of leaves are spotted with tiny black specks of excrement. Adult thrips are tiny, slender insects that are $1/25$ inch long and variously colored pale yellowish, black, or brown. They have four long, narrow wings fringed with long hairs. The larvae are usually wingless. Both gladiolus thrips (*Taeniothrips simplex*) and hollyhock thrips (*Liriothrips varicornis*) infest hollyhocks.

Since thrips burrow deeply into petal and leaf tissue, they are difficult to control, and early identification is necessary. Set out yellow sticky traps about four weeks after the last frost, as early warning devices. As soon as you spot thrips on a trap, spray plants with insecticidal soap every three days for two weeks. Prune away affected flowers and dip them in soapy water to kill burrowing thrips.

MOST COMMON DISEASES

Rust is by far the most serious disease problem of hollyhocks. In addition to the problems listed below, they are also occasionally afflicted with leaf spot diseases caused by several species of fungi, as well as root knot nematodes and a mosaic virus disease.

Leaves Have Brown Areas or Spots with Black Margins

Anthracnose

Anthracnose, a fungal disease, sometimes attacks hollyhocks, producing a browning or blotching of the leaves. The dead areas are marked by distinct black edges. Petals of infected flowers develop abnormally. Tiny black spore pustules appear in the spots.

Cultural controls can be used to combat anthracnose. Pick off and destroy any infected leaves as soon as they appear. Also, regularly clean up and destroy dead plant debris in the garden. Do not compost plant material you suspect to be infected. Rogue out and discard seriously infected plants, together with the soil in which they are growing. Disinfect garden tools with a liquid bleach solution (1 part bleach to 3 parts water) or 70 percent rubbing alcohol to avoid spreading the fungus from plant to plant. When watering, avoid wetting the foliage. A layer of mulch helps prevent fungal spores from splashing from the soil onto plants. If anthracnose is a particular problem in your area, spray at weekly to ten-day intervals with wettable sulfur or bordeaux mixture, particularly in rainy seasons. (Watch for leaf discoloration with the latter.)

Leaves with Pale Areas Above; Powdery Orange Spots Beneath

Rust

A variety of fungi cause rust disease in hollyhocks. They cause pale areas to appear on upper leaf surfaces, with powdery orange pustules or spots directly beneath on the undersides of the leaves. Rust is more prevalent in humid areas. It deforms infected stems, but does not harm hollyhock flowers.

The first line of defense in controlling rust is to plant hollyhocks in a location that has plenty of air circulation, and space plants far enough apart so that air can move between them. Also, avoid wetting the foliage when watering. Remove infected leaves as soon as possible, and destroy severely diseased plants. Clean up and destroy all plant material at the end of the season to prevent fungal spores from reinfecting the garden the following year. Rust can be prevented by periodic applications of wettable sulfur, begun several weeks before rust normally appears.

Hostas

Hosta spp.

DESCRIPTION

Hostas are indispensable, clump-forming perennials grown primarily for their bold, handsome foliage. They also produce attractive spikes of trumpet-shaped flowers in summer. There are about 40 species of hostas, and hundreds of cultivars from which to choose. Leaves may be variegated or plain. Size ranges from tiny dwarfs under 6 inches tall to 2-foot-tall plants such as *Hosta sieboldiana* whose leaves can be 1½ feet long and nearly as wide. Sometimes also called plaintain lilies or funkia, hostas are unparalleled perennials for shady areas. They can be used in borders, as ground covers, or specimen plants. Smaller species make excellent edging plants. Hostas are a good choice for areas that are sloped or difficult to reach because they require little care and also hold the soil well. They make fine companion plants for spring bulbs because when the bulbs finish flowering, emerging hosta foliage will hide the withering bulb leaves.

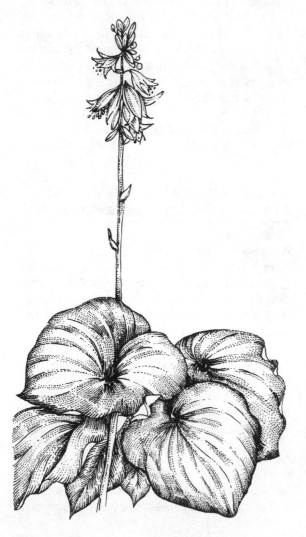

Height

Foliage height 1 to 2½ feet; dwarf cultivars, under 1 foot. The flower stalks rise another 1 to 1½ feet above their leaves.

Spread

Mature plants that have not been divided can spread to 5 feet, but most gardeners divide their hostas once the clumps are 1½ to 2 feet across.

Blossoms

Hosta flowers are tubular and borne in many-flowered spikes that generally rise above the foliage. Blooms may be white, lilac, or blue. They bloom along stalks that rise up from the leaves. *H. plantaginea*, commonly called fragrant plantain lily, is the only hosta species with fragrant flowers. Hostas bloom from mid- to late summer.

Foliage

Hostas have handsome, ribbed leaves that, depending on the species or cultivar, are oval with a heart-shaped base or narrow and lance shaped. Depending on the cultivar, leaves can be narrow and as short as 1 inch, or very broad and up to 1½ feet in length. Leaves can range from light to dark green or blue-green and may be variegated with yellow, light green, cream, and/or white.

ENVIRONMENT

Hardiness

Most hostas are hardy to USDA Zone 4.

Light

Hostas grow best in light to deep shade. For all but a few cultivars, a location in full sun will cause the foliage color to bleach out and brown, and sun-burned spots to appear in the foliage.

Soil

Plant hostas in moist, well-drained soil that is rich in organic matter. A slightly acidic pH from 6.0 to 6.5 is ideal.

PLANTING AND PROPAGATION

Planting

Most species of hostas can be grown from seed, but they take two to three years to make large, flowering-size plants. Most of the named cultivars (*H. sieboldiana* 'Frances Williams', for example) must be propagated by division, for they do not come true from seed. Seed can be sown outdoors or indoors. Outdoors, sow where the plants are to grow in spring or summer, up to two months before the last frost date of autumn. Indoors, sow from early spring to summer. Germination takes 15 to 20 days, and temperatures of 70°F are ideal. Plants sown indoors can be planted out in late summer or transplanted to pots, held in a cold frame through the first winter,

and planted out the following spring.

Purchased, pot-grown plants can be sown in spring or early summer. Dormant plants can be planted in fall. Set the plants in the ground so the crowns are level with the surface of the ground. Space smaller-leaved hostas 12 to 15 inches apart; large-leaved species, such as *H. sieboldiana,* should be spaced 2 to 3 feet apart.

Propagation

The best way to propagate hostas is by division in the spring or late fall after the plants have died back for the season. Hostas don't need regular dividing, however, and can be left undisturbed for many years. Small divisions will reach full size in three to five years.

Container Gardening

Hostas can be grown in containers that are large enough to keep the soil cool and moist—half-barrels are a suitable size.

PLANT MANAGEMENT

General Care

These handsome and useful plants are virtually care-free. Properly sited and planted, they require very little special attention from year to year. The flower stalks can be removed once the blossoms have faded. The foliage should be cut back at the end of the season, and clumps can be divided every five years or so.

Water

Hostas need ½ to 1 inch of water per week from watering or rainfall. They can tolerate some drought once established, however.

Feeding

A spring application of compost or a slow-acting, general-purpose fertilizer will serve the basic needs of hostas all season. For exceptional performance, give plants supplemental, light feedings (side-dressings or foliar spray) monthly from spring to midsummer.

Cutting Fresh Flowers

Hosta flowers can be added to arrangements, and their ornamental leaves are very useful for this purpose as well.

MOST COMMON CULTURAL PROBLEMS

Leaves Have Brown Edges; Foliage Is Scorched or Bleached; Plants Stunted

Improper Planting Location; Drought

Hostas that develop dry, brown leaf edges or have scorched or bleached areas in the centers of the leaves usually have been planted in a location that receives too much sun. Dry soil, which can be caused by lack of rainfall or by soil that does not hold water well because of low organic matter content, can also cause these symptoms. Hostas are shade-loving plants that prefer evenly drained soil that is moist and rich in organic matter. Plants growing in hot sun or under drought conditions will wilt frequently. Leaf size and growth rate is often stunted under these conditions as well. To correct this condition, add plenty of organic matter to the soil when planting, mulch plants to keep the roots cool, and select a location that is shaded, especially during the hottest part of the day.

MOST COMMON INSECT PESTS

Ragged Holes in Leaves; Trails of Slime on Plants

Slugs and Snails

Hostas are particularly vulnerable to slugs and snails.

Plants that have ragged holes in the leaves are probably infested with slugs or snails. Trails of slime on the foliage and around the plants are further confirmation of the presence of these pests. Slugs are active only at night, when they feast on plants by rasping holes in the foliage with their filelike tongues. During the day, they hide under boards, mulch, or leaf litter. Slugs are similar to snails except that they have no shells. Both are generally 1 to 2 inches long, although some species of slugs grow up to 8 inches in length. Either pest may be white, gray, yellow, or brown-black in color. They are attracted to moist, well-mulched gardens and are most destructive in shaded gardens and during rainy spells. During winter and in dry seasons, slugs burrow into the ground to wait for more favorable weather.

A multifaceted approach to control is best. Remove boards, rocks, clippings, and other debris to cut down on the places where these pests hide during the day. Or, check daily under favorite hiding places, handpick snoozing slugs, crush them or seal them into a jar full of water and kerosene or insecticidal soap, and discard them. Inverted flowerpots, pieces of grapefruit peel, and cabbage leaves will lure slugs and can be used to trap them. Handpicking at night with a flashlight can be effective if started early in the spring. Traps baited with beer or yeast and water are also effective. To make an effective trap, cut a 2-inch hole in the lid of a coffee can or a small plastic container and bury the container flush with the soil. Slugs are attracted to the yeast in the beer, climb down through the hole in the lid, and drown. The key is to begin trapping very early in the season in order to prevent the population from building up. Surrounding plants with barriers of sand, ashes, or copper sheeting will discourage slugs from invading your plantings.

MOST COMMON DISEASES

Hostas are bothered by few diseases, provided their few basic cultural requirements are met. They require well-drained soil; waterlogged soil, which prevents air from getting to the roots, encourages disease. Heavily packed mulch can encourage problems as well. Specimens with any physical damage are most vulnerable to disease because infectious fungi and bacteria can enter the plant through those wounds. Prune away damaged foliage, and be sure to mark plantings carefully to avoid inadvertently digging into the clumps when they are dormant. In addition to crown rot, discussed below, they are also occasionally attacked by fungi that cause leaf spot.

Stems Turn Black at Base; Leaves Turn Yellow and Wilt; Plants Collapse

Crown Rot
Although ultimately caused by fungi and bacteria that attack the crowns of the plants, crown rot is a cultural as much as a disease problem. Hostas are susceptible to crown rot when grown in soil that is not well drained. Damaging the crown of a plant by inadvertently digging into it, for example, can also lead to rot. Crown rot is especially a problem during the winter months; suspect it if no shoots appear in spring. Moist soil around the crowns of the plants leads to attack by both bacteria and fungi. The roots and crowns may be blackened, rotten, and covered with white fungal threads. The whole plant dies in a few days.

Cultural practices are very helpful in preventing crown rot in hostas. When planting, select a site with well-drained soil, or improve the drainage of the site by incorporating compost and other organic material into the soil. Keep winter mulch away from the crowns of the plants. This helps reduce moisture and prevents rotting during the winter dormant season. Thoroughly cultivating around plants also helps dry out the soil and discourages the spread of the organisms that cause this problem. Since hostas emerge late in spring, be sure to mark plantings to avoid accidentally digging into them and damaging the crowns. Remove and discard afflicted plants and the soil immediately surrounding them; do not compost.

PERENNIAL *Irises* *Iris* spp.

DESCRIPTION

Irises are one of the delights of spring. The genus is appropriately named for the Greek goddess of the rainbow, Iris, for their flowers come in almost every color combination. These striking perennials have swordlike leaves and come in a wide variety of sizes and forms. The genus is divided into two groups: species that grow from a rhizome (a fleshy underground stem, or rootstock) and those that arise from bulbs. (For more information, see the entry on bulbous irises, beginning on page 239.) Rhizomatous irises are further divided according to flower structure and size into such classes as Tall Bearded, Border Bearded, Intermediate Bearded, and Standard Dwarf Bearded. There are also classes of miniature iris suitable for rock gardens and reblooming iris that provide spring as well as autumn bloom. *Iris kaempferi* (Japanese iris) and *I. sibirica* (Siberian iris) are also popular, clump-forming irises with grasslike leaves. *I. cristata* (crested iris) is a diminutive native American wildflower suitable for wildflower gardens. Another group of native irises, prized in areas where the summers are hot and humid, are the Louisiana irises. There are irises for borders, beds, rock gardens, edging, ground covers, and the moist edges of ponds. They also make outstanding cut flowers.

Height

I. cristata (crested iris), 3 to 4 inches

I. kaempferi (Japanese iris) and *I. sibirica* (Siberian iris), about 2 feet

Border Bearded, 2 to 3 feet

Intermediate Bearded, 15 to 28 inches

Standard Dwarf Bearded, 10 to 15 inches

Tall Bearded iris and Louisiana irises, 3 to 4 feet

Spread

All irises will spread to form large clumps, but most gardeners dig and divide them regularly to keep them vigorous and disease-free. Clumps generally are kept about equal to the height of the plants.

Blossoms

All irises have unique, six-petaled flowers. Three of the petals, called standards, are erect; the other three, called falls, hang down or point outward. So-called bearded irises have fuzzy, caterpillar-like tufts of hairs, or beards, running down the top of the falls. Crested irises, including *I. crestata, I. kaempferi, I. sibirica,* and the Louisiana irises, have a crest instead of a beard on the falls. Bearded irises and Louisiana irises come in nearly all colors of the rainbow, and many cultivars with striking color combinations have been developed. Crested irises have a somewhat more limited color range, which includes lavender-blue, purplish blue, orchid rose, and white. With the exception of the reblooming irises, which are hardy only in the South, irises are spring-blooming plants. By selecting a variety of different plants from several groups, they can provide a long season of garden bloom. *I. cristata* blooms in early spring. Tall Bearded and Border Bearded irises bloom in mid-spring; Intermediate Bearded bloom somewhat earlier than the Tall Bearded. *I. kaempferi* and *I. sibirica* bloom in late spring.

Foliage

Iris leaves are smooth, green, and sword-shaped. They may be from 4 to 16 inches long, depending on the type. They grow directly from the rhizome at the soil surface and provide texture and drama all season long.

ENVIRONMENT

Hardiness

I. cristata and *I. sibirica,* USDA Zone 3
I. kaempferi, Zone 4

Bearded irises, Zone 4
Louisiana irises, Zone 5

Light

Irises should be grown in full sun, with the exception of *I. cristata*, which grows best with light shade. Most will tolerate light shade, but will not bloom as well as plants grown in full sun.

Soil

Bearded irises and *I. cristata* will tolerate a wide range of soil types, from sandy loam to heavy clay, provided the soil is well-drained. They prefer a neutral pH of 7, but will tolerate a range from slightly acidic to alkaline, pH 6 to 8. *I. kaempferi, I. sibirica*, and the Louisiana irises grow best in rich, moist but well-drained soil that is acid in pH. The Louisiana irises need soil that is especially rich in organic matter. All irises require soil that is very well drained in winter.

PLANTING AND PROPAGATION

Planting

Most of these irises are purchased as pot-grown plants or as divisions, since seed produced by the cultivars does not come true, and can be planted from spring to early fall. For best results, prepare the soil deeply, for although the rhizomes creep along the surface of the soil, roots can extend deeply into the soil. Plant the rhizomes on the surface of the soil, leaving about one-third of the rhizome above the soil surface. Space plants 1 to 2½ feet apart, depending on their ultimate height.

Propagation

Division is the best way to propagate all of the rhizomatous irises, and since they should be divided regularly to keep them disease-free and blooming at their best, this is a procedure you'll need to perform regularly. Do this either in the spring after the plants finish blooming, or early fall. Carefully dig up the gnarled clumps of rhizomes and wash them off with a hose. Inspect them carefully for signs of disease, slice the clumps into sections with a clean, sharp knife, and discard any portions that are old or show signs of disease or insect infestations. Either let these rhizomes dry off in the sun for a few hours or dust them with sulfur to ward off disease. Then replant the most vigorous sections. When dividing in the fall, trim back iris foliage for easier handling. Newly divided clumps of iris may not bloom the following season. With good soil conditions and an annual application of fertilizer, most clumps will return to full vigor the second season after dividing.

PLANT MANAGEMENT

General Care

Irises must be divided regularly because the clumps become crowded in the center and deteriorate. Divide plants as soon as crowding is apparent, generally every four or five years, anytime from flowering to early fall. Cut back iris flower stems after the flowers have faded. Do not, however, cut the leaves back severely after flowering. The plants need their leaves to store up energy for next year. However, in fall it is also a good idea to cut the foliage back by about two-thirds, and completely remove any diseased or dead foliage.

Bearded iris rhizomes benefit from exposure to sun, so it's not necessary to mulch iris during the growing season. However, mulching in winter helps minimize soil heaving and disturbance of the shallowly planted rhizomes. Rake away the mulch in the spring to allow sunlight to reach the rhizomes and carefully cultivate the soil. Because they prefer moister soils, *I. kaempferi, I. sibirica, Iris cristata*, and the Louisiana irises benefit from summer mulch.

Water

All irises benefit from abundant moisture just before

and during the flowering season, but most bearded irises are quite drought resistant during other times of the year. Newly planted specimens should get 1 inch of water a week from rain or by watering to help them become established. After that, bearded irises only need water during spells of hot, dry weather. *I. kaempferi, I. sibirica, I. cristata,* and the Louisiana irises should never be allowed to dry out completely.

Feeding

A spring application of compost or a slow-acting, general-purpose fertilizer will serve the basic needs of iris all season. For exceptional performance, give plants supplemental, light feedings (side-dressings or foliar spray) monthly from spring to midsummer.

Cutting Fresh Flowers

Cut irises for indoor display in the early morning. Choose stalks with barely opened blossoms and cut them with a sharp knife. Add a teaspoon of sugar per quart of water in the container in which they are arranged to prolong their freshness.

MOST COMMON INSECT PESTS

In addition to the pests listed below, irises are sometimes attacked by aphids, which cause curled and distorted leaves; beetles and caterpillars, which chew holes in flowers and foliage; and slugs, which also chew holes in flowers and foliage and leave behind slimy trails. The C-shaped grubs of Japanese beetles also sometimes feed on the roots of irises.

Irregular Tunnels in Leaves; Rhizomes Damaged

Iris Borers
Iris foliage that is disfigured with irregular tunnels or mines in the lower portion of the leaves is probably infested with iris borers, undoubtedly the most serious pest of irises, especially bearded irises. The

caterpillars emerge in April or early May when the leaves are 5 to 6 inches high. They climb the foliage and enter the leaves through pinpoint-size holes drilled a few inches above the ground. They excavate slender feeding channels that resemble the burrows of leafminers, working their way downward toward the rhizomes. Areas of the leaves may also appear water soaked. By midsummer, the borer larvae attack iris rhizomes. By this time, they are fat, pink to flesh-colored with brown heads, and 1½ to 2 inches long. They eat out the center of the rhizomes, then pupate in the soil. The adults appear in late summer (August to October) and are night-flying moths with purplish front wings and yellow-brown hind wings. The pest overwinters as eggs on foliage and debris at the base of plants. The eggs are creamy white with a greenish tinge at first; later they are lavender in color. A serious side effect of these insects' chewing is the introduction of the bacteria that cause soft rot of the rhizomes.

Preventive measures are helpful in controlling this pest. To eliminate overwintering eggs, cut iris bloom stalks and leaves at the base in the fall and burn them, as they are the primary overwintering site for these pests. Thoroughly clean up and discard any other plant material in the garden that may harbor eggs. Watch the base of the plants for signs of infestation in early spring, and if you see any larvae before the plants flower, pinch them in their mines to kill them. Then, dig infested specimens after flowering and cut out all infested portions of leaves and rhizomes, kill the larvae, and discard or burn diseased plants. Spread pyrethrum dust around the base of the plants in the spring to kill the hatching larvae that emerge from the soil to climb the foliage.

Holes in Seedpods

Iris Weevils
Iris weevils are snout-nosed beetles that are ⅕ inch long and black with white and yellow scales. The larvae are small, fat grubs that feed on the seeds and then pupate inside the seedpods. The adults emerge when the seedpods open. These pests destroy

iris seeds, but can be easily controlled by picking and discarding the flower heads as they fade.

Flower Buds Die or Petals Are Distorted

Thrips

Several species of thrips occasionally infest iris. *I. kaempferi* is especially susceptible to iris thrips (*Iridothrops iridis*). This pest feeds by rasping the folds of the leaves, which leaves the plants open to infection by fungi. Iris thrips cause stunted growth and russet or sooty areas on the leaves. The tops of the plants eventually turn brown and die out. Serious infestations can kill nearly all of the roots as well. Iris thrips feed from spring to fall and overwinter as adults near the leaf buds in the shelter of the old leaf bases. The larvae are tiny white pests; adults are wingless and dark brown. Both gladiolus thrips (*Taeniothrips simplex*) and flower thrips (*Frankliniella tritici*) also infest iris. These pests feed on buds, stem tips, and flowers. Infested plants have distorted blooms, petals and leaves are flecked with white, and leaf tips can wither, curl, and die. The undersides of leaves are spotted with tiny black specks of excrement. Adult thrips are tiny, slender insects that are 1/25 inch long and variously colored pale yellowish, black, or brown. They have four long, narrow wings fringed with long hairs. The larvae are usually wingless.

Since thrips burrow deeply into petal and leaf tissue, they are difficult to control, and early identification is necessary. Iris thrips can be controlled by regular applications of insecticidal soap directed toward the base of the plants, every five to seven days until the infestation has been cleared up. Iris divisions can also be soaked in hot (120°F) water for 30 minutes to kill these pests. For flower and gladiolus thrips, set out yellow sticky traps about four weeks after the last frost, as early warning devices. As soon as you spot thrips on a trap, spray plants with insecticidal soap every three days for two weeks. Prune away affected flowers and dip them in soapy water to kill burrowing thrips.

MOST COMMON DISEASES

In addition to the diseases listed below, irises occasionally develop leaf spot, caused by several different species of fungi. Rust, another fungal disease, causes rust-red pustules on both sides of the leaves. In rainy weather, fungi can also blight or spot flowers. (See Fungal Disease, beginning on page 340.) They can also be infected with a mosaic disease caused by a virus. Infected plants, which should be destroyed, may be stunted and streaked with yellow.

Rhizomes Rotted and Soft; Odor Present

Bacterial Soft Rot

Soft, pulpy rhizomes accompanied by an offensive odor and withered leaf tips are the most obvious signs of this disease. Bearded irises, especially the tall ones, are most likely to become infected. Crowded conditions and shady locations increase susceptibility, as does a borer infestation. The bacteria (*Pectobacterium carotovorum*) enter the plants through wounds—those made in the leaves by iris borers or caused by careless cultivation. Once they enter the plants, they multiply rapidly, causing water-soaked streaks on the leaves. The rhizomes eventually rot and collapse, and leaves wilt and die.

Controlling iris borers is the first line of defense (see Iris Borers above). Cut out infected growth as soon as it is detected. Dig up severely infected rhizomes, cut out and discard badly affected portions, and dip the healthy parts in a household bleach solution (1 part bleach to 3 parts water). Dip tools in a solution of 70 percent denatured alcohol to avoid transferring bacteria from plant to plant.

Irises grown in soil that is not well drained is also susceptible to a rhizome rot caused by the fungi *Botryotinia convoluta*. This disease is common in cool, wet weather and is often responsible for plants that die in early spring. To prevent rhizome rot, plant irises in well-drained soil, and do not bury the rhizomes too deeply. Dig and destroy afflicted portions of the plant.

Leaves Turn Brown; Soft Rot of Rhizomes

Crown Rot

Although ultimately caused by the fungi *Pellicularia rolfsii,* crown rot of iris is a cultural as much as a disease problem, for crowded plants that have not been regularly divided are most susceptible. The fungi enter the plants at the base of leaves and flower stalks, and then invade the rhizomes, where they cause a dry rot. The fungi cover the rhizomes with white, threadlike mycelia followed by tiny, brown or black fruiting bodies.

Dig and discard afflicted plants, together with the soil in which they are growing. Take care not to spread infected soil beyond the planting site. Discard plant material and soil that is infected; do not compost. Regularly divide irises to prevent the plants from becoming overcrowded.

PERENNIAL Peonies *Paeonia* spp.

DESCRIPTION

Peonies have been garden mainstays for generations. Perennials that endure for years, even decades, in the yard and garden, they are valued for their sturdy constitutions and their huge, showy spring flowers. Common Peony (*Paeonia officinalis*) and Chinese Peony (*P. lactiflora*), collectively referred to simply as herbaceous peonies, are the most familiar of the many species of this popular plant. Peonies can be used in beds and borders and also make striking specimen plants when used alone. Their enormous, white, pink, yellow, or red blooms make striking cut flowers, either in arrangements with other flowers or when displayed alone. Many cultivars are very fragrant.

Height

3 to 4 feet

Spread

3 feet or more

Blossoms

Peonies bear magnificent flowers that range from 3 to 5 inches across in late spring to early summer. Cultivars are classified as early-, midseason, or late-blooming, and individual plants remain in bloom one to two weeks. The fragrant blossoms can be rose, light pink, deep red, white, or even creamy yellow. Flowers come in several types, including singles, which have a few broad petals with a cluster of stamens in the center; semidoubles; and doubles. Japanese- and anemone-flowered cultivars have clusters of petal-like stamens in the center surrounded by broad petals.

Foliage

The deeply divided leaves are a deep green and remain attractive all season long. They are 6 to 8 inches long.

ENVIRONMENT

Hardiness

Peonies are hardy to USDA Zone 5.

Light

For best bloom, plant peonies in full sun. They will tolerate light shade, but will not bloom as well and may have weak stems. In deep shade, the foliage will come back year after year, but plants will fail to bloom.

Soil

Peonies tolerate a wide range of soil types, but for best results, plant them in rich, well-drained soil that is deeply prepared and contains plenty of organic matter. Ideal pH is nearly neutral (7), but plants will tolerate pH ranging from 6 to 8. Since these plants can be left where planted for years without dividing, take extra care to dig the soil deeply, and add plenty of organic matter such as compost or leaf mold. If drainage is a problem, build peony beds higher than the surrounding soil surface or add lots of organic matter to improve drainage.

PLANTING AND PROPAGATION

Planting

Peonies are available as pot-grown plants throughout the season, or as bare-root divisions in fall. Pot-grown specimens can be planted in early spring, but the best time for planting peonies is late summer or early fall at least six weeks before the ground freezes. Since peonies do not like to be disturbed once they are planted, choose the site carefully. Once established, peonies can stay in place for 15 to 20 years. A spot that provides some shelter—a wall, fence, or building—is desirable to protect heavy peony flowers in bloom from wind.

Remarkably adaptable in most things, peonies are very fussy about how deeply they are planted. Set the crown, from which the pointed red buds peak in the fall, an inch or so above the soil surface. Tops of budding shoots must be no more than 1 to 2 inches below the soil surface. Planting too deeply is the most common reason for failure to bloom. Space plants about 3 feet apart so they will have plenty of room to expand and won't crowd or need dividing for several years. It takes about three years for roots to become fully established and for the plants to begin flowering. Extend the display in your yard over 6 weeks by planting early, midseason, and late cultivars.

Peonies are hardy to quite cold temperatures, but mulch them the first winter after planting. Do this after the ground freezes in November or December to keep soil temperatures even and prevent heaving of the ground caused by the freezing and thawing process.

Propagation

Peony clumps need not be disturbed for as long as 10 or even 20 years, but can be divided to provide more plants. Fall is the ideal time to divide plants. Gently dig the clumps and, with a sharp knife, cut it into sections, leaving at least three "eyes," or growing points, on each section. Replant each section immediately at the proper depth in a prepared bed.

PLANT MANAGEMENT

General Care

Well-established peony clumps, and especially those plants with very large flowers, will probably need staking to keep the heavy blooms from bending over to the ground. Sometime before the buds begin to break open, set four stakes into the ground around the clump, taking care not to damage the roots, and lace heavy twine or wire back and forth among the tops forming a lattice through which blossom-bearing peony stems can grow and be supported. Or, use ready-made metal staking rings. Be sure the stakes are tall enough to support the stems—4-foot-long stakes that are pushed 1 foot into the soil are fine. To get bigger blossoms on your plants, remove side buds early in their development, leaving those at the end of stems to benefit from maximum nutrition and grow very large. Remove faded flowers regularly during the bloom period. Also cut out damaged stems or unhealthy looking leaves. Cut the foliage to the ground in late fall and compost it or, if leaf spot or other diseases have been a problem, discard it.

Water

Ideally, peonies should get about 1 inch of water a week from rain or by watering.

Feeding

A spring application of compost or a slow-acting, general-purpose fertilizer will serve the basic needs of peonies all season. For exceptional performance, give plants supplemental, light feedings (side-dressings or foliar spray) monthly from spring to midsummer.

Cutting Fresh Flowers

Peonies make superb cutting flowers. Cut just-opened blossoms early in the morning with a sharp knife. Plunge the stems into warm water for an hour or two before arranging them for display. Add a teaspoon of sugar to the water in the vase to prolong the bloom.

MOST COMMON CULTURAL PROBLEMS

Buds Fail to Open

Bud Blast

Peony plants that produce buds that develop to the size of a small pea but fail to grow or open into flowers have been afflicted with bud blast, a condition that can be caused for a variety of reasons. Drought, low temperatures in early spring when the buds are forming, and lack of potassium in the soil all can cause bud blast. Peonies planted too deeply or that are growing in shade can also exhibit this condition. Finally, infestation by root knot nematodes has been linked to bud blast.

Plants Fail to Form Buds or Flowers

Crowns Planted Too Deeply; Excessive Shade

There are several reasons why peonies fail to bloom, the most common of which is that the crowns have been planted too deeply. Crowns should be no more than 1 to 2 inches below the soil surface. Clumps that have remained undisturbed for a decade or more may be so crowded that they fail to bloom. Plants growing in too much shade will also fail to bloom. If you suspect any of these reasons, dig and replant. Young plants, or divisions that have three or fewer "eyes" also won't bloom until they are older and larger. In the Deep South, peonies may not receive enough cold winter weather to initiate dormancy and bud formation. (Early-blooming cultivars may bloom under these conditions.)

MOST COMMON INSECT PESTS

In addition to the insects listed below, peonies are almost always infested with ants when they are in bud and flower. The ants feed on the sugary nectar on the buds, but do little, if any, other damage. They don't require controlling. Fall webworm, a caterpillar, and scale sometimes infest peonies late in the season.

Holes in Leaves and/or Flowers

Beetles

Rose chafer (*Macrodactylus subspinosus*), often called rose bug although it is a beetle, is a tan, 1/3- to 1/2-inch-long insect with a reddish brown head that feeds on peony flowers. Late-blooming peonies are also sometimes attacked by Japanese beetles (*Popillia japonica*), which are 1/2-inch-long beetles that are shiny, metallic green with copper-colored wing covers. The larvae of these beetles are C-shaped, grayish-white grubs with dark brown heads that can eat plant roots. Fully grown grubs can reach 3/4 to 1 inch long.

For the most part, all beetles are controlled the same way. Where possible, handpick and crush them or drop them into a pail of soapy water. If the infestation is light, this is all you will need to do. For heavier infestations, spray infested plants with a solution of pyrethrum and isopropyl alcohol, mixing 1 tablespoon of alcohol with every pint of diluted pyrethrum mixture. Apply this solution every three to five days until the problem is corrected. For long-term control, apply milky spore disease (*Bacillus popilliae*) to lawns and garden. It will kill the larvae of most beetles.

Japanese beetles can also be controlled by pheromone traps. Set up traps a week before the beetles are expected to emerge in your area, making sure traps are no closer than 50 feet from the peonies or any other plant vulnerable to beetle attack, such as roses.

Flower Buds Die or Petals Are Distorted

Flower Thrips

Flower thrips (*Frankliniella tritici*) occasionally infest peonies, feeding on buds, stem tips, and flowers. Infested plants have distorted blooms, and petals are flecked with white, brown, or red. Adult thrips are tiny, slender insects that are 1/25 inch long and variously colored pale yellowish, black, or brown. They have four long, narrow wings fringed with long hairs. The larvae are usually wingless.

Since thrips burrow deeply into petal and leaf tissue, they are difficult to control, and early identification is necessary. Set out yellow sticky traps about four weeks after the last frost, as early warning devices. As soon as you spot thrips on a trap, spray plants with insecticidal soap every three days for two weeks. Prune away affected flowers and dip them in soapy water to kill burrowing thrips.

Plants Stunted; Leaves Yellowed or Covered with Yellow-Brown Spots

Nematodes

Peonies are attacked by southern root knot nematodes (*Meloidogyne incognita*). Plants infested with root knot nematodes look sickly, wilted, or stunted and have yellowed or bronzed foliage. Their root systems are poorly developed, may have tiny galls or knots on them, and can even be partially decayed. Nematodes are not insects, but slender, unsegmented roundworms that are barely visible to the unaided eye.

Prevention is the best way to deal with them, since severely infested plants are best dug up and destroyed. Do not propagate from infested clumps. Thoroughly clean up all garden debris each fall and discard it to destroy overwintering nematodes. Do not compost soil or plant material that may be infested. (Soil that has been removed with infested plants can be heat pasteurized in an oven and then re-used, but this is a tedious process.) Organic matter in the soil helps to control root knot nematodes because it not only benefits the fungi and bacteria that feed on them, it also keeps plants healthy and better able to withstand mild infestations. Add lots of compost, especially leaf mold, to the bed before planting. Turn severely infested plots over to a thick planting of French marigolds for an entire season and dig the plant remains into the soil at season's end to discourage these pests. Crop rotation is also a good idea; don't grow susceptible plants on the same plot year after year.

MOST COMMON DISEASES

Peonies are bothered by few diseases, provided their few basic cultural requirements are met. They require well-drained soil, for waterlogged soil leads to the blight diseases discussed below as well as other rot diseases that can be dealt with in a similar manner. In addition, peonies are subject to a variety of leaf spot diseases caused by fungi. These disfigure the foliage but do little, if any, harm to the plant. They can also be afflicted with several virus diseases, which cause stunted plants and spindly shoots. Virus-infected plants should be destroyed.

Shoots Wilt and Collapse; Leaves Covered with Spots

Blight
The most common disease of garden peonies is botrytis blight, caused by a gray mold called *Botrytis*

paeoniae. The disease is first apparent in spring when peony shoots are about 1 foot tall. Shoots of afflicted plants wilt suddenly and fall over. Close inspection reveals that the base of the leaves and stems have turned brown or black and rotted and that the stalks are covered with a gray mold near the ground. The fungi shed many spores, which are transported from plant to plant by wind, insects, and unwary gardeners. On young leaves, the fungi cause leaf blight. Afflicted plants develop large, irregular brown patches. The fungi also attack and rot buds and opening flowers. The fungi cause bud blast; afflicted flowers and buds turn brown and eventually are covered with gray mold. The fungi overwinter as spores near the base of infected plants.

A second blight disease, downy mildew blight, is caused by the fungi *Phytophthora cactorum.* Symptoms of this disease closely resemble botrytis blight, but stems never develop the characteristic gray mold of that disease. Downy mildew blight causes entire shoots to turn black, and cankers develop on stems, which then fall over. Unlike botrytis blight, downy mildew blight often invades the crown of the plant, causing a wet rot and ultimately killing the entire plant.

Cultural practices are very effective in controlling botrytis blight. Remove and destroy infected plant parts as soon as they appear. Put them into a plastic bag before discarding to keep the spores from spreading. Each fall, cut and discard all above-ground refuse to prevent the fungi from overwintering. Do not compost plant material that may be infected. When planting, select a site with well-drained soil, or improve the drainage of the site at planting time by incorporating compost and other organic material into the soil. Peonies should not be planted in spots where drainage is poor. Do not allow manure to come in contact with stems. In the North, plants may need a winter mulch to protect them from freezing temperatures, but remove it in early spring so that the soil around the plants can dry out. To avoid spreading the fungi from plant to plant, disinfect tools with a solution of 1 part household bleach and 3 parts water or 70 percent rubbing alcohol. In severe cases, spray the plants in spring when shoots are 1 foot high with bordeaux mixture, and again two weeks later. (Watch for leaf discoloration when using.) If the fungi spread to leaves or cause buds to blast, make a third application.

The cultural controls discussed above also are effective ways to deal with downy mildew blight. However, seriously infected plants suspected of having downy mildew blight should be dug and discarded, together with the soil in which they are growing. The fungi invade the roots of the plant, where fungicides such as bordeaux mixture are ineffective.

PERENNIAL  *Phlox* spp.

DESCRIPTION

The perennial species of phlox are showy, long-flowering plants that produce clusters of trumpet-shaped flowers in a wide range of colors. They range from tall, erect plants to low-growing or trailing ones. There are perennial phlox for every part of the garden: Garden or summer phlox (*Phlox paniculata*) is the backbone of the summer perennial border; moss pink or moss phlox (*P. subulata*) is an early-spring bloomer perfect for edgings and in the rock garden; and creeping phlox (*P. stolonifera*) is a woodland native that makes a fine addition to wildflower gardens or as a ground cover in shady areas. For the most part, they are easy to grow and require little care.

Height

P. paniculata (garden or summer phlox), 3 to 4 feet
P. stolonifera (creeping phlox), 9 to 12 inches
P. subulata (moss pink or moss phlox), 5 to 6 inches

Spread

P. paniculata (garden or summer phlox), 2 to 3 feet
P. stolonifera (creeping phlox) and *P. subulata* (ground or moss pink), 3 to 4 feet if left undivided

Blossoms

Phlox bear terminal clusters of showy flowers in a wide variety of colors, including white, purple, pink, blue, and lavender. The individual blooms are trumpet- or funnel-shaped, 1 to 1½ inches across, and have five petals that open into a flat face. Many cultivars of *P. paniculata* and *P. subulata* are available; some have contrasting centers. There are both pink- and blue-flowered forms of *P. stolonifera*. *P. subulata* and *P. stolonifera* are spring blooming; *P. paniculata* blooms in mid- to late summer.

Foliage

P. paniculata and *P. stolonifera* leaves are about 3 inches long, lance-shaped, and light green in color. *P. subulata* is semi-evergreen and bears small, needlelike leaves.

ENVIRONMENT

Hardiness

All three species are hardy to USDA Zone 4.

poorer, sandier soil than *P. paniculata* or *P. stolonifera*. Perennial phlox will not grow well in heavy clay soil, but will a tolerate a broad pH range from 6 to 8.

PLANTING AND PROPAGATION

Planting

Perennial phlox are not generally grown from seed because popular cultivars must be propagated by division or some other asexual means, since seed does not come true from seed. For best results, grow these perennial species from divisions, pot-grown plants, or cuttings planted in spring.

Propagation

Perennial species of phlox are easiest to propagate by division, but they can also be propagated by root or stem cuttings.

PLANT MANAGEMENT

General Care

Remove the flowers of *P. stolonifera* and *P. paniculata* as they fade; shear or cut back clumps of *P. subulata* by half to encourage more bushy growth.

Water

As a general rule, phlox should receive ½ to 1 inch of water per week from rain or by watering.

Feeding

A spring application of compost or a slow-acting, general-purpose fertilizer will serve the basic needs of phlox all season. For exceptional performance, give plants supplemental, light feedings (side-dressings or foliar spray) monthly from spring to midsummer.

Light

P. paniculata and *P. subulata* grow best in full sun, but will tolerate light shade. *P. stolonifera* needs a location in light to full shade.

Soil

Grow phlox in rich, well-drained soil that is moist and high in organic matter. *P. subulata* will tolerate

MOST COMMON CULTURAL PROBLEMS

Flowers Change Color the Second Year or Over Several Seasons

Cultivars Don't Come True from Seed
Although creeping phlox such as *P. stolonifera* and *P. subulata* will produce the same color flowers year after year, hybrid forms of *P. paniculata* may not be so consistent. Seed-sown plants of *P. paniculata* very likely will bear flowers that resemble the predominant parent and produce mauve-pink flowers. If *P. paniculata* is allowed to set seed and self-sow, the seedlings will take over and in subsequent years the flower color and size of your phlox planting will change. To prevent this, remove the flowers as they fade, before the seed ripens.

MOST COMMON INSECT PESTS

P. stolonifera and *P. subulata* are bothered by few insects and can easily withstand attacks by most pests, provided the plants are healthy and vigorous. *P. paniculata* is attacked by several insects. In addition to the ones listed below, corn earworm, stalk borer, and scale sometimes infest *P. paniculata*.

Holes in Leaves and/or Flowers

Beetles
Several species of beetles chew holes in the foliage and flowers of *P. paniculata*. Asiatic garden beetles (*Maladera castanea*) are ½-inch-long, cinnamon brown beetles that feed only at night. Black blister beetles (*Epicauta pennsylvanica*) are black, ½-inch-long insects that also feed on flowers and leaves. June beetles (*Phyllaphaga* spp.) are red-brown, 1-inch-long beetles that are also called June bugs or May beetles. Like the Asiatic garden beetles, they feed at night. The larvae of the beetles are C-shaped, grayish-white grubs with dark brown heads

that can eat plant roots. Fully grown grubs are ¾ to 1 inch long.

Leaves perforated with dozens or hundreds of tiny holes may be victims of the potato flea beetle (*Epitrix cucumeris*). These shiny, black or brown pests are only 1/16 inch long and very active, jumping like fleas when disturbed. Flea beetles, which are especially a problem on younger plants, transmit viral and bacterial diseases. They overwinter as adults and generally feed on weeds in early spring, then move to the garden. The larvae are tiny grubs that feed on plant roots.

For the most part, all beetles are controlled the same way. Where possible, handpick and crush them or drop them into a pail of soapy water. (Wear gloves if you suspect you have blister beetles, for they can cause blisters if they are crushed on skin.) If the infestation is light, this is all you will need to do. For heavier infestations, spray infested plants with a solution of pyrethrum and isopropyl alcohol, mixing 1 tablespoon of alcohol with every pint of diluted pyrethrum mixture. Apply this solution every three to five days until the problem is corrected. Barriers such as floating row covers, like Reemay, can also be used to prevent beetles from gaining access to phlox. For long-term control, apply milky spore disease (*Bacillus popilliae*) to lawns and garden. It will kill the larvae of most beetles. Beneficial nematodes introduced into the soil will take care of the flea beetle larvae.

Leaves Covered with White or Light Green Spots

Bugs
The phlox plant bug (*Lopidea davisi*) is a member of the order Hemiptera, or true bugs, that infests garden phlox. Both juveniles and adults feed on the upper surfaces of new leaves and developing buds. Their feeding causes light green or whitish spots on the leaves. Damage is the result of the bugs feeding with their piercing-sucking mouthparts. Severe infestations can cause deformed growth and young shoots and buds that are dwarfed. Adults are

yellow-green and about ¼ inch long with four black stripes on their backs. Juveniles are red or orange.

Four-lined plant bugs (*Poecilocapsus lineatus*), which are primarily a pest of early summer, also attack phlox, feeding with piercing-sucking mouthparts. They are greenish yellow with four wide black stripes down their backs. Their nymphs are bright red with black dots. They generally cause round yellow to brown spots on the foliage.

Preventive measures are helpful in controlling these pests, several of which overwinter in garden refuse. Thoroughly clean up the garden in spring and fall to discourage overwintering adults and eggs. Handpicking adults, nymphs, or eggs and dropping them into a jar of soapy water is also effective if the infestation isn't too great. If that is not effective, spray the plants with insecticidal soap every three to five days for two weeks. Be sure to spray the undersides of the leaves. In severe cases, try three applications of pyrethrum laced with isopropyl alcohol, one every three days. Spray early in the morning when bugs are least active. If the infestation is heavy, dust plants with sabadilla.

Deformed Shoot Tips and Leaves; Swollen Stems; Plants Stunted

Bulb and Stem Nematodes

Phlox plants that develop swollen tissue and extremely distorted shoot tips and leaves may be infested with bulb and stem nematodes (*Ditylenchus dipsaci*). Infested plants may have narrow, threadlike leaves or ones that are curled or wrinkled. The tips of the stems may also be swollen. Growth is stunted, plants fail to flower, and eventually die. Bulb and stem nematodes also cause many buds to develop at the base of the plant, but the stems are bent sideways. Nematodes are not insects, but slender, unsegmented roundworms that are barely visible to the unaided eye. Bulb and stem nematodes overwinter in the soil or in infested plant material. They spread in the soil by swimming in the film of water on plants, by garden tools, and by animals who carry them from plant to plant. They enter the stomata of young shoots in early spring or summer and also can enter the stems at the base where new roots have emerged.

Dig up and destroy infested specimens along with the soil in which they are growing; do not compost. There is no cure once the plants are infested. Do not grow phlox in the same spot year after year if bulb and stem nematodes have been a problem. Do not propagate plants by dividing clumps. Instead, propagate by cuttings from healthy plants. Stems that emerge in very early spring are often free of nematodes, and root cuttings are also not infested. Thoroughly clean up all garden debris each fall and discard it to destroy overwintering nematodes. Do not compost soil or plant material that may be infested. (Soil that has been removed with infested plants can be heat pasteurized in an oven and then re-used, but this is a tedious process.) Mulching plants in spring may discourage nematodes from climbing up from the soil. Also, avoid spraying water on leaves when watering.

Leaves Stippled with Tiny Yellow Dots; Webby Foliage

Spider Mites

Leaves that are dry and stippled with tiny yellow dots are a sign that your phlox are infested with spider mites, tiny pests that suck chlorophyll out of the leaves. They also inject toxins into the foliage; this causes distorted or discolored growth. Leaves, stems, and flowers also may be swathed in fine webbing. As their name suggests, spider mites are related to spiders. These tiny creatures, which are about ¹⁄₅₀ inch long and barely visible to the naked eye, may be yellow, green, red, or brown. Two-spotted spider mites (*Tetranychus urticae*) attack phlox. Spider mites reproduce most rapidly during hot, dry weather. They are especially a problem on greenhouse-grown phlox plants; inspect purchased bedding plants carefully to avoid bringing home infested specimens.

Severely infested plants should be destroyed, or infested portions cut and disposed of, since infestations are difficult to control once they are well under way. Spider mites can be controlled by washing the plants, especially the undersides of the leaves. For best results, use a forceful spray of water once every other day to knock the mites off the plants; wash the plants at least three times. If that is not effective, spray the plants with insecticidal soap every three to five days for two weeks. To avoid spreading the mites from plant to plant, don't touch healthy plants after examining infested ones.

MOST COMMON DISEASES

P. subulata and *P. stolonifera* are undemanding plants that are bothered by few diseases. *P. paniculata* is affected by several diseases. In addition to the ones listed below, it is occasionally afflicted with rust, wilt, and several virus diseases, including aster yellows.

Stems Turn Black at Base; Leaves Turn Yellow and Wilt; Plants Topple Over

Crown Rot

Although ultimately caused by fungi and bacteria that attack the crowns of the plants, crown rot is a cultural as much as a disease problem. Phlox are susceptible to crown rot when grown in soil that is not well drained. Damaging the crown of a plant, by inadvertently digging into it, for example, can also lead to rot. Crown rot is especially a problem during the winter months; suspect it if no shoots appear in spring. Moist soil around the crowns of the plants leads to attack by both bacteria and fungi. The roots and crowns may be blackened, rotten, and covered with white fungal threads. The whole plant dies in a few days.

Cultural practices are very helpful in preventing crown rot. When planting, select a site with well-drained soil, or improve the drainage of the site by incorporating compost and other organic material into the soil. Keep winter mulch away from the crowns of the plants. This helps reduce moisture and prevents rotting during the winter dormant season. Thoroughly cultivating around plants also helps dry out the soil and discourages the spread of the organisms that cause this problem. Be sure to mark plantings to avoid accidentally digging into them and damaging the crowns. Remove and discard afflicted plants and the soil immediately surrounding them; do not compost.

Leaves Covered with Dark Spots or Blotches

Leaf Spot

Several different kinds of fungi cause unsightly spots on phlox foliage. Leaves may have transparent or brown or black spots, often with gray or nearly white centers. Some fungal spots are surrounded by flecks or black dots, which are the spore-bearing fruiting bodies. Often spots come together to form larger patches of dead tissue. These fungi thrive on moist leaf surfaces.

To control leaf spot, pick off and destroy infected leaves. Also, regularly clean up and destroy dead plant debris in the garden to reduce spore populations. These fungi overwinter as spores in such debris, so an end-of-season cleanup is especially important. Rogue out and discard seriously infected plants, together with the soil in which they are growing. A layer of mulch helps prevent spores from splashing from the soil onto plants. If leaf spot is a particular problem in your area, spray at weekly to ten-day intervals with wettable sulfur or bordeaux mixture, particularly in rainy seasons. (Watch for leaf discoloration with the latter.)

White Powder Covering Leaves

Powdery Mildew

Phlox leaves that are covered with a white or ash gray powdery mold probably have powdery mildew. Badly infected leaves become discolored and distorted, then drop off. Powdery mildew is caused by fungi that live primarily on the surface of the leaves, flowers, and stems of plants, not inside them.

Powdery mildew most commonly develops on plants grown close together where air circulation is restricted, especially on the lower leaves where humidity is higher and moisture is more abundant. Allow ample spacing between plants, and collect and discard all aboveground refuse in the fall. Spray affected plants thoroughly with wettable sulfur once or twice at weekly intervals starting as soon as the whitish coating of the fungus is visible.

PERENNIAL Poppy, Oriental *Papaver orientale*

DESCRIPTION

Like most old-fashioned garden favorites, oriental poppies are undemanding, easy-to-grow plants that provide showy bloom in return for very little care. Originally native to western Asia, these plants put on a yearly display of enormous blooms in late May or June. Although oriental poppies with shocking orange-red blooms are best known, plant breeders have selected cultivars with a wide range of vivid colors, including white, orange, pink, and red, usually with a black central blotch. Poppies are most often used in perennial borders. The plants die down in late summer, after flowering, so these plants are best paired with other perennials or annuals that will fill in after they fade. Oriental poppies make fine cut flowers, although stems, leaves, and roots exude a milky sap when cut.

Height

2 to 4 feet

Spread

Undivided clumps can spread several feet.

Blossoms

The flowers of oriental poppies range from 6 to 12

inches across and are borne one per stem atop tall stalks. The petals are crumpled when the buds open, and the full-blown flowers have a crepe paper-like texture. Flowers bloom in late spring or early summer. There are single- and double-flowered cultivars, and blooms may be white, pink, salmon, orange, or red. Many have central blotches of a second color, most commonly purple-black.

Foliage

Poppy foliage is basal, meaning borne at the base of the plant. It has deeply lobed margins and is hairy in texture. After the flowers fade, the foliage gradually dies down, disappearing completely by mid- to late summer. It generally reappears in fall and persists through the winter.

ENVIRONMENT

Hardiness

Poppies are hardy to USDA Zone 3.

Light

Grow oriental poppies in full sun or very light shade.

Soil

Oriental poppies will grow well in any ordinary garden soil, provided it is well-drained. Well-drained soil is essential for winter survival because the fleshy roots rot under soggy conditions.

PLANTING AND PROPAGATION

Planting

Most named cultivars of oriental poppies are grown from divisions, for the showy flower colors do not come true from seed. Purchased, pot-grown plants can be set in the garden in spring, but late summer to early fall, when the plants are dormant, is the best time for planting or dividing oriental poppies.

Established plants have deep taproots, and specimens transplanted or divided in spring will wilt and usually die. Set the crowns at a depth of 3 inches and mulch them during the first winter for protection. Be sure the mulch isn't packed around the foliage, which emerges in late fall or early winter.

Propagation

Oriental poppies can be propagated by division in late summer or early fall. They can also be propagated by root cuttings. To propagate in this manner, cut 4-inch lengths of root, dip them in sand to stop the milky sap that emerges, and plant them in pots held in a cold frame or in the garden. Be sure to set the cuttings right-side up—with the end that was nearest the plant closest to the soil surface. Plants propagated in this manner should be protected the first winter and will bloom the second spring after the cuttings are made.

PLANT MANAGEMENT

General Care

Once established, oriental poppies require little in the way of regular care. Since the plants are dormant in late summer, and thus easily damaged inadvertently, be sure to keep the plantings marked. A layer of mulch in summer will preserve soil moisture. Plants will need division about every five years to maintain vigor.

Water

Oriental poppies need ½ to 1 inch of water per week from watering or rainfall, especially when they are in bud and bloom. They have deep roots and can tolerate some drought once established, however.

Feeding

A spring application of compost or a slow-acting, general-purpose fertilizer will serve the basic needs of oriental poppies all season.

Cutting Fresh Flowers

Oriental poppies make excellent cut flowers, but the tips of the stems should be seared with a lighted match to prolong vase life.

MOST COMMON CULTURAL PROBLEMS

Foliage Dies Back in Summer

Summer Dormancy

Oriental poppies die back after flowering, generally by midsummer. Be sure to mark plantings carefully so you won't disturb them accidentally after they die back. Combine them with baby's-breath, hostas, or summer-blooming annuals that will fill in the gap once they die down for the summer.

MOST COMMON INSECT PESTS

In addition to the insect pests listed below, oriental poppies are subject to infestation by leafhoppers and root knot nematodes.

Pale or Yellow Spots on Leaves, Leaves Curled and Distorted

Aphids

Plants infested with aphids have distorted growth that may be curled, puckered, or stunted. Leaves may turn yellow or brown, and feeding can seriously damage flower buds or cause distorted flowers. Plants may also wilt under bright sunlight. Aphids are soft-bodied, pear-shaped sucking insects about the size of the head of a pin; they may be brown, green, yellow, or nearly black. They are often found clustered under leaves, and flower buds and stem tips may be covered with dense colonies of these insects. Ants, attracted by the aphids' honeydew secretions, wander over the plants, and black, sooty mold can develop on the honeydew as well. Several species of aphids infest oriental poppies. Bean aphid (*Aphis fabae*) is most common, but green peach aphid (*Myzus persicae*) and melon aphid (*Aphis gossypii*) also infest this host.

Light infestations of aphids can be controlled by washing the plants, especially the undersides of the leaves. For best results, use a forceful spray of water once every other day to knock the aphids off the plants; wash the plants at least three times. If that is not effective, spray the plants with insecticidal soap every three to five days for two weeks. If these pests become a very serious problem, make two applications of pyrethrum, three to five days apart.

Holes in Leaves and/or Flowers

Beetles

Rose chafer (*Macrodactylus subspinosus*), often called rose bug although it is a beetle, is a tan, ⅓- to ½-inch-long insect with a reddish brown head that feeds on poppy flowers. The larvae of these beetles are C-shaped, grayish white grubs with dark brown heads that can eat plant roots. Fully grown grubs can reach ¾ to 1 inch long.

For the most part, all beetles are controlled the same way. Where possible, handpick and crush them or drop them into a pail of soapy water. If the infestation is light, this is all you will need to do. For heavier infestations, spray infested plants with a solution of pyrethrum and isopropyl alcohol, mixing 1 tablespoon of alcohol with every pint of diluted pyrethrum mixture. Apply this solution every three to five days until the problem is corrected. For long-term control, apply milky spore disease (*Bacillus popilliae*) to lawns and garden. It will kill the larvae of most beetles.

Leaves and Flowers Deformed, Dwarfed, or Marked with Small Spots

Bugs

Two species of the true bugs (order Hemiptera)

infest oriental poppies. Their feeding can cause deformed growth and young shoots and buds that are dwarfed. Leaves and flowers may be marred with tiny yellow or brown spots. Damage is the result of the bugs feeding with their piercing-sucking mouthparts. Tarnished plant bugs (*Lygus ruguli-pennis*) and four-lined plant bugs (*Poecilocapsus lineatus*) both infest this host.

Tarnished plant bugs, which are the most serious of these pests, are active, ¼-inch-long bugs that are green to brown in color and mottled with white, yellow, and black. On either side of the insect near the back is a yellow triangle with a black dot at one corner. Tarnished plant bugs appear in early spring, and, if left uncontrolled, become increasingly numerous toward the end of summer. They feed by sucking sap from plants and also release a toxin when feeding that can deform foliage and shoots.

Four-lined plant bugs, which are primarily a pest of early summer, are greenish yellow with four wide black stripes down their backs. Their nymphs are bright red with black dots.

Preventive measures are helpful in controlling these pests, several of which overwinter in garden refuse. Thoroughly clean up the garden in spring and fall to discourage overwintering adults and eggs. Handpicking adults, nymphs, or eggs and dropping them into a jar of soapy water is also effective if the infestation isn't too great. If that is not effective, spray the plants with insecticidal soap every three to five days for two weeks. In severe cases, try three applications of pyrethrum laced with isopropyl alcohol, one every three days. Spray early in the morning when bugs are least active. If the infestation is heavy, dust plants with sabadilla.

MOST COMMON DISEASES

In addition to the diseases listed below, oriental poppies occasionally develop leaf spots caused by several species of fungi. They are also subject to infection by two virus diseases—beet curly top and tomato spotted wilt virus.

Water-Soaked Spots on Foliage; Foliage and Flowers Turn Black

Bacterial Blight
Oriental poppies that develop water-soaked spots on leaves, stems, and flowers are probably infected with bacterial blight, caused by *Xanthomonas papavericola*. The spots eventually turn black and other parts of the plant turn brown. Afflicted plants lose most of their leaves and eventually die when stems are girdled.

Remove and destroy infected plant parts as soon as they appear, and dig and destroy seriously infected plants, together with the soil in which they are growing. Since the bacteria remain in the soil, if problems persist, rotate poppy plantings to another part of the garden.

Leaves with Pale Patches Above, Mildew Beneath; Plants Fail to Flower

Downy Mildew
Poppy plants that develop pale spots on upper and lower surfaces of leaves that are usually covered by a white or gray mold probably have downy mildew, a fungal disease caused by *Peronospora arborescens*. Afflicted plants fail to flower and stems are distorted. Once the fungi spread to the base of the plant, the entire plant wilts and dies. This disease blights seedlings of annual poppies, for the fungus is thought to be carried in the seeds, but also can infect mature plants.

Plant poppies in a location that affords plenty of ventilation, full sun, and well-drained soil. Pick and destroy infected plant parts as soon as they appear. Dig and destroy heavily infected plants, together with adjacent soil. Do not compost plant material that may be infected. Collect and discard all aboveground refuse when the plants go dormant in late summer. Spray infected plants once or twice at weekly intervals with wettable sulfur, bordeaux mixture, or another copper fungicide when molds or mildews first appear on leaves. (Watch for leaf discoloration when using the bordeaux mixture). Several applications may be needed to stop the spread of the fungus. Do not save seed from infected plants.

PERENNIAL Yarrows *Achillea* spp.

DESCRIPTION

Yarrows are sturdy, vigorous perennials belonging to the daisy family, Compositae. Although they can be aggressive, somewhat weedy plants, like many other popular perennials, breeders have developed fine cultivars that make excellent subjects for perennial borders and beds. Blooms of the most popular garden yarrows produce large, tightly packed, flat-topped clusters. The individual flower heads are tiny, but they are borne in abundance. Yarrows, which have naturalized in fields and other neglected places where the soil is often infertile, also make fine additions to meadow gardens. Unless you are planning to use yarrows in a wild garden, it's best to select named cultivars. Most yarrows make fine cut or dried flowers.

Height

Achillea filipendulina 'Coronation Gold', 2 to 3 feet
A. millefolium 'Fire King', 1½ to 2 feet
A. ptarmica 'The Pearl' or 'Angels' Breath', 2 feet
A. taygetea 'Moonshine', 2 to 3 feet
A. tomentosa 'King Edward', 1 foot

Spread

Yarrows are vigorous plants and will spread as far as they are allowed.

Blossoms

Yarrows bear tiny flowers that are only about ¼ inch across. Most cultivars bear them in dense, flattened, 2- to 3-inch clusters atop tall stems. Flowers come in white, mustard to sulfur yellow, pink, salmon, and red. Cultivated forms of *A. ptarmica* have loose clusters of double, ½- to ¾-inch flowers that are white. Yarrows bloom from June to August or September.

Foliage

Yarrow leaves are delicately divided, featherlike, and green or gray-green. They are very aromatic when crushed.

ENVIRONMENT

Hardiness

Yarrows are hardy to USDA Zone 2 or 3.

Light

For best performance, plant yarrows in full sun.

Soil

Yarrows will grow well in average to somewhat poor garden soil, provided it is well-drained. They will tolerate very poor soil, but rich, highly organic soil will lead to weak, rank growth.

PLANTING AND PROPAGATION

Planting

Most cultivars of yarrow are propagated by division and are available as pot-grown plants. Purchased specimens can be planted in spring or fall. Space plants about 2 feet apart. However, some cultivars can be grown from seed as well. Seed can be sown indoors or out, but needs light for germination, so do not cover it when planting. Outdoors, sow seed in spring or summer, up to two months before the first frost of autumn. Indoors, sow anytime, and germinate at temperatures of about 70°F. Germination takes 10 to 12 days.

Propagation

Yarrows are most easily propagated by division, which can be done in early spring or fall, although spring is probably the best time to revitalize clumps. Dig the plant and cut the clump apart; divisions can be large or as small as several-inch-long sections of root. They can also be propagated by cuttings taken in midsummer.

PLANT MANAGEMENT

General Care

Yarrows need very little care. Because they are rampant growers, they do need controlling. Divide plants every three to four years to keep them in check and growing vigorously. When dividing, discard old, woody sections at the center of the clump. *A. ptarmica* and

A. tomentosa may need dividing annually. Some cultivars need staking to keep them from flopping over nearby perennials and so the flowers show to best advantage. Remove spent flowers before they set seed to prolong the blooming season and prevent them from self-sowing all over the yard.

Water

Yarrows should get 1 inch of water a week from rain or by watering until they're established, after which they can be left pretty much to themselves. One of their great virtues is their drought resistance.

Feeding

Yarrows have no trouble growing on poor soils, which is in fact their most valuable asset outside the garden. Rich soil or excessive fertilizer will cause rank, weak growth. A single application of a slow-acting, general-purpose fertilizer in spring is more than sufficient for fine performance.

Cutting Fresh Flowers

Yarrow blossoms make fine cut flowers, although they are most valued for drying.

Drying Flowers

Yarrows make outstanding dried flowers as well and can be easily air dried. The dried flower heads keep their color better if you cut them before the pollen forms. Strip off the leaves so that you have bare stems. Air dry them by hanging them upside down in a warm, dry place.

MOST COMMON CULTURAL PROBLEMS

Seedlings Appear Where They Are Not Wanted

Reseeding
Yarrows can reseed prolifically from year to year, and unexpected seedlings can become a nuisance. Picking or deadheading the flowers before they go to seed can reduce this problem. Their roots also can spread aggressively, so divide them regularly and discard unwanted plants.

MOST COMMON INSECT PESTS

Yarrows are easy-to-grow plants that are seldom bothered by insect pests. With the exception of aphids, they are not seriously bothered by any insects.

Pale or Yellow Spots on Leaves, Leaves Curled and Distorted

Aphids
Plants infested with aphids have distorted growth that may be curled, puckered, or stunted. Leaves may turn yellow or brown, and feeding can seriously damage flower buds or cause distorted flowers. Plants may also wilt under bright sunlight. Aphids are soft-bodied, pear-shaped sucking insects about the size of the head of a pin; they may be brown, green, yellow, or nearly black. They are often found clustered under leaves, and flower buds and stem tips may be covered with dense colonies of these insects. Ants, attracted by the aphids' honeydew secretions, wander over the plants, and black, sooty mold can develop on the honeydew as well. Artemisia aphid (*Macrosiphum artemisiae*) and leafcurl plum aphid (*Brachycaudus helichrysi*) both infest yarrow.

Light infestations of aphids can be controlled by washing the plants, especially the undersides of the leaves. For best results, use a forceful spray of water once every other day to knock the aphids off the plants; wash the plants at least three times. If that is not effective, spray the plants with insecticidal soap every three to five days for two weeks. If these pests become a very serious problem, make two applications of pyrethrum, three to five days apart.

Plants Stunted and Wilted; Foliage Yellowed

Root Aphids

Yarrows that seem to stop growing or turn yellow and wilt under bright sunlight may be infested with root aphids. Root aphids are soft-bodied, pear-shaped insects about the size of the head of a pin. They are generally white, yellow, or dull green in color and each has a tuft of waxy cotton in the back. Both lettuce root aphid (*Pemphigus bursarius*) and sugar-beet root aphid (*P. populivenae*) infest yarrow. Winged forms emerge in fall, and the pests migrate to poplar trees to overwinter in galls on leaf stems. In addition to yarrow, they spend summers on asters, lettuce, and grasses.

Root aphids are extremely difficult to control once an infestation begins. The aphids migrate from poplars to their summer hosts in late June or July. Applications of insecticidal soap at weekly intervals may be of help. Once a bed has been infested with root aphids, replant the following year with plants that are not as susceptible.

MOST COMMON DISEASES

Yarrows are not seriously bothered by any diseases, provided their basic cultural demands are met. Most important is their demand for full sun and ordinary to somewhat poor soil that is on the dry side and very well drained. They occasionally develop powdery mildew, rust, and stem rot—all fungal diseases. If your plants develop problems, see Fungal Disease, beginning on page 340.

CHAPTER 3

Bulbs

If the word "bulb" came up in a word association test, nearly anyone would immediately respond with "daffodil," "tulip," or "crocus." But this group of plants is something of a catchall category that contains more than just the spring-flowering species with which we are so familiar. "Bulbs" includes plants that grow from true bulbs—lilies, daffodils, tulips, and hyacinths to name a few. But it also includes ones that arise from corms (such as crocuses), rhizomes (cannas), tubers (tuberous begonias), and tuberous roots (dahlias). See the illustration on page 383 for a comparison of these structures.

To confuse matters even further, bulbs are often grouped into two general groups: hardy bulbs and tender bulbs, a distinction made on the basis of the plant's ability to survive the winter outdoors all year round. Hardy bulbs, such as daffodils and crocuses, can be planted and left in the ground year after year, exactly like perennials. (In fact, all bulbs are actually perennials, regardless of whether they are hardy or not.) Tender bulbs can't withstand northern winters and must be dug up, stored indoors, and replanted in spring after danger of frost has passed, much like annuals.

In the individual plant entries that follow, you'll find that there are many ways to use bulbs in the garden. You'll also find extensive information on how to care for the many different kinds of bulbs and what steps to take to prevent problems that can occur.

Probably the best step you can take toward avoiding problems in your bulb plantings is to take time to carefully inspect any bulbs you buy. Healthy bulbs that have been properly stored should show no evidence of soft or dry rot on the scales or at the base of the bulbs. There also should be no signs of mold, mildew, shriveling, scrapes, or bruises. Don't buy bulbs that are damaged. They can harbor diseases, such as basal rot, or insects, such as bulb mites. They also won't grow and bloom as well as healthy ones. So, for the best value for your money, inspect before you buy.

If you have mice, voles, squirrels, or other rodents in your garden, they may be your biggest problems as far as your bulb plantings go. Such rodents love the taste of bulbs, especially in winter when food is scarce. They won't bother daffodil bulbs because they are poisonous. If rodents are chewing their way through your bulb beds, turn to chapter 7 to read about how to control them.

Begonia, Tuberous
Begonia × tuberhybrida

DESCRIPTION

Begonias are a large group of tropical plants that are very popular both as houseplants and in gardens, for they produce abundant, beautiful flowers and handsome foliage. Leaves, stems, and flowers are fleshy and succulent. The tuberous begonias commonly grown today, collectively called *Begonia × tuberhybrida,* are a group of hybrids developed by crossing several different species from the Andes in South America. The common name tuberous begonia stems from the fact that they arise from a somewhat cup-shaped, brown tuber, unlike the annual or wax begonia (*B. × semperflorens*), which is fibrous rooted. One look at the gorgeous flowers tuberous begonias produce is enough to convince almost any gardener to try a few. Plant breeders have developed many cultivars. These have been organized into divisions according to plant habit, which may be upright or trailing, and flower type. The single or double blooms usually resemble roses, camellias, or carnations. Tuberous begonias are ideal for growing in beds or containers.

Height

1 to 1½ feet

Spread

1 to 1½ feet

Blossoms

Tuberous begonias have showy, waxy blossoms that come in shades of red, pink, yellow, orange, or white. They may be single or double and can have bicolored blooms or petal edges that are ruffled or smooth. Like all begonias, these plants bear male and female flowers separately, but on the same plant. In areas with cool, moist summers, they bloom from summer right up until frost.

Foliage

The leaves of tuberous begonias are green and succulent. They are borne alternately on the somewhat brittle stems.

ENVIRONMENT

Hardiness

Tuberous begonias are tender bulbs that must be dug up and stored indoors over the winter. Day temperatures below 80°F and night temperatures below 60°F suit them best.

Light

Tuberous begonias grow best in partial shade.

Soil

Tuberous begonias must have a soil mixture that is rich and perfectly drained. They are best grown in raised beds or containers filled with a highly organic mixture—⅔ leaf mold or sphagnum peat and ⅓ sand is ideal—to ensure the drainage they require. Soil should be slightly acidic (pH 6.5). Loosen the soil to a depth of 1 foot when preparing beds for planting.

PLANTING AND PROPAGATION

Planting

Begonia tubers come in various sizes, from 1¼ to 3 inches or more in diameter. The largest tubers produce the largest plants and the most flowers. You can purchase already grown potted plants from garden centers, or start your own plants from dormant tubers, which can be held over and rebloomed year after year with proper care. Tuberous begonias can also be grown from seed, which is very tiny and dustlike. For information on growing from seed, see the entry on annual or wax begonias, beginning on page 26. Tuberous begonia seed can take up to eight weeks to germinate.

Start the tubers indoors in early spring (February or March) to give them a head start before transplanting to the garden after danger of frost has passed. To grow them, plant the tubers indoors in shallow, well-drained containers filled with 2 inches of peat or sphagnum moss. Place the tubers concave side up, cover them lightly with peat or sphagnum moss, and set the container in a warm (60° to 70°F), bright place. Water very sparingly at first—start with a light sprinkle of water on the surface each time the medium dries out. When the tubers begin to grow, water more frequently. When the shoots reach about 4 inches, the tubers are ready for transplanting to pots, planters, or beds.

Plant tubers 1 inch below the surface in a soil mixture that is rich in organic matter and very well drained. Transplant started plants after all danger of frost has passed. Select a site where plants will receive light shade or early morning or late afternoon sun only.

Propagation

These plants are most often propagated by dividing the tubers in spring at planting time. Cut the tubers into sections, making sure each piece has at least one "eye," or bud. Dust the sections with sulfur to prevent fungal rot, and plant.

Container Gardening

Tuberous begonias are superb in pots, hanging baskets, or window boxes. To provide adequate room for roots, select pots that are at least 10 inches wide and 6 inches deep. Planters that are 8 inches wide by 6 inches deep are fine.

PLANT MANAGEMENT

General Care

Most tuberous begonias will need staking, for their stems are brittle and easily broken. Insert stakes at least 3 inches away from the tubers to avoid damaging the roots, and tie stems to them with soft cloth strips. Regularly remove spent flowers and leaves that show signs of mildew to prevent disease problems. The tubers will need to be dug and overwintered indoors, as they are not frost hardy.

Overwintering

Dig the tubers in the fall before frost. Set the tubers, with the fading stems still attached, indoors in a dry, frost-free place. Let the tubers and plants dry thoroughly, then carefully remove the stems. Store the tubers over winter in paper bags in a cool, dry, frost-free place. When storing tubers, inspect them regularly and discard any that are not firm and clean.

Water

Tuberous begonias require a regular supply of water in order to perform adequately. They grow and flower best if the soil is evenly moist but dries out slightly between waterings. Plants kept in soil that is too wet or too dry will drop their flower buds. Check soil moisture regularly, especially in containers. If the soil is somewhat dry to the touch, it's time to water thoroughly. To avoid problems with mildew, water in the morning, and wherever possible, avoid sprinkling the foliage and flowers. Use a gentle soaker hose or cover the soil with a board to break the force of the water.

Feeding

Tuberous begonias are heavy feeders. Plant them in rich, organic soil, and feed every two to three weeks once they begin actively growing. A drench of liquid fertilizer such as manure tea or fish emulsion is ideal. Stop feeding when plant growth slows in the fall. Don't feed plants that have stopped growing, instead withold fertilizer, let them dry out slightly more than usual, and wait until growth resumes before resuming feeding.

MOST COMMON CULTURAL PROBLEMS

Buds Drop without Opening

Improper Moisture; Temperature Changes
Bud dropping may be caused by too much or too little water, especially if plants are allowed to completely dry out between waterings. Although tuberous begonias do best when the soil surface dries out slightly between waterings, try not to let them dry out completely. A sudden temperature change from hot to cold or vice versa also causes buds to drop.

MOST COMMON INSECT PESTS

In addition to the pests listed below, tuberous begonias are occasionally infested with mealybugs, whiteflies, aphids, spider mites, and scale. These pests are primarily problems with greenhouse-grown specimens, however. If you are buying started plants, inspect them carefully for signs of disease.

Plants Stunted; Leaves Yellowed or Covered with Yellow-Brown Spots

Nematodes
Tuberous begonias are attacked by both root knot nematodes and leaf nematodes. Nematodes are not insects, but slender, unsegmented roundworms that are barely visible to the unaided eye. Plants infested with root knot nematodes look sickly, wilted, or stunted and have yellowed or bronzed foliage. Their root systems are poorly developed, may have large galls or knots on them, and can even be partially decayed. Plants decline slowly and die. Southern root knot nematodes (*Meloidogyne incognita*) attack tuberous begonias.

Leaf nematodes (*Aphelenchoides olesistus*) cause irregular brown spots on the leaves. The spots gradually increase in size until the entire leaf curls up and drops. Infested plants are stunted and unsightly. Leaf nematodes overwinter in the soil, in infested leaves, or in the leaves of young plants.

Prune away and destroy any stems or leaves infested with leaf nematodes; do not compost. At the end of the season, when you dig the tubers, look for galls or knots that signal infestations of root knot nematodes. Tubers infested with either species can be treated by immersing dormant tubers in hot (120°F) water for 30 minutes. Replant the following year in sterilized soil. Organic matter in the soil also helps to control root knot nematodes because it not only benefits the fungi and bacteria that feed on them, it also keeps plants healthy and better able to withstand mild infestations. Add lots of compost, especially leaf mold, to the bed before planting.

Leaves Covered with Irregular, Red-Brown Lines or Spots

Thrips

Several species of thrips can infest tuberous begonias. These pests feed by rasping buds, stem tips, and flowers. Infested plants have distorted blooms, petals and leaves are flecked with white, and leaf tips can wither, curl, and die. The undersides of leaves are spotted with tiny black specks of excrement. Adult thrips are tiny, slender, 1/25-inch-long insects and are variously colored pale yellowish, black, or brown. They have four long, narrow wings fringed with long hairs. The larvae are usually wingless.

Since thrips burrow deeply into petal and leaf tissue, they are difficult to control, and early identification is necessary. Inspect purchased plants carefully to avoid bringing home infested specimens. Set out yellow sticky traps as early warning devices about four weeks after the last frost. As soon as you spot thrips on a trap, spray plants with insecticidal soap every three days for two weeks. Prune away affected flowers and dip them in soapy water to kill burrowing thrips. Thrips can overwinter on tubers. Dust the tubers with pyrethrum when storing if thrips have been a problem.

MOST COMMON DISEASES

Leaves Covered with Spots or Blotches

Bacterial or Fungal Leaf Spot

Both bacteria and fungi cause leaf spots on tuberous begonias. These diseases generally do not threaten the life of the plant, but do make the leaves unsightly. The bacteria *Xanthomonas begoniae* cause small, blisterlike spots on the leaves, which enlarge and look transparent. The spots emit slimy colonies of bacteria and leaves eventually die. Fungi that thrive on moist leaf surfaces, including *Cercospora* spp., *Gloeosporium* spp., *Penicillium bacilosporium,* and *Phyllosticta* spp. also cause leaf spots on tuberous begonias. Leaves may have transparent or brown or black spots. Some fungal spots are surrounded by flecks or black dots, which are the spore-bearing fruiting bodies. Often spots come together to form larger patches of dead tissue.

Cultural controls are effective ways to combat both bacterial and fungal leaf spot. Pick off and destroy any infected leaves as soon as they appear. Also, regularly clean up and destroy dead plant debris in the garden. Do not compost plant material you suspect to be infected. Rogue out and discard seriously infected plants, together with the soil in which they are growing. A layer of mulch helps prevent fungal spores from splashing from the soil onto plants.

If fungal leaf spot is a particular problem in your area, spray at weekly to ten-day intervals with wettable sulfur or bordeaux mixture, particularly in rainy seasons. (Watch for leaf discoloration with the latter.) If you suspect bacterial leaf spot, disinfect garden tools with 70 percent denatured alcohol or liquid bleach after handling each plant, to avoid transmitting bacteria from plant to plant. Spray afflicted plants weekly during rainy spells with a copper-based bactericide. Control insects (such as aphids) that may transmit disease organisms. Increase air circulation by spacing plants far enough apart for air to move between them, and remove the lower 4 to 6 inches of foliage to avoid contact with wet soil.

White Powder Covering Leaves

Powdery Mildew

Tuberous begonias are nearly always attacked by this fungal disease, which causes leaves to be covered with a white or ash gray powdery mold. Badly infected leaves become discolored and distorted, then drop off. Powdery mildew is caused by fungi that live primarily on the surface of the leaves, flowers, and stems of plants.

Powdery mildew most commonly develops on plants grown close together where air circulation is restricted, especially on the lower leaves where humidity is higher and moisture is more abundant. Allow ample spacing between plants, and collect and discard all aboveground refuse in the fall. Spray afflicted plants thoroughly with wettable sulfur once or twice at weekly intervals starting as soon as the whitish coating of the fungus is visible.

Roots and Stems Turn Black and Rot; Plants Topple Over

Stem Rot

Tuberous begonias are occasionally attacked by a stem rot caused by *Pythium ultimum*. Stems of infected plants rot at the base and subsequently collapse. The fungus can also invade the tubers and destroy them.

Preventive measures are very helpful in controlling this problem. Plant tuberous begonias in well-drained soil, avoid overwatering, avoid overcrowding the plants, and keep mulch away from the base of plant stems. Remove and discard infected plants, together with the surrounding soil, or cut away affected plant parts with a clean, sharp knife or razor blade. (Cuttings taken from the tops of afflicted stems are generally healthy and can be used to propagate plants stricken with stem rot.) Do not compost infected plants or soil; discard it. Disinfect tools with a solution of 1 part household bleach and 3 parts water or 70 percent rubbing alcohol to avoid spreading the disease. For long-term prevention, lighten heavy soil with a mixture of perlite, vermiculite, and/or peat moss, and provide good drainage.

BULB Canna   *Canna × generalis*

DESCRIPTION

Cannas are tall, heat-loving plants of tropical descent that boast lush towers of banana-like leaves and bright flowers that resemble gladioli or orchids. The garden cannas we grow today are the result of complex breeding programs, thus their botanical name *Canna × generalis*. Perennials only in the Deep South and in southern California where winters are mild, these showy plants are grown as annuals in the North. Fortunately, northerners enjoy them over and over again by digging and storing the fleshy, tuberous roots over the fall and winter and replanting them in the spring. Cannas are planted in beds and borders.

Height

4 to 8 feet; dwarf cultivars, 1½ to 2 feet

Spread

Plants grown as perennials in the South and Southwest will form large clumps. In the North, plants grown as annuals will spread 1½ to 3 feet or more, depending on the size of the rhizome planted in spring.

Blossoms

Canna flowers somewhat resemble gladiolus blooms.

They are about 4 inches across and cluster at the ends of tall, canelike stems. Vividly colored, they may be red, yellow, orange, pink, white, variegated, or speckled. The showy part of the flowers are actually sterile, petal-like stamens. The true petals are small and greenish in color. Canna flowers bloom in mid- to late summer or early fall.

Foliage

Canna leaves may be green, purplish, or bronzy red. They are broad and somewhat paddle shaped. Typically they are 6 inches wide and from 1½ to 2 feet long.

ENVIRONMENT

Hardiness

Cannas are heat-loving plants that cannot tolerate frost. In USDA Zones 9 and 10, and with a thick winter mulch in Zone 8, they can be grown outdoors year-round. They will die to the ground each winter, but the rhizomes will persist. In the North, they must be grown as summer bedding plants, since the roots cannot withstand frost.

Light

For best performance, grow cannas in full sun.

Soil

Cannas grow best in soil that is moist, rich in organic matter, and very well drained. They are often grown in mounded or raised beds to ensure proper drainage. A slightly acidic pH ranging from 6.0 to 6.5 is ideal.

PLANTING AND PROPAGATION

Planting

Cannas are planted in spring as dormant rhizomes or rootstocks. Each section should have two to five "eyes," or buds, on it. For earliest bloom, start these roots indoors four weeks before the last spring frost, and plant them in a sunny location outdoors only after danger of frost has passed. Or, plant tubers directly in the ground well after the last frost date and when the soil temperature is at least 65°F. This will be about the same time for planting corn and tomatoes. Plant the tubers 3 to 4 inches deep and 1½ to 2 feet apart.

Propagation

Cannas can be propagated by division of the rhizomes in spring or fall, at planting time, or when they are being dug for winter storage. Cut the rhizomes into sections with a sharp knife, making sure each section has three to five "eyes."

Container Gardening

Cannas can be grown in very large pots or tubs on the patio or terrace.

PLANT MANAGEMENT

General Care

Once established, cannas require very little care. Very tall plants growing in exposed locations may need staking to prevent damage from wind or rain.

Overwintering

In fall, once the tops of the plants have been killed by the first light frost, cut away most aboveground growth, leaving 6- to 8-inch stalks attached to allow convenient handling of the rootstocks. Carefully dig up the rhizomes, shake the dirt off them, and allow them to dry for several hours in the sun. Discard any diseased or old, woody portions. Store them over the winter in dry sand or vermiculite in a cool, dark place at 40 to 50°F. In spring, divide the rhizomes into pieces, each with at least three to five "eyes," and start the cycle again.

Water

Cannas need 1 inch of water a week from rain or by watering. Avoid wetting the foliage to reduce the risk of diseases. Cannas do well in hot weather as long as they're kept well watered.

Feeding

A spring application of compost or a slow-acting, general-purpose fertilizer will serve the basic needs of cannas all season.

MOST COMMON INSECT PESTS

In addition to the pests listed below, cannas, especially those grown in the Deep South, can be infested with several species of scale as well as mealybugs.

Holes in Leaves and/or Flowers

Beetles

Cannas are a particular favorite of Japanese beetles, which chew holes in foliage and flowers. Japanese beetles (*Popillia japonica*) are ½-inch-long beetles that are shiny, metallic green with copper-colored wing covers. Severe infestations can completely skeletonize plants. The larvae are C-shaped, grayish white grubs with dark brown heads that can eat plant roots. Fully grown grubs are ¾ to 1 inch long.

Spotted cucumber beetle (*Diabrotica undecimpunctata*) also infests cannas. It is a slender, ¼-inch-long insect that is greenish yellow with 12 black spots on its back. It feasts on petals, buds, and leaves and seems especially drawn to light-colored flowers in late summer. Adults overwinter at the base of weeds or other plants and lay eggs in spring. This pest is also commonly called southern corn rootworm because the yellowish, wormlike, ½- to ¾-inch-long larvae feed on roots.

Beetles can be controlled by handpicking, provided the infestation is not too large. Where possible, handpick and crush them or drop them into a pail of soapy water. For heavier infestations, spray infested plants with a solution of pyrethrum and isopropyl alcohol, mixing 1 tablespoon of alcohol with every pint of diluted pyrethrum mixture. Apply this solution every three to five days until the problem is corrected. For long-term control, apply milky spore disease (*Bacillus popilliae*) to lawns and garden. It will kill the larvae of most beetles.

Japanese beetles can also be controlled by pheromone traps. Set up traps a week before the beetles are expected to emerge in your area, making sure traps are no closer than 50 feet from the cannas or any other plant vulnerable to beetle attack, such as roses.

Holes in Leaves; Chewed Edges

Caterpillars

Two species of leaf-eating caterpillars chew holes in canna foliage. Yellow woolly bear (*Diacrisia virginica*) is a 2-inch-long caterpillar covered with yellowish and brownish hairs. Saddleback caterpillar (*Sibine stimulea*) is a reddish caterpillar with a purple-brown patch edged in green on the back. It can sting and has spines along the sides and at both ends.

Mild infestations are easily controlled by hand-picking caterpillars and dropping them in a jar of soapy water. Be sure to wear gloves if you suspect saddleback caterpillars, for their sting is severe. To control serious infestations, apply Bt (*Bacillus thuringiensis*) at three- to five-day intervals until the caterpillars disappear. Dust or spray both sides of the leaves, and reapply after rain. Also, regularly clean up and dispose of garden debris throughout the season to reduce future generations.

Leaves Stuck or Rolled Together with Silk; Foliage Ragged or Discolored

Leafrollers or Leaftiers

Aptly named, leafrollers protect themselves while feeding by rolling terminal leaves into tubes and binding them with strands or webs of silk. Leaftiers feed in a similar manner by fastening leaves together with strands of silk. Both cause foliage that is ragged or skeletonized, turns brown, and dies.

Larger canna leafroller (*Calpodes ethlius*) is a 1¾-inch-long caterpillar that is green with a dark orange head. It feeds by cutting strips of the leaves and folding them over to hide in. As it grows, it eats ever-larger holes in the foliage. The adult is a small brown butterfly with white spots.

Lesser canna leafroller (*Geshna cannalis*) is a 1-inch-long species that is yellowish white with a greenish tinge. It feeds by fastening young leaves together before they have unrolled. The adult is a light brown moth.

Greenhouse or celery leaftier (*Udea rubigalis*) also infests cannas. The larvae are ⅜- to ¾-inch-long caterpillars that are light green or cream to yellow in color with a white stripe down their backs and a green line down the center of the stripe. Adult leaftier moths, which are active only at night, are brown or gray and ¼ to ½ inch long. They lay eggs that resemble fish scales on the undersides of leaves.

Handpicking of eggs and larvae is usually an effective way to control this pest, since infestations are usually light. Remove any rolled or folded leaves, for they shelter caterpillars, or crush the pests in their rolled hideouts. Bt (*Bacillus thuringiensis*) also is an effective control. Apply as a powder or spray every two weeks until the larvae disappear. A thorough end-of-season cleanup is also a helpful control, since the pests overwinter in leaves and other debris.

MOST COMMON DISEASES

Water-Soaked Streaks on Leaves; Flower Buds and Stalks Rot

Canna Bud Rot

This bacterial disease produces water-soaked streaks and spots on new, unfolding canna leaves as well as older leaves. The spots run together or give the leaves a striped appearance. They may be whitish at first, but eventually turn black. It then spreads to the flowers, which turn black and die before opening. On older leaves, the bacteria cause yellowish spots with margins that look water soaked. The disease can spread down the stalks, eventually killing them. A gummy sap may bleed from diseased areas on stalks.

Destroy the rhizomes of diseased plants. Select healthy tubers and dip these in a copper-based bactericide before planting. The condition is aggravated by overwatering, overcrowding, and poor aeration.

Leaves with White Areas Above; Whitish or Rust-Colored Pustules Beneath

Rust

Rust is occasionally a problem on cannas. It causes pale areas on upper leaf surfaces, with powdery, rusty or whitish pustules directly beneath. *Puccinia thaliae* is the fungus that causes rust on cannas.

Rust is rarely a serious problem on cannas. Remove and destroy infected leaves, or in severe cases entire plants, as soon as possible. Collect and destroy all infected garden debris before growth starts in the spring. Control weeds in and around the garden, for they may also harbor rust fungi. To ensure good ventilation, space plants far enough apart so that air can circulate between them. Also, avoid wetting the foliage when watering. Rust can be prevented by periodic applications of wettable sulfur, begun several weeks before the problem normally appears.

Leaves Greenish Yellow or Curled and Deformed; Shoots Spindly or Stunted

Virus Diseases

Cannas are susceptible to two virus diseases—mosaic and aster yellows. Virus-infected plants have spindly, stunted shoots and yellowed foliage. Leaves may be marked with ring spots, lines, pale areas, or mottling, and dead spots may appear on the foliage of infected plants. Stunted growth, dense "rosettes," and small flowers are also signs of virus disease. Aster yellows causes leaves that are greenish yellow and spindly, along with stunted or dwarfed growth. Young plants that are infected show a slight yellowing along leaf veins. Shoot tips branch abnormally and tend to develop into witches'-brooms; secondary shoots are usually spindly. Flowers are deformed and may be aborted entirely. Regardless of the normal bloom color of the cultivar, flowers are often sickly yellow-green. Virus diseases are spread by sucking insects such as leafhoppers. Afflicted plants eventually wilt and die.

There is no cure for virus-infected plants. Remove and destroy them; do not compost. Do not save the rhizomes of plants you suspect to be infected. To control the insects that transmit these diseases, spray remaining plants with a mixture of insecticidal soap and isopropyl alcohol. Make this mix by adding 1 tablespoon of alcohol to each pint of insecticidal soap solution. Spray at three- to five-day intervals, making three applications. The virus overwinters in various perennials and weeds such as daisies, plantain, and gaillardia. Infected plants are not necessarily killed by the disease, but should be dug up and destroyed, since they continue to infect nearby plants via leafhoppers. Disinfect garden tools with a solution of 1 part household bleach and 3 parts water or 70 percent rubbing alcohol to avoid spreading virus diseases from plant to plant. Also, wash your hands after handling infected plants.

BULB *Colchicums*   *Colchicum* spp.

DESCRIPTION

Colchicums are small bulbs with showy white, rose-purple or yellow flowers that resemble the popular spring-blooming crocuses. The flowers are borne in spring or fall, although the fall-blooming species and cultivars are most common. The leaves are grasslike and may appear in spring or fall, depending on the species. Despite the fact that colchicums are commonly called autumn crocuses, they are not related to the popular, true crocuses, *Crocus* spp. *Colchicum* spp. belong in the lily family, Liliaceae, while *Crocus* spp. are in the iris family, Iridaceae. However, both grow from corms and make fine additions to rock or wildflower gardens; they also can be planted under trees. *Colchicum autumnale,* common autumn crocus or meadow saffron, is the best-known species, but many cultivars have been developed as well. Cultivars have large flowers that may be single or double. The corms are poisonous if eaten.

Height

6 to 10 inches

Spread

3 to 4 inches

Blossoms

Colchicum flowers range from 3 to 4 inches long and 3 to 4 inches wide in full bloom. They're flaring or funnel shaped, have six petals, and rise directly from the corm on a tubelike, slender stalk. There are from 4 to more than 20 flowers per corm. Flower colors include white, rose-pink, lilac-mauve, and violet. Most colchicums bloom in fall.

Foliage

The leaves are dark green, lush, and somewhat coarse in texture. They are narrow and grasslike, reaching 8 to 10 inches in length. Each corm produces four to six leaves. The leaves of *C. autumnale* appear in spring and die back by early summer.

ENVIRONMENT

Hardiness

Colchicums are hardy to USDA Zone 4.

Light

Plant colchicums in full sun or light shade.

Soil

Grow colchicums in rich, well-drained soil. Slightly acid soil (pH 6.0 to 6.5) is fine.

PLANTING AND PROPAGATION

Planting

Plant colchicums in a sunny location as soon as you buy them during their brief dormant period in July and August. Place the corms so the tops are 3 to 4 inches below the surface and space plants 3 to 4 inches apart. The corms have pointed growing tips, which should be placed right-side up. Cover the plants with mulch to protect the soil from extreme variations in temperature, which may cause it to heave and disturb the bulbs. Since the leaves appear in spring, select a site where their foliage won't detract from spring-blooming bulbs. They can be planted with ground covers such as *Vinca minor*, commonly called creeping myrtle.

Propagation

Each year after flowering, colchicums produce a new corm atop the old corm, which shrivels and dies as the foliage fades. In addition, they also produce several small cormels that arise near the parent corm each year. Although these plants can be left undisturbed in the soil for years to grow and multiply without attention, they can be propagated by digging the corms and dividing them. Plants can be dug when in flower, but are best dug when dormant, then divided and replanted. Replant immediately so the roots do not dry out. Discard the old, shriveled parent corm and replant the new full-size corm as well as the cormels. Cormels will bloom in one to two years.

PLANT MANAGEMENT

General Care

Like most bulbs, colchicums require very little care. It is important to allow the leaves that appear in the spring to age and die naturally so that the corm can acquire and store energy through them for blooming in the fall.

Water

Colchicums generally receive all the moisture they require from natural rainfall.

Feeding

Although colchicums will flower for years without any special care, they do benefit if fed twice a year. Feed with compost or a slow-acting, general-purpose fertilizer in the early fall prior to blooming and again in the early spring before their leaves appear.

MOST COMMON CULTURAL PROBLEMS

Plants Disappear or Fail to Bloom after One or More Seasons

Foliage Cut Down Too Early; Rodents

If your colchicums disappear entirely or produce leaves but no foliage after a season or two, you may have cut the foliage down too early. If the corms are to produce enough food to bloom in subsequent years, the foliage must be allowed to remain until it dies back naturally. Plan on planting colchicums where the ripening foliage won't be unsightly, and mark the plantings so you won't disturb them by accident. Rodents such as mice, voles, gophers, and squirrels all will eat colchicum corms, and they also may be the cause for your plants' disappearance. Wet, clayey soils will generally cause the corms to rot and die. Finally, although colchicum corms are often depicted blooming in a shallow saucer of water, or on other surfaces without any soil, corms treated in this manner generally will not bloom again.

MOST COMMON INSECT PESTS

Colchicums are seldom bothered by insect pests. It is a good idea to inspect bulbs carefully before buying them to look for signs of infestation.

Foliage Yellowed or Distorted; Plants Fail to Flower; Corms Decayed

Bulb Mites

Colchicums that fail to flower or produce yellowed or distorted foliage may be infested with bulb mites. If you suspect these pests, you'll need to dig the corms and look closely for them. Bulb mites are about $\frac{1}{50}$ inch long and are whitish in color. They have four pairs of legs, piercing-sucking mouthparts, and cluster in tight colonies on bulbs. They favor damaged, rotting bulbs, but can also burrow into healthy specimens. Their feeding causes corky, brown spots on bulbs, which eventually turn to a dry, crumbly pulp. Mite damage also opens the way for bacteria and fungi to attack. They travel from planting to planting by attaching themselves to insects, rodents, or other soil organisms.

Dig and destroy all seriously infested corms, together with the soil in which they are growing; do not compost. Don't plant new bulbs in soil that has been infested. The mites can be killed by dipping the corms in hot (120°F) water for a few minutes. Inspect bulbs carefully for signs of infestation when you purchase them.

MOST COMMON DISEASES

Colchicums are bothered by few diseases, provided their few basic cultural requirements are met. Waterlogged soil, which prevents air from getting to the roots, encourages disease, and heavily packed mulch can encourage problems as well. Inspect corms carefully when you buy them to look for rotted or damaged tissue. Corms should be solid and fleshy, not shriveled, dry, or wet looking.

BULB **Crocuses** *Crocus* spp.

DESCRIPTION

Traditional harbingers of spring, each year the brightly colored, cup-shaped blooms of crocuses emerge from lawns and gardens to celebrate the end of winter. Flowers are held close to the ground and may be white, yellow, pink, lilac, or deep purple. All are about 3 to 6 inches tall, have grasslike leaves, and arise from corms. In addition to the common or Dutch crocus, *Crocus vernus,* there are many other species and cultivars from which to choose. *C. biflorus,* or Scotch crocus, and *C. chrysanthus* both bloom in very early spring before the blooms of *C. vernus* appear. Surprisingly, there are also autumn-flowering species in this genus, including *C. medius* and *C. sativus,* or saffron crocus. True crocuses (*Crocus* spp.) belong to the iris family, Iridaceae, and should not be confused with *Colchicum* spp., the autumn crocuses, which are in the lily family, Liliaceae. Cultivars of Dutch crocuses have larger blooms than most and are favorites for forcing indoors. Crocuses are narrow, upright plants. Plant crocuses at the front of beds and borders, in rock gardens, in woodland gardens, and around deep-rooted trees such as oaks.

Height

3 to 6 inches, some large-flowered cultivars reach 8 inches.

Spread

About 2 inches, but clumps can develop if left undisturbed

streaked in the throat. The stigmas in the centers of the blooms are also brightly colored. The flowers last about ten days, but by selecting a wide variety of species and cultivars, you can plan for several weeks of bloom.

Foliage

Crocus leaves emerge from a basal crown. They are narrow, grasslike, and dark green, often with a silvery stripe down the center of each leaf. Length ranges from 4 to 6 inches. Some species produce the leaves after the flowers; others bear their leaves with the flowers.

ENVIRONMENT

Hardiness

Most crocuses are hardy to USDA Zone 4. *C. biflorus* is hardy to Zone 5. *C. sativus* is hardy to Zone 6.

Light

Crocuses prefer full sun, although they will do fine in areas under deciduous trees and shrubs that are bare in the early spring.

Soil

Crocuses will grow in most any soil as long as it is well drained, but for best results, grow them in sandy or gritty soil. Like most bulbous plants, crocuses do poorly in wet, clayey soils. To improve drainage, add lots of organic matter to your soil, or plant in raised beds. Crocuses will tolerate a wide range of soil pH (from 6 to 8).

PLANTING AND PROPAGATION

Planting

Plant crocuses in fall. For best results, dig the soil to a depth of about 6 inches when planting, and incor-

Blossoms

Crocuses bear cup- or funnel-shaped flowers that range from 2 to 5 inches long and arise directly from the corm or are borne on a very short stalk. They bloom from early to midspring, generally in late February or early March. Those planted in a protected location, such as near a building or other sunny, sheltered area, may flower two weeks earlier than specimens planted in the open. Depending on the species or cultivar, flowers may be white, yellow, blue, lavender, or purple; many are bicolored or

porate organic matter such as well-rotted compost and bonemeal into the soil. Set the corms with the bases 3 to 4 inches below the surface, keeping the pointed growing tips right-side up.

Propagation

Each year after flowering, crocuses produce a new full-size corm atop the old corm, which shrivels and dies as the foliage fades. In addition, they also produce several small cormels that arise near the parent corm each year. Although these plants can be left undisturbed in the soil for years to grow and multiply without attention, they can be propagated by digging the corms after the foliage turns brown in summer. Shake the soil off the roots, separate the cormels from the parent corm, and replant. Discard the old, shriveled parent corm and replant the new full-size corm as well as the cormels. Cormels will bloom in one to two years.

Container Gardening

Common crocuses can be grown outdoors in tubs or pots, but may not survive the winter in the northernmost parts of their ranges. They can also be forced for indoor bloom.

PLANT MANAGEMENT

General Care

Crocuses, like most bulbs, require very little care. It is important to allow their leaves to age and die naturally, so that the corms can make enough energy to produce flowers for the following season. Once planted, they can remain in the ground undisturbed for years. If they are planted in the lawn, be prepared to leave the area unmowed until the crocus foliage has died. Plan on replacing crocuses planted in lawns, or any other location where they must compete with plants other than shallow-rooted annuals, every few years. Although crocuses benefit from a layer of mulch applied after the ground freezes in

fall, be sure to remove the thick coverings of fallen leaves that may fall on plantings at the end of the season. Leaves can become matted so tightly that crocuses can't emerge in spring.

Water

Crocuses generally receive all the moisture they require from natural rainfall.

Feeding

Although crocuses will flower for years without any special care, they do benefit from an annual feeding either in spring just before the blooms appear or in early fall. Use compost or a slow-acting, general-purpose fertilizer.

MOST COMMON CULTURAL PROBLEMS

Plants Disappear or Fail to Bloom after One or More Seasons

Foliage Cut Down Too Early; Rodents

If your crocuses disappear entirely or produce leaves but no foliage after a season or two, you may have cut the foliage down too early. If the corms are to produce enough food to bloom in subsequent years, the foliage must be allowed to remain until it dies back naturally. Plan on planting crocuses where the ripening foliage won't be unsightly. Rodents such as mice, voles, gophers, and squirrels all will eat crocus corms, and they also may be the cause for your plants' disappearance. Finally, wet, clayey soils will generally cause the corms to rot and die.

MOST COMMON INSECT PESTS

Crocuses are seldom bothered by insect pests, although several species of aphids have been reported on them. It is a good idea to inspect bulbs carefully for signs of infestation before buying them.

Foliage Yellowed or Distorted; Plants Fail to Flower; Corms Decayed

Bulb Mites

Crocuses that fail to flower or produce yellowed or distorted foliage may be infested with bulb mites. If you suspect these pests, you'll need to dig the corms and look closely for them. Bulb mites (*Rhizoglyphus echinopus*) are about $1/50$ to $1/25$ inch long and are whitish in color. They have four pairs of legs, piercing-sucking mouthparts, and cluster in tight colonies on corms. They favor damaged, rotting bulbs, but can also burrow into healthy specimens. Their feeding causes corky, brown spots on bulbs, which eventually turn to a dry, crumbly pulp. Mite damage also opens the way for bacteria and fungi to attack. They travel from planting to planting by attaching themselves to insects, rodents, or other soil organisms.

Dig and destroy all seriously infested corms, together with the soil in which they are growing; do not compost. Don't plant new corms in soil that has been infested. The mites can be killed by dipping the corms in hot (120°F) water for a few minutes. When buying crocuses, look carefully for signs of infestation.

MOST COMMON DISEASES

Crocuses are bothered by few diseases, provided their few basic cultural requirements are met. Water-logged soil, which prevents air from getting to the roots, encourages disease, and heavily packed mulch can encourage problems as well. Inspect corms carefully when you buy them to look for rotted or damaged tissue. Corms should be solid and fleshy, not shriveled, dry, or wet looking. Crocuses are occasionally attacked by two diseases that are more common on gladiolus corms—scab and dry rot. Discard any corms that show signs of rot, such as sunken leisions, black or water-soaked spots, mold, or dry scabs. Corms that are unusually light in weight may have dry rot and also should be destroyed. They also are occasionally attacked by fungi, which rot the corms, and mosaic virus disease.

BULB *Daffodils*   *Narcissus* spp.

DESCRIPTION

Daffodils are probably one of the most familiar of the spring-flowering bulbs. They are easy to grow, require little care, have few pests, tolerate a wide range of environmental conditions, and once planted, provide color each spring for years. There are only about 26 species in the genus *Narcissus*, which belongs to the amaryllis family, Amaryllidaceae, but plant breeders have developed literally hundreds of cultivars with a wide variety of flower forms. Most daffodils produce nodding, white or yellow flowers that are borne alone or several per stem. Experts have organized the species and cultivars into 11 different divisions based on flower form and hybrid origin. All arise from bulbs and have narrow, strap-shaped leaves. Whether called daffodils, narcissus, or jonquils, these care-free plants are perfect for adding spring color to beds, borders, rock gardens, wildflower gardens, or naturalized areas. They can be forced for indoor bloom and also make beautiful additions to spring bouquets.

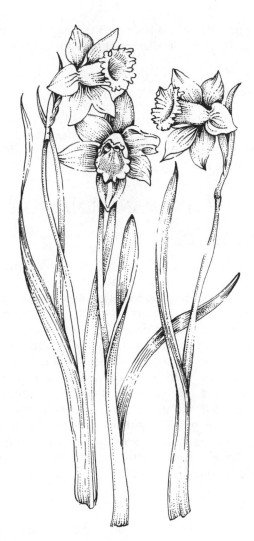

central "cup," called a corona, in the center that is either long and trumpet-shaped or short and cup-shaped. Six petal-like segments, collectively called the perianth, surround the corona, which may have a frilly edge. Daffodil colors range from white to yellow to orange to pink, and many are bicolored. The flowers of the most commonly grown daffodils are typically 1 to 2 inches long and as much as 3 to 4 inches wide. They are borne singly or in clusters. Many are very fragrant. Daffodils bloom in spring. Cultivars are classified according to bloom time, with most sellers indicating whether they bloom in early, mid-, or late spring. By selecting a variety of cultivars with different bloom times, you can extend the flowering season in the garden.

Foliage

Most daffodils have stiff, flattened, straplike leaves that range from 1 to 1½ feet long and about ¾ inch wide. They are smooth and bluish green to green. The tiny species types typically have grasslike leaves that are only 2 to 4 inches long and less than ½ inch wide.

ENVIRONMENT

Hardiness

Most daffodils are hardy to USDA Zone 4. South of Zone 8, where winter temperatures seldom dip below 20°F, gardeners will need to purchase special pre-chilled bulbs in order to get them to bloom. Tazetta hybrid daffodils will grow in Zones 7 to 10 without special treatment.

Light

Grow daffodils in a spot with full sun or light shade in early spring when the foliage is present. A site under high-branched deciduous trees is fine.

Soil

Daffodils grow best in soil that is rich in organic

Height

1 to 1½ feet; dwarf species and cultivars, 6 to 8 inches

Spread

About 6 inches; will produce new bulbs each year and can form large clumps if left undivided

Blossoms

There's no mistaking daffodil flowers—they have a

matter, and they must have good drainage, for the bulbs will rot in damp soil. Like all bulbs, daffodils will not grow well in wet, clayey soils. They will tolerate a wide range of soil pH, from 6 to 8.

PLANTING AND PROPAGATION

Planting

Plant daffodils in the fall by mid-October, or at least a month before the ground freezes. The bulbs need time to grow roots before the soil freezes completely. If possible, loosen the soil 1 foot deep when preparing the bed for planting and add plenty of compost. These plants can be left undisturbed for many years after planting, and the added care at planting time will improve performance. As a general rule, set the bulbs at a depth equal to 1½ times the height of the bulbs, that's 6 to 9 inches deep for most daffodils. Space them 6 inches apart. Measure the depth from the top of the bulb as it rests in the hole, not from the bottom of the hole. If they are not quite at the proper depth, daffodil bulbs tend to adjust their own depth. Be sure each bulbs' pointed growing tip is right-side up. Fill the holes with soil and cover the bed with mulch to protect it from heaving due to temperature fluctuations during the winter.

Propagation

Daffodil bulbs produce smaller bulbs, or offsets, which are attached to the parent bulb, each year. These reach flowering size, and the plantings increase in size each year. (When buying bulbs, look for these double- or triple-"nosed" bulbs. They'll produce more flowers than single-"nosed" ones.) Daffodils can be left undisturbed for years, but as more and more offsets are produced, clumps can get crowded and need dividing. Plants that are crowded will produce smaller flowers and weak, spindly-looking plants. To divide, dig the bulbs after the foliage turns brown in mid- to late summer. Shake the soil off the roots and put them in a basket in a shady spot to dry off for a couple of days. Then gently

separate the offsets from the parent bulbs and replant them all. Smaller offsets will not bloom for a year or two.

Container Gardening

Daffodils can be grown outdoors in tubs or pots, but may not survive the winter in the northernmost parts of their range. They can be forced for indoor bloom as well.

PLANT MANAGEMENT

General Care

Daffodils, like most bulbs, require very little care. After they have bloomed, pinch off the dead flowers, leaving the stems and leaves to gradually die back. If they are planted in lawns, delay mowing until well into June, when the daffodil leaves have yellowed. While the leaves are not very attractive during this period, they are storing nutrients and energy for next season's bloom. If they are planted among other green shrubs, ground covers, or perennials, the dying leaves are less obvious. Double-flowered forms have extra-heavy blooms and may need staking or other support to keep them from scraping in the dirt after rains. For the largest blooms, plan on digging and dividing clumps about every four years.

Water

Daffodils generally receive all the moisture they require from natural rainfall.

Feeding

Although daffodils will flower for years without any special care, they do benefit from an annual feeding either in spring just before the blooms appear or in early fall. Use compost or a slow-acting, general-purpose fertilizer.

Cutting Fresh Flowers

Daffodils make spectacular large bouquets and fine

additions to arrangements. Cut new, barely opened flowers in early morning with a clean, sharp knife. Plunge them into a pail of warm water for several hours or overnight. Add 1 teaspoon of sugar per quart of water in the vase to prolong freshness. The flowers will last four to six days.

Drying Flowers

Daffodils are not commonly dried, but they can be dried with silica gel. To dry in silica gel, cut flowers in full bloom, leaving 1-inch stems. Place flowers, stems down, in a coffee can or other sealable container partially filled with silica gel. Carefully sift silica gel over the blooms until they are completely covered, making sure not to crush the cups.

MOST COMMON CULTURAL PROBLEMS

Plants Disappear or Fail to Bloom after One or More Seasons

Foliage Cut Down Too Early
If your daffodils disappear entirely or produce leaves but no foliage after a season or two, you may have cut the foliage down too early. If the bulbs are to produce enough food to bloom in subsequent years, the foliage must be allowed to remain until it dies back naturally. Tying or braiding the foliage also reduces the amount of food the plants can manufacture. Plan on planting daffodils where the ripening foliage won't be unsightly. Daffodil bulbs are poisonous, so they generally aren't bothered by rodents. Overcrowded plants may produce few blooms or fail to bloom altogether. Finally, wet, clayey soil, which can cause the bulbs to rot and die, may also be the cause of your bulbs' disappearance.

MOST COMMON INSECT PESTS

Daffodils are seldom bothered by insect pests, but it is a good idea to inspect bulbs carefully before buying them to look for signs of infestation.

Plants Fail to Grow and/or Flower in Spring; Swollen Spots on Leaves

Bulb and Stem Nematodes
Infestations of bulb and stem nematodes (*Ditylenchus dipsaci*) cause plants that fail to grow in spring or fail to form flowers. Leaves that are infested are deformed, have yellow-green spots, and small swollen places that can be felt when they are pulled through the fingers. To confirm the infestation, cut across a bulb to look for the dark circles or yellow-brown blotches, which the nematodes cause when they feed on the bulb scales.

Nematodes are not insects, but slender, unsegmented roundworms that are barely visible to the unaided eye. Dig and destroy bulbs that are infested, together with the soil in which they are growing. Bulb and stem nematodes are a particular problem in wet soil. Valuable cultivars that are infested can be treated by soaking the bulbs in hot (120°F) water for several hours. Bulbs treated in this manner should be dried for several weeks after digging.

Bulbs Softened; Plants Fail to Appear in Spring

Bulb Flies
Bulbs that feel soft at planting time, or those that fail to appear in spring, may have been infested with either bulb fly (*Lampetia equestris*) or lesser bulb fly (*Eumerus tuberculatus*). The adult bulb fly is a hairy insect that resembles a bumblebee; lesser bulb fly is a blackish green insect that is about ⅓ inch long. Both lay eggs near the base of bulb leaves. The eggs hatch into larvae that bore into the bulbs. Damage done by the ½- to ¾-inch-long grubs often lead to bacterial or fungal rot.

When buying bulbs, inspect them carefully, looking for signs of infestation such as entry holes or softness caused by feeding or rot. Destroy any bulbs that feel soft before planting.

Foliage Yellowed or Distorted; Flowers Disfigured or Absent; Bulbs Decayed

Bulb Mites

Daffodil bulbs infested with bulb mites produce sickly looking growth. Leaves are stunted or deformed, and flowers may be disfigured or do not appear at all. If you suspect these pests, you'll need to dig the bulbs and look closely for them, or you'll discover them in bulbs that you buy or have stored for forcing. Bulb mites (*Rhizoglyphus echinopus*) are about 1/50 to 1/25 inch long and are whitish in color. They have four pairs of legs, piercing-sucking mouthparts, and cluster in large colonies on bulbs. They favor damaged, rotting bulbs, but can also burrow into healthy specimens. Their feeding causes corky, brown spots on bulbs, which eventually turn to a dry, crumbly pulp. Mite damage also opens the way for bacteria and fungi to attack. They travel from planting to planting by attaching themselves to insects, rodents, or other soil organisms. They are most active when conditions are warm (60° to 80°F) and humid. Bulb scale mites (*Steneotarsonemus laticeps*) cause bulbs that are mushy and rotted and are mostly discovered when bulbs are dug or planted.

Dig and destroy all seriously infested bulbs, together with the soil in which they are growing; do not compost. Don't plant new bulbs in soil that has been infested. The mites can be killed by dipping the bulbs in hot (120°F) water for a few minutes. When buying bulbs, look carefully for signs of infestation.

MOST COMMON DISEASES

Although daffodils can be infected by a variety of rot diseases, most problems can be avoided by inspecting bulbs carefully before purchase and handling them carefully until planting. Avoid bulbs that are shriveled, discolored, or show signs of dry or soft rot on the bulb scales or the base of the bulbs. Healthy bulbs that have been properly stored should show no evidence of rot, mold, mildew, shriveling, or other damage. The papery bulb coat should also be intact. Plant daffodils in well-drained soil and avoid sites where other plants have been killed by rot diseases.

Stunted Plants, Deformed Flowers

Basal Rot or Crown Rot

Basal rot is a fungus disease caused by *Fusarium oxysporum* forma *narcissi* that attacks bulbs, beginning at the roots or at the base of the bulb scales. The fungi cause soft, brown, rotted tissue and spread up through the center of the bulb. Infected plants are stunted and produce few flowers. Crown rot, which can be caused by two different fungi, *Pellicularia rolfsii* and *Sclerotium delphinii*, cause similar symptoms aboveground. Infected bulbs are covered with white mold.

Carefully examine bulbs to look for signs of disease when you are purchasing them. Dig bulbs that produce stunted or diseased-looking growth and look carefully for diseased-looking roots or rotted or moldy bulbs. Dispose of infected plants, together with the soil in which they are growing. Do not compost plant material or soil that you suspect is infected. Handle bulbs carefully at planting time; the fungi are most likely to infest bulbs that have been cut or scraped. Don't plant daffodils in sites where these diseases have been a problem.

Foliage Covered with Streaks or Spots; Flowers Rot

Fire, Leaf Spot, or Scorch

Daffodils are subject to several fungal diseases that cause streaked or spotted foliage that dies prematurely. The first sign of the fungal disease called fire, caused by *Sclerotinia polyblastis*, is red-brown spots on the leaves that may be covered with spores. As the disease spreads, the leaves are destroyed and the flowers rot. Fire doesn't rot the bulbs. It is especially a problem in hot, humid weather.

Daffodil leaves that develop large blotches or spots after the flowers fade may have leaf spot, caused by the fungus *Didymellina macrospora*. Afflicted leaves wither and die before the plants can manufacture enough food for the following year. Consequently, the bulbs don't ripen properly.

Stagonospora curtisii causes the disease called scorch. The leaves of afflicted plants develop brownish spots that are surrounded by yellowed tissue. The fungi infect the top of the bulb scales and the leaves carry them to the surface as they emerge. Gardeners in the Pacific Northwest may see daffodils that develop white mold, caused by *Ramularia vallisumbrosae*. Afflicted plants have white or tan powdery spots near the tips of the leaves. The spots are surrounded by unusually dark green tissue. White mold spreads quickly, killing foliage and flower stalks.

Cultural controls are very helpful in controlling all of these diseases. Pick and destroy any leaves that appear infected as soon as they appear, and clean up and destroy all foliage as soon after it fades as possible. Do not compost plant material that may be infected; destroy it. During wet or humid spring weather, spray plants regularly with a fungicide such as bordeaux mixture or a fungicidal soap to control the fungus. Add a small amount of soap to bordeaux mixture as a spreader-sticker to ensure even coverage. (Watch for leaf discoloration when using the bordeaux mixture.)

Leaves and Flowers Streaked or Mottled with Greenish Yellow; Foliage Spindly or Deformed

Virus Diseases

Daffodils are susceptible to several virus diseases. Virus-infected plants have spindly, stunted shoots and yellowed, streaked or mottled foliage. Regardless of the normal bloom color, flowers are often sickly yellow-green. Virus diseases are spread by sucking insects such as leafhoppers. Afflicted plants eventually wilt and die.

There is no cure for virus-infected plants. Remove and destroy them; do not compost. Do not save the bulbs of plants you suspect to be infected. To control the insects that transmit these diseases, spray remaining plants with a mixture of insecticidal soap and isopropyl alcohol. Make this mix by adding 1 tablespoon of alcohol to each pint of insecticidal soap solution. Spray at three- to five-day intervals, making three applications. The virus overwinters in various perennials and weeds such as daisies, plantain, and gaillardia. Infected plants are not necessarily killed by the disease, but should be dug up and destroyed, since they continue to infect nearby plants via leafhoppers. Disinfect garden tools with a solution of 1 part household bleach and 3 parts water or 70 percent rubbing alcohol to avoid spreading virus diseases from plant to plant. Also, wash your hands after handling infected plants.

BULB *Dahlias* *Dahlia* spp.

DESCRIPTION

Dahlias are tender, tuberous-rooted perennials native to Central and South America. In this country, they are most often grown as annuals and are dug, overwintered indoors, and returned to the garden year after year. Members of the daisy family, Compositae, they produce flower heads that consist of showy ray florets, or "petals," that encircle buttonlike centers consisting of tiny, tightly packed, ray florets. All of the dahlias grown in gardens today are hybrids that descend mostly from crosses between *Dahlia pinnata* and *D. coccinea*. There are literally hundreds of cultivars from which to choose, with flowers ranging from daisylike to very double, and dainty to the size of dinner plates. So many different flower forms have been developed that experts have classified them into groups according to the type of bloom. Gardeners looking for dwarf plants should remember that the term *Miniature Dahlias* signifies cultivars that have flowers less than 4 inches across, regardless of the size of the plant. So-called dwarf dahlias are small in stature, but depending on the cultivar, these plants can range from under 1 to 3 feet in height. In exchange for a minimum of care, dahlias will provide a riot of colorful bloom from midsummer to frost. They also make fine, long-lasting cut flowers.

Height

3 to 8 feet in height; dwarf cultivars, 1 to 3 feet

Spread

2 to 3 feet

Blossoms

Dahlia blossoms come in a wide range of colors and forms. Colors include shades of yellow, red, orange, pink, rose, purple, and white, and many have bicolored blooms. Flower forms include small, daisylike blooms; dainty, ball-shaped pompons; and enormous, curly-petaled wonders. Cactus-flowered dahlias have double flowers with long, quill-shaped petals that curve inward. Anemone-flowered cultivars have pincushion-like centers surrounded by one or more rows of ray florets. Flower size can range from 1 to as much as 15 inches across. Dahlias begin flowering in early summer and continue until the first hard frost in autumn.

Foliage

Dahlia leaves are compound and somewhat coarse in texture with prominent veins and toothed edges.

They are usually medium green. Some have bronze or purplish foliage.

ENVIRONMENT

Hardiness

Dahlias are tender perennials that cannot withstand any frost. Their tuberous roots must be dug up and stored over the winter in all but USDA Zones 9 and 10.

Light

For best results, plant dahlias in full sun. They will also tolerate light shade.

Soil

Grow dahlias in light, rich, well-drained soil. They will do poorly in wet, clayey soils. Planting in raised beds and/or incorporating plenty of organic matter into the soil will improve drainage. Dahlias will tolerate soil pH ranging from 6 to 8.

PLANTING AND PROPAGATION

Planting

Most dahlias are grown from tuberous roots, although some cultivars can be grown from seed. They are very susceptible to frost and should only be planted outdoors after all danger of frost has passed and the soil has warmed in spring. Prepare the soil to a depth of at least 1 foot when planting, incorporating plenty of organic matter and making sure that the site is well drained. Dahlias are good choices for raised beds, since they require well-drained soil. The plants should be spaced anywhere from 8 to 24 inches apart, depending on the ultimate height of the cultivar. Tuberous roots can be planted in much the same way as bulbs. Orient them in the soil so that the "eyes," or buds, point upward and the fleshy roots spread out in the planting hole, about 6 to 8 inches below the surface of the soil. At first, cover the buds with about 3 inches of soil, then gradually fill in as the shoots grow.

Seeds should be sown indoors six to eight weeks before the last frost date. Germination takes five to ten days and plants can be moved to the garden after all danger of frost has passed.

Propagation

The easiest way to propagate dahlias is to divide the tuberous roots, which are dug for overwintering at the end of the season. Divide the tuberous roots in spring before planting, with a sharp knife, making sure that each tuber has a piece of the stem with a bud attached. A dusting of garden sulfur on the fleshy roots will help prevent diseases and insect pests.

Container Gardening

Dwarf dahlias can be grown in tubs or large pots, but they must be watered faithfully, for once they are allowed to dry out, dahlias are extemely difficult to coax into bloom again.

PLANT MANAGEMENT

General Care

All but the shortest cultivars of dahlias will require staking. It's best to drive stakes into the ground before planting. Use rags or yarn to tie the growing plants to these stakes. It's also a good idea to pick off faded flowers. To encourage extra large flowers, leave the bud at the end of the stem, but pinch off side buds and branches growing below this terminal bud. For bushier plants with more flowers, pinch out the central stem after four to six leaves form, so many sideshoots will develop.

Overwintering

To store the tuberous roots of dahlias over the winter, dig them after the tops of the plants have been blackened by the first frost of autumn. Shake the soil off the roots, and leave them to dry for several hours in the sun. After drying, cut the tops off and store the tuberous roots in a cool, dry place over winter. They should be stored dry, but check them every few weeks to make sure they do not dry out so much that they shrivel. Plants that begin to grow during winter storage are receiving too much heat and/or light.

Water

Dahlias need at least 1 inch of water a week from rain or by watering. For best bloom, the soil should never dry out completely, although plants will not tolerate wet, soggy soil. Mulch heavily to retain soil moisture.

Feeding

Dahlias are heavy feeders. Work plenty of compost into the soil at planting time and provide established plants with a handful of slow-acting, general-purpose fertilizer in spring. In addition, provide monthly supplemental feedings throughout the growing season—side-dressings are ideal.

Cutting Fresh Flowers

Dahlias are ideal cut flowers. All the types are gorgeous in both informal bouquets or formal arrangements. Cut them when the flowers are fully opened. Store them overnight in a bucket of cold water in a cool room. When you transfer them to their container, strip off all leaves that would fall below the waterline. Cut dahlias will last seven to ten days.

Drying Flowers

Dahlias are not generally used as dried flowers, but they can be dried with silica gel. Small- to medium-size blooms are the most successful. To dry in silica gel, cut flowers in full bloom, leaving 1-inch stems. Place flowers, stems down, in a coffee can or other sealable container partially filled with silica gel. Carefully sift gel over blooms until they are completely covered.

MOST COMMON INSECT PESTS

In addition to the pests listed below, dahlias occasionally can become infested with tarnished and four-lined plant bugs and whiteflies.

Pale or Yellow Spots on Leaves, Leaves Curled and Distorted

Aphids

Plants infested with aphids have distorted growth that may be curled, puckered, or stunted. Leaves may turn yellow or brown, and feeding can seriously damage flower buds or cause distorted flowers. Plants may also wilt under bright sunlight. Aphids are soft-bodied, pear-shaped sucking insects about the size of the head of a pin; they may be brown, green, yellow, or nearly black. They are often found clustered under leaves, and flower buds and stem tips may be covered with dense colonies of these insects. Ants, attracted by the aphids' honeydew secretions, wander over the plants, and black, sooty mold can develop on the honeydew as well. Several species of aphids infest dahlias, including bean aphid (*Aphis fabae*), green peach aphid (*Myzus persicae*), and leafcurl plum aphid (*Brachycaudus helichrysi*).

Light infestations of aphids can be controlled by washing the plants, especially the undersides of the leaves. For best results, use a forceful spray of water once every other day to knock the aphids off the plants; wash the plants at least three times. If that is not effective, spray the plants with insecticidal soap every three to five days for two weeks. If these pests become a very serious problem, make two applications of pyrethrum, three to five days apart.

Stems or Stem Tips Wilt or Break Off; Leaves Wilt

Borers

If dahlia stems break and leaves wilt, look closely for small, round holes in the stems, from which borers may have expelled their castings. Three species of borers infest dahlias, but European corn borer (*Ostrinia nubilalis*) is the most serious pest. Its larvae are pinkish caterpillars that darken with age and have two rows of dark spots down the sides. Adults are yellow-brown moths with dark wavy bands on the wings. There are at least two generations in the North, the most serious of which occurs in late summer. The larvae feed on buds, flowers, and new leaves immediately after hatching, causing stem tips to turn brown. They then bore into the stalks, where their feeding causes stem tips to wilt. Burdock borer (*Papaipema cataphracta*) is a pale brown caterpillar with three white stripes. Adults are small moths. Stalk borer (*Papaipema nebris*) is a long, slender caterpillar marked with a dark brown or purple band around the middle and several conspicuous stripes running the length of the body. Adults are grayish brown moths. Both of these feed by boring into the stalks.

Preventive measures are most effective when dealing with these pests. Clean up all weeds, especially those that are susceptible to borer infestations, and cut and burn any plant stalks that may harbor overwintering eggs or pupae. Rotating the location of your dahlia plantings can also help control this pest. Make several applications of Bt (*Bacillus thuringiensis*) at weekly intervals early in the season just as the borers are entering the plants and again in midsummer to catch the second generation of European corn borers. Infestations of burdock and stalk borers can be controlled by inserting a wire through each entry hole and killing the larvae.

Leaves Turn Yellow, Then Brown and Become Brittle; Growth Stunted

Leafhoppers
These pests feed on foliage, causing the leaf margins to turn yellow, then brown. Eventually, the entire leaf turns brown and becomes brittle. Severe infestations will cause plant growth to be stunted. Leafhoppers are often strikingly colored, ⅛- to ¼-inch-long insects that are wedge shaped with wings held in a rooflike position above their bodies. They're very active, moving sideways or hopping suddenly when disturbed. Nymphs and adults suck juices from leaves, buds, and stems. Some species may spread virus diseases such as aster yellows, which they pick up in spring when feeding on infected wild plants. Potato leafhopper (*Empoascus fabae*),

a small, slender, pale green insect about ⅛ inch long, is the species that most commonly infests dahlias.

To control serious infestations, spray infested plants with a mixture of insecticidal soap and isopropyl alcohol. Make this mix by adding 1 tablespoon of alcohol to each pint of insecticidal soap solution. Spray at three- to five-day intervals, making three applications. If leafhoppers are a common problem in your backyard, place a barrier such as floating row covers, like Reemay, over plants in early spring. Also, apply preventive sprays of insecticidal soap solution or pyrethrum at four- to five-day intervals for the first month of growth.

Plants Stunted; Leaves Yellowed or Covered with Yellow-Brown Spots

Nematodes
Dahlias are attacked by root knot nematodes, which cause plants to look sickly, wilted, or stunted and have yellowed or bronzed foliage. Their root systems are poorly developed, may have large galls or knots on them, and can even be partially decayed. Plants decline slowly and die. Southern root knot nematodes (*Meloidogyne incognita*) and northern root knot nematodes (*M. hapla*) both attack dahlias. Nematodes are not insects, but slender, unsegmented roundworms that are barely visible to the unaided eye.

At the end of the season, when you dig the tuberous roots, look for galls or knots that signal infestations of root knot nematodes. Plants infested with either species can be treated by immersing dormant tuberous roots in hot (120°F) water for 30 minutes. Replant the following year in sterilized soil. Organic matter in the soil also helps to control root knot nematodes because it not only benefits the fungi and bacteria that feed on them, it also keeps plants healthy and better able to withstand mild infestations. Add lots of compost, especially leaf mold, to the bed before planting. Turn severely infested plots over to a thick planting of French marigolds for an entire season and dig the plant remains into the soil at season's end to discourage these pests. Crop rotation is also a good idea; don't grow susceptible plants on the same plot year after year.

Leaves Stippled with Tiny Yellow Dots; Webby Foliage

Spider Mites

Leaves that are dry and stippled with tiny yellow dots are a sign that your dahlias are infested with spider mites, tiny pests that suck chlorophyll out of the leaves. They also inject toxins into the foliage; this causes distorted or discolored growth. Leaves, stems, and flowers also may be swathed in fine webbing. As their name suggests, spider mites are related to spiders. These tiny creatures, which are about 1/50 inch long and barely visible to the naked eye, may be yellow, green, red, or brown. Two-spotted spider mites (*Tetranychus urticae*) are the most common species to attack dahlias. Spider mites reproduce most rapidly during hot, dry weather.

Severely infested plants should be destroyed, or infested portions cut out and disposed of, since infestations are difficult to control once they are well under way. Spider mites can be controlled by washing the plants, especially the undersides of the leaves. For best results, use a forceful spray of water once every other day to knock the mites off the plants; wash the plants at least three times. If that is not effective, spray the plants with insecticidal soap every three to five days for two weeks. To avoid spreading the mites from plant to plant, don't touch healthy plants after examining infested ones.

Irregular, Whitish Strips on Petals

Thrips

Several species of thrips can infest dahlias. These pests feed by rasping buds, stem tips, and flowers. Infested plants have distorted blooms marred by whitish strips or lines, petals and leaves are flecked with white, and leaf tips can wither, curl, and die. The undersides of leaves are spotted with tiny black specks of excrement. Adult thrips are tiny, slender, 1/25-inch-long insects that are variously colored pale yellowish, black, or brown. They have four long, narrow wings fringed with long hairs. The larvae are usually wingless.

Since thrips burrow deeply into petal and leaf tissue, they are difficult to control, and early identification is necessary. Inspect purchased plants carefully to avoid bringing home infested specimens. Set out yellow sticky traps as early warning devices about four weeks after the last frost. As soon as you spot thrips on a trap, spray plants with insecticidal soap every three days for two weeks. Prune away affected flowers and dip them in soapy water to kill burrowing thrips. Dust the roots of infested specimens with pyrethrum before storing them for the winter. Before planting, corms can also be soaked in a solution of Lysol and water for 3 hours to rid them of thrips. Mix 1¼ tablespoons of Lysol per gallon of water.

MOST COMMON DISEASES

Plants Wilt Suddenly; Stems Rot at Soil Line

Bacterial Wilt

Dalhias that wilt suddenly and appear to have rotted at the base of the stems may have been afflicted by bacterial wilt. Two species of bacteria cause this disease in dahlias: *Pseudomonas solanacearum* causes a soft, wet rot at the base of the stems, and yellow masses of bacteria ooze out when the stems are cut; *Erwinia cytolytica* causes the stems to turn brown and soften at the base, cut stems will appear black inside, and the rotted stems will have an unpleasant odor. The latter will invade the tuberous roots as well as stems.

Preventive measures are helpful in controlling bacterial wilt. Plant dahlias in well-drained soil, avoid overwatering or overcrowding plants, and keep the garden clear of old plant debris. Remove and discard infected plants, together with the surrounding soil, or cut away affected plant parts with a clean, sharp knife or razor blade. Discard infected plant material; do not compost. Disinfect tools with a solution of 1 part household bleach and 3 parts water or 70 percent rubbing alcohol to avoid spreading the disease. The bacteria overwinter in the soil, so avoid planting susceptible plants in heavily infested soil, and rotate dahlia plantings. Also, avoid planting vulnerable plants near solanaceous vegetables such as potatoes, tomatoes, eggplant, and other plants subject to the same disease.

Flowers Turn Brown and Rot

Blight

During wet, cloudy weather, a fungus disease caused by *Botrytis cinerea* can cause dahlia flowers to turn brown and decay. The fungi can spread and rot buds and cover afflicted plants with a powdery gray mold.

Pick off and destroy blighted flowers as soon as you spot them; do not compost. Spray plants with wettable sulfur to prevent the spread of the disease.

Soft Galls at Base of Plants

Crown Gall

Dahlias occasionally develop large, soft galls near the base of the plants. The galls, which are caused by the bacterium *Erwinia tumefaciens*, can stunt plant growth and eventually envelop the stem and kill the plants.

Destroy dahlias that develop galls as soon as they are discovered, together with the surrounding soil. The bacteria can be killed by dipping the roots in a copper-based bactericide at planting time. Don't propagate plants infested with these galls. Discard infected plant material; do not compost. Disinfect tools with a solution of 1 part household bleach and 3 parts water or 70 percent rubbing alcohol to avoid spreading the disease.

White Powder Covering Leaves

Powdery Mildew

Dahlia leaves that are covered with a white or ash gray powdery mold probably have powdery mildew. Badly infected leaves become discolored and dis-

torted, then drop off. Powdery mildew is caused by fungi that live primarily on the surface of the leaves, flowers, and stems of plants, not inside them. Powdery mildew is unsightly, but does not cause any permanent damage to the plants.

Powdery mildew most commonly develops on plants grown close together where air circulation is restricted, especially on the lower leaves where humidity is higher and moisture is more abundant. Allow ample spacing between plants, and collect and discard all aboveground refuse in the fall. Spray affected plants thoroughly with wettable sulfur once or twice at weekly intervals starting as soon as the whitish coating of the fungus is visible.

Leaves with Round, Yellow-Green Spots That Later Turn Brown

Smut

During spells of hot, humid weather, the fungus *Entyloma dahliae* can cause roundish, yellow-green spots on dahlia foliage. The spots eventually turn brown, dry out, and fall out, creating leaves filled with holes. A close inspection with a hand lens may reveal the fruiting bodies of the fungi in the spots.

Pick and destroy all afflicted leaves as soon as they are apparent, and discard all aboveground refuse in the fall. Spray affected plants thoroughly with wettable sulfur once or twice at weekly intervals starting as soon as the spots appear.

Leaves Greenish Yellow, or Curled and Deformed; Shoots Spindly or Stunted

Virus Diseases

Dahlias are susceptible to mosaic virus diseases and tomato spotted wilt virus. Mosaic diseases cause leaves that have light green bands or yellowish blotches or spots. Leaves and plants are stunted. Tomato spotted wilt virus causes ring spots, lines, pale areas, mottling, or dead areas to appear on the foliage of infected plants. Afflicted plants may not show symptoms the first year, but will develop spots and exhibit stunted growth the second year.

There is no cure for virus-infected plants. Remove and destroy them; do not compost. Do not save or propagate roots of infested specimens. Small stem tip cuttings can be made from infected plants if necessary because the virus does not move readily toward the growing tips. Disinfect garden tools with a solution of 1 part household bleach and 3 parts water or 70 percent rubbing alcohol to avoid spreading virus diseases from plant to plant. Also, wash your hands after handling infected plants. To control the insects that transmit the disease, spray remaining plants with a mixture of insecticidal soap and isopropyl alcohol. Make this mix by adding 1 tablespoon of alcohol to each pint of insecticidal soap solution. Spray at three- to five-day intervals, making three applications. The virus overwinters in various perennials and weeds such as daisies, plantain, and gaillardia.

Stems Turn Black at Base; Leaves Turn Yellow and Wilt; Plants Topple Over

Wilt and Stem Rot

A variety of soil-dwelling fungi can attack dahlias at the base of the plants, causing stems to turn black from the base upward and rotting the crowns of the plants. Afflicted plants wilt and die suddenly. Grayish white mold may be present at the base of the plant, and discolored, water-soaked lesions eventually girdle the stems. Once these fungi have girdled stems or rotted crowns or roots, the leaves turn yellow and wilt, stems or plants topple over, and the plants eventually die. Plants are most susceptible to rot when grown in soil that is not well drained.

Preventive measures are very helpful in controlling rot and wilt. Plant dahlias in well-drained soil, avoid overwatering and overcrowding, and keep mulch away from the base of plant stems. Remove and discard infected plants, together with the surrounding soil, or cut away affected plant parts with a clean, sharp knife or razor blade. Discard infected plant material; do not compost. Disinfect tools with a solution of 1 part household bleach and 3 parts water or 70 percent rubbing alcohol to avoid spreading the disease. Keep the garden clear of old plant debris. For long-term prevention, lighten heavy soil with a mixture of perlite, vermiculite, and/or peat moss, and provide good drainage.

BULB *Gladiolus* *Gladiolus* spp.

DESCRIPTION

Gladioli, most commonly referred to simply as glads, are showy, summer-blooming plants in the iris family, Iridaceae, that arise from corms. Since they are only hardy in the South, these plants are planted outdoors in spring and then dug and overwintered indoors. The common or garden gladioli (*Gladiolus × hortulanus*) are often referred to simply as glads.

Plant breeders have developed many spectacular cultivars from which gardeners can choose. The flaring or trumpet-shaped blooms are borne along tall spikes and come in many colors, including yellow, orange, red, maroon, pink, rose, and white. They are often bicolored. Glads are grown in beds and borders and make excellent cut flowers. *G. tristis,* commonly called eveningflower gladiolus, has white or yellowish flowers that are very fragrant.

Height

G. × *hortulanus* (common or garden gladiolus), 2 to 4 feet

G. tristis (eveningflower gladiolus), 20 to 24 inches

Spread

Plants are erect, spreading only about 6 to 8 inches.

Blossoms

The flowers are showy, six-petaled, and funnel-shaped. They are arrayed up the side of erect, unbranched stems. Individual flowers open separately, starting at the bottom of the stalk. Bloom size ranges from 2 to 5 inches. Petals may be frilled, ruffled, or smooth and come in all colors of the spectrum. Many are bicolored with interesting markings. Available flower colors include white, cream, light yellow, orange, light and deep salmon, scarlet, light red, deep red, black-red, light and deep rose, shades of violet to lavender to purple. Only *G. tristis* is known for its sweet scent. The flowers last about a week, but by planting corms at two-week intervals starting in spring, the bloom season can be extended from June to October.

Foliage

The leaves are narrow and sword-shaped with smooth margins. They are medium green in color and grow from 1 to 1½ feet long.

ENVIRONMENT

Hardiness

Glads are considered tender bulbs. *G.* × *hortulanus* is only hardy in USDA Zones 9 and 10; *G. tristis* is hardy to Zone 7.

Light

Grow glads in full sun for best results.

Soil

Although glads tolerate many soil types, they are

happiest in soil that is well-drained, rich in organic matter, sandy, and slightly acidic (pH 6.5 to 7.0).

PLANTING AND PROPAGATION

Planting

In the South, glad corms can be planted any time. In the North, they can be planted from early spring, after the danger of frost has passed, to midsummer. Be sure to allow three months to bloom and store nutrients before the first killing frost arrives in the fall. Plan to make several plantings at two-week intervals to extend the blooming season.

For best results, prepare the soil to a depth of 1 foot at planting time and add plenty of organic matter to improve drainage. Planting depth varies with corm size: Plant small corms (½-inch diameter or less) 3 inches deep; medium corms (up to 1 inch), 4 to 5 inches deep; and large corms (1¼ inches and up), 6 to 8 inches deep. The depth is measured from the top of the corm as it sits in the hole. When planting, cover the corms with part of the soil and then gradually fill in the holes to cover them completely as the plants grow. Space plants in groups 6 to 8 inches apart, or in rows 6 inches apart. Be sure their pointed growing tips point upward. Don't feed the corms at planting time, but provide a side-dressing of a slow-release, general-purpose fertilizer when the plants emerge from the soil and again when the flowers show color.

Propagation

Each year after flowering, a new full-size corm is produced atop the old corm, which shrivels and dies as the foliage fades. In addition, they also produce several small cormels that arise near the parent corm each year. When the plants are dug at the end of the season, separate the cormels, store them with the full-size corms, and replant the following year. Discard the old, shriveled parent corms. Cormels will bloom in one to two years.

PLANT MANAGEMENT

General Care

Provided their basic cultural requirements are met, glads need very little attention. Their tall flower stalks will need staking, however. If they are in rows, simply stretch a string along the row on both sides of the plants and stake it at each end. For individual plants, drive a stake into the soil nearby, being careful not to harm the corm, and loosely tie the glad flower stalk to it with string or cloth strips. Allow the leaves to yellow and die back for about six weeks after the flowers are finished. After this, corms may be dug up to winter over inside.

Overwintering

In the South, corms can be left in the ground for several years before they must be dug up. In the North, they must be dug and stored indoors each year before hard frost. About six weeks after they bloom, once the leaves begin to turn yellow, carefully lift the corms with a spading fork. Gently shake the soil off. Cut off the dying stems just above the top of the corms, and burn or discard them to destroy any pests that may be present. Allow the corms to dry out of direct sun, then dust them with a copper-based fungicide to kill fungi that might rot the corms. Dust with pyrethrum to destroy any thrips that might overwinter on the corms.

Store the corms in a cool (40°F), dry, well-ventilated place. Store corms in single layers in flats or ventilated trays (if stacked, place blocks between them to permit air circulation). They can also be stored in paper bags; in shallow boxes covered with dry sand, soil, shavings, or vermiculite; in open-mesh bags; or in paper cartons.

Water

Ideally, glads should get roughly 1 inch of water a week from rain or by watering. During hot, dry weather, water thoroughly once a week. Avoid spraying water on the flowers once the stems have gotten tall to avoid causing them to tip over.

Feeding

For best results, feed the corms twice, once when the plants emerge from the soil and again when the flowers show color—side-dressing is ideal.

Cutting Fresh Flowers

Cut flowering glad stems for indoor display in the early morning. Use a clean, sharp knife, and harvest when the lowest bud on the spike is just starting to open. Leave at least five leaves behind on the corm to allow it to continue developing. Plunge flower spikes into a pail of warm water for several hours or even overnight. Arrange them in a container, adding a teaspoon of sugar per quart of water to prolong their freshness.

MOST COMMON INSECT PESTS

Pale or Yellow Spots on Leaves, Leaves Curled and Distorted

Aphids

Plants infested with aphids have distorted growth that may be curled, puckered, or stunted. Leaves may turn yellow or brown, and feeding can seriously damage flower buds or cause distorted flowers. Plants may also wilt under bright sunlight. Aphids are soft-bodied, pear-shaped sucking insects about the size of the head of a pin; they may be brown, green, yellow, or nearly black. They are often found clustered under leaves, and flower buds and stem tips may be covered with dense colonies of these insects. Ants, attracted by the aphids' honeydew secretions, wander over the plants, and black, sooty mold can develop on the honeydew as well. Melon aphid (*Aphis gossypii*) is the most common species found on this host.

Light infestations of aphids can be controlled by washing the plants, especially the undersides of the leaves. For best results, use a forceful spray of water once every other day to knock the aphids off the plants; wash the plants at least three times. If

that is not effective, spray the plants with insecticidal soap every three to five days for two weeks. If these pests become a very serious problem, make two applications of pyrethrum, three to five days apart.

Foliage Yellowed or Distorted; Plants Fail to Flower; Corms Decayed

Bulb Mites

Glads that fail to flower or produce yellowed or distorted foliage may be infested with bulb mites. If you suspect these pests, you'll need to dig the corms and look closely for them. Bulb mites (*Rhizoglyphus echinopus*) are about $1/50$ to $1/25$ inch long and are whitish in color. They have four pairs of legs, piercing-sucking mouthparts, and cluster in tight colonies on corms. They favor damaged, rotting bulbs, but can also burrow into healthy specimens. Their feeding causes corky, brown spots on bulbs, which eventually turn to a dry, crumbly pulp. Mite damage also opens the way for bacteria and fungi to attack. They travel from planting to planting by attaching themselves to insects, rodents, or other soil organisms.

Dig and destroy all seriously infested corms, together with the soil in which they are growing; do not compost. Don't plant new corms in soil that has been infested. The mites can be killed by dipping the corms in hot (120°F) water for a few minutes. When buying corms, look carefully for signs of infestation.

Irregular, Whitish Gray Streaks on Petals

Thrips

Several species of thrips can infest glads. These pests feed by rasping buds, stem tips, and flowers, as well as the corms while they are in storage. Infested plants have distorted blooms marred by whitish gray strips or lines that seem to glisten. Infested flowers and foliage eventually turn brown, and the undersides of leaves are spotted with tiny black specks of excrement. Seriously infested plants may fail to flower altogether. Corms that have been infested during the winter become sticky and rough in texture and are generally darker than healthy corms. Adult thrips are tiny, slender, 1/25-inch-long insects that are variously colored pale yellowish, black, or brown. They have four long, narrow wings fringed with long hairs. The larvae are usually wingless. There are several generations per year.

Since thrips burrow deeply into petal and leaf tissue, they are difficult to control, and early identification is necessary. Set out yellow sticky traps as early warning devices about four weeks after the last frost. As soon as you spot thrips on a trap, spray plants with insecticidal soap every three days for two weeks. Prune away affected flowers and dip them in soapy water to kill burrowing thrips. Dust the roots of infested specimens with pyrethrum before storing them for the winter. This will also take care of other pests, including tulip bulb aphid (*Dysaphis tulipae*) and grape mealybug (*Pseudococcus maritimus*), that may crop up in storage. Before planting, corms can also be soaked in a solution of Lysol and water for 3 hours to rid them of thrips. Mix 1¼ tablespoons of Lysol per gallon of water.

MOST COMMON DISEASES

Corms are subject to several fungus diseases that develop during storage. Fortunately, proper handling can go a long way toward averting these problems. Dig the corms carefully, dry them completely before separating the old, shriveled corm from the new one, and dust them with a copper-based fungicide before storage. Avoid damaging the corms, for cuts and scrapes can leave them open to invasion by fungi. Discard any corms that show signs of rot, such as sunken leisions, black or water-soaked spots, mold, or dry scabs. Corms that are unusually light in weight may have dry rot and also should be destroyed. Don't add infected plant material to the compost heap; discard or destroy it. Inspect stored corms periodically during the winter, so that fungi don't spread undetected. Corms that are mildly infected may not show signs of rot at planting time, but sprout and then turn yellow and/or wilt suddenly after planting. In addition to these problems, bacteria can cause similar symptoms. Glads are also subject to virus diseases that cause streaked or distorted flowers. Corms of infected plants should be destroyed.

BULB *Hyacinth*   *Hyacinthus orientalis*

DESCRIPTION

A favorite among the spring bulbs, hyacinths are grown for their colorful, heavily scented flowers that appear in spring. Members of the lily family, Liliaceae, they arise from bulbs and produce stiff, football-shaped spikes of flowers and strap-shaped leaves. These plants are commonly referred to as garden, common, or Dutch hyacinths. They can be planted in beds and borders and also are fine for forcing indoors. Hyacinths also make excellent cut flowers.

Height

10 to 12 inches

Spread

6 to 9 inches

Blossoms

Heavily scented hyacinth flowers are tubular or bell-shaped with six waxy petals that curve backward. Flowers appear in spring and are carried in dense, blunt spikes that stand erect on thick stalks. Each bulb produces only one such spike. Colors include white, pink, and lilac-blue.

Foliage

Leaves are narrow and straplike with smooth edges. They grow up to 1 foot long and ¾ inch wide.

ENVIRONMENT

Hardiness

Hyacinths are hardy to USDA Zone 5. Mulch them heavily in the northern part of their range to protect the shoots that emerge in early spring.

Light

Hyacinths do best in full sun.

Soil

Like all bulbs, hyacinths require soil that drains well. They do best in well-drained soil that is rich in organic matter and won't tolerate wet, clayey soils. The pH can range from 6 to 8.

PLANTING AND PROPAGATION

Planting

Plant hyacinths in the fall by mid-October, or at least a month before the ground freezes. The bulbs need time to grow roots before the soil freezes completely. If possible, loosen the soil 1 foot deep when preparing the bed for planting and add plenty of compost. Plant hyacinth bulbs 5 to 6 inches deep and 6 to 8 inches apart. Measure the depth from the top of the bulb as it rests in the hole, not from the bottom of the hole. If they are not quite at the proper depth, bulbs tend to adjust their own depth.

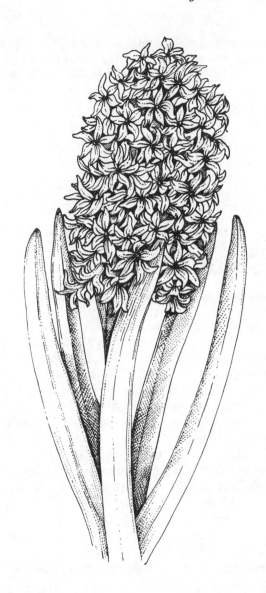

Be sure each bulb's pointed growing tip is right-side up. Fill the holes with soil and cover the bed with mulch to protect it from heaving due to temperature fluctuations during the winter.

Propagation

Hyacinths are difficult to propagate and don't generally multiply the way daffodils do. However, they can be propagated by cutting an X in the base of the bulb; do this in the fall when the bulbs are planted. Small bulblets will form along the cut. The following spring, after the flowers fade, dig the bulbs. Then separate and replant the bulblets. They will bloom in two to three years.

Container Gardening

Hyacinths are easy to force for indoor bloom.

PLANT MANAGEMENT

General Care

Hyacinths, like most bulbs, require very little care. However, because they are tall and top-heavy when in bloom, they may need staking in blustery spring weather. Try to select a site that is protected from strong wind. Be sure not to damage the bulb when staking plants, and use yarn or rags to tie the brittle stems. Also, cut off the flower heads after blooming to prevent seeds from forming and direct the plant's energies toward producing food for next season's flowers. Leave the stalk and the leaves to age and die naturally. While the leaves are not very attractive during this period, they are storing nutrients and energy for next season's bloom. Large, newly planted bulbs will produce extra-large flower clusters the first season after planting, smaller clusters thereafter. Although hyacinths, more than other bulbs, tend to "wear out" and need to be replaced, a regular fertilizing program will keep them vigorous for several years.

Water

Hyacinths generally receive all the moisture they require from natural rainfall.

Feeding

Although hyacinths will flower for years without any special care, they do benefit from an annual feeding either in spring just before the blooms appear or in early fall. Use compost or a slow-acting, general-purpose fertilizer.

Cutting Fresh Flowers

Hyacinth flowers make sturdy, fragrant additions to floral arrangements. Cut them just as they are coming into bloom. Use a sharp knife and cut the stalk down near the soil.

MOST COMMON INSECT PESTS

Hyacinths are seldom seriously bothered by insect pests, but it is a good idea to inspect bulbs carefully before buying them to look for signs of infestation.

Pale or Yellow Spots on Leaves, Leaves Curled and Distorted

Aphids

Plants infested with aphids have distorted growth that may be curled, puckered, or stunted. Leaves may turn yellow or brown, and feeding can seriously damage flower buds or cause distorted flowers. Aphids are soft-bodied, pear-shaped sucking insects about the size of the head of a pin; they may be brown, green, yellow, or nearly black. They are often found clustered under leaves, and flower buds and stem tips may be covered with dense colonies of these insects. Ants, attracted by the aphids' honeydew secretions, wander over the plants, and black, sooty mold can develop on the honeydew as well. Both bean aphid (*Aphis fabae*) and green peach aphid (*Myzus persicae*) infest hyacinths, and these pests carry virus diseases to the plants.

Light infestations of aphids can be controlled by washing the plants, especially the undersides of the leaves. For best results, use a forceful spray of water once every other day to knock the aphids off the plants; wash the plants at least three times. If that is not effective, spray the plants with insecticidal soap every three to five days for two weeks. If these pests become a very serious problem, make two applications of pyrethrum, three to five days apart.

Plants Fail to Grow and/or Flower in Spring; Swollen Spots on Leaves

Bulb and Stem Nematodes

Infestations of bulb and stem nematodes (*Ditylenchus dipsaci*) cause plants that fail to grow in spring or fail to form flowers. Leaves that are infested are deformed, have yellow-green spots, and small swollen places that can be felt when they are pulled through the fingers. To confirm the infestation, cut across a bulb to look for the dark circles or yellow-brown blotches, which the nematodes cause when they feed, on the bulb scales.

Nematodes are not insects, but slender, unsegmented roundworms that are barely visible to the unaided eye. Dig and destroy bulbs that are infested, together with the soil in which they are growing; do not compost. Bulb and stem nematodes are a particular problem in wet soil. Valuable cultivars that are infested can be treated by soaking the bulbs in hot (120°F) water for several hours. Bulbs treated in this manner should be dried for several weeks before planting or storing.

Bulbs Softened; Plants Yellowed or Fail to Appear in Spring

Bulb Flies

Bulbs that feel soft at planting time, or those that fail to appear in spring, may have been infested with lesser bulb fly (*Eumerus tuberculatus*). The adult is a blackish green insect that is about ⅓ inch long. It lays eggs near the base of bulb leaves. The eggs hatch into larvae that bore into the bulbs. Damage done by the ½- to ¾-inch-long grubs often leads to bacterial or fungal rot.

When buying bulbs, inspect them carefully, looking for signs of infestation such as entry holes or softness caused by feeding or rot. Destroy any bulbs that feel soft before planting.

Foliage Yellowed or Distorted; Bulbs Decayed

Bulb Mites

Hyacinth bulbs infested with bulb mites produce sickly looking growth. Leaves are stunted or deformed, and flowers may be disfigured or do not appear at all. If you suspect these pests, you'll need to dig the bulbs and look closely for them, or you'll discover them in bulbs that you buy or have stored for forcing. Bulb mites (*Rhizoglyphus echinopus*) are about ¹⁄₅₀ to ¹⁄₂₅ inch long and are whitish in color. They have four pairs of legs, piercing-sucking mouthparts, and cluster in large colonies on bulbs. They favor damaged, rotting bulbs, but can also burrow into healthy specimens. Their feeding causes corky, brown spots on bulbs, which eventually turn to a dry, crumbly pulp. Mite damage also opens the way for bacteria and fungi to attack. They travel from planting to planting by attaching themselves to insects, rodents, or other soil organisms.

Dig and destroy all seriously infested bulbs, together with the soil in which they are growing; do not compost. Don't plant new bulbs in soil that has been infested. The mites can be killed by dipping the bulbs in hot (120°F) water for a few minutes. When buying bulbs, look carefully for signs of infestation.

MOST COMMON DISEASES

Although hyacinths can be infected by a variety of rot diseases, most problems can be avoided by inspecting bulbs carefully before purchase and handling them carefully until planting. Avoid bulbs that are shriveled, discolored, or show signs of dry or soft rot on the bulb scales or the base of the bulbs. Healthy bulbs that have been properly stored should show no evidence of rot, mold, mildew, shriveling, or other damage. The papery bulb coat should also be intact. Plant hyacinths in well-drained soil, and avoid sites where other plants have been killed by rot diseases. In addition to the rot diseases listed below, hyacinths are sometimes attacked by gray mold during cold, wet weather. This disease rots the flowers. It can be controlled by destroying diseased flowers and spraying with a fungicide such as bordeaux mixture. (Watch for leaf discoloration when using.)

Plants Fail to Flower or Flowers Are Deformed; Stalks Rot

Soft Rot
Hyacinth bulbs that fail to flower altogether, or that produce disfigured, irregularly shaped flowers, may be infected with the bacterial disease soft rot, caused by *Pectobacterium carotovorum*. Infected plants produce stalks that rot and collapse, and bulbs develop a thick, slimy rot that is foul smelling. Soft rot can be a problem if hyacinths are grown in wet, poorly drained soil, or if bulbs have been stored improperly.

Inspect bulbs carefully when buying them, and don't buy hyacinths that may be infected. Plant in well-drained soil, and don't water the plants excessively. Dig and destroy any infected bulbs, together with the soil in which they are growing. Do not compost material you suspect to be infected. Disinfect tools with a solution of 1 part household bleach and 3 parts water or 70 percent rubbing alcohol to avoid spreading the disease.

Leaves and Flowers Streaked or Mottled with Greenish Yellow; Foliage Spindly or Deformed

Virus Diseases
Hyacinths are susceptible to mosaic virus disease. Virus-infected plants have spindly, stunted shoots and yellowed, streaked or mottled foliage. Regardless of the normal bloom color, flowers are often sickly yellow-green. Virus diseases are spread by sucking insects such as leafhoppers. Afflicted plants eventually wilt and die.

There is no cure for virus-infected plants. Remove and destroy them; do not compost. Don't save the rhizomes of plants you suspect to be infected. To control the insects that transmit these diseases, spray remaining plants with a mixture of insecticidal soap and isopropyl alcohol. Make this mix by adding 1 tablespoon of alcohol to each pint of insecticidal soap solution. Spray at three- to five-day intervals, making three applications. The virus overwinters in various perennials and weeds such as daisies, plantain, and gaillardia. Infected plants are not necessarily killed by the disease, but should be dug up and destroyed, since they continue to infect nearby plants via aphids or leafhoppers. Disinfect garden tools with a solution of 1 part household bleach and 3 parts water or 70 percent rubbing alcohol to avoid spreading virus diseases from plant to plant. Also, wash your hands after handling infected plants.

Flower Stalks Water Soaked; Stripes on Leaves

Yellow Rot
Yellow rot is a bacterial disease caused by *Xanthomonas hyacinthi,* which primarily attacks hyacinths that have been grown in wet, poorly drained soil. The leaves develop water-soaked stripes at the tips, which eventually turn brown and die. Flower stalks also develop water-soaked splotches that turn brown. Bulbs have rotted spots at first and then rot completely. The disease is spread by wind, by splashing rain, and by carrying the bacteria from plant to plant on tools.

Carefully examine bulbs to look for signs of disease when you are purchasing them. Plant in well-drained soil, and don't water the plants excessively. Dig and destroy any infected bulbs, together with the soil in which they are growing. Do not compost material you suspect to be infected. Disinfect tools with a solution of 1 part household bleach and 3 parts water or 70 percent rubbing alcohol to avoid spreading the disease.

BULB *Irises* *Iris* spp.

DESCRIPTION

Irises belong to a large genus that contains stately perennials that arise from stout rhizomes, as well as species that arise from bulbs and add color to the spring garden. Both types have swordlike leaves and come in a wide variety of colors. Bulbous irises,

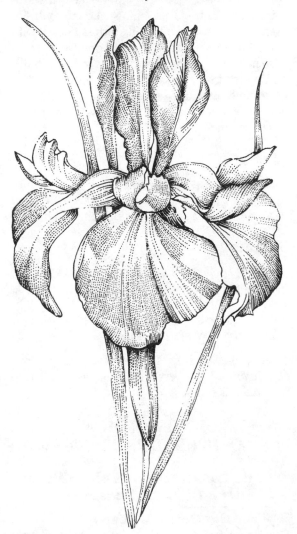

the species that are treated here, are used in rock gardens and in borders and can be overplanted with small, shallow-rooted annuals. They also can be forced indoors in pots. (For information on the rhizomatous species, see the entry on perennial irises, beginning on page 179.) Perhaps the best known of the bulbous species are the so-called Dutch irises, which were developed by plant breeders from crosses between several species, primarily *Iris xiphium*, Spanish iris. For this reason, Dutch irises are generally included with *I. xiphium*. The taller-growing species of bulbous irises make attractive additions to spring bouquets.

Height

I. danfordiae, 2 to 4 inches at flowering time; leaves lengthen to 1 foot after flowering

I. reticulata, 8 to 10 inches at flowering time; leaves lengthen to 1½ feet after flowering

I. xiphium (Spanish and Dutch irises), 20 to 24 inches

Spread

I. danfordiae, 4 to 6 inches

I. reticulata, 4 to 6 inches, but plants will spread and develop small clumps after several seasons

I. xiphium (Spanish and Dutch irises), 4 to 6 inches

Blossoms

All irises have unique, six-petaled flowers: three of the petals, called standards, are erect; the other three, called falls, hang down or point outward. *I. danfordiae* has 1-inch-long flowers with falls that are yellow spotted with olive green. The standards are erect, bristlelike structures. *I. reticulata* bears

3½-inch flowers that usually are violet-purple with a yellow crest. Selections with pale blue and deep purple flowers are available.

Foliage

The bulbous irises have leaves that are narrow and grasslike. *I. danfordiae* and *I. reticulata* have leaves that are four-sided. *I. xiphium* has leaves that are nearly round.

ENVIRONMENT

Hardiness

The bulbous irises are generally hardy to USDA Zone 5.

Light

Irises should be grown in full sun.

Soil

Plant bulbous irises in well-drained soil that is rich in organic matter. They will not grow well in wet, clayey soil. They prefer a neutral soil (pH 7).

PLANTING AND PROPAGATION

Planting

Bulbous irises are planted in fall. For best results, prepare the soil to a depth of about 6 inches and plant the bulbs 3 to 4 inches deep. Planting *I. danfordiae* at least 4 inches deep helps discourage the bulbs from producing many nonflowering size bulblets. Space plants 3 to 5 inches apart.

Propagation

Plants of *I. reticulata* can be propagated by digging the clumps in the fall, separating the bulbs, and replanting. Although *I. danfordiae* tends to produce many small bulblets, it and *I. xiphium* tend to die out after one or two seasons.

PLANT MANAGEMENT

General Care

As with all bulbs, the foliage of these plants must be allowed to mature and ripen naturally if the plants are to bloom the following year. Plants of *I. reticulata* will return year after year, provided the foliage isn't cut back and the soil is well drained. However, the other bulbous irises tend to die out after the first season, and many gardeners replace them each year. Try protecting Spanish and Dutch irises in winter by planting them in a sheltered, south- or west-facing site and mulching with salt hay or with cut evergreen branches. Spanish and Dutch irises also need to remain dry during the summer; bulbs can be left in the ground after the foliage dies, or they can be dug, dried for several hours in the sun, stored in open boxes during the summer, and replanted in fall.

Water

Bulbous irises generally receive all the moisture they require from natural rainfall. Spanish and Dutch irises should not be watered during the summer.

Feeding

A spring application of compost or a slow-acting, general-purpose fertilizer will serve the basic needs of these plants all season.

Cutting Fresh Flowers

Spanish and Dutch irises can be cut for arrangements. *I. danfordiae* is a very short-stemmed species; *I. reticulata* is stemless.

MOST COMMON CULTURAL PROBLEMS

Plants Disappear or Fail to Bloom after One or More Seasons

Foliage Cut Down Too Early

If your irises disappear entirely or produce leaves

but no foliage after a season or two, you may have cut the foliage down too early. If the bulbs are to produce enough food to bloom in subsequent years, the foliage must be allowed to remain until it dies back naturally. *I. reticulata* will return year after year, provided this condition is met and the soil in which it is growing is well drained. However, *I. danfordiae* and *I. xiphium* are not so accommodating. They tend to die out after a season or two in most gardens. *I. danfordiae* often will produce many small bulbils, which produce foliage but no flowers. One reason may be that these species require hot, dry conditions in summer after the foliage fades. Try digging, storing, and replanting the bulbs.

MOST COMMON INSECT PESTS

In addition to the pests listed below, bulbous irises can be attacked by the same pests that infest the rhizomatous species. (See the perennial iris entry, beginning on page 179.)

Bulbs Softened; Plants Yellowed or Fail to Appear in Spring

Bulb Flies

Bulbs that feel soft at planting time, or those that fail to appear in spring, may have been infested with lesser bulb fly (*Eumerus tuberculatus*), a blackish green insect that is about 1/3 inch long. It lays eggs near the base of bulb leaves. The eggs hatch into larvae that bore into the bulbs. Damage done by the 1/2- to 3/4-inch-long grubs often leads to bacterial or fungal rot.

When buying bulbs, inspect them carefully, looking for signs of infestation such as entry holes or softness caused by feeding or rot. Destroy any bulbs that feel soft before planting.

Foliage Yellowed or Distorted; Flowers Disfigured or Absent; Bulbs Decayed

Bulb Mites

Iris bulbs infested with bulb mites produce sickly looking growth. Leaves are stunted or deformed, and flowers may be disfigured or do not appear at all. If you suspect these pests, you'll need to dig the bulbs and look closely for them, or you'll discover them in bulbs that you buy or have stored for forcing. Bulb mites (*Rhizoglyphus echinopus*) are about 1/50 to 1/25 inch long and are whitish in color. They have four pairs of legs, piercing-sucking mouthparts, and cluster in large colonies on bulbs. They favor damaged, rotting bulbs, but can also burrow into healthy specimens. Their feeding causes corky, brown spots on bulbs, which eventually turn to a dry, crumbly pulp. Mite damage also opens the way for bacteria and fungi to attack. They travel from planting to planting by attaching themselves to insects, rodents, or other soil organisms.

Dig and destroy all seriously infested bulbs, together with the soil in which they are growing; do not compost. Don't plant new bulbs in soil that has been infested. The mites can be killed by dipping the bulbs in hot (120°F) water for a few minutes. When buying bulbs, look carefully for signs of infestation.

MOST COMMON DISEASES

Although irises can be infected by a variety of rot diseases, most problems can be avoided by inspecting bulbs carefully before purchase and handling them carefully until planting. Avoid bulbs that are shriveled, discolored, or show signs of dry or soft rot on the bulb scales or the base of the bulbs. Healthy bulbs that have been properly stored should show no evidence of rot, mold, mildew, shriveling, or other damage. The papery bulb coat should also be intact. Plant irises in well-drained soil, and avoid sites where other plants have been killed by rot diseases. In addition to the rot diseases listed below, bulbous irises are sometimes attacked by gray mold during cold, wet weather. This disease rots the flowers. It can be controlled by destroying diseased flowers and spraying with a fungicide such as bordeaux mixture. (Watch for leaf discoloration when using.) They also can be attacked by the same diseases that infest the rhizomatous species. (See the perennial iris entry, beginning on page 179.)

Plants Stunted; Flowers Deformed

Basal Rot or Crown Rot

Basal rot is a fungus disease caused by *Fusarium oxysporum* that attacks bulbs beginning at the roots or at the base of the bulb scales. The fungi cause soft, brown, rotted tissue and spread up through the center of the bulb. Infected plants are stunted and produce few flowers. Crown rot, caused by *Pellicularia rolfsii*, causes similar symptoms aboveground. Infected bulbs are covered with white mold.

Carefully examine bulbs to look for signs of disease when you are purchasing them. Dig bulbs that produce stunted or diseased-looking growth and look carefully for diseased-looking roots or rotted or moldy bulbs. Dispose of infected plants, together with the soil in which they are growing. Do not compost plant material or soil that you suspect is infected. Handle bulbs carefully at planting time; the fungi are most likely to infest bulbs that have been cut or scraped. Don't plant irises in sites where these diseases have been a problem.

Leaves Covered with Round, Grayish to Brown Spots

Leaf Spot

Irises that develop round, gray spots edged in brown on the leaves are probably infected with fungal leaf spot. The spots generally appear at the tops of the leaves. They begin as tiny brown spots with water-soaked margins, but eventually run together and cause the leaves to die early in the season. Similar symptoms are caused by a bacteria as well. Although these diseases don't work their way down to infest the bulbs, the leaves die early, which weakens the plants.

Remove any leaves that develop spots as soon as you discover them. Clean up and destroy all foliage after it fades to prevent the fungus from overwintering. In severe cases, spray with a fungicide such as bordeaux mixture. If leaf spot is a particular problem in your area, spray at weekly to ten-day intervals with wettable sulfur or bordeaux mixture, particularly in rainy seasons. (Watch for leaf discoloration with the latter.)

BULB **Lilies** *Lilium* spp.

DESCRIPTION

True lilies, *Lilium* spp., are spectacular, summer-blooming bulbs that have trumpet- or bell-shaped flowers borne singly or in many-flowered clusters. The bulbs consist of loose, fleshy scale, and the flowers are borne on erect, leafy stems. The genus *Lilium* is a large one—it contains between 80 and 90 species. Plant breeders have hybridized them extensively to develop hundreds of hybrids that are generally easier to grow than the species. Species lilies are listed by their botanical names in most gardening books, while the many mixed-parent hybrids have been organized into divisions according to their origins. These groups are further divided according to flower form. Examples of hybrid groups include Aurelian Hybrids, sometimes called Trumpet or Olympic Hybrids, which bear fragrant, trumpet- or bowl-shaped flowers that may be 8 inches long. Candidum Hybrids are descended from *L.*

candidum (Madonna lily). Lilies make fine additions to borders, can be planted in clumps as specimen plants, and also are used for naturalizing. Lilies make spectacular cut flowers, but when cutting and using them, be aware that their pollen stains permanently.

Height

Height varies according to species or hybrid group. For example, American Hybrid Lilies, which include

the 'Bellingham' cultivars, are 4- to 6-foot plants. Asiatic Hybrid Lilies are 2 to 5 feet tall. Aurelian Hybrids can range from 3 to 8 feet. Oriental Hybrid Lilies can be as short as 2½ feet or as tall as 7 feet.

Spread

1 to 2 feet, depending on the species or cultivar

Blossoms

Lily flowers have six petal-like segments called tepals that curve backward at the tips and may be white, yellow, orange, red, maroon, or purple. The flowers have six stamens, and many species and cultivars are spotted on the inside. Some species bear only one flower per plant, but most hybrids produce many-flowered spikes.

Foliage

Lily leaves are narrow, 4 to 7 inches long, and dark green with smooth edges.

ENVIRONMENT

Hardiness

Hardiness varies from species to species. American, Asiatic, and Aurelian Hybrid Lilies are hardy to USDA Zone 4; Candidum and Oriental Hybrid Lilies to Zone 5.

Light

Hybrid lilies prefer a location in full sun or light shade, but the flowers may fade prematurely if exposed to hot sun. Some of the species lilies need partial shade.

Soil

Plant lilies in light, well-drained, loamy soil that is slightly acidic (pH 6). Like most bulbs, lilies dislike wet, clayey soils. To improve drainage, add organic material to the soil at planting time.

PLANTING AND PROPAGATION

Planting

Lilies grow best in a site where the soil remains moist and cool at all times. A site where the base of the plants remain shaded is ideal, and lilies can be successfully planted with small rhododendrons or azaleas, tall ferns, or other somewhat shallow-rooted perennials. These companion plants will shade the roots without providing too much competition. Mulch also helps keep the soil moist and cool. Also, select a site protected from strong wind.

Plant lilies in early spring or in fall. The bulbs are fleshy and very fragile and, unlike other bulbs, should have some fleshy roots attached. There may be roots at the base of the bulbs as well as at the base of the stalks that arise from the top of the bulbs. Handle the bulbs with care, for they bruise and are damaged easily. When planting, dig beds to a depth of at least 1 foot and add a generous amount of compost, humus, or other organic matter. It's a good idea to dust the bulbs with a fungicide before planting to prevent rot. Most lilies should be set in the ground with the base of the bulb three times as deep as the bulb is high. (A 4-inch-tall bulb should be planted with the base 1 foot below the surface, for example.) The one exception to this rule is that *L. candidum* and the Candidum Hybrid cultivars should only be planted in late summer or early fall and with no more than 1 inch of soil over the tops of the bulbs.

Propagation

Lilies can be propagated in a variety of ways. Most will produce seed, and depending on the species or cultivar involved, they will form small bulbils in the axils of the leaves or small bulblets near the base of the stalk or just under the surface of the soil. Seed, bulbils, or bulblets can all be harvested at the end of the season when ripe, planted, and grown into new plants. Seed-grown lilies, which are the result of sexual reproduction, will not produce lilies that are identical to the parents. Plants grown from bulbils or bulblets will be identical to the parent plants. Lilies can also be propagated by gently pulling a few scales from the base of the bulb, dusting them with fungicide and planting them in moist vermiculite or other sterile potting media. The scales will produce tiny bulblets, which will grow into plants identical to the parents. Finally, some lilies can be propagated by simple division. In fact, plants that develop crowded-looking clumps will need to be divided. Dig the clumps after the foliage turns brown late in the summer, shake the soil off the roots, and carefully separate the bulbs. Discard any unhealthy-looking bulbs and then replant the healthy ones as soon as possible. If you can't replant the bulbs right away, be sure to wrap them in a plastic bag of barely moist peat moss to keep the roots from drying out, and store them in the refrigerator or other cool place. (Unlike many other bulbs, those of lilies are never really dormant.)

PLANT MANAGEMENT

General Care

Tall plants may require staking; be sure to keep stakes well away from the base of the plants to avoid damaging the bulbs. Lilies resent disturbance and should not be dug or divided unless absolutely necessary. Many lilies are susceptible to virus diseases, which are transmitted by aphids. There is no cure for infected plants, so it is important to control aphid populations and destroy any infected plants. Streaked, spotted, or stunted foliage; dwarfed plants; or distorted, misshapen flowers are all indications of virus disease. Dig and discard any infected plants. After the flowers have bloomed, remove them to prevent them from going to seed. Cut the stalk just below the lowest flower. Leave the remaining stem and all its leaves to gradually wither and turn brown after it has collected nutrients for the bulb for next year.

Water

Lilies need soil that remains moist at all times

without being wet. Ideally, about 1 inch of water a week from rain or by watering is fine, but check the soil under the mulch regularly to see if you need to water. Use a soaker hose and avoid splashing the leaves, which encourages disease.

Feeding

Feed lilies twice a year, once in early spring when growth first emerges and again just before the flowers open.

Cutting Fresh Flowers

There's nothing more stunning than a vase of freshly cut lilies. For indoor display, cut them in the early morning with a clean, sharp knife. Plunge them into a pail of warm water for several hours or overnight. When you've arranged them in their container, add a teaspoon of sugar per quart of water to prolong freshness. Wear an old shirt or smock when cutting lilies because the pollen will stain permanently.

MOST COMMON CULTURAL PROBLEMS

Plants Fall or Blow Over

Low Potassium Level in Soil
Although many of the new hybrid lilies are bred to have short, sturdy stalks that don't need staking, plants may still fall over. If this happens, check the level of potassium, or potash, in the soil. Also, select a site that is protected from winds.

MOST COMMON INSECT PESTS

In addition to the pests listed below, lilies sometimes can be attacked by stalk borers. When buying bulbs, look for signs of infestation by thrips, which cause light brown, dried-out looking scales. Healthy lily bulbs are fleshy and generally white in color.

Pale or Yellow Spots on Leaves, Leaves Curled and Distorted

Aphids
Plants infested with aphids have distorted growth that may be curled, puckered, or stunted. Most importantly, aphids transmit virus diseases to which many lilies are extremely susceptible. Leaves may turn yellow or brown, and feeding can seriously damage flower buds or cause distorted flowers. Aphids are soft-bodied, pear-shaped sucking insects about the size of the head of a pin; they may be brown, green, yellow, or nearly black. They are often found clustered under leaves, and flower buds and stem tips may be covered with dense colonies of these insects. Ants, attracted by the aphids' honeydew secretions, wander over the plants, and black, sooty mold can develop on the honeydew as well. Crescent-marked lily aphid (*Neomyzus circumflexus*), foxglove aphid (*Acyrthosiphon solani*), green peach aphid (*Myzus persicae*), melon aphid (*Aphis gossypii*), and purple-spotted lily aphid (*Macrosiphum lilii*) all attack this host.

Light infestations of aphids can be controlled by washing the plants, especially the undersides of the leaves. For best results, use a forceful spray of water once every other day to knock the aphids off the plants; wash the plants at least three times. If that is not effective, spray the plants with insecticidal soap every three to five days for two weeks. If these pests become a very serious problem, make two applications of pyrethrum, three to five days apart.

Foliage Yellowed or Distorted; Bulbs Decayed

Bulb Mites
Lily bulbs infested with bulb mites produce sickly looking growth. Leaves are stunted or deformed, and flowers may be disfigured or do not appear at all. If you suspect these pests, you'll need to dig the bulbs and look closely for them, or you'll discover them in bulbs that have been stored and are offered for purchase. Bulb mites (*Rhizoglyphus echinopus*)

are about ¹⁄₅₀ to ¹⁄₂₅ inch long and are whitish in color. They have four pairs of legs, piercing-sucking mouthparts, and cluster in large colonies on bulbs. They favor damaged, rotting bulbs, but can also burrow into healthy specimens. Their feeding causes corky, brown spots on bulbs, which eventually turn to a dry, crumbly pulp. Mite damage also opens the way for bacteria and fungi to attack. They travel from planting to planting by attaching themselves to insects, rodents, or other soil organisms. They are most active when conditions are warm (60° to 80°F) and humid.

Dig and destroy all seriously infested bulbs, together with the soil in which they are growing; do not compost. Don't plant new bulbs in soil that has been infested. The mites can be killed by dipping the bulbs in hot (120°F) water for a few minutes. When buying bulbs, look carefully for signs of infestation.

Holes in Leaves and/or Flowers

Weevils and Beetles
Several species of weevils and beetles chew holes in the foliage and flowers of lilies. Fuller rose beetle (*Pantomorus cervinus*), which feeds on leaves at night, is a common species found on lilies. It is a gray-brown, ¹⁄₃-inch-long weevil with a broad snout and a white stripe on each wing cover. Control these pests, where possible, by handpicking and crushing them or dropping them into a pail of soapy water. Weevils can also be captured by covering the ground around lilies with a white cloth and shaking the plant lightly. The startled weevils will play dead and drop to the ground and can easily be scooped up. If the infestation is light, this is all you will need to do. For heavier infestations, spray infested plants with a solution of pyrethrum and isopropyl alcohol, mixing 1 tablespoon of alcohol with every pint of diluted pyrethrum mixture. Apply this solution every three to five days until the problem is corrected. For long-term control, apply milky spore disease (*Bacillus popilliae*) to lawns and garden. It will kill the larvae of most beetles.

MOST COMMON DISEASES

Although lilies can be infected by a variety of rot diseases, most problems can be avoided by inspecting bulbs carefully before purchase and handling them carefully until planting. Avoid bulbs that are shriveled, discolored, or show signs of dry or soft rot on the bulb scales or the base of the bulbs. Healthy bulbs that have been properly stored should show no evidence of rot, mold, mildew, shriveling, or other damage. They should have some roots that are intact and relatively undamaged. The scales should be fleshy. Plant lilies in well-drained soil, and avoid sites where other plants have been killed by rot diseases. In addition to the diseases listed below, lilies are occasionally infected by two other fungal diseases: Rust causes powdery pustules on leaves; stem canker rots and girdles the base of the stems. Control measures described for gray mold, below, are effective for both of these diseases.

Stems Rot Below Soil Surface; Plants Wilt and Topple Over

Foot Rot
Lily stems that rot just below the surface of the soil may be infected with foot rot, a fungus disease caused by *Phytophthora cactorum*. Infected tissue shrinks, and the stems are girdled, wilt, and fall over. The fungus can also attack and kill the tips of the shoots when they emerge in spring.

Dig and discard bulbs that may be infected, together with the soil in which they are growing. Do not compost plant material or soil that you suspect is infected. Handle bulbs carefully at planting time and when the new shoots emerge from the soil. Spray newly emerging shoots with bordeaux mixture or other copper-based fungicide to which a small amount of soap or other spreader-sticker has been added. (Watch for leaf discoloration when using bordeaux mixture). Plant lilies in well-drained soil, but avoid sites where these diseases have been a problem.

Shoots Wilt and Die Suddenly in Spring; Spots on Leaves; Flower Buds Rot

Gray Mold

The most common fungal disease of lilies is gray mold, caused by *Botrytis elliptica*. It causes a variety of symptoms; most commonly the tops of the shoots emerging in spring suddenly wilt and die. In the garden, the afflicted plants may or may not be covered by the characteristic gray moldy covering from which the disease gets its name. However, if you suspect gray mold, place a few leaves in a closed jar for a few days; the mold will develop in humid conditions. Other signs of this disease include yellow or red-brown spots on the leaves, that in wet, humid weather will run together and blight the entire leaf. Flowers and buds can also rot. The fungus is most active in wet weather.

Pick and destroy any leaves, stems, or flowers that appear infected as soon as they appear. Thoroughly clean up and destroy all plant material in fall, as soon after the foliage fades as possible. Do not compost plant material that may be infected; destroy it. During wet or humid spring weather, spray plants regularly with a fungicide, such as bordeaux mixture, or a fungicidal soap to control the fungus. Add a small amount of soap to bordeaux mixture as a spreader-sticker to ensure even coverage. (Watch for leaf discoloration when using bordeaux mixture.)

Leaves and Flowers Streaked or Mottled with Greenish Yellow; Shoots Stunted

Virus Diseases

Lilies are susceptible to several virus diseases. Virus-infected plants have spindly, stunted shoots and yellowed, streaked or mottled foliage. Regardless of the normal bloom color, flowers are often sickly yellow-green. Plants may also be stunted or form low-growing "rosettes." Virus diseases are spread by sucking insects such as aphids. Afflicted plants eventually wilt and die.

There is no cure for virus-infected plants. Remove and destroy them; do not compost. Don't save the bulbs of plants you suspect to be infected or propagate from them. To control the insects that transmit these diseases, spray remaining plants with a mixture of insecticidal soap and isopropyl alcohol. Make this mix by adding 1 tablespoon of alcohol to each pint of insecticidal soap solution. Spray at three- to five-day intervals, making three applications. Viruses can overwinter in various perennials and weeds such as daisies, plantain, and gaillardia. Infected plants are not necessarily killed by the disease, but should be dug up and destroyed, since they continue to infect nearby plants via aphids or leafhoppers. Disinfect garden tools with a solution of 1 part household bleach and 3 parts water or 70 percent rubbing alcohol to avoid spreading virus diseases from plant to plant. Also, wash your hands after handling infected plants.

BULB *Tulips* *Tulipa* spp.

DESCRIPTION

Tulips are members of the lily family, Liliaceae, that have been garden favorites for centuries. Botanists estimate that there are between 50 and 150 species, most native to the Mediterranean regions of Europe, the Near East, and Asia. Over centuries of growing and breeding, thousands of hybrids of mixed parentage have been developed, which today are more commonly grown than the species. Both species and hybrid tulips have been separated into 15 divisions according to bloom time, flower form, and parent species. The divisions have been further organized into four groups: Species Hybrids; Early; Midseason; and Late or May-Flowering. Species Hybrids include Kaufmanniana Tulips, Fosterana Tulips, and Greigii Tulips. Early Tulips include both Single and Double Early Tulips. Midseason Tulips, which bloom in mid- to late spring, include the Mendel, Triumph, and Darwin Hybrid Tulips. The Late or May-Flowering Tulips include Darwin, Lily-Flowered, Cottage (also called Single Late Tulips), Rembrandt, Parrot, and Double Late (also called Peony-Flowered) Tulips.

Keep these divisions in mind when selecting tulips. Most catalogs will refer to them when describing the cultivars they have to offer. By selecting plants from several divisions and each of the four groups, you can plan for a long spring display. Tulips are grown in beds, in borders, as edging plants, and in rock gardens. Most make fine cut flowers.

Height

Height depends on the cultivar and division. Kaufmanniana Tulips (commonly called water lily tulips) and Greigii Tulips are both 6 to 8 inches tall. Fosterana Tulips (best known for the cultivar 'Red Emperor') are 16 to 18 inches tall. Both Single and Double Early Tulips range from 9 to 16 inches. Midseason Tulips are all about 1 or 1½ to 2 feet in height. Late or May-Flowering Tulips generally range from 2 to 2½ feet.

Spread

6 to 8 inches

Blossoms

Most tulips bear solitary, cup-shaped blooms, each has six tepals (three petal-like sepals and three true petals) that are identical. There are double-flowered cultivars, as well as some bouquet tulips that bear several blooms per stalk. Blooms come in most colors, except true blue, and range from 1 to 4 inches long.

Foliage

Tulip leaves are thick, 6 to 8 inches long, and straplike to broadly oval. They are a bluish green color with smooth margins. Some, most notably the Species Hybrids, have foliage that is attractively mottled or striped with maroon.

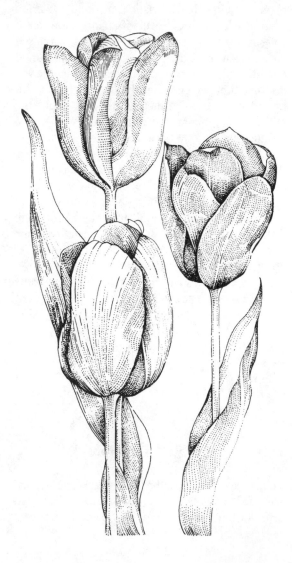

ENVIRONMENT

Hardiness

Most tulips can be grown as far north as USDA Zone 4. South of Zone 8, they may not receive enough cold winter weather in order to bloom.

Light

Grow tulips in full sun.

Soil

Tulips grow best in very well-drained soil that is somewhat sandy and rich in organic matter. For best results, dig a deep bed and enrich the soil with lots of organic matter such as compost, leaf mold, or peat moss to improve drainage. Soil that is slightly acidic (pH 6.5) is ideal.

PLANTING AND PROPAGATION

Planting

Plant tulips in mid- to late fall, in a sunny location, at least four weeks before the ground freezes, so their roots have time to develop. It's important that the bulbs are stored in a cool place until they are planted; bulbs exposed to temperatures above 70°F for even a short time will produce flowers that are one-half to one-third normal size. Don't buy bulbs from dealers who haven't stored them properly. Also, watch out for bulbs offered so early in the season that they have been exposed to high, late-summer temperatures.

Plant bulbs 4 to 8 inches deep, depending on the size of the bulb. (Small bulbs are planted closer to the surface than larger ones.) If planted deeper, up to 1 foot, tulip bulbs will produce fewer offsets, but will bloom for several years. Measure the depth from the top of the bulb to the surface, not from the bottom of the hole, and be sure the bulb's pointed growing tip is up and the rounded bottom is down.

Fill the hole with soil, firm it to be sure there is good contact with the soil, and cover the bed with mulch to protect it from heaving from temperature fluctuations during the winter.

Propagation

Tulips can be propagated by removing the offsets they produce. Dig the bulbs after their foliage turns brown early in the summer, shake the soil off the roots, and air dry them in a shady spot for a couple of days. Separate the offsets from the parent bulbs and replant.

Container Gardening

Tulips can be forced for bloom indoors, but not as easily as other types of bulbs, like hyacinths and daffodils.

PLANT MANAGEMENT

General Care

Tulips generally die out after a year or two of bloom, or produce many small offsets that do not flower. As a result, they are often treated as annuals. In this case, they are pulled or dug right after the flowers fade and are discarded, then replaced and replanted in fall. Planting bulbs at a depth of a foot or more can extend the number of years bulbs bloom. Species Hybrids tend to return more reliably than some of the other hybrids.

If you want to encourage tulips to bloom again, pick off the dead flowers before they go to seed, leaving the stems and leaves to gradually die back. Do not cut them until the leaves are yellowed. While they are not very attractive during this period, they are storing nutrients and energy for the next season.

Water

Tulips generally receive all the moisture they require from natural rainfall.

Feeding

Tulips benefit from an annual feeding either in spring just before the blooms appear or in early fall. Use compost or a slow-acting, general-purpose fertilizer.

Cutting Fresh Flowers

Cut barely open flowers for indoor display in the early morning with a clean, sharp knife. Plunge them into a pail of warm water for several hours or overnight. Add a teaspoon of sugar per quart of water in the vase to prolong freshness. Tulips are not terribly satisfactory in floral arrangements. They tend to flop over unless they are wired, and they drop their petals fairly quickly.

MOST COMMON CULTURAL PROBLEMS

Flowers Are Small or Misshapen, or Plants Fail to Bloom Entirely

Improper Storage and/or Planting

Tulip bulbs that are exposed to temperatures over 70°F for even a short period of time can produce flowers that are unusually small or that are misshapen. For best results, look for bulbs that have been stored at cool temperatures (around 40°F). Gardeners in the South and Southwest may find that their tulips are not as tall as they should be, or that they fail to bloom entirely. This is generally because the plants did not receive enough days of cold temperatures during the winter months to develop properly. Buy special cold-treated bulbs, or ask your local cooperative extension agent for a list of cultivars that are suited to the winter temperatures in your area. Bulbs planted in very late fall, or in wet or clayey soil, may not form roots before they become completely dormant. In spring, this can cause distorted shoots and flowers. Finally, tulips

are a favorite food of rodents, which dig and eat the bulbs. If these pests are a serious problem, plant the bulbs in wire mesh baskets (hardware cloth is fine) to keep the pests at bay.

MOST COMMON INSECT PESTS

It is a good idea to inspect tulip bulbs carefully when you are buying them. Tulip bulb aphids, which are waxy and gray, cluster under the papery bulb covering. Bulbs are also occasionally infested with bulb fly. This pest is discussed in the daffodil entry, beginning on page 218.

Pale or Yellow Spots on Leaves, Leaves Curled and Distorted

Aphids

Plants infested with aphids have distorted growth that may be curled, puckered, or stunted. Most important, aphids transmit virus diseases to which tulips are susceptible. Leaves may turn yellow or brown, and feeding can seriously damage flower buds or cause distorted flowers. Aphids are soft-bodied, pear-shaped sucking insects about the size of the head of a pin; they may be brown, green, yellow, or nearly black. They are often found clustered under leaves, and flower buds and stem tips may be covered with dense colonies of these insects. Ants, attracted by the aphids' honeydew secretions, wander over the plants, and black, sooty mold can develop on the honeydew as well. Crescent-marked lily aphid (*Neomyzus circumflexus*) attacks tulips.

Light infestations of aphids can be controlled by washing the plants, especially the undersides of the leaves. For best results, use a forceful spray of water once every other day to knock the aphids off the plants; wash the plants at least three times. If that is not effective, spray the plants with insecticidal soap every three to five days for two weeks. If these pests become a very serious problem, make two applications of pyrethrum, three to five days apart.

Foliage Yellowed or Distorted; Flowers Disfigured or Absent; Bulbs Decayed

Bulb Mites

Tulip bulbs infested with bulb mites produce sickly looking growth. Leaves are stunted or deformed, and flowers may be disfigured or do not appear at all. If you suspect these pests, you'll need to dig the bulbs and look closely for them, or you'll discover them in bulbs that have been stored and are offered for purchase. Bulb mites (*Rhizoglyphus echinopus*) are about 1/50 to 1/25 inch long and are whitish in color. They have four pairs of legs, piercing-sucking mouthparts, and cluster in large colonies on bulbs. They favor damaged, rotting bulbs, but can also burrow into healthy specimens. Their feeding causes corky, brown spots on bulbs, which eventually turn to a dry, crumbly pulp. Mite damage also opens the way for bacteria and fungi to attack. They travel from planting to planting by attaching themselves to insects, rodents, or other soil organisms. They are most active when conditions are warm (60° to 80°F) and humid.

Dig and destroy all seriously infested bulbs, together with the soil in which they are growing; do not compost. Don't plant new bulbs in soil that has been infested. The mites can be killed by dipping the bulbs in hot (120°F) water for a few minutes. When buying bulbs, look carefully for signs of infestation.

MOST COMMON DISEASES

Although tulips can be infected by a variety of rot diseases, most problems can be avoided by inspecting bulbs carefully before purchase and handling them carefully until planting. Avoid bulbs that are shriveled, discolored, or show signs of dry or soft rot on the bulb scales or the base of the bulbs. Healthy bulbs that have been properly stored should show no evidence of rot, mold, mildew, shriveling, or other damage. They are creamy yellow or white with no black specks, splotches, or scrapes. The papery bulb coat should also be intact. Plant tulips in deeply prepared, well-drained soil, and avoid sites where other plants have been killed by rot diseases.

Plants Stunted, Wilted, and Die Before Flowering

Basal Rot or Crown Rot

Basal rot is a fungus disease caused by *Fusarium oxysporum* forma *tulipae*, which attacks bulbs beginning at the roots or at the base of the bulb scales. The fungi cause soft, brown, rotted tissue and spread up through the center of the bulb. Infected plants are stunted, have reddish foliage, wilt, and generally die before flowering. Stored bulbs infected with this disease have dry, blackened bases and are dull white.

Carefully examine bulbs to look for signs of disease when you are purchasing them. Dig bulbs that produce stunted or diseased-looking growth and look carefully for diseased-looking roots or rotted or moldy bulbs. Dispose of infected plants, together with the soil in which they are growing. Do not compost plant material or soil that you suspect is infected. Handle bulbs carefully at planting time; the fungi are most likely to infest bulbs that have been cut or scraped. Don't plant tulips in sites where these diseases have been a problem.

Foliage Is Streaked or Spotted; Flowers Rotted

Blight or Fire

The fungal disease caused by *Botrytis tulipae*, commonly called blight or fire, is the most serious disease problem that affects tulips. The first sign of the disease is red-brown spots on the leaves or flowers that may be covered with spores. The spots turn grayish as the disease develops. Afflicted plants are stunted and turn pale yellow-green. The flowers fail to open, and stems may rot completely. The bulbs are marked with round, black or dark brown spots.

Pick and destroy any leaves or flowers that appear infected as soon as they appear, and try to dispose of them without scattering spores throughout the planting. (Placing them in a plastic bag is effective.) Dig and destroy stems, leaves, and bulbs of all afflicted plants, together with the soil in which they are growing. Do not compost plant material that may be infected; destroy it. Rotate tulip plantings to avoid growing them for several years in the same spot. During wet or humid spring weather, spray plants regularly with a fungicide such as a fungicidal soap, but stop spraying as soon as the buds begin to show color, for the fungicide will spot the flowers.

Leaves and Flowers Streaked or Mottled with Greenish Yellow; Foliage Spindly or Deformed

Virus Diseases
Tulips are susceptible to several virus diseases. Virus-infected plants have spindly, stunted shoots and yellowed, streaked or mottled foliage. Flowers may be marked irregularly with white or yellowish streaking. Virus diseases are spread by sucking insects such as aphids.

There is no cure for virus-infected plants. Remove and destroy them; do not compost. Don't save the bulbs of plants you suspect to be infected. To control the insects that transmit these diseases, spray remaining plants with a mixture of insecticidal soap and isopropyl alcohol. Make this mix by adding 1 tablespoon of alcohol to each pint of insecticidal soap solution. Spray at three- to five-day intervals, making three applications. Infected plants are not necessarily killed by the disease, but should be dug up and destroyed, since they continue to infect nearby plants via leafhoppers. Disinfect garden tools with a solution of 1 part household bleach and 3 parts water or 70 percent rubbing alcohol to avoid spreading virus diseases from plant to plant. Also, wash your hands after handling infected plants.

CHAPTER 4
Roses

No other flower epitomizes the beauty, scent, and romance of flowers like roses. They are the most widely known of plants, and a bouquet of them is synonymous with tenderness and affection. Growing roses has a different reputation. As garden plants, roses are notoriously touchy, supposedly requiring continual care and attention. In fact, roses are no more difficult than most other flowers. You do have to prune them, but on the other hand you won't ever have to divide them. With a basic understanding of their simple requirements, you can have a flower garden filled with beautiful roses.

DESCRIPTION

Over the years, roses have been divided into a variety of classes and sub-classes according to origin, bloom type, and habit. These groups include species, shrub, climbing, old garden, and miniature roses, as well as the familiar hybrid teas, grandifloras, and floribundas. Although you can grow gorgeous roses without having a clue as to their classifications, knowing them will help you choose those best suited to your flower garden.

Shrub roses look more like other flowering shrubs. Flowers are small to medium-size. Depending on the cultivar, plants may bloom once during the summer or all season. Shrub roses are usually very durable plants, often having superior hardiness and disease resistance.

Climbing roses have long, arching canes that reach 6 feet or more in length. This group is divided into several types, including large-flowered climbers, which bear large blooms singly or in clusters, and climbing hybrid teas, which are indeed climbing forms of hybrid tea cultivars. Both have thick, somewhat stiff canes and an upright growth habit; they bloom on and off all summer. Rambling roses have thinner, more flexible canes and clusters of small blossoms once in early summer. Climbing roses have no tendrils with which to hold onto trellises or arbors, so you will have to fasten the canes loosely to these structures.

Old garden roses have been regaining much-deserved popularity among gardeners. There is a great deal of variation in plant and flower size and type, as well as blooming period. Both shrub and old garden roses are further divided into many different sub-classes, based on growth habit and flower form as well as origin.

Miniature roses are diminutive versions of just about every other type of rose. As such, they can be used in many different ways in the flower garden, including as an edging and in container plantings. Most bloom nonstop throughout the summer and into fall.

Hybrid tea, floribunda, and grandiflora roses produce spectacular blooms all season long. These roses can be planted in masses or grown individually among your other flowers. Wherever they're grown, they create grand splashes of color. The grandifloras are generally taller and are excellent for use at the back of the flower border. Hybrid teas work well in the middle of the border, and the shorter floribundas can be used toward the front.

All of these roses are very adaptable in the garden, some providing flowers from late spring to late fall. Others have one spectacular blooming period. Growing a variety of types of roses among your other flowers enriches and enhances your garden. All make wonderful cut flowers. When planting a rose bed, greater impact is achieved when roses are planted in groups with three plants of the same cultivar in each group. If you plant roses by themselves in a bed rather than integrating them into your flower borders, consider bordering them with low annuals.

Height

Climbing Roses
Large-flowered cultivars, 6 to 15 feet
Rambling cultivars, 6 to 20 feet

Floribundas
2 to 3 feet

Grandifloras
Up to 6 feet

Hybrid Teas
3 to 5 feet

Miniature Roses
6 to 18 inches

Shrub and Old Garden Roses
2 to 8 feet; some cultivars 12 feet or more

Spread

Roses usually spread about two-thirds the height of the plant. Generally, roses will grow larger and wider the warmer the climate. A particular hybrid tea rose might have a spread of 2 feet in Boston but 4 feet in Seattle, where growing conditions are better. Climbing roses will spread as they are permitted, reaching coverage of up to 20 feet in mild climates, if unpruned.

Blossoms

It's the hybrid tea rose that most of us picture when we think of roses. This group has been bred specifically for large, spectacular, many-petaled blossoms borne singly on long, straight, sturdy stems. In contrast, the flowers of floribundas bloom in large clusters on compact plants.

Roses come in many colors—red, pink, orange to apricot and gold, white to cream, burgundy, and even lavender. Some roses have a classic scent, though many of the modern hybrids, bred for beautiful blossoms, have lost the strong familiar rose fragrance of their ancestors. Some roses bloom from early summer steadily into late fall. Others bloom in early summer and again in fall. Still others bloom only in late spring or early summer. Some roses produce showy red, orange, or yellow hips (seedpods). These colorful rose hips are excellent in fall arrangements and add color to the fall and winter landscape, as well as providing winter food for birds. They are also an excellent source of vitamin C.

Foliage

Roses are deciduous. Their leaves range in color from bronze-red to olive and near-chartreuse to dark green. Leaf texture may be smooth or rough. Some cultivars have shiny leaves, while others have leaves with more of a matte surface.

ENVIRONMENT

Roses thrive in a location with full sun and good air movement, which helps the dew and the rain to dry quickly, discouraging disease problems. Too much wind, however, can damage the foliage in summer and the canes in winter. If you live in a windy area, plant roses where they will get some protection, such as near a wall, fence, hedge, or other windbreak.

Hardiness

Most shrub roses and some old garden roses can survive the cruelest winters, while only some of the hybrid teas, grandifloras, and floribundas will make it without some winter protection. These are only generalizations; within each group, hardiness changes from cultivar to cultivar. Experts disagree on what rose is hardy where. Consequently, hardiness zones have not been assigned to specific cultivars. If you're not sure about the hardiness of a rose you want to plant, check with your local rose society or garden club to see if anyone's growing it and, if so, how it's doing.

Light

Roses need bright sun at least 5 to 6 hours a day. Most roses will tolerate filtered shade, but too much shade reduces the number of blossoms, encourages legginess, and invites rust and mildew problems. If you have a choice, locate your roses so that they receive sunlight early in the day. Roses prefer some shade from the scorching summer sun in the afternoon.

Soil

A well-drained but moist soil provides the best environment for rose roots. When planting roses, place them in a soil that contains at least 25 percent organic matter. The ideal mix consists of equal parts of loamy soil, organic matter (compost, leaf mold, peat moss, and so forth), and builder's sand. Get your roses off to an excellent start by adding 15 pounds of fish meal, 20 pounds of alfalfa meal, 20 pounds of gypsum, and 15 pounds of bonemeal per 100 square feet. Roses like slightly acid soil, with a pH range of 6.0 to 6.5, but will tolerate soils with a pH as high as 7.5.

PLANTING AND PROPAGATION

Unlike most flowers, roses are precise in their planting requirements. In the end, of course, if you place them in good soil and provide them with the proper environment, your planting techniques become secondary. Nevertheless, you will enjoy healthier, more vigorous roses if you plant them correctly.

Planting

All roses except miniatures are sold either as packaged, dormant, bare-root plants or as plants growing in containers. Both types are usually 2-year-old, field-grown plants. The bare-root plants are available by mail order or locally in retail nurseries and garden centers. The container-grown roses are offered only at local nurseries and garden centers. Miniature roses are available as potted plants, both by mail and from local sources.

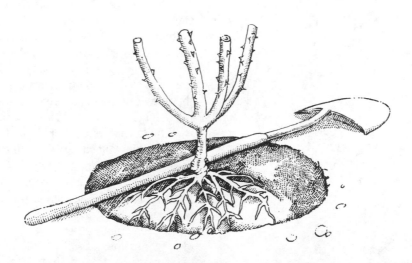

It's best to plant bare-root roses as soon as possible after you receive them in the mail or bring them home. When planting, prepare the soil deeply to accommodate their roots, and then spread the roots out evenly in the planting hole. The proper planting depth varies with your climatic zone. Where winter temperatures fall below freezing, place the plant so the bud union is about 2 inches below the surface of the soil, to protect it from winter cold. In milder climates, place the plant so the bud union is at the soil surface. Check for proper planting depth by placing a shovel across the planting hole and making sure the bud union is at the proper depth.

In most parts of the country, bare-root roses are planted in the early spring before the green buds leaf out, or about the time forsythia blooms. Container-grown plants can be planted anytime during the growing season. There is some risk in planting during the hottest part of the summer, but if you take care to water them well, they'll survive.

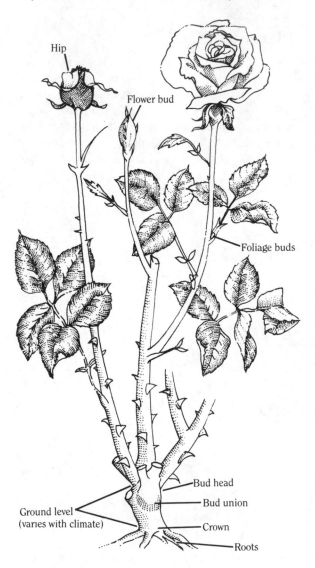

Anatomy of a rose.

It's best to get bare-root plants into the ground as soon as they arrive in the mail or as soon as you bring them home. Soak the roots in water overnight before planting. If you cannot plant them immediately, keep them dormant by making sure the roots are damp and storing the plants in a cool, dark place. They should be planted within a week.

The following are suggested planting times for dormant, bare-root roses: Pacific Northwest, February and March; Pacific Southwest coast, January and February; Southwest, late December and January; south central, late January and February; the mid-South, December and January; subtropical areas, December and January; north central, April and early May; eastern seaboard, March and early April; and Northeast, April and early May.

When planting roses, remember that rose roots eventually grow 16 to 18 inches long, so try to mix organic matter that deeply into the soil. When digging the hole for your roses, remove any rocks to give the roots plenty of good soil and room to spread.

Planting depth varies with your climatic zone. Determine it by the level of the bud union—the bulbous or swollen area just above the roots where the flowering stock was grafted to the rootstock. Where winter temperatures fall below freezing, place the plant so the bud union is about 2 inches below the surface of the soil to protect it from winter cold. In milder climates, place the plant so the bud union is at the soil surface. In very cold climates, you can position the plant so that the bud union is as deep as 4 inches.

Miniature roses have no graft or bud union, so you can set them at the same depth in the ground as they were in their original containers.

If you're planting a dormant rose bush, mound at least 6 inches of soil around and over it. This prevents canes from drying out and protects the roots from any sudden cold spells. When the weather warms and buds do begin to sprout, gradually remove the soil mound over a period of a week or two. Loosen the wire holding the plant's name tag so it does not constrict the cane to which it is attached.

About a month after the buds begin to sprout,

you should notice vigorous growth. Fertilize your plants according to the feeding instructions below. *Do not add fertilizer to the planting mix;* doing so delays growth and can injure the developing roots.

Spacing

The distance between rose plants and other flowers in your garden depends on the rose cultivar and your climate. The warmer the climate, the larger roses grow, so they need to be spaced farther from other plants. Hybrid tea and grandiflora roses should be set 20 to 30 inches from surrounding plants, with roses in colder climates needing the lesser spacing and those in warmer climates requiring the greater distance. The planting range for floribundas is 1½ to 2 feet. Shrub and old-fashioned roses vary greatly in their mature height; a good rule of thumb is to space them a distance equal to one-half their mature height for your area. Space miniature roses 6 to 12 inches apart, depending on their mature height.

Propagation

The easiest way to propagate roses is from softwood cuttings taken during the blooming season. You can also propagate them by budding, or grow them from seed.

Container Gardening

Some of the smaller hybrid roses can be grown in containers and should be planted in pots that are at least 14 inches deep and 18 inches wide. Miniature roses make fine container plants. They need pots that are 6 to 10 inches in diameter. Miniature roses can be set outdoors on decks or patios, and they grow very well indoors, too. When raising them indoors, use commercial soilless mixes to avoid fungal disease, which might be carried in soil from your yard. They need at least 4 to 5 hours of sunshine a day. Do not let them dry out. Container-grown roses that decorate the outside of your home need to be moved to unheated shelters when the temperature falls below 28°F.

PLANT MANAGEMENT

Roses are not low-maintenance plants. They require a fair amount of care in order to look their best, but they're worth it.

Water

Roses are thirsty plants and need a steady flow of moisture for peak performance. Do not let them dry out. In most soils and regions, about an inch of water a week suffices. In very sandy soil or in the South, roses may need as much as 2 inches of water every week. You want to keep roots moist but not standing in water throughout the growing season. Water must penetrate 16 to 18 inches to reach the roots of mature plants. That is why the best soil drains easily but also retains moisture. Watering is only necessary during the dormant season if conditions have been unusually dry.

The best system for watering roses uses drip irrigation placed under a layer of organic mulch. This puts water right into the soil and prevents any from splashing up onto the plants and bringing with it any fungal spores that might be on the soil surface. An alternative is to put a soaker attachment on the end of your hose and water each plant individually. Whatever method you use, water your roses in the morning so the plants can dry off quickly, inhibiting the development of fungal diseases.

Feeding

Because repeat-blooming roses work hard producing blooms for a long season, they do best with more than one feeding each year. The three key times are in the spring right after pruning, when they have developed the first flower buds, and again about two months before the first frost in your area. Gardens with fast-draining, sandy soil will need more frequent applications, and in climates with an extended growing season, additional applications are beneficial. The older cultivars of rose that bloom only once a year should be fertilized once in early spring.

Fertilize your roses with dehydrated or composted cow manure, bloodmeal, and bonemeal, applying 1 cup of each per plant for the first feeding in spring. Work it lightly into the soil surface. Use fish emulsion or manure tea for additional feedings. Some gardeners use a foliar feeding of diluted seaweed extract (1 tablespoon to a gallon of water) several times during the summer. Another suggestion is to mix 1 or 2 tablespoons of dry brewer's yeast with a gallon of water, and spray the mixture over the entire plant. Both mixtures will produce greener foliage, sturdier growth, and improved bloom.

Mulching

Roses benefit enormously from mulching. While it keeps weeds down, its greatest value is in reducing evaporation. It helps maintain moisture levels and keeps the soil cooler in the summer, when roses are vulnerable to heat stress. A thick organic mulch, freshly applied in early spring while the plant is still dormant, also helps to reduce fungal disease problems. It does this simply by covering infected soil and preventing any spores from being bounced up onto plants with splashing rain.

At least a month before the expected last frost in spring, spread 2 to 4 inches of organic mulch around the base of each rose bush, starting 2 inches away from the stems. Although the soil around the roses will warm up more slowly in spring, you will have fewer fungal disease problems to deal with later in the season. Use wood chips, shredded bark, pine needles, cottonseed or cocoa bean hulls, chopped leaves, ground corn cobs, or peat nuggets for mulch. Geotextile material makes an excellent first layer for mulching around roses. Lay the textile on the soil and then cover it with organic matter for a more attractive look.

Deadheading

Repeat-blooming roses, including climbers, will bloom more profusely if you remove faded blossoms. This encourages plants to put nutrients and energy into producing more flowers rather than into producing seeds. Dead flowers also provide a congenial environment for disease. The exceptions are the roses that are grown partially for their ornamental hips, such as *Rosa rugosa* and related hybrids, *Rosa pomifera*, 'Golden Wings', eglantine roses, and the new shrub rose 'Bonica'.

To properly deadhead roses, cut the stem back to an outward-facing bud or leaflet, cutting at a 45-degree angle just above a five-leaflet leaf. This encourages strong new growth away from the center of the plant. Try to avoid removing any more leaves than you have to. The leaves are the plant's food factory and are essential to the regrowth of new leaves and blossoms. At the same time, don't be so prudent that you snip off only the blossoms, because that favors the production of smaller leaf stems or buds.

Fall Cleanup

A thorough fall cleanup every year is essential to keep roses healthy. Remove any leaves that remain on the plant, and rake up and discard all old leaves, prunings, and any other debris on the ground or around the base of the plants. This will remove insect eggs or disease spores that overwinter on plant debris. After cleaning the bed, water the soil thoroughly; the roots of roses remain active long after winter begins.

Winterizing

How well your roses survive winter depends on which species or hybrids you are growing—some are hardier than others—and also on the health and vigor of the plants. But you can take measures to increase a plant's chances of passing through this sometimes harsh season completely unharmed.

Icy temperatures, vast fluctuations in temperature, and whipping winds are the three threats of winter. To protect your roses, your goals are to prevent the temperature around plants from dropping below a certain point, to steady that temperature so alternate freezing and thawing does not occur, and to keep branches from being thrashed by winds that loosen the entire plant from the ground.

The techniques of winter protection generally apply to all roses grown in all regions of the country. The extent of protection varies according to just how cold winters get. Timing also varies from region to region, but begin winterizing your plants just before hard-freezing weather sets in, which usually occurs about a month or two after the first frost.

Roses growing in an area where winter temperatures do not drop below 20°F really don't require winter protection, although it doesn't hurt to spray them with an antitranspirant to minimize water loss during the cool months. If your plants are located in a site that is exposed to drying winter winds, wrap the plants or build a wind barrier with burlap or floating row covers, such as Reemay. These materials allow air to get to the plant, but protect it from the drying effects of the wind. A more attractive option is to shield plants with a permanent fence or hedge; leave 10 feet between the fence and the rose bushes.

In areas where winter temperatures drop as low as 10° to 15°F for a two-week period or more, begin winterizing roses after the first hard frost. Mound fresh, loose soil or compost 6 to 8 inches high around the base of each plant. Do not pull up soil from the rose bed, but bring it in from another part of the garden so that roots aren't exposed. Prune the plants back to half their height and tie the canes together with twine. Spray the bushes with an antitranspirant, then lay 8 to 10 inches of organic mulch over the entire bed. Some gardeners surround their plants with a cylinder of chicken wire or netting to keep the mulch from blowing away in the wind.

If you live where temperatures dip to −15°F or lower, follow all of the steps mentioned earlier and enclose the entire plant under a protective shield such as a peach basket, tar-paper cone, or a commercially available rose cap or cone designed to protect roses in winter, pruning plants to fit.

When spring arrives, don't be too eager to remove this winter covering. As the mounds around the base of your roses thaw, gradually remove soil over a period of two to three weeks. Do this carefully to avoid breaking any stems that may have already begun to grow. Tender new growth can be easily killed by even a light freeze, so keep some straw or floating row covers, like Reemay, handy to spread around plants in the event of a late frost.

Climbing roses require a slightly different method of winter protection. If you live in an area where winter temperatures drop below −5°F, detach your large-flowered, repeat-blooming climbers from their supports and lay them on the ground. Carefully bunch the canes together and peg them to the soil with wooden or wire hoops of some kind. Finally, completely cover them with 4 to 6 inches of well-drained soil, compost, or organic mulch.

Pruning

Pruning roses is a routine maintenance chore, not something to be dreaded. It really isn't difficult. Prune roses to give them good form; to encourage new growth; to remove any diseased, damaged, or dead wood; and to generate larger blossoms.

Get your pruning shears out in early spring after the last frost, just before your roses break dormancy. You should be as certain as you can that freezing temperatures won't strike again. You don't want a late frost to damage the new growth that forms after pruning. In warm climates, you may begin as early as January. Where winters are severe, you may have to wait until April. The blooming of forsythia is a reliable signal that it is time to prune.

First, remove any dead wood down to the nearest healthy, dormant bud eye. A bud eye is a small bulge on the stem that has what looks like a tiny eye with a horizontal crease underneath it. Once dormancy has broken, or it has been stimulated by pruning, the bud eye will develop into a new shoot. Notice the direction in which bud eyes point. After pruning, the top bud on each cane should be facing away from the interior of the plant so that new canes don't all grow into the center, where they will tangle and compete for sunlight. Position your shears so that the cutting blade is on the lower end of the cut to ensure a clean cut. Make the cut at a 45-degree angle, at least 1 inch below the dead wood and about ¼ inch above the outward-facing bud. If cuts are made too high above the bud, the wood above the bud will die, providing a haven for pests and diseases. If the cane that you are pruning has no buds, remove the entire branch down to the union with the stem. Also completely remove any old, thick, and woody canes; they produce a profusion of twigs rather than strong stems.

After pruning the dead canes, remove all diseased wood. Cut any sickly canes down to a plump, healthy bud, at least 1 inch below the infected area.

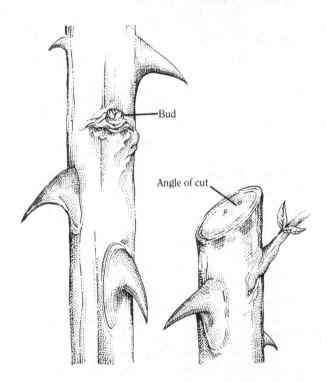

When pruning or cutting any type of rose, cut the stems at a 45-degree angle ¼ inch above a bud that faces toward the outside of the plant. This helps eliminate branches that cross and keeps the bush open at the center.

Next, remove all undesirable wood—the weak, spindly, and deformed growth and the doglegs (canes that grow straight out and then curve upward). Cut canes that are growing toward the center of the bush. If two branches cross, remove the weaker one.

Finally, remove all suckers or reversion growth (undersized shoots that come from the rootstock below the graft union). When cutting them out, take the entire base of the sucker from the crown area, along with a piece of the crown if necessary.

After you've finished pruning, consider spraying your plants with bordeaux mixture, a flowable sulfur fungicide, or a fungicidal soap to prevent the early onset of fungal diseases. Then spray with dormant oil as a final obstacle to insect eggs and disease spores that may have remained on the plant through the winter. This must be done before green leaves begin to emerge.

Pruning Specific Types of Roses

Although the technique and purpose of pruning are the same for all roses, consider specific methods for specific types to bring the best form, health, and vigor to the particular roses you are growing.

Shrub and Old Garden Roses. It is not true that shrub roses need no pruning. They do require far less pruning than hybrid teas, grandifloras, and floribundas, but you'll get more vigorous, healthy shrub roses if you give the plants some light attention with the pruning shears in the early spring.

Take a long-term approach when pruning shrub roses. You want to encourage strong new shoots to grow from the base of the plant by removing older, less vigorous wood that shades new growth. This is a process of gradual renewal rather than radical removal. After the second growing season, cut back any overly long, vigorous shoots by about 25 percent. During the third and subsequent dormant seasons, routinely remove one or two of the oldest shoots to favor the strong new canes. Trim growth to maintain the open, upright shape and cut back any excessively long shoots.

Climbing Roses. During the first two years, do not prune large-flowered climbers except to remove dead wood. Climbing roses produce better flowers on canes that grow horizontally rather than vertically. So the trick to managing a climbing rose is to thin out the oldest wood from time to time, keeping the total number of canes constant and securing the canes to the trellis so that they tend toward a more horizontal position. Do this major pruning in the winter, when the plant is dormant.

Prune the newer canes with some restraint in order to keep young shoots appearing throughout the bush. Cut them back to 6 to 8 inches, leaving three or four bud eyes on each stem. This pruning will allow your plants to produce more blossoms. Remember to guide those young canes to grow horizontally whenever possible. As the climber fills the space you have allotted it, you will want to do some pruning each spring, just after the bush begins to put out new growth.

When climbers become old and begin to outgrow their trellises, prune them vigorously, cutting back old canes to the ground.

Rambling Roses. Though you prune climbers during dormancy, you must prune ramblers immediately after flowering. Pruning is necessary to remove dead, diseased, or unsightly wood and to keep the plant under control. Since ramblers produce so many flowers along their stems, you do not need to be so concerned with finding buds against which to prune. Prune branches that stick out of the general shape of the plant and prune branches deep inside that are clearly dead or producing few leaves or flowers. Ramblers can be cut back severely —to just a foot or two—immediately after flowering, and will come charging back if fed and watered properly.

Miniature Roses. If you want to keep a miniature rose compact, prune it back severely every year, cutting canes to 6 to 8 inches. Otherwise, prune lightly as you would a floribunda bush rose.

Hybrid Teas and Grandifloras. The degree to which you prune these roses depends on the effect you want to achieve, as well as the state of your plants. In general, more pruning produces fewer but showier blossoms on smaller shrubs.

If you want to produce a few very showy blooms, or if your plants have become weak and need to be rejuvenated, remove all but three or four canes and cut those down to a height of 6 to 10 inches. This degree of pruning also reduces the chances for recurrence of any serious fungal diseases your roses had last year.

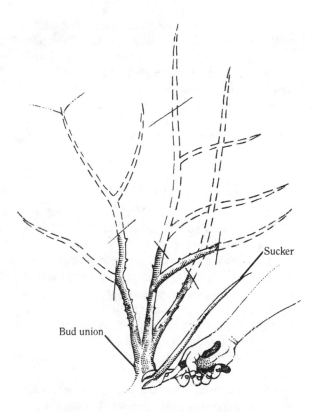

When pruning hybrid tea roses, cut dead wood down to the nearest healthy bud. Then cut out all weak, spindly growth and branches that grow toward the center of the bush. A properly pruned plant should have three or four main canes cut to about 10 inches above the soil line. Look carefully for any suckers that arise from below the bud union. If allowed to grow and flower, they will produce flowers that resemble the rootstock, not the cultivar you've purchased, which was budded or grafted on top.

If you want to create a larger, well-shaped bush with smaller but more numerous blossoms, prune moderately. Leave 5 to 12 canes and cut them down to 1½ to 2 feet. A third technique, light pruning, means that less than one-third of the plant is cut back, a practice that will produce an even larger bush covered with a profusion of short-stemmed flowers. The moderate approach produces the best look for most gardens.

Floribundas. Floribundas are not pruned as severely as hybrid teas, but you do need to remove all the dead and undesirable wood each year. Cut all the longer canes down to about half their former height to maintain the plant's good form. For healthier, more vigorous roses, cut the canes of the floribunda to within 6 inches of the ground every two to three years.

Cutting Fresh Flowers

We all want our cut roses to last as long as possible. With a few tricks, you can add days to the life of the blooms you bring indoors.

Cut blossoms when the air is cool, preferably at dusk or early morning. Roses cut during the heat of the day wilt quickly. Make sure you bring not only your sharp knife or shears to the rose bed, but a bucket full of tepid water for immersing cut stems. Select those flowers that are only partially opened. Single blooms will last longest if picked when they are barely starting to unfold.

When cutting flowers, leave at least two leaves above the main stem. Using a sharp knife or shears, make the cut at a 45-degree angle just above a leaf. New growth will originate from the base of this leaf, so choose a leaf that faces toward the outside of the plant. Immediately after you cut a stem, plunge the entire stem to the base of the blossom into the bucket of water.

Keep cut flowers in water in a cool place out of drafts until you are ready to arrange them; you can keep them in water in the refrigerator to retard the opening of buds.

Arranging Flowers

When cutting flowers for arrangements, select several in various stages of early blooming to give your arrangement a less uniform and more interesting appearance. Remove the foliage that will be below the surface of the water in the vase, but don't scrape the stem with a knife. At ½ inch or more above the end of each stem, make a fresh cut at a sharp angle to expose as much of the cut surface to water as possible. Then plunge stems deeply into warm (about 95 to 105°F) water. Leave the roses there for about 30 minutes, until the water cools; then set them, still in the water, in a cool place. Revive wilted roses with the same procedure.

Fill your vase with fresh water and add powdered floral preservative according to package directions, or add 1 teaspoon of sugar and several drops of household bleach to a quart of lukewarm water. Then arrange your roses. Keep the arrangement out of drafts and move it to a cool spot at night. Many gardeners feel it's worth the extra effort to change the water daily and make a new cut in the bottom of the stem every couple of days.

Drying Flowers

Dried rose petals are a staple of traditional potpourri. Pick rose blossoms after the morning dew is gone, but early enough so that the essential oils remain. For a dry potpourri, pull the petals from the blooms, spread them on a drying rack, and place them away from the light for four days to two weeks, or until they dry completely. You can also dry rose petals in the oven. Set the oven temperature to warm and place the petals on a cookie sheet in the oven, leaving the door ajar to allow moisture to escape. Stir the petals occasionally for even drying. This technique is faster, but the petals will lose the intensity of their color.

Rose blossoms can also be dried by air drying or in silica gel. To air dry, trim off broken stems and leaves, and hang stems upside down. Dry in a warm, dry, well-ventilated space like an attic or large closet. Handle carefully, as the stems are fragile. Both dried buds and small flowers are attractive in arrangements or in potpourri. To dry in silica gel, place flowers, stems down, in a coffee can or other sealable container partially filled with silica gel. Carefully sift silica gel over blooms until they are completely covered.

MOST COMMON CULTURAL PROBLEMS

Climbing Roses Flower Only on Ends of Canes

Improper Growing Habit

If your climbing roses produce blossoms only at the ends of the canes and not along their lengths, examine their growing habits. Many climbing roses produce more blossoms when the canes are growing horizontally or at a 45-degree angle to the ground. If the canes are growing vertically, the flowers will bloom only at the ends. Reposition your canes and secure them so that most of them have a more horizontal orientation.

Canes Blackened or Damaged after Early Fall Freeze

Plants Not Hardened Off for Winter; Lack of Winter Protection

Sudden changes in temperature in the fall, before the plant has hardened off for the winter, can be disastrous. Early freezes kill more canes than even colder winter temperatures. Damage occurs most often on tender new shoots, so avoid late summer feedings of nitrogen and hold back on water, which encourages new growth. If a very early cold spell is expected, cover the rose bush with floating row covers, like Reemay, overnight to give it some protection.

Plants Are Leggy; Fail to Flower

Not Enough Sun

If roses don't get 5 to 6 hours of full sun each day, they will become leggy and may not produce any blossoms at all. The only solution is to move the plants to a better location.

Blossoms Don't Open Fully

Overexposure to Cool Temperatures and Dampness

Cool nights or dark, damp days can cause balling—that's when blossoms open halfway and then stop. Cut off these blooms; when weather conditions improve, good growth will begin again. If you live in an area where cool or foggy summers are common, select rose cultivars that have fewer petals, and balling will occur less often.

Plants Wilt

Excessive Heat

Very hot weather fatigues a rose plant. At temperatures above 90°F, the plant uses food faster than the leaves can manufacture it. In hot climates, don't overprune roses. If the season is particularly hot and sunny, cover part of the rose garden with wooden lath shading to give some shade during the hottest part of the day. Move container-grown roses to partially shaded locations. Applications of antitranspirant sprays slow loss of water from the leaves and subsequent wilting.

New Foliage Dies

Overfertilizing

If the new foliage of your roses dies or is stunted and off-color, the soil may contain excessive salts from too much fertilizing. Fortunately, this condition is rare when organic fertilizers other than manure are used. Water the plant heavily to put the excessive salts into suspension. Water heavily again a day later to leach those salts from the soil. Avoid using fresh manure, which can cause burning, and stick to well-rotted, composted manure or other slow-acting, general-purpose fertilizers.

New Roses Grow Slowly

Plants Dried Out

New roses cannot be allowed to dry out either before or after you plant them or they will grow poorly. Soak bare-root plants 6 to 24 hours before planting. Water them very well when you plant them, and if it is unusually hot, protect the plants from drying out by shading them with some moist burlap or floating row covers, like Reemay. Leave the material on the plants until the weather cools or the plants become established.

MOST COMMON INSECT PESTS

Pale or Yellow Spots on Leaves, Leaves Curled and Distorted

Aphids

Aphids feed on the foliage and flowers of roses, sucking out the juices. The leaves turn yellow or brown, wilt under bright sunlight, and eventually curl and pucker. Flowers, too, can become malformed. You may find honeydew secreted by the aphids on leaves and flowers. Ants are attracted by this honeydew. Melon aphid (*Aphis gossypii*), green peach aphid (*Myzus persicae*), potato aphid (*Macrosiphum euphorbiae*), and rose aphid (*Macrosiphum rosae*) are among the species that attack roses. The aphids feed on the undersides of leaves. These insects are about the size of the head of a pin and have soft, pear-shaped bodies. Most species are green, but some species are pink or reddish. You will usually see them on the buds and leaves of garden roses in May and June, and they are common pests in greenhouses. Aphids multiply so rapidly that infested flower buds and stalks become covered with them.

Wipe the pests off by hand. This won't kill all of them because they reproduce so quickly, but it slows them down until you have time to take other actions. To control light infestations, spray the undersides of the leaves vigorously with water. Spray the water in the early morning, once every other day, for three days. For medium to heavy infestations, spray with insecticidal soap every two to three days until the aphids are gone. If these pests become a very serious problem, make two applications of pyrethrum, three to five days apart.

Holes in Leaves, Flowers, or Buds

Beetles

Beetles eat leaves or flowers of roses, leaving obvious holes. In large numbers, they can completely skeletonize leaves and destroy flowers. Sometimes the grubs of beetles attack the roots of roses. You won't see any immediate, obvious symptoms, but rather a general weakening of the plant. Some of the more troublesome pests of roses include fuller rose beetles, goldsmith beetles, Japanese beetles, rose chafer beetles, rose curculios, and rose leaf beetles.

Fuller Rose Beetles. See page 271.

Goldsmith Beetles. Common in the eastern United States and in the Southwest, this hairy, lemon yellow beetle (*Cotalpa lanigera*) is 1 inch long and looks like a June bug. The larvae resemble white grubs and attack the roots of roses.

Japanese Beetles. These ubiquitous pests (*Popillia japonica*) are familiar to most gardeners. The adult beetles are ½ inch long and shiny, metallic green with copper-colored wing covers. The larvae are grayish white grubs with dark brown heads. Fully grown, these plump pests measure ¾ to 1 inch long. They lie in the soil in a distinctive arc-shaped resting position.

Rose Chafer Beetles. Also known as the rose bug or rose beetle (*Macrodactylus subspinosus*), this pest is tan, has long legs, and measures ⅓ to ½ inch long. It skeletonizes foliage and damages flowers. Rose chafer beetles are common in the northeastern states and as far west as Colorado.

Rose Curculios. See page 271.

Rose Leaf Beetles. These small, oval, green or blue metallic-looking insects (*Hodonata puncticollis*) bore into rosebuds and partially opened flowers as well as foliage. Larvae sometimes damage the roots of roses.

Controlling Beetles

For the most part, all beetles are controlled the same way. First, pick them off the plants and drop them into a pail of soapy water. It's easiest to pick them in the early morning, before they dry out and become more mobile. If the infestation is light, this is all you will need to do; otherwise, move on to additional control measures. Spray infested roses with a solution of pyrethrum and isopropyl alcohol, mixing 1 tablespoon of alcohol with every pint of pyrethrum mixture. Apply this solution every three to five days until the problem is corrected. A rotenone spray or dust will also control beetles. Some gardeners have found that white geraniums are fatal to Japanese beetles and that the beetles prefer the deadly plants to their roses. If you're adventurous, you might experiment by underplanting your rose bushes with white geraniums.

You can kill the larvae of most of these beetles with milky spore disease (*Bacillus popilliae*). Tests in Ohio showed that Japanese beetles preferred to lay their eggs in low-pH (acidic) lawns and would avoid lime-rich soils. When pulverized dolomitic limestone was applied to a lawn at the rate of 100 pounds per 1,000 square feet, it served as a barrier on the soil surface and prevented the beetles from laying eggs in the lawn.

Japanese beetle traps are effective, but their lures often work too well for your garden's good. Recent tests have shown that they can draw more beetles to your garden than they trap. Unless you can site the traps far away from vulnerable plants—at least 50 feet downwind—you'd be better off letting the neighbors' traps lure *your* beetles than setting up traps for theirs.

Caterpillars

If the leaves or buds of your roses are chewed, it's very likely that some type of caterpillar has done the damage. The most common caterpillar pests of roses include the bristly rose-slug, the fall webworm, and the rose budworm.

Bristly Rose-Slugs. You wouldn't want to meet up with this insect in the middle of a dark night. Contrary to its name, the bristly rose-slug (*Cladius isomerus*) isn't a slug at all, but the ½-inch-long, hairy, slimy larva of a sawfly. These larvae chew on the undersides of rose leaves, skeletonizing them, and then eat holes clear through. They are active primarily at night. The adults eat entire leaves. If you handpick them, wear gloves because their bristles can irritate the skin.

Fall Webworms. These pale yellow or green caterpillars (*Hyphantria cunea*) are 1 inch long. The adult moth has white- to brown-spotted wings with a spread of 1½ inches. Caterpillars attack in August, when you'll find their webbed nests among the foliage. Inside the nests, you'll see leaves skeletonized from webworm feeding. Cut out or remove well-established nests. As soon as you spot webs forming, spray the entire rose bush with Bt (*Bacillus thuringiensis*). Spray every three to five days, making two or three applications.

Rose Budworms. Two types of budworm have been known to infest roses. One is whitish orange, about ⅛ inch long; the other is green, about ¾ inch long. They feed on rosebuds and leaves.

Controlling Caterpillars

Pick off caterpillars and their nests, and destroy the infested buds, leaves, or stems. Then spray the plant weekly with Bt (*Bacillus thuringiensis*) until the symptoms and the caterpillars disappear. Repeated applications of insecticidal soap can be used to control bristly rose-slugs.

Slugs and Snails

Large, ragged holes in the leaves of your roses and slimy trails on or around the plants are sure signs of slug and/or snail attack. These creatures are particularly attracted to damaged plants. They begin feeding at the bottom and work their way up. A moist, well-mulched garden with acidic soil is heaven to them. They're active at night, rasping holes in rose leaves with their filelike tongues. After a night of debauchery, they hide under boards or leaf litter during the day. Slugs and snails are always most destructive during rainy spells.

The best way to control slugs and snails in a rose bed is to keep them out. If your roses are regularly raided by slugs and snails, bar their paths with Snail-Barr, a 3-inch-wide band of thin, flexible copper sheeting. If you grow roses in raised beds that are edged with boards or railroad ties, attach Snail-Barr around the outside. Slugs and snails get an electric shock when their slimy bodies encounter the copper, and they don't stay around to prolong the encounter. Most of the companies listed under "Controls" in the source list at the end of this book offer flexible copper sheeting.

The needle-sharp crystals of diatomaceous earth also act as an effective barrier to soft-bodied insects such as slugs and snails. Spread diatomaceous earth around the plants you want to protect, and reapply after rain.

For roses growing in the landscape, as opposed to ones in formal rose beds, a multifaceted approach to control is best. Remove boards, rocks, clippings, and other debris to cut down on the places where these pests hide during the day. Or, check daily under favorite hiding places, handpick snoozing slugs, crush them or seal them into a jar full of water and kerosene or insecticidal soap, and discard them. Inverted flowerpots, pieces of grapefruit peel, and cabbage leaves will lure slugs and can be used to trap them. Handpicking at night with a flashlight can be effective if started early in the spring. Traps baited with beer or yeast and water are also effective. To make an effective trap, cut a 2-inch hole in the lid of a coffee can or a small plastic container and bury the container flush with the soil. Slugs are attracted to the yeast in the beer, climb down through the hole in the lid, and drown. The key is to begin trapping very early in the season in order to prevent the population from building up. Surrounding plants with barriers of sand, ashes, or copper sheeting will discourage slugs from invading your plantings.

Canes Girdled, Die Back; Leaves Wilt

Borers
Borers are the larvae of various insects. As their name implies, they bore into the canes of roses, causing new growth to wilt suddenly.

Carpenter Bee Larvae. Carpenter bees (*Ceratina* spp.) are ⅓-inch-long, black or metallic-colored bees that lay eggs in rose canes. Their larvae will bore out the pith (soft center) of rose canes, which causes serious wilting.

Raspberry Cane Borers. The adults of this pest (*Oberea maculata*) are slender beetles, striped black and yellow and about ½ inch long. The larvae make holes in canes and bore down through the canes to the crowns below the ground, where they pupate. This takes them from one to two seasons. They attack uninjured canes at a point 6 to 8 inches below the ends of the tips, causing them to droop and the leaves to wilt.

Rose Stem Girdlers. Girdler larvae (*Agrilus aurichalceus*) mine the canes of roses, traveling in a spiral up the stems as they go. The stems swell up, split, and often die. The adults are metallic green, ¼-inch-long beetles. They appear in June and July.

Rose Stem Sawflies. This wasplike insect (*Hartigia trimaculata*) has transparent wings. Its larvae are yellowish white worms with brown heads, which grow to ⅗ inch in length. They bore into the canes, causing them to wilt and die back.

Controlling Borers
As soon as you discover borer damage, prune the canes below the infested section. To keep the larvae from entering cut canes, insert a flat-headed tack in the end or plug the hole with grafting wax, putty, or paraffin. Some gardeners paint the end of a pruned cane with shellac or tree wound paint.

Leaves Stippled White

Leafhoppers
The nymphs and adults of leafhoppers suck juices from the leaves, buds, and stems of roses, leaving tiny white spots on the surfaces of the plants. Eventually, the leaves shrivel and drop off. You may also find secretions of honeydew on your plants, which foster the growth of sooty mold.

Rose leafhoppers (*Edwardsiana rosae*) are ¼- to ⅓-inch-long, wedge-shaped insects. They carry their wings in a rooflike position above their bodies.

They're very active, and, true to their name, they hop suddenly or move sideways when disturbed. Their eggs hatch in May, and young insects feed on leaf undersides. Potato leafhoppers (*Empoascus fabae*) also sometimes infest roses.

Spray infested plants with a mixture of insecticidal soap and isopropyl alcohol. Make this mix by adding 1 tablespoon of alcohol to each pint of insecticidal soap solution. You may need to make two applications, three to five days apart. If leafhoppers are a common problem in your backyard, consider covering your roses with floating row covers, like Reemay, in early spring to deny them access. Take the covers off when the air temperature under it exceeds 85°F.

Leaves Stuck or Rolled Together with Silk; Foliage Discolored

Leafrollers
The caterpillars of these insects protect themselves while feeding on roses by rolling leaves into tubes around themselves and binding them with strands or webs of silk. The leaves become skeletonized, turn brown, and die.

Roses are vulnerable to attack from a few different species, including fruit tree leafrollers (*Archips argyrospilus*), oblique-banded leafrollers (*Choristoneura rosaceana*), and red-banded leafrollers (*Argyrotaenia velutinana*). The caterpillars may be light to dark green or cream to yellow in color and ⅜ to 1¾ inches long. Adult moths are brown or gray and ¼ to ½ inch long.

Handpick the rolled leaves and destroy the caterpillars. To prevent problems with leafrollers, spray roses with Bt (*Bacillus thuringiensis*) just as the flower buds begin to emerge on the rose bush. This will kill any young caterpillars before they can begin feeding. A dormant oil spray applied in very early spring while your plants are dormant also reduces leafroller problems.

Leaves Yellowed; Plants Stunted

Nematodes
Nematodes feed on the roots of plants. As a result,

infested roses look sickly, wilted, or stunted and their foliage is yellowed or bronzed. They decline slowly and die. Root systems are poorly developed, even partially decayed, and have galls. The effects of nematode activity are most apparent in hot weather, when plants recover poorly from the heat.

The root knot nematodes *Meloidogyne hapla* and *M. incognita* attack roses. The former infests roses grown outdoors in the northern states; the latter is a common pest of greenhouse roses in the North and outdoor roses in the South. Nematodes are not insects, but slender, unsegmented roundworms that are barely visible to the unaided eye.

Control these pests by adding lots of compost—especially leaf mold—to the soil around your roses. This encourages beneficial fungi, which attack nematodes. Fertilize your plants with a drench of fish emulsion to repel nematodes.

Flower Buds and Leaves Turn Black and Die

Rose Midges
Midges (*Dasineura rhodophaga*) are microscopic insects, but they can blacken and kill rosebuds and leaves. It's the whitish maggots that are destructive. They usually hatch after the first bloom cycle and rasp tender plant tissue as they feed. Leaves and blossoms blacken and shrivel. Unchecked, a heavy midge infestation can eliminate all bloom from late spring through early fall. After feeding, the larvae drop to the soil where they pupate and emerge as reddish or yellowish brown flies within a week.

As soon as you spot midge damage, remove and destroy all the infected flower buds.

Leaves Discolored; Small Bumps on Leaves and Canes

Scale
The first sign of a scale attack is wilting and darkening of the leaves. This is followed by leaf drop, reduced growth, and stunted plants. Heavy infestations of scale can kill a plant. Some species excrete honeydew, which coats the foliage, attracting ants

and encouraging the growth of sooty mold. If you suspect scale, look for the pests themselves. Scale insects have rounded waxy coverings and are $1/10$ to $2/5$ inch in diameter, giving them the appearance of small bumps. You can find them on leaves and canes. Depending on the species, they may be white, yellow, brown, or black. The most common species to attack roses is the rose scale (*Aulacaspis rosae*). It is gray or brown and thickly infests older canes. Other species include San Jose scale (*Quadraspidiotus perniciosus*), black scale (*Saissetia oleae*), cottony-maple scale (*Pulvinaria innumerabilis*), and oyster-shell scale (*Lepidosaphes ulmi*). Scale outbreaks can be triggered by environmental stresses such as too much or too little water. Overfeeding roses with nitrogen also encourages scale populations by accelerating the growth of plants. Scales are attracted to the new, succulent, sugary shoots.

If you've caught the problem before many scale have infested your plants, simply scrape them off with your fingernail or with a cotton swab dipped in rubbing alcohol. For heavier infestations, spray plants with a mixture of alcohol and insecticidal soap every three days for two weeks. Make this mix by adding 1 tablespoon of alcohol to each pint of insecticidal soap solution.

Leaves Stippled with Tiny Yellow Dots; Webby Foliage

Spider Mites
Yellow stippling on rose foliage is a sign of spider mite infestation. Several species of spider mites, including two-spotted spider mites (*Tetranychus urticae*), attack roses. They spin webs across leaf surfaces and on new growth. As they continue to feed, leaves become spotted with red, yellow, or brown spots; then they curl and eventually drop off. Some floribunda roses are so susceptible to mites that they lose their leaves prematurely. You'll find mites on the undersides of leaves. They are about $1/50$ inch long (the size of a grain of pepper) and may be yellow, green, red, or brown.

As soon as you discover stippled leaves on your roses and have determined that mites are the cause, begin control measures. Spray plants in the early morning with a forceful stream of water, to knock the mites off the leaves. Repeat this once a day for three days. If mites are still present, spray with insecticidal soap every three to five days for two weeks. To avoid spreading the mites from plant to plant, don't touch healthy plants after examining infested ones.

Brown Edges on Blossoms; Buds Open Partially or Not at All

Thrips
If you see brown edges on your rose blossoms, and the buds open only partially or don't open at all, suspect thrips. These insects attack buds in their early stages, working among the unfurled petals. The buds become deformed and fail to open properly, and the damaged petals turn brown and dry. New growth may also be damaged in the same way.

Roses are vulnerable to flower thrips (*Frankliniella tritici*) and tobacco thrips (*F. fusca*). The adults are tiny, slender, $1/25$-inch-long insects and may be pale yellow, black, or brown. They have four narrow wings fringed with long hairs, and their legs are very short.

Since thrips burrow deeply between the petals, early identification and control is important. Set out yellow sticky traps about four weeks after the last frost. As soon as you spot thrips on the traps, spray your roses with insecticidal soap every three days for two weeks. Commercially available predatory mites, lacewings, ladybugs, and beneficial nematodes are effective backups to the soap spray. Thrips prefer a dry environment, so make sure plants are adequately watered.

Leaves Notched

Weevils
Weevils, commonly called snout beetles, are a distinctive type of beetle with long, prominent snouts.

Weevils that attack roses eat foliage and flower buds.

Japanese Weevils. These weevils (*Pseudo-cneorhinus bifasciatus*) chew along the margins of rose leaves, giving them a notched appearance. If abundant, they can defoliate plants. The beetles are about ¼ inch long and light to dark brown in color with striped wing covers. They feed at night and hide in soil and plant debris during the day. The larvae of Japanese weevils bore into the roots and stems of roses.

Fuller Rose Beetles. This gray-brown wee-vil (*Pantomorus cervinus*) is found mostly in the South and Southwest. It has a white stripe on each wing cover and is about ⅓ inch long. It feeds at night, chewing ragged edges around rose leaves. During the day, it rests on twigs or in foliage and can be handpicked. The yellowish, brown-headed larvae feed on the roots of roses.

Rose Curculios. The rose curculio (*Rhyn-chites bicolor*) is a curious-looking pest—a red wee-vil with a long, black snout. Adults eat holes in the buds of roses, which often prevent them from open-ing. The white larvae feed on flowers and seeds. This pest occurs throughout most of the United States but is most common in the northern states. Collect and burn the dried, infested buds before larvae have a chance to complete their development.

Controlling Weevils

Weevils play dead when disturbed, folding their legs and dropping to the ground. You can turn this to your advantage when trying to remove these pests from your roses. Spread a cloth on the ground beneath infested plants; then gently shake the limbs of the plant. Startled weevils will drop onto the cloth and you can easily gather them up and destroy them. As soon as you find weevils on your roses, begin spraying weekly with a pyrethrum-alcohol solution. Make this solution by combining 1 table-spoon of alcohol with a pint of pyrethrum mix. Apply the mixture at night, at least 2 hours after dark. For further control, apply a sticky substance, such as Tanglefoot, around the main stem of the rose to prevent adults from climbing up and eating the leaves. Introduce predatory nematodes to the soil to stop the reproduction of weevils.

Leaves Yellowed; Plant Grows Poorly

Woolly Apple Aphids

Woolly apple aphid (*Eriosoma lanigerum*) attacks the roots of roses. The damage it causes interferes with the flow of water and nutrients through the plant, which eventually retards and distorts plant growth. It is most severe in young rose plants recently placed in the garden. Early symptoms of root aphid damage are yellow or brown leaves, which may wilt in bright sunlight. If you looked at the roots, you would find them scarred or knotted. Often you will see ants going into holes in the soil around the base of the rose plant. They may be herding woolly apple aphids, as they do aphids aboveground. Like all aphids, woolly apple aphids have soft, pear-shaped bodies and are about the size of the head of a pin. Unlike other aphids, they are purplish and covered with a bluish white, cottony material.

Once woolly apple aphids have become estab-lished in the soil around your roses, there is no environmentally safe method of eradicating them. You can reduce their impact by spraying your roses and nearby deciduous shrubs, as well as rose family trees, such as apple and pear, with dormant oil before the buds break in late winter or early spring. The dormant oil will smother the aphids' eggs. Con-trolling the ants that accompany these aphids will also help to keep the population down.

GENERAL DISEASE PROTECTION

The three major disease threats to roses are black spot, powdery mildew, and rust. However, most rose growers will face only two of these, because whereas mildew occurs across the country, the territories of rust and black spot seldom overlap.

You can prevent diseases in your roses relatively well with some careful planning and care. Good air circulation reduces disease by eliminating warm, moist conditions that favor the growth of fungi and bacteria. So, avoid planting roses in walled-in or crowded areas and prune to keep the centers of the plants open. Water plants before noon and try not to splatter the foliage. Water that splashes up from the ground can carry disease spores from the soil onto the plants. Spreading an organic mulch around your roses also helps keep fungal spores off your roses simply by covering soil that might be infected. Removing and destroying diseased foliage throughout the season and giving the area a thorough fall cleanup will also help minimize disease.

Although no rose is absolutely immune to diseases, there are cultivars that have a high degree of resistance. Growing these cultivars and practicing preventive maintenance will give you an added advantage in growing healthy, vigorously blooming roses. Some cultivars to consider include 'Anabell', 'Aquarius', 'Bonica', 'Cherish', 'Confidence', 'Duet', 'Europeana', 'Gold Medal', 'Pascali', 'Precious Platinum', 'Pristine', 'Queen Elizabeth', and 'Sea Pearl'.

An Annual Spray Program

Your roses will have an excellent chance of avoiding disease altogether if you implement the following preventive spray program. This program is safe to the environment, to you, and to your roses. If you have the proper spray equipment, it takes little time to follow. All of the products last for years in storage, so buy everything you need for the whole year. The basic requirements are an antidesiccant spray, wettable or liquid sulfur fungicide, and a bottle of dormant oil. This program protects against the three most common fungal diseases (black spot, powdery mildew, and rust) and controls mites, thrips, and aphids. If you can't find wettable or liquid sulfur, use fungicidal soap or other sulfur-based or copper-based fungicides. Do not use this program with rugosa roses; sulfur damages them, and they are immune to fungal diseases so they don't need it.

To implement the spray program, follow these steps:

1. In late fall or early winter, at the end of the growing season, after fall cleanup but before the hard freeze sets in, spray each of your rose bushes thoroughly with an antidesiccant. Follow the manufacturer's directions for repeating applications. This protects plants from drying out in winter, but also presents a barrier to any spores that might land on your roses during warm spells.

2. Early in spring, when you finish your spring pruning but while the plants are still dormant, spray them with fungicidal soap or wettable sulfur fungicide and then cover them completely with dormant oil. The fungicide kills most of the spores; then the dormant oil suffocates any that remain. The oil also presents a barrier to airborne spores.

3. From the time when leaves first emerge, and every seven days thereafter until July 4, spray each plant again with fungicidal soap or a wettable sulfur fungicide. Remember, sulfur sprays should not be applied in hot sun or when temperatures exceed 85°F.

4. Continue to spray with the fungicidal soap or sulfur fungicide from July 4 until the first frost, making applications every ten days.

MOST COMMON DISEASES

Black Spots on Leaves

Black Spot

Not surprisingly, the fungal disease black spot (*Diplocarpon rosae*) produces black spots on the leaves of infected plants. These spots are surrounded with yellow. Eventually, leaves turn yellowish pink and fall off. In severe cases, this disease can defoliate a rose bush by midsummer.

Black spot thrives in moist environments and is most common in northeastern and southeastern states, and in some midwestern states where summers are warm and moist. Black spot begins to appear when the air temperatures approach 65°F and rain is abundant or humidity high. Infection begins on leaves low to the ground. Young leaves, 6 to 14 days old, are the first to go.

To control this disease, prune and destroy all the affected leaves immediately and begin weekly applications of fungicidal soap or a wettable or liquid sulfur spray, continuing applications throughout the season.

Hybrid tea roses that show superior resistance to black spot include 'Tropicana', 'First Prize', 'Miss All-American Beauty', 'Mister Lincoln', 'Tiffany', 'Portrait', 'Pink Peace', 'Pristine', 'Proud Land', 'Duet', 'Peace', and 'Electron'.

Grandiflora roses with resistance to black spot include 'Queen Elizabeth', 'Prominent', 'Montezuma', and 'Sonia'.

For black spot–resistant floribundas, consider 'Rose Parade', 'Razzle Dazzle', 'Gene Boerner', 'Europeana', 'First Edition', 'Ivory Fashion', 'Carrousel', and 'Angel Face'.

Buds Fail to Open

Blight
If the buds on your roses don't open but turn brown and decay instead, your plants have been infected with botrytis blight (*Botrytis cinerea* or *B. allii*). The fungus that causes this disease resides in old blooms and in winter-killed canes, so pick off and destroy the faded blooms. Spray shrubs weekly with a sulfur- or copper-based fungicide such as a fungicidal soap.

Plants Grow Poorly; Tumorlike Growth on Roots or Base of Plants

Crown Gall
If your roses look a little sickly, inspect them closely. You may find a rough, tumorlike growth near the base of the plant or on the roots. Such a growth indicates crown gall. This bacterial disease (*Agrobacterium tumefaciens*) often gains entry to a plant through wounds made when cultivating. The galls should be pruned off and the wound sealed with landscape paint or putty. Disinfect the knife between cuts to avoid spreading the disease.

White Powder Covering Leaves and Buds

Powdery Mildew
Powdery mildew is easily recognized by the thin, white, powdery growth of fungus (*Spaerotheca pannosa*) that grows on leaves and canes. This disease infects young leaves first. Raised, blisterlike areas develop, which cause the leaves to curl, then the infected leaves become covered with grayish white powdery fungus. This disease hits flowers, too, and you may find the unopened flower buds of infected plants white with mildew. The buds may not open at all.

Mildew prefers young, succulent growth. The mature tissue on the plant is usually not affected. The disease usually occurs during periods of cool nights, humid days, and no rain and is severe only in coastal areas, like the Pacific Coast, where temperatures are moderate, high cloud cover or fog is common, and summer rainfall is minimal.

As soon as you discover this disease on your roses, prune off the infected leaves or tips and spray the plants weekly with fungicidal soap or liquid or wettable sulfur. If powdery mildew is a common problem in your yard, take preventive measures and begin spraying roses in early spring while they are still dormant. Use the spray schedule described earlier in this section. Keep an eye on your roses when temperatures reach around 65°F and it hasn't rained in a while: These conditions favor the growth of the powdery mildew fungus.

Hybrid teas with resistance to powdery mildew include 'Tiffany', 'Pristine', 'Miss All-American Beauty', 'Futura', 'Pascali', 'Peace', 'Seashell', 'Pink Peace', 'Proud Land', 'Mister Lincoln', 'Tropicana', and 'Chicago Peace'.

'Queen Elizabeth' and 'Prominent' are grandifloras that show good resistance to powdery mildew.

The floribundas with a good track record include 'Europeana', 'Rose Parade', 'Charisma', 'Sarabande', 'Saratoga', 'Cathedral', 'Sunsprite', 'Razzle Dazzle', 'First Edition', and 'Evening Star'.

Raised Red-Orange or Yellow Pustules on Leaves

Rust
Small red-orange or yellow pustules on the leaves or canes of your roses indicate rust (*Phragmidium* spp.), a fungal disease. These spots usually develop on the undersides of leaves first and may be inconspicuous. Later, they pop up on the upper leaf surfaces and stems. Rose rust is primarily a problem in the western United States. Some cultivars will drop the infected leaves.

When you find rust spots, prune infected leaves and begin spraying your plants weekly with fungicidal soap or liquid or wettable sulfur, using the annual spray program described on page 272. If this disease commonly occurs on your roses, try to prevent it by spraying plants with fungicidal soap, liquid sulfur, or wettable sulfur in early spring, when temperatures optimal for rust coincide with heavy dew, rain, or periods of cloud cover or fog.

Canes Swollen and Discolored

Stem Canker
Swollen and discolored dead areas on rose canes can mean that the soft tissue just under the canes' surfaces is infected. Canes commonly split open, exposing underlying tissues and sometimes bleeding a gummy exudate. The cause is common canker or stem canker (*Leptosphaeria coniothyrium*), a fungal disease. Stem canker occurs in wounds on canes and in the cut ends of pruned canes, especially if the cut was not made close to a bud. Prompt pruning of infected canes is the best control.

PART 2

Problems in the Flower Garden

CHAPTER 5

Insects

Most of the insects you see in the flower garden are either harmless, adding a little color and diversity to the garden without threatening your plants, or beneficial, pollinating your flowers or eating pests. However, pest insects do visit the flower garden. Most of the time, their damage level is acceptable— you'd have to crawl within inches of your plants to see the few holes in the leaves. In these cases, the best policy is live and let live: Spraying would just disrupt the natural balance (which, after all, is keeping things under control) and waste your time and money. If you're threatened with an invasion, however, or if pests are making your garden look ragged and unsightly, it's time to reach for the controls.

Fortunately, flower gardeners have a variety of safe and effective controls for insect pests in the backyard. New botanicals, biologicals, and traps are being researched, tested, and marketed on a regular basis. Because more and more of these controls are effective only on one pest or a related group, and even broad-spectrum botanicals often work better on some pests than others, "know thine enemy" is the relevant commandment here. Identify your problem pest—*then* choose the appropriate control. An understanding of insects in general and how they identify and feed on various flowers will give you a better idea of how to use natural pesticides most effectively. (If it's a stomach poison, for example, you'll have to apply it to parts of the plant that the pest will eat.)

Of course, many of the pest problems you face in the flower garden can be prevented before they develop. The first line of defense is the plant's own built-in protections. If certain pests become problems almost every year, choose resistant cultivars whenever they're available. (Catalogs usually mention pest or disease resistance in their plant descriptions, and you can often get a listing from your cooperative extension agent.) By following good gardening practices and giving plants the care they need, you'll encourage all your plants' natural resistance to pests.

Insects themselves—the beneficial allies that prey on or parasitize pests—are your second line of defense. For that reason, there is no need to kill off every last pest insect on your property. The beneficial predators need some food to encourage them to stay around. A healthy balance of beneficial and pest insects tends to keep outbreaks under control.

Despite our best preventive efforts, however, occasionally pest insects appear in overwhelming numbers. At such times, the third line of defense is an environmentally safe pesticide. Many biological and botanical pesticides, as well as organic controls such as insecticidal soap and diatomaceous earth, are now available at garden centers and through mail order.

The best approach to pest control in the flower garden is a well-rounded strategy that includes good garden practices, prevention, and, when needed, safe controls. With such an approach, your garden can be beautiful and comparatively problem-free year after year.

IDENTIFYING THE PEST

Obviously, identification of invading insect pests is the key to sucessful prevention and control. Develop the habit of observing the leaves and buds of your flowering plants closely. As you become familiar with the look of the plant, you will be able to see symptoms of pest infestation as soon as they develop. Knowledge of characteristic symptoms will make it easier to identify the insect culprit. Then you can plan a control strategy.

Look for Symptoms

The signs of insect attack are easily recognized, although a few may resemble disease symptoms. Some of the most common symptoms of insect pest attack include the following:

- Leaves chewed from the outside edge
- Holes chewed in the leaves
- Complete defoliation of the plant
- Leaves wilted and discolored
- Discolored speckles on the leaves
- Leaves curled or puckered

Once you are alerted to the possibility of an insect pest problem, examine the affected plant for the culprit itself. In most cases, insect pests attack the plant's tender new growth, so look there first. Check the upper leaf surfaces, then the undersides of the leaves (where most insects and their eggs are located), and finally, the point where leaves attach themselves to the stem. Examine the buds and flowers. Although pests can also strike roots, and many pests—such as the dreaded slug—work at night, this daytime search will reveal most of the common culprits.

There are a number of good books for identifying pest insects. *Rodale's Color Handbook of Garden Insects; Rodale's Garden Insect, Disease, and Weed Identification Guide; The Healthy Garden Handbook;* and *The Golden Guide to Insect Pests* are particularly easy to use.

CONTROLLING INSECT PESTS

When you have found a pest or its damage, the next step is determining an effective control. Your goal is to suppress pest populations before they do measurable harm to the flower garden.

Traps and Mechanical Controls

Before you reach for sprays or dusts, even though they might be comparatively harmless botanical or biological controls, consider trapping or some other physical means of removing insect pests from plants. Often these solutions to the problem are the safest, surest, and least expensive.

Cover Traps
Some pests seek protection from the hot sun during daylight hours. Trap them by offering a simple piece of board or a length of empty garden hose for shelter. Slugs happily crawl under boards, and earwigs readily crawl into a piece of garden hose. Check these traps twice a day and discard any inhabitants in a can of water containing a little kerosene or soap.

Handpicking
Handpicking, though not for the squeamish, is one of the oldest methods of safe and effective insect control. Used in the early stages of infestation, it can forestall a population explosion. Pick off pests and squash them between your fingers, or just drop them in a can of kerosene or soapy water. Wear tight-fitting rubber gloves if you don't like the idea of handling insects.

Locating insects and then handpicking them is slow work. To speed things up, spray water on the plants. Disgruntled pests will crawl from their wet hiding places to the tops of the plants, where it's easier to pick them.

Sticky Traps
Sticky traps can be used to cut down on aphid and whitefly numbers. You can purchase them or make your own. To make a trap, take a 10″ × 10″ piece of

Insect infestations cause a variety of symptoms when they infest plants. Some signs to look for include (*a*) holes chewed in the flowers or foliage, (*b*) deformed leaves or flowers that may be curled or puckered, and (*c*) leaves rolled or stuck together. You'll have to look closely for aphids; they are tiny sucking insects that may cluster on buds or stem tips (*d*).

Masonite or other sturdy material that is colored school bus yellow and cover it with something sticky such as Tangle-Trap, TackTrap, Stickem, glycerine, motor oil, or petroleum jelly. Hang the traps so that they are adjacent to, but not above, susceptible plants, or attach them to stakes. Clean and recoat them periodically.

Water Spray

A forceful water spray will take care of some pests by itself. Drench infested plants with a hose, targeting the undersides of leaves where many insects live and lay their eggs. Aphids and spider mites can be controlled this way. Spraying plants with water several days in succession will disrupt the pests' breeding and hatching cycles and can eliminate the population altogether.

Spray plants early in the morning. Use a hose with a nozzle that emits a fine spray of water. Turn the water on high and thoroughly spray the infested plant. Spray at least twice more, either three days in a row or every other day. This will wash off the pests that are already feeding on your plants and eliminate their eggs.

Natural Sprays and Dusts

If handpicking and mechanical controls are not effective, try a spray or dust to get rid of insect pests. Most products can be applied in either form, but sprays are a little easier to use and generally provide more thorough and even coverage than dusts. You can use virtually any type of sprayer, from a plastic, hand-held bottle to a large garden sprayer, depending on the size of the plant or the garden area you need to cover. (Most of the companies listed under "Supplies" in the source list at the end of this book sell quality sprayers.) Listed below are several different types of sprays and dusts, with details on how to use them.

Insecticidal Soap

Insecticidal soaps, such as Safer's, are now widely available commercially. They have been specially formulated to kill certain pest insects, while spar-ing beneficial insects. Insecticidal soap is biodegradable and breaks down within 7 to 14 days, so it does not harm plants or the environment. It is safe to use around animals and people. While homemade soap sprays might be effective, only commercial soap spray is recommended for uniform performance. It is easy to use and is effective against many insect pests, including aphids, spider mites, and whiteflies.

If you are dealing with a heavy infestation, spray affected plants every two to three days for two weeks. Set the sprayer for medium droplet size and strong pressure to thoroughly wet all surfaces of the plant from top to bottom. Insecticidal soap is a contact insecticide, so it must directly contact the insect to be effective. Take care to spray the undersides of leaves, where you will find most of the pests.

Insecticidal Soap and Alcohol. Increase the effectiveness of insecticidal soap by mixing it with isopropyl alcohol. Make this mix by adding a tablespoon of alcohol to each pint of insecticidal soap solution. Alcohol alone can burn plants, but diluted in the soap spray, it penetrates an insect's waxy protective coating and carries the pesticide with it, bringing it in direct contact with the insect's body.

Garlic Spray

We're all cautious about eating garlic or onions when we're in the company of others, fearful that those we're talking with will turn and walk away at the smell of garlic breath. Apparently garlic has that effect on pest insects, too. Homemade sprays from garlic, onions, or chives have been found to effectively repel certain insect pests. To make the spray, mix ½ cup of finely chopped garlic cloves, onions, or chives with 1 pint of water; then strain out the particles and spray.

Researchers are working on a more potent brew made by soaking 10 to 15 finely minced garlic cloves in a pint of mineral oil for at least 24 hours. The oil is then strained. Two teaspoons of the oil are mixed with a quart of insecticidal soap solution and applied to infested plants. Some tests show the soap spray's effectiveness has been greatly improved by the garlic oil, even on pests not normally killed by the soap alone. However, the true effectiveness of this spray is still undetermined.

Diatomaceous Earth

Diatomaceous earth (often called D.E.) keeps pests from plants in the same way that hot coals would prevent most people from walking up to something. Diatomaceous earth is a powder made from the fossilized skeletons of diatoms—microscopic sea creatures composed primarily of silica. The granules of this fine powder are soft to us, but to insects they are very sharp; they cut the bodies of soft-bodied pests such as caterpillars on contact, causing them to dehydrate and die. D.E. is effective against aphids, caterpillars (including cutworms), fly maggots, grubs, mites, slugs, and the like. It does not harm earthworms.

When you buy D.E., make sure that it's designated for agricultural use, not for use in swimming pool filters. To apply, dust D.E. around the base of plants in the late evening, ideally after a light rain or after plants have been sprayed with a fine mist of water. Dust progressively upward from the ground, covering stems and leaves, especially the undersides of leaves. You can also spray it on plants. Put ¼ pound D.E. in a 5-gallon sprayer. Add 1 teaspoon of flax soap (available from paint supply stores) or insecticidal soap concentrate in a quart of warm water, then add more water, enough to make 5 gallons. Mix the solution well. Reapply after rain.

Biological Controls

The variety of beneficial insects, bacteria, and viruses that already reside in your yard will help protect your flowering plants from pest insects. Perhaps the best known of the biological controls are the predatory and parasitic insects that attack and destroy pests. There are also microscopic creatures—the viruses and bacteria—that are more than willing to enlist in your war against the troublesome insects in your flower garden. Two that are readily available for use against flower pests are Bt (*Bacillus thuringiensis*) and milky spore disease (*Bacillus popilliae*).

Bt (*Bacillus thuringiensis*)

Bt is a naturally occurring parasitic bacterium that attacks leaf-eating caterpillars. It invades their digestive systems and kills them within 24 hours. You can purchase commercially prepared Bt under a number of trade names, including Bactur, Biotrol, Dipel, and Thuricide. Bt is sold in both powder and liquid forms. The powder may be applied as a dust or diluted with water and sprayed on plants. The liquid is usually concentrated and should be diluted with water according to package instructions. The liquid Bt can only be stored for a year; in effect, you need to replace it each season. Stored in the container in a cool, dark place, powdered Bt will remain viable for three to five years.

Because Bt kills *all* caterpillars, it's important to make sure that you've got a problem before you apply it. Otherwise, you could kill the beautiful butterflies and lovely nocturnal moths that add such delight to the summer garden. Try to identify the moths and butterflies hovering over your flowers; most are colorful and harmless. Make sure you're not destroying the parsleyworm that tomorrow might be a gorgeous black swallowtail. If caterpillars are causing unsightly damage—say, if corn earworms are eating holes in your ageratum foliage or leaftiers are rolling your forget-me-not leaves—try handpicking before resorting to Bt. If you're confronted by a major infestation or have too many plants to handpick, Bt is an effective control.

The timing of Bt applications is critical because it must be eaten by the caterpillars to be effective. Generally, caterpillars are most active in the spring and late summer. Observe your plants closely during these times, and as soon as you see destructive caterpillars beginning to feed, spray or dust plants with Bt. Thoroughly cover all parts of the plant leaves, especially the undersides. When using the powdered form of Bt, wet plants before you dust them. Dusting the undersurfaces as well as the top surfaces of leaves keeps Bt active longer because the bacteria survive longer out of direct sunlight. Reapply the dust after each rain.

To make a foliar spray from powdered Bt, follow the directions on the container. Spray infested plants every 10 to 14 days until the pest is under control. To help the diluted powder adhere to plant leaves, add 1 tablespoon of fish emulsion to each gallon of spray. A little commercial insecticidal soap or light horticultural oil also works as an adherent. The liquid concentrate formulation of Bt adheres well to plants.

Keep in mind that Bt breaks down in sunlight. The powdered form remains viable for only seven days after application, and the liquid spray form for just 24 hours. Apply Bt each year as the pest caterpillars emerge.

Milky Spore Disease (*Bacillus popilliae*)

Like Bt, milky spore disease is a bacterial disease. It is applied to lawns to control beetle grubs—specifically, the white grubs of the Japanese beetle, a major pest of roses and other flowers. Milky spore takes 2 to 3 years to provide complete control of grubs, but it continues to be effective for up to 20 years, so that a single application provides long-term control. It is sold as a dust, in granular from, or as a wettable powder under the trade names Doom, Grub Attack, and Japidemic. Apply in spring or fall, when grubs are most active. Because beetles can emerge from surrounding lawns and migrate to your flowers, you'll get best control if your neighbors apply milky spore to their lawns when you treat yours. Unused milky spore remains viable for several years.

The Last Resort— Botanical Poisons

In spite of every precaution, sometimes pest insects overwhelm a flower bed. In these cases, the traps, sprays, and other methods discussed above can't control the situation fast enough and prized flowers are threatened. Under these rare circumstances, it may be necessary to resort to the last line of defense—the botanical poisons. These products include pyrethrum, rotenone, ryania, and sabadilla. Although these poisons have been extracted from various plants and are, therefore, natural substances, they are deadly to all insects. They will kill off the pest insects that infest your plants, but they will also kill nearby beneficial insects, including honeybees. These products require careful handling for user safety, as well. Use them as a last resort in situations where there is no alternative. Because these products do break down quickly, they do not pose a significant threat to the environment.

Minimize the impact of botanical poisons by using them carefully. If a botanical poison is necessary while honeybees are pollinating, use pyrethrum rather than rotenone, and spray at dusk, when bees are least active. Even though it's more toxic to bees, pyrethrum breaks down more quickly—within 6 hours if the temperature is 55°F or higher. Foliar sprays of either pyrethrum or ryania are less toxic to bees than dusts. If a heavy dew is predicted, do not spray; the insecticide will not break down before the bees begin feeding in the morning.

Pyrethrum

Made from the crushed dried flowers of the painted or pyrethrum daisy (*Chrysanthemum cinerariifolium*), pyrethrum paralyzes many insects on contact. It acts quickly, passing directly through the skin of the insect and disrupting its nerve centers. The insect becomes disoriented and stunned. However, if an insect receives less than a lethal dose, it will revive completely. Pyrethrum residues do not persist in the environment, and their impact on pests lasts only 6 hours. It must contact the insect directly to be effective. Usually, two applications to the threatened plant, three to four days apart, will successfully control a pest problem. Apply pyrethrum in the evening to avoid killing bees, and don't use it near streams or ponds—it's toxic to fish.

Do not confuse this botanical insecticide with synthetic pyrethrins, like allethrin, or with the synthetic pyrethroids, which are altogether more complex and persistent types of chemicals and have a much more devastating effect on beneficial insects and the environment.

Pyrethrum plus Alcohol. We've already

seen that alcohol boosts the effectiveness of insecticidal soaps; it can also make pyrethrum more effective. Again, it penetrates an insect's waxy protective coating, allowing the pyrethrum to paralyze and kill the pest more quickly. To make this solution, mix 2 parts alcohol with 1 part water, then add the pyrethrum in the concentration called for on the bottle. Do not get this mixture on your skin. If you do, wash immediately with soap and water.

Pyrethrum Blends. In crisis situations, when the life of an important plant is seriously threatened by insect infestation and no other control has worked, you can raise the ante even higher. Potent blends of poisons are available that combine pyrethrum with rotenone, ryania, or both. In a typical blend, the pyrethrum serves as the immediate knockdown agent, while the rotenone or the ryania kills insects over a longer period. Apply these blends at dusk, after honeybees have returned to the hive.

Timed-Release Pyrethrum. For longer-term effectiveness, purchase pyrethrum that has been encapsulated so that it functions as a time-released insecticide when sprayed onto plants. It adheres to the leaves of plants and remains potent for up to a week. Look for X-clude, by Whitmire Research Laboratory, 3568 Tree Court Industrial Boulevard, St. Louis, MO 63122.

Rotenone

Rotenone is refined from the roots of several tropical plants, including derris, cube barbasco, and timbo. Rotenone is a stomach poison. When used properly, it doesn't harm humans, wildlife (except fish), or pets, but it is a very powerful insecticide and should be used with respect. It will kill beneficial insects, including ladybugs and honeybees, as well as pests. You can apply rotenone as a dust; however, less is needed if you dilute it with water and spray it on plants. Use it only at dusk, after the bees have returned to the hive. A 1 percent solution will take care of most insects. If you are dealing with Japanese beetles or weevils, or if the 1 percent solution doesn't seem to be effective, increase the concentration to 5 percent. Rotenone remains potent

for two to three days. Spraying once every three days, making two or three applications, should control most troublesome insect pests. Because it is very toxic to fish, do not spray it around bodies of water.

Sabadilla

The seeds of a lily from South America and the Caribbean are the source of sabadilla. One of the safer botanical poisons, it has little effect on mammals, but is toxic to bees. It is available only as a dust. Wet plants before applying for better coverage. Apply it weekly on the undersides of the leaves of infested plants until the target pests are under control. A contact poison, it controls such pests as aphids, blister beetles, squash bugs, stink bugs, and caterpillars. Sabadilla isn't easy to find, but it is available through mail-order catalogs. One brand name is Red Devil. Unlike most pest controls, sabadilla actually becomes *more* effective in storage.

Insect Predators and Parasites

As mentioned earlier in this chapter, many species of resident beneficial insects devour thousands of insects each day. Learn to recognize these "good" insects and make them welcome in your landscape.

Because many beneficial insects emerge later in the season than pest insects do, gardeners may be more aware of pest problems early in the season than they are later. When the beneficials arrive, they must have a steady food supply, so resist the temptation to eradicate all insect pests immediately. Beneficial predatory insects will stay in your yard and police it only if there is something for them to eat. Your goal should be to maintain a balance of "good" and "bad" insects, so use pesticides sparingly early in the season before beneficials come on the scene.

Create the Best Environment

While you can buy beneficial insects and introduce them into your garden, it is far cheaper and probably more effective to simply encourage the beneficial species native to your area. Create the kind of environment they like. The more diverse the plantings in and around your yard and garden, the more attractive it will be to a wide variety of helpful insects. The more permanent plantings you have around the yard—perennial beds, woodland gardens, groupings of shrubs—the more stable the habitat you offer for beneficials to reside in year after year. Some homeowners go so far as to set aside a special nursery, or insectary patch, where weeds, brambles, and wildflowers are encouraged to thrive, providing a haven for "good" bugs. (A wildflower meadow would provide the same environment.) These special plantings are most effective within 25 to 50 feet of the plants you are trying to protect, but they provide some protection up to 150 feet away. Hedgerows, windbreaks, and wooded patches also serve as nurseries for beneficials.

As for specific plants, trichogramma wasps find food and winter shelter on buckwheat, dill, mustard, and tansy. Parasitic wasps and flies are especially fond of black-eyed Susans, daisies, goldenrod, and related flowers. General favorites include Queen Anne's lace and other members of the parsley or carrot family (Umbelliferae)—herbs like angelica, anise, caraway, chervil, dill, lovage, and parsley—plus flowers such as asters, bachelor's buttons, milkweed, and yarrow. Some evergreens provide a haven for all sorts of helpful insects. Ample supplies of nectar and pollen provide food for predators when pest populations are low and for many beneficial adult parasites. See the box, "Beneficial Insects and the Plants That Attract Them," on the opposite page for suggestions on specific plants to grow.

Clyde Robin Seed Company (see the source list at the end of this book for the address) offers a wildflower mixture, Border Patrol, which is specially designed to attract and support beneficial insects. This mix produces an attractive wildflower garden with a secret agenda of supporting a beneficial insect population in your landscape. It contains seeds of angelica, baby-blue-eyes, bishop's flower, black-eyed Susan, candytuft, evening primrose, nasturtium, strawflower, wild buckwheat, and yarrow. Border Patrol is also available through Gardener's Supply (again, see the source list for the address).

Entomologist Linda Gilkeson has observed in her research that water is as important to maintaining a beneficial insect population as food and shelter. Consider placing two birdbaths in the yard—one for insect-eating songbirds, the other for beneficial insects. To make a birdbath attractive to insects, stack several piles of small stones in it to allow the insects to drink water without the danger of drowning. Place this bath in among the flowers where birds are less likely to land. You don't want them eating the beneficial insects you are trying to attract. Put the other birdbath out in the open. Birds prefer to land in open areas so they can see cats or dogs approaching. Don't forget a dish of water for your other garden ally, the toad. A sunken dish, perhaps shaded by a low shelter of rocks and/or boards, will keep this companionable, long-lived amphibian eating pests in your garden throughout the season.

Beneficial Insects and Nematodes Available Commercially

If you don't want to plant a wildflower patch or set up a birdbath to attract beneficials, you can still purchase beneficial insects and release them in your backyard. While it is not quite as simple as it sounds, this is an effective alternative when time or space limits your ability to attract naturally occurring beneficial insects. It is important to follow directions carefully, lest your newly purchased insects promptly fly away. Make the effort to determine the right time to release these pest fighters and follow the technique correctly so commercial beneficial insects will settle down in your garden.

Timing is critical. Introduce predatory and parasitic insects before pests get out of hand, but not prematurely. There must be sufficient numbers of pests to keep the beneficials busy and well fed. Unless they find insects to eat and the right plants to shelter them, beneficials will go elsewhere. Consider the type of environment needed by the beneficials you plan to purchase. Alter your backyard habitat to make sure that water is available and to provide the types of flowers mentioned above. Fol-

Beneficial Insects and the Plants That Attract Them

To attract beneficial insects to your garden and encourage them to stay, grow the plants they prefer.

Lacewings. Members of the carrot family, oleander, and wild lettuce.

Ladybugs. Alfalfa, angelica, coffeeberry, evergreen euonymous, goldenrod, Mexican tea, morning-glory, oleander, and yarrow. Ladybugs also like ragweed, but you probably don't want to plant this hayfever source in your garden!

Parasitic wasps. Members of the carrot family, members of the daisy family, buckwheat, buttercup, goldenrod, oleander, strawberries, and white clover.

Syrphid flies and hover flies. Members of the daisy family.

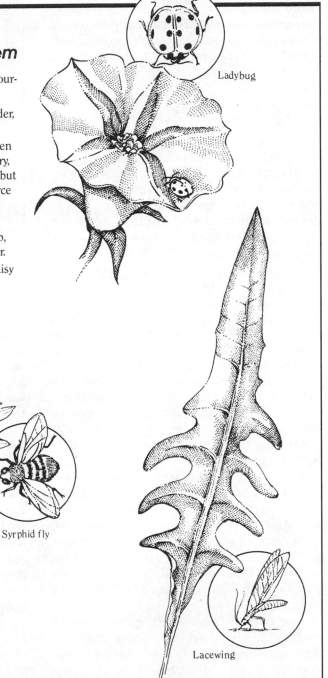

Ladybug

Syrphid fly

Lacewing

lowing are descriptions of the various predators and parasites that might be able to help you control the insect pests in your flower garden, along with information on how to introduce them into your backyard and keep them there.

Beneficial Nematodes

Not all nematodes are plant parasites. Certain species will help you control pests. These soil-dwelling, microscopic worms burrow inside pest grubs, soil-dwelling caterpillars (like cutworms), and maggots. They release bacteria, which usually kill the host insect within 48 hours. The nematodes then feed and reproduce within the dead insect.

Beneficial nematodes (the best known is *Neoaplectana carpocapsae*) attack black vine weevils, chinch bugs, cutworms, fall armyworms, fire ants, fungus gnats, Japanese beetle grubs, mole crickets, pine weevils, root maggots, rose chafers, sod webworms, strawberry weevils, white grubs, wireworms, and the larvae of cucumber beetles, flea beetles, gypsy moths, and squash vine borers. They will not harm beneficial insects or earthworms.

Beneficial nematodes are sold in packages of 1,000,000 and up. (Ten million—the amount in a box of BioSafe, one trade name for the nematodes—will treat up to 225 square feet.) They look like powder and can be stored in your refrigerator from two to six months. Mix them with water and use a sprayer or watering can to introduce them into the soil. Apply as soon as plants are up. An application of 50,000 nematodes per plant, for example, will control iris borers. To treat container-grown plants, apply roughly 5,000 nematodes to each gallon of soil. Water the nematodes into the soil around the base of your plants in the early spring. You should see effects within five days, but allow two months for maximum control.

Nematodes will overwinter in the soil as far north as Minnesota, but their survival rate is not high enough to provide effective insect control the following season, so reapply each year. Only the infective juvenile stage of the nematode is functional as an insect control.

Beneficial Insects Available Commercially

Beneficial nematodes
Green lacewing larvae
Ladybugs
Parasitic wasps
  Braconid wasps
  Chalcid wasps
  Ichneumon wasps
  Trichogramma wasps
Praying mantids
Predatory mites

Green Lacewing Larvae

Of all the beneficial insects you can buy through the mail, green lacewings (*Chrysopa* spp.) are probably the most effective all-purpose controls. Various species occur naturally throughout North America, but all have a slender body and long, delicate, transparent green wings. They are ½ to ¾ inch long and lay their tiny white eggs on threadlike stalks on the undersides of leaves. The adults eat pollen, nectar, and honeydew. It's the larvae, known for their voraciousness as aphid lions, that feed on pest insects. They are alligator-shaped, yellowish gray with brown marks and tufts of long hair, and they grow to about ⅜ inch long. Their most distinctive feature is a pair of long, thin jaws, which curve together like ice tongs. Three or four generations are produced each year. Lacewings pass the winter in the pupal stage in cocoons.

The insects lacewing larvae attack include aphids, leafhopper nymphs, mealybugs, mites, scale, whiteflies, and the eggs of caterpillars, mites, thrips, and other small pests. Ravenous little creatures, they can eat up to 60 aphids an hour. By boosting the natural lacewing population in your flower beds in the early summer, you can get a jump on these insect pests. Lacewings cannot bear the cold, so wait until the average air temperature is at least 70°F.

You can purchase lacewings in egg or larval form, although eggs are trickier to handle. Approximately 5,000 lacewing larvae will cover an area of about 2,500 square feet. They like to eat each other, so release them as soon as you receive them by placing them in different areas of the yard. Unlike other beneficial predators, lacewing larvae tend to stay in the area where they're released. But because their effective period is short—they become adults in one to three weeks—your best bet for control is to make three releases, one every five to seven days.

If you've ordered eggs, don't be surprised to find some larvae in the container; the eggs may have hatched in shipment. The eggs must be lodged gently in leaf and stem crevices, in spaces between petals, or in flower centers.

To encourage continued residence of newly introduced lacewings, place Wheast around the yard and garden. This is a sweetened dairy product sold as food for beneficial insects. Lacewing adults will also eat a honeydew-like mixture made from 1 part sugar and 1 part brewer's yeast in water and such commercially available versions as Bug Chow and BugPro, which should be mixed with enough water to give a molasses-like consistency. Put drops of this mixture on plants that are vulnerable to the pests you want lacewings to control. And don't forget to include nectar-rich flowers like oleander, Queen Anne's lace, and yarrow in your flower beds—adult lacewings will feel right at home.

Ladybugs

Ladybugs (*Hippodamia convergens*) are the beneficial insects that first come to mind for most of us. We learned in childhood that these rather endearing little orange-colored beetles with black spots are welcome in the garden. The reason is that both the larvae and the adults eat small insects. They can eat up to 40 aphids an hour—one adult may consume 5,000 aphids—and will also make meals of chinch bugs, mealybugs, scale, spider mites, thrips, whiteflies, and other soft-bodied pests, as well as various small larvae and insect eggs.

Ladybugs reverse their coloring from larval to adult stage. The ¼-inch-long beetles are orange to red with black spots, and the larvae are black with orange spots. The larvae are about ½ inch long and are usually covered with spines. The cylindrical eggs are yellow-orange. There is only one generation each year. In the East and Midwest, ladybugs overwinter in weedy areas or garden trash; in the West, they migrate to the mountains each fall.

Estimates differ, but plan on releasing about one ladybug per square foot—2 to 3 gallons of them per acre. Released too early in the season when their food supply is low, ladybugs will be forced to seek food in other yards. If you're not sure whether the pest population in your yard will support all the ladybugs you've bought, release only some of them and store the rest in the refrigerator, where they'll survive for up to three weeks. Release them late in the evening when the air has cooled off and dew has settled on the grass. If the ground is dry, lightly water the yard and garden. When releasing ladybugs, gently place handfuls of beetles at the base of your pest-ridden plants. Cover them immediately with damp straw or hay. They will soon climb the plant and begin to hunt for food. Walk 20 to 30 paces and release another handful near another group of infested plants. Handle ladybugs gently so as not to excite them into flight. Under normal conditions, they will mate within 48 hours and produce aphid-eating offspring in two weeks.

To encourage ladybugs to stay in your yard, grow pollen- and nectar-producing plants such as alfalfa, angelica, coffeeberry, evergreen euonymus, goldenrod, Mexican tea, morning-glory, oleander, and yarrow. Commercially available food attractants such as Bug Chow and BugPro, which should be mixed with water until molasses-like, then placed in droplets on the plants, also help newly released adults settle down.

Parasitic Wasps

These tiny insects, though a danger to insect pests,

do not sting gardeners. They willingly attack a variety of aphids and caterpillars. A few different types are available commercially through mail-order catalogs.

The adults of each of these parasites feed on nectar, which they obtain from weeds and wildflowers, particularly those in the daisy and carrot families. By planting some of these in your yard, you will encourage beneficial wasps to stay. Perhaps the best plant for all wasps is fennel. It seems to attract a large number of beneficial insects all season long.

Braconid Wasps. These wasps lay their eggs in the bodies of aphids, cucumber beetle grubs, cutworms, gypsy moths, hornworms, tent caterpillars, and various other larvae. The larvae hatch and grow inside their hosts, weakening and often killing them. Then they pupate on the backs of the hosts. These pupae are the "wasp eggs" so often seen on the backs of parasitized tomato hornworms.

Braconid wasps are sold commercially as eggs. The adults, which can be black, red, or yellow, are just $1/16$ to $5/8$ inch long. They prefer warm, humid conditions with temperatures above 59°F.

Chalcid Wasps. Chalcid wasps seek out aphids, asparagus beetles, leafhoppers, scale, whiteflies, and various caterpillars and other beetles. They lay their eggs in or on the pest. The larvae grow inside the pest, weakening and eventually killing it. Some adults also feed directly on the host. The adult chalcid is just $1/16$ to $3/8$ inch long, so you'll probably not see them unless you take pains to do so. Chalcid wasps are found throughout North America. Like the braconid wasps, chalcids prefer warm, humid conditions. One chalcid wasp of interest to flower gardeners, the trichogramma wasp (see below), is available commercially.

Ichneumon Wasps. Species of ichneumon wasp range in size from $1/8$ to 3 inches long and in color from yellow to brown and black. Adults lay eggs in borers, cutworms, eastern tent caterpillars, fall webworms, sawflies, and other larvae. Ichneumon wasps are not commercially available, but are found naturally throughout North America.

Trichogramma Wasps. The tiny ($1/45$-inch-long) trichogramma wasps kill the eggs of insect pests. The female wasp lays her eggs in the pest egg, and when the trichogramma egg hatches into a larva, it consumes its host. Among the 200 species of pest that trichogramma wasps parasitize are aphids, armyworms, cabbageworms, cutworms, fall webworms, gypsy moths, hornworms, leafrollers, loopers, mealybugs, scale, whiteflies, and various beetle larvae.

The release of trichogramma wasps is more effective when coupled with a spray of Bt (*Bacillus thuringiensis*) on infested plant leaves (see page 281); a sequence of three smaller releases is more effective than one large release. Make the three releases at two-week intervals so the wasps can parasitize host eggs as they're laid. The most effective species for protection of ornamentals is *Trichogramma minutum*, while the best species for general garden use is *T. pretiosum*. Trichogrammas are widely available commercially. Shipped in the egg, 20,000 will control host species on ½ acre.

Praying Mantids

These fearsome-looking creatures, the Darth Vaders of the insect world, are known for their voracious appetites for insects, including flies, mosquitoes, and moths. Various species are found throughout North America. They may be green or brownish and are about 2 inches long. They have papery wings and enlarged front legs adapted for grasping. Mantids overwinter in the egg stage. They deposit their eggs on twigs and grass stems in an egg case that looks like it was made from papier-mâché. Each case contains 200 or more eggs. One generation of mantids occurs each year.

When you buy praying mantis egg cases, you may get more than you bargained for. Unlike most of the other beneficials, the mantids prey on all insects, including each other. Each egg case may produce a couple of hundred hungry little mantids, but they will probably eat each other before they start working on your pest problem. The few that do survive will establish territories and drive off others of their kind. Regardless of how many egg cases you set out, by midsummer there will be only two or three mantids in a 20-by-40-foot flower garden. At this rate, those mantids will have cost you a couple of dollars each, and it is likely that you already have some in your backyard anyway.

If this hasn't discouraged you, and you still want to purchase mantids, try about three egg cases for 5,000 square feet of garden. To increase the young mantids' survival rate, put the egg cases in a screen-covered box. Check them every day after the trees begin to leaf out. Provide them with water, and, after two days, separate the newborns before they start eyeing one another. Scatter them around the garden. They will still drive off many of their brothers and sisters, but coverage should be fairly good, and you may even have a generation that will reproduce and help provide control next year.

Predatory Mites
Predatory mites will attack other mites, including spider mites and greenhouse mites. One release per season should provide continued control, since some mites will remain in the garden after the pest outbreak is stopped. You'll only need two predatory mites for each square foot or plant less than 2 feet tall; for larger plants, release two per large stem or branch. Mites flourish in warm weather with temperatures averaging between 68° and 86°F. If daytime temperatures are too low, their reproductive rate slows.

Animal Predators

In addition to naturally occurring spiders and beneficial insects like assassin bugs, ground beetles, robber flies, rove beetles, soldier beetles, and others that will police your yard for pests, you can count on help from larger beneficial creatures. Among these allies are bats, toads, songbirds, and lizards, all of which will eagerly gobble up grubs or binge on beetles. Of course, some of these animals can make pests of themselves, as well. For instance, skunks are voracious eaters of grubs and larvae, but they may inadvertently tear up your seedlings while looking for them. A few seasons of experience will indicate which ones are most valuable for your pest control problems and which ones need to be denied entry.

This inventory of pest-eating insects and animals that reside in a balanced, active backyard ecosystem provides a persuasive argument against the use of garden chemicals that might harm these friends of the garden. If you attract and encourage beneficial insects and predatory animals, you will find that most of your insect problems will be reduced considerably. The process may take a few years, but the results will be worth the effort. Once you have achieved a flower garden where a variety of plants, insects, and animals are in balance, no pest problem should get out of control. Remember, too, that when you have a system in which all the elements are balancing and controlling each other, you'll have less work to do.

Bats
Bats suffer from bad press. Stories of vampires, bites in the neck, and, lately, rabies obscure the ways in which bats offer very real benefits to the gardener. These unobtrusive mammals do not bother humans unless they are cornered or provoked. They venture out in the early evenings to make a meal of insects. A single bat can eat over 1,000 mosquitoes a night. And they produce bat guano, an excellent source of organic nitrogen. So, if you have a multitude of night-flying pests, you'd be better off putting up bat houses (now readily available from suppliers that offer a wide selection of birdhouses and feeders) than putting out the garlic.

Birds
Songbirds are seldom credited for all their help in controlling flower garden pests. Although many adult songbirds eat seeds, they also harvest tens of thousands of insects during the weeks when they raise their young. Baby birds cannot digest seeds and must be fed fresh insects. Increase your yard's bird population and you'll reduce the pest population.

Feeding birds during the winter months contributes significantly to maintaining a good-size bird population in your area. To encourage them to stay around over the summer, continue supplemental feeding at the feeder. Put out less food, less often. This will encourage them to stay in your yard

without making them entirely dependent on the feeder.

Provide an inviting backyard habitat for birds. Landscape with plants that offer tasty seeds and berries. *Echinacea* and *Rudbeckia* are favorite seed producers, and roses that produce large hips are good for winter nourishment. In addition, provide trees and shrubs where birds can take shelter and hide from the neighborhood cats and dogs. A supply of water year-round is a necessity: Sometimes water is more important than food. Remember to put the birdbath or water dish in the open where birds can see cats and dogs coming. Consider providing birdhouses and nesting platforms; then you'll be sure to have many parent birds collecting insects for their young.

Some of the best pest patrollers are house wrens, northern (formerly Baltimore) orioles, and chickadees, but many other birds will help you control insect pests. Even the lowly starling and the pugnacious English sparrow devour literally thousands of pest insects or insect larvae each season.

Frogs and Toads

Frogs and toads are princes when it comes to pest control. In a toad's eight-month active season, it can eat 24,000 insects—think of its 30-year lifetime average! Unfortunately, they don't discriminate between pests and beneficial insects. They'll happily gobble up large numbers of cutworms or potato beetles, but they're just as likely to eat helpful spiders or ladybugs. Frogs are particularly fond of sow bugs, and toads will devour ants, aphids, caterpillars, cutworms, grasshoppers, slugs, spiders, and squash bugs, but in general, what they eat depends on what happens to be in your yard. Unless you have a pond or water garden, you shouldn't attempt to keep frogs, but a half-buried water dish and a few hiding places will spell home to a toad. You can encourage toads to stay by leaving the door or driveway light on at night—they'll relish all those moths and beetles on the screen door.

Lizards

If you live in the southern or western states, the lizards you see lolling about on some sunny rock or warm patch of ground will help keep the insect population down. Lizards prefer stony, open terrain. Vertical surfaces like trees, stone walls, fences, and walls of abandoned buildings are favorite haunts, though anoles (our American chameleons) seem to like hedges, and beautiful, blue-lined skinks enjoy sunning on patios and chimneys. Lizards are harmless, amusing reptiles that can provide hours of leisurely observation as you go about your garden chores or indulge in a bit of sunning yourself. They should be encouraged to call your yard their home.

Common Birds and the Insects They Eat

You can attract some of the following insect-eating birds to your garden by providing them with an inviting habitat. Seed-producing annuals and perennials, roses that produce edible hips, and shrubs and trees that bear berries and provide shelter all will help encourage birds to stay in your garden. In addition, birdhouses and a source of drinking and bathing water, such as a birdbath, will provide even more encouragement.

Bluejays. Cutworms.

Blackbirds. Cutworms.

Chickadees. Aphids, Colorado potato beetles, flea beetles, and leafminers.

Purple finches. Aphids, Colorado potato beetles, cucumber beetles, flea beetles, leafhoppers, and leafminers.

Robins. Cabbage loopers, Colorado potato beetles, cutworms, leafminers, and slugs.

Sparrows. Cabbage loopers, cucumber beetles, cutworms, and leafhoppers.

Starlings. Cabbage loopers, imported cabbageworms, and Japanese beetles.

Warblers. Aphids, cucumber beetles, and flea beetles.

Wrens. Cutworms and leafhoppers.

You can encourage toads to make a home in your garden by providing them with a half-sunken water dish in a sheltered area.

Skunks

Skunks eat a wide variety of food, including chicken eggs, mice, snakes, and yellow jackets, but their favorite fare is plant-eating insects and larvae lurking in flower beds and lawns. They are particularly good at rooting out grubs and cutworms. Of course, they also love fruit, but they usually gather pieces that have fallen to the ground. So, if you see a skunk waddling across the lawn, don't chase it, especially since it will probably spray you with a fragrance you won't enjoy wearing.

Snakes

While certain parts of the country are plagued by genuinely dangerous snake species, most snakes that find their way into your backyard only represent a threat to garden pests. Garter snakes and the like prey on rodents and snap up bugs and beetles. Try to overcome any antipathy you may harbor to-

ward these creatures and permit them to hunt in and around your flower beds. They will return the courtesy by consuming pest insects for you and curbing the population explosion of bulb-eating voles and mice.

PREVENTING PEST DAMAGE

Of course, keeping insects pests away from your plants means even less work for you. You can discourage pests by following good gardening practices. Take a few precautionary steps before and after the growing season to foster plant vigor, because healthy plants are less susceptible to attack. Just a little more effort up front will save hours of labor later on.

Yard and Garden Cleanup

Perhaps the most important step you can take to maintain a pest-free and disease-free garden is to keep the yard and garden neat and clean. Fallen, decaying leaves and twigs shelter slugs, snails, and other pests that hide out during the day. Rotting weeds and plants, as well as soggy leaves and twigs, harbor pest insects and disease spores over the winter. Keeping your yard free of clutter and plant debris is essential to keeping down populations of insect pests next season.

Fall Cleanup

Clean up thoroughly in the fall. When all leaves and twigs have dropped from the shrubs and trees, and annuals and perennials have faded and died, collect all this organic material and compost it. However, refuse from diseased plants, as well as organic mulch that has been used during the growing season and may harbor disease, should be trashed. Get down to bare soil in all your gardens where annuals have been, around perennials, and under all shrubs.

Once your garden soil is cleared, cultivate it by raking thoroughly, if possible. In perennial beds and under shrubs, cultivate only 1 or 2 inches to avoid damaging the shallow root systems. This fall cultivation buries those insects that normally overwinter on the surface of the soil and brings to the surface those that prefer to snuggle a little deeper in the earth. The former suffocate; the latter will be eaten by birds.

This is also a good time to improve soil texture by incorporating humus-rich materials like shredded leaves and compost, and to add amendments like lime, greensand, or fresh manure that need a season to break down. By spring, the nutrients will be available to your plants.

About two to three weeks after that first deep cultivation, shallowly rake cleared gardens and bare areas again. This exposes more larvae to birds and other predators. Then leave the soil bare until it freezes hard.

Once the soil has frozen hard, lay a 2- to 6-inch layer of organic mulch over all the bare soil in the garden and around the shrubs. In those areas of the South where there is no freeze, leave the soil bare for at least a month before mulching it. Leaves chopped in a shredder, or shredded by running the lawn mower back and forth over them, are ideal mulching material. In the fall, leaves are plentiful and make excellent composting material next spring when they are removed before planting.

Spring Cleanup

After a major fall cleanup, spring preparation is simple. Remove the winter mulch from any areas where spring bulbs and early-blooming perennials have been planted. Leave the mulch around the shrubs and supplement it later in the season.

Barriers

Barriers are effective in preventing pest infestations in flower beds. There are a variety of barriers that will discourage pests from attacking ornamental plants by denying them access throughout the season.

Mulch

Among its other benefits, mulch can block some insect pests from reaching your plants, especially those that overwinter just under the surface of the soil. At the very least, it controls weeds, which may harbor pests. Black plastic mulch or any of the new agricultural fabric (geotextile) mulches laid on bare soil will prevent many larvae from emerging. Agricultural or landscape fabric mulch effectively prevents soil-dwelling insects like weevils from climbing up from the soil and attacking the foliage of flowering plants. Cut a circle of material wide enough so that it extends half again wider than the width of the plant all the way around. Fit the fabric mulch snugly around the stem of the plant and fasten it firmly to the soil. This makes a barrier, preventing the weevils from emerging from the soil.

Flexible Copper Sheeting

If your flowers are regularly raided by slugs and snails, bar their path, with Snail-Barr, a 3-inch-wide band of thin, flexible copper sheeting. You can wrap it around the outside edge of a window box or planter, or around the lip of a barrel or flower pot. If you grow flowers in raised beds that are edged with boards or railroad ties, attach Snail-Barr around the outside. Slugs and snails get an electric shock when their slimy bodies encounter the copper, and they don't stay around to prolong the encounter. Most suppliers listed under "Controls" in the source list at the end of this book offer flexible copper sheeting.

Diatomaceous Earth

The needle-sharp crystals of diatomaceous earth act as an effective barrier to soft-bodied insects, like slugs and snails. For more on how to use this natural deterrent, see page 281.

Resistant Plant Varieties

One of the best ways to prevent pest problems is to grow plants that simply aren't bothered by insects. Over the years, researchers have developed flower cultivars that are resistant to specific insect pests. There aren't yet as many insect-resistant ornamentals as there are vegetables, but researchers are breeding new insect- and disease-resistant flowers every season. Keep your eye on the market for new developments, and check seed catalogs for the resistant cultivars that will grow best in your area.

Learn Insect Emergence Times

Learn when a specific pest insect is likely to appear in your garden. Timing is crucial. If you are prepared at the right time with the right control, you can stop a problem before it has begun. Each species of insect has its own fairly predictable pattern of birth, feeding, maturity, reproduction, wintering, and death. If you can learn these patterns and how they coincide with your yard and garden calendar, you'll be able to predict when problems might arise. To facilitate preventive measures, it's especially important to know when overwintering pests are due to emerge in your flower garden.

The emergence times of insects vary from region to region, even neighborhood to neighborhood. Air temperature, moisture, and the availability of food all affect an insect's schedule. Check with your cooperative extension agent for a rough idea of when the problem insect typically appears, then record these times. More important, observe your garden and mark down the date when you begin to see each pest arrive. To make these emergence times easier to remember, connect them with some other garden-related event, such as the budding or blooming of lilacs in the spring, or jot them down in a garden diary.

Guide to Insect Pests

While there are hundreds of insects that damage flowers, most of them won't do any serious damage to your garden. A few unknowns may occasionally turn up in your backyard, but for the most part, a relatively small group of insects commonly occur on ornamental plants.

The following pest profiles will tell you a lot about the looks and lifestyles of these common insect pests. You'll find tips on the best methods of control, as well as several additional suggestions for removing the most common pests or preventing their attack. The recommended control might not be the best one for your particular situation. You may have to try others to find which works best in your yard. Trial and error will determine which is the most effective method in your flower garden. For more on how these pests affect your flowers, see the individual plant entries in part 1.

<u>INSECT</u> *Aphids*

DESCRIPTION

Aphids occur throughout the United States. They are quite tiny, ranging from ⅕ to 1/12 inch long. They have soft, pear-shaped bodies, and depending on the species, may be green, brown, black, purplish, red, or pink. They have long antennae and two tubelike projections at the rear of their abdomens. Some species have wings, while others are wingless. Aphids overwinter as eggs. They produce many generations a year. Descriptions of many different kinds of aphids are included in the individual plant entries in part 1.

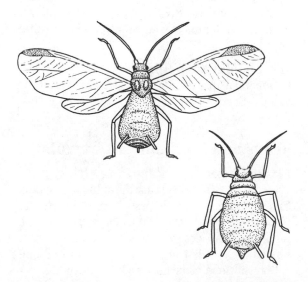

Aphid problems may be a symptom of too much nitrogen fertilizer or extravagant use of pesticides that kill off aphid predators and parasites. Switching to organic, slow-release fertilizers and nontoxic pesticides, and encouraging the natural enemies of aphids, are important steps in reducing aphid problems.

MOST OBVIOUS SYMPTOMS

Aphids suck the juices from leaves and stems. The foliage of infested plants will show pale or yellow spots. Whole leaves may turn yellow or brown. Leaves may be curled, puckered, or stunted. Flower buds may be seriously damaged, and flowers may be distorted. Plants may wilt under bright sunlight. Worse, aphids carry many viral diseases, such as mosaic. In addition, they excrete honeydew, which supports the growth of black, sooty mold and attracts ants. They can do a lot of damage to seedlings and tender ornamental plants like nasturtiums. Check the undersides of leaves for small groups of aphids. You may also find them clustered on the new buds, stems, and young leaves of your flowers.

Certain species, such as the corn root aphid (*Aphis maidiradicis*), live in the soil and attack roots, bulbs, and corms. If you suspect this soil-dwelling form is damaging your plants, the only way to verify it is to examine the roots of your plants for knots caused by the aphids. Ants often bring these soil-dwelling aphids to your plants. They will carry young aphids through their tunnels to plant roots and will nurse aphids' eggs through the winter. Besides the knotted roots, plants infested with root aphids show the same symptoms as those attacked by aboveground aphids—stunted and wilted with curled, yellowed foliage. Suspect root aphids if your plants seem to stop growing.

BEST CONTROL STRATEGY

Light infestations of aphids are easy to control. Simply spray infested plants vigorously once every other day, in the early morning, to knock the pests off your plants; wash the plants at least three times. Make sure the undersides of the leaves get their share of forceful spray. If this doesn't take care of them, use insecticidal soap every three to five days for two weeks. As a last resort, spray with pyrethrum once every three to five days, making two applications.

If your plants are infested with root aphids, the only way to effectively control them is by controlling the ants that herd them. Thorough spading in the fall disturbs ant nests and any caches of aphid eggs in them. Once a bed has been infested with root aphids, replant the following year with plants that are less susceptible.

MONITORING APHIDS

Emergence Time

In warmer climates, aphids reproduce continually. In the North, the eggs overwinter on bark or in ground litter, and the larvae emerge at the end of May or early June. Look for them on the undersides of leaves. If you see ants crawling on or around your plants, watch them to see if they are herding groups of aphids.

Early Warning Devices

Sticky Traps

You can buy or make yellow sticky traps, which will attract aphids and let you know when they have arrived. Place them on or near vulnerable plants a week or two before you expect aphids to appear.

Trap Crops

Nasturtiums can be used as a trap crop to spot early infestations of aphids, provided they fit in with your garden design. Grow them in the garden, or within 10 to 15 feet of it. Aphids are attracted to nasturtiums, so if these pests are in your yard, they'll show up on the nasturtiums, which you can then destroy.

OPTIONS FOR CONTROLLING APHIDS

Natural Sprays

A variety of natural pesticides are effective against aphids. See the beginning of this chapter for more information on making and using some of the following sprays.

Garlic Spray

Homemade sprays made with garlic have been found to effectively repel aphids. To make the spray, mix ½ cup finely chopped garlic cloves with 1 pint water; then strain out the particles.

Hot Pepper Spray

Hot pepper spray can be an effective insect control. Mix ½ cup finely chopped or ground hot peppers with 1 pint water. Strain the mixture to form a clear solution, then use this solution on your plants. Wear gloves to protect your skin from the burning pepper oils.

Insecticidal Soap Spray

Commercial insecticidal soap effectively controls aphids. Spray infested plants every three to five days for two weeks.

Traps and Mechanical Controls

Handpicking

Handpicking will help reduce the aphid population. Simply squeeze the little pests in your fingers. Try to destroy the first generation, before eggs are laid. Monitor plants closely to spot the earliest arrivals immediately—if left undiscovered, rapid multiplication will soon make handpicking impossible.

Sticky Traps

If you don't mind the appearance of them hanging in the flower beds, yellow sticky traps can provide another effective means of controlling aphids.

Botanical Poisons

See the beginning of this chapter for more information on the following botanical poisons.

Pyrethrum

Pyrethrum is most effective if it is mixed with iso-propyl alcohol, which helps the pyrethrum penetrate the aphids' skin. Add 1 tablespoon alcohol to 1 pint prepared pyrethrum. This mix must come in direct contact with the aphids to work.

Rotenone

Rotenone can be sprayed or dusted on plants; a 1 percent concentration should kill aphids.

Insect Predators and Parasites Available Commercially

Green lacewings, ladybugs, aphid midges, and braconid or chalcid wasps all feed on aphids.

PREVENTING APHID DAMAGE

Fall Cleanup

A thorough cleanup of your flower beds in the fall eliminates aphid eggs that might be overwintering on leaf litter or twigs of trees and shrubs. It is an important step in preventing future infestations of aphids.

Barriers

Diatomaceous Earth

If aphids visit certain flowers repeatedly, dust whole plants with diatomaceous earth.

Wood Ashes

Root aphids can sometimes be kept away from your plants by adding a small amount of wood ashes in the planting holes when you set plants out in spring.

Animal Predators

Winter songbirds eagerly search the bark of trees and devour as many aphid eggs as they can find. These birds include chickadees, chipping sparrows, nuthatches, purple finches, and warblers.

Insect Predators

Assassin bugs, bigeyed bugs, chalcid wasps, damselflies, dance flies, ground beetles, hover flies, ladybugs, minute pirate bugs, predatory thrips, soldier beetles, spiders, the orange larvae of predatory midges, and the sluglike larvae of flower flies all help to keep populations of aphids down.

Other Preventive Steps

Make sure the air can circulate around vulnerable plants. Stagnant air around plants creates a more attractive environment for aphids.

PLANTS AFFECTED

The following popular flowering plants are especially attractive to aphids.

- Bean aphid: dahlia, hyacinth, nasturtium, poppy.
- Crescent-marked lily aphid: annual aster, columbine, delphinium, larkspur, lily, nasturtium, salvia, tulip.
- Foxglove aphid: bellflower, chrysanthemum, columbine, geranium, lily, pansy, salvia, verbena.
- Green peach aphid: annual aster, chrysanthemum, dahlia, delphinium, forget-me-not, geranium, hyacinth, larkspur, lily, marigold, nasturtium, poppy, rose, snapdragon, verbena.
- Melon aphid: annual aster, chrysanthemum, columbine, cosmos, gladiolus, marigold, poppy, rose, snapdragon, sunflower, verbena.
- Root aphid: annual aster, cosmos, sunflower, yarrow.
- Tulip bulb aphid: gladiolus, tulip.
- Other aphids: annual aster, bachelor's button, balloon flower, black-eyed Susan, chrysanthemum, columbine, coreopsis, cosmos, crocus, dahlia, delphinium, geranium, hollyhock, impatiens, iris, larkspur, lily, nasturtium, perennial aster, rose, sunflower, tuberous begonia, verbena, yarrow, zinnia.

INSECT *Beetles*

Beetles make up 40 percent of all insects—a tremendous diversity of potential pests. Fortunately, only a few species of beetle are major pests of flowering plants. These include the Asiatic garden beetle, the blister beetle, the flea beetle, the Japanese beetle, and the rose chafer, which are given special sections below. Although weevils are also beetles, their mode of operation and appearance is so different that they are treated in a separate entry. For information on weevils, including fuller rose beetles, see page 330.

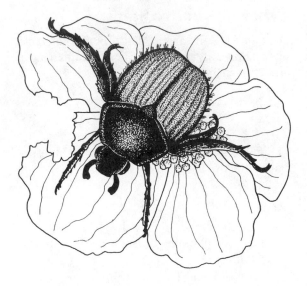

DESCRIPTION

Beetles come in a variety of colors, shapes, and sizes, but in general, all have hard, opaque wing covers that meet in a straight line down the middle of their backs. This characteristic gives beetles an armored appearance. Descriptions of different kinds of beetles are included in the individual plant entries in part 1.

MOST OBVIOUS SYMPTOMS

Beetles will eat leaves, stalks, and flowers. You may find damage ranging from small holes in the leaves of infested plants to large chunks ripped off the edges of leaves to defoliation of the entire plant. Some, like the Japanese beetle (*Popillia japonica*), will concentrate on the flower, burrowing in at the base where the petals are attached to the stem. Soil-dwelling beetle larvae, called grubs, eat plant roots.

BEST CONTROL STRATEGY

Light infestations can be controlled by handpicking. Crush the beetles or drop them in a pail of soapy water. A major infestation requires repeated handpicking, sometimes two or three times a day at its peak. As a last resort, spray infested plants with a solution of pyrethrum and isopropyl alcohol, mixing 1 tablespoon of alcohol with every pint of diluted pyrethrum mixture. Apply this solution every three to five days for two weeks, or until the problem is corrected.

For long-term control, spread milky spore disease (*Bacillus popilliae*) to lawns and garden. It will kill the larvae of most beetles, but it takes a few years to be completely effective. Cultivate your garden soil in the fall and again in the spring to expose beetle eggs, larvae, and pupae to the weather and to predatory birds.

OPTIONS FOR CONTROLLING BEETLES

Barriers

Floating Row Covers
Barriers such as floating row covers, like Reemay, can also be used to prevent beetles from gaining access to the plants, but this will look unsightly.

PREVENTING BEETLE DAMAGE

Animal Predators

Many songbirds, toads, and rodents feed on beetles.

Insect Predators

Spiders also feed on beetles.

PLANTS AFFECTED

Popular flowering plants enjoyed by beetles include black-eyed Susan, canna, coreopsis, cosmos, hollyhock, iris, lily, petunia, phlox, salvia, snapdragon, sunflower, and verbena. Special preferences of Asiatic garden beetles, blister beetles, flea beetles, Japanese beetles, and rose chafers are listed below.

Asiatic Garden Beetles

DESCRIPTION

The Asiatic garden beetle (*Maladera castanea*) is ½ inch long. It is cinnamon brown all over, but otherwise looks like the Japanese beetle. This nocturnal beetle is the one you're most likely to see at the back door light on summer nights. The C-shaped, grayish grubs are ¾ inch long with light brown heads and spines arranged in a semicircle on the underside of the last abdominal segment. Like Japanese beetle grubs, they live in the soil, feeding on grass roots. There is one generation a year. Adults are active from mid-July to mid-August, when they lay their eggs in the soil at the base of plants. Adults feed on ornamentals and can skeletonize leaves and flowers. These pests are common along the Atlantic seaboard.

BEST CONTROL STRATEGY

As for Beetles, opposite page.

PLANTS AFFECTED

Popular flowering plants favored by Asiatic garden beetles include annual aster, chrysanthemum, cosmos, delphinium, perennial aster, petunia, phlox, and zinnia.

Blister Beetles

DESCRIPTION

Blister beetles, like the black blister beetle (*Epicauta pennsylvanica*), are slender and about ¾ inch long, with soft, flexible wing covers. The entire body is black or dark gray, and the wing covers may be marked with white stripes or have white margins. Blister beetles are very active and frequently appear in large numbers in the latter part of June and July. The adult chews foliage and fruit. It is poisonous, causing blisters if you touch a crushed beetle. The larvae feed on grasshopper eggs. The larvae of blister beetles overwinter in the soil. Blister beetles are found in eastern North America and the central United States.

BEST CONTROL STRATEGY

As for Beetles, page 298. Wear gloves when handling blister beetles; they can cause blisters when crushed on the skin.

PLANTS AFFECTED

Popular flowering plants favored by black blister beetles include annual aster, chrysanthemum, phlox, and zinnia.

Flea Beetles

DESCRIPTION

Flea beetles, like the potato flea beetle (*Epitrix cucumeris*), are shiny, black beetles about the size of a pinhead ($1/16$ inch long). Some species have yellow or white markings. They are very active and jump like fleas when disturbed. Females lay eggs near the base of plants. These hatch in about one week, and the larvae feed on the roots of plants for two to three weeks before pupating and emerging as winged adults to attack foliage. Flea beetles transmit viral and bacterial diseases, including early blight and bacterial wilt. These insect pests are found throughout the United States.

BEST CONTROL STRATEGY

As for Beetles, page 298. Beneficial nematodes introduced to the soil will take care of the larvae.

Sticky Traps. White sticky traps, often used to indicate the arrival of flea beetles, will also reduce their numbers in your yard, but need to be supplemented with stronger measures as soon as the beetles begin turning up.

Diatomaceous Earth. Sprinkle diatomaceous earth (D.E.) around the base of vulnerable plants to discourage flea beetles, or dust whole plants with D.E. Other materials used by gardeners to repel flea beetles include lime and coffee grounds, which have a similar effect on flea beetles. Spread them in a circle around each plant.

Floating Row Covers. To protect vulnerable seedlings in the spring, you might want to cover them with floating row covers, like Reemay, or with netting, fabric, cheesecloth, or some similar material as soon as you plant them. Seal the edges of the fabric with soil. These materials permit sunlight, air, and water to reach the plant, but deny flea beetles access to it. When the plants have grown and become well established, remove the cover.

PLANTS AFFECTED

Popular flowering plants favored by flea beetles include annual aster, forget-me-not, nasturtium, petunia, and phlox.

Japanese Beetles

DESCRIPTION

The Japanese beetle (*Popillia japonica*) is about ½

inch long. It is shiny, metallic green and has copper-colored wings. The grub is grayish and has a dark brown head. Two rows of spines form a V on the underside of the grub's last abdominal segment. When full grown, the grub is plump and if it were to stretch out, it would measure ¾ to 1 inch in length; however, most of the time you'll find these chubby larvae curled in a C shape. The female beetles lay their white eggs in the soil. Adults eat foliage and fruit. They can fly a distance of up to 5 miles and go out only in the daytime. Larvae feed on grass roots. Japanese beetles have a one- or two-year life cycle. They overwinter in the soil at the larval stage. Japanese beetles are found primarily in the eastern half of the United States but are moving westward.

BEST CONTROL STRATEGY

As for Beetles, page 298.

Pheromone Traps. Japanese beetles can also be controlled with pheromone traps that lure them with food and sex attractants. The attractants are attached to a slick, narrow-necked, plastic bag that the beetles cannot climb out of once they fall in. Set traps a week or so prior to the emergence of adults in your area (usually late spring or early summer). Hang one or more about 5 feet off the ground and never place the traps any closer to a vulnerable plant than 50 feet, or beetles may be drawn to the plant instead of the trap.

Trap Crops. Borage is a common trap crop for Japanese beetles. White geraniums, grape vines, and zinnias, especially white or light-colored ones, can be used as trap crops to spot early infestations of Japanese beetles. Japanese beetles also love to feed on the evening primrose (*Oenothera* spp.), which grows as a weed everywhere. Locate trap crops within 10 to 15 feet of the plants routinely threatened by the beetles. Handpick the beetles from the trap crop before they move on to your flowers.

PLANTS AFFECTED

Popular flowering plants favored by Japanese beetles include annual aster, astilbe, canna, cosmos, daylily, delphinium, four-o'clock, hollyhock, iris, marigold, peony, perennial aster, rose, and zinnia.

Rose Chafers

DESCRIPTION

Rose chafers (*Macrodactylus subspinosus*), also called rose bugs or rose beetles, are tan-colored, long-legged beetles, about ¼ inch long. This pest can be distinguished readily from other rose-infesting beetles by its color and its sluggish movements. They'll feed on flowers for about four weeks, after which the creamy white, reddish brown–headed larvae attack the roots of lawn grasses, where they can do considerable damage. Rose chafer larvae are easily mistaken for Japanese beetle grubs.

Rose chafers are most common in the northeastern states, but make trouble as far west as Colorado. They breed abundantly in sandy soils. Suburban homeowners rarely have problems with rose chafers, but they often infest roses that are grown near fallow fields. Cultivated crops make better neighbors for roses.

BEST CONTROL STRATEGY

As for Beetles, page 298.

PLANTS AFFECTED

Popular flowering plants favored by rose chafers include chrysanthemum, hollyhock, peony, poppy, and rose.

INSECT Borers

DESCRIPTION

Borers are the larvae of many kinds of moths and beetles. They range in length from ½ to 2 inches. Usually they are white or pink with brown heads. Descriptions of different kinds of borers are included in the individual plant entries in part 1.

MOST OBVIOUS SYMPTOMS

When borers tunnel into the soft stem of a flowering plant, they weaken the stem and often break it.

If you notice that plants are bent over, or that their leaves have wilted suddenly, check the stems for small, round holes, which might have been made by borers. Around the edges of the holes, you will often see sawdustlike castings, called frass, which have been expelled by the borers. If your bearded irises have borers, the foliage will be disfigured with irregular tunnels or mines in the lower portion of the leaves. Areas of the leaves may also appear water soaked. The centers of the rhizomes may be eaten out, leading to bacterial soft rot.

BEST CONTROL STRATEGY

Prevention is most effective when dealing with borers, since by the time symptoms appear, it's usually too late to save the flower stalks. Clean up all weeds, especially those that are susceptible to borer infestation, and cut and burn any plant stalks that may harbor overwintering eggs or pupae. Rotating the location of vulnerable plants can also help control this pest. Parasitic nematodes mixed with water and sprayed on the soil according to package directions will control borers if applied in spring before the borers emerge from the soil. Bt (*Bacillus thuringiensis*) is effective if applied early in the season just as the borers are entering the plants. Make several applications at weekly intervals. If your plants are infested with European corn borers (*Ostrinia nubilalis*), apply Bt again at midsummer to catch the second generation. You can also inject Bt into infested stems 1 inch above the borer hole. Infestations of burdock and stalk borers (*Papaipema cataphracta* and *P. nebris*) can be controlled by inserting a wire through each entry hole and killing the larvae. For some plants, especially those with

302

thick stems, slitting the stems lengthwise, removing the borers, and binding the stems together is effective. However, this is tedious work if you have a large planting.

MONITORING BORERS

Emergence Time

Look for all borers in spring. Watch the base of bearded iris plants for signs of infestation in early spring.

OPTIONS FOR CONTROLLING BORERS

Mechanical Controls

Cutting Infested Parts
If borers have infested your flowering plants, slit each affected stem lengthwise in the area of the borer hole. Remove the insect and bind the stem together with green twine, which is available from garden centers and nurseries.

Squashing Iris Borers
If you see any borer larvae in bearded iris foliage before the plants flower, pinch them in their mines to kill them. Then dig infested plants after flowering and cut out all the infested portions of leaves and rhizomes, kill the larvae, and discard or burn diseased plants.

Botanical Poisons

Pyrethrum
Spread pyrethrum dust around the base of plants to kill the hatching borer larvae that emerge from the soil to climb the foliage.

PREVENTING BORER DAMAGE

Fall Cleanup

Keep your garden clean by gathering and destroying weeds and any stems that might harbor eggs or pupae through the winter. Cut bearded iris bloom stalks and leaves at the base and burn them, as they are the primary overwintering site for iris borers. The adult columbine borer (*P. purpurifascia*) scatters its eggs on the ground near vulnerable plants, so scraping the soil around the plants can destroy its eggs.

PLANTS AFFECTED

The following popular flowering plants are especially attractive to borers.

- Burdock borer: dahlia, delphinium, hollyhock.
- European corn borer: annual aster, chrysanthemum, cosmos, dahlia, hollyhock.
- Iris borer: iris.
- Stalk borer: annual aster, chrysanthemum, columbine, cosmos, dahlia, delphinium, hollyhock, lily, marigold, salvia, snapdragon, zinnia.
- Other borers: columbine, rose.

INSECT Bugs

DESCRIPTION

Bugs can range from 1/16 to 1/2 inch long. They come in an amazing variety of colors and patterns, from light green and speckled through red-and-black mottled to brown with a checkered border. Many of them are shield shaped. Crushed bugs—especially stink bugs—often emit a peculiar or offensive odor. Descriptions of many different kinds of bugs are included in the individual plant entries in part 1.

MOST OBVIOUS SYMPTOMS

The first sign of bug damage on flowering plants is leaves covered with white or light green spots. Leaves and flowers can be marred with small, sunken spots

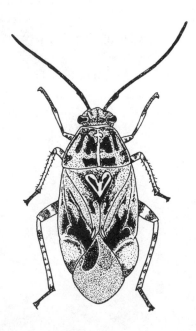

that may be tan, yellow, or brown. Severe infestations can cause deformed growth and dwarfing of young shoots and buds. Shoot tips of severely infested plants may wilt. Lace bugs, such as chrysanthemum lace bugs (*Corythucha marmorata*), cause tiny yellow or brown spots on leaves, which then develop a bleached appearance. They can also cause stem damage. Chrysanthemum lace bugs leave telltale resinous, dark droppings on the undersides of foliage.

BEST CONTROL STRATEGY

Handpicking adults, nymphs, and eggs and dropping them into a jar of soapy water will take care of light infestations. Don't crush them in your hands—many will stink! For heavier infestations, spray the plants with insecticidal soap every three to five days for two weeks. Especially with the chrysanthemum lace bug, be sure to spray the undersides of the leaves.

OPTIONS FOR CONTROLLING BUGS

Botanical Poisons

Pyrethrum
In severe cases, try three applications of pyrethrum laced with isopropyl alcohol, one every three days. Spray early in the morning when bugs are least active.

Sabadilla
If the infestation of bugs is heavy, dust the plants with sabadilla.

PREVENTING BUG DAMAGE

Spring and Fall Cleanup

Thoroughly clean up the garden in spring and fall to discourage overwintering adults and eggs in garden refuse.

PLANTS AFFECTED

The following popular flowering plants are especially attractive to bugs.

- Four-lined plant bug: chrysanthemum, coralbells, coreopsis, dahlia, phlox, poppy, snapdragon, sunflower.
- Harlequin bug: chrysanthemum, sunflower.
- Lace bug: chrysanthemum, hollyhock, perennial aster.
- Tarnished plant bug: annual aster, chrysanthemum, cosmos, dahlia, hollyhock, impatiens, marigold, nasturtium, poppy, salvia, snapdragon, sunflower, zinnia.
- Other bugs: hollyhock, phlox, snapdragon, sunflower.

INSECT *Caterpillars*

Caterpillars come in all shapes, sizes, and colors, and they can be found anywhere in North America.

There are diamondback caterpillars, hornworms, woolly bears, and red-humped caterpillars. All of these and many more share a fondness for plant foliage. Fortunately, the methods for controlling caterpillars are basically the same for all species. When selecting control measures for caterpillars, take time to identify the ones that are larvae of the beautiful butterflies and lovely nocturnal moths that add such delight to the summer garden. Try to identify and protect the larvae of these species; most are colorful and harmless.

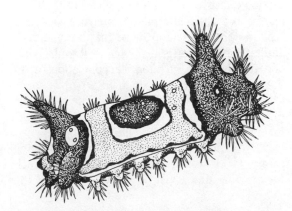

DESCRIPTION

Caterpillars are the wormlike larvae of moths and butterflies. They may be only ¼ inch long or more than 2 inches long. Some are fuzzy; others are smooth. Many are either green or brown, but others are brightly colored and have beautiful markings. Descriptions of many different kinds of caterpillars are included in the individual plant entries in part 1. Cutworms, a group of caterpillars that fell young transplants and seedlings, have their own entry beginning on the opposite page.

MOST OBVIOUS SYMPTOMS

Caterpillars will eat the foliage and stems of just about any plant in your garden. Holes in leaves and chewed leaf edges are typical signs of caterpillar attack. Another telltale clue is leaves that are rolled up or fastened with silk. In a very short period of time, caterpillars can defoliate a plant.

BEST CONTROL STRATEGY

Handpicking makes a sizable dent in most populations of caterpillars and can keep them from getting out of hand if you catch the infestation right away. Butterfly lovers must reconcile the danger posed to their flowers by the caterpillar with the obvious depletion of butterflies if control methods are too effective. The best way to avoid this is to learn to recognize caterpillars by using a good field guide and only picking those that become drab adults. Handpicking is ideal because it controls but does not obliterate the caterpillar population. Crush the caterpillars or drop them in a pail of soapy water. Wear gloves if you suspect saddleback caterpillars; their sting is severe. Remove any rolled or folded leaves, since they shelter caterpillars.

Bt (*Bacillus thuringiensis*) kills most leaf-eating caterpillars if it is applied to the leaves on which they are feeding. Dust or spray all parts of the leaves, especially the undersides, at three- to five-day intervals until the caterpillars cease to be a problem. Reapply after rain.

OPTIONS FOR CONTROLLING CATERPILLARS

Botanical Poisons

Pyrethrum or Rotenone

If the caterpillar infestation gets out of control, spray all sides of the leaves with pyrethrum or a 1 percent solution of rotenone. Usually, two applications, one every three to four days, will solve the problem.

PREVENTING CATERPILLAR DAMAGE

Garden Cleanup

Regularly clean up and dispose of garden debris throughout the season to reduce the size of future generations. A thorough end-of-season cleanup is also beneficial.

Insect Predators and Parasites

Many insects prey upon or parasitize caterpillars, including fireflies, ground beetles, soldier beetles, stink bugs, and tachinid flies.

PLANTS AFFECTED

- Cabbage looper and imported cabbageworm: nasturtium.
- Corn earworm: ageratum, nasturtium.
- Fall webworm: peony.
- Sunflower moth: sunflower.
- Columbine skipper: columbine.

- Tobacco budworm: ageratum.

- Yellow woolly bear and saddleback caterpillar: canna.

- Other caterpillars: annual aster, black-eyed Susan, chrysanthemum, geranium, hollyhock, iris, marigold, petunia, snapdragon, sunflower, sweet alyssum.

INSECT *Cutworms*

DESCRIPTION

Several different species of cutworm occur throughout North America. These pests are plump, softbodied, dull grayish or brownish caterpillars that are 1 to 2 inches long. You'll usually find them in a curled position—that is, if you find them. They feed at night and hide in the soil during the day. Cut-

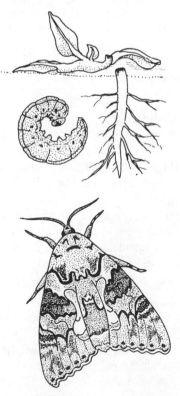

worms develop into moths. The females lay their eggs in the soil during the growing season. Cutworms overwinter in either the larval or pupal stage. Up to five generations can occur in one year.

MOST OBVIOUS SYMPTOMS

Cutworms work quickly and invisibly. One day all the young plants in your flower garden will look great; the next day they will be leveled. Cutworms generally attack seedlings, severing the stems at or below the level of the soil. They work at night, so you won't catch them in the act of hacking down your flowering plants. Examine any toppled plants closely. If they look like they've been mowed, cutworms have probably been at work. If the cut is angled, rabbits might be the culprits. Sometimes cutworms attack plants from below the soil, damaging the root systems and causing the plants to wilt and collapse.

BEST CONTROL STRATEGY

You can't save seedlings or transplants once they've been attacked, so if cutworms are an annual problem in your yard, use a barrier to deny them access to your plants. See below for several different methods that work well and are easy to use.

MONITORING CUTWORMS

Emergence Time

Most cutworms attack plants in early spring; however, many species produce new generations throughout the year, though their damage is less apparent as the season progresses.

OPTIONS FOR CONTROLLING CUTWORMS

Traps and Mechanical Controls

Cornmeal or Bran Meal Traps

After putting out transplants, sprinkle ½ teaspoon cornmeal or bran meal around each plant. Apply it in a circle with a trail leading away from the stem of the plant. Cutworms will eat the meal, which will then absorb moisture, swell, and kill them.

Handpicking

You can handpick cutworms at night. Look for them near the base of plants and just under the soil surface.

Biological Controls

Bt (*Bacillus thuringiensis*)

Bt effectively controls some species. Dust seedlings and transplants at the soil level.

Insect Predators and Parasites Available Commercially

Beneficial nematodes are an effective long-term control. Introduce them into the soil around your seedlings or transplants, using the rate specified on the package. Braconid and trichogramma wasps also prey on cutworms.

PREVENTING CUTWORM DAMAGE

Fall Cleanup

The adult moths lay eggs in the fall in weeds and grass, and the larvae or pupae overwinter in the soil. Clearing the yard of weeds and mowing the lawn closely in the fall are important steps in preventing cutworms from appearing next spring.

Barriers

While using barriers to keep cutworms away from young plants is perhaps the best way to control cutworm damage, not all methods are effective. Placing matchsticks or toothpicks in a ring around the stems of seedlings does not prevent cutworm damage. The various methods described here are all effective.

Diatomaceous Earth

Dust diatomaceous earth around the base of each plant. It will scratch the cutworms and keep them from reaching your seedlings.

Milk Cartons

To protect vulnerable seedlings, plant them in half-gallon paper milk cartons. When you transplant them outside, merely cut out the bottom of the carton and plant the whole carton, leaving the top rim sticking out of the soil about an inch. Cutworms will be unable to climb over the protruding carton to get to the plants.

Paper Collars

Protect individual transplants and seedlings by putting a 3-inch collar made from stiff paper or plastic around them. Sections of paper towel rolls or toilet paper rolls are ideal. Push the collar 1 to 2 inches into the ground.

Paper cups can also be used for paper collars. Cut the bottom out of a paper cup. Press the cup into the soil, upside down, around the stem of the plant you want to protect. Be sure to push the rim of the cup 1 to 2 inches deep into the soil.

Wood Ashes

Sprinkle two handfuls of wood ashes around the base of each transplant after you put it in the ground. Don't let the ashes touch the plant. Alternatively, make a trench around each plant, 3 to 4 inches wide and a few inches deep, and fill it with wood ashes. Cutworms don't like to crawl over them.

Animal Predators

Swallows and bats eat the adult moths. The cutworms provide a fine meal for blackbirds, bluejays, brown thrashers, meadowlarks, chickens, robins, sparrows, and wrens, as well as moles, shrews, snakes, and toads.

Insect Predators

Any of the caterpillar eaters prey upon cutworms.

These include fireflies, ground beetles, soldier beetles, stink bugs, and tachinid flies.

PLANTS AFFECTED

Any transplant or seedling is vulnerable to cutworms. Popular flowering plants that the pests seem to specially favor include annual aster, bachelor's button, delphinium, dianthus, and pansy.

INSECT *Leafhoppers*

DESCRIPTION

Leafhoppers are wedge-shaped, ⅛- to ¼-inch-long insects. They carry their wings in a rooflike position over their bodies, which accounts for their unusual shape. They may be green, brown, or yellow and

often have colorful markings. Leafhoppers hop suddenly, move sideways, and are very active. Their life cycles vary depending on the species; some overwinter as eggs, others as adults. Eggs are laid on the undersides of leaves. Some species, such as the aster leafhopper (*Macrosteles fascifrons*), spread viral diseases such as aster yellows. Leafhoppers occur throughout the United States. Descriptions of different kinds of leafhoppers are included in the individual plant entries in part 1.

MOST OBVIOUS SYMPTOMS

Nymphs and adults suck juices from plant leaves, buds, and stems. Foliage often appears distorted and discolored, mottled with white or yellow spots. Leaves eventually shrivel and drop off. The plants weaken. The large amounts of honeydew excreted by leafhoppers give plants a glazed appearance. Black, sooty mold may grow on this honeydew.

BEST CONTROL STRATEGY

Spray infested plants with a mixture of insecticidal soap and isopropyl alcohol. Make this mix by adding 1 tablespoon alcohol to each pint of insecticidal soap solution. Make three applications, spraying once every three to five days.

MONITORING LEAFHOPPERS

Emergence Time

Nymphs appear in early spring.

OPTIONS FOR CONTROLLING LEAFHOPPERS

Natural Sprays

Insecticidal Soap and Alcohol Spray
To control serious infestations of leafhoppers, spray infested plants with a mixture of insecticidal soap and isopropyl alcohol. Make this mix by adding 1 tablespoon of alcohol to each pint of insecticidal soap solution. Make three applications, spraying once every three to five days.

Mechanical Controls

Handpicking
Leafhoppers move very quickly and are difficult to catch, but if you move quickly, you can catch and crush them.

Botanical Poisons

Pyrethrum
Pyrethrum will kill leafhoppers, but it must come in direct contact with the insects in order to be effective. If leafhoppers are a particular problem in your area, it can be used as a preventive spray. Apply at four- to five-day intervals for the first month of growth.

PREVENTING LEAFHOPPER DAMAGE

Fall Cleanup

Adults like to hibernate in weeds, but dislike perennial grasses. So by cleaning up the garden in fall and having an area of weed-free turf around your garden beds, you can discourage these pests.

Barriers

Floating Row Covers
If leafhoppers are a common problem in your garden, place a barrier such as Reemay or other floating row covers over the plants in early spring. After a month, remove the covers. If you don't want to cover the plants, try a natural spray.

Animal Predators

Chickadees, purple finches, sparrows, swallows, titmice, and wrens eat leafhoppers.

Insect Predators

Assassin bugs, bigeyed bugs, damselflies, and syrphid flies are important predators of leafhoppers. Parasitic wasps are also valuable in controlling these pests.

Other Preventive Steps

Weed control is effective in reducing egg-laying sites. It is especially important to get rid of thistles, plantain, and dandelions.

PLANTS AFFECTED

Popular flowering plants preferred by leafhoppers include the following:

• Aster leafhopper: annual aster, baby's-breath, marigold, nasturtium.
• Other leafhoppers: coreopsis, cosmos, dahlia, marigold, petunia, poppy, rose, salvia, zinnia.

INSECT *Leafminers*

DESCRIPTION

Leafminers are the larvae of various insects: small black flies, moths, sawflies, or beetles. Adults will usually lay eggs on the undersides of leaves. The larvae that hatch are green or black and about ⅛ inch long. Upon emerging, they tunnel into the leaves between the upper and lower surfaces to feed on the inner part. Several generations develop each summer, and these pests pass the winter in a cocoon in the soil. Leafminers carry black leg and soft rot diseases. Many species occur throughout North America. Descriptions of different kinds of leafminers are included in the individual plant entries in part 1.

MOST OBVIOUS SYMPTOMS

The foliage looks discolored or diseased. Leaves will show light green to brown serpentine mines or tunnels between the upper and lower leaf surfaces. Large, blotchy areas of the leaves may turn brown or tan. About two weeks after the infestation begins, affected leaves may turn completely brown and collapse. Careful observation will reveal dark specks of excrement within the mines, and the tiny white maggots are often visible through the leaf tissue.

BEST CONTROL STRATEGY

To remove leafminers from your plants, pick off and destroy all infested leaves. If necessary, prune back stems until only uninfested growth remains. The larvae can sometimes be repelled by spraying plants with several weekly applications of insecticidal soap in late June or early July. Do not compost soil or plant material that may be infested. If leafminers are a problem year after year, consider covering vulnerable plants in spring with floating row covers, like Reemay, or some other material that will prevent these pests from getting to your plants.

MONITORING LEAFMINERS

Emergence Time

Leafminers emerge from the soil in early spring.

Egg laying continues through the summer as new generations mature.

OPTIONS FOR CONTROLLING LEAFMINERS

Mechanical Controls

Handpicking

Handpick leafminer eggs. Turn the leaves over and look for the chalky white, $1/16$- to $1/8$-inch-long eggs. Three to five eggs will be lined up in a row. Scratch them off the leaf and destroy them. Flies will continue to lay eggs, so repeat this process once a week for three to four weeks. If the eggs have already hatched, the upper surface of the leaves will have grayish blisters. Cut off the blisters; it's not necessary to cut off the entire leaf. The plants will survive and grow quickly if you leave as much healthy tissue as possible. Destroy all the infested leaf parts you cut from the plant.

PREVENTING LEAFMINER DAMAGE

Fall Cleanup

Leafminers overwinter in the soil and emerge in early spring; consequently, a thorough fall cleanup will help control them. Cultivate the soil around your plants in late fall to expose these insects to birds and other predators. Leave the soil bare until it freezes solid, then lay down a winter mulch. Remove weeds, especially lamb's-quarters.

Preventive Spray Programs

The key to controlling leafminers is to try to catch the adult—whether it is a fly, moth, or beetle—before it lays eggs on the target plant. Try to find out, within a day or two, the expected emergence date of the adult insect; then spray vulnerable plants with insecticidal soap at that time. This would be about May 1 in most parts of the country. In a cold spring, you can delay the first application about a week or so. For best results, spray at seven- to ten-day intervals, making two applications. To control a second brood of leafminers, spray plants again about July 1 and July 10. Spray only the target plants to avoid hurting too many beneficial insects in the area.

Barriers

Floating Row Covers

The surest way to prevent leafminer damage on your plants is to screen them out. Floating row covers, like Reemay, are effective barriers, allowing sun, air, and rain to reach the plants while preventing leafminers from laying their eggs on them.

Animal Predators

Chickadees, purple finches, and robins eat leafminers.

Insect Predators

Ladybugs eat the eggs of leafminers.

PLANTS AFFECTED

The following popular flowering plants are affected by leafminers.

- Columbine leafminer: columbine.
- Larkspur leafminer: delphinium, larkspur.
- Other leafminers: chrysanthemum, hollyhock, nasturtium, verbena.

INSECT *Leafrollers*

DESCRIPTION

Leafrollers are the caterpillars of moths. They may be light to dark green or cream to yellow in color and grow to a length of ⅜ to 1¾ inches. The adult moths are small—¼ to ½ inch long—with brown or gray wings. Often, two generations occur in a year, one in spring and the other in late summer. They pass the winter in their pupal stage in plant debris under trees. These insect pests roll leaves around themselves for protection while they are in their pupal stage. Some of the more common pests are the oblique-banded leafroller (*Choristoneura rosaceana*) and the red-banded leafroller (*Argyrotaenia semipurpurana*). Descriptions of different kinds of leafrollers are included in the individual plant entries in part 1.

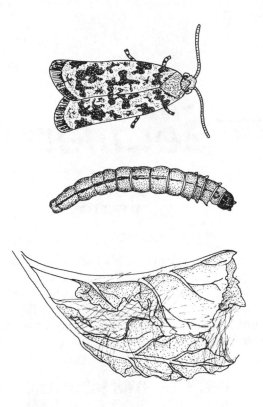

MOST OBVIOUS SYMPTOMS

You'll probably first notice an infestation when you see that the leaves on your flowers are rolled up. Leafrollers protect themselves inside rolled leaves, which they bind with strands of silk. Once they've built little homes for themselves, they'll go out and chew holes in flower buds and leaves. These pests have healthy appetites and may skeletonize leaves, which will turn brown and drop in late summer.

BEST CONTROL STRATEGY

Crush leafrollers as you find them, and spray plants with Bt (*Bacillus thuringiensis*). If leafrollers are a common problem in your yard, spray vulnerable plants with Bt just before you expect the caterpillars to begin feeding.

MONITORING LEAFROLLERS

Emergence Time

Leafrollers overwinter as pupae in garden debris, and the moths appear in spring.

OPTIONS FOR CONTROLLING LEAFROLLERS

Botanical Poisons

Pyrethrum and Rotenone
A mixture of equal parts pyrethrum and rotenone

powder can be dusted over plants to control leaf-rollers. Dust the plants twice, 30 minutes apart. However, infestations are rarely heavy enough to warrant the use of botanical poisons.

PLANTS AFFECTED

Popular flowering plants preferred by leafrollers include annual aster, canna, geranium, and rose.

INSECT # *Leaftiers*

DESCRIPTION

Leaftiers are ⅜- to ¾-inch-long caterpillars that are light green or cream to yellow in color with a white stripe down their backs and a green line down the center of the stripe. The adult moths have gray or brown wings and are about ¼ to ½ inch long. Descriptions of other kinds of leaftiers are included in the individual plant entries in part 1.

MOST OBVIOUS SYMPTOMS

Leaftiers attack the terminal buds of plants. They bind leaves around these buds with strands of silk to create a shelter for themselves while they feed. These leaves will become ragged and unsightly, turn brown, and die.

BEST CONTROL STRATEGY

Infestations are usually light and are easily controlled simply by handpicking the caterpillars. Remove any rolled or folded leaves, which will shelter the leaftiers. Infested leaves should be destroyed, since the pests pupate and overwinter in them. Bt (*Bacillus thuringiensis*) is also an effective control. Apply it as a powder or spray every 10 to 14 days

while the caterpillars are actively eating, until the pests are gone. If leaftiers infest your plants year after year, start spraying with Bt just before you expect the caterpillars to begin feeding.

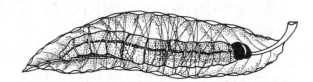

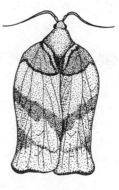

MONITORING LEAFTIERS

Emergence Time

Leaftiers overwinter as larvae and resume feeding the following spring.

OPTIONS FOR CONTROLLING LEAFTIERS

Botanical Poisons

Pyrethrum and Rotenone

A mixture of equal parts pyrethrum and rotenone powder can be dusted over plants to control leaftiers. Dust the plants twice, 30 minutes apart. However, infestations are rarely heavy enough to warrant the use of botanical poisons.

PLANTS AFFECTED

Popular flowering plants favored by leaftiers include the following:

• Greenhouse or celery leaftier: ageratum, canna, forget-me-not, geranium, marigold, pansy, snapdragon.
• Other leaftiers: chrysanthemum, nasturtium, salvia.

INSECT Nematodes

DESCRIPTION

Actually, nematodes aren't insects. They are microscopic wormlike organisms. They have whitish, translucent, unsegmented bodies covered by a tough cuticle. Most nematodes are innocuous, living out their lives in fresh water or salt water or in soil. Some are beneficial, parasitizing a long list of pest insects. But unfortunately for gardeners, a number of nematodes are plant pests. These include bulb and stem nematodes, foliar nematodes, and root knot nematodes, which are given special sections below.

MOST OBVIOUS SYMPTOMS

Pest nematodes attack all plant parts—stems, leaves, buds, roots, bulbs, and corms. Generally, it is difficult to diagnose nematodes just by looking at a plant. Very often the only sign of a nematode problem is weakened plants that don't look healthy and vigorous. The exceptions are the root knot nematodes (*Meloidogyne incognita* and *M. hapla*), which form galls or swellings on plant roots. Other nematodes produce leaf discoloration, stunting, or dieback.

In general, plants infested with nematodes look sickly, wilted, or stunted. Their foliage turns yellow or bronze, and they decline slowly and die. If the root system has been attacked, it will develop poorly and may even decay, and if infested by the root knot nematode, it will show galls. Effects of nematode activity are most apparent in hot weather; plants will recover poorly from the heat.

BEST CONTROL STRATEGY

If you find that your plants are infested with nematodes, add compost to the soil, which will attract beneficial fungi that will then attack the nematodes. If you are planning a flower garden in soil that you know is nematode infested, consider a colorful bed of marigolds the first season. Plant a solid bed of African, French (like 'Tangerine'), and golden marigolds, or 'Nemagold' marigold mix. In addition to producing plenty of flowers, the plants will help control nematodes in the bed. The marigolds act as a trap crop. The nematodes enter their roots, and once inside, they seem to be unable to reproduce. In addition, marigolds release a substance that suppresses nematode populations. Till them into the soil at season's end. The following year, you shouldn't have any problems with nematodes. Some species of chrysanthemum (in particular, *Chrysanthemum coccineum* and *C. parthenium*) also reduce harmful nematodes in the soil.

If nematodes are a recurring problem in your flower bed, plant early in the season and use resistant cultivars. Space plants so that the leaves do not touch. Avoid wetting foliage, since nematodes swim up the stems and enter leaves through the stomata (pores).

MONITORING NEMATODES

Nematodes are always present in the soil. It's just that sometimes they get a little out of hand. If you suspect that nematodes are causing damage, there are a couple of tests you can use to determine if they indeed are harming your plants.

Check the soil for root knot nematodes by taking some soil from the location you think might be infested. Plant cucumber seeds in a small pot of this soil. After the first true leaves appear, pull up the seedlings and carefully wash the soil away from the roots. If nematodes are present, you will see small, beadlike knots on the roots.

Another test uses radishes instead of cucumbers. Collect soil samples at a depth of 3 inches below the surface from various sites in the garden. Mix these together and fill four small pots with the soil. Freeze two of the pots for 48 to 72 hours to kill any nematodes that might be present; then plant radishes in all four pots. Radishes are quite sensitive to nema-

todes. Examine the seedlings after six days. If the radishes grown in the soil that was frozen look much better than those in the untreated soil, your garden soil probably contains too many pest nematodes.

OPTIONS FOR CONTROLLING NEMATODES

Natural Sprays and Soil Additives

Chitin

A non-toxic nematocide, ClandoSan, has been shown in university tests to be superior to chemical nematocides. ClandoSan's active ingredient is chitin, found in the shells of shellfish. Tilled or watered into the soil, it stimulates populations of nematode-suppressing microorganisms. One application a year of 4½ to 14 pounds per 100 square feet, according to package directions, is sufficient to control nematodes in your yard or garden.

Fish Emulsion

Crops fertilized with fish emulsion suffer less nematode damage than those fertilized in other ways. Researchers suspect that some component of the fish oil may be toxic or offensive to the nematodes. A combination of fish emulsion and an extract from the yucca plant, available commercially as Pent-a-Vate, provides even more effective control.

Kelp Meal

Certain soil fungi that kill root knot nematodes are made more potent by the presence of kelp meal in the soil. Add about 1 pound of meal to every 100 square feet of garden. This treatment is particularly effective if you also add compost to the soil.

Seaweed Extract

Whether used as a foliar spray or as a soil drench, seaweed extract will reduce root knot nematode infestations of ornamental plants. Natural hormones in the seaweed, called cytokinins, help the plants increase their resistance to nematode invasion. Fewer larvae penetrate the roots, and those that do are inhibited in their development. As a side benefit, the seaweed extract produces bigger roots and stems and better yields. Mix 1 tablespoon liquid seaweed in 2 gallons water.

PREVENTING NEMATODE DAMAGE

Fall Cleanup

In the fall, clear away decayed vegetation and put a mulch of peat moss or some other organic material around plants. This helps prevent infestation of the lower leaves of plants by nematodes that overwinter in old, infested leaves.

Soil Solarization

If a particular garden bed suffers consistently from serious nematode problems, you might want to consider digging it up and solarizing it. This technique has been effective in controlling nematodes in the warmer southern and western states. To solarize the soil, plow or till it deeply during hot weather. Soak the ground thoroughly with water and cover it with clear plastic. The hot temperatures that develop under the plastic will destroy nematodes and other harmful pests and diseases.

Insect Predators

Predatory mites and springtails do an excellent job of controlling nematodes.

Other Preventive Steps

Fallow Soil
If you garden in an area that has hot, dry summers, you can control nematodes easily by letting the infested area lie fallow and by withholding water during the hottest months. Turning the soil occasionally during this time exposes nematode eggs, many of which die in the sun. Of course, this method depends on your willingness to abandon a flower bed for a season.

Garden Hygiene
To avoid transferring nematodes to healthy plants, clean all tools and garden shoes that have been in contact with infested soil. Make a disinfectant solution from 1 part household bleach and 3 parts water. Thoroughly wet the surfaces of greenhouse benches, bins, flats, and containers with this solution. Clean soil and algae from tools with a scrub brush and soak the tools in the bleach solution overnight.

Organic Material
Make sure the soil has plenty of organic matter, which encourages nematode predators such as springtails and carnivorous fungi. Rich soil stimulates sturdy root growth, which withstands the effect of nematode damage. In addition, decomposing organic matter is thought to generate nematode-toxic compounds. Soil amendments such as leaf mold, grass clippings, castor pomace (a by-product of castor oil production), and manure have been known to suppress nematodes under the right conditions. Research indicates that leaf mold compost suppresses populations of harmful nematodes. Compost releases fatty acids, similar to those used as pest-control agents, which reduce nematode populations. Many plant leaves also are toxic to nematodes. Laboratory tests have shown pine needles to be particularly potent. For best results, mix compost into the garden soil.

PLANTS AFFECTED

Nematodes aren't too selective when it comes to attacking flowers. Some of those most commonly affected are listed in the specific nematode entries below.

Bulb and Stem Nematodes

MOST OBVIOUS SYMPTOMS

Symptoms of bulb and stem nematodes include deformed shoot tips and leaves and stunted plants.

Plants may have narrow, threadlike leaves or leaves that are curled or wrinkled. The tips of stems may also be swollen. Plants fail to flower and eventually die.

BEST CONTROL STRATEGY

Dig up and destroy infested specimens, together with the soil in which they are growing, for there is no cure once the plants are infested. Do not compost infested plants or soil. (Soil can be heat pasteurized in an oven and reused, but this is a tedious, smelly process.)

PREVENTING BULB AND STEM NEMATODE DAMAGE

Do not grow plants in the same spot year after year if nematodes have been a problem. Don't propagate infested plants by dividing clumps; instead, propagate by cuttings from healthy plants. Thoroughly clean up all garden debris each fall and discard it to destroy overwintering nematodes. Mulching plants in spring may discourage nematodes from climbing up from the soil. Finally, avoid spraying water on the leaves when watering.

PLANTS AFFECTED

Popular flowering plants attacked by bulb and stem nematodes include daffodil, hyacinth, and phlox.

Foliar Nematodes

MOST OBVIOUS SYMPTOMS

If your plants have foliar nematodes, you'll know by the yellow-brown spots covering the leaves, starting on leaves at the base of the plant and gradually moving up the stems. The spots eventually run together and cover the entire leaf, which dies, turns brittle, and falls off. Serious infestations can kill the entire plant.

BEST CONTROL STRATEGY

Remove leaves and stems infested with foliar nematodes. Dig up and destroy seriously infested specimens, together with the soil in which they are growing. Don't compost infested plants or soil.

PREVENTING FOLIAR NEMATODE DAMAGE

Do not grow plants in the same spot year after year if nematodes have been a problem. Don't propagate infested plants by dividing clumps; instead, propagate by cuttings from healthy plants. Thoroughly clean up all garden debris each fall and discard it to destroy overwintering nematodes. Mulching plants in spring may discourage nematodes from climbing up from the soil. Finally, avoid spraying water on the leaves when watering.

PLANTS AFFECTED

Popular flowering plants that fall victim to foliar nematodes include chrysanthemum, coralbells, delphinium, and tuberous begonia.

Root Knot Nematodes

MOST OBVIOUS SYMPTOMS

Root knot nematodes inject saliva into root tissues as they feed, introducing toxins and bacteria that cause plant tissues to rot. Afflicted cells enlarge, forming a tiny gall (the root knot) around the nematodes. The galls interfere with nutrient transport and inhibit the growth of the plants. As a result, plants are stunted and look sickly or wilted with yellowed or bronzed foilage. The root systems are poorly developed and can be partially decayed.

BEST CONTROL STRATEGY

Organic matter in the soil helps to control root knot nematodes because it not only benefits the fungi and bacteria that feed on them, it also keeps plants healthy and better able to withstand mild infestations. Add lots of compost and leaf mold to the flower bed before planting.

Turn severely infested plots over to a thickly planted cover crop of marigolds for an entire season, and dig the plant remains into the soil at season's end to discourage these pests. Rotation is also effective; don't grow susceptible plants on the same plot year after year.

PREVENTING ROOT KNOT NEMATODE DAMAGE

If your plants have foliar nematodes, you'll know by the yellow-brown spots covering the leaves, starting on leaves at the base of the plant and gradually moving up the stems. The spots eventually run together and cover the entire leaf, which dies, turns brittle, and falls off. Serious infestations can kill the entire plant.

PLANTS AFFECTED

Popular flowering plants favored by nematodes include the following:

• Southern root knot nematode: annual aster, cockscomb, dahlia, delphinium, four-o'clock, geranium, hollyhock, impatiens, pansy, peony, petunia, rose, sweet alyssum, tuberous begonia.

• Other root knot nematodes: dahlia, daylily, geranium, nasturtium, pansy, poppy, rose.

INSECT **Scale**

DESCRIPTION

Scale insects are related to mealybugs and aphids. They resemble tiny limpets, ranging from $\frac{1}{12}$ to $\frac{1}{5}$ inch in length. Scales cover plants with cottony white masses or clusters of somewhat flattened, reddish-brown, grayish, white, yellow, brown, or black bumps. Safe under their rounded, waxy shells, the pests insert threadlike sucking mouthparts into the plant and suck the sap. Some species excrete honeydew, which mars foliage, attracts ants, and encourages the growth of sooty mold.

The insects either lay eggs or bear live nymphs under the shells. Newly hatched nymphs (called crawlers) disperse to other parts of the plant and settle down to form their own shells. One to seven generations may be completed in a single year, depending on the length of the season.

Scale outbreaks can be triggered by pesticides used against other pests or by environmental stresses such as too much or too little water. Overuse of nitrogen fertilizer can encourage the growth of scale populations by accelerating the growth of plants. Scales are attracted to the succulent new shoots.

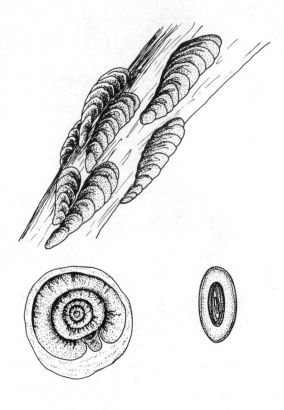

MOST OBVIOUS SYMPTOMS

The leaves of scale-infested plants turn yellow and may drop. On roses, leaves wilt and turn dark. This is followed by leaf drop, reduced growth, and stunted plants. A shiny or sticky material (honeydew) may cover the leaves of any infested plant. The scale, which are immobile, are also easy to spot. Heavily infested plants may be covered with a solid layer of overlapping, waxy shells. Heavy scale infestations can kill plants.

BEST CONTROL STRATEGY

If caught early on, the pests can be scraped off plant surfaces with a dull knife or even a fingernail. Another effective control for light infestations is a cotton swab dipped in rubbing alcohol. Make sure the alcohol contacts the scale insects. Spray infested plants with a mixture of isopropyl alcohol and insecticidal soap every three days for two weeks as described below. The crawlers are unprotected by the waxy scales that make adults difficult to kill, so sprays timed to coincide with the crawler stage are most effective.

MONITORING SCALE

Emergence Time

Scale insects generally overwinter as adults or eggs on host plants. The eggs hatch in spring, and the nymphs begin feeding on new growth.

OPTIONS FOR CONTROLLING SCALE

Natural Sprays

Horticultural Oil Spray
Light horticultural oil, also called superior horticultural spray oil, is lighter and less viscous than the dormant oils traditionally used. Traditional dormant oils had a viscosity rating of 100 to 220 and evaporated less quickly than the light or superior oils used today, which have a viscosity rating of 60 to 70. The lower viscosity allows these new oils to evaporate much more quickly from leaves and stems, thus making them less toxic to plants while retaining their effectiveness against pest insects. It can be used during the growing season to control scale. Use a 2 to 3 percent solution, and make sure you spray it directly on the scale insects because the oil works by suffocating them. Before spraying, remove heavily infested plant parts, if possible.

Insecticidal Soap and Alcohol Spray
Mix 1 cup of isopropyl alcohol and 1 tablespoon of insecticidal soap concentrate in 1 quart of water, then apply the mixture every three days for two weeks. The soap kills the crawlers, but the alcohol penetrates the adult scale insects' shells.

Botanical Poisons

Pyrethrum

Pyrethrum paralyzes scale on contact. It must be applied directly on the scale to kill the pests. Combine pyrethrum with isopropyl alcohol, mixing 1 tablespoon of alcohol with every pint of diluted pyrethrum mixture to increase its effectiveness. Usually two applications, each made three to five days apart, will control scale.

Insect Predators and Parasites Available Commercially

Green lacewings, lacewings, and various parasitic wasps will attack scale insects. The wasps *Comperiella bifasciata* and *Aphytis melinus* parasitize red scale; *Metaphycus helvolus* parasitizes black scale; and *Aphytis lepidosaphes* attacks purple scale.

PREVENTING SCALE DAMAGE

Fall Cleanup

Remove scale-infested annuals from the garden and destroy them. Cut off badly infested rose canes and infested stems of bulbs and perennials. Throw them out; do not compost scale-infested material. Check trees and shrubs near the garden for scale infestations. If you find scale, apply dormant oil sprays in late winter, but make sure the plants you're spraying aren't oil sensitive.

Animal Predators

Chickadees and woodpeckers eat scale insects.

Insect Predators and Parasites

Chalcid wasps are natural foes of scale insects.

PLANTS AFFECTED

Popular flowering plants attacked by scale include canna, geranium, peony, rose, tuberous begonia, and wax begonia.

INSECT *Slugs and Snails*

DESCRIPTION

Slugs and snails are land-dwelling mollusks related to clams, mussels, and oysters. Slugs are snails without shells. They have flabby, slimy bodies, usually 1 to 2 inches long, although some have been known to grow to 8 inches. Their colors vary from white to gray to yellow to brown-black, often cunningly patterned. Snails have soft bodies covered with sticky slime, which are protected inside coiled shells. Their bodies can be charcoal gray, cream, brown, or even pinkish. The markings on the shells vary considerably from species to species.

Slugs and snails can almost always be found in moist, well-mulched gardens that have acidic soil. They're active at night, rasping holes with their filelike tongues in all kinds of plants. During the day, they sleep under boards or leaf litter. Slugs and snails simply love moisture and become particularly destructive in shaded gardens and during rainy spells. No matter where you live in the United States, you may have occasion to meet up with these pests.

MOST OBVIOUS SYMPTOMS

Plants attacked by slugs display large, ragged holes in their leaves, flowers, and stems. Leaves may be completely eaten away. You may also see the slimy trails left by the creatures on the leaves or on the soil around your plants. Slugs begin feeding at the bottom of plants and work their way up. They first attack plants that have been damaged in some way, but they will eat healthy plants as well.

BEST CONTROL STRATEGY

The best way to control slugs is to set up a barrier, such as Snail-Barr, to keep them off vulnerable plants or out of the garden. Surrounding plants

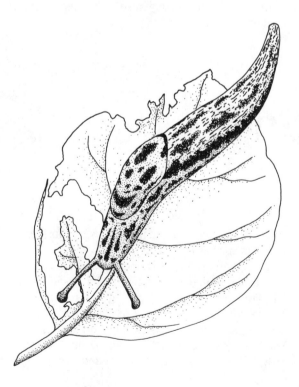

with barriers of ash, sand, or copper sheeting will also discourage slugs from invading your plantings. Handpicking will help—scouting expeditions at night with a trowel and flashlight are especially fruitful—but it's unlikely to provide complete control if you live in slug- or snail-infested areas. Fortunately, a number of traps provide effective control (see below). The key is to begin trapping very early in the season to prevent the population from building up.

MONITORING SLUGS AND SNAILS

Emergence Time

Slugs and snails will arrive in your garden in early spring.

Early Warning Devices

Slug Bar Trap

These commercial traps are small, covered, rectangular boxes. Filled with beer and strategically placed in the flower bed, they lure nearby slugs to their doom. Use them early in the season to determine when the first slugs have arrived and all year to reduce the slug population. Remember to dump the victims and replenish the beer every day or two.

Other Early Warning Devices

Snails will crawl under upturned clay flower pots, flat stones, and boards. Check beneath them regularly for early arrivals. If using a flower pot, place it on the north (shady) side of the plant and elevate one edge to make it easy for the snails to crawl inside. Check these traps twice a day and remove and destroy the pests.

OPTIONS FOR CONTROLLING SLUGS AND SNAILS

Traps and Mechanical Controls

Beer Traps

Perhaps the most common, and one of the most

effective, controls for slugs and snails is the beer trap. To make an effective trap, cut a 2-inch hole in the lid of a coffee can or a small, straight-sided, plastic container and bury the container flush with the soil. Attracted by the yeast in the beer, slugs will dive in and drown. Replace the beer every few days or after rain. Some gardeners report that 1 teaspoon baker's yeast in 3 ounces water is even more effective than beer, and tests have shown that "near beer" is most effective of all.

Cover Traps

Anything that produces a cool, shady environment can be used as a cover trap for slugs. Lay pieces of old board, carpet, stone, plantain, or cabbage leaves in discreet parts of the garden, where they won't detract from its appearance. Check these cover traps twice a day and remove and destroy the pests.

Place hollowed halves of grapefruit, hollow side down, in the garden, and check them several times a day to remove the slugs. The effectiveness of these rinds lasts only two to three days. You can also use cantaloupe rinds.

Handpicking

If you don't mind grabbing their fat, slimy bodies, handpicking makes a sizable dent in the slug population right away, particularly if combined with trapping. Go out at night, armed with a flashlight and a can half full of kerosene or soapy water. Check plants, boards, mulched areas, and walkways for the slimy creatures. You can use tweezers, a pair of wooden chopsticks, a pair of doctor's forceps, or plastic gloves if you prefer not to touch these pests with your fingers. Sprinkle table salt on slugs and snails if you want to kill them without picking them up, or bisect them with a trowel.

PREVENTING SLUG AND SNAIL DAMAGE

Fall Cleanup

Remove boards, rocks, clippings, and other debris, as well as cover traps put out during the growing season, in the fall to deny slugs and snails a ready shelter for the winter.

Preventive Spray Programs

The primitive plant horsetail (*Equisitum arvense*), which grows wild throughout most of North America, contains substances that repel slugs. To make a solution from horsetail, place 1 to 2 ounces of the dried herb in a pot with a gallon of water. Bring the water to a boil and then simmer for 20 minutes. For a little extra punch, add cayenne peppers to the pot. Cool the solution and strain it; then spray it on vulnerable plants.

Barriers

Diatomaceous Earth

The sharp-edged grains of diatomaceous earth will cut the soft bodies of slugs and snails. One step on this stuff and slugs and snails will turn around and head in the other direction. So spread diatomaceous earth around flowering plants you want to protect. Reapply after rain.

Eggshells

Eggshells have the same effect as diatomaceous earth. Slugs and snails won't wander over the sharp shells. Spread crushed eggshells thickly around plants you want to protect.

Flexible Copper Sheeting

Another development in the battle against slugs is the use of a strip of flexible copper sheeting. (The commercial product is called Snail-Barr.) If you have boxed raised flower beds, tack a 2-inch strip of this material around the outside boards, about 1 inch from the the tops of the beds. The cause of copper's success as a slug and snail barrier is that it always carries a very mild electric charge. Although we can't detect it, it gives a shock to slugs and snails on contact. This product is available from most of the companies listed under "Controls" in the source list at the end of this book.

Hardware Cloth

For gardens in boxed raised beds, tack hardware cloth with sharp points onto the outside boards of the box. Make sure the hardware cloth extends 2 inches above the boards. Slugs won't crawl over this mini-fence. Copper sheeting is even more effective —it shocks as well as blocks slugs and snails.

Sand

Although mature slugs and snails aren't bothered by sand, it does irritate baby slugs. Spread it around flowering plants in spring when slugs are tiny.

Seaweed Mulch

Slugs and snails seem to be repelled by seaweed. If you have access to fresh seaweed, rinse it well with fresh water and spread it around plants or around the outside of flower beds. It will also add nutrients to the soil as it decomposes.

Wood Ashes

Wood ashes also act as a barrier to slugs. Sprinkle two handfuls of wood ashes around the base of each plant when plants are 4 to 5 inches tall, or dig a trench a few inches deep and 3 to 4 inches wide around vulnerable plants, and fill it with ashes. Keep ashes from contacting the plants.

Animal Predators

Downy woodpeckers, robins, and other garden birds are happy to bite into a nice juicy slug. Garter snakes are also important predators. Other slug enemies include grass snakes, salamanders, shrews, toads, and turtles. Chickens don't usually care for slugs, but ducks will eat them.

Insect Predators

Black rove beetles, centipedes, firefly larvae, ground beetles, and soldier beetles all prey on slugs or slug eggs.

Other Preventive Steps

Eliminate Hiding Places

Slugs take up residence and breed in cool, dark places such as under boards, under leafy ground covers, in weedy patches, and among rubble. If slugs are a problem in your backyard, consider removing the mulch on garden paths, the boards around raised beds, and other potential shelters.

Prevent Nitrogen Deficiencies in Plants

Slugs prefer to eat soft, slightly rotting leaves. When plants are deficient in nitrogen, their lower leaves turn yellow and gradually decay, making them quite vulnerable to slug attack. Keep your plants well fed, and if they are beginning to look a little undernourished, give them a quick boost with manure tea.

PLANTS AFFECTED

Ageratum, balloon flower, bellflower, bleeding-heart, daylily, delphinium, geranium, hollyhock, hosta, iris, marigold, nasturtium, pansy, petunia, salvia, snapdragon, and wax begonia are among the many popular flowering plants beset by snails and especially slugs.

INSECT **Spider Mites**

DESCRIPTION

Spider mites are not true insects; they are relatives of spiders and belong to the arachnid family. You will barely be able to see them because they are so small. They have four pairs of legs and piercing-sucking mouthparts. Spider mites attack many kinds of plants, feeding on the undersides of leaves, and on flowers, bulbs, and corms. As they feed, they inject toxins into plant tissues, which causes discoloration and distortion.

Spider mites love hot, dry conditions, especially in greenhouses. The hotter it is, the more rapidly they develop from egg to adult and the more eggs they lay. And they can reproduce rapidly—the two-spotted spider mite (*Tetranychus urticae*) will produce a new generation every two weeks if conditions are right.

Outdoor plants repeatedly sprayed with pesticides are most likely to develop bad spider mite infestations because the sprays kill off the pests' natural enemies, such as predatory mites, green lacewings, ladybugs, and damsel bugs. Repeated spraying has also made mites immune to most of the chemical pesticides in use today. Virtually no garden plant is safe from their attack. Spider mites occur throughout the United States. Many species are known; some of the more common mites are the cyclamen mite (*Stenotarsonemus pallidus*), the broad mite (*Polyphagotarsonemus latus*), and the two-spotted spider mite (*Tetranychus urticae*). The bulb mite (*Rhizoglyphus echinopus*) is a pest of most bulbous plants. Descriptions of different kinds of mites are included in the individual plant entries in part 1.

MOST OBVIOUS SYMPTOMS

If you see white or yellow stippling, tiny yellow dots, or red spots on the upper surfaces of leaves, your plant is probably infested with mites. The undersides of leaves will be speckled with the tiny pellets of excrement and cast skins of mites, and you'll find the mites themselves. Leaves, shoots, and flowers may be swathed in fine webbing. Overall yellowing of the leaves begins along the veins and then spreads over the entire leaf surface. The leaves will dry out, and growth may be distorted or discolored.

If you suspect that one of your plants is infested with mites, examine the undersides of the leaves with a magnifying glass. Tap a few leaves or a small branch tip against a sheet of white paper and look for mites crawling on the paper.

Bulbs infested with bulb mites have stunted or deformed, sickly, yellowed foliage. Flowers are disfigured; plants may not bloom at all. The bulbs are decayed with corky, brown spots and eventually turn to dry, crumbly pulp. Bulb mite damage also opens the way for bacterial and fungal attack.

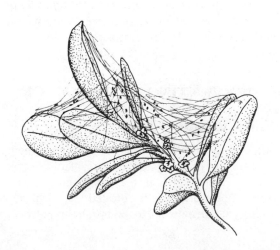

BEST CONTROL STRATEGY

Start control measures as soon as you notice the

first stippling of leaves. Light infestations can be controlled if you spray infested plants once every other day in the early morning with a forceful spray of water to knock the mites from the leaves. Make sure you spray the undersides of the leaves. Wash the plants at least three times. If spider mites are still around or the infestation is heavy, spray with insecticidal soap every three to five days for two weeks. If the infestation is severe, destroy infested annuals or cut infested portions and dispose of them, since infestations are difficult to control once they're well under way.

If your bulbs have mites, dig and destroy all seriously infested bulbs, together with the soil in which they are growing. Don't compost infested bulbs or soil. The mites can be killed by dipping bulbs in hot (120°F) water for a few minutes. Don't plant new bulbs in soil that has been infested.

MONITORING MITES

Emergence Time

The adult mites overwinter in plant debris below the surface of the soil and emerge in late spring. They complete their life cycle in about two weeks. Check leaf undersides weekly for mites and mite damage.

OPTIONS FOR CONTROLLING MITES

Natural Sprays

Garlic Spray
Some homeowners have reported successful control of mites by treating plants with a garlic spray. To make the spray, mix ½ cup finely chopped garlic cloves with 1 pint water; then strain out the particles.

Water Spray
Spider mites prefer a warm, dry environment. Discourage them by shading plants and misting daily with water. This creates a cooler microclimate around plants and helps keep mite populations from exploding. Once the mites are under control, reduce the misting to avoid promoting disease.

Botanical Poisons

See the beginning of this chapter for more information on some of the poisons listed below.

Pyrethrum
Pyrethrum paralyzes mites on contact. For best results, apply twice at three- to four-day intervals.

Rotenone
A spray of 1 percent solution will take care of most mite problems.

Sabadilla
Apply sabadilla weekly on the undersides of the leaves of mite-infested plants.

Triple-Plus
Triple-plus is a product that combines rotenone, pyrethrum, and ryania. When using it against spider mites, apply it in early June, and repeat applications two or three times at ten-day intervals.

Insect Predators and Parasites Available Commercially

Green lacewings and ladybugs prey on spider mites, and certain predatory mites will attack their pest relatives. The predatory mites include *Phytoseiulus persimilis* and *Amblyseius californicus*. One release per season should help control pests.

PREVENTING MITE DAMAGE

Fall Cleanup

Mites move readily from plant to plant—by themselves and by hitching rides on transplants, or even on your tools and hands. Don't touch mite-free plants after working with infested ones. Dip your tools in rubbing alcohol to remove stowaways. Keep the garden free of weeds and remove all plant debris after the growing season. Promptly trim off yellowed leaves and spent blossoms with sharp, clean tools. Destroy the trimmings immediately.

Preventive Spray Programs

On plants most vulnerable to mites, begin a biweekly preventive spray program using commercial insecticidal soap mixed with very dilute seaweed extract. Spray this solution on the undersides of all new growth. Make two or three applications every two weeks in the beginning of the growing season, followed by a monthly application just on those plants most vulnerable to mites.

Barriers

Diatomaceous Earth
Spread diatomaceous earth around the base of affected plants or dust whole plants with it, beginning from the ground and moving upward to cover all stems and leaves. Remember to dust the leaf undersides.

Insect Predators

Ambush bugs, bigeyed bugs, damsel bugs, dance flies, firefly larvae, ladybugs, pirate bugs, predatory midges, and predatory thrips will help you keep mites out of the yard. These insects occur naturally in many yards. Encourage them to stay around. Wild brambles offer a nice residence for many of these beneficial insects.

Other Preventive Steps

Close Inspection
Examine bedding plants carefully before you bring them home from the garden center or nursery, and pass up any that show signs of mites or mite damage. When buying bulbs, look carefully for signs of infestation. If you find any, look elsewhere.

Spacing Plants
Mites will crawl from plant to plant where the leaves form bridges. By spreading plants out so that they don't touch each other, you will slow down the infestation. If possible, move infested plants to an area away from healthy plants.

PLANTS AFFECTED

Popular flowering plants preferred by mites include the following:

• Bulb mite: bulbous iris, colchicum, crocus, daffodil, gladiolus, hyacinth, lily, tulip.

• Cyclamen mite: ageratum, delphinium, larkspur, snapdragon, zinnia.

• Two-spotted spider mite: ageratum, cockscomb, dahlia, delphinium, impatiens, larkspur, nasturtium, pansy, petunia, phlox, rose, snapdragon, zinnia.

• Other mites: chrysanthemum, dianthus, geranium, marigold, petunia, rose, salvia, snapdragon, tuberous begonia, wax begonia, zinnia.

INSECT *Thrips*

DESCRIPTION

Only ¹/₂₅ inch long, thrips are very difficult to spot. You can observe them by shaking infested flowers over a sheet of paper. Thrips' dark fecal pellets and the whitened, desiccated tissue that results from their mass feedings will be visible on the paper. These insects are very active and hop or fly away like little bits of confetti when disturbed. Adult females lay eggs on the leaves or stems of plants. Nymphs hatch and begin feeding on the host plants. They will remain on the plant throughout adulthood. A generation of thrips is normally completed in about two weeks, and several generations occur in a year. Many species occur throughout North America. Thrips most often attack dry, stressed plants. Descriptions of different kinds of thrips are included in the individual plant entries in part 1.

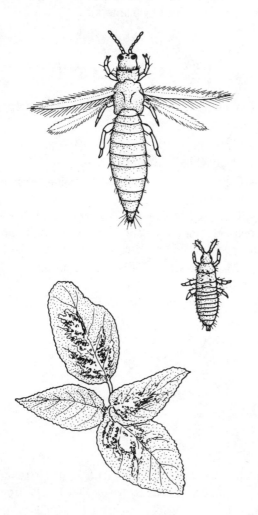

MOST OBVIOUS SYMPTOMS

The chief targets of thrips attack are flowers. They rasp and puncture petals to feed on the juices, leaving flowers discolored, flecked with white, and disfigured. Infested flower buds turn brown and die. In severe cases, the flower stalks may fail to develop altogether. Some species, especially flower thrips, are color sensitive and are particularly attracted to white, yellow, and other light-colored blossoms. There are thrips that will attack only flowers, but some also feed on leaves, which become flecked with white. Leaf tips can wither, curl, and die. The undersides of affected leaves will be spotted with tiny black specks of excrement. New growth will be distorted. Heavy infestations destroy blossoms and leave foliage looking scorched. Stems may develop corky lesions that extend over several inches.

Iris thrips produce stunted growth and russet or sooty areas on leaves. The tops of infested plants eventually turn brown and die out. Serious infestations can kill nearly all of the roots as well. Because iris thrips feed by rasping the folds of the leaves, the plants are vulnerable to fungal infection as well.

BEST CONTROL STRATEGY

Since thrips burrow deeply into petal and leaf tissue, they are difficult to control, and early identification is necessary. As soon as you spot thrips, spray infested plants with insecticidal soap every three days for two weeks. Prune away affected flowers and dispose of them; do not compost them. Thrips prefer a dry environment, so make sure plants are adequately misted and watered.

To control iris thrips, direct regular applications of insecticidal soap spray at the base of each plant. Apply the spray every five to seven days until the infestation has been controlled. You can also soak iris divisions in hot (120°F) water for 30 minutes to kill these pests.

MONITORING THRIPS

Emergence Time

Thrips are active in greenhouses throughout the year. Outdoors, they emerge from hibernation in the spring and will find their way onto plants by early summer.

Early Warning Devices

Sticky Traps

It's vital to detect thrips early. Set yellow sticky traps out in the flower beds about four weeks after the last frost in spring to catch the first thrips of the season and thus signal their arrival. Start spraying your plants as soon as you see thrips on the traps.

OPTIONS FOR CONTROLLING THRIPS

Natural Sprays

Garlic Spray

Garlic is a definite second-best to insecticidal soap in the flower garden, since part of the pleasure of flowers is their fragrance. However, if you've run out of soap, homemade sprays made from garlic have been found to effectively repel thrips. To make the spray, mix ½ cup finely chopped garlic cloves with 1 pint water; then strain out the particles. Spray every few days for a week or two.

Botanical Poisons

See the beginning of this chapter for more information on the poisons listed below.

Pyrethrum

Pyrethrum paralyzes thrips on contact; it must actually touch them to be effective.

Rotenone

A 1 percent solution of rotenone can be used to fight thrips.

Insect Predators and Parasites Available Commercially

Both the adults and larvae of green lacewings and ladybugs are effective thrips destroyers. Predatory mites (*Amblyseius cucumeris* and *A. mckenziei*) attack the egg and larval stages of thrips. They may require as long as two months to establish control, but they will be effective. Soil-dwelling nematodes will seek out thrips in the soil, burrow inside them, and reproduce. The nematodes release bacteria that will kill thrips.

PREVENTING THRIPS DAMAGE

Fall Cleanup

In the fall, cultivate the soil to 2 inches around your plants. Cultivate shallowly again in early spring to catch thrips that have dropped to the ground to pupate and overwinter.

If you leave gladiolus corms in the ground from year to year, they may host a population of gladiolus thrips. Dig these corms early in the fall before they are mature, and cut off the tops. The pests will be carried away in the cut portion. As a final measure, burn the tops. Preventing early infestation is necessary, since it's nearly impossible to reach the insects with sprays once they've settled between flower petals.

In general, pick off and destroy infested buds and flowers. Don't compost them because the larvae mature in the compost pile and fly back to your plants.

Barriers

Aluminum Mulch

If you can stand their appearance in your flower beds and borders, aluminum foil and aluminum polyethylene mulches will reduce the number of thrips on your plants.

Diatomaceous Earth

Diatomaceous earth spread around plant stems creates a barrier to thrips. You can also dust whole plants, beginning from the ground and working upward.

Organic Mulch

Spreading 4 to 6 inches of heavy organic mulch beneath plants keeps adult thrips from emerging in early spring. It may also prevent thrips that pupate in the soil from finding suitable pupation sites later in the season.

Insect Predators

Some species of thrips are actually beneficial insects, preying upon other thrips and small insect pests. Other naturally occurring beneficials that control thrips include damsel bugs, ground beetles, minute pirate bugs, and syrphid flies.

Other Preventive Steps

Soaking Corms in Cold Storage

To fight gladiolus thrips, just before planting gladiolus corms, soak them in a solution of 1¼ table-spoons Lysol in a gallon of water. Storing corms at 40° to 45°F also effectively eliminates remaining thrips. Generally, trouble with gladiolus thrips is much less serious when bulbs are planted early rather than late. Don't leave corms in the ground from one year to the next, particularly if your neighbors grow gladiolus. Dig them early in the fall, before they're mature, and cut off the tops, which harbor most of the pests.

PLANTS AFFECTED

Popular flowering plants preferred by thrips include the following:

- Flower thrips: daylily, iris, peony, rose.
- Gladiolus thrips: hollyhock, iris.
- Other thrips: annual aster, dahlia, gladiolus, hollyhock, iris, lily, rose, tuberous begonia, wax begonia.

INSECT **Weevils**

DESCRIPTION

Weevils, which are actually a type of beetle, are distinguished by their long, slender snouts that end in mouths. Also sometimes called snout beetles, they have tear-shaped, black, brown, or gray bodies that are covered with a hard shell, and they are ¹/₁₀ to ¼ inch long. The adult weevils feed at night and rest under plant debris during the day. Most species will "play dead" when disturbed, folding their legs and dropping to the ground. The larvae also feed on plants. They are legless, about ½ inch long, and white to pink in color with brown heads.

The weevils comprise a large group of insects; about 2,500 occur in North America. You won't have to worry about all of them, though. Two of the most common, the fuller rose beetle and the rose curculio, are given special sections below. Descriptions of different kinds of weevils are included in the individual plant entries in part 1.

MOST OBVIOUS SYMPTOMS

Adult weevils eat holes or notches in leaves; some species roll or curl them. When abundant, they can

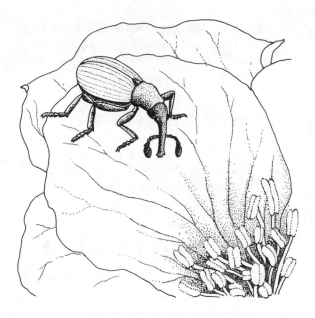

solution of one of the botanical poisons such as pyrethrum or ryania, once in the early spring and again in midsummer. Dig and discard badly infested specimens, together with the soil in which they are growing. Do not compost this material; discard it. Iris weevils feed on iris seeds and pupate in the seedpods; control them by picking and discarding flower heads as they fade.

MONITORING WEEVILS

Emergence Times

Weevils will begin to show up in your yard in late spring—April and early May in most parts of the country.

OPTIONS FOR CONTROLLING WEEVILS

Traps and Mechanical Controls

Cardboard Traps

Two or 3 hours after dark, when the weevils have moved up onto the plant, place a strip of cardboard coated with a sticky material, such as Tanglefoot, around the stem. The next morning, when the weevils crawl down the stem, the Tanglefoot will trap them. Make sure the cardboard fits snugly around the stem or the weevils will crawl underneath it.

Botanical Poisons

Rotenone

If you are using rotenone, a 5 percent solution will be necessary to control weevils.

Sabadilla

Apply sabadilla weekly on the undersides of leaves of infested plants.

Insect Predators and Parasites Available Commercially

One of the best techniques for controlling a heavy

defoliate plants. The larvae carve zigzag paths into roots, crowns, and stems. Crowns of plants blacken and die, are very stunted, or are eaten away. Infested plants wilt and will pull out of the ground easily.

BEST CONTROL STRATEGY

Weevils are difficult to control once plants are infested, but since the adults are unable to fly, moving healthy plants to another part of the garden is an effective way to keep them from spreading. Because of their habit of dropping to the ground when startled, you can remove many weevils from infested plants by spreading a cloth beneath the plants and shaking them. The weevils will drop onto the cloth, where you can gather them and destroy them in a jar of soapy water or kerosene. In addition, spray infested plants weekly with a solution of pyrethrum and isopropyl alcohol. Make this solution by combining 1 tablespoon of alcohol with a pint of pyrethrum mixture. Apply the solution at night, at least 2 hours after dark. For heavier infestations, drench the crowns of infested plants with a infestation of weevils or preventing a weevil attack is to introduce parasitic nematodes into your garden. Release them early in the season, around planting time.

PREVENTING WEEVIL DAMAGE

Garden Cleanup

Weevils make themselves at home among dead plants, so keep your garden clean. Clean up plant debris and cut away the foliage of infested plants to prevent the pests from overwintering (as both adults and larvae) in leaf litter and around the crowns of the plants. They will also feed on various weeds, including cocklebur, Joe-pye weed, morning-glory or bindweed, ragweed, and thistle. Remove these from your yard and you'll have fewer problems with weevils.

Animal Predators

Bluebirds, warblers, wrens, and other birds eat weevils. Scraping the soil near the plants in early spring to expose eggs to birds may be an effective control.

Insect Predators

Spiders catch adult weevils.

PLANTS AFFECTED

Popular flowering plants preferred by weevils include coralbells, iris, lily, and rose.

Fuller Rose Beetles

DESCRIPTION

This nocturnal weevil is about 1/3 inch long and is gray-brown with a broad snout and a white stripe on each wing cover. Its larvae are yellowish grubs with brown heads. Fuller rose beetles occur outdoors in the South and Southwest. They are serious greenhouse pests in the North, where they are most abundant in December.

MOST OBVIOUS SYMPTOMS

Fuller rose beetle larvae feed on roots and girdle flower stems, while the adults chew around the edges of leaves at night, making them ragged. Plants turn yellow and die.

BEST CONTROL STRATEGY

The weevils hide on twigs and in foliage during the day. Hunt them out and handpick them, crushing them or dropping them into a pail of soapy water. Weevils can also be captured by covering the ground around infested plants with a white cloth and shaking the plants lightly. The startled weevils will drop to the ground and "play dead," and can easily be scooped up. For heavy infestations, spray them directly with a solution of pyrethrum or rotenone laced with isopropyl alcohol every three to five days until they are gone. Make the solution by mixing 1 tablespoon of alcohol with every pint of diluted pyrethrum or rotenone mixture. For long-term control, apply milky spore disease (*Bacillus popilliae*) to lawns and garden to kill the larvae.

PLANTS AFFECTED

Popular flowering plants favored by fuller rose beetles include chrysanthemum, lily, and rose.

Rose Curculios

DESCRIPTION

The rose curculio adult is 1/4 inch long with a red

body and a long, black snout. The white larvae feed on seeds and flowers, then drop to the ground to pupate and hibernate. Rose curculios occur throughout the United States, but are most common in northern, colder regions; North Dakota, in particular, experiences severe infestations.

MOST OBVIOUS SYMPTOMS

Curculios chew holes in the buds of roses, and as a result, the buds often fail to open.

BEST CONTROL STRATEGY

Control these insect pests by handpicking adults and larvae. Collect and destroy the damaged, dried buds, which may be harboring larvae. If the infestation is heavy, spray roses with rotenone or pyrethrum. Throughout the year, clean up garden debris to remove any pests that might be hiding there.

PLANTS AFFECTED

Roses are the favorites of rose curculios.

INSECT **Whiteflies**

DESCRIPTION

These pests are tiny, mothlike, white, winged insects. When shaken from a plant, they look like flying dandruff. The yellowish nymphs are legless, flat, and oval and may resemble scale insects at certain stages. Females lay yellow, cone-shaped eggs on the undersides of leaves. Both nymphs and adults attack plants. Whiteflies occur throughout the United States. In the North, they are common greenhouse pests. Many generations occur in a year. In western states, leafhoppers are also called whiteflies. See the entry on leafhoppers, beginning on page 309.

MOST OBVIOUS SYMPTOMS

Whiteflies suck juices from plant leaves, buds, and stems, weakening the entire plant. The leaves will turn yellow and die, and the growth of the plant will be stunted. Honeydew may cover foliage, and this in turn encourages the growth of sooty, black mold, especially on the undersides of leaves. Tiny white-flies are clearly visible on plants, and you will easily be able to make an accurate diagnosis if these pests have infested any of your annuals or perennials—just brush the plants and watch for the white cloud.

BEST CONTROL STRATEGY

Inspect purchased bedding plants carefully to avoid bringing home infested specimens. Whiteflies are difficult to control once they have infested your garden plants. Spray lightly infested plants with insecticidal soap as soon as you spot whiteflies. Apply it directly to the whiteflies every two to three days for two weeks. Make sure you spray the undersides of the leaves. For very serious infestations, you may have to resort to pyrethrum, but try the soap spray first. Destroy heavily infested annuals as soon as you detect the problem, for whiteflies will quickly spread throughout the garden if infestations are not controlled.

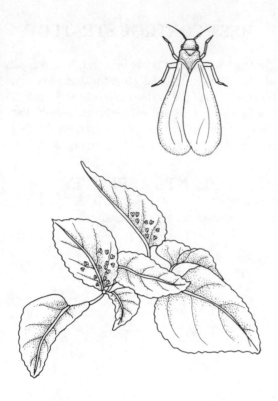

MONITORING WHITEFLIES

Emergence Times

In the South, the nymphs hibernate throughout the winter and emerge in spring when air temperatures are above 65°F. In the North, whiteflies are a greenhouse pest in winter and are often brought home on infested bedding plants or transplants. Whiteflies can't overwinter outdoors in the North.

Early Warning Devices

Sticky Traps

Yellow sticky traps will catch the earliest of the whiteflies in your backyard. In addition to letting you know that these pests are around, these traps help control the infestation, if you don't mind the

sight of them hanging in your flower garden. Use them as controls for only three to four weeks—any longer and they'll trap beneficials as well.

OPTIONS FOR CONTROLLING WHITEFLIES

Natural Sprays

Insecticidal Soap and Alcohol Spray

Isopropyl alcohol mixed with water and insecticidal soap can be completely effective in controlling whiteflies. Make the solution by combining 1 cup of alcohol and ½ tablespoon insecticidal soap in 1 quart of water. Two applications, a week apart, should remove all the whiteflies.

Water Spray

If you spray plants vigorously with water, you can knock many whiteflies from the leaves. It's best to do this early in the morning, when the whiteflies are sluggish. Use a nozzle that will produce a fine spray of water, and be sure to spray the undersides of the leaves as well as the top surfaces. Spray at least three times—three days in a row or every other day—to get the whiteflies that will hatch from eggs laid before you began spraying.

Botanical Poisons

Pyrethrum

Pyrethrum paralyzes whiteflies on contact. Apply it directly to the whiteflies. Be sure to spray the undersides of the leaves as well as the tops. Spray once every five days, making three applications, to control the problem.

Ryania

You can also spray infested plants with ryania. Several applications are usually needed.

Insect Predators and Parasites Available Commercially

Green lacewings are probably the most effective

insects you can buy to control whiteflies, but lady-bugs and chalcid and trichogramma wasps will also attack these pests. Use wasps only in a greenhouse; they'll be wasted outdoors.

PREVENTING WHITEFLY DAMAGE

Preventive Spray Programs

On plants most vulnerable to whiteflies, follow a biweekly preventive spray program using insecticidal soap. Begin by spraying seedlings you start indoors, covering the undersides of the leaves. Continue to spray plants every two weeks throughout the first month after transplanting them outdoors.

Animal Predators

Gnatcatchers, kinglets, phoebes, and swallows are some of the common songbirds that eat whiteflies.

PLANTS AFFECTED

Popular flowering plants beseiged by whiteflies include ageratum, annual aster, chrysanthemum, dahlia, geranium, salvia, and tuberous begonia.

CHAPTER 6

Diseases

If you're like most gardeners, you fight disease backward. You'll encounter a disease problem in your flower bed, *then* seek out control measures. Only after the crisis has passed will you think in terms of prevention. That's too bad, because prevention, as you'll see below, is the best disease-fighting technique. But whether you approach disease control with a "prevention first" attitude or wait until something goes wrong, this chapter will help you identify and solve your disease problems. It provides information on the most common ornamental plant diseases and discusses backyard management of plant disease, including controls and preventive tactics. Since there is very little variation in treatment techniques between the specific diseases within each type of disease—all fungal diseases respond well to the same techniques, for example—there are no individual disease entries. For more specific treatments, refer to the plant entries in part 1.

You have fewer tools for fighting disease in your flower garden than there are for use against insect and animal pests. Often, by the time a disease makes its presence known, it's too late to save infected plants. You have little choice but to consign sick plants to the trash. However, the removal of infected plants does serve as an important control of disease in your flower garden and landscape as a whole.

Luckily, there are some cases where this all-or-nothing approach is unnecessary. A number of fungal diseases cause spots or some yellowing, but are not lethal to the plant or seriously detrimental to the flowering of that plant in your garden. So don't panic at first sight of a single yellow leaf on your delphinium. Look at the general vigor of the plant. If it looks healthy otherwise, watch it closely for a few days or even weeks to see if in fact you have a serious problem. Most fungal diseases spread slowly. If your plants are deteriorating very rapidly (within a few days), it is more likely a sign of a viral or bacterial disease, and in that case the infected plants should be removed and destroyed immediately.

CONTROLLING DISEASE

The first step in controlling diseases in the flower garden is to spot and identify them. Look for symptoms. Examine your plants for changes in their general appearance. Many, if not most, of the problem symptoms you will find on your plants are caused by insects rather than disease. By reading the descriptions given for diseases and insect pest problems in this book, and with some experience, you will learn to distinguish insect damage from disease damage. (Read chapter 5 to familiarize yourself with the symptoms of insect problems.)

Once you've decided that the problem is caused by a disease rather than an insect pest, you will need to determine the type of disease that has infected your plants. Unfortunately, not every disease exhibits a distinctive pattern of symptoms. If you can narrow down the problem to one of the types covered in this chapter—fungal, bacterial, or viral, as well as cultural disorders and symptoms of nematode infestation—you can generally determine the best way to treat it. Again, the descriptions of

symptoms provided in part 1 of this book will be of help in narrowing down your choices and identifying a cure. (See the box, "Symptoms of Disease," below for help in identifying the symptoms of cultural disorders; fungal, bacterial, and viral diseases; and nematode infestation.)

Symptoms of Disease

The following list of symptoms and causes will help you decide whether you have a cultural disorder; fungal, bacterial, or viral disease; or if your plants may be infested with nematodes.

Cultural Disorders

A variety of conditions can cause cultural disorders, including nutrient deficiencies, improper pH, poor soil drainage, under- or overfertilization, and improper light exposure. The symptoms of these problems generally cause chlorosis, or yellowing, of the leaves. Chlorotic areas in most cases eventually turn brown or die. Look closely to see if the yellowing affects all of the leaves or only the youngest or oldest ones. Cultural disorders can also result in yellowed or browned leaf edges, yellowing between the veins of the leaves, or in irregular or mosaic spots or patterns.

Fungal Diseases

Plants infected with fungi can develop a variety of symptoms, depending on the type of disease involved. Look for pale patches on the leaves that may or may not be associated with rust-colored, powdery-looking patches on the upper or lower surface; round or irregular spots or blotches of chlorotic (yellowed) tissue that darken with time and dead spots or blotches on leaves are other signs of fungal diseases. Also look for water-soaked or greasy-looking spots on leaves or stems, or black, rotted-looking streaks or blotches. In this case, once the fungi have rotted all the way around the stem (girdle it) the afflicted stem will wilt and die. Seedlings that die suddenly, rotting at the soil surface and falling over, probably have been afflicted with a common fungal disease called damping-off.

Bacterial Diseases

Plants that exhibit the following may have a bacterial disease of some kind: rotted leaves, stems, branches, or tubers, often accompanied by a foul odor. When cut, afflicted plant parts often exude sticky-looking, yellowish or whitish masses of bacteria. Other symptoms of bacterial diseases include wilted leaves or stems, or large, irregularly shaped galls near the soil line on roots and stems.

Viral Diseases

There are many different viral diseases, all of which cause slightly different symptoms. Look for some or all of the following symptoms if you suspect your plants may be infected with a viral disease. Virus-infected plants generally exhibit overall poor plant performance, specifically, small, stunted plants, leaves, and blossoms. Blossoms and leaves may be disfigured, or the plant may develop shoots that branch abnormally, creating witches'-brooms. Many viral diseases cause a yellow-and-green mottling pattern on leaves, stems, or even blossoms. Also look for puckered, rolled, or extremely narrow ("shoestring") leaves and chlorosis (yellowing of leaves), specifically irregular yellow spots on leaves, often accompanied by leaf curling or excessive branching.

Nematode Infestation

Nematode-infested plants are stunted and grow poorly. Root knot nematodes form galls or swellings on plant roots, which you will find if you dig the plants to examine the roots. Other species cause deformed leaves or stems. Put nematodes at the bottom of your list of suspects. If no other explanation seems to fit, check the possibility that your plants have nematodes.

Diseaselike problems in the flower garden can be divided into five broad categories: cultural disorders, fungal diseases, bacterial diseases, viral diseases, and symptoms of nematode infestation. It's not always easy to decide which category your plant problem falls under, though, not only because many symptoms are characteristic of several diseases, but also because a plant may have more than one disease at the same time. Nevertheless, some problems are more common than others. You'll learn to diagnose disease problems from your experience of what has happened in your flower garden in previous years. Although there is some overlap, each type of disease can be recognized by a general set of symptoms.

There are a number of good books for identifying diseases; *Rodale's Garden Insect, Disease, and Weed Identification Guide,* Cynthia Westcott's *Plant Disease Handbook,* Time-Life's *Pests and Diseases,* and Pascal P. Pirone's *Diseases and Pests of Ornamental Plants* are particularly easy to use.

If you have just begun to work with a flower garden, you will find that most of your disease problems will actually be disorders caused by cultural conditions (watering, feeding, location, and so forth) rather than true diseases. The most common actual disease problems will be fungal diseases. Bacterial and viral diseases and the symptoms of nematode infestation occur less often.

CULTURAL DISORDERS

The environment surrounding a plant above and below the ground is crucial to its health. Disruptions or changes in environmental conditions can cause certain disorders in otherwise healthy plants. Above the surface of the soil, the vagaries of wind, rain, light, air temperature, and humidity cause such problems as dieback, leaf scorch, and sunscald. Environmental conditions below the surface of the soil, such as the tilth of the soil, nutrient deficiencies or excesses, moisture content, soil temperature, and an inappropriate pH, cause other disorders.

Cultural disorders can weaken a plant and lead to real pathogenic disease. For example, anthracnose and powdery mildew are fungal diseases encouraged by hot, dry summer weather. Planting flowers that love good drainage, like lilies and bearded irises, in waterlogged plots will lead to root rot.

The causes of cultural ailments most frequently fall into one of five categories: soil deficiency, which includes pH problems and basic mineral imbalances; improper watering; problems with light intensity, which can be caused by inadequate hardening off as well as by putting a plant in the wrong place; improper fertilization, which involves the quantity and balance of nutrients you add to the existing soil environment; and physical injury to the stem or roots.

Of the five groups of plant diseases and diseaselike problems, cultural disorders are the easiest to correct once they have been properly diagnosed. Making a proper diagnosis, however, takes some skill and experience. The most common symptoms are general weakening of the whole plant or some color change in the leaves, such as yellowing or reddening.

Symptoms and Causes of Cultural Disorders

The following list of symptoms and causes will help you identify the cultural problems in your flower garden.

Chlorosis
Chlorosis is the yellowing of leaves. Its appearance on your plants will differ, depending on the type of problem your plants have.

On All Leaves. This may be caused by a lack of nutrients, extremely bright light, or high temperatures.

On Youngest Leaves. A lack of iron or manganese, or insufficient light, may cause yellowing of the youngest leaves.

On Older Leaves. Chlorosis on older leaves may only mean that the soil lacks nitrogen or potassium, or it may need aeration.

On Leaf Edges. This is often a sign of a deficiency in both magnesium and potassium.

Between Leaf Veins. This may indicate a deficiency in iron or manganese, or there may be sulfur dioxide in the air.

As Irregular Spots. Cold water can cause irregular yellow spots on leaves.

As Mosaic Pattern. Cold water can also cause a mosaic pattern of yellow spots on leaves.

Dead Areas on Leaves

Cultural disorders are often signaled by the rotting of areas on leaves.

On Leaf Edges or Tips. This could indicate a potassium deficiency, boron excess, fluoride excess, excessive heat or cold, or insufficient water.

As Spots or Sections. Cold water can cause dead areas on leaves.

On Edges and Inner Sections. This may be caused by too much light, cool temperatures, or cold water.

With Water-Soaked or Greasy Appearance. Excessive heat or cold, or cold water on the foliage, may produce this effect.

Control of Deficiency Disorders

Nutritional disorders can usually be quickly remedied by applying the appropriate foliar spray to a weakening plant, then correcting the soil deficiency or imbalance that caused the problem. Soil tests can be extremely helpful, providing a profile of your garden soil's strengths and weaknesses. However, you can also take long-term measures to control environmental problems without ever pinpointing the specific cause. Simply follow these steps:

1. Make sure the soil is healthy, with the proper pH level, nutrient balance, and drainage, and has sufficient water-holding capacity for the plants you're growing.

2. Make sure the plants get the right amount of water.

3. Make sure the plants get the right amount of fertilizer.

For example, if you spread an inch of compost on the soil throughout the garden every year, you will be correcting many of the soil deficiencies most commonly found in the new flower garden. If you spray your plants once or twice a season with a kelp extract, your plants will get the necessary micronutrients, even if there are some deficiencies in the soil. If you make sure that the plants get a consistent level of water (about 1 inch a week) from rain or by watering, you eliminate over- or underwatering. And finally, if you add an appropriate amount of slow-acting, general-purpose fertilizer (roughly 1 cup per 25 square feet of garden) once a season, you will eliminate most nutritional problems. So even though it may be difficult to identify the specific cultural cause of a problem, these easy steps will help to remedy the current problem and prevent any potential cultural disorders from becoming garden realities.

FUNGAL DISEASE

Disease fungi are microscopic plants that take nourishment from the plants on which they live—in other words, they are parasites. Fungal diseases exhibit a number of distinctive symptoms, often indicated by their names. Downy mildew and powdery mildew create pale patches on the leaves of infected plants. Rusts can be identified by their rusty color on leaves. Leaf spot causes round, yellow spots on diseased leaves; the spots darken over time. Many fungal diseases can be controlled or even eliminated by proper gardening practices. When you spot a problem in a plant, rule out possible cultural problems before looking for a fungal cause. And remember, not all fungal diseases are found in all parts of the country.

Symptoms of Fungal Disease

The following symptoms may indicate a fungal disease of some kind.

- Pale patches on leaves

- Chlorosis (yellowing of leaves), specifically round spots or irregular yellow-green spots that darken with time
- Dead spots or sections on leaves
- Water-soaked or greasy appearance on leaves or stems
- Rust-colored spots
- Sudden death of small seedlings

Fungal diseases tend to spread over the entire plant somewhat slowly, occurring over weeks rather than days, whereas problems caused by viruses or bacteria spread quite quickly. However, this does not mean you should wait to confirm that you have a fungal problem; once a fungal disease has spread throughout the plant, it can be difficult to control, and the plant may be too severely damaged to survive. This is especially true of stem and crown rot or wilt diseases that rot the base of the plant.

Control of Fungal Disease

Treatment of fungal disease varies depending on the specific disease. In some cases, removing the affected leaves is all you'll need to do. However, in most cases, you should leave the plant alone and begin some control strategy using fungicidal sprays or dusts. The individual plant entries in part 1 offer more specific control steps for diseases. But in general, once you've decided your plant has a fungal disease, such as rust or black spot, it often can be arrested by the application of an appropriate organic fungicide.

How to Use Organic Fungicides

Organic fungicides are much less effective once a disease has become well established, so for best results, apply them early in the season—even before there is evidence of plant damage if a particular disease has consistently been a problem in your garden. This means, of course, that you must remember when a fungal disease struck a particular perennial or annual last year so you can anticipate its arrival at about the same time this year. Generally, you should repeat fungicide treatments every week or ten days throughout the growing season to prevent a fungal disease from developing or to keep it controlled.

Remember, whether you use a dust or a spray, only those parts of the plant that are actually coated with the fungicide are protected; that is why some kind of "sticker" material should be included in any spray mixture. Problems on individual plants can be handled with a fungicide sold in its own applicator bottle. If you have many infected plants or larger plants you may need to use about ½ to 1 gallon of spray. The organic fungicides listed below are safe to use in the flower garden, but handle them with respect. Wash your hands thoroughly after using these materials.

A single organic fungicide will not control all fungal diseases. Fortunately, your flower garden will not be attacked by many different fungal diseases, requiring a shelf full of different control products. All homeowners should have a sulfur-based fungicide such as a fungicidal soap spray on their shelves, since it does control several fungal problems. You can add other products to your store as they become necessary.

Types of Organic Fungicide

Although there are many powerful fungicides on the market that will control most fungal diseases, only a few are considered totally safe to the environment. These are recommended here for safe application in the flower garden.

Antitranspirants. Researchers at Texas Tech University, in Lubbock, found that antitranspirants sprayed on zinnias kept these highly susceptible plants free of powdery mildew—in fact, the antitranspirants worked better than a chemical fungicide. The plants were sprayed with antitranspirant five times during the growing season. The researchers concluded that antitranspirants controlled the mildew because the antitranspirant film on the leaves repelled the fungus organism, and it also prevented the coat of water necessary to the fungus's development from forming. An added benefit was increased vigor and flowering, due to increased water and nutrient content in the plant cells. Anti-transpirants are available under a number of trade names, including Cloud Cover, Vapor Gard, and Wilt-Pruf.

Baking Soda. Japanese researchers have found that baking soda (sodium bicarbonate) controls powdery mildew and other mildews when sprayed on plants at weekly intervals at a concentration of 1 level teaspoonful per 2 quarts of water. Not only does the soda prevent fungal spores from germinating and stop development of the disease, but it even appears to help the plants repair fungus-damaged tissue.

Bordeaux Mixture. This fungicide is a mixture of salts of copper and hydrated lime and has a very low level of toxicity. It works by burning the spores of fungal diseases. Do not mix it with other materials. When combined with Bt (*Bacillus thuringiensis*), other materials make the Bt ineffective. Do not use bordeaux mixture during cool, wet weather; it will damage your plants. It can be used to control anthracnose, black rot, leaf spot, and other fungal diseases. Wherever bordeaux mixture is recommended, you may safely substitute one of the fixed-copper compounds below. Bordeaux mixture is corrosive to iron and steel.

Fixed-Copper Compounds. The fixed-copper compounds, such as basic copper sulfate, copper oxychloride, and cuprous oxide are effective in controlling various fungal and bacterial diseases. These compounds are sold under various trade names and should be used only as directed on the labels. Do not use them during cool, wet weather or they may damage your plants. They help to control anthracnose, bacterial leaf spot, downy mildew, early blight, late blight, leaf spot, powdery mildew, and other fungal diseases.

Among the fixed-copper fungicides on the market are Basic Copper Sulfate, Basi-Cop, Bonide, Copper 53 Fungicide, Microcop, T B-C-S 53, Top Cop, and Tribasic Copper Sulfate. Others include Bordo, Bordo-Mix, C-O-C-S, Coprantol, Kocide 101, Miller 658, and Ortho Copper Fungicide.

Fungicidal Soap Spray. Safer has developed a fungicidal soap spray made from sulfur in a soap base. Simply follow the package directions for application. It is available in a ready-to-use form, Safer Garden Fungicide, and a concentrate called Safer Fungicide Concentrate. Fungicidal soap will control such common fungus problems as black spot, rust, and powdery mildew. Most of the companies listed under "Controls" in the source list at the end of this book offer this product.

Garlic Spray. Garlic's antiseptic properties make it an effective control for mildews and other fungi. Apply it as a spray. To prepare a solution, chop enough garlic cloves to fill ½ cup. Mix the garlic with 1 pint of water and let it steep for a few minutes, then strain out the chopped cloves. Remember garlic's other claim to fame—its pungent odor—and try another control if you're growing flowers for their fragrance. If you want cut flowers for the house, make sure you spray stems and foliage well below the level of the flowers.

Sulfur. Sulfur is one of the best natural fungicides available and has a very low toxicity. Applied to the surface of leaves, ground elemental sulfur will prevent the germination of certain fungal spores that fall on a treated leaf. The finer the grind, the more even the coverage and the better the adhesion. The finest form is micronized sulfur. You can also buy sulfur as a wettable powder and spray it on your plants at a rate of 1 tablespoon per gallon of water. Note that sulfur is also available in convenient, easy-to-use, liquid form combined with a soap-based material as the carrier (sold as fungicidal soap). The liquid sticks to the undersides of leaves better than the powder.

Use sulfur at two-week intervals as a preventive method during periods when you expect fungal infections to occur. Do not apply it when air temperatures are over 80°F. Sulfur fungicides will help control these fungal diseases, among others: anthracnose, black spot, leaf spot, powdery mildew, and rust.

Water Spray. Experiments at Laredo Junior College in Texas showed that spraying plants daily with a garden hose equipped with a spray nozzle provided effective control against powdery mildew. Protection was as great as that provided by a chemical fungicide, and the fungicide had an added drawback: When treatment was discontinued, the fungicide-treated plants quickly succumbed to fungal disease, while water-sprayed plants displayed more resistance.

Preventing Fungal Disease

As they say, the best defense is a strong offense. Fungal disease may be hard to get rid of, so the best control is to prevent infection of your plants in the first place. There are a number of good gardening practices that, combined, make a winning team against fungi.

Resistant Cultivars

The best way to prevent fungal diseases in your yard and garden is to use cultivars of plants that have been bred to be resistant to or tolerant of those diseases. (Resistant plants have a strong ability to withstand or repel a disease; tolerant plants can survive and produce flowers in spite of infection.) Resistant and tolerant cultivars are not always available, but when they are, try them and see how you like them. These cultivars are something of an event in the plant world and are almost always called out in catalogs, so they're easy to spot. Examples include 'Rose Pinwheel' zinnia, 'Bonica' rose, and 'Peachblush' and 'Red Carpet' lilies. Some cultivars, like 'Gold Rush' and 'Prelude' lilies, are notoriously susceptible to certain fungal diseases and should be avoided if those diseases are problems in your flower garden.

Mulching

Most fungal spores are spread by the wind and by rain bouncing them up onto plants from the soil. Using mulch in your flower garden prevents this by acting as a barrier. Use drip irrigation to avoid the splashing of water that occurs with overhead watering. If you must use a sprinkler or hold a hose over your plants, water before noon so the sun will dry off the moisture on the leaves, eliminating the moist environment the spores need to multiply. Try to aim the water at the ground around plants rather than on the plants themselves. And don't work in your garden in humid, rainy weather or when your plants are wet, or you might carry spores from plant to plant.

Correct Spacing

If fungal diseases are a serious problem in your area, and especially if you live in a hot, humid climate, provide maximum spacing between the plants in your flower garden to encourage good air circulation around them. Fungal diseases thrive in hot, damp areas with poor air circulation. The better the air circulation, the faster the plants will dry after rain or after overhead watering.

Cleanup

A regular program of garden cleanup is an essential part of your disease-fighting efforts. Seriously infected plants should be regularly dug and destroyed, or the diseased portions removed, before they can affect other plants in the garden. Critical to preventing any serious fungal disease is a very thorough yard and garden cleanup in the fall, which reduces the overwintering sites for fungal spores. Conscientiously pull up infected annuals and take up the leaves of infected perennials and dispose of them. Resist the urge to compost any plant material you suspect to be diseased—spores could survive composting. When disposing of diseased plant matter, it's also a good idea to immediately put it in a plastic bag or other container right where the plants are growing. That way, you won't spread any more spores around the garden than absolutely necessary.

Sulfur

Use a sulfur-based fungicide or a fungicidal soap at two-week intervals as a preventive method during periods when you expect fungal infections to occur. Do not apply it when air temperatures are over 80°F, as it can damage leaves at high temperatures.

Solarization

Soil solarization is a technique that has proven effective in reducing fungal disease in the garden. If you're starting a flower bed in a site that you know is troubled with fungal disease, or if your annual garden is plagued with fungus problems, this technique can give the soil a fresh start. For information on how to solarize your soil, see page 349.

Keeping Tools Clean

It is always wise to keep your tools clean, especially if fungal diseases are a problem anywhere in your yard or garden. Some gardeners keep handy a covered 5-gallon pail with a household bleach solution (1 part bleach and 3 parts water) or a copper fungicide solution mixed according to the directions on the container. Dip spades, forks, trowels, scissors, pruners, and other tools in either of these solutions after working in the garden around vulnerable or infected plants. After disinfecting your tools, coat them with oil to keep them from rusting.

Plants Affected

Some flowering plants are susceptible to specific fungal diseases. If you're growing or want to grow a plant that's prone to a fungus problem, this list can alert you early enough to take preventive measures. This is only a guideline; more plants are susceptible than are listed, but these are the most common. For more specifics, see the individual plant entries in part 1.

- Anthracnose: hollyhock, pansy, snapdragon.
- Blight: dahlia, iris, marigold, peony, snapdragon, rose, tulip, zinnia.
- Canker: annual aster, cosmos, lily.
- Club root: sweet alyssum.
- Crown rot: baby's-breath, balloon flower, bellflower, black-eyed Susan, bulbous iris, columbine, coreopsis, daffodil, delphinium, hosta, iris, larkspur, pansy, phlox, snapdragon, tulip.
- Damping-off: annual aster, cockscomb, delphinium, impatiens, petunia, salvia, sweet alyssum, verbena, wax begonia.
- Downy mildew: annual aster, bachelor's button, forget-me-not, perennial aster, poppy, salvia, sweet alyssum.

- Gray mold (botrytis): annual aster, baby's-breath, bulbous iris, hyacinth, lily, snapdragon.
- Leaf spot: annual aster, balloon flower, bellflower, black-eyed Susan, bulbous iris, chrysanthemum, cockscomb, columbine, coralbells, coreopsis, cosmos, daffodil, daylily, four-o'clock, geranium, hollyhock, hosta, impatiens, iris, marigold, nasturtium, pansy, peony, perennial aster, phlox, salvia, sunflower, tuberous begonia, wax begonia.
- Powdery mildew: ageratum, annual aster, astilbe, black-eyed Susan, balloon flower, bellflower, coralbells, cosmos, dahlia, delphinium, larkspur, perennial aster, phlox, rose, salvia, sunflower, tuberous begonia, wax begonia, yarrow, zinnia.
- Rhizome rot: iris.
- Root rot: ageratum, bachelor's button, balloon flower, bellflower, columbine, cosmos, four-o'clock, geranium, iris, lily, pansy, snapdragon, zinnia.
- Rust: ageratum, annual aster, bachelor's button, balloon flower, bellflower, black-eyed Susan, canna, chrysanthemum, coreopsis, dianthus, four-o'clock, hollyhock, iris, lily, pansy, perennial aster, salvia, snapdragon, sunflower, sweet alyssum, yarrow.
- Smut: dahlia, pansy.
- Stem rot: balloon flower, bellflower, black-eyed Susan, bleeding-heart, coralbells, cosmos, dahlia, dianthus, geranium, impatiens, marigold, pansy, petunia, snapdragon, sunflower, tuberous begonia, wax begonia, zinnia.
- Wilt: annual aster, astilbe, bachelor's button, bleeding-heart, dahlia, dianthus, forget-me-not, marigold, sunflower, sweet alyssum.

BACTERIAL DISEASE

The bacteria that attack flowering plants are carried to those plants in running or splashing water or in transported soil. They can enter a plant through wounds or through the tiny natural openings in the epidermis. Once inside, bacteria travel short distances in the sap of the plant.

Symptoms of Bacterial Disease

Disease bacteria are microscopic organisms that cause trouble when they live in flowering plants. Pathogenic bacteria operate in a number of harmful ways. The bacteria that cause rots release an enzyme that dissolves cell walls in leaves, stems, and tubers. Wilts are caused by bacteria that block a plant's vascular system. Crown gall occurs when bacteria invade through plant wounds or bruises, then exude substances that promote abnormal growth in the host plant. The following symptoms may indicate a bacterial disease of some kind.

- Rotted leaves, stems, branches, or tubers, often accompanied by a foul odor
- Wilted leaves
- Large, irregularly shaped galls near the soil line on roots and stems

Control of Bacterial Disease

Bacterial diseases cannot be cured. *Remove all infected plants immediately and put them in the trash, even if they have only slight symptoms of a bacterial disease.* Do not place diseased plants in your compost pile, even if you maintain an active pile that heats up.

Preventing Bacterial Disease

Prevent the spread of a bacterial disease by cleaning your tools after cutting a diseased plant. There are a number of disinfectants used by professional gardeners. Isopropyl alcohol is an excellent disinfectant for tools. Use it between cuts to prevent the spread of plant diseases. Or, you can use a disinfectant spray such as Lysol, which is effective and easy to use. Just give tools a spritz between cuts. Some professionals use a bleach solution made up of 1 part household bleach and 3 parts water. After disinfecting your tools, coat them with oil to prevent rusting. Wash your hands after handling infected plants, not because they are dangerous to you, but because your unwashed hands could transmit the disease to healthy plants.

Plants Affected

Some flowering plants are particularly susceptible to bacterial infections. If you are growing or want to grow these plants, mulch them to keep water from splashing up and contaminating them. Work carefully around the plants so you don't injure them, creating entryways for bacteria. The following list will give you a general overview of bacterial diseases and the common annuals and perennials that are prone to them. For specifics, look under the individual plant entries in part 1.

- Bacterial leaf spot: geranium, nasturtium, tuberous begonia.
- Bacterial soft rot: daffodil, hyacinth, iris.
- Bacterial wilt: nasturtium.
- Blight: marigold, peony, poppy, zinnia.
- Crown gall: baby's-breath, dahlia.
- Stem rot: bleeding-heart, coralbells, petunia, wax begonia.
- Wilt: astilbe, bleeding-heart, cosmos, dahlia, marigold, nasturtium, dianthus, sweet alyssum.

VIRAL DISEASE

Viruses are basically protein packets with DNA or RNA inside. They are parasites, multiplying inside their hosts or, if no host is available, lying inactive—but viable—in dead plant material for up to 50 years while waiting for a new victim.

Viruses are spread from plant to plant in a number of ways. Insects, especially aphids, leafhoppers, mealybugs, and whiteflies, often carry them. Aphids are the worst offenders; the green peach aphid (*Myzus persicae*) can carry more than 50 different plant viruses. Viruses can also be carried on your hands and on garden tools. Smokers can transmit a mosaic virus from their cigarettes. Cuttings taken from infected stock plants will result in infected progeny, and viruses can also be carried by seeds.

Symptoms of Viral Disease

The following symptoms may indicate a viral disease.

• Poor plant performance, characterized by small, stunted foliage or small, off-color blossoms

• Sudden death of a plant

• Chlorosis (yellowing of leaves), specifically irregular yellow spots on leaves, often accompanied by leaf curling or excessive branching

• Mosaic yellow-and-green mottling pattern on leaves, stems, or even blossoms

• Dead areas on leaves

• Puckered, rolled, or extremely narrow ("shoestring") leaves

Control of Viral Disease

Viral diseases cannot be cured. Remove and destroy the infected plants—remember, dead plant matter left in the garden continues to harbor the disease. As with bacterial diseases, *remove all infected plants,* even if symptoms are mild. Do not place diseased plants in your compost pile, and clean your hands and tools with a bleach solution made up of 1 part household bleach and 3 parts water.

Plants Affected

If an annual, perennial, or bulb you want to grow is prone to a particular virus, buy certified disease-free seed or stock when available, and grow resistant cultivars when you can find them. A list of common flowering plants that are virus-prone follows. For more information, consult the individual plant entries in part 1.

• Aster yellows: annual aster, baby's-breath, bachelor's button, balloon flower, bellflower, canna, chrysanthemum, coreopsis, cosmos, delphinium, forget-me-not, marigold, nasturtium, petunia, salvia, sweet alyssum.

• Beet curly top: cockscomb, coreopsis, cosmos, delphinium, four-o'clock, geranium, nasturtium, petunia, zinnia.

• Mosaic: canna, chrysanthemum, crocus, dahlia, delphinium, dianthus, hollyhock, hyacinth, iris, petunia.

• Other viruses: chrysanthemum, cosmos, daffodil, dahlia, delphinium, dianthus, geranium, gladiolus, lily, nasturtium, pansy, peony, petunia, poppy, tulip, zinnia.

NEMATODES

Nematodes are tiny parasitic worms that feed on and reproduce in plants. Although they are actually pests and are dealt with in chapter 5, the problems they cause are included with diseases because their symptoms are similar to those caused by diseases, and the symptoms continue for the life of the plant, as do those of the pathogenic diseases.

Generally, it is difficult to diagnose nematodes just by looking at a plant. Very often the only sign of a nematode problem is weakened plants that don't look healthy and vigorous. The exceptions are the root knot nematodes (*Meloidogyne incognita* and *M. hapla*), which form galls or swellings on plant roots. Put nematodes at the bottom of your list of suspects when you are trying to identify a disease. If no other explanation seems to fit, check the possibility that your plants have nematodes. (See the nematode entry, beginning on page 315.)

GENERAL DISEASE-PREVENTION PRACTICES

Because they often work fast and are difficult to control, the best way to fight plant diseases is to prevent them from getting a foothold in the first place. Fortunately, prevention is easier than fighting a plant disease that is established in your garden. A few simple garden maintenance steps will go a long way toward prevention. For example, by simply spreading compost, using seaweed extract sprays, and watering properly, you can significantly reduce the incidence of cultural disorders. Using mulch reduces the spread of fungal and bacterial diseases that are often transported to the plant in rain or irrigation water splashing up from the soil. Viral diseases can often be prevented by controlling insect pests such as aphids, which carry these diseases. These and many other commonsense care practices can keep your flower garden almost disease free.

Flower Garden Management

The best approach to garden-wide disease prevention is to follow some general gardening practices that help prevent *all* disease. You might think building healthy soil with compost or adding mulch around your plants is simply extra effort, but such practices expend less energy than trying to combat a disease once it has taken hold in the flower garden—to say nothing of eliminating disappointment over favorite plants looking hideous or even dying. In addition, many of these garden-management practices prevent other potential problems, such as soil deficiencies, pest infestations, and poor drainage. Remember, a healthy flower garden is your strongest ally in disease prevention. Vigorous plants can withstand many diseases on their own.

Steps for Disease Prevention

1. Build healthy soil.
2. Use compost.
3. Plant resistant species and cultivars.
4. Use preventive foliar sprays.
5. Use mulch.
6. Eliminate the method of transmission.
7. Water early in the day.
8. Keep tools clean.
9. Clean up the flower garden in fall.
10. Solarize the soil.
11. Use drip irrigation to prevent fungal disease.
12. To avoid spreading fungal disease, don't work with plants when they are wet.

Build Healthy Soil

Soil that has a minimum content of 5 percent organic matter (more than 10 percent is even better) has a pH of around 6.5, contains at least five earthworms per cubic foot, and gets an annual 1-inch layer of compost will prevent diseases as effectively as any other disease-fighting tool or technique except genetic resistance. A healthy soil maintains a balance between beneficial bacteria, fungi, and other microorganisms and those pathogens that can cause disease if allowed to multiply. The most common disease-causing bacteria and fungal spores in your neighborhood are usually present in the soil. However, beneficial microorganisms keep those diseases under control as long as the soil is healthy. (See page 373 for more information on soil management.)

Use Compost

Compost benefits the garden in many ways, and one of the benefits it offers is disease control. Recent research by Safer Agro-Chem, in Wellesley, Massachusetts, has shown that compost produces certain fatty acids that are toxic to fungal diseases and to certain bacterial diseases of plants. Decomposing rye and timothy grasses, among others, release fatty acids that control parasitic nematodes.

Research by the Ohio Agricultural Research and Development Center has shown that compost, especially the kind that is made by simply piling compost materials and leaving them to decompose, suppresses harmful root-invading fungi, which can cause such diseases as root rot and damping-off. Certain beneficial bacteria are present in compost. These bacterial allies produce substances called siderophores that tie up iron, depriving harmful organisms of this necessary element. Beneficial fungi found in compost, particularly species of *Trichoderma* and *Pythium*, are antagonistic to pathogenic fungi. For example, they will attack rhizoctonia root rot fungi and some water mold fungi. The more of these beneficial bacteria and fungi present in the soil, the fewer disease problems will occur.

Compost produced by chopping and turning the materials in your compost pile, with its high temperatures, has less disease-suppressive ability than a low-temperature compost made without turning because beneficial microorganisms are killed by the high heat. "Seeding" high-temperature compost with small amounts of mature compost made at moderate temperatures (about 80°F) restores its ability to fight disease-causing organisms. (See page 376 for more information about compost.)

Use Preventive Foliar Sprays

A number of natural fungicides made from sulfur suspended in liquid soaps, such as Safer's Fungicidal Soap, are available commercially. Use them to prevent as well as control diseases. When mixed with a seaweed extract, these fungicides can be especially effective in stopping fungal diseases in their tracks. Use this mixture as a preventive spray every two weeks during the early part of the growing season on those plants that are vulnerable to fungal disease. (Roses are good candidates for this treatment.) Wait at least four days after applying any pesticide spray before using these fungicides to avoid a conflict between the two products.

Use Mulch

Organic mulches can also help prevent disease. For example, research is beginning to suggest that organic mulches such as chopped leaves may mitigate the harmful effects of certain soil fungi and nematodes by creating a chemical environment that either repels those pathogens or kills them outright. (See page 386 for more information about mulch and mulching systems.)

Eliminate the Method of Transmission

If you know that the plants in your flower garden are vulnerable to certain diseases, or if you simply want to take all possible measures to prevent disease in your yard and garden, consider the ways in which disease is transmitted to plants and remove those means of transmission.

Virtually all of the fungal diseases are transmitted by the movement of microscopic spores that travel to the plant by wind, water, or a carrier (such as yourself or an animal) that has picked up spores

in its travels. Water splashing up from the ground during rains or through overhead watering commonly carries fungal disease up to the plant from the ground. One way to prevent this is to spread black plastic or geotextile mulch over the soil early in the season, even before the soil thaws from the winter freeze. Most fungal spores do not emerge from the soil until air temperatures are in the seventies. If you have black plastic or geotextile mulch in place on your flower beds by midspring, you'll prevent spores from bouncing up onto the plants. Unfortunately, this trick won't work on established perennial beds or on flower beds that have spring bulbs in them, since these plants begin emerging early.

Using drip irrigation to water your flower garden instead of an overhead sprinkler or hose is another way to eliminate the splashing of water that carries spores and bacteria with it. A drip irrigation system laid under the black plastic mulch benefits the plants by providing constant soil moisture while reducing fungal disease problems.

Finally, don't handle plants that are wet. Handling wet plants, or for that matter working in the garden when it's wet or the humidity is very high, can transfer pathogens from plant to plant.

Water Early in the Day

One of the easiest ways to reduce the incidence of plant disease, especially bacterial and fungal disease, is to water your garden in the morning. This allows the plants to dry thoroughly before nightfall, denying these diseases the moist, damp conditions they thrive in.

Keep Tools Clean

If disease is a problem in your flower garden, it is especially important to keep your gardening tools cleaner and more sterile than you normally might. Hoes, rakes, shovels, trowels, and other tools can carry fungal spores, bacteria, and viruses and spread those pathogens to other plants in your garden. Keep a 5-gallon pail containing bleach solution (1 part household bleach and 3 parts water) handy. Then, as a matter of routine, you can dip your tools in the solution to disinfect them after you've scraped off the soil. Be sure to oil them afterward to prevent rust.

Clean Up the Garden in Fall

Fall cleanup is one of the most important steps you can take to reduce both insect and disease problems in your flower garden. It is essential that all debris from infected plants be removed from the yard and garden and placed in the trash. Other organic material, such as weeds, fallen leaves, and even compost, should be removed and composted. Diseases overwinter on plant residues, so even healthy annual plants left in the garden provide a favorable environment for any diseases that might be carried into the garden by air, water, insects, or animals.

Solarize the Soil

In the past, it was assumed that if certain disease pathogens, such as verticillium wilt and fusarium wilt, were present in the soil, they would remain there and you would always have problems with them. Over the past ten years, a technique called solarization has been developed that may solve many garden disease problems. Solarization was developed in Israel and has since been tested at a number of universities across the United States. It is a process that produces very high levels of heat and humidity in the soil. This process pasteurizes the soil, destroying harmful bacteria, fungi, some nematodes, virtually every type of insect larvae, and weed seeds near the surface. Solarization is an effective control for a number of chronic disease problems found in the flower garden.

An unexpected and unexplained bonus of solarization is that it also enhances the soil's ability to grow especially robust and healthy plants. Plants perform splendidly in beds that have been solarized. Solarization destroys harmful organisms, but it seems that certain beneficial organisms are not harmed. Jim DeVay, chairman of the plant pathology department at the University of California at Davis, says, "While many fungi, bacteria, and other pathogens are killed, certain fungi that play an important role in utilization of plant nutrients and crop development withstand the heat and survive."

Solarization's drawbacks are that you can only use it on a new or empty bed (one that has no plants growing in it) and that it's most effective during the growing season. That means if you try it, you'll have an unsightly bed of plastic for a month or more instead of flowers. For most gardeners, the sacrifice is only worthwhile if their gardens are seriously infected with a soilborne disease year after year. The reason you can't solarize an existing perennial or bulb bed is that the technique would kill the plants as well as pathogens. The best time to solarize soil is during July and August, when temperatures are highest and days are sunny. The procedure for solarizing all or part of a bed is fairly straightforward. Simply follow these steps:

1. Loosen up the top foot or so of soil with a fork, U-bar digger, or tiller.

2. Water the soil heavily so that it is soaking wet—wetter than if you were simply watering your plants. Then let the bed sit overnight.

3. The next day, cover the bed or part of the bed with 3- to 6-mil, clear, plastic film. Do not use black plastic because it will not produce the desired greenhouse effect.

4. Seal the plastic film along all edges with soil, and keep the soil tightly covered for four to six weeks.

It is likely to rain during the four- to six-week solarization period, leaving puddles on the plastic. Take a broom and sweep the puddles away because they reduce the effect of the sunlight striking the film. Do not punch holes in the plastic to drain the water because that will let the heat escape.

After the solarization process is finished, you can plant anything you want in that area right away. Try not to disturb the soil very much when you put in the new plants. The weed seeds near the surface have been killed, but the seeds 4 or more inches down could still germinate if brought to the surface.

CHAPTER 7

Animal Pests

Unlike insects, which are usually less troublesome in the flower garden than in the vegetable patch, animals can wreak havoc wherever they turn up. A dog can demolish a flower bed in pursuit of a rabbit; a cat can decide that there's no litter box like your carefully worked soil. Tulip bulbs are caviar to voles, and deer think the greatest delicacies are flower buds, denuding everything from roses to phlox and asters. And unlike vegetable gardens, which can be effectively fenced off and strewn with Mylar ribbons, aluminum pie plates, hawk kites, and other colorful deterrents, your flower garden is a focal point in the landscape. It's supposed to draw the eye by its beauty, not look like a flea market.

Unfortunately, there are no quick, surefire solutions to any serious animal pest invasion. You have three basic choices in almost all cases: You can trap the pest to kill or remove it; you can set up a barrier of some kind that will effectively deny the pest access to your yard or garden; or you can put repellents on or around your plants to keep pests away from them. This chapter will focus first on the most effective control measures available for your use and then it will address various preventive measures. The chapter ends with a pest-by-pest description of the most effective management methods.

CONTROLLING ANIMALS

Effective animal pest control depends on three primary factors: timing, persistence, and diversity.

Timing. In managing animal pests, good timing is crucial. Install barriers *before* you expect an animal to make its appearance, and start control measures at the very first indication of damage. Unlike most insects, animals can wipe out an entire planting or even the whole garden in a very short time if the problem is left unattended.

Persistence. Some animals, such as squirrels and deer, are ingenious in foiling your attempts to thwart them. A single try at establishing a barrier may not do the job. You will have to keep trying until you come up with a control or combination of controls that finally outsmarts the wily marauders.

Diversity. No single control method or preventive step is always satisfactory, even if it worked last year. Typically, a variety of strategies and devices are required, often used in combination. Placement of traps and barriers must be shifted frequently to ensure success against persistent pests.

In many cases, the only realistic option you have in controlling a pest after it has discovered your yard is trapping. Biological controls have lim-

351

ited effectiveness, and poisons pose hazards to the environment, pets, and children. In this section, you'll find control steps ranging from those with the least impact to those with greater impact on the environment.

Traps

Most people are unhappy about having to kill any living creature, so they prefer to use what are called live traps, which catch the animal without harming it. Once caught, the culprit is taken out to the countryside and released.

Livetrapping animal pests isn't the best control, simply because the animal might not survive in its new environment. Any given area already has an established population of wildlife, and adding a new member puts a little more demand on the available food, water, and habitats. Using barriers to prevent pests from getting to your plants in the first place is perhaps the best solution, but if it doesn't work effectively in your backyard, you may have to resort to trapping if you want to protect your flower garden.

Box traps are the safest design for livetrapping garden pests. *Do not* use leg-hold and snare traps. They are nonspecific and will trap and kill pets as well as pests. Also, these traps can maim an animal instead of killing it and could seriously hurt unwary children (or adults) as well. Limit trapping in your yard to humane live traps. Box traps are available for many of the most troublesome animal pests, including chipmunks, gophers, groundhogs, mice, moles, rabbits, and squirrels. (See the opposite box, "The Best Traps for the Worst Pests," for recommended sizes.)

Using Traps

Set the traps in sheltered areas near or around the place where you have spotted a pest in action. Do not set the traps out in the open. Conceal them with leaves, sticks, and/or grass clippings so that they look a bit more natural. To avoid raising the suspicion of the animals you want to catch, try not to leave your own scent on the traps any more than you have to. You can boil traps with pine cones, dried leaves, or other natural materials to mask your scent. Handle the traps and the bait with gloves—preferably rubber gloves just out of the package. Follow the directions that come with the traps to set them up correctly with bait in place. After that, check the traps every day to renew the bait and see if you have trapped the culprit. Once you have trapped the animal, consult your local cooperative extension agent for advice on where to take it.

The Best Traps for the Worst Pests

Chipmunks
$5'' \times 5'' \times 15''$ box trap. Bait with peanuts or other nut meats.

Gophers
Standard wooden-based rattrap, two-pronged pincher trap (called the Macabee trap), or squeeze-type box trap. Bait with a large amount of grains, sunflower seeds, peanuts, or other nut meats.

Groundhogs
$12'' \times 12'' \times 36''$ box trap. Bait with nut meats or pieces of fruit.

Mice
$5'' \times 5'' \times 15''$ box trap, standard wooden-based mousetrap, or glue boards especially designed for mice. Bait with nut meats, dried fruit, or bacon.

Moles
Choker or harpoon-type trap. No bait needed.

Rabbits
$10'' \times 12'' \times 30''$ box trap. Bait with fresh greens, carrots, or fresh clover.

Squirrels
$8'' \times 8'' \times 24''$ box trap. Bait with peanuts, sunflower seeds, walnuts, almonds, oats, or melon rinds.

Biological Controls

Compared with the wide range of predators and parasites available for insects, there aren't many biological controls available for animal pests. While badgers eat gophers and mountain lions eat deer, people do not generally have these predators in their backyards. However, a couple of less unnerving biological controls may already be there.

Many homeowners have found that animal pests tend to be less troublesome when there are dogs or cats outside much of the time. Most rabbits, for example, do not feel very comfortable eating while a dog or cat is on the prowl. Male dogs and cats will mark their territories with scent; these boundary marks can sometimes keep rabbits from venturing into your flower garden. Of course, you want to make sure that your pets don't become pests in the flower bed in turn. Restrict their patrols to the garden perimeter. If you let your pets play or stay in the yard, make sure their rabies shots are up-to-date.

Poisons

There are no poisons that are not in one way or another potentially dangerous to pets and children. *Do not* use poisons to control animal pests in the flower garden.

PREVENTING ANIMAL PROBLEMS

Over the years, desperate homeowners and gardeners have resorted to a number of ingenious tactics in the battle against animal pests. Here are some of the most successful preventive measures, from fences to bars of soap.

Barriers

If you know from past experience that an animal pest is likely to attack your flower garden, then the best approach to control is to deny access in the first place. There are a number of techniques for preventing access, some more effective than others.

If you want to use a barrier, that usually means building some kind of fence.

Fences

You may have, or want to design, a lovely, formal or semi-formal, colonial flower garden with beds and paths neatly enclosed in a white picket fence. But if your idea of the ideal flower garden is a series of bright, informal island beds "floating" in a sea of lawn, or undulating borders running along the edges of your property, you need to fence the *yard,* not the flowers. This is the most expensive—and effective—control option, but a creative approach can help curb costs. For example, you can fence only the backyard, side yard, or front yard, and site your flower garden there. Or you can disguise a less expensive wire fence with vines.

The size of the fence depends on which pest or pests you are trying to thwart: Make sure your fence is high enough to be effective. To keep deer out, it must be at least 7 to 8 feet high, unless you're setting up a double-layer fence. In this case, each fence can be 4 feet tall, and they should be 5 feet apart. A 3-foot fence will keep out gophers, groundhogs, and rabbits. Even if burrowing pests are not currently a problem, if you are going to the trouble of erecting a permanent fence, it is a good idea to bury at least 6 inches of it in the ground to forestall any future subterranean invasions. Finally, be sure your fence is a solid barrier—spacings between boards or other materials should be less than 2 inches. (Remember that various animals can jump, dig, and squeeze through small places and that deer are less likely to jump a fence if they can't see what's on the other side.) The actual design of your fence and the materials you use will ultimately depend on how much time and money you wish to spend.

Repellents

For many years, gardeners have been trying to find substances that will keep animals out of their yards and gardens. Several products are now available that promise to successfully ward off various animal pests, including birds, rabbits, raccoons, and deer.

In addition, there are dozens of home remedies invented by frustrated gardeners under siege from some troublesome animal. These products work better for some gardeners than others, and no one product seems to be foolproof all of the time in all areas of the country. If you prefer not to put up a fence, then you may wish to experiment with one or more of these repellents; however, be prepared for variable effectiveness.

Repellents come in two general forms—those that repel by odor and those that repel by some audio, visual, or tactile characteristic.

Scent Repellents

Various animal repellents are sold commercially in many garden centers and through mail-order catalogs. Hinder, Big Game Repellent, and Ro-Pel are a few examples. The success of the scent repellents is quite spotty. Some homeowners swear by them; others find they don't work at all. (Most companies listed under "Controls" in the source list at the end of this book carry various repellents.) In addition, dozens of home remedies have been reported in gardening magazines, and several scent repellents seem to be particularly popular.

Cat Litter. Many gardeners find that used cat litter repels rabbits when it's sprinkled around ornamentals and repels moles and gophers when it's buried. To try it, sprinkle well-used litter around vulnerable plants, replacing it each week and after each rain. For moles and gophers, dump the litter right into the holes of the active burrows. But use caution when handling and distributing litter: Cat feces may contain toxoplasmosis parasites, which can infect humans. *Do not* use litter around edible plants or if you have young children who might come in contact with it. Pregnant women should also avoid contact with cat litter.

Hair. Lots of homeowners report that they have kept deer away by hanging human hair from the trees around their flower garden. Use mesh bags with a ⅛-inch or smaller mesh. Place at least two large handfuls of hair in each bag and hang them from the branches of trees and shrubs at a height of about 30 inches. They should be no farther than 3 feet apart. This method works best if you replace the hair every four days, which means that you really need to be friends with a barber or hairdresser to make this system work.

Pepper. Pepper is organic, so it doesn't harm the soil, and it's very inexpensive. Sprinkle black or hot pepper all over and around plants. It reportedly repels rabbits and squirrels. Reapply the pepper after rain.

Soap. Deer are also repelled by strongly scented soap. Use bars of deodorant soap, keeping them in their wrappers so they'll last longer. String them on wires and hang them about 30 inches above the ground (deer-nose height) on the branches of the trees or shrubs nearest to your flower garden. Space them no farther than 3 feet apart. Be aware that decking your trees and shrubs with soap, while effective, is hardly ornamental. A subtler means of protection would be more appropriate for the flower garden unless you're really desperate.

Audio, Visual, and Tactile Repellents

A host of audio, visual, and tactile tricks that keep pests away have been tried and recommended. The following is frequently recommended. Though no scientific research supports its effectiveness, its popularity suggests that it might be worth a try.

High-Tech Vibrations. The Go'pher It II Rodent-Repelling Garden Stake is a 1-foot-long, 1-pound commercial device that emits a sound inaudible to humans and pets but highly irritating to rodents. It is battery powered and vibrates at 15-second intervals to repel burrowing rodents, including gophers, moles, and voles, over a distance of 50 feet in all directions. Thus, one Go'pher It II could protect a 100-foot-long flower bed. Unfortunately, this gadget carries a hefty price tag of $50. (Most companies listed under "Controls" in the source list at the end of this book carry Go'pher It II.)

Other Repellents

While gardeners have tried many other materials, such as ammonia, vinegar, bloodmeal, and manure from zoo carnivores, to repel animals through noxious odors, none have been proven uniformly effective. Because of this, we hesitate to recommend them as repellents for animal pests.

These schemes just scratch the surface of the long list of home remedies for animal pests. In the rest of this chapter we will look at individual animal pests and the best prevention and control measures for each. Keep in mind that if you have neither the time nor the inclination to experiment, or lack the patience to try multiple approaches, then the most reliable control device for small animals is a trap, and the best prevention for all animals is an effective barrier.

Guide to Animal Pests

People create lovely flower gardens for their pleasure and enjoyment. However, a property with a colorful flower garden, a lovely lawn, and a variety of trees and shrubs will also, inevitably, attract animal pests. While many of these animals are appealing in nature, they are seldom welcome in the garden. As they go about raising a family, eating, and sleeping, they can inadvertently damage plantings. What follows in this section are profiles of the most troublesome pests and options for controlling them and preventing problems. Some of these solutions have been proven more effective than others; you'll need to try them to see how they work in *your* flower garden.

ANIMAL Chipmunks

Chipmunks are territorial animals. Males and females live apart rather than in communal burrows. They have a keen sense of smell and a strong sense of curiosity. In the course of gardening, your scent is transferred to plants, bulbs, or seeds that may be planted in the chipmunk's territory. The chipmunk feels its territory has been invaded; curiosity overcomes caution and the animal digs up the plant.

SIGNS OF CHIPMUNK DAMAGE

Plants and bulbs are dug up, especially just after they have been planted in the soil. Bulbs tend to be the most commonly bothered.

BEST CONTROL STRATEGY

Traps are about the only effective control for chipmunks. Use a 5″ × 5″ × 15″ box trap, baited with peanuts or other nut meats.

STEPS TO PREVENT CHIPMUNK DAMAGE

Barriers

Once any type of plant that has previously been bothered by chipmunks is in the ground, cover it with a piece of screening or fencing. Ordinary window screening or fence with a mesh of up to 1 × 2 inches will suffice. Place the screening on top of the plant, securing it with stones. The plant may be slightly flattened, but will recover in a few days. On bigger plants, place the screen flat on the ground around the base (you don't need to secure heavier fencing). The screening discourages chipmunks from coming near the plant. Leave it in place for about a week, until your scent dissipates and the plant has established itself. Screening works over bulb beds as well.

Repellents

Ro-Pel repels chipmunks by odor and taste. Spray it on bulbs, seeds, and flowering plants before planting them. Be sure to wear gloves and a mask; the label warns that you should avoid skin contact and inhalation of the fumes. Ro-Pel is available from Burlington Bio-medical & Scientific Corporation and Ringer Corporation (see the source list at the end of this book for the addresses).

Antitranspirants

Recent research suggests that spraying bulbs with an antitranspirant spray (usually applied to the foliage of broad-leaved evergreens to keep them from dehydrating and wilting in winter) masks the human scent, so the chipmunk will overlook them. Commonly available antitranspirants include Wilt-Pruf, ForEver Green, Pro-Tec, and VaporGard. These products are widely available in garden centers and nurseries.

NATURAL PREDATORS

Any owls and snakes on your property will help keep the chipmink population under control. And of course, one of the best rodent controls known is the house cat.

ANIMAL **Deer**

Deer can spell disaster for a flower garden. They usually feed in the late evening or early morning, when no one is around. One or two deer can virtually destroy an ornamental garden in one night. Far from finicky eaters, they devour almost everything found in the flower garden, as well as foliage and bark from trees and shrubs. Various species of deer thrive throughout the United States and Canada.

SIGNS OF DEER DAMAGE

Deer can chew annuals and perennials to the ground. On roses, azaleas, and other flowering shrubs, deer will eat flower buds, leaves, and shoots.

VULNERABLE PLANTS

Deer will eat almost anything: fruits, vegetables, flowers, and foliage. A flower garden planted near fruit trees—a notorious favorite—will be more vulnerable than one that is not. Look for signs of deer runs (narrow tracks) on your property, often clearly visible in snow. Deer are creatures of habit, following the same trails rather than branching out. If you find a run, site your flower garden well away from it.

BEST CONTROL STRATEGY

The most effective way to control deer is with a wall or fence.

STEPS TO PREVENT DEER DAMAGE

Barriers

A 6-foot solid wood or masonry wall will deter deer, even though they could jump over it, because they are less likely to try to jump when they can't see where they'll land. For small areas, homeowners

have had success with a double woven wire fence 8 to 10 feet tall. Don't skimp on fence height—a wire fence *must* be that tall to be effective. For a less forbidding look but excellent protection, you can put up a double fence. Deer-plagued homeowners have kept their gardens pest free with two 4-foot-high fences spaced 5 feet apart. The fences are made of 12½ gauge fencing with 2" × 4" mesh, attached to metal stakes spaced 5 feet apart. Deer can't jump both fences at once, and the 5-foot enclosure between fences doesn't give them enough clearance to get over the second fence if they clear the first. They apparently realize this and keep out. Though not exactly a garden accent, the effect of the fences can be minimized by painting them a neutral color like brown and planting vines or shrubs to disguise them.

Repellents

Many times, a particular odor will repel deer. However, it *must* be kept fresh to be effective. One handy trick is to mix your repellent agent with an anti-transpirant such as Wilt-Pruf, ForEver Green, Pro-Tec, or VaporGard to give it season-long effectiveness.

Hair
Human hair, available from beauty parlors and barber shops, provides some protection if the deer aren't desperate for food. If you have a shade garden edged by trees, you can hang bags of hair. Use mesh bags with ⅛-inch or smaller mesh, and fill each with at least two large handfuls of hair. Hang them from outer tree branches about 30 inches from the ground and no more than 3 feet apart. In tests on deer damage to evergreens, hair reduced damage by 34 percent. Excellent control was provided for vegetable crops in Alabama tests by hanging bags of hair 2 feet high and 5 feet apart around the garden perimeter. But remember, while not as visible as soap bars, hair bags won't do much for garden aesthetics.

Soap
Deodorant soap has been proven a very effective deer repellent. If your garden is bordered by trees and you care more about deer control than appear-

ances, you can give it a try. For soap to work well, string bars on wires and hang them on outer tree branches about 30 inches from the ground and no farther than 3 feet apart. Leave soap wrappers on so the soap will last longer. If you have no trees around the flower bed, soap hung 30 inches from the ground on poles set around the garden itself might also work.

Eggs
An invisible but effective control is an egg spray. Louisiana researchers found that a spray of 18 eggs in 5 gallons of water protected an acre of soybeans from deer. The deer were repelled by the smell of decomposing eggs, which in that dilution was too faint for humans to detect. If you'd rather not mix your own, a commercial egg spray, Big Game Repellent (see below), has also been very effective in tests.

Hot Sauce Spray
Another remedy is a homemade hot sauce spray or spray of Tabasco sauce. Mix 1 to 2 tablespoons Tabasco sauce and 2 tablespoons antitranspirant in 1 gallon water. Spray vulnerable ornamental plants with this mixture. Be sure to respray after it rains. Commercial hot sauce sprays have reduced deer damage on evergreens by 15 percent in tests.

Garlic Spray
Recent research has shown that selenium, which gives off a garlicky odor, prevents deer from eating tree shoots and seedlings. Since the selenium in garlic is the component responsible for the notorious "garlic breath," spraying a garlic solution on flowering plants might have a similar repellent effect. Like hot sauce, it would have to be reapplied after rain. And remember, you might be repelled by your garlicky plants, too! An alternative is planting a time-release garlic capsule (available at health-food stores) at the base of each large perennial or clump of flowers.

Commercial Repellents
If home remedies don't work, there are many commercial products that may be worth a try.

Big Game Repellent (Deer Away). This product is made from eggs; the deer are repelled by the smell of them decomposing. It's a highly effective repellent, coming out tops in deer control in tests on evergreens (even so, control was just over 50 percent). Reapply after rain.

Bonide Rabbit-Deer Repellent and Bulb Saver. One taste of this stuff and rabbits and deer should walk away. Spray or brush it on plants. When you mix this product with an anti-transpirant, it is said to prevent basal rot and decay on bulbs while it deters animal pests. An application of Bonide Repellent will last three to six months. It is available from Bonide Chemical Company, 2 Wurz Avenue, Yorkville, NY 13495.

Chew-Not. This product also repels by taste. Spray or brush it on plants. Chew-Not's disadvantage is that it leaves an unattractive white residue on the plants due to its egg-white consistency. It is available from Nott Manufacturing Company, Pleasant Valley, NY 12569.

Hinder. This spray contains ammonium soaps of fatty acids and repels by odor. It must be reapplied after heavy rains. Tests have shown that it can reduce deer damage by 50 percent, but it can also damage new leaf growth. It comes as a spray and is available from most of the companies listed under "Controls" in the source list at the end of this book.

Ro-Pel. The taste of Ro-Pel repels pests. And no wonder—it contains denatonium saccharide, the most bitter compound on earth. It also is an odor repellent. Spray it on both sides of the leaves of flowering plants. Be sure to wear gloves and a mask when using it. Results from Ro-Pel have been mixed; some fruit growers have found it ineffective against deer. Ro-Pel is available from Burlington Bio-medical & Scientific Corporation and Ringer Corporation (see the source list at the end of this book for the addresses).

ANIMAL Gophers

Gophers range in length from 6 to 12 inches. They have thick bodies with small eyes and ears. Their sense of smell is excellent. They are seldom found aboveground. Once gophers arrive in your yard, they resemble a small invasion force. One acre can feed and house 16 to 20 gophers, so it is easy to see why they can be a very serious problem. Gophers range from Indiana west to the Pacific Ocean. The most common is the pocket gopher.

SIGNS OF GOPHER DAMAGE

Gophers push soil out of their holes, creating distinctive fan- or crescent-shaped mounds on the surface of the ground. After digging a mound, they may close up the entrance hole with a soil plug. One

gopher can create several mounds a day. Gopher tunnels, about 2 inches in diameter, follow no pattern, running from a few inches to 2 feet below the soil. You know you have gophers when your plants are damaged in areas where there are fan-shaped mounds. Sometimes plants simply disappear—one morning you'll look out and find that a gopher has yanked your pansies down into its tunnel.

VULNERABLE PLANTS

Gophers eat the underground parts of flowering plants and a wide variety of other roots, bulbs, tubers, grasses, and seeds. They can damage lawns, flowers, vegetables, vines, and trees. Their mounds sometimes smother small plants.

BEST CONTROL STRATEGY

A sure way to drive this pest away is to determine the location of all the entrances to its tunnel system and then fumigate. Find a piece of hose material that can be attached to the exhaust of a power lawn mower. Stick one end of the hose into the gopher's tunnel, then seal the opening with soil. Next, drop some oil onto the inside of the hot exhaust pipe to create smoke, and attach the other end of the hose to the smoking pipe. After a few minutes, you should see smoke coming from all other entrances to the tunnel system. You may see gophers emerging as well.

Once you identify all the entrances to the tunnel system, you have several choices. You can seal them with piles of soil and continue to blow exhaust from the power mower into the tunnel, killing the inhabitants with poisonous carbon monoxide fumes, or you can put sulfur into the holes and seal all the entrances. The cheapest source of sulfur is one of the emergency highway flares that come with auto safety kits or are found in auto supply stores. Cut through an emergency flare with a sharp knife (not a saw). Dig into the runway, then pour the flare powder directly into the tunnel. Cover this hole, as well as all the exit holes that you have discovered. The more airtight the tunnel system is, the more anxious the gophers will be to leave. Once you are sure that the gophers are gone, seal the tunnels securely with soil. You'll know the gophers are gone when you no longer see fresh mounds around your property.

Another option is to place small, ammonia-soaked sponges into each gopher hole and then seal them all. Gophers will abandon their burrows in a hurry. The best time to use all these controls is in early spring when the gopher tunnel complex is least developed.

OTHER OPTIONS FOR CONTROLLING GOPHERS

Flooding

Locate the main gopher burrow by probing the soil with a long screwdriver or similar probe. When the probe hits the main tunnel, it should suddenly drop about 2 inches. Once you've located the main tunnel, insert a garden hose into it. When you turn the water on, it will flow in both directions throughout the tunnel system. The gopher will try to escape by exiting from one of the mounds. It can then be trapped as described below.

Traps

Trapping can effectively eliminate gophers. Place standard wooden-based rattraps in shallow pits near

burrow entrances. Cover the trap trigger with a thin layer of soil and lure your victims to the traps by sprinkling small amounts of grain on the soil.

You can also trap gophers with a Macabee or other pincher trap, or with a box trap such as the Gopher Getter. You'll need two or more traps. Set them with special care. Wear gloves to prevent human scent from contaminating the devices. If you inadvertently touch the traps, you can wash them in soapy water. Open up the main burrow enough to allow you to insert two traps, one facing in each direction. The gopher will run over the trigger mechanism, regardless of the direction in which it is moving. Attach strong twine or rope between the trap and a stake driven into the ground. This prevents the rodent from pulling the trap deep into the burrow. Use a wooden board, cardboard, or other sturdy material to cover the hole you dug to place the traps, and be sure to sift dirt around the edges of the covering to exclude light. If the gopher sees light coming from the top of the tunnel, it will push soil toward it, tripping the trap without being caught. If you don't catch any gophers within three days, pull out the traps and reset them in a new location.

STEPS TO PREVENT GOPHER DAMAGE

Barriers

Bulb beds and individual large perennials can be protected with ½-inch mesh wire if it is laid on the bottom and sides of the planting hole. Be sure to place the wire deep enough so that it does not restrict root growth.

Repellents

Cat Litter
Dump several scoops of well-used cat litter right into each burrow entrance. As mentioned at the beginning of this chapter, do not use this trick in the food garden. It is an option for the flower garden if children won't be playing in the soil.

Repellent Plants
You might try circling the garden with plants such as oleander (*Nerium*) and squill (*Scilla*) that are unpalatable to gophers. Foraging gophers that encounter oleander roots might be deterred from tunneling into the garden.

Commercial Repellents
Ro-Pel. A commercial product, Ro-Pel can be used to keep gophers away. Both the odor and taste of this product repel these rodents. Spray it on both sides of the leaves of flowering plants. Be sure to wear gloves and a mask when using it. Ro-Pel is available from Burlington Bio-medical & Scientific Corporation and Ringer Corporation (see the source list at the end of this book for the addresses).

Go'pher It II. Go'pher It II is a battery-powered, sound-emitting device that you can insert into the lawn or garden. It emits sound waves every 15 seconds and will keep gophers out of areas up to 100 feet in diameter. The sound waves cannot be detected by humans or nonrodent pets. (Go'pher It II is available from most companies listed under "Controls" in the source list at the end of this book.)

NATURAL PREDATORS

The gopher has a number of natural predators that could help you in your battle to rid the yard of these persistent pests. Certain snakes of the *Pituophis* genus (bull snakes, gopher snakes, and pine snakes) relish gophers. Other predators include cats, dogs, king snakes, skunks, barn owls, badgers, hawks, and coyotes.

ANIMAL Mice and Voles

A number of different types of mice and voles may nibble on your flowers. Voles, such as the meadow vole, are chunky in build with small ears that are almost concealed in fur. They also have small eyes and short tails. Meadow voles are white underneath and gray-brown on top. The house mouse, which is less likely to damage your flowering plants, is gray all over with large, distinct ears. The white-footed mouse and related deer mouse range over most of the continent. In addition to whitish underparts, legs, and feet, they have large eyes and ears, and their tails are over 2 inches long.

SIGNS OF DAMAGE

Mice and voles are known to move into mole tunnels and use them to gain access to plant roots. They create surface trails through long grass, weeds, and brush and can also burrow underground. They are most damaging in winter, when they may overwinter in the mulch placed around perennial flowers, where they chew on the roots. They are generally active all year round.

VULNERABLE PLANTS

The roots of flowering plants in the garden are fair game for mice and voles. These rodents also gnaw on the roots of young trees and shrubs, as well as on bark buried under the snow during the winter months.

BEST CONTROL STRATEGY

The traditional mousetrap still works. The most effective way to reduce rodent populations through trapping is to buy a large number of snap-traps and set them all at once, one or two nights in a row. Buying a few traps to catch these pests over a long period of time does not work as well. Bait the traps with a tiny dab of peanut butter or bacon, or a 50/50 mix of peanut butter and uncooked oatmeal. A good technique is to bait the traps for two or three nights without setting them. Then when you finally do set the traps, you'll catch the mice by surprise.

A steel drum with bait inside makes a very simple homemade mousetrap. The mice scramble into the standing drum, and once they are inside, they can't climb out. You'll have caught them red-handed.

OTHER OPTIONS FOR CONTROLLING MICE AND VOLES

Vitamin D Bait

A vitamin D_3-pelleted bait causes a calcium imbalance in the pest's blood, which causes it to stop

feeding after eating the pellets and die in two to four days. This bait is toxic only to rodents. It is available from Necessary Trading Company and Natural Gardening Research Center (see the source list at the end of this book for the addresses).

STEPS TO PREVENT MOUSE AND VOLE DAMAGE

Barriers

Though far from decorative, galvanized hardware cloth makes a durable barrier that can be left on all year. Buy ¼-inch mesh in a 24-inch width. Cut the hardware cloth long enough to completely encircle the flower bed. Bury this little fence at least 2 inches deep to keep mice and voles from digging under it. Make sure the top of the fence extends above the snow line.

Repellents

These pests do not like the taste of Ro-Pel. Spray it on both sides of the leaves of landscape plants. Be sure to wear gloves and a mask when using it. Ro-Pel is available from Burlington Bio-medical & Scientific Corporation and Ringer Corporation (see the source list at the end of this book for the addresses).

Other Options

Good sanitation is one way to discourage these pests from visiting your yard. Clean up all possible food sources, such as vegetables left in the garden at season's end and fallen apples, crab apples, or other fruit. Be sure to use rodent-proof containers of metal or glass to store seeds and birdseed, and keep birdseed swept up.

Don't mulch perennials until the ground freezes hard. Putting mulch down early invites mice and voles to set up housekeeping and gives them easy access to roots in unfrozen soil.

Keep an area of at least 3 feet clear around trees, removing tall grass, weeds, and shrubby growth. Mice and voles do not like to come out in the open and will hesitate to cross that bare space to gnaw on the trees.

NATURAL PREDATORS

Any owls and snakes on your property will help keep the mouse and vole populations under control. And of course, one of the best rodent controls known is the house cat.

ANIMAL # Moles

Moles do not eat plants, but they do eat lots of grubs, beetles, earthworms, and other soil dwellers. The problem is that moles can harm the root systems of young plants when they tunnel through the soil in search of food. This damage is compounded by the fact that they can spread disease from plant to plant. In addition, other pests that are more harmful, like field mice, use mole runs. Several mole species are known; they are found throughout the United States.

SIGNS OF MOLE DAMAGE

In their search for food, moles make an extensive network of tunnels, many of which are used only once. They are solitary animals, and it is likely that only one or two moles are responsible for all the damage to your lawn or garden. Moles are active all year long. When cold weather comes, they follow the earthworms deep into the soil below the frost line.

It's easy to tell if your garden has been invaded by moles or gophers: Mole tunnels are smaller in diameter than most gopher tunnels and they don't have the fan-shaped dirt piles around the entrance and escape holes that characterize gopher tunnels.

VULNERABLE PLANTS

Lawns rich in grubs and earthworms are most likely to be riddled with molehills. Seedlings can be harmed in spring by moles tunneling in search of grubs and other insects.

BEST CONTROL STRATEGY

Traps can be effective, but you have to be persistent. The best time to trap is in early spring when the first mole ridges appear. To find out which runs are used as "travel lanes," step lightly on a small section of several tunnels so that you disturb but do not completely collapse them. Mark these sections with stones or garden stakes. In two days, note which ones are raised—those are active runs and good locations for setting a trap. You can restore the turf over unused tunnels with a lawn roller or by treading on them.

Choker traps (such as the Nash mole trap), scissor-jawed traps (such as the Out of Sight mole trap), and harpoon traps (such as the Victor mole trap) do catch moles when used properly. Install these traps according to the instructions that come with them. They all basically work by springing when a mole sets off the trigger as it attempts to raise a flattened portion of its run.

No evidence exists to support claims that castor beans or mole plants (*Euphorbia lathyris*) keep moles away, or that daffodil bulbs or dandelions work either. Furthermore, castor beans, mole plants, and daffodil bulbs are all poisonous and pose a threat to curious children.

OTHER OPTIONS FOR CONTROLLING MOLES

Digging

As an alternative to trapping, you can try digging out moles. Because moles may be active at any time of the day, it is often possible to see the soil ridging up as the mole moves along. Put a shovel into the soil right behind the mole and flip the animal out into a bucket, which you can then fill with water to drown the culprit.

Flooding

A technique that's effective when mole runs are

short is to flush the little animals out with water. Just open the main run, insert a garden hose, and turn on the water. When the water spreads through the tunnels, adult moles will try to escape through other exits, where you can kill them with a shovel. If you flood the runs in spring, you may also drown the young in their nest.

STEPS TO PREVENT MOLE DAMAGE

Get Rid of Grubs

Beetle grubs feed on plant roots and in turn are eaten by moles. Remove the grubs and your lawn will be less attractive to moles. Kill Japanese beetle grubs in your soil with applications of milky spore disease (*Bacillus popilliae*), commercially available as Doom and Grub Attack, among other trade names. Other beetle grubs can be controlled with beneficial nematodes (sold as Bioquest by most of the companies listed under "Controls" in the source list at the end of this book).

Barriers

Moles will avoid hard, stony soil, which is difficult to dig through. You can create an effective barrier by digging a trench 2 feet deep and 6 inches wide around vulnerable areas. Fill the trench with heavy clay and stony and/or compacted soil and keep it dry. You can pave or mulch the barrier to create an attractive path around the lawn or garden.

Repellents

Cat Litter
You might achieve success with the strong odor of well-used cat litter. Dump several scoops of litter right into the mole's burrow. Don't use cat litter in food gardens or where small children may come in contact with it. Pregnant women should also avoid contact with cat litter. A sprinkling of tobacco or red pepper into each burrow may also deter moles.

Windmills
Place windmills (available commercially through garden centers and catalogs) in mole runs. The windmills create vibrations that seem to deter moles. A less expensive alternative is to insert a child's pinwheel into the tunnel ridge. Empty glass soda bottles work along the same principle. Set a bottle in the mole run, open end up. The wind blowing across the opening of the bottle creates vibrations that spread along the mole tunnel.

Commercial Repellents
Mole Evictor. The Mole Evictor is a battery-operated vibrating device that you set in the soil. The vibrations emanating from it supposedly drive moles away for good. Most companies listed under "Controls" in the source list at the end of this book.

Go'pher It II. Go'pher It II produces battery-powered vibrations that clear moles within a 100-foot radius. (It is available from most companies listed under "Controls" in the source list at the end of this book.)

Rodent Rocks. Rodent Rocks are porous lava stones that have been soaked in an organic repellent containing onions and garlic. When the rocks are buried 6 inches deep and 2 to 4 feet apart, their odor is claimed to effectively repel moles for 4 to 12 months. Circle the lawn with Rodent Rocks for best effectiveness. You can buy a package of about 60 Rodent Rocks from Gardener's Supply Company (see the source list at the end of this book for the address).

NATURAL PREDATORS

Cats and dogs are natural predators. They'll kill moles, but they won't eat them because of their bad taste.

ANIMAL Rabbits

Rabbits have shown themselves to be extremely adaptable to human environments. Cottontails are active mainly from dusk until midmorning, and spend the warmer part of the day in shaded areas. They may hide under thick shrubs or beneath garden sheds. The Eastern cottontail is the species usually found nibbling in the yard and garden, but various species of rabbit are found throughout the United States and Canada.

SIGNS OF RABBIT DAMAGE

Herbaceous plants, especially young ones, will be nibbled down to the base. In winter, rabbits remove a considerable amount of bark from young trees, and they chew the new shoots.

VULNERABLE PLANTS

Rabbits' favorite foods include carrots, geraniums, grasses, lettuce, marigolds, peas, raspberry canes, strawberries, tulip shoots, weeds, and the bark of young shrubs and trees, particularly euonymus, honey locust, and sumac.

BEST CONTROL STRATEGY

Trapping is the most effective way to control rabbits. Commercial box traps measuring $10'' \times 12'' \times 30''$ are recommended. Rabbits are more likely to enter a dark trap than one that's well lighted, so put a tarpaulin over the trap.

STEPS TO PREVENT RABBIT DAMAGE

Barriers

Ordinary chicken-wire fence can rabbit-proof the flower garden, but it isn't very attractive. Bury the fence 6 inches into the soil and extend it at least 2 feet aboveground. Make sure the holes in the mesh are smaller than 2 inches—1 to 1½ inches is ideal.

Wire Guards
You can put wire guards around individual plants if you don't mind the look and have the time and patience to make them. Make a cylinder around each plant with hardware cloth, attaching it to stakes to keep it upright. Make the guards higher than 1½ inches so a rabbit can't stand up on its hind legs to reach its lunch.

Repellents

Repellents may help you reduce rabbit damage. As

mentioned in the beginning of the chapter, these vary in effectiveness. In the case of rabbit control, taste repellents are often more effective than scent repellents. You can choose from a wide range of scent repellents to keep rabbits away from your plants.

Bloodmeal

Rabbits tend to avoid anything that smells of blood. Sprinkling dried bloodmeal on the soil around vulnerable plants may keep rabbits away, but you'll have to reapply it after each rain.

Vinegar

Vinegar may also ward off rabbits. Save a few corn cobs after a meal and cut the cobs in half. Soak them in vinegar for 5 minutes, then scatter them throughout the flower or vegetable garden. Two weeks later, soak them again in the same vinegar. You can keep reusing this vinegar; just keep it in its own labeled bottle.

Commercial Repellents

No Nib'l. Commercial taste repellents include No Nib'l, which can be dusted or sprayed on plants. To make a spray, mix the contents of the 6-ounce can with 2½ gallons of water.

Ro-Pel. Another commercial product, Ro-Pel, works in the same fashion. These repellents are available from Burlington Bio-medical & Scientific Corporation and Ringer Corporation (see the source list at the end of this book for the addresses).

Hinder. Products containing Hinder provide effective control.

Other Repellents

Other rabbit repellents reported effective by some homeowners include lion and tiger manure (sold by some zoos as ZooDoo), a solution of cow manure and water applied as a spray, onions interplanted among crops, and bonemeal. Sprinkle or place repellents immediately around the target plants.

You can purchase a commercial taste repellent or make one at home. During the growing season, discourage rabbits by spraying nicotine sulfate on your garden. Prepare the spray by mixing ½ teaspoon of 40 percent nicotine sulfate in 1 quart of water. An even easier repellent to use is black or hot pepper. Simply sprinkle it all over and around plants.

Inflatable or cast plastic snakes and owls look lifelike and are readily available from most mail-order garden catalogs. These pseudo-predators will frighten rabbits away from the tree or garden area they're placed in. Move them every few days so the rabbits won't catch on.

Antitranspirants

A combination antitranspirant and pest repellent is Bonide Rabbit-Deer Repellent and Bulb Saver, available from Bonide Chemical Company, 2 Wurz Avenue, Yorkville, NY 13495. Spray or brush it on vulnerable plants. The repellent effect will last three to six months.

Eliminate Daytime Cover

One way to reduce the rabbit population in the yard is to remove brush piles, one of their favorite daytime resting places. Clear out overgrown walls, fences, and ditches. Lack of cover will discourage rabbits from hanging around. Anything you can do to eliminate sanctuaries will help solve the rabbit problem; however, if you live next to a wooded area, there may be too many hiding places to deal with in this manner. Fortunately, nearby big trees may help, since they will encourage predators such as owls and hawks.

ANIMAL Squirrels

Eight species of squirrels live in the United States. The most common are the eastern gray squirrel and the fox squirrel, which can make nuisances of themselves at bird feeders and cause occasional problems in the flower garden.

SIGNS OF SQUIRREL DAMAGE

Squirrels eat crocuses and other bulbs. They are particularly troublesome when they eat the foliage of newly emerged crocuses right to the soil line. They often make holes in the lawn or garden as they search for nuts buried earlier in the season.

VULNERABLE PLANTS

In the flower garden, squirrels are most interested in crocuses and other hardy bulbs coming up in the spring. (They will not eat daffodils because the bulbs are poisonous.) Squirrels also eat nuts (including green and ripe walnuts and almonds), fruits (such as oranges, apples, and avocados), buds, and bark. They love birdseed.

BEST CONTROL STRATEGY

You can catch a squirrel in a medium-size box trap baited with fruit, nuts, or peanut butter.

STEPS TO PREVENT SQUIRREL DAMAGE

Barriers

To keep squirrels out of bird feeders, put a baffle on the pole beneath the bird feeder or on the wire it's strung on. Baffles are available from the same com-

panies that sell bird feeders and supplies. You can also make your own from stovepipe.

Repellents

Commercial Repellents

Ro-Pel. Ro-Pel, a commercial product, smells and tastes awful to squirrels. Soak bulbs in Ro-Pel before planting them, and squirrels will leave them alone. This repellent is available from Burlington Bio-medical & Scientific Corporation and Ringer Corporation (see the source list at the end of this book for the addresses).

The Squirrel. The Squirrel, also commercially available, is a sheet of paper coated with gel. The unpleasant sensation of gel on their feet discourages squirrels from encroaching on the protected area. This paper is available from J. T. Eaton & Company, 1393 East Highland Road, Twinsburg, OH 44807.

PART 3

Garden Management

CHAPTER 8

Flower Gardening Basics

From the beginning, the real story of this book has been how to prevent problems in the garden before they occur, and throughout the book, we've provided tips and hints about the basic good gardening practices that will help you do just that. This chapter sums up the basic principles of good gardening that will help you grow better, healthier flowering plants—annuals, perennials, bulbs, and roses. They are also principles that will improve your gardening techniques in any part of the landscape.

PLANNING

The planning process can be as simple or as complex as you want to make it. You may want to plant masses of annuals for a season-long show of brilliant color, to naturalize daffodils along the edges of your yard, or to plan a border of annuals, perennials, and bulbs that provides a progression of colors and textures that changes from season to season. Several of the books listed in the recommended reading section on page 393 contain helpful discussions of design principles, such as using color and texture in the garden and combining plants of various heights, blossom types, and foliages attractively.

All too often the role of problem solving is neglected in the rush to plan and plant a garden. There are hundreds of tips and suggestions for eliminating or reducing cultural, pest, and disease problems in parts 1 and 2. Try to keep them in mind when you start selecting plants out of a glossy, full-color catalog or at your local nursery. It's all too easy to get caught up in the beautiful colors and textures of plants, but keeping an eye out for potential problems can save you work and disappointment in the future. In addition, if you keep a few basic principles in mind while selecting and planting the plants you'd like to grow in your flower garden, you'll be well on the way to preventing problems that might otherwise crop up.

Knowing Your Garden

Take time to really examine what kind of environment your garden provides for the plants you want to grow. What are the general environmental conditions of the region in which you live—weather, rainfall, and USDA hardiness zone? What type of soil do you have? Is it sandy and dry; clayey; or deep, rich, and loamy? Finally, is your garden sun-baked, shady, or somewhere in between?

You probably have a good idea of what the climate is like in your area—how much rainfall is average, how hot the summers are, and how cold the winters can get. You also may or may not know which hardiness zone you live in. These environmental factors are important because they determine what plants will naturally grow and thrive in your area. If you live in a region with cool, damp summers, you'll find that some plants—snapdragons and delphiniums, for example—are particularly suited to your climate. On the other hand, in regions with hot, dry summers, plants that prefer heat and dry soil such as cosmos and yarrow are perfect choices. The entries in part 1 provide plenty of information on what types of environmental conditions suit the plants best. You can also tell a lot about what grows well in your area by looking at the plantings at local botanical gardens and visiting the gardens of friends and neighbors. Don't be afraid to ask questions, either!

Then, when you're ready to start planning, picking out plants, and planting, you'll have a good idea of what would naturally do well in your garden. That doesn't mean you can't grow any plants not exactly suited to your environment, it just helps to identify which ones will thrive with little care. It also helps to identify what extra steps you can take to help less well-suited plants to flourish.

Siting Plants

Once you really start to look at the conditions your garden provides for plants, you'll quickly realize that there are many potential microclimates available, all of which provide opportunities for plants to grow and thrive. Keep these microclimates in mind when planning your garden and picking the planting sites for each of the plants you'd like to grow. For example, since pansies prefer cool temperatures, try planting them on the north side of your house so they'll be protected from the hot sun. If you'd like to have an especially early display of daffodils or

crocuses, look for a hot, south-facing spot, preferably next to a building that will hold heat. For tall plants that might require staking, look for a site that is protected from prevailing winds. Planting in large clumps can also help many taller plants such as cosmos to support each other, perhaps eliminating problems with staking. If you don't have a protected spot, consider adding a hedge or fence to provide some wind protection.

Proper siting can also extend the life of the blooms in your garden. For example, the flowers of many plants will last longer if protected from hot noonday sun, and a few hours of dappled shade (such as that provided by high-branching trees) will save the flowers without reducing the bloom of most sun-loving plants. Another way to extend the life of individual flowers is to design borders that run north and south rather than east and west. Plants growing in a north-south border get sun from each side and are less likely to burn than ones planted on the south side of a border that runs east and west.

Light

Light, of course, is critical to plant growth. When deciding what plants to grow and where to grow them, it's important to carefully consider how sunlight falls around your yard. A spot that seems like a lovely sunny space in early spring may be shaded by a canopy of trees later in the season. Your home also casts shadows on the landscape, and exactly where they fall depends on the time of the year and the time of day.

Once you've evaluated the availability of sunlight in your landscape, consider the light requirements of the plants you'd like to grow and then match the right plant to the right place in your yard. A plant that needs full sun will not bloom in shade and will generally produce spindly growth; shade-loving plants will burn and produce stunted growth in full sun. Plants whose cultural requirements are matched to the site will be healthier and develop fewer problems with insects and diseases than mismatched ones.

Full Sun

A plant that requires full sun needs unfiltered, uninterrupted sunlight from sunrise to at least 3:00 P.M. Morning sun is better than late afternoon sun because it warms the plants faster.

Partial Sun

Plants preferring partial sun need 5 to 6 hours of direct sunlight, with shade or filtered sun the rest of the day.

Partial Shade

One might assume that partial shade and partial sun mean the same thing, but they don't. Plants that like partial shade belong in an area that gets dappled sun all day long, or dappled sun interrupted for up to 4 hours by either direct sun or full shade. Partial shade also refers to conditions under tall trees, the branches of which form a high canopy over the garden and filter the sunlight. This is also referred to as indirect light.

Full Shade

This is solid, sunless shade such as that provided by a building or a dense overhang of foliage.

Soil

The type of soil you have will determine both what kinds of plants will grow well for you and what kinds of soil-improvement programs you'll want to undertake. Surprisingly, knowing the texture and structure of your soil is as important as knowing its pH. That's because they determine how well the soil drains, how it holds nutrients and water, and how easy or difficult it is to till. Soil texture refers to the sizes of the individual mineral particles in soil. Structure refers to the way the individual particles are arranged.

All soils are made up of different percentages of sand, silt, and clay. The percentage of each of these particles determines the soil's texture. Sand particles are the largest and most irregular of the three; clay particles are small enough they can't be seen with an ordinary microscope; silt particles fall somewhere in between. While sand functions as the soil's skeleton, helping keep it permeable and well aerated, clay particles (along with organic matter such as humus) act as storage reservoirs for water and nutrients. That's why clay soils are usually more fertile than sandy ones.

You can get a general idea of what kind of soil you have by picking up a sample, wetting it slightly, and rubbing it in your palm with your fingers. Sandy soil feels gritty; silty soil feels smooth, like moist talcum powder; and soil that is high in clay will feel harsh when its dry and sticky or slippery when its wet.

Then try measuring plasticity—soils that are high in clay can easily be molded into a ribbon or "worm" when wet. You can form a moist clay soil (60 percent clay, 20 percent sand, and 20 percent silt) into a long, durable ribbon, ⅛ inch thick. Clay loams (30 percent sand, 35 percent silt, and 35 percent clay) can also be molded, but not quite as well. An excellent way to determine your soil type is to perform an at-home soil fractional analysis test. For directions, see the box, "Soil Fractional Analysis," on page 374.

Structure and Pore Space

The structure of the soil and the soil pore space determine how well water moves through the soil and how easy it is to work. Structure develops when sand, silt, clay, and organic matter in the soil clump together, ideally forming a loose, crumbly mass. Soils that have good structure have plenty of large pores, which generally contain air, and small pores, which hold water in the soil. For example, a good topsoil is made up of about half minerals (sand, silt, and clay) and half pore space. Half of the pore space of a good loam soil is made up of large pores filled with air. The other half is small pores that can hold water in the soil. Sandy soils have large particles and plenty of pore space, but the spaces are so large, water drains through the soil very quickly. They also generally have very few clay and other particles to hold nutrients in the soil. Clay soils are the other extreme. They can hold plenty of water and nutrients, but have few large pores to allow water to drain through. Thus, they waterlog easily, and they hold water very tightly in small pores, so plants can't extract it easily.

Soil Fractional Analysis

For an easy way to find out what the texture of your soil is try a soil fractional analysis on a sample of dry soil. You'll need the following supplies:

  1 clear glass quart jar with a tight-fitting lid

  1 teaspoon of nonsudsing dishwashing detergent

  a watch or clock

  a crayon or grease pencil

  1 cup of dry, finely pulverized soil (To get a soil sample that represents your whole garden, take tablespoon-size samples from several locations and depths, mix them, dry them thoroughly, and then pulverize them with a rolling pin or mallet.)

Start by filling the jar two-thirds full of water. Then, add the soil and detergent, fasten the lid securely, and shake it vigorously for 10 to 15 minutes. Set the jar down somewhere it can be left undisturbed for several days.

The following formula will determine the percentage of each type of particle: A equals the thickness of the sand level; B equals the thickness of the silt level; C equals the thickness of the clay level; D equals the thickness of all three deposits. So, to determine the percentage of sand in your soil, multiply A times 100 and divide by D; for the percentage of silt, multiply B times 100 and divide by D; for the percentage of clay, multiply C times 100 and divide by D.

The texture triangle below shows the many combinations of sand, silt, and clay that make up soil texture types. Use it to determine the type of soil you have. A clay soil contains about 60 percent clay, 20 percent sand, and 20 percent silt. Loam, the most desirable texture for garden soil, contains 40 percent sand, 40 percent silt, and 20 percent clay. Loam and silt loam soils are desirable because they have enough clay in them to store adequate amounts of water and plant nutrients, but not so much that the soil is poorly aerated or difficult to work.

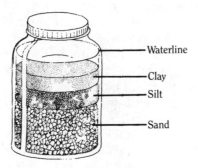

Waterline
Clay
Silt
Sand

Sand particles are largest and heaviest particles in soil and will settle out of the sample within 1 minute. At the end of a minute, use the crayon or grease pencil to mark the level of sand. Silt particles are next smallest and take about 2 hours to settle. Make a second mark on the jar after 2 hours to indicate the level of silt. Clay particles are extremely small and will remain in suspension for several days. You'll know they've settled out once the water is clear. Then, make a third mark to indicate the level of clay particles.

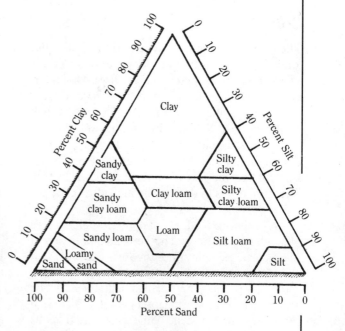

Soil that has been walked on repeatedly will generally become compacted, meaning it will have smaller pore space and won't drain as well. Soil under paths or where garden equipment or cars are driven will become very compacted. The more clay you have in your soil, the more it will tend to compact. (That's why raised beds are such a good solution for gardeners with extremely clayey soils. They can be worked from the outside without walking on or compacting the soil in the beds.) Tilling or digging soil when it's wet can also destroy structure. That's why clay soils form such rock-hard clods if they're worked too wet. Another way to protect the structure of the soil in your flower beds is to avoid walking on them. Set aside grass or stepping-stone pathways to direct traffic to where you want it.

Soil Improvement

So, what do structure, texture, and pore space have to do with your flower garden and how many problems your plants might have? They determine how well your soil holds water and nutrients, how well it drains, and what kinds of cultural techniques will best help your flowers grow and thrive. Ironically, soil-improvement practices are the same for all types of soil because organic matter improves the structure of all types of soil.

Organic matter can be added to the soil in many forms, including seaweed, peat moss, or chopped leaves, but compost is the ideal soil conditioner. Compost and other types of organic matter improve soil structure and, thus, both tilth and aeration. It helps hold nutrients and water in the soil and makes them available to growing plants. Organic matter also helps attract earthworms and other beneficial soil dwellers. In clay soils, it improves drainage and aeration by helping to create large pores that can fill with air, and it helps sandy soils hold nutrients and water.

So, plan on adding plenty of organic matter to your soil by working composted organic matter into the soil when you prepare a bed or border, and every year thereafter.

Soil Tests

Soil tests are another way to gain useful information about your soil. You can be a very successful gardener without ever determining the pH of your soil or how much potassium or phosphorus it contains, but such information can help point your soil-improvement and fertilization programs in the right direction.

Soil tests reveal how acidic or alkaline your soil is and also estimate how much of the major plant nutrients are contained in your soil. The soil pH, which measures soil acidity or alkalinity, matters because it determines the chemical availability of vital nutrients to plants. In very alkaline soils, iron and other vital minerals such as boron, copper, manganese, and zinc are chemically tied up and plants can't absorb them; phosphorus is the most important nutrient tied up in acid soil.

The pH scale ranges from 1 to 14. Readings below 7 are acidic, above 7, alkaline. Seven is neutral. A pH level that is slightly acid to neutral—between 6 and 7—is fine for most flower and vegetable gardens because at that level, the essential plant nutrients are most readily available. Most plants will tolerate a fairly wide pH range, especially if the soil is rich in organic matter.

The two most common ways to test your soil are home test kits or sending a soil sample to the cooperative extension service. (Home soil tests are available from most of the companies listed under "Supplies" in the source list at the end of this book.) See the city or county listings in the telephone directory to find your local cooperative extension service. Most kits provide solutions and guides for determining the approximate content of the three major soil nutrients: nitrogen (N), phosphorus (P), and potassium (K), as well as soil pH.

Taking the Sample

In order to get an accurate picture of your soil, be sure to take a series of samples from several different spots. Then, mix them together and spread them out to dry in a box or on newspapers. Damp or wet soil can give false test readings. Once the sample is completely dry, rub it through a screen to remove any lumps.

Adjusting pH

Soil pH can be adjusted by adding ground limestone to raise it (make it less acid) or by adding sulfur to lower it (make it less alkaline). Soil texture affects how easy or difficult it is to change the pH of any given soil. For example, it's much easier to change the pH of a sandy soil than a loam soil. That's because a loam soil has more clay particles and more organic matter, which make it more buffered or resistant to change. Before you rush out to buy limestone or sulfur, however, consider the fact that soil organic matter is the great equalizer as far as pH is concerned. Organic matter such as compost or humus will tend to lower the pH of alkaline soils and raise the pH of acid soils. See the box, "Changing pH," below for general guidelines on raising or lowering pH.

Changing pH

You can change the pH of your soil by adding lime to raise the pH of acid soil or ground sulfur to lower the pH of alkaline soil. The quantities you'll need will depend on the type of soil you have.

To raise the pH of acid soil about one point, add the following quantities of ground limestone per 100 square feet:

Sandy soil, 3 to 5.5 pounds

Sandy loam, 5 to 7 pounds

Loam, 7 to 10 pounds

Heavy clay, 7 to 8 pounds

To lower the pH of an alkaline soil one point add the following quantities of ground sulfur per 100 square feet:

Sandy soil, 1 pound

Heavy clay, 2 pounds

Organic Matter and pH

Organic matter can also be used to bring the pH of both alkaline and acid soil closer to neutral. Sawdust, composted oak leaves, wood chips, leaf mold, cottonseed meal, and peat moss are especially effective in lowering the pH of alkaline soils. Pine needles and wood chips from coniferous trees are acidic and also will lower pH. Wood ashes, especially those from slow-growing hardwoods such as oaks and hickories, as well as bonemeal, crushed marble, and crushed oyster shells, are effective for raising the pH of acid soils.

Making Compost

We've already learned what an important role compost can play in the quality of the soil—its structure, pH, nutrient- and water-holding capacity, as well as its role in improving soil. But what is compost and how is it made?

Compost is organic matter that has been decomposed by microorganisms such as bacteria and fungi. These organisms secrete enzymes and acids to dissolve cell walls and release the contents of the plant cells. Eventually, huge populations of microorganisms build up in a compost pile, and their activity can generate so much heat that interior temperatures can exceed 130°F, which is high enough to kill most weed seeds and disease organisms. Humus is the end product of the composting process, although it, too, is still actively decomposing. Humus helps hold nutrients in the soil and release them to plants as they need them. It also contains beneficial microorganisms that enhance plant growth.

Compost is made from many different types of organic matter, including grass clippings, leaves, sawdust, wood chips, manure, and vegetable parings from the kitchen. The easiest way to make compost is to make a pile of different types of organic matter in a corner of your yard and leave it for a few years. But there are several steps you can take to speed the process. Start with a layer of brush to hold the pile off the ground and aerate it, and be sure the pile is in full sun so it will heat up more quickly. Then pile on alternating layers of slow-decaying materials such as leaves, wood chips, and sawdust, and fast-decaying material such as grass clippings, manure, and food wastes. You can speed the process up even more by chopping or shredding all the materials that go into the pile and then digging or turning the pile every few days. For more on speeding the process, see the box, "Quicker Compost," on the opposite page.

If you prefer something neater than a pile, consider one of the commercially available compost bins (see "Supplies" in the source list at the end of this book) or make one of your own. Bins can be made of lumber, chicken wire, hardware cloth, bricks, concrete blocks, hay bales, or railroad ties—just use what's handy. It's a good idea to build two bins, one for finished compost, the other for the "working" pile. Finished compost looks just like the dark, almost black material you find under the layer of leaves on the forest floor. It looks and feels much like a potting soil mix you might buy from your local gardening store, and it has little odor.

What to Compost

Feed your pile with nearly anything that once was alive—grapefruit rinds, leaves, grass clippings, eggshells, plant remains from the vegetable garden, dried seaweed, manure, kitchen parings. However, don't add fats and meat scraps because they decompose slowly and will attract rats. It's also not a good idea to add cat or dog manure, because it can transmit parasites to humans. To keep from spreading plant diseases, don't add diseased plant materials. Also avoid any weeds that might have seeds. (A good compost pile will heat up enough to destroy most weed seeds, but who wants to take the chance?) If you have very alkaline or acid soil, see the box, "Changing pH," on the opposite page for a list of materials that will help you adjust your pH in the proper direction.

Another way to speed the process is to learn the carbon to nitrogen (C/N) ratios of the organic materials you're using. Organic matter with ratios of 25 or 30 parts carbon to 1 part of nitrogen decompose most quickly. Mature sweet clover, with a nearly ideal ratio of 23 to 1, breaks down very rapidly. Sawdust, with a ratio of 500 to 1, decomposes slowly. Why? because microorganisms working away on sawdust use up the available nitrogen, which stops the decomposition process. (For a list of some common materials and their C/N ratios, see the opposite box, "Quicker Compost.") Then, plan on using layers of materials that compost quickly along with slow-to-compost materials such as sawdust and wood chips. The closer the average C/N ratio of all the organic matter in your pile is to 25 or 30 to 1, the faster the materials will decompose.

Compost and other organic matter worked into the soil will help you attain the gardener's ultimate goal of a rich, well-drained soil in which many different plants can grow and thrive. Since compost improves soil structure, promotes drainage in clayey

Quicker Compost

There are three tricks that will speed up the composting process:

1. Put materials you are planning to compost through a shredder or chipper before adding them to the pile. Leaves can be chopped in a lawn mower. They will decompose much faster than unchopped material.

2. Layer in a variety of materials so that the overall carbon to nitrogen ratio is close to 25 or 30 to 1. You can use the list that follows to determine the various ratios of the materials you have on hand. If you have an abundance of slow-to-compost materials, add bonemeal or bloodmeal, cottonseed meal, or manure to provide extra nitrogen to the mixture.

3. Turn the pile every week to 10 days. By mixing the material, you bring more oxygen into the pile, which serves as fuel for the microorganisms that are actually breaking down the organic materials.

Carbon/Nitrogen Ratios of Composting Materials

Alfalfa, 13 to 1

Cornstalks, 60 to 1

Fruit wastes, 35 to 1

Grass clippings, 19 to 1

Humus, 10 to 1

Leaves, from 40 to 1 to 80 to 1

Legume and grass hay, 25 to 1

Manure, rotted, 20 to 1

Paper, 170 to 1

Sawdust, 500 to 1

Sewage sludge

   Activated, 6 to 1

   Digested, 16 to 1

Straw, 80 to 1

Sweet Clover

   Green, 16 to 1

   Mature, 23 to 1

Table scraps, 15 to 1

Wood, 700 to 1

soils, helps sandy ones retain water and nutrients, and also neutralizes pH, you can hardly work too much into the soil.

Substitutes for Homemade Compost

Perhaps your yard doesn't offer a good place for making compost, or maybe even the fastest method of making this material isn't fast enough. Well, you can find other means of obtaining compost, or you can use other materials in its place. First, check to see if your community has a large-scale composting system. Often these sites are open to the public, and compost or leaf mold is free for the taking. If you can't get your hands on any compost at all, you can purchase peat humus and processed cow manure at most garden centers and mix them into the soil. Remember that peat *humus* is different than peat *moss*. Peat moss is more acidic than peat humus, with a pH of 3.2 to 4.5; peat humus has a pH between 4 and 7.5. Some gardeners are fortunate to live near mushroom farms, where they can obtain composted mushroom soil—another excellent source of organic matter. Usually, farmers sell this mushroom soil at a very reasonable price. Let the mushroom soil sit for at least six weeks before adding it to the soil in your garden.

PLANTING AND PROPAGATION

The plant entries in part 1 contain extensive information on the best way to plant and propagate the individual annuals, perennials, bulbs, and roses in this book. Getting plants off to a good and healthy start is crucial to helping them perform at their best. That's why we've stressed the importance of examining plants before you buy them to look for signs of insects and diseases. Careful handling is also important, whether you are transplanting seedlings you've grown yourself or settling in pot-grown or bare-root perennials. Bruised, scraped, or otherwise damaged tissue is open to attack by diseases and insects. Plants that are unnecessarily stressed by underwatering or sudden environmental changes at planting time are also vulnerable. The following

suggestions will help you make sure your plants have a smooth and easy transition, whether you are planting them for the first time or propagating plants for yourself or gardening friends.

Growing from Seed

Most annuals and many perennials are easy to grow from seed. (The individual entries in part 1 provide sowing information for each plant that is easy to grow from seed.) Seed can be sown inside and then transplanted outdoors when the weather permits, or outdoors directly where the plants are to grow. All but the hardiest annuals are generally started indoors in late winter or early spring and transplanted outdoors after danger of frost has passed. Or they can be sown outdoors where they are to grow after the last frost date. Many perennials and hardy annuals can be sown outdoors where they are to grow in spring or summer up to two months before the last frost date.

Starting Seeds Indoors

Timing is tricky. A common mistake is to sow seeds too early in the spring, which can result in large, spindly, overgrown plants or ones that have had to be transplanted several times. Most seed packets give recommended starting dates, which are based on the number of weeks before the last average frost date. They also offer transplanting guidelines based on that date. If you don't know what your average last frost date is, start by calling your local cooperative extension agent. Most seedlings should be about six to eight weeks old at transplant time. Some of the slower growers will need more time (again check the seed packet and the recommendations in part 1). If you start the seeds later than recommended, no harm is done and the plants are sure to thrive. If you start too early and the roots start to outgrow their containers, you'll need to transplant the seedlings into bigger containers so they can continue to grow before being moved outdoors.

Like plants in the garden, seedlings started indoors need just the right amount of light, nutrients, and water. Indoors, where the environment is designed to please people, not plants, providing these essentials can be challenging.

Seedlings and Light

Seedlings grown indoors often get spindly because they don't get enough light. You can start seedlings on a windowsill of a south-facing window or in a greenhouse, but in late winter, the days are still relatively short, so there is not really enough light to produce compact, healthy transplants. The sturdiest seedlings are grown under fluorescent lights. For most situations, just one shop light fixture with two 48-inch fluorescent tubes is sufficient to get started raising seedlings. Be sure the fluorescent light fixture is adjustable so that it can be moved either up or down, or that the plants can be moved up and down under it. It is important to maintain the proper distance between plants and light as the plants grow.

Basements are ideal locations for setting up fluorescent lights for starting seedlings. Temperatures there are usually pretty constant, holding between 60° and 75°F throughout the whole year. Most basements have water available, which makes caring for the seedlings convenient. Gardeners without basements might consider building a seedling bench that harmonizes comfortably with the other houseplants in the living space.

The keys to growing seedlings successfully under lights are the duration of light and the distance of the light from the top leaf of the plant. Have your lights on for 14 to 16 hours a day, every day. Anything less will not produce the best growth. Use an automatic timer to turn the lights on and off. When seedlings are just little sprouts, hang the lights no more than 3 inches above them. As the plants get their first true leaves, move the lights up to about 4 inches above them. You can set the lights at 6 inches when the seedlings are several inches tall so that the light shines evenly on all the plants, even those on the edge of the shelf.

Choosing Containers

In choosing a container for your seedlings, con-

sider not only convenience but also how much damage might occur to seedling roots at transplant time. Seedlings whose roots are torn or broken during transplanting will stop growing while they recover from their injuries. Flats of seedlings that must be untangled or cut apart may take a week or more to recover.

To reduce transplant shock to plants, start seeds in individual containers. Seedlings can be started in Styrofoam coffee cups, egg cartons, peat pots, and dozens of other containers. There are also a wide variety of seed-starting systems available commercially.

Whatever type of containers you choose, be sure they have a hole in the bottom for good drainage. The key is to provide the seedlings with a growing medium and container that drains well while simultaneously retaining moisture. Commercial, ready-mixed, seed-starting medium is available at any garden center. If you wish to make your own, the standard recipe is 1 part vermiculite, 1 part perlite, and 2 parts sterilized compost or potting soil.

Watering

Seedlings need an even supply of moisture, but many are subject to damping-off and other diseases if they are overwatered. For best results, water seedlings from the bottom. You can stand the containers in water until it rises to just below the surface of the soil, and then take them out and let them drain. Don't leave seedlings standing in water longer than necessary. There are also commercially available systems that provide automatic watering via a capillary mat upon which the seedlings sit. These are available from Gardener's Supply Company (see the source list at the end of this book for the address).

Humidity

Seedlings germinate best when provided with high humidity, so loosely cover the containers until germination occurs. After that, it's best to gradually remove the covering. Seedlings grown in very high humidity tend to be too succulent and spindly to make good transplants.

Hardening Off

Before they are ready to go outdoors permanently, seedlings require a little time to become acclimated to the outdoor weather. To condition or harden off seedlings, set them outdoors in a sheltered spot for a few hours each day when the temperature is over 40°F. Try not to set them in the direct sun, and shelter them from too much wind. A porch, under shrubs, or a similarly protected place is ideal. Gradually increase the exposure over a week or so, leaving them out longer and exposing them to more sun and breeze. Bring them indoors each night at first, but after about a week, leave them outdoors for 24 hours. Be sure to water regularly; they'll need more water during this hardening off process than they did when they were indoors. Then, transplant to the garden.

Outdoor Sowing

Many kinds of seeds can be sown outdoors into a prepared seedbed where the plants are to grow. Lightly cultivate the garden soil with a rake or tiller and rake it fairly smooth. The soil may feel cold, but it should not feel wet or lumpy. The general rule of thumb for sowing seeds is that they need to be covered at a depth of about three times the seed's thickness, but there are exceptions to this rule. Some seeds require light to germinate; others require darkness. Again, use the recommendations in part 1 and on the seed packets to determine the best technique for each type. After sowing, firm the soil to make sure that contact is made between the seeds and the damp soil.

A common mistake of beginning gardeners is planting too closely. Seeds are usually so small that it is hard to believe they'll ever grow into the large plants described on their packets. Crowded seedlings develop into undersized plants and are more likely to be attacked by some diseases and insects. Resign yourself to thinning the seedlings if sprouts are too crowded. It's also important to keep direct-sown plantings carefully weeded because weeds can quickly crowd out more desirable plants.

Other Options

There are several other options to sowing seeds indoors or outdoors where they are to grow. Of course, you can use a greenhouse for germinating most plants, but if you don't have one, a cold frame or hotbed is the next best thing. You can sow seeds in pots in fall or early spring and raise them in the frame. This technique can be used with hardy perennials and some hardy annuals such as pansies. Seed sown in fall won't germinate until early spring but will sprout in very early spring and get a good start on the growing season.

Another alternative is to sow seeds of perennials in a nursery bed. A nursery bed really isn't any different from any other bed into which seeds are direct-sown, but it's used to sow and raise plants that will eventually be moved elsewhere in the garden. The advantage is that all your perennial seedlings can be cared for at one time and in one place. If you use a raised bed, your weeding chores will be easier.

Buying Plants

Of course, you can buy annuals and potted perennials at garden centers and nurseries. When you buy plants, look for healthy green foliage that shows no evidence of scorching from sun or wilting because they've been poorly cared for. Also take time to look carefully for signs of insects or diseases. Whiteflies, spider mites, and aphids are three common pests you can carry home on purchased plants. Although plants that are already in flower are most appealing, they don't necessarily make the best transplants. You're better off with sturdy plants that have not yet formed flowers because they'll be able to put energy into growing roots before they need to support flowers. Handle the plants carefully to minimize the shock of transplanting and they'll be well on their way.

When buying bare-root perennials—or when you inspect a shipment that has arrived in the mail—you'll want to look for signs of rot or other damage. Perennials often arrive from mail-order nurseries with their roots wrapped in wood shavings in a plastic bag. Roses also are often shipped this way.

Open the box immediately. If there are any leaves on the plants, stand them up in the box to keep the air circulating around them. Keep the roots covered and moist so they don't dry out. If you receive a small box of young, dormant perennials, you can hold them temporarily in the refrigerator. In any case, make an effort to get these plants in the garden as soon as possible.

It's also important to inspect bulbs carefully when you buy them. Many problems can be avoided by inspecting bulbs carefully before purchase and handling them carefully until planting. Avoid bulbs that are shriveled, discolored, or show signs of dry or soft rot on the bulb scales or the base of the bulbs. Also look closely for signs of bulb mites and other insect pests. Healthy bulbs that have been properly stored should show no evidence of rot, mold, mildew, shriveling, or other damage. The papery bulb coat should also be intact. Lily bulbs should have their fleshy roots attached as well.

Planting

Bed Preparation

Whether you're planting annuals, perennials, bulbs, or roses, you'll need to prepare the bed by working organic matter into the soil and digging or tilling the soil. Especially with perennials, bulbs, and roses that will be around for many years to come, take extra time to provide them with a deep, well-prepared bed in which to grow. Deeply dug soil enriched with plenty of organic matter, such as compost, will drain efficiently, providing a healthy environment for plant roots. It encourages plants to develop extensive and deep root systems, which will improve drought tolerance and overall health.

In your eagerness to get started in spring, don't make the mistake of working the soil when it's too wet. Working wet soil destroys the structure and compresses pore space, which in turn affects drainage and aeration. This is especially important if you have a soil that is high in clay because it compacts so easily. To see if it's ready to work, take a handful of soil and squeeze it into a ball. If the ball crumbles easily when dropped, the soil is ready to work. If it forms a soggy lump, it's too wet.

When it's ready to work, dig the soil deeply and incorporate plenty of compost as you go. For best results, till at least the top 1 foot of soil. For deep-rooted perennials that will be permanent residents, dig the soil to a depth of 2 feet or so.

Planting Pot-Grown Plants

The best time to transplant seedlings, purchased bedding plants, or pot-grown perennials into the garden is on a cloudy day, in the late afternoon, or early evening. The transplanting process is hard enough on the plants without their having to cope with bright, hot sun on their first day in the ground. Do everything you can to minimize damage to the root system of each seedling and to reduce any other unnecessary shock to the plants.

Dig a hole big enough to contain the root ball. Make sure the crown of the plant is at the same depth that it was in the container. If you haven't already added plenty of organic matter to the soil, add it at planting time. Whenever possible, handle seedlings by their leaves rather than risk bruising their stems. Water the plants as you go rather than waiting and watering them all at the end, so the roots don't dry out accidentally.

Young perennial plants purchased from garden centers are usually in containers. To plant them, gently remove each plant from its container and untangle or loosen the mass of roots that may have developed while the plant was growing in the pot. If the plant has been in the container so long that it has become root bound, the roots will be tightly wrapped around each other with virtually no dirt on them. Slice through these roots with shallow, vertical cuts at three or four spots around the circumference of the root mass to encourage branching and loosen the roots. Dig a planting hole slightly larger than the diameter of the loosened root mass. Make sure the crown of the plant is at the same depth that it was in the pot. Cover the roots with compost-enriched soil, press down snugly, and water generously.

Planting Bare-Root Perennials

When planting bare-root perennials, dig a hole large enough to spread the roots comfortably without crowding them. If you haven't already added plenty of organic matter to the soil, add it at planting time. Build a mound of soil in the bottom that comes almost up to the top of the hole. As you set the plant in place, spread the roots over this mound. You must position the plant so that the place where the roots come together (the crown) is just below the soil line. When leaves begin to emerge, they will be right there, ready to push above the soil. Fill the hole with soil that has been enriched with compost, and water thoroughly.

Planting Bulbs

Hardy bulbs such as crocuses, daffodils, and tulips are planted in fall, two to four weeks before the ground freezes (from October 1 to November 1 in most northern areas). Later planting may result in short stems and smaller flowers. (Colchicums are planted in late August, if possible, or as soon as you can get them in the fall.) If you forget to plant your bulbs until late fall, it's better to plant them late than to wait until spring because they're likely to dry out and die if you try to hold them through the winter. Tender bulbs such as dahlias and tuberous begonias are planted in spring, much like annuals. You'll find specific instructions for planting these, as well as lilies, tender cormous plants such as gladiolus, and canna rhizomes in the individual plant entries in chapter 3. See the opposite page for an illustration of what these different structures look like.

Hardy bulbs can be planted in individual holes made with a bulb-digging tool or a trowel. For mass plantings, the beds can be dug to the proper depth, the bulbs set in place, and then covered with soil en masse. Either way, good soil preparation is essential to healthy bulbs. Make sure the soil is well drained by adding plenty of compost or other organic matter. (Don't use fresh manure around bulbs at planting time, though.) If your soil is very poorly drained or very clayey, consider growing your bulbs in raised beds. If you are digging a complete bed, loosen or till the soil down to 1 foot, then spread a handful of bonemeal or a small handful of rock phosphate near where each group of bulbs will be planted. Cover with a thin layer of soil that has been amended with organic matter, then set the bulbs in rows or small groups. Cover them with soil, water, and mulch them for winter.

If you dig individual holes for each bulb, add a tablespoon or so of bonemeal or rock phosphate to the soil that you dig up, mixing it thoroughly. Set the bulb in the hole and fill in around and above it with this enriched soil. Once the bulbs are planted, cover the area with a protective layer of mulch. You'll find details for determining proper planting depths and other tips for improving your results in the individual bulb entries in chapter 3.

Propagation

It's easy to get hooked on propagating your own plants because many are very easy to grow from stem cuttings or division. Common annuals such as impatiens and begonias will even produce roots when you stick a 3- to 5-inch-long cutting in a glass of water and set it in a well-lit window. When making cuttings, it's best to to remove all flowers and buds, as well as all but the top two or three leaves. This way, the cutting will direct its energy toward root growth. Cuttings can be potted up as soon as some roots are showing, but be sure to keep them shaded for the first three or four days.

A better way to root cuttings is to stick them in a soilless rooting medium such as vermiculite. Thoroughly moisten the vermiculite and dip the end of each cutting in a commercial rooting hormone before sticking it down into the medium. Keep the vermiculite moist but not wet. Roots should appear in about two to three weeks. It's also a good idea to loosely cover the cuttings with plastic to raise the humidity so they don't dry out too much while they are forming roots. See the individual plant entries in part 1 for information on which plants can be propagated in this manner.

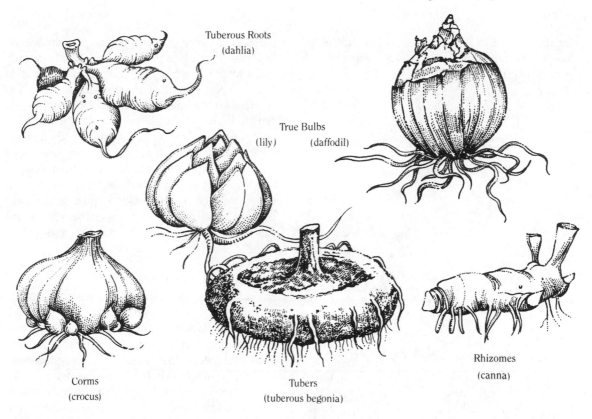

Tuberous Roots
(dahlia)

True Bulbs
(lily)   (daffodil)

Corms
(crocus)

Tubers
(tuberous begonia)

Rhizomes
(canna)

Dividing Perennials

For perennials, the easiest way to propagate is by division. Many perennials need dividing periodically to prevent overcrowding and to revitalize clumps that tend to die out in the center. If you grow perennials, you'll probably be propagating them this way regularly. The individual plant entries in part 1 will give you an idea of how often you'll need to divide your plants, but you can generally divide them anytime if you need a plant to give a fellow gardener or want a bit more color in a corner of your yard.

For best results, divide perennials in early spring or in fall a month or two before the ground freezes for winter. Although many plants will withstand dividing in late spring or summer, moving plants at a time of year when temperatures can soar is riskier. Also, new divisions don't have the deep root systems needed to withstand heat and drought. Divisions made in late fall can be subject to frost heaving because they haven't been given time to develop root systems sufficient to anchor them in soil that freezes and thaws repeatedly. Apply a deep layer of mulch after the ground freezes to help keep soil temperatures constant. Again, timing details and exceptions to these general guidelines are mentioned in the individual plant entries in part 1.

Perennials can withstand fairly rough treatment in the division process. Once you've dug the clump that's to be divided, you can pry the crowns apart by using two spading forks back to back, split the clump with a spade, or cut off the divisions with a sharp knife. Some perennials will separate easily, without such strong-arm tactics. Use your own judgment, and be as careful as you can. Obviously, the goal is to minimize disturbance to the roots' development and the plants' bloom cycle. The fewer roots and buds that are cut or damaged, the quicker the divisions will recover. Be sure each division has at least one or more growing points, and look carefully for rot or signs of insects. Discard any unhealthy-looking portions along with the older, woody growth from the center of the clump.

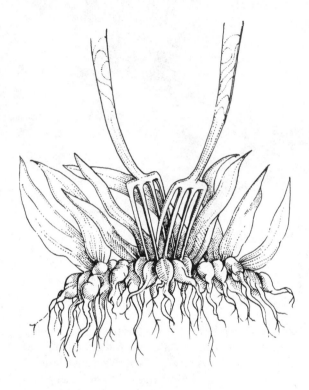

Replant divisions as soon as possible, firming the soil around them and thoroughly watering them. Be sure to plant them at the same depth they were growing at previously. If you can't plant them right away, wrap the roots in damp newspaper or pack them in moist peat moss, and keep them out of direct sun until you can get them in the ground. You can also plant them temporarily and move them to a more permanent location later.

Propagating Bulbs

As long as your hardy bulbs continue to flower satisfactorily, it's best not to worry about splitting them up; leave them undisturbed. However, poor flower development is a sign that the bulbs should be lifted, divided, and replanted. Daffodils can frequently become overcrowded, but in the case of tulips, poor bloom generally means the bulbs should be replaced. It is best to divide and transplant hardy bulbs after the foliage has turned brown or died back completely in the spring or early summer. You can replant the bulbs right away or store them and replant them in the fall. If you're storing the bulbs, gently remove soil on them and dry them thoroughly by spreading them out in a very shady spot for a week. (Be sure they're protected from rodents, which will eat all but daffodil bulbs.) Store them in paper bags or nylon stockings (not plastic bags because they don't breathe). Keep them in a warm (65° to 70°F), dry place out of the sun, and replant in fall.

Storing Tender Bulbs

In the North, tender, summer-flowering plants such as dahlias, gladiolus, and cannas are dug in fall when the leaves turn yellow or after the first frost. Use a spading fork to lift the bulbs from the ground. You'll find specific instructions for storing and propagating these plants in the individual plant entries in chapter 3. Keep in mind that it's best to store these plants in paper bags, loose-weave sacks, or old stockings. Plastic bags don't breathe and will lead to rot. Bags can be hung from the ceiling or walls in a cool, dark, dry location such as a basement. Store large numbers of bulbs on trays with screen bottoms. Separate the bulbs by species or cultivar before storing them, so that you know which ones are which. Be sure air can circulate around your stored bulbs. Never store bulbs more than two or three layers deep; deep piles of bulbs generate heat and will decay. Check them several times during the winter and remove those that are rotted and diseased. In the spring, inspect them carefully for signs of disease. Keep only healthy bulbs that are firm and free of spots.

PLANT MANAGEMENT

General Care

Most of the good general gardening practices that

help prevent problems in your garden have been discussed thoroughly in previous sections of this book, both in the individual plant entries in part 1 and in the chapters on insects, diseases, and animal pests in part 2. By now, you already know that regular cleanup and removal of spent flowers, insect-infested plants or plant parts, and diseased-looking tissue should become a part of your regular care routine, regardless of the flowers you're growing. You'll also want to add a thorough annual fall cleanup to your regular garden maintenance routine.

There are a few other techniques and basic plant management practices that will improve your results and put you well on your way to a healthy and flourishing flower garden.

Staking

Many flowers support themselves without assistance. But those that are taller than about 2 feet will often need staking. Zinnias, for example, may fall over from the weight of their blossoms or from heavy rains or winds. The same is true of peonies, dahlias, lilies, and delphiniums, to name a few. These plants will look more attractive if they're supported or staked in some fashion, and the stems won't be broken by wind or rain. You can rig your own staking system with bamboo sticks and string, or you can purchase ready-made staking devices that are sold in some garden centers and through catalogs. There are two approaches to staking flowers—individual stakes for single-stemmed plants like larkspurs or dahlias; group staking for multistemmed plants like peonies or lilies. The best technique for single plants is to wrap yarn or string around the stake once, then circle it lightly around the plant before coming back to the stake to tie the knot. Tie the plant to the stake about two-thirds to three-quarters of the way up the stem. Avoid using stakes that are taller than the plant because they ruin the look of the garden.

When you need to stake a clump of flowers, don't simply run some string around the outside of the clump; that won't look natural and will detract from your garden's appearance. Charles Cresson, a horticulturist in the Philadelphia area, has developed a special staking technique that he has used successfully for years. Insert several bamboo stakes about 8 inches apart around the outside edge of a clump of plants that needs staking. Angle them outward from the plant slightly. Using a ball of green twine that fits comfortably in your hand, tie the end to a stake and pass it through the middle of the clump, then wrap it around the opposite stake a couple times before passing it through the plants to another stake on the opposite side. Do this until all the stakes are connected by a web of string.

The final step is to loosely circle the clump by connecting the stakes around the perimeter. This matrix of string supports the clump in a very natural fashion from the middle as well as from the sides. The leaves should hide the stakes and twine. Cresson recommends that you set up this support system right before the plants start to flop over (probably as the flower buds show color) or just before bad weather, which can knock over the plants, is expected.

Deadheading

It's a good idea to get in the habit of removing blossoms that are past their prime. Deadheading, the process of removing faded blossoms from plants, not only keeps a garden looking neat, it also encourages repeat bloom and prevents plants from self-seeding. Many plants are stimulated to blossom longer and more profusely when their old flowers and forming seedpods are removed. Deadheading can also be used to prevent plants from reseeding. Deadhead by pinching off spent blossoms with your fingers, or snip them off with scissors.

Bulbs also benefit from deadheading because making seeds unnecessarily drains energy from them. However, it is very important to leave the foliage of hardy bulbs and allow it to yellow and die naturally after bloom. During this period, these plants look scraggly and unattractive, but it is essential that the leaves be permitted to produce energy for next year's bloom. When the leaves of early spring bulbs have begun to turn yellow, you can plant annuals right on top of the bulbs. Or, use hostas as companion plants; their foliage will emerge and hide the yellowing bulb foliage.

Mulching

In summer, a 1- or 2-inch layer of some organic material such as chopped leaves, shredded bark, compost, or wood chips helps control weeds, conserves soil moisture, and keeps dirt and soil-borne diseases from splashing up on the flowers. In the winter, a heavier protective layer of mulch applied after the ground freezes will minimize damage to the plant from soil heaving due to fluctuations in winter temperatures. Winter mulching materials include hay, chopped leaves, shredded bark, or straw. As a general rule, keep mulch away from the crowns of perennials to avoid such problems as crown rot.

It is wise to rake newly fallen leaves off beds in late fall because unchopped leaves can become a sodden mass that can smother plants as they sprout in the spring and encourage rot diseases. Instead, chop newly fallen leaves with a shredder or lawn mower and compost them or use them as a winter mulch after the ground freezes. Remove this mulch a few weeks before expected last frost.

Watering

Obviously, water requirements vary from plant to plant. If you've matched plants to the environment in your garden, incorporated plenty of organic matter into your soil, and provided your plants with a moisture-retaining layer of mulch, your plants may do fine with the water naturally available from rainfall. You'll need to water new transplants until they become established and if weekly rainfall is inadequate.

Of course, the amount of watering you need to do will also depend on your soil type. If you have sandy soil that is unable to hold much water in reserve for plants, you'll need to water more often than if you have loamy or clayey soil that can hold plenty of moisture.

A plant reacts very simply to too little or too much water—it wilts. Wilting that occurs during the heat of a midsummer day is common and temporary; don't be alarmed by it. However, wilting that extends beyond the heat of day, especially if it occurs in the morning, is a signal that the plant is suffering a serious water shortage.

Keeping track of rainfall helps you avoid overwatering or underwatering your flower garden. The best way to do that is to mount a rain gauge someplace in or around your property. Remember to empty the gauge after each rainfall. Keep track of the rainfall on a weekly basis. If, after a few days, less than ½ inch of rain has fallen, you should think about watering, particularly the annuals or new transplants. You don't have to keep precise records on paper. Just keeping rough track in your head is all that is needed to use this easy system.

Because annuals lack the extensive root systems that most perennials and hardy bulbs have, it's important to pay attention to their watering needs. Most annuals need about an inch of water each week from rain and/or by watering. If annuals are allowed to dry out to the point of visible wilting, this stress will take its toll on their health. Their blossoms will be dull and small, and they will not last as long as annuals that have been properly watered.

Perennials are generally deeper rooted and more drought tolerant than annuals, but they are vulnerable to both overwatering and underwatering. Generally, they need ½ to 1 inch of water a week either by watering or from rainfall. To keep perennials happy when you do water, be sure to moisten the soil to a depth of 1 foot or so. With plants that are subject to diseases such as crown rot, only water when the soil is dry.

Hardy bulbs need no more water than most other plants in your ornamental garden. The only critical period is the few weeks following the bloom period, if rainfall has not been adequate. For water requirements of summer-flowering bulbs, see the individual plant entries in chapter 3.

How to Water

Most people water from above, using an oscillating sprinkler or a handheld hose or watering can of some sort. This has several disadvantages. In the first place, it takes a considerable amount of time.

Also, when you water this way, you can lose as much as 30 to 40 percent of the water from evaporation and runoff. Overhead watering causes another, more serious problem. It encourages disease. Fungi like moist conditions and may find the wet leaves of your plants very enticing. Of course, leaves do get wet when it rains, but if you can avoid wetting the leaves every time you water, you will definitely reduce the chances of disease infecting your garden plants.

If you do use overhead watering methods, use these techniques for best results. First, always water deeply so that the soil is moistened at least 1 foot down. If possible, water in the morning, so foliage has a chance to dry. This minimizes disease problems. And last, avoid watering at midday because too much water will be lost to evaporation. Consider using soaker hoses or a drip system, especially if you water frequently or live in an area where water is at a premium. They use much less water than traditional sprinklers. Water from a drip system has no chance to evaporate or run off because it is completely absorbed by the soil. These systems also help fight disease, since they prevent water and soil-borne fungi from splashing up on the plants.

FEEDING THE FLOWER GARDEN

Taking good care of your soil is one of the best ways to have a healthy and trouble-free flower garden. If you've conditioned the soil with compost at planting time, many of the annuals, perennials, and bulbs listed in this book will need little else beyond an annual application of a slow-acting, general-purpose fertilizer to keep them looking their best.

You can choose from a number of different organic fertilizers, depending on the needs of your backyard. They all provide nutrients in varying degrees, but they differ in cost, availability, method of application, and duration of effectiveness.

Organic Fertilizers

Packaged fertilizers—chemical or organic—carry a three-part number that indicates the percentages of nitrogen (N), phosphorus (P), and potassium (K) contained in the fertilizer. For example, a fertilizer with the formulation 3-2-1 contains 3 percent nitrogen, 2 percent phosphorus, and 1 percent potassium. One main feeding each year provides most annuals, perennials, and bulbs with all they need to thrive. Some plants benefit from supplemental feedings; there are exceptions, however, and the individual plant entries in part 1 provide information about which plants do. See the box, "Using Organic Fertilizers," beginning on page 388 for guidelines on what to use for feeding your plants.

Compost is often thought of as a soil conditioner, but it also is a perfectly good general-purpose fertilizer, containing some nitrogen, phosphorus, and potassium as well as almost the entire range of micronutrients. (It's a good idea to add rock phosphate directly to your compost pile or mix it into the garden if you are going to use compost as your only fertilizer, though.)

Nitrogen

Nitrogen is essential to all stages of plant growth, and it must be readily available throughout the season. Since this nutrient is rapidly depleted from the soil, it must be replaced almost continuously. Bloodmeal and cottonseed meal are good sources of nitrogen, and they release it slowly to the garden. Well-rotted manure, fish meal, fish emulsion, and compost are also good sources of nitrogen.

Plants that are deficient in nitrogen will grow slowly and be stunted. Leaves will be smaller than normal and turn pale, beginning at the tips. Eventually, the whole leaf will turn yellow. Lower leaves are affected first. In severe deficiencies, the underside of the stems and leaves turn bluish purple. The plants become spindly and drop older leaves. The blossoms are small and highly colored when open. Because nitrogen is so soluble, nitrogen deficiencies are common in sandy soils, where more leaching occurs. It can occur also in soils with a high organic content when soil temperatures are around 40°F.

(continued on page 391)

Using Organic Fertilizers

If you depend on natural materials such as compost and manure for soil nutrients, keep in mind that the best way to maintain or build soil fertility is to do it slowly with annual applications. Use the table below to determine which types of fertilizers you'd like to use and which nutrients they supply. You can also mix the ingredients listed. For example, a mixture of 2 parts bloodmeal, 1 part rock phosphate, and 4 parts wood ashes will make a balanced mixture with a nitrogen-phosphorus-potassium (N-P-K) ratio of 4-5-4.

Organic Fertilizers Catalog

Fertilizer	Nutrients Supplied	Rate of Application	Uses and Comments	Sold as
Bloodmeal, dried blood	Bloodmeal: 15% N, 1.3% P, 0.7% K Dried blood: 12% N, 3% P, 0% K	Up to 3 lbs. per 100 sq. ft. (more will burn plants)	Source of readily available N; add to compost pile to speed decomposition; also repels deer and rabbits. Lasts 3–4 months.	Bloodmeal, dried blood
Bonemeal	3% N, 20% P, 0% K; 24–30% calcium	Up to 5 lbs. per 100 sq. ft.	Excellent source of P; raises pH. Best on bulbs and flower beds. Steamed bonemeal breaks down faster, but raw bonemeal still contains gelatin, which is rich in N. Lasts 6–12 months.	Raw bonemeal, steamed bonemeal
Colloidal phosphate	0% N, 18–22% P, 0% K; 27% calcium; 1.7% iron; silicas; 14 other trace minerals	Up to 10 lbs. per 100 sq ft.	More effective than rock phosphate on neutral soils; P availability higher (2% available immediately) than rock phosphate's because of small particle size of colloidal clay base; half the pH-raising value of ground limestone. Use in fall. Lasts 2–3 yrs.	Colloidal phosphate, soft phosphate, Lonfosco
Composted cow manure	2% N, 1% P, 1% K	40 lbs. per 50–100 sq. ft. as soil conditioner; 2 parts manure to 6–8 parts loam as potting mix	Low level of nutrients and slow release makes it most valuable as a soil conditioner.	Composted cow manure, Longhorn

Fertilizer	Nutrients Supplied	Rate of Application	Uses and Comments	Sold as
Cottonseed meal	6% N, 2-3% P, 2% K	2-5 lbs. per 100 sq. ft.	Acidifies soil, so it's best for crops that prefer low pH. Lasts 4-6 months.	Cottonseed meal
Fish emulsion, fish meal	Fish emulsion: 4% N, 4% P, 1% K Fish meal: 10% N, 4-6% P	Fish emulsion: dilute 20 parts water to 1 part emulsion Fish meal: up to 5 lbs. per 100 sq. ft.	Fish emulsion: apply as a foliar spray in early morning or evening. Fish meal: use in early spring, at transplanting, and any time plants need a boost. Lasts 6-8 months.	Fish emulsion, fish meal, fish solubles
Granite dust	0% N, 0% P, 3-5% K; 67% silica; 19 trace minerals	Up to 10 lbs. per 100 sq. ft.	Very slowly available; releases potash more slowly than green-sand; improves soil structure; use mica-rich type only. Lasts up to 10 yrs.	Granite dust, granite meal, crushed granite
Greensand	0% N, 1% P, 5-7% K; 50% silica; 18-23% iron oxide; 22 trace minerals	Up to 10 lbs. per 100 sq. ft.	Slowly available; loosens clay soils; apply in fall for benefits next season. Lasts up to 10 yrs.	Greensand, Jersey greensand, glauconite
Guano (bat)	8% N, 4% P, 2% K average, but varies widely; 24 trace minerals	Up to 5 lbs. per 100 sq. ft; 1 lb. per 5 gal. water for manure tea	Caves protect guano from leaching, so nutrients are conserved.	Quik Start, Bloomin' Wonder, Super Bat, Full Circle Bat Guano, Natural Bat Guano
Guano (bird)	13% N, 8% P, 2% K; 11 trace minerals	3 lbs. per 100 sq. ft.	Especially good for roses and bulbs.	Plantjoy
Hoof and horn meal	14% N, 2% P, 0% K	Up to 4 lbs. per 100 sq. ft.	High nitrogen source, but much more slowly available than bloodmeal. Good for fall-planted perennials; smelly. Takes 4-6 wks. to start releasing N, but lasts 1 yr.	Hoof and horn meal

(continued)

Using Organic Fertilizers—Continued

Organic Fertilizers Catalog—*Continued*

Fertilizer	Nutrients Supplied	Rate of Application	Uses and Comments	Sold as
Kelp meal, liquid seaweed	1% N, 0% P, 12% K; 33% trace minerals, including more than 1% calcium, sodium, chlorine, and sulfur, and about 50 other minerals in trace amounts	Kelp meal: up to 1 lb. per 100 sq. ft. Liquid seaweed: dilute 25 parts water to 1 part seaweed for transplanting and rooting cuttings; 40 parts water to 1 part seaweed as booster	Contains natural growth hormones, so use sparingly. Best source of trace minerals. Lasts 6–12 months.	Thorvin Kelp, FoliaGro, Sea Life, Maxicrop, Norwegian SeaWeed, kelp meal, liquid kelp
Langbeinite	0% N, 0% P, 22% K; 22% sulfur; 11% magnesium	Up to 1 lb. per 100 sq. ft.	Will not alter pH. Use when there is abundant calcium and sulfur; magnesium and potassium are needed.	Sul-Po-Mag, K-Mag
Rock phosphate	0% N, 33% P, 0% K; 30% calcium; 2.8% iron; 10% silica; 10 other trace minerals	Up to 10 lbs. per 100 sq. ft.	Releases P best in acid soils below pH 6.2. Slower release than colloidal phosphate; will raise pH 1 point or more.	Rock phosphate, phosphate rock
Sulfur	100% sulfur	1 lb. per 100 sq. ft. will lower pH 1 point. Dilute at 3 Tbs. sulfur to 1 gal. water as fungicide	Lowers pH in alkaline soils; increases crop protein; ties up excess magnesium.	Sulfur, Dispersul
Wood ashes	0% N, 0–7% P, 6–20% K; 20–53% calcium carbonate; trace minerals such as copper, zinc, manganese, iron, sodium, sulfur, and boron	1–2 lbs. per 100 sq. ft.	Nutrient amounts variable. Highest in young hardwoods; will raise soil pH. Put on soil in spring and dig under; do not use near young stems or roots; avoid using ashes of colored paper or painted trees; these may contain lead. Coal or coke ashes may contain sulfides. Protect ashes in winter. Lasts 1 yr. or more.	Wood ashes

SOURCE: Adapted from "Understanding Organic Fertilizers," *Rodale's Organic Gardening*, vol. 33, no. 2, February 1986.

Phosphorus

Phosphorus is available from rock phosphate, a slow-release source that can be incorporated with compost or alone. For a quick-release source of phosphorus, spray with diluted fish emulsion. Plants can easily absorb the needed phosphorus from the liquid spray through their leaves.

Phosphorus strengthens stems and is necessary for proper fruiting, flowering, seed formation, and root branching. Phosphorus deficiencies cause all of the plant's leaves, especially the undersides, to develop as a reddish purple color. Leaf veins and stems also turn color. The young leaves will be unusually small and dark in color. As they mature, they become mottled and may turn bronze. Plants may produce very thin stems.

A phosphorus deficiency is more likely to occur in acid soils than in alkaline. Sometimes it is a temporary condition caused by cold, wet soil. Phosphorus is less soluble in cold soil, and the acids that break it free from other elements need heat to function. In addition, phosphorus uptake can be enhanced by soil microbes, and unless the temperature and moisture content are hospitable, the microbes won't develop. A temporary deficiency is most likely to occur in early spring when soil is cold and wet and the small plant roots have less ability to absorb this nutrient.

Potassium

Like phosphorus, commercial potassium fertilizers come in slow-acting and quick-acting forms. The slow-acting potassium fertilizers include granite dust and greensand. Both can be worked into the soil alone or added to compost. Dilute fish emulsion provides a quick source of potassium. Another solution is to spread wood ashes around the base of the plant.

Plants use potassium, or potash, to form sugars, starches, and proteins. Potassium promotes the action of certain enzymes and boosts the cold hardiness of many plants. It enhances the color of some plants and is necessary for the development of root systems.

Plants that are deficient in potassium develop gray-green leaves, starting with the oldest leaves at the bottom of the plant. The leaves may also have yellowed or mottled margins. Eventually, they turn brown and take on a scorched appearance. Potassium deficiencies can also cause bronze-colored leaves and curling and drying of leaf margins. A plant suffering from a potassium deficiency shows poor resistance to disease, heat, and cold. Its blossoms may be misshapen and small. Potassium leaches out of very light, sandy soils. It is most likely to be deficient in the upper layers of soil, since plants remove it from these levels.

Supplemental Feedings

Many plants benefit from periodic feedings throughout the growing season. (See the individual plant entries in part 1 to see which plants this benefits.) Dry fertilizers can be applied as side-dressings, by working the fertilizer lightly into the soil around the plants. For quicker results, you can apply liquid fertilizers as a foliar spray or soil drench. Fish emulsion is ideal for liquid feeding because it contains a broad spectrum of nutrients and micronutrients. Be sure to apply according to package directions. Use a very dilute solution for foliar feeding, so you are sure not to burn the plants.

If you use any liquid fertilizer as a drench (pouring it directly into the soil) rather than as a foliar spray, apply it right after rain or immediately after you have watered the garden. The fertilizer will spread more evenly in the moist soil and will be more readily accessible to roots. The best time for foliar fertilizing is in the early morning on a cloudy, humid day. If you spray in the evening, the leaves of your plants will remain wet overnight; this could create disease problems. Set the sprayer to as fine a spray as possible.

Sources for Equipment and Supplies

A major source of information for this section came from *Gardening by Mail 2,* by Barbara J. Barton, Tusker Press, 1987.

CONTROLS

The following companies offer controls for insects, diseases, and animal pests, including animal repellents and traps, organically safe pesticides and fungicides, insect traps, and beneficial insects and diseases.

Agrilite
P.O. Box 12
93853 River Rd.
Junction City, OR 97448

Bountiful Gardens
19550 Walker Rd.
Willits, CA 95490

W. Atlee Burpee Co.
300 Park Ave.
Warminster, PA 18974

Charley's Greenhouse Supply
1569 Memorial Hwy.
Mt. Vernon, WA 98273

The Clapper Co.
1121 Washington St.
W. Newton, MA 02165

Down to Earth Distributors
850 W. 2d St.
Eugene, OR 97402

Earlee, Inc.
2002 Hwy. 62
Jeffersonville, IN 47130

Evans BioControl
895 Interlocken Pkwy. Unit A
Broomfield, CO 80020

Gardener's Supply Co.
128 Intervale Rd.
Burlington, VT 05401

Green Earth Organics
9422 144th St. E
Puyallup, WA 98373

Harmony Farm Supply
P.O. Box 451
Graton, CA 95444

Hydro-Gardens, Inc.
P.O. Box 9707
Colorado Springs, CO 80932

Orol Ledden & Sons
Center & Atlantic Aves.
P.O. Box 7
Sewell, NJ 08080-0007

Liberty Seed Co.
128 First Dr. SE
P.O. Box 806
New Philadelphia, OH 44663

Mellinger's
2310 W. South Range Rd.
North Lima, OH 44452-9731

The Natural Gardening Co.
217 San Anselmo Ave.
San Anselmo, CA 94960

Natural Gardening Research
Center
Hwy. 48
P.O. Box 149
Sunman, IN 47041

Nature's Control
P.O. Box 35
Medford, OR 97501

Necessary Trading Co.
703 Salem Ave.
New Castle, VA 24127

North Star Evergreens
P.O. Box 253
Park Rapids, MN 56470

Ohio Earth Food
13737 Duquette Ave. NE
Hartville, OH 44632

Organic Pest Management
P.O. Box 55267
Seattle, WA 98155

Peaceful Valley Farm Supply
Co.
P.O. Box 2209
Grass Valley, CA 95945

Plow and Hearth
301 Madison Rd.
Orange, VA 22960

Pony Creek Nursery
P.O. Box 16
Tilleda, WI 54978

Ringer Corp.
9959 Valley View Rd.
Minneapolis, MN 55344

SUPPLIES

The following companies offer a wide range of gardening supplies, including sprayers, drip irrigation supplies, composting equipment, floating row covers, meters, and other instruments.

Brookstone Co.
127 Vose Farm Rd.
Peterborough, NH 03458

W. Atlee Burpee Co.
300 Park Ave.
Warminster, PA 18974

Charley's Greenhouse Supply
1569 Memorial Hwy.
Mt. Vernon, WA 98273

Earlee, Inc.
2002 Hwy. 62
Jeffersonville, IN 47130

Gardener's Supply Co.
128 Intervale Rd.
Burlington, VT 05401

Green Earth Organics
9422 144th St. E
Puyallup, WA 98373

Harmony Farm Supply
P.O. Box 451
Graton, CA 95444

Orol Ledden & Sons
Center & Atlantic Aves.
P.O. Box 7
Sewell, NJ 08080-0007

A. M. Leonard, Inc.
P.O. Box 816
Piqua, OH 45356-0816

Liberty Seed Co.
128 First Dr. SE
P.O. Box 806
New Philadelphia, OH 44663

Mellinger's
2310 W. South Range Rd.
North Lima, OH 44452-9731

Necessary Trading Co.
703 Salem Ave.
New Castle, VA 24127

Peaceful Valley Farm Supply
Co.
P.O. Box 2209
Grass Valley, CA 95945

Ringer Corp.
9959 Valley View Rd.
Minneapolis, MN 55344

Smith & Hawken
25 Corte Madera
Mill Valley, CA 94941

Recommended Reading

Books   Ball, Jeff, and Charles O. Cresson. *The 60-Minute Flower Garden*. Emmaus, Pa.: Rodale Press, 1987.

Barton, Barbara J. *Gardening by Mail 2*. Sebastopol, Calif.: Tusker Press, 1987.

Bubel, Nancy. *The New Seed-Starters Handbook*. Emmaus, Pa.: Rodale Press, 1988.

Carr, Anna. *Rodale's Color Handbook of Garden Insects*. Emmaus, Pa.: Rodale Press, 1979.

Cox, Jeff, and Marilyn Cox. *The Perennial Garden*. Emmaus, Pa.: Rodale Press, 1985.

Cravens, Richard H. *Pests and Diseases*. Alexandria, Va.: Time-Life Books, 1977.

Crockett, James Underwood. *Crockett's Flower Garden*. Boston: Little, Brown and Company, 1981.

Hill, Lewis, and Nancy Lewis. *Successful Perennial Gardening*. Pownal, Vt.: Storey Communications, 1988.

Lima, Patrick. *The Harrowsmith Perennial Garden*. Camden East, Ontario.: Camden House Publishing, 1987.

Loewer, Peter. *The Annual Garden*. Emmaus, Pa.: Rodale Press, 1988.

——. *A Year of Flowers*. Emmaus, Pa.: Rodale Press, 1989.

Logsdon, Gene. *Wildlife in Your Garden*. Emmaus, Pa.: Rodale Press, 1983.

Mother Earth News. *The Healthy Garden Handbook*. New York: Simon & Schuster, 1989.

Reilly, Ann. *Park's Success with Seeds*. Greenwood, S.C.: Geo. W. Park Seed Company, 1978.

Smith, Miranda, and Anna Carr. *Rodale's Garden Insect, Disease, and Weed Identification Guide*. Emmaus, Pa.: Rodale Press, 1988.

Taylor, Norman. *Taylor's Guide to Annuals*. rev. ed. Edited by Gordon P. DeWolf, Jr. Boston: Houghton Mifflin Company, 1986.

——. *Taylor's Guide to Bulbs*. rev. ed. Edited by Gordon P. DeWolf, Jr. Boston: Houghton Mifflin Company, 1986.

——. *Taylor's Guide to Perennials*. rev. ed. Edited by Gordon P. DeWolf, Jr. Boston: Houghton Mifflin Company, 1986.

Westcott, Cynthia. *The Gardener's Bug Book*. 4th ed. Garden City, N.Y.: Doubleday & Company, 1973.

——. *Plant Disease Handbook*. 3d ed. New York: Van Nostrand Reinhold Company, 1971.

Wyman, Donald. *Wyman's Gardening Encyclopedia*. New York: Macmillan Publishing Company, 1977.

Yepsen, Roger B., Jr., ed. *The Encyclopedia of Natural Insect and Disease Control*. Emmaus, Pa.: Rodale Press, 1984.

Magazines and Newsletters

American Horticulturist, American Horticultural Society, P.O. Box 0105, Mt. Vernon, VA 22121

Avant Gardener, P.O. Box 489, New York, NY 10028

Common Sense Pest Control Quarterly, Bio-Integral Resource Center (BIRC), P.O. Box 7414, Berkeley, CA 94707

Fine Gardening, The Taunton Press, 63 S. Main St., P.O. Box 355, Newtown, CT 06470

The Green Scene, Pennsylvania Horticultural Society, 325 Walnut St., Philadelphia, PA 19106

Horticulture, Horticulture Limited Partnership, 20 Park Plaza, Suite 1220, Boston, MA 02116

Hort Ideas, Greg and Pat Williams, Rte. 1, Box 302, Gravel Switch, KY 40328

IPM Practitioner, Bio-Integral Resource Center (BIRC), P.O. Box 7414, Berkeley, CA 94707

National Gardening, National Gardening Association, 180 Flynn Ave., Burlington, VT 05401

Rodale's Organic Gardening, Rodale Press, 33 E. Minor St., Emmaus, PA 18098

Hardiness Zone Map

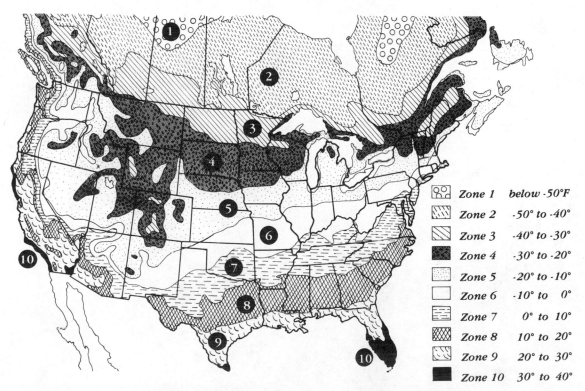

Zone 1	below -50°F
Zone 2	-50° to -40°
Zone 3	-40° to -30°
Zone 4	-30° to -20°
Zone 5	-20° to -10°
Zone 6	-10° to 0°
Zone 7	0° to 10°
Zone 8	10° to 20°
Zone 9	20° to 30°
Zone 10	30° to 40°

Average Minimum Temperatures for Each Zone

Index

Page references in boldface indicate boxes and tables.

Rodale Press, Inc., publishes RODALE'S ORGANIC GARDENING,
the all-time favorite gardening magazine.
For information on how to order your subscription,
write to RODALE'S ORGANIC GARDENING, Emmaus, PA 18098.